Investment Management For Insurers

Edited by

David F. Babbel, Ph.D.
Professor of Insurance and Finance
The Wharton School
University of Pennsylvania

and

Frank J. Fabozzi, Ph.D., CFA
Adjunct Professor of Finance
School of Management
Yale University

Published by Frank J. Fabozzi Associates

Cover design by Scott C. Riether

© 1999 By Frank J. Fabozzi Associates
New Hope, Pennsylvania

ISBN: 1-883249-47-3

About the Editors

David F. Babbel is Professor of Insurance and Finance at the Wharton School, University of Pennsylvania. Prior to joining the Wharton faculty in 1985, he was a finance professor at the University of California at Berkeley, beginning in 1978. He has served as Vice President of Insurance and Pensions at Goldman, Sachs and as Senior Economist, Financial Sector Development at the World Bank. He has published six books and monographs and 80 articles on insurance-related subjects and serves on the Valuation Task Force of the American Academy of Actuaries. Professor Babbel specializes in insurance liability valuation and fixed income investments.

Frank J. Fabozzi is editor of the *Journal of Portfolio Management*, an Adjunct Professor of Finance at Yale University's School of Management, and a consultant in the fixed-income and derivatives area. From 1986 to 1992, he was a full-time professor of finance at MIT's Sloan School of Management. Frank is a Chartered Financial Analyst and Certified Public Accountant who has edited and authored many books in finance. He is on the board of directors of the BlackRock complex of funds and the Guardian Life family of funds. He earned a doctorate in economics from the City University of New York in 1972 and in 1994 received an honorary doctorate of Humane Letters from Nova Southeastern University. He is a Fellow of the International Center for Finance at Yale University.

The Wharton Financial Institutions Center

The Wharton Financial Institutions Center provides a multi-disciplinary research approach to the problems and opportunities facing the financial services industry in its search for competitive excellence. Our research focuses on the issues related to managing risk at the firm level as well as ways to improve productivity and performance.

The Center was established in 1992 with a generous grant from the Alfred P. Sloan Foundation. The Sloan Foundation's continuing support, together with project sponsorship from participating financial service firms, facilitate the Center's ability to meet the evolving needs of the academic and industry constituents.

The Center consists of a community of faculty, visiting scholars and Ph.D. candidates whose research interests complement and support its mission. We work closely with industry executives and practitioners to ensure that our research is informed by the operating realities and competitive demands facing industry participants as they pursue competitive excellence.

Those who would like to learn more about the Center or become members of our research community are referred to our active website, http://fic.wharton.upenn.edu/fic, for further information. This includes a calendar of events, copies of other research papers and related activities.

Anthony M. Santomero
Richard K. Mellon Professor of Finance
Director, Wharton Financial Institutions Center

Table of Contents

Contributing Authors

Faye S. Albert	Albert Associates
Mark J. P. Anson	OppenheimerFunds, Inc.
David F. Babbel	University of Pennsylvania
Oren Cheyette	BARRA, Inc.
Roger G. Clarke	Analytic/TSA Global Asset Management
Harindra de Silva	Analytic/TSA Global Asset Management
Kenneth B. Dunn	Miller Anderson & Sherrerd, LLP
Frank J. Fabozzi	Yale University
Peter Fitton	Neuristics Corporation
H. Gifford Fong	Gifford Fong Associates
Sunita Ganapati	Lehman Brothers
C. Douglas Howard	Baruch College, CUNY
Bruce I. Jacobs	Jacobs Levy Equity Management
Ronald N. Kahn	BARRA, Inc.
Robert C. Kuberek	Wilshire Associates Incorporated
Wai Lee	J.P. Morgan Investment Management Inc.
Kenneth N. Levy	Jacobs Levy Equity Management
Graham Lord	Lord Consulting
Greg M. McMurran	Analytic/TSA Global Asset Management
James F. McNatt	The Eager Street Group, Inc.
Yiannos A. Pierides	University of Cyprus
Paul Puleo	Lehman Brothers
Shrikant Ramamurthy	Prudential Securities Incorporated
Robert R. Reitano	John Hancock Mutual Life Insurance Company
Mark Retik	Lehman Brothers
Anthony M. Santomero	University of Pennsylvania
Roberto M. Sella	Miller Anderson & Sherrerd, LLP
Beth Starr	Lehman Brothers
Robert Stricker	Citicorp
Brent T. Tran	Asset Strategy Consulting
Irwin T. Vanderhoof	New York University
Oldrich A. Vasicek	Gifford Fong Associates
Stavros A. Zenios	University of Cyprus

Preface

The objective of this book is to provide comprehensive coverage of all aspects of the investment management process for insurers. There is coverage of the economic framework for managing an insurer's funds, the products (cash market and derivatives) in which an insurer may invest, the economic valuation of an insurer and individual assets and liabilities, risk measurement and control, and performance measurement.

The book is divided into five sections. Section I sets forth the general issues and analytical framework for the sections that follow. The insurance industry has turned to risk management techniques as a means for improving performance. Chapter 1 explains the various types of risk insurers face and then describes the current methodologies insurers use for risk management, identifying the shortcomings of these methodologies. It is suggested that all risk management practices should focus on how firm value is affected. Chapter 2 explains the relationship between owners' equity and the various components that contribute to that value, thereby providing a conceptual framework for estimating the value of insurance liabilities. Moreover, any benchmark an insurer uses to facilitate performance measurement must be designed in a manner that is consistent with a focus on the firm's value. In Chapter 3, a performance measurement system designed for insurers is explained. The asset allocation of a property and casualty company's funds among major asset classes should integrate the insurer's assets, liabilities, and underwriting results, subject to regulatory and rating agency capital adequacy requirements and tax considerations. Chapter 4 suggests an optimization model for a property and casualty insurer that takes all of these factors into account.

Section II describes the cash market products in which insurers may invest and derivative instruments that can be used in risk management. Chapter 5 covers Treasury securities, agency securities, corporate bonds, medium-term notes, municipal securities, and Eurobonds. Structured products — mortgage-backed securities and asset-backed securities — are the subject of Chapter 6. Derivative instruments can be used to control interest rate risk and credit risk. These instruments include futures, forwards, options, caps, floors, and swaps. Derivative instruments used to control interest rate risk are explained in Chapter 7. The relatively new instruments for controlling credit risk are covered in Chapter 8. An emerging class of structured insurance risk products is the catastrophe-linked security. This product is described in Chapter 9.

The five chapters in Section III deal with valuation. We believe that the key to investment strategies, risk measurement, and performance measurement is the ability to develop good models for valuing the assets, liabilities, and derivatives of an insurer. Valuation is needed to assess how an insurer's economic surplus will change when interest rates change. Therefore, it is impossible to discuss interest rate risk management without a good valuation model. Valuation is also the key to assessing investment strategies and the selection of undervalued securities and the avoidance of overvalued securities. Chapters 10 and 11 cover stochastic interest rate models. Chapter 12 shows how to value path-dependent securities. The procedure for valuing interest rate derivatives is explained and the problems associated with valuation are discussed in Chapter 13. Monte Carlo simulation is commonly used to value complex interest rate derivative instruments. In Chapter 14, sampling techniques designed to reduce the computational time and improve the accuracy of Monte Carlo-type valuations are outlined.

The measurement and control of interest rate risk is the subject of Section IV. The first chapter in this section provides various definitions of risk for fixed income securities, some key attributes of risk, several approaches to modeling risk, and risk models. Term structure factor models are used to identify interest rate risk and are described in Chapter 16. In this chapter, the major types of factor models and the application of factor models to risk management are explained. Duration is a single measure of the interest rate risk of an asset or liability assuming a parallel shift in the yield curve. As such, it is a commonly used estimate of the interest rate sensitivity of an insurer's economic surplus. In Chapter 17, the proper way to measure duration for assets and liabilities with embedded options is explained. This measure, called effective duration, is superior to the traditional measure (Macaulay or modified duration) which ignores any embedded options. Chapter 18 focuses on managing risk exposure to changes in the shape of the yield curve. A framework for hedging the interest rate risk exposure of corporate securities using cash market Treasuries and Treasury derivative instruments is provided in Chapter 19. Hedging interest rate risk for mortgage-backed securities is complicated by prepayment risk. Chapters 20 and 21 suggest how to hedge positions in mortgage-backed securities. Chapter 22 returns to the question of risk measurement by showing how value-at-risk measures and stress testing should be used to quantify risk for a portfolio of complex investments. Finally, a key input into any valuation model and any value-at-risk measurement system is the estimated interest rate volatility. Measuring and forecasting this volatility is the subject of Chapter 23.

Because the major holdings of insurers are fixed income securities, a major focus of the book is on the valuation of these securities, their risk attributes and measurement, and the use of derivatives to control their risk. Section V covers equity portfolio management. The first two chapters in this section, Chapters 24 and 25, describe equity investment management and analysis. The use of equity derivatives for managing equity portfolios is the subject of the final chapter in this book, Chapter 26.

We believe this book will be a valuable addition to the library of anyone associated with the management of the funds of insurance companies. We wish to thank the authors of the chapters for their contributions. A book of this type by its very nature requires the input of specialists in a wide range of technical topics and we believe that we assembled some of the finest in the industry.

David F. Babbel
Frank J. Fabozzi

Section I:

General Issues

Chapter 1

Risk Management by Insurers: An Analysis of the Process

David F. Babbel, Ph.D.
Professor of Insurance and Finance
The Wharton School
University of Pennsylvania

Anthony M. Santomero, Ph.D.
Richard K. Mellon Professor of Finance
The Wharton School
University of Pennsylvania

INTRODUCTION

The past decade has seen a dramatic rise in the number of insolvent insurers. The ostensible causes of these insolvencies were myriad. Some of the insolvencies were precipitated by rapidly rising or declining interest rates. Others resulted from losses on assets such as junk bonds, commercial mortgages, CMOs, real estate, and derivatives. Mispricing of insurance policies, natural catastrophes, and changes in legal interpretations of liability and the limits of coverage hurt still others. The "churning" of policies by unscrupulous sales agents, insolvencies among the reinsurers backing the policies issued, noncompliance with insurance regulation, and malfeasance on the part of officers and directors of the insurance companies affected some as well. But despite the numerous and disparate apparent causes of these insolvencies, the underlying factor in all of them was the same: inadequate risk management practices. In response to this, insurers almost universally have embarked upon an upgrading of their financial risk management and control systems to reduce their exposure to risk and better manage the amount they accept. In short, the industry has turned to financial risk management techniques as a way to improve performance.

Coincidental to this activity, and, in part, because of our recognition of the industry's vulnerability to financial risk, the Wharton Financial Institutions

An abbreviated version of this chapter appeared in the *Journal of Risk and Insurance*, June 1997.

3

Center, with the support of the Sloan Foundation, has been involved in an analysis of financial risk management processes in the financial sector. From 1995 through 1996, on-site visits were conducted to review and evaluate the risk management systems and the process of risk evaluation that is in place.

In the insurance sector, system evaluation was conducted covering a number of prominent life/health and property/casualty insurers, both in the United States and abroad. The information obtained on the philosophy and practice of financial risk management comes primarily through intensive interviews of these insurance firms, conducted by a team of researchers from the Wharton Financial Institutions Center.[1] Measured in terms of admitted assets, these firms range in size from $7 billion to well over $100 billion. They are organized as stock, reciprocal, or mutual insurers. Some firms restrict their activities to life insurance and pensions; the others are multi-line insurers, selling the full range of property/casualty and life/health products. These visits were augmented by interviews conducted with additional large insurance firms domiciled in Japan and Europe as well as North America. As was the case above, these firms include life companies, property/casualty companies, and a multi-line company. (See Exhibit 1.)

Our information was then supplemented by five recently published surveys. Three of these were the 1994, 1995, and 1996 "Insurer CIO Surveys," conducted by Goldman, Sachs & Co.[2] These surveys were based on responses from 58-79 companies, depending on the survey, with approximately two-thirds from the life lines and one-third from the property/casualty lines. The response rate in these surveys was roughly 40%. Over 90% of the responding companies had assets in excess of $1 billion. Another pair of surveys was conducted by Joan Lamm-Tennant.[3] Her surveys were of a much more extensive set of insurers, ranging in assets from $75 million to over $100 billion. There were 119 and 144 respondents to her 1995 and 1996 surveys, respectively, representing a response rate between 11% and 20% of the firms surveyed. The business mix of these firms was split about equally between life/health and property/casualty insurance.

The purpose of this chapter is to outline the results of this investigation. It reports the state of risk management techniques in the industry — questions asked, questions answered, and questions left unaddressed by respondents. This chapter cannot recite a litany of the approaches used within the industry, nor can

---

[1] Members of the team included Anthony Santomero (leader), David Babbel, Yuval Bar-Or, Richard Herring, Paul Hoffman, Susan Kerr, Spencer Martin, Steve Pilloff, Jeffrey Trester, and Sri Zaheer.

[2] See J. N. Alexander, P. J. Bouyoucos, M. H. Siegel, and A. Gola, "The Goldman Sachs Insurer CIO Survey," *Industry Resource Group,* May 1994; M. H. Siegel, M. J. Millette, and D. Pouraghabagher, "The Goldman Sachs Insurer CIO Survey," *Industry Resource Group,* April 1995; and, M. J. Millette, A. J. Levinson, and J. A. Oleinick, "The Goldman Sachs Insurer CIO Survey," *Industry Resource Group*, May 1996.

[3] See J. Lamm-Tennant, "Survey and Commentary on Investment Policies and Practices of the U.S. Insurance Industry," Chalke, Chantilly, Virginia, 1995, and J. Lamm-Tennant and D. Gattis, "Survey and Commentary on Investment Policies and Practices of the U.S. Insurance Industry," SS&C, Bloomfield, Connecticut, 1996.

it offer an evaluation of each and every approach. Rather, it reports the standard of practice and evaluates how and why it is conducted in the particular way chosen. But even the best practice employed within the industry is not good enough in some areas. Accordingly, critiques will also be offered where appropriate. The chapter concludes with a list of questions that are currently unanswered, or answered rather unsatisfactorily in the current practice employed by this group of relatively sophisticated insurers. Here, we discuss the problems which the industry finds most difficult to address, shortcomings of the current methodology used to analyze risk, and the elements that are missing in the current procedures of risk management.

Exhibit 1: Outline of On-Site Discussions

I. Firm Level Perspectives

    1.1 Profile of the Company

        A. Size/relative position in the market

        B. Key lines of business

        C. Three year performance - key ratios

        D. Importance of risk management in creating value in key lines of business

        E. How risk management is integrated into business and performance planning

    1.2 Risk Management Organization - Firm Perspective

        A. Primary risks firm manages/monitors

        B. Organization of risk management responsibilities

        C. Decision process and decision bodies

        D. Risk planning process

        E. Risk monitoring process

        F. Firm level analytics

        G. Firm level reporting

    1.3 Risk Management Philosophy

        A. General risk appetite

        B. Key features believed to drive the risk management culture

        C. Stated risk management goals/philosophy

II. Management of Individual Risks

    II.1 Investment Risk Management

        A. Definition

        B. Organization of decision process

        C. Analytics (approaches, tools, procedures)

        D. Reporting (philosophy, frequency of mark-to-market)

        E. Limits on desired portfolio structures

        F. Checks and balances

        G. Strategic importance

        H. Performance management/incentives

        I. Tolerance testing

        J. Forecasting/planning

        K. Competitive intelligence

    II.2 Liquidity Risk

        A. Definition

        B. Organization of decision process

Exhibit 1 (Continued)

```
        C. Analytics
        D. Reporting
        E. Strategic importance
        F. Limits on desired portfolio structures
        G. Performance management/incentives
        H. Tolerance testing
        I. Forecasting/planning
        J. Competitive Intelligence
    II.3 Actuarial Risk
        A. Definition
        B. Organization of decision process
        C. Analytics
        D. Reporting
        E. Strategic importance
        F. Limits on desired portfolio structures
        G. Checks and balances
        H. Performance management/incentives
        I. Tolerance testing
        J. Forecasting/planning
        K. Competitive intelligence
    II.4 Other Important Risk Management Practices
        A. Definitions
        B. Strategic importance
        C. Analytics for management
        D. Incentive/performance management
III. Emerging Issues
IV. Firm Idiosyncrasies
V. Overall Firm Assessment
```

WHY MANAGE RISK — SOME GENERIC ANSWERS

It seems appropriate to begin our analysis of risk management techniques with a review of the reasons given for firm level concern over the volatility of financial performance. The finance literature on why firms manage risk at all is usually traced back to 1984. In that year Stulz first suggested a viable reason for objective function concavity, and his contribution is widely cited as the starting point of this burgeoning literature.[4] Doherty provides the first comprehensive treatment of this topic in a finance framework.[5] Since that time a number of alternative theories and explanations have been offered. Recently, Santamero presented a useful review of these explanations upon which we shall draw here.[6]

---

[4] R. Stulz, "Optimal Hedging Policies," *Journal of Financial and Quantitative Analysis* (June 1984).

[5] N. A. Doherty, *Corporate Risk Management: A Financial Exposition* (New York: McGraw Hill, 1985).

[6] A. Santomero, "Financial Risk Management: The Whys and Hows," *Financial Markets, Institutions, and Instruments*, December 1995.

The goal, as noted above, is to offer viable economic reasons for firm managers, who are presumed to be working on behalf of firm owners, to concern themselves with both expected profit and the distribution of firm returns around their expected value. The rationales for risk aversion can usefully be segmented into four categories: (1) managerial self interest, (2) the non-linearity of taxes, (3) the cost of financial distress, and (4) the existence of capital market imperfections.

In each case, the economic decision maker is shown to face a non-linear optimization because of the reason offered, and this leads the decision maker to be concerned with the variability of returns. In the first case the objective function itself is concave, while in the others the effect of some feature of the economic environment is to lead firm managers to behave in a risk averse manner. We begin with an explanation of each theory.

Managerial Self Interest

As mentioned above, the managerial self interest rationale is generally attributed to the work of Stulz. There, it was argued that firm managers have limited ability to diversify their own personal wealth position, associated with stock holdings and the capitalization of their career earnings associated with their own employment position. Therefore, they prefer stability to volatility because, other things equal, such stability improves their own utility, at little or no expense to other stakeholders. In truth, this argument can be traced back to the literature on the theory of agency. In this area, the relationship between firm performance and managerial remuneration is clearly developed in several works.[7]

Objections have been offered, however, to this line of reasoning. Some find the theory unconvincing, because it offers no reason for the manager to hedge his/her risk within the firm, rather than directly in the market. According to this view, managers with highly non-linear employment contracts could enter the financial market to offset the effect of such agency agreements on their own wealth position. By taking a short position in the firm's stock, the stocks of competitors, or the market, managers could obtain any level of concentration in firm-specific profitability.

However, this argument misses at least three important features of the employment relationship. First, it is illegal for senior management to take a short position in the firm's stock and problematic for them to be seen divesting themselves or systematically diversifying the investments that are correlated with firm performance. Yet, such a public divestiture would be required to properly hedge management's personal investment profile. Moreover, in the case of mutual insurers, it is even more difficult to offset a long position in firm-specific performance risk. Second, to the extent that some outcomes, defined as financial distress, lead to termination of the contract, it may be in the best interest of managers to con-

---

[7] See S. Ross, "The Economic Theory of Agency: The Principal's Problem," *American Economic Review* (May 1973), and S. Ross, "The Determination of Financial Structure: The Incentive Signaling Approach," *Bell Journal of Economics* (Spring 1977).

strain firm-level outcome, if only not to lose the future value of the employment earnings. More will be said about this later. Third, arguments in favor of expected value managerial decisions neglect the fact that managerial ability itself is not directly observable. Therefore, as Breeden and Viswanathan[8] and DeMarzo and Duffie[9] argue, observed outcomes may influence owner perception of managerial talent. This would, in turn, favor reduced volatility, or at least the protection of firm specific market value from large negative outcomes that may be found within the distribution of possible returns. For all, or any one of these reasons, therefore, there appears to be ample justification for the assumption that managers will behave in a manner consistent with a concave objective function.

The Non-Linearity of Taxes

Beyond managerial motives, firm level performance and market value may be directly associated with volatility for a number of other reasons. The first is the nature of the tax code, which both historically and internationally is highly non-linear. This point was brought to our attention by Smith and Stulz[10] and Gennotte and Pyle.[11] It has recently been emphasized in Nance, Smith, and Smithson[12] and Fite and Pfleiderer[13] as a key rationale of risk reduction. In each case, the authors indicate that, with a non-proportional tax structure, income smoothing reduces the effective tax rate and, therefore, the tax burden shouldered by the firm. By reducing the effective long term average tax rate, activities which reduce the volatility in reported earnings will enhance shareholder value.

However, two points are worth mentioning in this context. First, with the advent of more proportional tax schedules, particularly in the United States, the arguments here are somewhat mitigated. In fact, one should observe, *ceteris paribus,* a decline in the interest in risk management by American firms over the last decade because of the reduced progressivity of U.S. tax schedules. No one, however, has suggested that such is the case. Second, the tax argument rests on reported income, not true economic profit. To the extent that accounting principles permit tax planning, this argument may favor tax motivated reporting, and more careful management of the difference between book and market value of profits. For example, in the financial sector there is a long literature on tax plan-

---

[8] D. Breeden and S. Viswanathan, "Why Do Firms Hedge? An Asymmetric Information Model," Working Paper, Duke University, 1990.

[9] P. DeMarzo and D. Duffie, "Corporate Incentives for Hedging and Hedge Accounting," Working Paper, Northwestern University, 1992.

[10] C. W. Smith and R. Stulz, "The Determinants of Firm's Hedging Policies," *Journal of Financial and Quantitative Analysis* (December 1985).

[11] G. Gennotte and D. Pyle, "Capital Controls and Bank Risk," *Journal of Banking and Finance* (September 1991).

[12] D. Nance, C. W. Smith, and C. Smithson, "On the Determinants of Corporate Hedging," *Journal of Finance* (March 1993).

[13] D. Fite and P. Pfleiderer, "Should Firms Use Derivatives to Manage Risk?" in W. Beaver and G. Parker, (eds.), *Risk Management Problems and Solutions* (New York: McGraw Hill, 1995).

ning that speaks to this distinction between reported and operating profit. Greenawalt and Sinkey[14] document the existence of substantial income smoothing through the use of the loan loss provision expense item, while Scholes, Wilson, and Wolfson[15] present evidence of portfolio selection which accomplishes the same end. However, the argument here is that real economic decisions are affected by the tax code, not just their reporting. To the extent that significant discretion exists in tax reporting, tax consideration may not motivate actual decision making nearly as much as this theory suggests. Evidence on these points for the insurance industry is provided by Cummins and Grace[16] and Lamm-Tennant and Rollins.[17]

The Cost of Financial Distress

Firms may also be concerned about volatility of earnings because of the consequences of severely negative deviations from expected value and their implications for corporate viability. It is known that corporate debt creates a fixed cost that can be used as a competitive weapon in gaming models.[18] In such models, severely negative outcomes cause disruption and bankruptcy. To the extent that the bankruptcy state — or any set of specific states — is associated with a discrete increase in costs, the firm will be forced to recognize this fact in its choice calculus. In such cases, the firm behaves as if it had a concave objective function, because its payoff structure is non-linear across states.

The literature is filled with such stories. The classic paper by Warner[19] was the first to present empirical evidence of this cost, but more recent studies, such as Weiss[20] continue to reinforce its importance. As a result, standard corporate finance textbooks make clear reference to the cost of bankruptcy in their analysis of the investment decision. Smith and Stulz use this same argument to justify a desire for reduced volatility.

The cost is, perhaps, more important in regulated industries, however. In these cases, large losses may be associated with license or charter withdrawal and the loss of a monopoly position. For example, in the banking literature, Marcus

---

[14] M. Greenawalt and J. Sinkey, "Bank Loan Loss Provisions and the Income Smoothing Hypothesis: An Empirical Analysis," *Journal of Financial Services Research* (December 1988).
[15] M. Scholes, G. P. Wilson, and M. Wolfson, "Tax Planning, Regulatory Capital Planning and Financial Reporting Strategy for Commercial Banks," *Review of Financial Studies* (December 1990).
[16] J. D. Cummins and G. Grace, "Tax Management and Investment Strategies of Property-Liability Insurers," *Journal of Banking and Finance* (January 1994).
[17] J. Lamm-Tennant and T. Rollins, "Incentives for Discretionary Accounting Practices: Ownership Structure, Earnings and Taxation," *Journal of Risk and Insurance* (September 1994).
[18] See J. Brander and T. Lewis, "Oligopoly and Financial Structure: The Limited Liability Effect," *American Economic Review* (December 1986), and V. Maksimovic, "Capital Structure in Reported Oligopolies," *Rand Journal of Economics* (Autumn 1988).
[19] J. Warner, "Bankruptcy Costs: Some Evidence," *Journal of Finance* (May 1977).
[20] L. Weiss, "Bankruptcy Resolution: Direct Costs and Violation of Priority Claims," *Journal of Financial Economics* (October 1990).

makes this same argument for financial firms subject to charter review by regulatory agencies,[21] and Santomero[22] and Herring and Santomero[23] used this story to justify corporate separation for financial services firms. Staking and Babbel provide empirical support for its application to the insurance industry.[24] In all cases, however, the cost of financial distress must be non-linear, as linear cost functions do not lead to the required behavior.

Yet, the authors are on firm ground here, as there is ample evidence that financial distress leads to substantially increased costs associated with bankruptcy proceedings, legal costs, and perhaps most importantly the diversion of management attention from creating real economic value.[25]

Capital Market Imperfections

Recently the above argument has been extended in the work of Froot, Scharfstein, and Stein.[26] They accept the basic paradigm of the financial distress model above, but rationalize the cost of bad outcomes by reference to Myers' debt overhang argument.[27] In their model, external financing is more costly than internally generated funds due to any number of capital market imperfections. These may include discrete transaction costs to obtain external financing, imperfect information as to the riskiness of the investment opportunities present in the firm, or the high cost of the potential future bankruptcy state. In the case of mutual insurers, who have little access to the capital market, this line of argument is particularly compelling.

At the same time, the firm has an investment opportunity set which can be ordered in terms of net present value. The existence of the cost imperfections results in underinvestment in some states, where internally generated funds fall short of the amount of new investment that would be profitable in the absence of these capital market imperfections. Stated another way, the volatility of profitability causes the firm to seek external finance to exploit investment opportunities when profits are low. The cost of such external finance is higher than the internal funds due to the market's higher cost structure associated with the factors enumerated above. This, in turn, reduces optimal investment in low profit states.

---

[21] A. Marcus, "Deregulation and Bank Financial Policy," *Journal of Banking and Finance* (December 1984).

[22] A. Santomero, "The Changing Structure of Financial Institutions: A Review Essay," *Journal of Monetary Economics* (September 1989).

[23] R. Herring and A. Santomero, "The Corporate Structure of Financial Conglomerates," *Journal of Financial Services Research* (December 1990).

[24] K. B. Staking and D. F. Babbel, "The Relation between Capital Structure, Interest Rate Sensitivity, and Market Value in the Property-Liability Insurance Industry," *Journal of Risk and Insurance,* December 1995.

[25] For an extended discussion of costs, see C.W. Smith, C. Smithson, and D. Wilford, *Strategic Risk Management* (New York: Harper & Row, 1990).

[26] K. Froot, D. Scharfstein, and J. Stein, "Risk Management: Coordinating Investment and Financing Policies," *Journal of Finance* (December 1993), and K. Froot, D. Scharfstein, and J. Stein, "A Framework for Risk Management," *Harvard Business Review* (November 1994).

[27] S. C. Myers, "Determinants of Corporate Borrowing," *Journal of Financial Economics* (November 1977).

The cost of volatility in such a model is the forgone investment in each period that the firm is forced to seek external funds. Recognizing this outcome, the firm embarks upon volatility reducing strategies, which have the effect of reducing the variability of earnings. Hence, risk management is optimal in that it allows the firm to obtain the highest expected shareholder value.

The authors can support their theory with reference to evidence offered by Fazzari, Hubbard, and Peterson[28] and Hoshi, Kashyap, and Scharfstein,[29] who present evidence that internal cash flow is, in fact, correlated to corporate investment. In addition, Smith, Smithson, and Wilford regale us with anecdotes that further support this contention.[30]

Summary of Rationales

Together, the stories work fairly well. Firm managers are interested both in expected profitability and the risk, or variability, or reported earnings or market value. The latter can be rationalized by the existence of non-linear costs across the range of profit states associated with any given expected value. The non-linearity is associated with managerial incentive effects, the tax structure, the costs of crisis, and/or forgone investment opportunities. In any or all of these cases, the firm is led to treat the variability of earnings as a choice variable that it selects, subject to the usual constraints of optimization. How it proceeds to manage the risk position of its activity is the area to which we now turn.

RISK AS A CENTRAL INGREDIENT IN THE INDUSTRY'S FRANCHISE

The Role of Insurers in the Financial Sector

Insurers are in the risk business. In the process of providing insurance and other financial services, they assume various kinds of actuarial and financial risks. Over the last decade much has been written of the role of insurers within the financial sector.[31] This literature will not be reviewed in detail here. Suffice it to say that market participants seek the services of insurers because of their ability to provide actuarial risk pooling through their major product lines of life, property/casualty and health insurance, pension products, annuities, and other financial instruments. At the same time, they are major providers of funds to the capital

---

[28] S. M. Fazzari, R. G. Hubbard, and B. C. Petersen, "Financial Constraints and Corporate Investment," *Brookings Papers on Economic Activity,* 1988.

[29] T. Hoshi, A. Kashyap, and D. Scharfstein, "Corporate Structure, Liquidity, and Investment: Evidence from Japanese Industrial Groups," *Quarterly Journal of Economics* (February 1991).

[30] Smith, Smithson, and Wilford, *Strategic Risk Management.*

[31] See, for example, R. C. Merton, "On the Application of the Continuous-Time Theory of Finance to Financial Intermediation and Insurance," *Geneva Papers on Risk and Insurance* (July 1989), especially pp. 242-258.

market — particularly to the fixed income sectors. In performing these roles they generally act as a principal in the transaction. As such, they use their own balance sheet to facilitate the transactions and to absorb the risks associated with them. Therefore, it is here that the discussion of risk management and the necessary procedures for risk control has centered. Accordingly, it is in this area that our review of risk management procedures will concentrate.

What Risks Are Being Managed?

The risks contained in the insurer's product sales, i.e., those embedded in the products offered to customers to protect against actuarial risk, are not all borne directly by the insurer itself. In many instances the institution will eliminate or mitigate the actuarial and financial risk associated with a transaction by proper business practices; in others it will shift the risk to other parties through a combination of reinsurance, pricing and product design. Only those risks that are not eliminated or transferred to others are left to be managed by the firm for its own account. This is the case because the insurance industry recognizes that it should not engage in business in a manner that unnecessarily imposes risk upon it, nor should it absorb risks that can be efficiently transferred to other participants. Rather, it should only manage risks at the firm level that are more efficiently managed there than by the market itself or their owners in their own portfolios. In short, it should accept only those risks that are uniquely a part of the insurer's array of services.

Elsewhere it has been argued that risks facing all financial institutions can be segmented into three separable types from a management perspective.[32] These are:

1. risks that can be eliminated or avoided by standard business practices
2. risks that can be transferred to other participants
3. risks that must be actively managed at the firm level

In the first of these cases, the practice of risk avoidance involves actions to reduce the chances of idiosyncratic losses from standard insurance activity by eliminating risks that are superfluous to the institution's business purpose. Common risk avoidance practices include at least three types of actions. The standardization of process, insurance policies, contracts and procedures to prevent inefficient or incorrect financial decisions is the first of these. Another is the construction of portfolios on both sides of the balance sheet that benefit from diversification and the application of the Law of Large Numbers and Central Limit Theorem, which reduce the effects of any one loss experience. Finally, the implementation of incentive compatible contracts with the institution's management to require that employees be held accountable is the third. In each case, the goal is to rid the firm of risks that are not essential to the financial service provided, or to absorb only an optimal quantity of a particular kind of risk.

---

[32] See G. Oldfield and A. Santomero, "The Place of Risk Management in Financial Institutions," *Sloan Management Review* (Fall 1997).

There are also some risks that can be eliminated, or at least substantially reduced through the technique of risk transfer. Markets exist for many of the risks borne by the insurance firm. Actuarial risk can be transferred to reinsurers. Catastrophe risk can be offset somewhat by undertaking a position in catastrophe futures and perhaps even in catastrophe bonds. Interest rate risk can be hedged or transferred through interest rate products such as swaps, caps, floors, futures, or other derivative products. Insurance policies and lending documents can be altered to effect a change in their duration and convexity. Equity market risk can be reduced with an appropriate futures position in equities. In addition, they can offer products which absorb some financial risks, while transferring some of these risks to the purchaser. Defined contribution pension plans and variable universal life policies are clear examples of this approach. Finally, the insurer can buy or sell financial claims and reinsurance to diversify or concentrate the risk that results from servicing its client base. To the extent that the actuarial and financial risks of the insurance policies underwritten by the firm are understood by the market, they can be sold in part or in whole at their fair value. Unless the institution has a comparative advantage in managing the attendant risk and/or a desire for the embedded risk they contain, there is no reason for the insurer to absorb such risks, rather than transfer them.

However, there are two classes of activities where the risk inherent in the activity must and should be absorbed at the insurance firm level. In these cases, risk management must be aggressive and good reasons exist for using firm resources to manage insurance-level risk. The first of these includes actuarial exposures where the nature of the embedded risk may be complex and difficult to communicate and transfer to third parties. For example, Progressive Insurance Co. has a definite niche in the high risk auto insurance business owing to its concentration of underwriting activities, and Lutheran Brotherhood has a natural advantage for writing life insurance to its clientele. A similar situation may arise on the asset side of the business where the insurer holds private placements and other complex, proprietary assets that have thin, or even non-existent, secondary markets. Communication in such cases may be more difficult or expensive than hedging the underlying risk. Moreover, revealing information about the customer may give competitors an undue advantage. The second case includes risk positions that are central to the insurer's business purpose and are absorbed because they are the *raison d'être* of the firm. Actuarial risk inherent in the key insurance lines where the insurer may enjoy a competitive advantage or a market niche is a clear case in point. In all such circumstances, risk is absorbed and needs to be monitored and managed efficiently by the institution. Only then will the firm systematically achieve its financial performance goal.

How Are These Risks Managed?

In light of the above, what are the necessary procedures that must be in place to carry out adequate risk management for those risks that are essential ingredients to the insurer's franchise? What techniques are employed to both limit and manage the different types of risk, and how are they implemented in each area of risk management? It is to these questions that we now turn.

In general, the management of an insurance firm relies on a variety of techniques in their risk management systems. However, it appears that common practice has evolved such that four elements have become key steps to implementing a broad based risk management system. These include:

1. standards and reports
2. underwriting authority and limits
3. investment guidelines or strategies
4. incentive contracts and compensation

These tools are established to measure risk exposure, define procedures to manage these exposures, limit exposures to acceptable levels, and encourage decision makers to manage risk in a manner that is consistent with the firm's goals and objectives. To see these four parts of basic risk management achieve these ends, we elaborate on each part of the process below. Later in this chapter we illustrate how these techniques are applied to control each of the specific risks facing the insurance community.

Standards and Reports

The first of these control techniques involves two different conceptual activities, i.e., standard setting and financial reporting. They are listed together because they are the *sine qua non* of any risk management system. Underwriting standards, risk classification, and standards of review are all traditional tools of risk control. Consistent evaluation and rating of exposures of various types are essential for management to understand the risks on both sides of the balance sheet, and the extent to which these risks must be mitigated or absorbed.

The standardization of financial reporting is the next ingredient. Obviously, outside audits, regulatory reports, and ratings agency evaluations are essential for investors to gauge asset quality and firm level risk. But the types of information collected and the manner in which it is assembled and presented in statutory accounting reports are inadequate for the purposes of managing an insurance company. For instance, it is difficult to discern the magnitude and import of options insurers have effectively written on both sides of the balance sheet, e.g., call and prepayment options and loan commitments on the asset side, lapse, loan and surrender options on the liability side, by relying merely on statutory accounting reports. It is also difficult to estimate interest rate risk and default risk from the information provided there.

The statutory accounting reports have long been standardized, for better or worse. However, the need here goes beyond public reports and audited statements to the need for management information on actuarial risk, asset quality and overall risk posture. Such internal reports need similar standardization but much more frequent reporting intervals, with daily, weekly and monthly reports substituting for the quarterly statutory accounting periodicity. Thus, the collection and presentation of sufficient data to adequately manage the risk exposure of a company is a starting point.

Underwriting Authority and Limits

A second technique for internal control of active management is the use of position limits, and/or minimum standards for participation. In terms of the latter, the domain of risk taking is restricted to only those customers or assets that pass some prespecified quality standard. Then, even for those that are eligible, limits are imposed to cover exposures to counterparties, credits, and overall position concentrations relative to various types of risks. In general, each person who can commit capital, whether on the asset or liability side of the ledger, will have a well-defined limit. This applies to underwriters, portfolio managers, lenders, and traders. Summary reports show limits, as well as current exposure by business unit on a periodic basis. In large organizations, with thousands of positions maintained, accurate and timely reporting is difficult, but even more essential.

Investment Guidelines or Strategies

Investment guidelines and recommended positions for the immediate future are the third technique that is commonly in use. Here, strategies are outlined in terms of concentration and commitments to particular areas of the market, the extent of desired asset/liability mismatching or exposure to interest rate risk, and the need to hedge against systematic risks of a particular type. These limits lead to passive risk avoidance and/or diversification, because managers generally operate within position limits and prescribed rules. Beyond this, guidelines offer firm level advice as to the appropriate level of active management, given the state of the market and the willingness of senior management to absorb the risks implied by the aggregate portfolio. Such guidelines extend to firm level hedging and asset/liability matching. In addition, securitization and even derivative activity are rapidly growing techniques of position management open to participants looking to reduce their exposure to be in line with management's guidelines.

Similar guidelines are required on the liability side of the balance sheet. Underwriting standards and strategies are needed to ensure that the risks accepted conform to the parameters that the insurer is capable and willing to accept. They also foster better pricing of products, and prevent any one underwriter from compromising the future solvency of the firm.

Incentive Schemes

To the extent that the firm can enter incentive compatible contracts with senior management, line managers, and sales agents and make compensation related to the risks borne by these individuals, then the need for elaborate and costly controls is lessened. However, such incentive contracts must be consistent with the insurers' financial goals and require proper internal control systems. Such tools, which include underwriting risk and loss analysis, investment risk analysis, the allocation of costs, and the setting of required returns to various parts of the organization is not trivial. Notwithstanding the difficulty, well designed systems align the goals of managers with other stakeholders in a most desirable way. In fact, most financial debacles can be traced to the absence of incentive compatibility. For instance, the linkage of compensation to sales can lead to reckless and dangerous growth and poor underwriting or mispricing of risks. The linkage of managerial compensation to book earnings can lead to the acquisition of investments with negative convexity, duration mismatch risk, liquidity risk and credit risk, whose book yields are higher than their expected returns.

RISKS IN PROVIDING INSURANCE SERVICES

How are these techniques of risk management employed by the insurance sector? To explain this, we must begin by enumerating the risks which the insurance industry has chosen to manage, and illustrate how the four step procedures outlined are applied to risk control in each area.

The Actuarial View of Risks

As a starting point, most of the insurers interviewed classified their risks by adapting a framework which was proposed years ago by the Society of Actuaries' Committee on Valuation and Related Problems. Even though the Society of Actuaries is focused on life insurance and pensions, the property/casualty insurers interviewed also had adapted the same risk classification paradigm. The various categories of risks are dubbed C-1, C-2, C-3, and C-4, deriving these names from the Committee assigned to make recommendations on these issues.[33] We begin our review of the perceived risks with an explanation of the industry's own definitions.

C-1 risks are *asset risks*, which arise from the possibility that borrowers of insurer funds may default on their obligations to the company, or that the market value of an insurer's investment assets may decline. They include interest rate risk, credit risk, market risk, and currency risk.

C-2 risk is *pricing risk*, which stems from uncertainty about future operating results relating to items such as investment income, mortality and morbidity, frequency and severity of claims and losses, administrative expenses, sales and lapses. If an insurer's pricing is based on assumptions that prove inadequate, it may not be able to meet its obligations to policy owners.

C-3 risk is *asset/liability matching risk*, which springs from the impact of fluctuating interest and inflation rates on the values of assets and liabilities. If the impact of fluctuating rates is different on assets than on liabilities, the values of assets and liabilities will change by different amounts, and could expose the insurer to insolvency.

---

[33] Our discussion of these risks follows that of K. Black Jr. and H. D. Skipper Jr., *Life Insurance*, 12th ed. (Englewood Cliffs, N.J.: Prentice Hall, 1994).

C-4 risks are *miscellaneous risks*, generally thought to be beyond the ability of insurers to predict and manage, but they nevertheless represent real risk to the company. These risks include tax and regulatory changes, product obsolescence, poor training of employees and sales agents, and malfeasance, malversation, or misconduct of managers or other employees. Also included is the risk that laws or legal interpretations will change in a way that will alter the firm's obligations *ex post*. Another manifestation of C-4 risk is that there will be an unforeseen downgrade of acquisitions that could lead to a "run" on the assets of the insurance company. One firm referred to C-4 risk as "stupidity risk" — failure to employ and retain good people.

Two firms wryly referred to a new category of risk, dubbed *C-5* risk, which is the havoc that arises when a person who has strong political ambitions or is running for higher political office is appointed to be state insurance commissioner.

The use of the Society of Actuaries' risk classification taxonomy was viewed merely a useful point of departure by some of the insurance firms we interviewed, while others viewed it as satisfactory for their purposes. In our view, none of the risk classification schemas we saw was completely satisfactory. However, most of the conceivable risks that would impact insurers were included somewhere on the lists that we saw. (See Exhibit 2.) In most cases, however, the industry was straining to define the inherent financial risks as part of the C1 through C4 paradigm that had been developed years ago. In addition, it appeared that most schemas had undue focus on risks in isolation, rather than on their contribution to overall firm risk.

The Financial View of Risks

As an alternative to the actuarial decomposition of risk which is unique to the insurance industry, standard financial risk definitions are increasingly being proposed in the industry. For the sector as a whole, these risks can be broken into six generic types: actuarial, systematic, credit, liquidity, operational and legal risks. Briefly, we will discuss each of these risks facing the insurance institution; in a later section we will indicate how they are managed. Our focus will be on the financial risks, which include the first four of the risks listed below. Of course the risks associated with the provision of insurance services differ by the type of service rendered.

Actuarial risk is the risk that arises from raising funds via the issuance of insurance policies and other liabilities. It is the risk that the firm is paying too much for the funds it receives, or alternatively, the risk that the firm has received too little for the risks it has agreed to absorb. If an insurer invests its funds in efficiently traded securities, it should expect to have, on average, a zero net economic profit. If the insurer pays too much for these funds it cannot expect to earn a satisfactory profit in the long run. Another aspect of actuarial risk is that during any given time period, the underwriting losses will be in excess of those projected. This could happen for two reasons. First, the expectations themselves may be based on an inadequate knowledge of the loss distribution. Second, the losses may exceed their expectations in the normal course of business simply because losses fluctuate around their mean. The degree to which they deviate from the mean will depend, of course, on the characteristics of the loss distribution, which depend on the nature of the risks insured.

Exhibit 2: A List of Risks Facing Insurers

Corporate	Liability Side
Capital Utilization	Pricing
Expense Control, Overhead Burden	Pricing Adequacy
Regulatory Compliance	Expense Margin
Ethics & Employee Behavior	Unrealistic Competition
Accountability	Policy Lapses
Meritocracy	Long Tail of Liabilities
Quality of Management	Inflation Risk
Quality of Training	Actuarial
Quality of Workforce, Service	Mortality
Management Succession	Morbidity
Recruitment/Retention	Longevity
Industry Reputation	Subsidized Early Retirement
Industry Concentration	Disintermediation
Company Reputation	Secular Trend
Teamwork Over Turf	Utiliization of Covenants
Coping With Change	Antiselection
Technological Breakdown	Natural Catastrophe
Nontraditional Ventures	Moral Hazard
Guaranty Fund Assessments	Fraudulent Information
Tax Law Changes	Fraudulent Claims
Uninsured Pure Firm Losses	Morale Hazard
Information Systems Problems	Product Development
Legal Risk	Product Design
Financial Disclosure Risk	Product Appeal
	Consumer Misunderstandings
ASSET SIDE	Distribution
Credit	Cost of Distribution
Public Bonds	Agent Recruitment
Private Placements	Agent Productivity
Mortgages	Agent Retention
Collateral Risk	Policy Churning
Counter Party Risk	Regulatory Environment
Reinsurer Insolvency	Compliance
Systematic Risks: Interest Rate Risk	Loss of Tax Benefits
Call Risk - Callable Bonds	Health Care Reform
Prepayment Risk - MBS & CMO	Other Regulatory Changes
Duration, Convexity, Drift	Financial Reporting
Change in Interest Volatility	Surplus Strain
Yield Curve Shape, Twist	GAAP for Mutuals
Systematic Risks: Other	FAS 115
Equity Market Risk	Unsound Reporting
Basis Risk	Mark-to-Market Risk
Inflation Risk	Reputation
Liquidity	Ethics & Compliance
Cash Mismatch	Quality of Service
Disintermediation	Corporate Image
Run on the "Bank"	Market

Exhibit 2 (Continued)

Maturity Extension	Uncontrolled Growth
Mortgage Refinancing	Untested Markets
Loss of Equity Value	Market Saturation
Real Estate	Bank Competition
Stocks	Globalization
Subsidiaries	Liability Insurance
Derivatives	Political & Currency
Diversification	Foreign Exchange Risk of Claims
Asset Allocation	Profits Repatriation
Industry and Geographical Risk	Political Risk
Unstable Covariances Risk	
Political & Currency	SURPLUS
International Investments	Capital Adequacy
Foreign Exchange Risk	Funding Risk

Systematic risk is the risk of asset and liability value changes associated with systematic factors. It is sometimes referred to as market risk. As such, it can be hedged but cannot be diversified completely away. In fact, systematic risk can be thought of as undiversifiable risk. All investors assume this type of risk whenever assets owned or claims issued can change in value as a result of broad economic factors. Systematic risk comes in many different forms. For the insurance sector, however, three are of greatest concern, viz., variations in the general level of interest rates, basis risk, and (especially for property/casualty insurers) inflation.

Because of the insurers' dependence on these systematic factors, most try to estimate the impact of these particular systematic risks on performance, attempt to hedge against them, and thus limit the sensitivity of their financial performance to variation in these undiversifiable factors. To do so, most will both track and manage each of the major systematic risks individually. The first of these is undoubtedly *interest rate risk*. Here, they measure and manage the firm's vulnerability to interest rate variation, even though they cannot do so perfectly. At the same time, insurers with large corporate bond, mortgage and common stock holdings closely monitor their *basis risk*. Here the concern is that yields on instruments of varying credit quality, liquidity, and maturity do not move together, exposing the insurer to market value variation that is independent of liability values. In this case too, they try to manage, as well as limit, their exposure to it. Finally, to the extent that the frequency and severity of claims are influenced by *inflation risk*, expected losses will also be affected. This is particularly the case where insurance policies are written on a replacement cost basis. The inflation of concern can be general inflation, affecting repair costs, medical costs, and the like, or specific and localized inflation, like the quadrupling of certain building materials costs in southern Florida shortly after hurricane Andrew. All three of these systematic risks will be recognized as sources of performance variation.

Credit risk is the risk that a borrower will not perform in accordance with its obligations. Credit risk may arise from either an inability or an unwillingness on the part of the borrower to perform in the pre-committed contracted manner. This can affect the investor holding the bond or lender of a loan contract, as well as other investors and lenders to the creditor. Therefore, the financial condition of the borrower, as well as the current value of any underlying collateral is of considerable interest to an insurer who has invested in the bonds or participated in a direct loan.

The real risk from credit is the deviation of portfolio performance from its expected value. Accordingly, credit risk is diversifiable but difficult to eliminate completely, as general default rates themselves exhibit much fluctuation. This is because a portion of the default risk may, in fact, result from the systematic risk outlined above. In addition, the idiosyncratic nature of some portion of these losses remains a problem for creditors in spite of the beneficial effect of diversification on total uncertainty. This is particularly true for insurers that take on highly illiquid assets. In such cases, the credit risk is not easily transferred, and accurate estimates of loss are difficult to estimate.

Liquidity risk can best be described as the risk of a funding crisis. While some would include the need to plan for growth, the risk here is more correctly seen as the potential for a funding crisis. Such a situation would inevitably be associated with an unexpected event, such as a large claim or a write down of assets, a loss of confidence or a legal crisis. Because insurers operate in markets where they may receive clustered claims due to natural catastrophes, or massive requests for policy withdrawals and surrenders due to changing interest rates, their liabilities can be said to be somewhat liquid. Their assets, however, are sometimes less liquid, particularly where they invest in private placements and real estate. Given this situation, it is important for an insurer to maintain sufficient liquidity to easily handle any demands for cash. Otherwise, an insurer that would be solvent without a sudden demand for cash may have to sell off illiquid assets at concessionary prices, leading to large losses, further demands for cash, and potential insolvency.

Operational risk is associated with the problems of accurately processing claims, and accurately processing, settling, and taking or making delivery on trades in exchange for cash. It also arises in record keeping, processing system failures and compliance with various regulations. As such, individual operating problems are small probability events for well-run organizations but they expose a firm to outcomes that may be quite costly.

Legal risks are endemic in financial contracting and are separate from the legal ramifications of credit and operational risks. New statutes, court opinions and regulations can put formerly well established transactions into contention even when all parties have previously performed adequately and are fully able to perform in the future. For example, changes in the application of statutes of limitations for filing suits have affected the losses arising from property/liability policies. Similarly, the change to joint and several liability rules has also altered the distribution of risks that may be covered by insurance policies.[34]

---

[34] See P. W. Huber, *Liability: The Legal Revolution and Its Consequences* (New York: Basic Books, 1988).

Another type of legal risk arises from the activities of an institution's management, employees and agents. Fraud, violations of regulations or laws, and other actions can lead to catastrophic loss. Even a situation where the insurer legally fulfills all of its contract obligations can result in massive litigation if some policy owners had different expectations or understandings about the performance of their policies than what was specified in the contracts.

Every insurer faces a different exposure to each of these risks, depending on its business mix. In all its activities, an insurer must decide how much business to originate, how much to finance, how much to reinsure, and how much to contract to agents. In so doing, it must weigh both the return and the risk embedded in the asset and liability portfolios. Management must measure the expected profit and evaluate the prudence of the various risks enumerated above to be sure that the result achieves the stated goal of maximizing shareholder value, in the case of a stock insurer, or maximizing ownership interests, in the case of a mutual or reciprocal insurer. If the product's expected profit warrants the risk, then the activity is added to the insurer's balance sheet, and the risk must be managed. This risk management is achieved through the four step process outlined above. How this is implemented for each of the key financial risks enumerated above is the focus of our next section.

INSURANCE RISK MANAGEMENT SYSTEMS

Actuarial Risk

The risk of paying too high a price to raise funds is an important risk, particularly in light of the fact that insurers raise few funds in the competitive capital market. Most of their debt is raised in the form of issuing insurance policies. Policies are written today in exchange for lump sum or periodic premiums, but the amounts and timing of the repayment of these funds are often unknown and may occur within a month or more than 80 years later. Because the pricing of the policies reflects not only expected losses but also the yields an insurer can earn on the funds between the inception of a policy and its termination or the payment of benefits, the interest assumption used in developing insurance prices is of critical importance. Two things complicate this process. Forward interest rates cannot be synthesized to lock in a spread, for the insurer has no way of knowing if future periodic premium payments will be forthcoming. Also, the loss distributions can undergo substantial evolution over time, as more information is revealed and as the economic environment changes.

Insurers are typically quite skilled in managing actuarial risk. The manner in which this is done is described in insurance and actuarial textbooks.[35]

---

[35] See Black and Skipper, *Life Insurance*; R. E. Beard, T. Pentikäinen, and E. Pesonen, *Risk Theory,* 3rd ed. (New York: Chapman and Hall, 1984); H. U. Gerber, *An Introduction to Mathematical Risk Theory* (Homewood, Illinois: Richard D. Irwin, Inc., 1979); and J. D. Cummins and R. A. Derrig, *Financial Models of Insurance Solvency* (Boston: Kluwer Academic Publishers, 1989).

Therefore, here we will focus on what developments have occurred during the past decade that improve an insurer's ability to price and manage this risk.

Until recently, life insurance prices were developed using conservative static assumptions regarding loss distributions and interest rates. While this approach was satisfactory for much of the past century, it was ill-equipped to accommodate the interest rate volatility that began during the late 1970s. Life insurance policies are replete with options — settlement options, policy loan options, over-depositing privileges, and surrender or renewal privileges, on the part of the insured, and discretionary dividend and crediting rate options on the part of the insurer. Indeed, some have even viewed a life insurance policy as little more than a package of options.[36] In stable interest rate environments, policy owner utilization of these options is often predicated on individual or family circumstances. Hence, in the aggregate, utilization rates are fairly steady and amenable to forecasting.

However, when interest rates are volatile, the options gain in value and their utilization rates can fluctuate wildly. Traditional actuarial methods, which depended upon stability, were incapable of correctly valuing these options; hence, many policies were woefully underpriced.[37] Today the standard valuation methods that have been adopted by most of the sophisticated life insurers explicitly value these embedded options. Thus, insurers now can estimate the cost of the various option-like provisions of all kinds of life insurance policies. Most life insurers we interviewed were using the PTS software of Chalke, Inc. (now SS&C, Inc.). This software, and competing software offered by Tillinghast and others, use modern stochastic valuation techniques, familiar in the pricing of fixed income and mortgage-backed securities, to estimate the values of insurance policies in a manner consistent with that used to value the assets. Needless to say, this represents a big advance in the tools with which insurers can practice risk management.

Lest our enthusiasm for this advance be misconstrued as euphoria, we hasten to add that all is not well here. First, the stochastic valuation methodology most commonly used relies on a single stochastic factor. Most fixed income and mortgage-backed security valuation models are based on at least two stochastic factors. Without two factors, one tends to produce model values that are too highly correlated, and whose movements in value are perfectly correlated. Also, the speed of the software is sufficiently slow that it is difficult to implement more than a handful of path simulations in arriving at "option-adjusted" values. Moreover, it is unrealistic to attempt to model a prepayment feature or a call feature, which may be triggered by changes in long-term yields, while using the short-term rate paths to value the instrument. The second drawback is perhaps even more serious. Most insurers have

---

[36] See M. L. Smith, "The Life Insurance Policy as an Options Package," *Journal of Risk and Insurance* (September 1982).

[37] The value of the policy loan option by itself could account for 20%-45% of the present value of all future insurance premiums, if the option were used optimally. When factoring in the suboptimal utilization of this option, the estimated cost to an insurer of providing this option was in the 8%-12% range. Yet insurers had historically charged *nothing* for this option. Indeed, it was simply mandated that insurers begin to offer this option.

inadequate data collected and assembled with which to reliably model the interest sensitivity of policy option utilization. Accordingly, the valuation models really allow an insurer only to quantify better the impact of its guesses about what those utilization functions might look like. We encountered much frustration among life insurers that even though the valuation software had taken a long time to develop, the data requirements of the valuation software have still not been met. The third drawback is in how insurers interpret the data analyses provided by "black boxes."

We found that in some companies, there is neither an understanding nor an appreciation for the risk measures produced. There is often such shallow understanding of the underpinnings of the methodologies employed to measure risk that the computer output is either disregarded or uncritically accepted. Over time, as insurer personnel receive more training in stochastic methods and the meaning of the risk measures, they will be able to use the software to greater advantage in measuring and managing their risks.

Nonetheless, the availability of valuation software that is consistent with modern valuation principles is an important step forward, and software that is currently under development will remedy the shortcomings of being based on a single stochastic factor and producing value estimates, dare we say, at a relaxed pace. With this software, actuaries produce pricing estimates based on a dozen or so scenarios. However, they typically also test their prices using hundreds and thousands of additional scenarios, albeit not in an option-adjusted framework.

In the property/casualty sector, there is no counterpart to the modern valuation software for pricing liabilities. However, option-adjusted arbitrage-free valuation tools may be overly powerful given the imprecision associated with many of the risks that are insured. There are few options that compare with those available in life policies, and nominal values are often not guaranteed; guarantees are sometimes in terms of covering repair costs, replacement costs, medical costs, and so forth. Even when there are nominal maximum amounts of coverage, the losses below the maximum are subject to additional uncertainty because of inflation.

The use of reports and standards for underwriting life/health and property/casualty risks is routine. It is common to have dozens, and sometimes over a hundred "cells" in which to classify the risks. Base rates can be related to a number of factors, such as age, gender, occupation, schooling, health status and history, property characteristics, nature of business, and so forth. These base rates are then adjusted to reflect experience factors (e.g., past claims, driving behavior). While the fair premiums will be a function of interest rates, in practice the premiums charged will not adjust to reflect current interest rates very often. This is because it is administratively cumbersome to alter insurance premium schedules every time the interest rates change.

Underwriting limits are commonly established. Authority is limited to a certain amount. While insurance agents may have temporary binding authority, it is a common practice to have a party who is not involved in the policy sale to review the underwriting and make a determination whether the risk will ultimately be accepted and insured. Insurers are typically better at keeping track of sales commissions than in tracking losses to a particular sales agent or underwriter. However, many of the leading life/health and property/casualty insurers are carefully tracking the experience of their sales and underwriting personnel. If the experience falls outside the norm, it is common to place restrictions on further sales or more severe limitations on underwriting; alternatively, the activities of these sales agents and underwriters could be subject to greater oversight.

Perhaps the area of greatest concern in the area of actuarial risk is the misalignment of incentives between owners of the insurance firm and its sales and marketing staff. Much can be done to improve it. The typical arrangement is to pay commissions for sales of new policies, with the commissions on a multiperiod contract heavily front-loaded, particularly for life/health products. This creates a tremendous incentive for agents to sell as much business as possible, whether it is profitable for the company or not. It also creates strong incentives to replace existing policies, whose commission rates have dwindled to the low single digit percentage range, with new policies that pay commissions ranging from 20 to 100% of first year premiums. Sales managers and marketing personnel are also often rewarded based on volume of sales. Even senior management may sometimes have their compensation tied to sales growth.

Experience has shown that rapid growth is one of the factors most commonly associated with insolvency. It is useful to remember here that what is growing most rapidly is the accumulation of liabilities, not assets. One way to foster rapid growth is to underprice liabilities. Employees and agents whose compensation is tied to sales growth are therefore strong proponents of more "competitively-priced" insurance policies. Senior management often comes from a sales background, and is sympathetic with the notion that what is good for the insurance agents is good for the company. Pricing actuaries, who are supposed to be the watchmen and gate keepers in this area, are often placed under tremendous pressure to alter their assumptions so that the company's products can be priced more competitively. Of course, over time it will become apparent if the insurance policies are mispriced, but that is weighed against the immediate benefits of higher commission earnings and growth.

The sales side has one powerful club in this battle for determining policy prices. Sales agents often work for a number of insurers and can shift new business toward them. Worse, they can take existing business away from the firm, before it breaks even from heavy initial policy costs, and direct it elsewhere if they can demonstrate satisfactorily that policy illustrations or prices appear to be more favorable elsewhere. Many firms in the insurance industry are well aware of this misalignment of interests, yet feel thwarted by regulations about commission schedules.

In the long run, of course, insurers offering non-economic policies will go bankrupt. But the long run can take a long time to arrive; hence, the insurer who is trying to rationally price its policies faces a quandary. Does it succumb to the uneconomic pricing temporarily and hope to survive beyond the irrational players, and then restore sensible pricing, or does it choose to write very little current business and lose its distribution force? Neither choice is an attractive alternative.

Systematic Risk

Systematic Risk of Liabilities

No area in financial risk management of insurance has evolved as much as the analysis of systematic risk of liabilities during the past decade. This is, in large measure, due to the fact that insurers feel an increased sense of urgency in applying the tools of asset/liability management to measure and manage interest rate risk. We note that the two most recent Goldman Sachs surveys of life insurance Chief Investment Officers ranked asset/liability management (ALM) at the top of the list of their concerns, whereas the topic did not surface in the top four rankings in their earlier surveys. Property/liability companies are also giving greater attention to the area.

The increased importance given to ALM was echoed in the 1995 and 1996 surveys of Lamm-Tennant, who found it near the top of the factors that influence investment policy. Her findings are notable because they combine the results of both life/health and property/casualty insurers, and cover companies that are much smaller than those in the Goldman Sachs surveys. When contrasted with the earlier surveys of Babbel and Lamm-Tennant,[38] Babbel and Klock,[39] Lamm-Tennant,[40] and Bouyoucos and Siegel,[41] the increased importance of interest rate risk and ALM during the past few years is remarkable. All of the life/health and property/liability insurers we interviewed perceived this source of risk to be crucial to understand, measure and manage. However, the insurers we interviewed ran the gamut from naive to very sophisticated when it came to measuring interest rate risk.

On the liability side of the balance sheet, most of the life insurers were using PTS software developed by Chalke, Inc. to measure the effective duration and convexity of their liabilities.[42] The others were using TAS from Tillinghast, or some internally developed software. Most of the life insurers who were using the

---

[38] D. F. Babbel and J. Lamm-Tennant, "Trends in Asset/Liability Management for Life Insurers," *Insurance Perspectives,* Goldman Sachs (November 1987).

[39] D. F. Babbel and D. R. Klock, "Insurance Pedagogy: Executive Opinions and Priorities," *Journal of Risk and Insurance* (December 1988).

[40] J. Lamm-Tennant, "Asset/Liability Management for the Life Insurer: Situation Analysis and Strategy Formulation," *Journal of Risk and Insurance* (September 1989).

[41] P. J. Bouyoucos and M. H. Siegel, "The Goldman Sachs Insurer CIO Survey," *Industry Resource Group* (October 1992).

[42] Measures of interest rate sensitivity which take into account the interest-sensitive cash flows of an asset or liability stream are referred to as "effective duration and convexity," or alternatively, "option-adjusted duration and convexity." Measures of interest rate sensitivity which assume all cash flows are fixed, or at least insensitive to movements in interest rates, include "modified duration and convexity" and "Macaulay duration."

commercially available software packages had implemented some of their own customized enhancements to meet better their needs, capabilities, focus and concerns.

The use of effective duration and convexity measures represents a quantum leap from what the practice was only a few years earlier. Prior to 1992, virtually none of the insurers had access to a commercially available software package that could compute measures of effective duration and convexity for their liabilities. Even the PTS, TAS (formerly CALMS) and Milliman and Robertson software packages available at that time would not produce measures of effective duration and convexity. Rather, the duration numbers, in those cases where they were produced, were simple modified or Macaulay measures, which assume that all cash flows are fixed. Yet, liabilities are virtually all interest sensitive to some degree. They produce errors so large as to lead to reckless investment decisions, while imbuing such decisions with a veneer of analytical and quantitative credibility.[43] Back then, insurers who were concerned about interest rate risk relied heavily upon simulations. Indeed, duration estimations were considered so primitive that they were generally eschewed in favor of simulations, and rightfully so in our opinion. This is because many of the duration estimates that we saw then did not fully incorporate the interest rate sensitivity of cash flows for either assets or liabilities.

Today, convexity measures are also produced by the PTS software that is most commonly used. We found that insurers placed less confidence in the convexity numbers produced than in the duration numbers. This is because convexity numbers are much more sensitive to lapse assumptions than are duration numbers; while a misspecification of the interest rate sensitivity of lapses and other options can cause a large error in effective duration estimates, it will cause an even greater error in the estimates of convexity. Most insurers feel that they do not have enough reliable data on which to specify the relation of lapses and policy surrenders to interest rate movements. The lack of confidence they have in this crucial input to convexity estimates translates into a lack of confidence in the convexity estimates themselves. However, most companies did pay some attention to convexity estimates, but placed wide ranges around those estimates. The most common way to grasp the impact of convexity was in toggling the lapse/surrender sensitivity parameters in numerous simulations. The standard among the companies we interviewed was to perform simulations of between 500 and 10,000 paths to capture the impact of changing interest rate levels on policy lapses/surrenders.

While life insurers have more interest than confidence in the convexity estimates, they have progressed a long way over the past few years. Prior to 1992, the commercially available software did not even produce convexity estimates for life insurance liabilities. Instead, firms relied almost entirely on simulations. Many

---

[43] For example, we estimated the duration on a block of participating whole life policies for one mutual company. Its Macaulay duration was around 22 years, while its effective duration was approximately 5.6. See J. Lamm-Tennant, "Asset/Liability Management for the Life Insurer: Situation Analysis and Strategy Formulation," for a revealing survey of the level of sophistication in understanding and applying duration and Chapter 17 by David Babbel for a discussion of the pitfalls in using the older duration measures.

firms used only the seven highly artificial scenarios required of New York's Regulation 126. Prior to its passage, some insurers did not use the simulation method at all. Rather, they relied simply on their "best point estimates" and static lapse assumptions. Even today, there are insurers who use nothing more than the seven scenarios required under Regulation 126 to assess their exposure to interest rate risk.

The property/casualty insurers with whom we spoke had less concern about interest rate risk than their life/health counterparts. Nonetheless, they manifested greater understanding of the problem than a few years earlier. All of them were well aware of the importance of measuring duration of assets, producing in-house estimates of duration, or acquiring them from outside vendors, for most of their fixed income assets. More problematic was the estimation of duration for their real estate and equity portfolios. However, an analysis of the duration of their liabilities was generally missing. They had a notion that the duration was relatively short — perhaps a couple of years or so — but no more specific information.[44] Convexity was even less of a concern for these property/casualty insurers. Nonetheless, there appears to be at least some interest rate sensitivity in the payments made to satisfy property/casualty claims. For example, it is well known that workers' compensation claims tend to increase during periods of unemployment, as fraudulent claims seem to be filed with greater frequency. Similarly, fires and arson tend to occur with greater frequency when insured values exceed market values. To the extent that these and other situations are linked to interest rate levels, it can be supposed that some property/ casualty liabilities are interest sensitive. Available evidence on this front is scant, however.[45] Where the sensitivity is measurable, it tends to be more closely linked to inflation than to nominal interest rates. Therefore, the influence of inflation on their liabilities was deemed more important.

It would be fair to say that most property/casualty insurers paid little attention to the duration of their liabilities. It is generally thought that interest rate risk accounts for only a small portion of the change in the value of liabilities over time, and that other risks, such as actuarial risk, price regulation, legal risk, underwriting risk, inflation risk, and event or catastrophe risk swamp the influence of interest rate movements on the pricing and valuation of property and casualty insurance liabilities.

Systematic Risk of Assets
Insurers are concerned with interest rate risk more than other systematic risk factors, and rightly so. Over the past two decades, it has been the source of much of the fluctuation in the value of fixed income assets, which constitute the majority

---

[44] See D. F. Babbel and D. R. Klock, "Measuring the Interest Rate Sensitivity of Property/Casualty Insurer Liabilities," in S. G. Gustavson and S. E. Harrington (eds.), *Insurance, Risk Management, and Public Policy* (Boston: Kluwer Press, 1993).

[45] See J. H. Choi, "Estimating Market Value of Loss Payments of Property/Liability Insurance Companies Using Modern Valuation Technology," Working Paper, Wharton School, 1992.

of their assets. However, while it is the crucial systematic risk on the life insurance liability side, and of some importance for property/casualty liabilities as well, it is prominent but less dominating on the asset side of the balance sheet. This is because asset values are perceived to be affected not only by general interest rate levels, but also by basis risk, default risk, liquidity risk, call risk, prepayment risk, extension risk, sinking fund options, convertibility, real estate and equity risk. Yet, several of these risks are simply different manifestations of interest rate risk, making accurate measurement of paramount importance.

The measurement of interest rate risk on the asset side of the balance sheet is generally well done, although some insurers have a long way to go. Many insurers use the actuarial software mentioned earlier to estimate the durations and convexities of their investments. Some use software and pricing services like GAT and Bloomberg that are oriented strictly toward the asset side of the balance sheet. Several have developed their own, more sophisticated in-house programs for estimating values of both sides of the balance sheet. We noted that it was common to use more than a single source to assess the duration and convexity of assets. One stated reason for this was the divergence of opinion between the various programs and pricing services.

We did not encounter any property/casualty insurers who carefully measured the interest rate risk of both sides of their balance sheet. What was more common was for the focus to be on the interest rate risk of only the assets. Here the tools of duration and convexity measurement were applied, and insurers took steps to manage the overall exposure of their assets to interest rate risk and keep it within some targeted range. It was common for property/casualty insurers to use interest rate futures, swaps, and options to moderate this risk to acceptable levels. Options and futures were also used to hedge equity market risks, where the insurer maintained a large position in common stocks. The hedges were put in place, and then removed, as market conditions changed and the insurers' appetites for equity risk waxed and waned.

Asset/Liability Management

Asset/liability management typically did not go far beyond an assessment of the impact of interest rate movements on the value of the firm. Other systematic risks were usually dealt with in a more piecemeal fashion. The standard practice is to produce estimates of liability durations and convexities for each line of business, as well as for each asset class. These estimates are then weighted by the fair value of liabilities, or market value of assets, to arrive at overall asset and liability duration and convexity estimates. After factoring in leverage, the insurers are able to obtain measures of surplus duration and convexity. Examples of product level and firm level analyses are given in Exhibits 3 and 4.

The frequency for providing analysis of interest rate risk varies widely. Some firms provided weekly summaries of their asset durations and convexities, and monthly or quarterly summaries of their liabilities. In the case of interest rate futures and options, reports were more frequent, owing to their tremendous impact on overall interest rate risk. Some firms assessed their liability interest rate risks only on an annual basis, and among the property/casualty companies, liability durations were often not measured at all, nor was the interest rate sensitivity taken into account in liability simulations.

Many companies coupled this kind of analysis with one that shows the distribution of the future market value, or more typically, book value of surplus, based on hundreds of scenarios. An example is provided in Exhibit 5. This approach is conceptually fine, although we caution that when looking at distant future values of surplus, the values produced are extremely sensitive to slight variations in assumed yield spreads, which can get compounded for 30 years, and often are overly optimistic. Rarely are these approaches implemented with sufficient skill to account for the various correlations and patterns that can be observed in practice.

Exhibit 3: Option Adjusted Duration/Convexity
Life Product XX

	Assets			Liabilities			Surplus		
Int. Rate Shift (b.p.)	Option-Adjusted Value	Effective Duration	Convexity	Option-Adjusted Value	Effective Duration	Convexity	Option-Adjusted Value	Effective Duration	Convexity
−200	1,600	2.9	N/A	1,545	4.1	N/A	55	−30.8	N/A
−150	1,500	3.0	−66	1,405	2.9	60	95	4.5	−3,000
−100	1,400	3.1	−85	1,330	2.1	450	70	22.1	−25
−50	1,300	3.3	−176	1,243	1.8	700	57	36.0	−125
0	1,200	3.5	−190	1,151	1.5	680	49	50.5	−10,000
50	1,100	3.8	−121	1,061	1.4	390	39	69.1	−8,555
100	1,000	4.2	−50	975	1.2	85	25	121.2	−6,000
150	900	5.0	0	901	1.1	20	−1	−3,508.9	100
200	800	5.9	N/A	845	1.0	N/A	−45	−86.1	N/A

Exhibit 4: XYZ Insurance Company
Surplus Duration Analysis

Asset Class	Market Value	Effective Duration	Liabilities	Fair Value	Effective Duration	Economic Surplus	Effective Duration
Bonds	10,000,000	6.5	SPDA 1	8,500,000	3.2		
Mortgage-Backed Securities	5,000,000	4.2	SPDA 2	4,000,000	2.0		
Preferred Stock	200,000	8.1	Universal Life	400,000	7.9		
Common Stock	3,000,000	2.1	Term Life	300,000	1.3		
Mortgage Loans	6,000,000	5.7	Whole Life	12,000,000	6.8		
Equity Real Estate	2,000,000	1.0	Endowment	500,000	8.5		
Short-Term & Cash	1,500,000	0.8					
Totals	27,700,000	4.74		25,700,000	4.85	2,000,000	3.36

Exhibit 5: Distribution of Surplus Accumulation
Results of 99 Random Samples

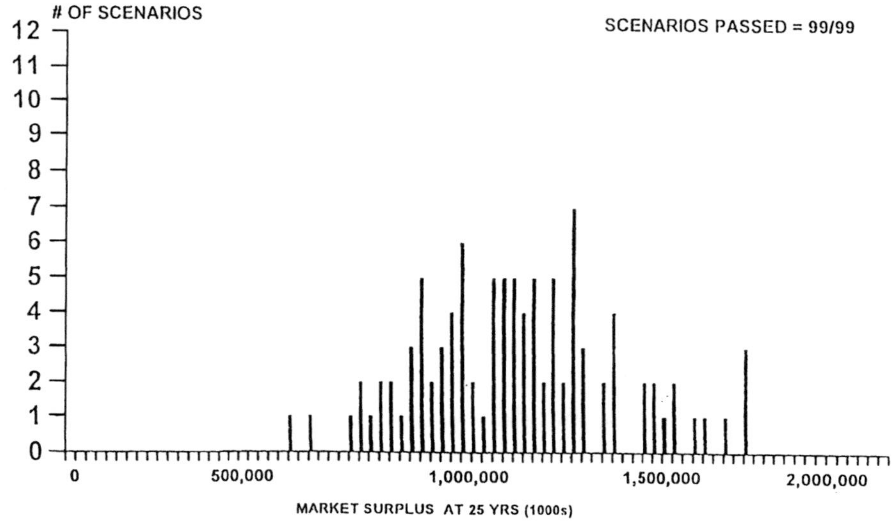

OF SCENARIOS   SCENARIOS PASSED = 99/99

MARKET SURPLUS AT 25 YRS (1000s)

Although many firms use the same general frameworks for analysis, when it comes to implementation we begin to see divergence in the quality of inputs and practice. By relying on a number of outside sources to provide the estimates of interest rate sensitivity for assets and liabilities, a number of insurers have injected another risk into the mix: divergent technologies and assumptions. We believe that for the purposes of asset/liability management, it is a misdirected effort to obtain the most credible measures of interest sensitivity of certain assets or liabilities. It is far more important to get measures of interest rate sensitivity that are calibrated similarly. After all, the absolute values are of less importance here than their relative values and the implication these have for the volatility of equity.

We saw a number of practices that invite problems. One prominent insurer used effective duration and convexity estimates for the liability side of the balance sheet, and modified Macaulay duration measures for the asset side. Another insurer did exactly the opposite. Some insurers base their aggregate duration and convexity numbers on book value weights, rather than market value weights. More than one insurer was frustrated that their actuarial departments relied entirely on simulations and provided no duration or convexity measures whatsoever. The actuarial scenarios run were based on completely random interest rate paths, inconsistent with any financial theory or history of interest rates. Several insurers relied on liability duration estimates based on only one interest rate factor, but on asset duration estimates based on two factors. Some insurers used duration measures for corporate bonds and mortgage-backed securities supplied by Wall Street that were based on different volatility parameters and processes than those used for other asset and liability categories. Some estimates were based on lattice models, while others were based on simulation models, or simulating through lattices. Only one insurer we know of is attempting to correct the duration measures on corporate bonds for the basis risk between corporate and government bonds.[46] Some insurers took the basis risk between movements in long-term versus short-term interest rates into account, but many did not. Some took into account all kinds of potential twists in the yield curve, while others allowed only for parallel shifts.

In setting limits on the amount of systematic risk the company desires to retain, a common approach is the one used by a leading multi-line insurer. The company places limits on its desired portfolio structure to reflect the variety of risks to which it is exposed. Limits are set on individual asset holdings, on industry concentration, and on asset type including mortgage-backed securities and collateralized mortgage obligations, all in a risk-based capital context. However, nowhere did we observe a methodology to derive such limits, or even a standardized approach across business lines.

For the balance sheet as a whole, limits are employed in two different ways. One approach is to impose a limit on the amount of duration mismatch allowed, either for particular product lines or for aggregating across all assets and liabilities. For instance, one company applies these restrictions on a product segmentation basis, allowing up to a year duration mismatch on participating whole life products, but only 1/10 of a year on GICs. Another company does not place restrictions on duration mismatches on a product by product basis, but on an aggregate portfolio basis. In our view, although most companies we interviewed used some sort of product segmentation approach, it is not necessary to do so. The advantage of a segmentation approach is the discipline it imposes on the pricing process, so that long term yields do not get used for pricing short term liabilities, and so forth. However, if this same discipline can be achieved in the pricing of insurance policies without a segmentation of assets into various product groupings, it seems that advantage would disappear. On the other hand, valuable resources would not be consumed in notionally dividing up the general account into the various segments, and it could be managed on an aggregate basis. This would avoid the costly duplication of efforts, where one product manager is selling an asset and another is buying the same or a similar asset, incurring transaction costs. Some firms simply transfer the assets between portfolio segments and use some sort of internal transfer pricing mechanism. Assets are acquired by the firm and then allocated to each product group according to perceived needs. This is done to foster a better sense of accountability and used in performance evaluation. But to reward a product group for producing net profits between liability costs and rates of return on assets which they had no responsibility in acquiring or divesting seems to be rewarding them for risks over which they had no control.

---

[46] For an explanation of the correction procedure, see D. F. Babbel, C. B. Merrill, and W. Panning, "Default Risk and the Effective Duration of Bonds," *Financial Analysts Journal* (January/February 1997).

While we appreciate the need for pricing discipline and control, we feel this could be achieved more simply and that the asset portfolios can be managed better on an aggregate basis.

The other limit is a restriction on the amount of scenarios that are allowed to reveal losses due to asset/liability mismatches. These limits are typically placed not only on the distribution of final simulated results, but also on the evolution of solvency over time associated with the simulations. One firm has almost no tolerance for scenarios showing negative profitability due to interest rate risk exposure. Because it is persuaded that interest rates are virtually impossible to forecast, and over which it has no control, it has decided to avoid interest rate risk of any kind, to the extent possible.

At the firm that decided to avoid as completely as possible interest rate risk, portfolio managers are not rewarded in any way for taking interest rate risk and trying to "time" the market. Indeed, their job could be lost if they stray outside narrow boundaries. Some firms purport to eschew interest rate risk, yet reward their investment department personnel if they achieve investment income or total rates of return above some benchmark level. By measuring only periodically the interest rate risk of assets, this invites the portfolio managers to "game" the system and attempt to improve their returns by incurring interest rate risk for brief periods of time. Some firms have duration targets but ignore convexity, leading portfolio managers to try barbell, ladder, or bullet maturity approaches to achieve higher investment income, depending on the shape of the term structure.

But by in large, the major difference between investment practices that we saw during this study, compared to what was occurring less than a decade ago, was that there was far less emphasis on yield and more on total rate of return. As recently as five years ago a survey of the American Council of Life Insurance revealed that two-thirds of chief investment officers did not even consider total rate of return as an investment objective. Yield was the primary focus. This was an impediment to effective asset/liability management but is beginning to dwindle. Nonetheless, we observed more concern with book yield than we feel is appropriate, given its lack of importance to the true economic performance of the firm.

Credit Risk

In addition to the credit risk that reveals itself as basis risk in the systematic risk factors listed above, there is also the risk of default on significant firm investments. While it may be idiosyncratic risk to the market as a whole, it is not idiosyncratic risk to the insurer maintaining a significant position in an asset that goes into default.

Insurance firms are generally very focused on credit risk, as are rating agencies and regulatory authorities. They produce weekly and monthly reports that monitor the credit risk of their assets. They rely on outside rating agencies, such as Moody's, Standard and Poor's, Duff & Phelps, and Dunn and Bradstreet. In addition, virtually all of their investments are assigned credit ratings by the Securities Valuation Office of the National Association of Insurance Commissioners, which are used for statutory reporting purposes. These ratings are not always viewed as sufficient measures of credit risk for those insurers who feel that absorbing credit risk is an important part of their franchise. Many insurers have their own due diligence requirements to meet before they will take on an investment that has credit risk. They undertake internal credit risk ratings, in some ways quite similar to those of Moody's or Standard and Poor's, although with different weightings on the risk factors. Moreover, they are prone to update their internal credit risk ratings promptly as important information bearing on the creditworthiness of a major investment position is revealed.

Insurers produce "Watch Lists" of firms they feel are in financial jeopardy, likely to be downgraded or become insolvent. They often have a dual track credit risk assessment, one for the asset itself, and another for the underlying collateral. They place limits on the portfolio exposure by industry, by geographic region, by business (e.g., real estate prohibited), and by company. They also have lists of approved counterparties for brokerage, settlement and swaps.

In Exhibits 6 and 7 we provide an example of one set of investment guidelines, with general and specific authorizations and limits that we feel are representative of the industry. However, there is substantial variation in the practices that we have seen. Perhaps the poorest approach we saw was a firm that used Moody's ratings, and assigned numerical values to each rating class. For instance, 1.0 was assigned to a rating of Aaa, 2.0 was assigned to Aa, 3.0 to A, 4.0 to Baa, 5.0 to Ba, 6.0 to B, 7.0 to Caa, 8.0 to Ca, 9.0 to C, and 10 to D. Adjustments are made to accommodate the modifiers of 1, 2, and 3 that Moody's often uses to designate relative quality within a ranking class. The company then has a target number of 3.0 to achieve in its overall credit risk plan. One problem with this approach, which they recognize, is that default rates and volatility of default rates do not grow linearly as rating is decreased step by step. Coupled with an incentive structure that rewards portfolio managers for the investment yields they book, this system leads to a credit barbell approach, as shown in Exhibit 8, because the portfolio manager can achieve superior yields by doing so.

The best approach we saw included a more refined ranking of credit risk, not by letter but by default probability coupled with standard deviation of defaults for each ranking. Covariance of asset returns was also taken into account, and the entire credit risk problem was cast in a surplus oriented mean-variance model. Diversification guidelines were incorporated through constraints on the optimization. Liquidity risk was reflected by reducing the expected returns by a number of basis points that was deemed appropriate from historical experience.

Liquidity Risk

Although insurance companies are faced with liquidity risk, most of the insurers we interviewed had little concern for it. Only one was concerned about having too little liquidity, and one was concerned about having too much liquidity. The others did not seem to be concerned, believing their situation to be well managed.

Exhibit 6: Investment Guidelines

General Authorizations

These general authorizations are to remain in effect until January 1997 unless modified or canceled.

The total investment in any one credit (total of bonds, preferred stock, convertible securities and common stock) is limited to 1% of net admitted assets, with the exception of direct U.S. Treasury and full faith and credit obligations and U.S. government-sponsored enterprise obligations, as further specified below.

The following authorizations specify which transactions the Investment Officers of the Company are authorized to conduct that their discretion.

Fixed Income Securities — Non Convertible*

A. Purchase U.S. Treasury and full faith and credit obligations in unlimited amounts.

B. Purchase U.S. Government sponsored enterprise obligations. Such purchases to be limited to 3% of net admitted assets per government sponsored enterprise, and an aggregate limitation of 10% of net admitted assets.

C. Purchase corporate bonds, or municipal bonds, or Canadian or other foreign bonds but only those denominated in U.S. dollars which are rated in the Baa category or better; purchase private placement issues rated in the Baa category or better, or its equivalent. (Equivalent rating to be the Investment Officer's judgment where an external rating is not available.)

D. Purchase mortgage-backed securities and collateralized mortgage obligations consistent with Investment Committee limitations and the Specific Authorizations.

E. Purchase asset-backed securities consistent with Investment Committee limitations and the Specific Authorizations.

F. Purchase preferred stocks of companies whose bonds or preferred stocks are rated in the Baa category or better, or its equivalent. (Equivalent rating to be the Investment Officer's judgment where an external rating is not available.)

G. New issues rated in the Baa category or better may be purchased up to 33 1/3% in excess of the amounts authorized, either at the issue or the market price.

Short Term Fixed Income

H. Purchase commercial paper (with maturities not exceeding 270 days), certificates of deposit or bankers acceptances which are rated wither A-1 or better by Standard & Poor's or P-1 by Moody's. Such purchases to be limited to 1% of net admitted assets per credit.

Repurchase Agreements

I. Repurchase agreements may be purchased with banks or security dealers as designated in the Specific Authorizations if they have all of the following characteristics: at least 102% of principal and interest collateralized by U.S. Treasury or Agency obligations; for periods not exceeding 60 days; and, all collateral not to exceed 5 years in maturity.
Total amount outstanding to be limited overall to 5% of net admitted assets and with any one counter party to 2% of net admitted assets.

* "Baa category should be interpreted to mean having a rating no lower than either Baa3 (by Moody's) or BBB- (by Standard & Poor's).

Exhibit 6 (Continued)

Reverse Repurchase Agreements

J. Reverse repurchase agreements may be transacted with banks or security dealers as designated in the Specific Authorizations.

Total amount outstanding to be limited to 5% of net admitted assets and per counter party to 2% of net admitted assets.

Dollar Rolls

K. Enter into dollar roll transactions with banks or security dealers designated in the Specific Authorizations.

Total amount outstanding to be limited to 5% of net admitted assets and per counter party to 2% of net admitted assets.

Other

L. Enter into CMO residual commitments as specified in the Specific Authorizations.

M. Use financial futures contracts and interest rate options (exchange traded and over-the-counter) to reduce interest rate risk exposure.

N. Sell securities held in the portfolio. Any purchaser or transfer agent of such a security need not inquire into the authority for such sale upon the Secretary's certification that it is made under this subdivision "N".

Convertible Securities**

O. Under the limits specified for non convertible bonds, purchase convertible bonds of companies with issues rated in the Baa category or better, or of companies with lower or non rated issues according to the following schedule:

Moody's (or S&P) Rating	Authorized Limit per Issuer as Percentage of the Convertible Portfolio
Ba1 (BB+) to Ba3 (BB-)	2.0%
B1 (B+) to B3 (B-)	1.0%
No Rating	1.0%
Caa (CCC+) to C (D)	0.5%

Purchases must not cause the aggregate statement value of convertible debt rated less than 2 by the NAIC to exceed the following percentages of the convertible debt portfolio:

NAIC Rating	Restrictions
3 3Z 6 6Z	60.0%
4 4Z 6 6Z	40.0%
5 5Z 6 6Z	7.5%
6 6Z	2.5%

P. Purchase of medium or lower grade bonds must not cause the aggregate statement value of bonds, including convertible debt, rated less than 2 by the NAIC to exceed the following percentages of net admitted assets:

NAIC Rating	Restrictions
3 3Z 6 6Z	10.0%
4 4Z 6 6Z	5.0%
5 5Z 6 6Z	3.0%
6 6Z	1.0%

** At market value: includes debentures and preferreds.

Exhibit 6 (Continued)

Q. No more than 25% of the portfolio's bonds rated less than 2 by the NAIC can be obligations of companies within a single industry nor should these issues in aggregate be imprudently weighted with companies that only conduct business within one narrow geographic region. The duration of these issues as a group should be viewed in the context of the total bond portfolio, and be governed under the overall investment strategy regarding duration.

R. Purchase convertible preferred stocks under the limits specified for non convertible preferred stocks of companies with issues rated in the Baa category or better, or of companies with lower or non rated issues according to the following schedule:

Moody's (or S&P Rating	Authorized Limit per Issuer as Percentage of the Convertible Portfolio
Ba1 (BB+) to Ba3 (BB-)	2.0%
B1 (B+) to B3 (B-)	1.0%
No Rating	1.0%
Caa (CCC+) to C (D)	0.5%

Common Stock

S. The Investment Officers are authorized to purchase common stocks of any United States or Canadian corporation or any foreign corporation whose shares are included in the S&P Common Stock Index in amounts consistent with the Investment Policy Statements as approved by the Committee subject to these additional restrictions. Specifically, the Investment Officers may not:

1. Invest in the equity securities of closed end funds, investment companies, limited partnerships or real estate investment trusts without specific authorizations

2. Make any purchase of common stock which would result in more than 5% of the value of the common stock portfolio being invested in the securities of one issuer

3. Purchase a common stock if as a result thereof more than 25% of the assets of the common stock portfolio will be invested in a particular industry

4. Purchase a common stock if as a result more than the authorized limit of the assets of the common stock portfolio will be invested in common stock of that particular issuer. The authorized limit per issuer will be a function of the issuer's common stock market capitalization in accordance with the following schedule:

Market Capitalization of Issuer of Common Stock	Authorized Limit per Issuer as % of the overall Common Stock Portfolio
$0-$25 million	0%
$26-$50 million	0.25%
$5 -$100 million	0.50%
$101-$200 million	1.00%
$201-$500 million	2.00%
$501-$1,000 million	3.00%
$1,001-$2,000 million	4.00%
more than $2,000 million	5.00%

Furthermore, the Investment Officers will make a quarterly presentation to the Investment Committee on the performance of the common stock portfolio and its risk characteristics in relation to appropriate benchmarks.

Exhibit 6 (Continued)

T. The Investment Officers are authorized to use stock index futures and options contracts (exchange traded and over-the-counter) to reduce stock market risk exposure.

Real Estate/Commercial Mortgages

U. The Investment Officers are authorized to:

1. *Commercial Mortgages*
Consummate transactions for the purchase, sale, exchange and disposition of real estate loans, up to $2.5 million with the approval of any three of the following officers of the Company:

Chairman of the Board, President, Chief Investment Officer and Senior Real Estate Investment Officer.

All transactions completed under this authority will be reported to the Real Estate Subcommittee of the Investment Committee of the Board of Directors

2. *Real Estate Equity*
Consummate transactions for the purchase, sale, exchange and disposition of real estate equities up to $2.5 million without leverage, with the approval of any three of the following officers of the Company:

Chairman of the Board, President, Chief Investment Officer and Senior Real Estate Investment Officer.

All transactions completed under this authority will be reported to the Real Estate Subcommittee of the Investment Committee of the Board of Directors.

Note:
The credit quality ratings provided by the NAIC have approximate correspondence to the Moody's and Standard & Poor's ratings as given in the table below:

NAIC Designation	Moody's Rating	S&P Rating
1, 1Z	Aaa, Aa, A	AAA, AA, A
2, 2Z	Baa	BBB
3, 3Z	Ba	BB
4, 4Z	B	B
5, 5Z	Caa, Ca, C	CCC, CC, C
6, 6Z	Caa, Ca, C, D	CCC, CC, C, D

Exhibit 7: Investment Guidelines
Specific Authorizations

The following specific authorizations for the purchase of securities to be executed at the discretion of the Officers of the Company were renewed by the Committee:

1. Bonds
   None
2. *Common Stocks*
   a. *Domestic*
      None

	Authorization Percent
b. *Foreign Companies*	
DeBeers Consolidated Mines (ADR)	1.0%
Sea Containers Ltd.	1.0%

3. *Convertible Subordinated Debentures*
   None
4. *Convertible Preferred Stock*
   Sea Containers Ltd.   1.0%
5. *Short Term Investments*
   None
6. Repurchase Agreements, Reverse Repurchase Agreements and Dollar Roll Transactions
   Banks and security dealers authorized for repurchase agreements and reverse repurchase agreements and dollar roll transactions are as follows:

   Barclays de Zoete Wedd Securities Inc.
   Bear Stearns Companies, Inc.
   Chase Securities Inc.
   Chemical Securities Inc.
   Citicorp Securities Inc.
   CS First Boston Corporation
   Donaldson, Lufkin & Jenrette Securities Corporation
   Goldman, Sachs & Co.
   J. P. Morgan Securities Inc.
   Lehman Brothers Inc.
   Merrill Lynch & Co. Inc.
   Morgan Stanley Group, Inc.
   Nomura Securities Co. Ltd.
   Paine Webber Inc.
   Salomon Brothers Inc.
   State Street Bank & Trust Company

7. *Hedging Transactions*
   A. *The following officers of the Investment Department are hereby authorized to execute hedging transactions in accordance with the guidelines:*
      Executive Vice President & Chief Investment Officer
      Senior Vice President, Vice President, and Second Vice President, Equity Securities
      Senior Vice President, Vice President, and Second Vice President, Fixed Income
      Assistant Vice President, Equity Trader

Exhibit 7 (Continued)

B. *The following banks and brokerage firms are hereby approved for the establishment of futures trading accounts:*
Bear Stearns Companies, Inc.
Citicorp Securities, Inc.
CS First Boston Corporation
Goldman, Sachs & Co.
Merrill Lynch & Co., Inc.

C. *Maximum amount which may be hedged is 5% of admitted assets.*

8. *Residual Commitments*
As approved by paragraph L of the General Authorization, the maximum amount of CMO Residual commitments is limited to $100 million.

9. Mortgage-Backed Securities Commitments
In the aggregate, the maximum amount of FHLMC, FNMA, and whole loan commitments is limited to $750 million at book value.

10. Asset-Backed Securities
In the aggregate, the maximum amount of ABS is limited to $250 million at book value.

11. Short Term Borrowing
Up to a maximum amount of $100 million, such maximum amount not to exceed $50 million with any one bank or financial institution
To require the personal signature or veritable authorization of any two of the following officers:
Chairman of the Board or Chief Executive Officer
President
Executive Vice Presidents
Treasurer
Vice President, Financial Management & Control

Exhibit 8: Five-, 10-, 15-, and 20-Year Cumulative Default Rates: 1970-1995

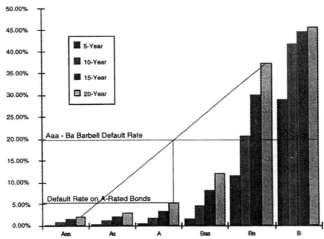

Liquidity is not as big a concern with many insurance firms as it is in other financial institutions for one good reason: most of their policies are less liquid than their assets. Life insurance companies issue policies that commonly feature high surrender charges. These charges are either explicitly stated, or implicit in the schedule of cash build-up. For example, a single premium deferred annuity, with annual crediting rate reset and a seven year maturity, may feature surrender charges beginning at 7%-10% during the first year, and declining in steps toward zero at maturity. Similarly, universal life and whole life products often have very low surrender values during the first year or two of a policy, and begin building up rapidly after that point. Other policies, such as variable universal life, have surrender provisions that act much like a mutual fund, where the amount received depends on the value of the underlying fund.

A decade or so ago, the problem of illiquidity was more pronounced. Policy surrenders for some companies approached a 60% rate, and massive amounts of policy loans were withdrawn. The industry has managed this problem in two ways. First, much of the new business written is sensitive to market rates of interest, so that there is not as wide a divergence between crediting rates on life policies and annuities versus market rates of interest. Thus, the incentive to surrender a policy is lessened. Second, policy loans are now offered mostly at variable rates that track market rates of interest, rather than the fixed policy loan rates of yore. An alternative to the variable rates charged on loans is a process known as "direct recognition," whereby the schedule of cash value build-up is altered if policy loans are incurred. The tax environment has also changed, and interest paid on policy loans is now no longer a deductible expense for tax purposes. Thus, the interest rate arbitrage incentive has virtually disappeared.

Not long ago, however, several well known life insurance companies, such as First Capital Life, Fidelity Bankers Life, Executive Life of California, Executive Life of New York, and Mutual Benefit experienced severe liquidity problems. But in each of these cases, there were other factors that precipitated a "run on the bank" phenomenon. The run in each case was caused, in part, by well publicized investment performance problems. In the case of the first four of the above mentioned companies, there were vast sums of policies in force with minimal, and even zero surrender charges. Some of the policies had been marketed through Wall Street brokerages, and were therefore of the "hot money" variety. Although the first four of these companies had large amounts of liquid assets, the withdrawal rates were so high that even these liquid resources were strained. Generally, however, life insurers are managed in such a way as to avoid these runs on the bank, either through policy design, sales channel, investment policy, or level of surplus.

Another problem that was more prevalent a decade ago was that all bonds were essentially reported at amortized book values. If a bond was sold prior to maturity, any capital gain or loss would need to be recognized. Many insurers, particularly during the early 1980s, could not afford to have the large capital losses appear on their books and impact their surplus. Today, however, a large portion of fixed income holdings are placed in accounts available for sale or trading, and are therefore already marked to market. Therefore, whether they are sold or not does not impact the reported values or the surplus as much.

On the property/casualty side of the business, the liquidity risk comes mostly from event risk or catastrophe risk. Most policies do not feature cash values that are easily accessible through surrender, although some policies will allow insureds to cancel prior to maturity and receive a portion of their premium. Moreover, the policies are typically very short term, renewable annually. With the relatively large surplus positions of most property/casualty insurers, most policyholders are willing to ride out a storm, knowing that renewal time will approach in just a few months.

In terms of the accounting policies of property/casualty companies, they tend to mark-to-market a larger portion of their fixed income securities than life companies, and also tend to hold more liquid, shorter term securities on average. Thus, their liquidity concerns almost always stem from event risk or catastrophe risk. They can avoid some of these risks by reinsuring portions of their books of business, and by broadly diversifying their risk portfolios geographically, by industry, and by type of risk. Alternatively, they can hold large amounts of liquid surplus assets. One leading property/casualty company attempts to keep enough surplus on hand to accommodate a "once in 500 years" event.

We provide some tables that are representative of the practice of liquidity risk measurement and management. The company defines liquidity risk as the risk of having inadequate net cash flows to meet expenses, benefits, withdrawals, and loan payments. It views product liquidity risk as the fluctuations in cash flows outside of the ranges that are expected. It first ranks assets by relative liquidity. It then projects its cash flows over a multiple year horizon on both sides of the balance sheet using a form like Exhibit 9. For those firms that maintain segmented accounts by product line, these liquidity reports are generated by product, as in the case of Exhibit 10.

Exhibit 9: Asset Liquidity Profile
(Ranking of liquid assets only, from most to least liquid)

Cash & Short Term*
Government and Government-Backed Securities
Investment Grade Public Bonds maturing in one year or less
Other Investment Grade Public Bonds
Private Placements in NAIC class 1 or 2 maturing in one year or less
Other Liquid Assets (see below)

Other Liquid Assets:

    Separate Account Assets
    Private Placements in NAIC Class 1 or 2 maturing in one to three years
    Private Placements in NAIC Class 1 or 2 maturing in three to five years
Public Unaffiliated Preferred Stock**
Public Unaffiliated Common Stock
Investment in Company Sponsored Mutual Funds

---

* Includes money market mutual funds, which are classified as Common Stock on th eStatutory Statements.
** Includes all Preferred Stock Schedule D Statement Value.

Exhibit 10: Liquidity Report
Life Product XXX Projected Cash Flows

Period	Asset Cash Flow	Liability Cash Flow	Net Cash Flow
1996			
1997			
1998			
1999			
2000			
2001			
2002			
2003			
2004			
2005			
2006			
2007			
2008			
2009			
2010			
2011			
2012			
2013			
2014			
2015			
2016			
2017			
2018			
2019			
2020			
2021			
2022			
2023			
2024			

A company's asset/liability committee is typically responsible for measuring and managing liquidity risk. Despite the lack of concern regarding this risk, there is still a large amount of analysis that is done to guard against illiquidity. In this regard, liquidity risk decisions are part of the analytics and scenario testing used by the company. In its investment plan, management of liquidity risk is two-fold. First, the company uses corporate and Regulation 126 modeling to measure net cash flow under various interest rate scenarios. Second, control is achieved by imposing constraints on investment. One such constraint includes ensuring that over 50% of the assets are held in "marketable securities."

Many companies use PTS for most of their analysis and stress testing. The scenario testing includes about 50-100 scenarios which shift the yield curve, both parallel and slope changes. For each path created by the scenario, net cash flows must be positive. Solvency of the company is also determined along each path. Reports are used for each product, and cash flows are projected out for about 30 years under each of the scenarios. By aggregating across products for each scenario, the company has an idea of the distribution of liquidity at the firm level. (See Exhibit 11.)

After all the scenario tests, the results have little impact on immediate decisions. For instance, if net cash flows were negative for a large portion of the stress tests, this would not imply that asset composition would change immediately. Suggestions would of course be made, but there is no guarantee that the portfolio would change immediately. Similarly, concentrations are not altered unless there are modifications to limits which would only occur quarterly or annually.

Exhibit 11: Relative Liquidity of Assets and Liabilities
Life Product XXX

LIABILITIES*

	Current Quarter	Prior Quarter -1	Prior Quarter -2	Prior Quarter -3
Level 1 Liquidity				
Level 2 Liquidity				
Level 3 Liquidity				
Level 4 Liquidity				
(Levels 1+2)÷Total				

*Liabilities are net of Policy Loans

ASSETS

	Current Quarter	Prior Quarter -1	Prior Quarter -2	Prior Quarter -3
Level 1 Liquidity				
Level 2 Liquidity				
Level 3 Liquidity				
Level 4 Liquidity				
(Levels 1+2)÷Total				

SUMMARY

	Current Quarter	Prior Quarter -1	Prior Quarter -2	Prior Quarter -3
Level 1 (Assets) ÷ Level 1 (Liabilities)				
Level 1 -2 (Assets) ÷ Level 1-2 (Liabilities) Guideline				
Level 1 -3 (Assets) ÷ Level 1-3 (Liabilities)				

NOTE:	Level 1	Level 2	Level 3	Level 4
Liabilities Surrender is at:	Book SChg<2%	Int Grnty Expires + Scheduled Ann Paymts, Next 12 months	Market; Market & SChg; Book, SChg>2%	Now Allowed
Assets	Cash, STI Inv Grade Bonds with aggregate market loss < IMR; Other	Mtg amort NII over Next 12 months	Inv Grade Bonds with aggregate market loss in excess of IMR	Mtg.; Below Inv Grade Bonds; Affil; VC: Other

In addition to running these scenario tests, there is also a "worst case scenario." This includes cash outflows of over 300% over a 2-3 year period and a lapse rate of 45%. For comparison, the highest lapse rate the company has ever experienced is 18% when it decided to decrease significantly dividends after a long history of either increasing or maintaining dividend payments.

There are no managers at the companies studied whose performance is based on the management of liquidity risk. Although it would be difficult to base everyday compensation on unlikely events, the company may benefit in the future from having a clearer line of responsibility with regard to liquidity management. The general procedure is that any ongoing problems with liquidity would be brought to the attention of the Chief Financial Officer. Any changes to the company's credit ratings which could potentially affect liquidity demands are very much a concern of the auditing group.

Other Risks Considered But Not Modeled

Beyond the basic four financial risks, viz., actuarial, systematic, credit and liquidity, insurers have a host of other concerns, as was indicated above. Some of these, like operating risk, are a natural outgrowth of their business and insurers employ standard risk avoidance techniques to mitigate them. Standard business judgment is used in this area to measure the costs and benefits of both risk reduction expenditures and system designs, as well as operational redundancy. While generally referred to as risk management, this activity is substantially different than the management of financial risk addressed here.

Yet there are still other risks, somewhat more amorphous, but no less important. In this latter category are legal, regulatory, reputational and environmental risk. In each of these risk areas substantial time and resources are devoted to protecting the firm's franchise value from erosion. As these risks are less amenable to *a priori* financial measurement, they are generally not addressed in any formal, structured way. However, they are not ignored at the senior management level of the insurance firm.

In passing from this topic it is worthwhile and timely to pause to consider one of the legal risks now encroaching upon the life industry. During the course of our interviews, a number of firms had been sued in the area of misrepresentation of insurance products by insurance agents. At the time of this writing, 44 class action lawsuits had been filed against firms for their so-called "vanishing premium" policies whose premiums did not vanish, as illustrated, owing to a prolonged decline in market interest rate levels. New class action lawsuits were being filed at the rate of one every three days. The damages claimed are staggering for some of the companies.

The manner in which insurers are responding to these lawsuits ranges from attempts to gain a quick and comprehensive settlement to attempts to have the arguments heard in court. Some insurers are merely biding their time to see how other firms fare in the struggle. But more interesting is how insurers are acting to avoid future problems stemming from alleged agent misrepresentation. One of the larger firms has established a department of compliance to train and monitor the behavior of its sales agents. All of its sales and promotional literature is undergoing careful scrutiny by the legal department.

Another firm has created an auditing division to oversee compliance from a central location, computerizing each transaction. Management is concerned with five components of compliance: customer satisfaction, new products, stable earnings, expansion capabilities, and corporate miscellaneous. They are building controls into the centralized computer system. Should an agent exceed the allotted number of address changes, disbursements, lapses, or sales, the computer will not process the policy until the auditing department has had a chance to investigate further. These stop measures are not announced to either the customer or the sales agent. The director of auditing indicated that the system is intended to prevent problems rather than react to them.

A compliance division has been introduced to complement the role of the internal audit group. This division is responsible for insuring the field force and also providing training to sales agents so they will better be able to represent the company's products. This division is currently sending out surveys to its customers to find out if they really understand the products they now hold. It is hoped that these measures will mitigate any class action suits in the future.

AREAS WHERE FURTHER WORK WILL IMPROVE METHODOLOGY

Thus far, the techniques used to measure, report, limit, and manage individual risks have been presented. In each of these cases, a process has been developed, or at least has evolved, to measure the risk considered, and techniques have been deployed to control each of them.

The insurance industry is clearly evolving to a higher level of risk management techniques and approaches than had been in place in the past. Yet, as this review indicates, there is significant room for improvement. Before the areas of potential value added are reviewed, however, it is worthwhile to reiterate an earlier point. The risk management techniques reviewed here are not the average, but the techniques used by firms at the higher end of the market. The risk management approaches at smaller institutions, as well as larger but relatively less sophisticated ones, are less precise and significantly less analytical. In some cases they would need substantial upgrading to reach the level reported here. Accordingly, our review should be viewed as a glimpse at best practice, not average practices. Nonetheless, the techniques employed by those that define the industry standard could use some improvement. By category, recommended areas where additional analytic work would be desirable are discussed below.

Actuarial Risk

There remains too much disagreement in the most fundamental area of actuarial science — namely, what discount rate or rates does one use to value insurance liabilities.[47] With such broad disagreement about what insurance is worth, or what it will cost the insurer, it is little wonder that we encounter difficulties when it comes to managing risk. On the bright side, it must be acknowledged that there is a flurry of activity taking place directed toward solving this conundrum. In our opinion, as the scope of what exactly is being valued is more carefully defined, there is a convergence in the estimates produced by the alternative valuation methods.[48]

During the past decade, tools have been developed that can take into account the interest rate sensitivity of policy cash flows. However, many insurers have not employed these tools. Among those who have, there is a severe problem with the data inputs that are necessary to produce useful output. Insurers have not tracked or organized their lapse, surrender and claims data in a manner that allows them to accurately model their interest rate sensitivity. While the models are capable of accommodating virtually any functional form of this behavior, including the effects of policy seasoning, channel of distribution, and so forth, little data exist to estimate the functional form. Of course, this was also the case with regard to the modeling of mortgage-backed securities prepayment a decade ago, but since that time data were collected and analyzed, allowing for the enlightened application of the valuation tools that we see today in that sector. We expect that the same will be true for insurers in a few more years.

Another area where we expect to see rapid improvement is in the versatility of the actuarial software and its speed. Currently, only single-factor stochastic models are being widely used. This results in output that is inconsistent with the other side of the balance sheet, where two or more factors are typically used. Moreover, the speed of processing is so slow that insurers make undesirable compromises when it comes to modeling their products fully. Emerging computer technology undoubtedly will remove this impediment to better policy pricing and risk analysis.

Systematic Risk

Tremendous progress has already been made over the past five years in this arena. Most of it has been directed toward interest rate risk management, which is appropriate given its importance to insurers. An important area for further development is the incorporation of basis risk and equity risk. Another important advance will be a consistent valuation methodology for both sides of the balance sheet.

While simulation studies have substantially improved over the past few years, the use of book value accounting measures and cash flow losses continues

---

[47] See I. T. Vanderhoof and E. I. Altman (eds), *The Fair Value of Insurance Liabilities* (Boston, MA: Kluwer Academic Publishers, 1998).

[48] See D. F. Babbel, "Financial Valuation of Insurance Liabilities," in *The Fair Value of Insurance Liabilities.*

to be problematic. Movements to improve this methodology will require increased emphasis on market-based accounting. Such a reporting mechanism must be employed on both sides of the balance sheet, however, not just the asset portfolio.

The simulations also need to incorporate the advances in dynamic hedging that are used in complex fixed income pricing models. As it stands, these simulations tend to be rather simplistic, and scenario testing is rather limited.

Credit Risk

The evaluation of credit rating continues to be an imprecise process. We note divergence between the NAIC ratings assigned to particular public and private placements versus the ratings assigned by the Wall Street ratings agencies. We should never expect to see a complete convergence here, as there is no single set of weights to apply to the risk factors across all industries and firms. However, we do expect to see less divergence over time, as more becomes known about the factors that lead to default.

We also expect to see more enlightened practices when it comes to aggregating credit risks. A sensible aggregation scheme would take into account default rates, default losses, and the shape of the distribution of losses across all ratings categories. In time we may even see a move toward market-based default measures, at least on publicly traded debt instruments. We anticipate that credit risks will soon be evaluated in a framework consistent with other financial risks. Some insurers are already moving in this direction.

Liquidity Risk

For the life companies, this seems to be the least of their major financial risks. Most companies are doing a satisfactory job of managing this risk. With the advent of mark-to-market accounting, the problems for liquidity caused by the fiction of book accounting will gradually subside. Most life insurers model this risk well. In the property/casualty sector, it remains a large risk. Crisis models need to be linked better to operational details. In addition, the usefulness of such exercises is limited by the realism of the environment considered.

If liquidity is to be managed, the price of illiquidity must be defined and built into illiquid positions. While this logic has been adopted by some institutions, this pricing of liquidity is not commonplace.

Risk Aggregation and Knowledge of Total Firm Exposure

The quest for an estimate of aggregate firm risk has been a stumbling block for the insurance industry. The extent of the differences across risks of different types is quite striking. Actuarial risk is carefully modeled, but reported at infrequent intervals. There is often a lack of follow-up to see whether, based on the insurer's experience, the actuarial assumptions have been appropriate. Systematic risk, particularly interest rate risk, is typically measured by life insurers on both sides of the balance sheet, and by property/casualty insurers at least on the asset side. Interest rate risk exposure is discerned using measures of effective duration and convexity, scenario simulations, or a combination of the two. For assets it may be reported as often as weekly or monthly, but for liabilities it is generally reported only quarterly or annually. The credit risk process is a qualitative review of the performance potential of different bonds and borrowers. It results in a rating, periodic re-evaluation at reasonable intervals through time, and on-going monitoring of various types or measures of exposure. Liquidity risk, on the other hand, more often than not, is dealt with as a planning exercise, although some reasonable work is done to analyze the effect of adverse events that affect the firm.

The analytical approaches that are subsumed in each of these analyses are complex, difficult and not easily communicated to non-specialists in the risk considered. The insurer, however, must select appropriate levels for each risk and select, or at least articulate, an appropriate level of risk for the organization as a whole. How can and is this achieved?

The simple answer is "not very well." Senior management often is presented with a myriad of reports on individual exposures, such as specific credits, and complex summaries of the individual risks, outlined above. The risks are not dimensioned in similar ways, and management's technical expertise to appreciate the true nature of both the risks themselves and the analyses conducted to illustrate the insurer's exposure to them is limited. Accordingly, over time, the managers of specific risks have gained increased authority and autonomy. In light of recent losses, however, things are beginning to change.

At the organizational level, overall risk management is being centralized into a Risk Management Committee, headed by someone designated as the Senior Risk Manager. The purpose of this institutional response is to empower one individual, or group, with the responsibility to evaluate overall firm-level risk, and determine the best interest of the company as a whole. At the same time, this group is holding line officers more accountable for the risks under their control, and the performance of the institution in that risk area. Activity and sales incentives are being replaced by performance compensation which is based, not on business volume, but on overall profitability.

At the analytical level, aggregate risk exposure is receiving increased scrutiny. To do so, however, requires the summation of the different types of risks outlined above. This is accomplished in two distinct, but related ways. In the first approach, risk is measured in terms of variability of outcome. Where possible, a frequency distribution of net returns is estimated, from historical data, and the standard deviation of this distribution is estimated. Capital is allocated to activities as a function of this risk or volatility measure. Then, the risky position is required to carry an expected rate of return on allocated capital, which compensates the firm for the associated incremental risk. By dimensioning all risk in terms of loss distributions, and allocating capital by the volatility of the proposed activity, risk is aggregated and priced in one and the same exercise.

The second approach is similar to the first, but depends less on a capital allocation scheme and more on cash flow or earnings effects of the implied risky position. This approach can be used to analyze total firm level risk in a similar manner to the first approach. Again, a frequency distribution of net returns from any one type of risk can be estimated from historical data. Extreme outcomes can then be estimated from the tail of the distribution. Either a worst case historical example is used for this purpose, or a three or four standard deviation outcome is considered. Given the downside outcome associated with any risk position, the firm restricts its exposure so that, in the worst case scenario, the insurer does not lose more than a certain percentage of its surplus or current income. Therefore, rather than moving from volatility of equity value through capital, this approach goes directly to the current earnings implications from a risky position. The approach, however, has two very obvious shortcomings. It is cash flow based, rather than market value driven; and it does not necessarily directly measure the total variability of potential outcomes through *a priori* distribution specification. Rather, it depends upon a subjectively pre-specified range of the risky environments to drive the worst-case scenario.

Both measures attempt to treat the issue of trade-offs among risks using a common methodology to transform the specific risks to firm-level exposure. In addition, both can examine the correlation of different risks and the extent to which they can, or should be viewed as offsetting. As a practical matter, however, only two of the insurers interviewed that were using these approaches viewed the array of risks as a standard portfolio problem. Rather, they separately evaluate each risk and aggregate total exposure by simple addition. As a result, much is lost in the aggregation. Perhaps over time this crucial issue will be addressed more widely.

The ability of insurance companies to estimate and manage firm level risk is a long way off. To reach this goal requires much more precision in the estimation and management of the individual risks within the firm. Aggregation only has meaning to the extent that the individual elements can be aggregated. This presumes that they are measured correctly, dimensioned in a similar manner, and incorporated in a unified framework of risk. When this is accomplished, risks of different types will be contrasted and compared, and trade offs will become possible. However, to achieve this requires a significant amount of work on the individual risks within the industry before any reasonable aggregation can transpire.

Chapter 2

Components of Insurance Firm Value, and the Present Value of Liabilities

David F. Babbel, Ph.D.
Professor of Insurance and Finance
The Wharton School
University of Pennsylvania

INTRODUCTION

In this chapter we discuss the relation between the market value of insurance company owners' equity and various components that contribute to that value. The effect of firm insolvency risk on each component of value is discussed in turn. One natural consequence of this analysis is a conceptual framework for estimating the value of insurance liabilities.

RISK AND THE COMPONENTS OF EQUITY VALUE

The market value of insurance company owners' equity is defined as the difference between the market value of assets and the market value of liabilities. For purposes of valuation, it is helpful to partition more finely the components of equity value. In this chapter, we will partition the value of insurance company owners' equity, or stock in the case of a stock company, into its four major components: franchise value, market value of tangible assets, present value of liabilities, and put option value. (See Exhibit 1.)

This chapter synthesizes and clarifies portions of four separate publications: D. Babbel, "Financial Valuation of Insurance Liabilities," in *Fair Value of Insurance Liabilities*, I. Vanderhoof and E. Altman, eds. (Kluwer Academic Publishers, 1998); "The Market Value of Insurance Liabilities," *North American Actuarial Journal* (October 1997); "A Perspective on Model Investment Laws for Insurers," *C.L.U. Journal* (September 1994); and D. Babbel and C. Merrill, "Economic Valuation Models for Insurers," *North American Actuarial Journal* (July 1998). The presentation in this chapter has benefited from helpful discussions with Arnold Dicke, Craig Merrill, Algis Remeza, and David Sandberg.

Exhibit 1: Market Value of Insurance Equity

Market Value of Equity = Market Value of Assets + Market Value of Liabilities

$$\text{Market Value of Equity} = \text{Franchise Value} + \text{Market Value of Tangible Assets} - \text{Present Value of Liabiliities} + \text{Put Option}$$

These components have the following elements. The franchise value stems from what economists call "economic rents." It is the present value of the "rents" that an insurer is expected to garner because it has scarce resources, scarce capital, charter value, licenses, a distribution network, personnel, reputation, and so forth. It includes renewal business.[1] Franchise value is dependent on firm insolvency risk. The less insolvency risk there is, the more likely the firm is to stay solvent long enough to capture all the available economic rents arising from its renewal business, its distribution network, its reputation, and so forth.

The next two of these components can be netted together, producing what we will call "net tangible value." This value is simply the market value of tangible assets, less the present value of liabilities.[2] This net tangible value is independent of what *kind* of assets an insurer has, but does depend on the *amount* of assets it holds. For instance, if the firm swaps Treasury securities worth $5 billion for junk bonds worth the same (but with higher coupons and/or face values), or swaps them for $5 billion worth of pork belly futures, the market value of tangible assets is the same. Similarly, the present value of the *promised* cash flows to insurance consumers remains the same (although the quality of the promise has changed — more will be said about this later). Therefore, the net tangible value of the firm at any given moment is unaltered by the kind of assets the firm holds. Moreover, it is completely independent of firm insolvency risk, although how this value evolves over time will depend on risk.

Put option value arises from the limited liability enjoyed by equityholders when their firm issues debt (i.e., insurance policies, the major debt of an insurance company). It is the value to equityholders of capturing the upside earnings while not incurring all the downside costs of default. The insolvency put option increases in value as the insurer takes on more risk. If the insurer faces minimal insolvency risk, there may be little benefit inuring to it from this component of value; but if it is a risky firm, the implicit insolvency put option may be of considerable value.

---

[1] It is reduced (usually slightly) by the present value of payments that the solvent insurer is expected to pay to state insurance insolvency guaranty programs, to the extent that these payments are not fully offset by state and federal tax reductions.

[2] Elsewhere this has been referred to as "liquidation value." However, because that expression is laden with connotations that are unhelpful in this context, we prefer to use the expression "net tangible value" here. In an actual liquidation, assets are sometimes unloaded at "fire sale" prices. This reduction in value may or may not be more than offset if the liquidator is able to extract favorable terms from assumption reinsurers, because the book of business transferred may still have some renewal value.

In what follows, we will use the more compact notation to represent the equations in Exhibit 1:

$$MV(E) = MV(A) - MV(L) \tag{1}$$

$$MV(E) = FV + MV(TA) - PV(L) + PO \tag{2}$$

At this point it is useful to pause and consider these juxtaposed equations. It is clear that the right-hand-sides of both equations must be equal to each other. It is equally clear that the market value of liabilities differs from the present value of liabilities unless the market value of assets is defined as the sum of the franchise value, market value of tangible assets, and put option (i.e., unless $MV(A) \equiv FV + MV(TA) + PO$).

But this broad definition of the market value of assets is not universally used and, therefore, neither is the associated equivalence of market value of liabilities with present value of liabilities. For instance, oftentimes people will think of the market value of liabilities as being the same thing as the market value of debt from an investor's point of view. Thus, if a bond that is subject to credit risk has been issued, its market value is reduced below that of an otherwise comparable default-free bond. Accordingly, the market value of liabilities is reduced when the debt becomes risky. This is ironic from an insurance regulatory perspective. If the insurer is likely to default on its insurance policies, it would suggest that the liabilities are worth less than they would be if they were secure. The riskier a firm is, the lower would be the market value of its liabilities. Therefore, were the insurer to report this market value of liabilities to regulators, the lower market value could suggest the insurer is in better financial health than if the insurer were to report a present value of liabilities that is not reduced by the prospect of insolvency.[3]

From a financial economics perspective, a firm issuing a default-prone bond has issued a combination of a default-free bond along with a default put option. The value of the bond is reduced by the value of the put. The investor is long a default-free bond and short a put.[4] The issuer is short a default-free bond and long a put. This put option would normally be on the asset side of an "economic balance sheet," although it appears nowhere on the typical accounting statement.

In Exhibit 2, each of these components of value is displayed separately as a function of firm insolvency risk. When these value elements are displayed together, as in Exhibit 3, we can see how the overall market value of the firm is related to its risk exposure. As the firm increases in insolvency risk, firm market value increases, and as it decreases in risk, again there is an increase in firm value.

---

[3] Executive Life Insurance Company of California, a $16 billion insurer which bet heavily on junk bonds until its demise in 1991, is an example of a company whose market value of liabilities (under this definition) would have been reduced far below the present value of its promised cash flows to policyholders.

[4] This notion was introduced by R. C. Merton, "On the Pricing of Corporate Debt: The Risk Structure of Interest Rates," *Journal of Finance* (May 1974), pp. 449-470, and "An Analytic Derivation of the Cost of Deposit Insurance and Loan Guarantees: An Application of Modern Option Pricing Theory," *Journal of Banking and Finance* (June 1977), pp. 3-11

This equity market value premium over net tangible value stems either from franchise value or from put option value, or from some combination of the two. This is not merely a theoretical construct. It has been accepted wisdom in the financial institutions literature for decades. Empirical research suggests the effect is pronounced in the case of insurance firms.[5] These insights will be helpful as we proceed to consider the valuation of insurance liabilities.

Exhibit 2: Insolvency Risk and the Components of Equity Value

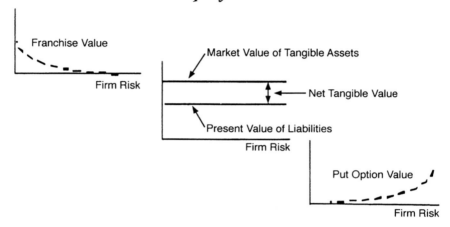

Exhibit 3: Components of Equity Value Combined

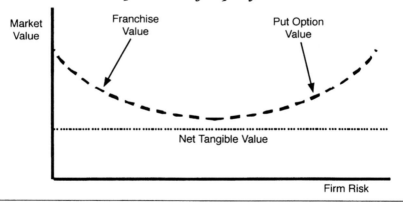

[5] D. Babbel and K. Staking, "The Market Reward for Insurers that Practice Asset/Liability Management," *Financial Institutions Research*, Goldman Sachs (November 1989); "It Pays to Practice A/L M," *Best's Review, Property/Casualty Edition* (May 1991); K. Staking and D. Babbel, "The Relation between Capital Structure, Interest Rate Sensitivity, and Market Value in the Property-Liability Insurance Industry," *Journal of Risk and Insurance* (December 1995); "Insurer Surplus Duration and Market Value Revisited," *Journal of Risk and Insurance* (March 1998).

THE VALUATION OF INSURANCE LIABILITIES

When it comes to the valuation of insurance liabilities, the driving intuition behind the two most common valuation approaches — arbitrage and comparables — fails us. This is because, for the vast majority of insurance liabilities, there are neither liquid markets where prices can be disciplined by the forces of arbitrage and continuous trading, nor are there close comparables in this market. We are left in a predicament, but not an impasse. If we can re-focus our attention from "market value" to "present value," progress can be made.

A useful question to begin our valuation of liabilities is: "How much money would I need today to satisfy completely, on an expectations basis, the obligations imposed on me through the insurance policies I have written?" It turns out that this is not only a good starting point, but a strong case can be made that it is also a good ending point insofar as liability valuation is concerned. The actuarial profession can best serve insurance management, financial markets, regulators, and investors by addressing that question. It can then be left for others to argue about the value of the default put option, franchise value, and the spin-off values of certain lines of business.

Direct versus Indirect Approach

If the focus is on determining the amount of assets necessary to satisfy, on an expectations basis, the obligations imposed by the liabilities, the next issue is how best to estimate that amount. We could take an indirect or a direct valuation approach. In the case of insurance companies, it becomes readily apparent that the indirect method of valuing liabilities may be quick, but is inefficient in addressing the question posed in the previous paragraph. Under the indirect method, tangible assets are valued and the market value of owners' equity is subtracted, presumably resulting in an estimate of the market value of liabilities. The problem with this approach, as can be seen by rearranging the terms of the equations in Exhibit 1, is that the equity value embraces the net value of default put options, franchise value, spin-off values, and perhaps other options, as well as the net tangible value; yet the market value of tangible assets (as distinguished from the market value of assets), omits one or more of these. Accordingly, the implied value of liabilities will be entangled with various options that are best relegated to the asset side of the balance sheet, as shown below:

$$PV(L) = FV + MV(TA) + PO - MV(E)$$
$$\neq MV(TA) - MV(E) = PV(L) - FV - PO$$

As can be seen to the right of the inequality above, subtracting the market value of equity from the market value of tangible assets will *understate* the present value of liabilities by the amount of franchise value and the default put option. While it is possible to estimate the values of the various options and add them to the value of the investment portfolio before subtracting the equity value to arrive at the present value of liabilities, this operation invokes several layers of subjective judgment and controversy that render the resulting liability calculation rather dubious.

With a more direct approach to the valuation of liabilities,[6] we can avoid a number of the pitfalls associated with the indirect approach, provided that we focus our attention on addressing the question posed in the second paragraph of this section. The present value of liabilities tells us the amount of tangible assets needed today in order to satisfy, on an expectations basis, our liabilities. (We may be able to satisfy them with fewer assets, if we get lucky, by taking interest rate, equity, or low credit quality bets, but *hope* should not be confused with *expectation*.) This present value, properly computed by means of Treasury-rate-based lattices or simulations properly calibrated to current Treasury security prices, takes into account any interest rate sensitivities in the cash flows.[7] Mortality and morbidity are factored in only on an expectation basis, although interest rate sensitivities are included to the extent that, with interest-sensitive policy surrenders and lapses, adverse selection is expected. (In practice, most companies do not currently take into account interest rate sensitivities of mortality and morbidity. As more reliable data become available, we suspect that they will.) Reserves and surplus needed to cushion variations from these interest-sensitive projections are not included in the present valuation of liabilities.

Reserves and Surplus

In insurance parlance, our present value of liabilities measure is analogous to the "actuarially fair value" concept developed by actuaries many decades ago. The major difference is that our measure modernizes it by explicitly accounting for stochastic interest rates and the cash flows that relate to them. Because we know, through modern finance valuation principles, how the stochastic nature of interest rates impacts value, it is a natural extension to incorporate. It also provides more meaningful value estimates of liabilities than those that ignore this source of randomness. The resulting present value estimates have, in essence, stripped out any insurer-specific C-1 risk (asset default) and C-3 risk (interest rate risk). Because the valuation lattices or simulation paths are calibrated to Treasury securities before applying them to insurance policies, we can be assured that the resulting liability estimate can be satisfied, on an expectation basis and, in principle, along all interest rate paths, with a properly engineered portfolio of Treasury securities and derivatives on Treasury securities. C-2 risk (mispricing of mortality/morbidity risk or of other pure risks) and C-4 risk (qualitative management issues) remain and are accounted for at their expected present values.

Now, if an insurer were to set aside reserves equal to the present value of liabilities, would this be adequate under most circumstances to satisfy the liabilities? The answer is a resounding "no." This is easy to demonstrate with an example. To be concrete, consider an insurer with a closed block of business. If assets were

---

[6] A good example of this approach is given by M. Asay, P. Bouyoucos, and T. Marciano, "On the Economic Approach to the Valuation of Single Premium Deferred Annuities," in Stavros Zenios (ed.), *Financial Optimization* (Cambridge: Cambridge University Press, 1993), pp. 132-135.

[7] These valuation models are discussed in Section III of this book. A thorough discussion of the models is available in D. Babbel and C. Merrill, *Valuation of Interest-Sensitive Financial Instruments*, Society of Actuaries, Frank J. Fabozzi Associates, 1996; and "Economic Valuation Models for Insurers," *North American Actuarial Journal* (July 1998).

set aside in an amount equal to the present value of that closed block of liabilities, and the block were left in a run-off mode, these assets would usually be inadequate to fund them. This is true whether the assets are duration and convexity matched to the liabilities or mismatched, because there can always be a deviation in the timing of a claim from what is expected. More often than not, the insurer would run out of assets before the final dollar of liabilities is paid, even though the assets were equal to the expected present value of the liabilities at the outset.[8] However, if the insurer were able to dip into surplus during those periods of shortfalls and reimburse with interest the surplus during periods of excess asset values, by the time the final dollar of liabilities is due, the insurer would have 50-50 odds of retaining sufficient assets remaining in the closed block to satisfy the final liability payment.

Clearly, a prudent insurer would need to set reserves greater than the present value of liabilities in order to have hopes of survival. Reserves, as usually computed, have a conservative bias is them designed to increase the probability of insurer solvency over time. Additionally, surplus is required in order to cushion against any shortfalls should the reserves prove to be inadequate.

In an economic sense, we need not focus on accounting concepts such as reserves, surplus, and risk-based capital. From a managerial viewpoint, these are best viewed as merely regulatory constraints. What is needed to cushion the liabilities against inadequate assets is actual money, as measured by the net tangible value — the excess market value of tangible assets over the present value of liabilities. The amount of net tangible value needed to provide an adequate cushion will depend on the amount and behavior of the present value of liabilities. A certain amount will be needed to handle actuarial risk, i.e., deviations from expected claims. More will be needed if there is model risk, i.e., the risk that experience will deviate from the functional relationships expressed as assumptions (e.g., interest-sensitive lapse functions) in our valuation models. If the insurer retains asset default risk, asset liquidity risk, and interest rate risk, additional net tangible value will be needed. Yet all of these calculations will depend on the amount and riskiness of the present value of liabilities and the desired level of insolvency risk.

Discussion

Occasionally, an objection is raised against our notion of the present value of liabilities by comparing it to readily observed market values of certain insurance liabilities. This objection is handled by keeping in mind that the present value should be formulated in a context of keeping the insurance business on the primary carrier's books, and for some good reasons.

Consider a situation in which an insurer has tangible assets worth $105 and a present value of liabilities of $100. Suppose that the net value of its put option to

---

[8] The reason that the probability of having enough assets is not simply 50-50 is that the expectation concept used in defining the present value of liabilities does not take into account the paths that the asset and liability values follow over time. Therefore, there will be many paths that would generate adequate asset returns by the final payment date to satisfy the remaining liabilities, yet inadequate returns over many paths prior to that final date.

default together with its franchise value is $2, and while not carried explicitly on its balance sheet, this value enhances the market value of its assets and equity.

Now, suppose that the insurer's liabilities are all GICs, and that it can repurchase and retire them in the open market for only $98. Alternatively, if it leaves them outstanding, it will require $100, in present value, to satisfy them ultimately. If one looks only at the cash price to retire the GICs, it looks like an attractive deal. But the *full* cost includes not only the $98 cash price but also the lost value of options ($2) associated with dropping that business.

Next, suppose that the insurer can transfer the liabilities to another insurer. Again, the true cost for the insurer is not only the value of tangible assets that must be transferred to the other insurer, but also the lost value of its options. The acceding insurer may require less than the $100 of present value needed to fully satisfy the liabilities but that does not mean that it costs less than $100 to fully satisfy them on an expectation basis. The acceding insurer may charge less because it gains the value of renewals or increases the value of its own default put option. After all, the transferred business will affect the acceding insurer's franchise and default put option values differently than that of the cedant. In fact, even the interest rate sensitivity (and therefore the value) of some of the liability cash flows may itself change when the business is transferred to a new carrier with a different kind of marketing force, crediting strategy, and financial strength. The acceding insurer may charge more simply because it can get more through negotiations. Yet these factors should not be misconstrued as impacting the present value of funds required for the primary carrier to satisfy fully, on an expectations basis, the retained liabilities.

Another objection against the present-value-of-liability concept is sometimes raised that the valuation models are fashioned to be arbitrage-free, yet the insurance liabilities, because of randomness surrounding claims and lapses, cannot be subject to the forces of arbitrage. But here we are reminded that it was not long ago when the mortgage-backed securities market emerged. Pricing was not subject to the forces of arbitrage due to the uncertainty surrounding the prepayment speeds, and there were no close comparables traded in the market. Nonetheless, satisfactory pricing algorithms were eventually developed based on two-factor, stochastic interest rate models. Consequently, option-adjusted spreads,[9] correctly calculated, have narrowed considerably and all but disappeared in some segments of that market. This suggests that even though these valuation models cannot rely on the forces of riskless arbitrage, they can still approximate value closely.

It would appear that similar pricing algorithms should be used to value insurance liabilities. These liabilities are also subject to considerable uncertainty.

---

[9] An option-adjusted spread is a "fudge factor" of sorts to capture in the interest rate lattices or paths the mispricing of the security based on the model price versus the market price. (See D. Babbel and S. Zenios, "Pitfalls in the Analysis of Option-Adjusted Spreads," *Financial Analysts Journal* (July/August 1992), pp. 65-69.) It is common to calculate option-adjusted spreads based on some fixed level of volatility for purposes of historical charting, but when pricing the securities, the volatility assumed should relate to the future period over which the mortgages will be repaid.

Some of the uncertainty, such as the incidence of lapse and surrender, devolves from the vacillation of future interest rate levels and paths. This uncertainty can be modeled in a fashion similar to mortgage-backed security prepayments. Uncertainty stemming from mortality, morbidity, accident experience, and some base levels of lapses and surrender may not be related directly to interest rates and can be reflected directly in the expected cash flows input into the valuation model.

In life insurance, there is a need to model the dividend and crediting rate practices of the insurer. These practices are often difficult to codify because a committee may declare a set of numbers to be used that is not related, through a simple formula, to the level and evolution of the stochastic Treasury rates used in the valuation models. Nonetheless, the decision process can usually be approximated by some formula tied to these interest rates. The actual process may rely more on realized portfolio yields and returns than on Treasury rates, yet on an *ex ante* basis, the stochastic Treasury rates may be used because they serve as certainty-equivalent rates of return on the portfolio subject to credit and liquidity risk. This should suffice for liability valuation purposes.

It is entirely another question, albeit an interesting one, to model the optimal dividend or crediting rate strategy. If a firm is not following such optimal strategies in certain lines of its business, it might be reflected in a higher spin-off value. Another separate question is whether the insurer is following sound asset/liability management practices. The present value of an insurance liability is not dependent on what assets the insurer holds nor on how its portfolio is structured. Rather, it depends simply on how much in default-free securities would be required today to meet its expected liability payments over time. Again, the present value must account for any interest rate sensitivities in the liabilities.

It is an important, but separate, issue how much in reserves and surplus is needed to ensure, with an acceptable degree of probability, that a sufficient cushion of assets is in place to handle any adverse deviations in liability payments from those expected. The amount of reserves and surplus required will, of course, depend on the structure of the investment portfolio and the probability distribution of state-contingent liability payments (where the states are defined by the levels and evolution of interest rates).

Our narrower definition of liability values, while unlikely to produce value estimates that precisely match those market values of liabilities which are actually traded in the marketplace, nonetheless has some merit. First, it is simpler to compute for most insurance liabilities than would be the case of a more expansive definition of market value, which would impound in some way the values of put options and franchise value. Second, it is subject to less controversy by relegating to the other side of the balance sheet some of the most troublesome areas of valuation. Third, it provides a useful number as a starting point to regulators and to the insurers themselves, who need to know how much it should take to fully defease the liabilities that the insurer has underwritten. Fourth, it provides a number that is more easily compared among insurers. Fifth, as discussed in Section IV of this book, it is particularly helpful in firm risk assessment, particularly if the liabilities are valued using models that feature the same drivers of uncertainty as used on the asset side of the economic balance sheet. Finally, as explained in the next chapter, it can serve as the basis for financial performance measurement.

Chapter 3

A Performance Measurement System for Insurers

David F. Babbel, Ph.D.
Professor of Insurance and Finance
The Wharton School
University of Pennsylvania

Robert Stricker
Vice President
Citicorp

Irwin T. Vanderhoof, Ph.D., FSA
Clinical Professor of Finance and Insurance
Stern School of Business
New York University

INTRODUCTION

One of the most basic tenets of modern financial theory is that managers should act in a manner consistent with maximizing the value of owners' equity. While there are theoretical conditions under which this tenet may not always apply, for practical purposes companies usually espouse it as a financial goal. If an insurer accepts this maxim as a company goal, it follows that the firm should view the performance of insurance managers and operatives in terms of whether it helps to promote higher firm value.[1] Any benchmarks the firm uses to facilitate performance measurement must be designed in a manner that is consistent with a firm value focus.

 The appropriate benchmark against which to measure performance will depend on the level within the organization of the individual whose performance is being measured. Senior investment management, responsible for establishing broad investment strategies and overall asset allocation, should be judged on how well those strategies meet the overall needs of the firm. On the other hand, the actual portfolio managers — who may invest only in a subset of the bond universe, such as corporate bonds or mortgage securities within a stated duration and credit quality

---

An earlier version of this chapter appeared as a Goldman, Sachs monograph.

range — should be judged against the performance of comparable securities. Their business objective should be to outperform an unmanaged portfolio of permitted investments. Generally, others in the organization will be responsible for defining which investments are permitted. Therefore, an ideal performance measurement system must have the flexibility not only to appropriately measure overall investment performance against firm goals, but also to include performance attribution.

Theoretically, the value of owners' equity in an insurance company should be the fair market value of its assets (mostly financial assets, but also its put option value[2] to default on financial obligations, and its intangible "going concern" value) minus its liabilities (mostly insurance policies and other financial liabilities). Typically, however, the focus is on accounting statements that are based on book values rather than market values. (Changes in market value generally are not recognized for mortgages, insurance liabilities, and most bonds.) Consequently, insurance companies have traditionally relied on yield as the primary performance measurement criterion. They have collected yield data on new investments and compared these yields with other insurers' results or against a specified passive index.

But there has been a growing disenchantment with the use of yield measures. High yields that a company achieves on new investments may merely reflect the fact that its investments have more credit risk, less liquidity, more call risk, greater foreign currency exposure, or a worse duration mismatch than those of a company showing a lower yield. Recent years have witnessed an increase in interest rate volatility, the growth of the high yield market where yield can be traded off for credit quality, the expansion of the mortgage securities market where yield can be traded off for prepayment risk, and the proliferation of other new security types with complex risk/reward tradeoffs. In this environment, looking at yield on new investments alone, without adjusting for the various risks associated with each security, is misleading. Indeed, the development of modern valuation technologies, described elsewhere in this volume, for mortgages, corporate bonds, and insurance liabilities has been motivated by the fact that yield and return are not the same thing. These models attempt to measure the cost (or expected loss) associated with yield curve, option, and credit risks.

---

[1] For the stock insurer, this goal translates directly into maximizing the firm's stock price. For the mutual insurer, the translation is more complex, as the policyowner is both the debt holder (in the form of issued policies) and equity owner. Therefore, certain actions that maximize current equity value may do little more than transfer wealth from one pocket to another of the same person (if surplus is distributed to policyowners). Or, if surplus is accumulated for future expansion, this may transfer wealth only from the current group of policyowners/equity holders to a succeeding generation of policyowners/equity holders. Because our focus will be on the investment management process, we will avoid this complication in large measure. Given a schedule of intended policy dividend payouts, an increase in investment performance beyond that anticipated can only add to surplus or enhance dividend levels. Thus, the policyowner would be at least as well off. In general, therefore, we can say that maximizing firm value enhances policyholder value today or in the future.

[2] See Chapter 2.

Comparing portfolio yields even among insurers with similar investment strategies and risk profiles can also be misleading. Timing differences in insurance cash flows, in conjunction with swings in interest rates, can result in one insurer having more money to invest when rates are high and another having more money to invest when rates are low. This results in different portfolio yields for reasons beyond the investment manager's control.

A yield focus can spawn accounting games and foster book-value-based portfolio reshuffling, yet have very little to do with promoting higher firm value. There has been growing recognition among insurers, therefore, of the need to adopt a performance measurement system that is compatible with the insurer's objective of increasing firm value. In this chapter, we propose a system designed to accomplish just that.

ENHANCING FIRM VALUE

We can identify four areas within the finance domain where portfolio managers can act to increase firm value:

- investing in projects or financial securities with positive net present values (NPVs), i.e., finding undervalued assets
- altering the firm's financial structure
- altering the firm's duration and convexity mismatches
- outperforming the firm's liabilities

Investing in Projects or Financial Securities with Positive NPVs

For the typical industrial firm, this is undoubtedly the area with the most potential for enhancing firm value. Insurers and other financial intermediaries, however, face quite a different situation. Their comparative advantage — indeed, their *raison d'etre* — is in issuing customized liabilities. Their aim is to issue these liabilities, be they in the form of property/liability insurance or life/health insurance, more cheaply than they could by raising funds in the public and private debt markets.

With the funds collected, they invest mostly in financial securities, not in projects with positive NPVs. Because publicly traded securities, according to believers in the efficient market hypothesis, are generally assumed to trade at fair prices, their NPVs are zero. Their prices are equal to the present values of expected future cash flows, discounted at the appropriate rates to reflect their relative riskiness. Even if one finds a security that appears to be underpriced, its NPV, as far as the market is concerned, remains zero until it is shown that the market is wrong; thus, buying the security will have no immediate repercussions on firm market value. When the market finally is convinced of its earlier mispricing, the price will quickly adjust so that NPV returns to zero. This change in equilibrium asset price will then have a positive impact on firm market value.

It is also possible that investments with positive NPVs can be found in the private placement market. However, these generally have less liquidity than publicly traded securities, and the market charges higher yields for this illiquidity. Therefore, as insurers acquire investments in this area, they may find that their firm values do not increase as much as might be expected based on yields alone, if indeed they increase at all in the short run. Only over time will the higher yields contribute to firm value.

There are other areas where the firm might be an active participant in undertaking a business or developing real estate property with a positive NPV. The market may recognize the attractiveness of the project and reward the company forthwith, and this reward will show up in the firm value.

Altering Financial Structure

An area in finance theory that has long been a center of controversy is the impact of financial structure — leverage — on the value of the firm. Empirical evidence is largely consistent with the notion that higher leverage, at least to a point, is associated with higher stock prices. Research by Staking and Babbel confirms this finding for insurers.[3] An aspect of the leverage issue that is particularly perverse with insurers is the influence of the insurance insolvency guarantee programs in most states, which protect policyholders against the consequences of insurer insolvencies. These programs, which assess the responsible, healthy insurers to cover the losses of the insolvent insurers, create obvious incentives for excess leverage, especially among the lower-tier companies.

Altering the Duration and Convexity Mismatches

There is a growing body of evidence that the market recognizes the importance of asset/liability management among life/health and property/liability insurers. Those insurers exhibiting greater mismatches between the interest rate sensitivity (duration) of market values of assets and liabilities generally had greater volatility in their stock prices occasioned by interest rate fluctuations. The early research was not oriented toward the impact of better asset/liability matching on the level of firm value; rather, its focus was restricted to the impact of a mismatch on changing firm values produced by interest rate moves.

A more interesting question is whether better asset/liability matching can enhance the *level* of firm value. Here, the studies by Staking and Babbel give us the first evidence. These studies showed that better matched companies commanded higher stock prices relative to the liquidation value of their surplus.[4] This

---

[3] See Kim B. Staking and David F. Babbel, "The Relation between Capital Structure, Interest Rate Sensitivity, and Market Value in the Property-Liability Insurance Industry," *Journal of Risk and Insurance* (December 1995), and Kim B. Staking and David F. Babbel, "Insurer Surplus Duration and Market Value Revisited," *Journal of Risk and Insurance* (March 1998).

[4] The liquidation value of their surplus was measured by marking to market the tangible assets of the company and subtracting the present value of the liabilities. The study showed that companies with assets well matched to liabilities had stock prices that were two and three times higher, relative to their liquidation value, than those of companies with average mismatches.

finding was particularly significant during years of high interest rate volatility and among companies that were not precariously leveraged. One reason for this premium is market recognition that an insurer has going concern value, and a company operating with a better match between assets and liabilities is more likely to be around to capture that extra value. Indeed, the studies found that a better match resulted in higher relative stock prices for all but the marginal companies, which exhibited higher stock prices by being less well-matched. The value of a mismatch to this latter group arises from the option to default (i.e., to "put" the liabilities to the state); this option increases in value as the business becomes more volatile.

Outperforming the Firm's Liabilities

In addition to taking measures that can have an immediate impact on the stock price or market value of owners' equity, a company can take a number of actions that will affect firm value only over time. Whenever a firm earns more on its assets than it pays on its liabilities, the excess will accrue to economic surplus. To the extent that these incremental additions to surplus are greater than the required return on equity, the economic value of surplus will rise.

This increment to surplus value derives from two principal sources. The operations side may be issuing liabilities on favorable terms and through cost-efficient distribution networks. Alternatively, the investment department may be experiencing favorable returns (relative to the product pricing assumptions) through superior market timing, securities selection, or asset allocation. Sometimes these two sources of value creation work together. For example, a prolonged pattern of superior investment performance will aid the sales force in attracting additional clients on favorable terms. In such a case, part of the credit for sales should go to the investment department.

STRUCTURING A PERFORMANCE MEASUREMENT SYSTEM

An evaluation of the financial and investment performance of a company should include activities undertaken in any of the aforementioned categories. Actions taken by the firm such as finding and investing in positive NPV securities or projects, altering leverage, and altering the duration and convexity mismatches can have swift repercussions on the firm value, to the extent that information regarding these actions is made publicly available. Accordingly, it is relatively straightforward to measure the impact of such actions. If a firm's stock is publicly traded, it requires determining only how its price changed, after factoring out the broad stock market, interest rate, and insurance industry influences on its price movement. For the mutual firm, it entails the difficult task of measuring the conversion (demutualization) value both before and after the actions are taken.

Other actions, which we have grouped under the heading of "Outperforming the Firm's Liabilities," can be evaluated only over longer periods of time.

These actions include strategic allocation of investments among broad asset classes, selection of individual assets within a broad class, timing of investment in anticipation of market moves, and so forth.[5] Our proposed performance measurement system is intended to focus on this area for enhancing firm value. It seeks to measure the performance over time of the insurer's assets relative to its liabilities (i.e., its spread over its cost of funds).

Establishing a Liability Benchmark

To determine whether its assets have outperformed its liabilities, an insurer must first determine how its liabilities have performed. Because the liabilities are not traded on an organized public exchange, it is not possible to monitor their behavior directly on a continual basis. Therefore, a liability benchmark must be devised, based on traded securities, that will mirror changes in values of the liabilities.[6]

Two characteristics of a liability benchmark are of utmost importance. First, the benchmark must be based on traded securities for which there is an active market. This will allow a firm to get reliable quotes on a timely basis. Second, and more important, the benchmark must behave in a manner that closely parallels the market value of the liabilities over time and under disparate economic circumstances. For example, it should exhibit duration, convexity, and sensitivity to other broad market forces in which one can take an investment position similar to that of the liabilities. The difficulty of evaluating complex insurance liabilities should not be underestimated. Nonetheless, it must be the starting point for developing an appropriate investment strategy from an asset/liability management perspective.

Asay, Bouyoucos, and Marciano provided a methodology to measure the costs of various policyholder options and the interest rate risk inherent in single premium deferred annuities and other interest-sensitive life policies.[7] A similar

---

[5] They also include some of the activities mentioned earlier, which are undertaken in anticipation of changes in market conditions in a particular direction. For example, an insurer may extend the maturity of its assets, creating a deliberate duration mismatch between assets and liabilities, in anticipation of a decline in interest rates beyond that implied by the current term structure. The market will not supply any immediate reward to these actions. Indeed, it may penalize such adventurism. Only time will reveal the wisdom of attempting to "out-guess" the market.

[6] Not every variable influencing the value of a given firm's liabilities can be closely mirrored by action in the capital markets. In life insurance, the mortality risk cannot be so mirrored. A similar situation exists for fire insurance, though transactions in the reinsurance markets could allow the transfer of some risk. Recent developments in the capital markets, such as insurance risk futures, can help allay general insurance market risks and may some day be sufficiently evolved that we can use them to impute market prices to pure insurance risks. A related possibility could occur if the insurance contract under study provided the possibility of transfer from a fixed book value account to a stock market account. If the stock market rose, it is possible that an increased rate of such transfers would occur and the value of the liability would change. While it would be theoretically possible to mirror many different conceivable variables, including the stock market, we do not advocate this. We will work only with the impacts of changes in the Treasury yield curve because the known effects of those changes overwhelm any of the more esoteric factors we could hypothesize. The extra complexity would not be worth the effort.

[7] Michael Asay, Peter Bouyoucos, and Tony Marciano, "An Economic Approach to the Valuation of Single Premium Deferred Annuities," Goldman, Sachs & Co., April 1989.

valuation method is now employed in actuarial software such as SS&C. The valuation methods are based implicitly on replicating the cash flows of the policy with capital market instruments and pricing the resulting replicated portfolios with market prices. This technology gives a company the ability to translate its non-traded liabilities into equivalent capital market portfolios for which there are active markets and therefore reliable price quotes. Consequently, it is possible to track the market value of an insurer's liabilities over time, even though they are not traded. This process differs from the usual approach of calculating only a yield and a duration of the liabilities as benchmarks for the asset portfolio characteristics. The mimicking portfolio has the desirable properties that (1) returns reflect the shape of the yield curve and the cost of embedded options, and (2) the effects of important sources of interest rate risk other than just duration — such as convexity and volatility — are directly incorporated. As noted, many companies may depend upon duration as the only characterization of the changes in the value of liabilities. However, our approach allows a richer representation of the risk and return properties of liabilities.

Using a liquid, traded securities portfolio that mimics the liabilities allows for a straightforward computation of a liability total rate of return index against which the performance of the assets can be measured. Outperforming this liability index ensures that the asset managers are, in fact, acting in a manner consistent with increasing the value of the firm. The current practice of measuring asset managers against an arbitrary index (even with the correct duration) does not ensure this result.

While a well-constructed portfolio that mimics a mature book of business should not vary dramatically over time, its composition may change as policies age and new policies are written. Consequently, it is necessary to reevaluate the liabilities periodically and adjust the liability benchmark if appropriate.

Levels of Performance Measurement

Armed with the concept of liability benchmarks, we are now prepared to measure whether our assets are outperforming our liabilities. We recommend that insurance investment managers measure their performance on a total rate of return basis and compare their performance to the total rate of return on a liability benchmark carefully constructed to reflect the costs of their liabilities. As Messmore has stated "From an investment perspective, total return in excess of liability-based benchmarks is the most meaningful measure of progress in the creation of economic wealth."[8] Recognizing that yield is an important consideration in many insurance products, especially interest-sensitive products, yield could be an important constraint in managing an insurance portfolio. However, because in today's capital markets it is so easy to enhance yield by taking on one or more

---

[8] Thomas Messmore, "Measuring Investment Performance Attribution," presentation at a conference on Performance Measurement and Management of Insurance Company Portfolios, Infoline, New York City, 1989.

risks — e.g., credit risk, duration risk, call risk, prepayment risk, liquidity risk, currency risk, etc. — total return is the better objective to measure because it implicitly accounts for all the risks in the portfolio at each point in time.

Ideally, insurers should calculate total returns on a daily basis, as do mutual funds. In practice, however, recognizing the time, expense, and effort required, it should be sufficient for insurance companies to calculate returns on a monthly basis. An assumption would be required for handling intramonth cash flows. Typically, these are assumed to occur in the middle of the month. Chaining together monthly total returns allows the insurer to calculate a time-weighted rate of return over any long-term horizon. It eliminates the impact of the actual timing of insurance cash flows over which the investment manager has no control. This allows for unbiased comparisons of performance.

Merely calculating the total rate of return on the assets and comparing it with any of the widely available generic bond indexes is not sufficient. It is extremely unlikely that such an index would mirror the insurer's actual liabilities. Indeed, even if firm investments substantially outperform a generic index, the result could be insolvency. This is because a bond market index couldn't be expected to match the duration of the insurer's liabilities, not to mention their convexity characteristics or other measures of interest rate sensitivity (e.g., to the yield curve or volatility). Hence, it is necessary to create a customized liability benchmark for each insurer's particular book of business. For the same reason, it would probably be inappropriate to compare the total return earned by one insurer on its investment portfolio with that of other insurers, unless all their liabilities were identical — a highly unlikely occurrence.

Using a liability benchmark is appropriate for asset portfolios funding the insurer's reserves. The proper benchmark for the assets funding capital and surplus, however, should be based on management's return objectives and risk tolerance. It could reflect a weighted average of indexes for diverse asset classes, such as stocks, bonds, real estate, and international securities.

A comprehensive performance measurement system will provide for evaluation of performance at several levels. We depict these levels in Exhibit 1. It will also allow performance attribution, i.e., the determination of ingredients contributing to relative performance.

Structuring a Performance Measurement System

Level I. The first step is to characterize each of the liabilities or liability groupings issued in terms of its market characteristics — duration, convexity, volatility, etc.

Level II. Next we set up benchmark asset portfolios we call sub-liability benchmarks (SLBs), to mirror the behavior of each kind of liability. Our central focus here will be on the total return of the SLB at each point in time, which should mimic the total cost of the particular line of business or group of policies for which it is acting as proxy.

Exhibit 1: Structuring a Performance Measurement System

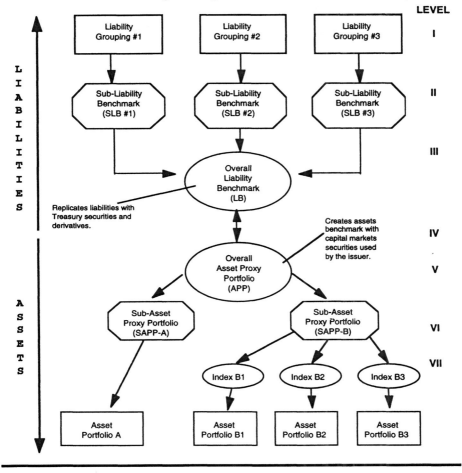

In designing a portfolio of securities to serve as a sub-liability benchmark, we recommend selection of U.S. Treasury securities, their derivatives, and other securities of minimal default risk. There are several reasons why we favor the inclusion and predominance of these securities:

- They are liquid and widely traded, and price quotes are easily obtained.
- They are typically the benchmark used for valuing other asset classes and are starting to be used as a benchmark for valuing insurance liabilities as well.
- Their diversity of characteristics allows them to be combined into portfolios that can emulate the market value behavior of almost any default-free cash flow stream.

- Insurance policies are very close to being considered default-free from the consumers' standpoint. Because policies are backed by the surplus and reserves of state-licensed and solvency-regulated companies, and in most cases are also backed by state insolvency guarantee programs, we can reasonably impute to them near default-free standing.
- Given this near default-free standing, consumers should not expect their insurance premiums to reflect interest rates that are any higher than those on similar, near default-free securities, after factoring in reasonable loads for distribution, administrative, and capital costs.[9] To the extent the insurer must offer a premium for competitive reasons, it can add an appropriate spread to the return of the sub-liability benchmark portfolio.
- For reasons discussed elsewhere,[10] it is preferable to model separately the portion of economic surplus derived through the default put option and the franchise or going concern value.

We should note here that there will come a day when we no longer need to rely on asset portfolio returns to proxy for liability costs. The economic behavior and costs of insurer liabilities will be modeled directly and the attributes of those costs over time will be able to be inspected on a daily or moment-to-moment basis. But for now, we believe the approach described above is the most practical alternative available.

Level III. These SLBs can then be aggregated into an overall liability benchmark (LB) if the insurer does not segment its portfolio. The weights used in aggregating the SLBs should reflect their relative shares of the total liabilities issued, where these shares are measured in market value units. (Note that the weights are not based on surplus allocated to a particular line of business.) The weights applied to each SLB will change over time as the proportions of business represented by each line or policy grouping change.

Level IV. Given the aggregate LB, the insurer can address the asset side. The first step is an asset allocation optimization where, for example, the LB becomes a constraint to the problem: maximizing total rate of return of the assets subject to outperforming the liabilities. This optimization could be a purely mathematical or an empirical exercise. Alternatively, investment managers could exercise their views about the likely relative performance of various sectors of the market. In the former approach, managers could perform a classic asset allocation optimiza-

---

[9] A sales force should not be rewarded for selling policies that reflect higher interest rates than these. If a company feels it must offer policies reflecting higher yields, then either it must be saddled with extraordinary distribution, administrative, or capital costs, or it may be marketing to a clientele that is seeking its products primarily for their investment characteristics rather than their insurance component, so they must compete with noninsurance investment alternatives with lower cost loadings. In either case, the company is following a practice that will reduce the value of surplus.

[10] See Chapter 2.

tion.[11] In the latter approach, investment managers define the asset allocation to set up an asset proxy portfolio (APP) that reflects their desires regarding asset allocation and timing. To achieve target profit margins, they will probably include risky assets in the APP rather than limit it to just the very high quality, liquid assets of the LB. To the extent that results for their target APP differ from the LB, these investment strategists are responsible and their decisions may be evaluated over time. For example, the APP may have more credit risk, call risk, or interest rate risk than the LB, based on their view of market conditions or bets on the economy. It is important to make allowances for their strategic views in this process.

Levels V and VI. The APP can be divided into several smaller sub-asset proxy portfolios (SAPPs), or indexes, that could serve as benchmarks to individual portfolio or investment managers. While each SAPP could correspond to a particular SLB, it may be more convenient to have the investment professionals organized according to various classes of investments (e.g., corporates, mortgages, municipals, equities, high yield bonds, etc.).[12] An important characteristic of these SAPPs is that they must aggregate to the overall APP both in terms of investment characteristics and total rate of return. Some SAPPs may be sufficiently large that it will be convenient to subdivide them even further, providing indexes of total return on asset groupings as targets for the ultimate investment managers to achieve or outperform (e.g., Index B1, B2, etc.).

Level VII. Finally, we get to the people charged with actually implementing the investment program. These individuals do the investing, and the total return and risk characteristics of their investments must be tracked over time. As their universe of permitted investments will generally be constrained, their actual performance should be measured against a passive portfolio with similar investment constraints. Alternatively, their performance could be gauged against an optimized portfolio meeting the investment constraints. Appropriate constraints might include liquidity, duration, convexity, credit quality, and minimum yield requirements.

Investment Income Allocation

Comparing the total return of the asset portfolio against a benchmark related to the requirements of the liabilities is the best single measure of relative investment performance. It does not, however, reflect either the timing of cash flows or short-

---

[11] This would use as inputs the returns and covariances between various asset classes. The result would be a mean-variance efficient asset portfolio that beats the liabilities on an expected basis (or in various scenarios). Alternatively, managers could optimize over a different objective function (e.g., minimize risk), using excess asset returns over liabilities as the input.

[12] SAPPs are lettered, rather than numbered, to connote an indirect connection between them and the actual liability groupings.

term accounting results. Thus, if one product line grows rapidly when interest rates are high while another grows rapidly when rates are low, the former product line should have a higher yielding portfolio and more investment income, even though they both might have the same total return performance. It may thus be desirable to develop an alternative benchmark for purposes of income allocation and tracking accounting results.

This can be accomplished by creating a benchmark portfolio to mirror the future liability flows under all likely future interest rate paths. This is not an easy task. To be done correctly, it requires a sophisticated modeling system that can generate an appropriate set of interest rate paths and then forecast asset and liability cash flows for each path, taking care to handle the embedded options properly.

Taxation and the Liability Benchmark

Taxation of investment and underwriting income is a complex consideration to incorporate in a performance measurement system, particularly for a property/liability company in light of the alternative minimum tax. In highly regulated states, any taxes incurred by an insurance enterprise on investment income are supposed to be passed along to the ultimate consumers of insurance policies. The theoretical justification has been that the equity owners of insurance companies could invest directly in the securities held by insurers without undergoing an extra layer of taxation. Therefore, fair pricing demands that the incremental taxes be added to the policy premiums.[13] How well this works in practice is open to question, however, and an insurer minimizing the taxes to be passed along in the form of higher insurance prices may be at a competitive advantage.

In less highly regulated states, the tax issue is even more important. Much uncertainty surrounds the ultimate level of losses and the evolving nature of tax law. Therefore, it is difficult for an investment manager to optimize the tax position of the enterprise by choosing an appropriate mix of taxable and tax-exempt bonds. Nonetheless, the manager can make some judgments about the appropriate mix and can adjust the liability benchmark to reflect that mix, allowing performance to be measured on a pre-tax basis.

Realized capital gains and losses arising out of portfolio management also have tax implications. Given that the marginal tax rates on interest income and capital gains are different, the impact goes beyond simply a timing difference in income recognition. (A capital gain results when yields have declined, so future income will be reduced on the reinvested proceeds.) However, the book recognition of capital gains and losses can be managed in practice to optimize their impact on taxes. We therefore recommend measuring investment total rates of return on a pre-tax basis.

---

[13] See J. David Cummins and Scott A. Harrington (eds.), *Fair Rates of Return in Property-Liability Insurance* (Kluwer Nijhoff Publishing, 1987).

PERFORMANCE ATTRIBUTION

By setting up our performance measurement system in a tiered structure as depicted in Exhibit 1, we have also made it easier to attribute performance correctly. There are people responsible at the various levels of performance measurement to ensure that the system operates smoothly.[14]

Performance attribution requires first a measure of performance so that there is something to attribute! A useful starting point is to compare the spread between the actual total rate of return on the combined investment portfolios (Level VII) and the total rate of return on the overall liability benchmark (Level III).

We refer to this as a starting point because it measures actual investment return against a proxy for liability costs. It is important to periodically perform economic valuations of the liabilities themselves and see whether their realized behavior has been well reflected by the asset portfolios that are used as proxies for them. If not, there are three areas where the discrepancy could have arisen. The first would be at Level I, where the actuaries may have improperly characterized the nature of the liabilities in terms of their investment characteristics (e.g., duration, convexity, lapse, drifts). It is possible that the actuaries correctly characterized the investment attributes of the liabilities, yet estimated poorly other attributes (e.g., mortality, frequency or severity of losses) that would produce the aberrant behavior. If all is well at Level I, the problem may have arisen at Level II, where a financial technician has taken the input from actuaries and incorrectly created proxy asset portfolios (liability benchmarks) intended to exhibit the same investment characteristics. The third area where a problem may have arisen is at Level III, where the separate liability groupings benchmarks are weighted and combined into an overall liability benchmark. If the market value weightings of the books of business implied by the overall liability benchmark were incorrect, or evolved over time in a manner inconsistent with that assumed in the schedule for devising the benchmark, there could be a discrepancy between the actual behavior of the benchmark and the aggregate liabilities that it represents.

If the periodic examinations of the suitability of the overall liability benchmark prove satisfactory, we can then focus with confidence on the total rate of return spread between Levels III and VII, as indicated earlier. This total spread can then be attributed to performance achieved at Levels IV, V, VI, and VII.

The individuals responsible for corporate investment strategy can be evaluated on the basis of how their overall asset proxy portfolio performed relative to the overall liability benchmark. If the strategic plan is a good one, it should show up over time by having the APP outperform the LB. It is possible that the strategic view is satisfactory but the implementation is not. The persons responsible for implementing the strategic view may demonstrate poor asset selection, or deviate from the plan on their own recognizance. It is also possible that the strate-

---

[14] In some firms, especially smaller insurers, the same individual may perform two or more of the functions identified.

gic plan is a poor one, but that the persons responsible for implementing it may exceed their targets, with the result that assets outperform liabilities. This could occur at Levels V, VI, and VII.

Assuming that the SAPPs have been designed correctly, so that they aggregate to the APP, we are next ready to measure the performance of the portfolio managers against their targets (Levels V and VI). To the extent that the portfolio managers acquire securities that differ in composition from their SAPPs, or invest their available funds at different times than that assumed in the SAPPs, their performance will differ from projections.

At times the need to achieve a minimum yield spread over Treasuries will conflict with a portfolio manger's perception of relative value in the market, and therefore with his expected total return performance over the short run. In part to account for this conflict, while at the same time recognizing the annual planning and compensation cycle at most companies, we recommend that performance be measured over both a 1-year and a rolling 3-year period.

The typical portfolio manager will have a cohort of specialists helping to acquire the investments desired on favorable terms. These specialists will be looking for undervalued assets and may exercise some discretion about the nature of assets they acquire at any time, while working over time to achieve their part of the balance desired by the portfolio manager. They may be charged with investing to beat a particular index. If they outperform their target indexes, we can undertake further investigation to determine how this was achieved. For example, did they demonstrate superior asset selection or superior timing, or did they deviate from their risk norms and win their bets?

By summing the various components of performance attribution, we should arrive again at the total rate of return spread between Levels III and VII. The information collected from this endeavor will enable us to determine more fairly which members of our investment team have contributed best toward achieving our objectives and help us readjust our investment plans for future periods.

CONCLUSION

We recommend that insurers switch from yield to total return for performance measurement. Incremental yield can always be achieved by accepting more of one or more types of risks. Only total return implicitly and fairly accounts for all of the risks in a portfolio. For those insurance products where yield is an important component, it should be a *constraint* on the investment process rather than the primary objective.

Performance should be measured relative to a benchmark index created to reflect risk and return characteristics of the liabilities. We can construct this index using the modern valuation techniques referred to in this chapter. Given the liability index, members of the investment team can manage assets with the objective of outperforming this index. This ensures that both asset and liability managers have coordinated incentives consistent with increasing the value of the firm. In general, the liability benchmark will be composed of Treasuries and their derivatives (e.g., options), unless the insurance liability is closely linked to some particular sector of the stock or bond market.

Traditional accounting does not require that bonds be marked to market. Thus, in the short run, accounting results can diverge from economic total return results. Nonetheless, over time they must converge. The evidence suggests that rating agencies, equity analysts, and the market in general consider the market value of the firm's assets when trying to value it. Furthermore, there are growing pressures on insurance companies to mark their bond portfolios to market.

In the long run, the time, effort and expense required to measure total return — and to reward performance that enhances it — should increase the ultimate value of the firm and thus justify the expense involved.

Chapter 4

Asset Allocation for Property and Casualty Insurers

Brent T. Tran, CFA
Director, Quantitative Research
Asset Strategy Consulting

INTRODUCTION

This chapter presents an asset allocation model developed for property and casualty insurers. The model provides a convenient framework from which insurers can make decisions regarding their asset allocation. The framework integrates the insurer's assets, liabilities, and underwriting results. Additionally, the model provides a framework for analyzing the impact of asset allocation on the firm while constrained by regulatory and rating agency capital adequacy requirements. Further, the model considers insurer performance after the effects of federal income taxes.

This model is introduced at a time of greater competition and consolidation among insurers. More sophisticated approaches to asset management and asset liability management are going to be expected. For example, at a recent conference, A.M. Best indicated that "avoiding investment crises" is not evidence of a sophisticated asset management strategy. Therefore, asset allocation models, such as the one presented here, may provide insurers assistance as they seek competitive advantages.

The chapter's objective is to outline a conceptual framework for evaluating asset allocation decisions in the context of returns and risks to economic surplus. Economic surplus is essentially the market value of assets minus the present value of liabilities. While this notion of economic surplus is not currently the basis for either generally accepted accounting principles (GAAP), statutory accounting principles (SAP) or tax accounting, the model builds on the belief that economic surplus is a better measure of the insurer's long-run fiscal health.

The model specifications are as follows:

- Building on an investment asset return and risk base, the model provides a total surplus return and risk framework for analyzing impacts on the whole

The author wishes to thank Peter C. Gunder for his comments in developing this model.

of the insurance company. This process entails integrating the firm's investment assets, liabilities, and underwriting results.

- The model provides a method to analyze the impact of asset allocation decisions on the firm's surplus, asset growth, and investment income.
- The model provides a framework for analyzing the impact of the asset allocation decision on Risk Based Capital.
- Firm-specific investment policies are easily incorporated.
- The analysis can be performed on a pre-tax and after-tax basis.
- Broader policy issues such as insurance leverage are addressed.

THE ASSET ALLOCATION MODEL

This section discusses an integrated approach for establishing a strategic asset allocation for property & casualty insurance companies. This approach is illustrated schematically in Exhibit 1.

Exhibit 1: Integrated Asset Allocation

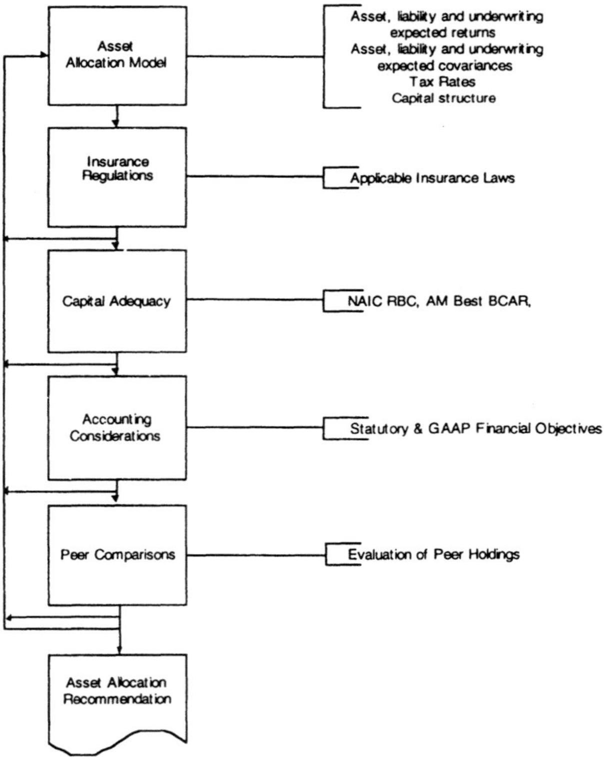

Economic Surplus

Insurance companies often focus solely on statutory surplus, the difference between statutory assets and liabilities. In statutory accounting, some assets (e.g., stocks) are carried at market value, while bonds are generally recorded at amortized cost. On the liability side, reserves are booked at the actuarially expected cost of claims and any costs associated with settling those claims, usually on an undiscounted basis. The insurance company generally does not discount its liability, even though the liability might be realized only in the distant future.[1]

While the focus of the model is on the economic surplus of the insurer, considerable emphasis must be maintained on statutory surplus, for it is this accounting figure that is generally more transparent for insurance regulators, rating agencies, and investors. Therefore the maximization of the economic surplus of the firm can be achieved while managing the constraint of a statutory surplus position.

Economic surplus is defined as the difference between the market value of assets and the present value of liabilities. Computing the present value of liabilities requires discounting the statutory liabilities by a market interest rate consistent with the duration of the liabilities.[2] Once a company's economic surplus is defined, investigation of those factors that contribute to the growth of economic surplus can begin.

Return on Surplus

To maximize the economic wealth of an insurer, the focus is on the growth of the economic surplus of the firm. This growth is measured by the return on surplus.

Return on surplus (ROS) has three major components: the *return on assets* (ROA), *return on liabilities* (ROL) and the *return on underwriting* (ROU). In equation form, the annualized ROS is expressed as:

$$\text{ROS} = \frac{A}{S}\text{ROA} - \frac{L}{S}\text{ROL} + \frac{P}{S}\text{ROU} \tag{1}$$

where

ROS	=	return on surplus
ROA	=	total return on assets
ROL	=	return on liability
ROU	=	return on underwriting
A	=	market value of assets
L	=	present value of liabilities
S	=	economic surplus
P	=	premiums earned

---

[1] Certain lines of business may be presented on a discounted basis for statutory purposes.

[2] A company's liability duration is assumed to equal the duration of its loss reserves. Many adjustments are made, however. For example, reinsurance recoverables and unearned premiums on potential future cash flows.

The total investment assets of the insurance company add to surplus through the total rate of return of the assets multiplied by investment leverage, or the ratio of assets to surplus. The liabilities of the insurer and their net change will diminish surplus by the rate of growth of liabilities multiplied by financial leverage, or the ratio of liabilities to surplus. The insurer's underwriting operations will add to surplus through the rate of return on underwriting multiplied by insurance leverage, or the ratio of premiums to surplus.

All of these three major components affect surplus. In order for the insurer to maximize the risk adjusted rate of growth to surplus based on asset allocation decisions, optimization techniques are employed to identify those investment portfolios that will maximize return on surplus for a given level of surplus risk.

Surplus risk can be defined as the volatility (or variance) of the surplus. Based on the three contributors to return on surplus, the risk to surplus is composed of the volatility of each of these factors and their diversification effects. Annualized surplus risk is expressed in equation form as:[3]

$$\sigma_{ROS}^2 = \left(\frac{A}{S}\right)^2 \sigma_{ROA}^2 + \left(\frac{L}{S}\right)^2 \sigma_{ROL}^2 + \left(\frac{P}{S}\right)^2 \sigma_{ROU}^2 - 2\left(\frac{AL}{S^2}\right) \text{cov}(ROA, ROL)$$

$$+ 2\left(\frac{AP}{S^2}\right) \text{cov}(ROA, ROU) - 2\left(\frac{LP}{S^2}\right) \text{cov}(ROL, ROU) \tag{2}$$

The variance of combination of three variables is the weighted sum of their variances offset by their covariances. In this case, surplus risk is the weighted sum of variances of ROA, ROL and ROU, with the leverage ratios as their weights.

Thus the volatility of surplus can be affected by up to six factors. For example, a firm that has high asset volatility may be able to mitigate such volatility through decreased investment leverage or low covariances with the liabilities or underwriting results.

Objective Function

Having defined the return and risk to surplus, standard quadratic programming techniques can be applied to solve for optimal portfolios. The decision variables are the weights of the investment assets and the amount of insurance leverage.

The model assumes that the return of liabilities, return on underwriting, investment leverage and financial leverage are beyond control and thus not true parameters. In practice, the three major return components and the leverage ratios are all decision variables. Thus the model can be extended to help insurers make optimal asset allocation and capital utilization decisions.

---

[3] While the model uses a variance framework, semivariance could easily be substituted into the model.

The objective function is expressed as:

$$\text{minimize } \sigma_{\text{ROS}}^2 \text{ for ROS}_n = (r_1, r_2, r_3, ..., r_n) \tag{3}$$

subject to:

$$\sum_1^n x_i = 1$$

$x_i \geq 0$ for any i

$$\frac{A}{S} - \frac{L}{S} = 1$$

The objective function minimizes the variance of the portfolio in surplus space for a given level of surplus return. This process, similar to Markowitz's mean-variance optimization,[4] produces an efficient frontier of surplus efficient portfolios.

Input Estimation

Before moving on to demonstrate how the model can be used as a decision-making tool, commentary on the estimation of the inputs of the model is in order.

To represent each asset class, an expected return and variance estimate must be assigned. Many methods exist to forecast returns, but for the purposes of this chapter, time series of expected return data on capital market assets are used to represent the ROA.

Any proxy of the expected return for liabilities across time would be based upon market values as opposed to statutory values. Highly simplified approximations on the behavior of the liabilities exist. For example, one method approximates the liability return as the change in the present value of the liability (discounted at the current rate of interest consistent with the duration of the liabilities) caused by interest rate movements. With this method, the negated expected return of a Treasury bond with the same duration as the liabilities can be used as a proxy. Further, innovative techniques in liability based benchmarking have suggested building a portfolio of capital market instruments that seek to replicate the behavior of the liabilities.[5] For the purposes of this chapter, the single Treasury security method was chosen for simplicity.

Analysis of the underwriting results in property and casualty insurers centers around three key ratios: the loss, expense and combined ratios. The conventional interpretation of the combined ratio is an accounting rate of return equal to the calendar-year losses divided by net premiums earned (loss ratio), plus the expense ratio. The incurred losses which underlie the loss ratio are the sum of all loss payments plus any changes in the loss reserves during that calendar year. This provides only an accounting rate of return, not an economic measure of the rate of return. A measure

---

[4] Harry M. Markowitz, "Portfolio Selection," *Journal of Finance* (March 1952).

[5] Key rate duration estimates of liabilities can be used to create a basket of securities that exhibit the approximate interest rate sensitivity of the liabilities.

closer to the economic rate of return from underwriting can be calculated by adjusting for the periodicity of loss payments to the year that the loss event occurred. An accident-year combined ratio matches loss payments and changes in reserve estimates to the year the event occurred, thereby providing an approximation of the economic rate of return of the underwriting operations of the insurer. A historical underwriting return series can be calculated by subtracting one from the accident-year combined ratio. Aside from the periodicity problem in the loss ratio, another problem exists for which no apparent adjustment is available. The loss reserves of the insurer may incorporate intentional reserving errors meant to stabilize reported underwriting results. This smoothing of loss reserves, while undertaken sometimes for tax purposes or other financial reporting, will downwardly impact the volatility of underwriting results.[6] Errors in reserves are calculated as the difference between ultimate losses and the original estimate for incurred losses in each year. Based on the magnitude and pattern of these reserve errors, adjustments can be made for more meaningful estimates of true underwriting results. Until insurance liability portfolio trading is widespread in the capital markets, the accident year combined ratio approach, mindful of reserving errors, is a reasonable representation of underwriting returns.

The estimation of the asset, liability, and underwriting covariance matrix can be based on the historical time series derived above. However, using historical data to represent behavior, explicitly assumes that past results are indicative of future results. New techniques in volatility forecasting may provide a more predictive covariance matrix than one obtained solely from historical time series.[7]

The integration of a company's tax status is a crucial element of any investment plan. Federal income taxation codes for P&C insurance companies include the calculation of the regular tax and the Alternative Minimum Tax (AMT). Current theory suggests that the optimal taxable/tax-exempt mix is determined when the regular tax and the AMT tax are equivalent.[8] At this point the profitability of the company's investment and underwriting activities is maximized.[9] However, the code creates the ability for an insurer to build and use an AMT credit. Such credits are accrued in years that an insurer is an AMT payer and applied in subsequent years to offset regular tax. Thus the existence of an AMT credit allows us to assume that the insurer will forever be a marginal regular tax payer. Thus a simplifying assumption is that the insurer pays regular taxes.

Analysis of capital utilization focuses around the insurance leverage ratio,[10] which measures the amount of policies written per unit of surplus on the

---

[6] Mary A. Weiss, "A Multivariate Analysis of Loss Reserving Estimates in Property-Liability Insurers," *Journal of Risk and Insurance* (June 1985).

[7] Methods which should be considered, if they are properly specified, are ARMA and GARCH models.

[8] Alfred Weinberger and Vincent Kaminski, "Investment Strategy for Property/Casualty Insurance Companies: The Fixed Income Portfolio After Tax Reform," *Salomon Brothers Research*, 1991.

[9] The Tax Reform Act of 1986 stipulates that an insurance company must pay the greater of the regular or alternative minimum tax; thus by minimizing the amount of taxes paid, income is maximized.

[10] J. David Cummins and David J. Nye, "Portfolio Optimization Models for Property-Liability Insurance Companies: An Analysis and Some Extensions," *Management Science* (April 1981).

insurer's balance sheet. While higher leverage can improve a company's profitability, it can also attract the unwanted attention of insurance regulators and rating agencies. On the other hand, low insurance leverage can indicate that the insurer may be too conservative in its policy writing, therefore under-utilizing its capital.

Applying surplus returns and surplus standard deviation to classic mean-variance techniques generates the efficient frontier, maximizing surplus return for a given level of surplus risk. In the normal application of mean-variance optimization, returns (without borrowing) can never be negative; however, in surplus space, the difference between asset returns and liability returns can be negative.

Risk Tolerance

One flaw in asset allocation models is that they provide no guidance for choosing the optimal asset allocation. Utility theory comes in handy and can provide a structure for choosing the optimal portfolio. Estimating the utility function of the insurer is equivalently estimating the risk aversion factor. For example, insurers with stable operating results and steady cashflow may have a low risk aversion factor, and can afford a more aggressive investment program. On the other hand, insurers with poor operations may have higher risk aversion and tend to favor more conservative investment portfolios.

AN ILLUSTRATION

A demonstration of the application of the asset allocation model to the hypothetical investment portfolio of a personal automobile liability insurer is presented in Exhibit 2.

Insurance Company A writes automobile insurance for qualified insurers. The insurer's latest rating from AM Best was A++(Superior), reflecting the company's outstanding underwriting performance, conservative operating strategy, and substantial capital adequacy. Company A's profitability has been consistently superior over the past five years. With an average combined ratio of 97,[11] the company maintains a competitive cost advantage over its competitors. There are no foreseeable reasons for Company A not to continue in the same fashion in the future.

Exhibit 2: Asset Allocation as of 6/30/97 ($MM)

Company A	$Value	Percent
Cash	380	7.3
Treasuries	1380	26.6
Corporates	9	0.2
Municipals	3,130	60.5
Equity	185	3.6
Real Estate	94	1.8
	5,178	100.0

[11] For this example, Company A's calendar-year and accident-year combined ratios equate.

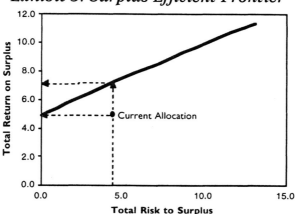

Exhibit 3: Surplus Efficient Frontier

Exhibit 4: Surplus Efficient Mixes

Asset Allocation	Return on Surplus	Risk to Surplus
Current Alloc.	4.92	4.41
Mix 1	5.05	0.37
Mix 2	5.76	1.56
Mix 3	6.47	2.98
Mix 4	7.18	4.42
Mix 5	7.88	5.86
Mix 6	8.59	7.30
Mix 7	9.29	8.74
Mix 8	10.00	10.18
Mix 9	10.70	11.63
Mix 10	11.41	13.13

The majority of Company A's investment assets are concentrated in tax-exempt bonds. The remainder is split among cash, government securities, and equities. Corporate debt represents an insignificant part of the portfolio. There is a small real estate allocation representing the land and building in which its headquarters are housed.

Using the information obtained by Company A's annual statements and AM Best Reports, the inputs of the model can be computed.

Exhibits 3 and 4 present the surplus optimization results subject to the constraints imposed by the Model Investment Law.[12] This was chosen to define

[12] The defunct Model Investment Law, now a part of Appendix A-280, placed specific limits on investment asset sectors such as common stocks, foreign stocks, and fixed income credit sectors. Some of the general constraints of the Model Investment Law were: up to 40% of assets can be invested in Canadian government bonds, up to 10% in government money market mutual funds, up to 20% in NAIC 3 or lower rated debt, up to 20% in foreign securities, up to 25% in common stocks, and up to 20% in preferred stocks. Additionally, the Model Investment Law had provisions for derivatives, mortgage backed securities, and an all encompassing "basket clause."

the investment constraints, not because it is prescriptive of optimal allocations, but rather because it is a standard publicly available constraint set that is useful for the example.

With the current asset allocation, Company A is earning an after-tax surplus return of 4.92% at a surplus risk (standard deviation of return on surplus) of 4.41%. While the current mix has provided sufficient earnings to Company A, it lies below the efficient frontier. By traveling towards the efficient frontier, a portfolio that maximizes return for risk can be found. Mix 4 incurs approximately the same risk to surplus with considerably more return on surplus than the current mix — adding 226 basis points of incremental return.

To arrive at Mix 4, shown in Exhibit 5, Company A would need to reduce its Treasury and municipal holdings. Allocations to short-term bonds and equity would be increased. Real estate is constrained at 1.82%, since the allocation represents the company's building.

AN EXTENDED ILLUSTRATION

As noted earlier in this chapter, the major components of return on surplus are based on investment, reserving and underwriting activity. This section will demonstrate that by changing the insurance leverage of the firm, the insurer can increase return with relatively small increases in risk.

Using the scenario developed in the previous section, a comparison of the minimum risk portfolios under various insurance leverage levels will illustrate the profound effect that this decision variable can have. Exhibit 6 plots three efficient frontiers with insurance leverage set to 1.03, 1.5, and 2.0.

The effect of the increase of insurance leverage is dramatic, as shown in Exhibit 7. For example, a change from a 1.03 ratio to a 1.50 ratio increases the return on the minimum risk portfolio by 180 basis points with a 10 basis point rise in risk.

The implication to surplus maximizing insurers is that in addition to the investment allocation decision, insurers can increase the amount of premiums generated per unit of surplus to leverage the return (if positive) that the underwriting activities contribute to surplus.

Exhibit 5: Implementation of Efficient Portfolio

Asset Allocation	Mix 4	Change from Present
Short Bonds	43.8%	+36.5%
Interm. Treas.	21.5%	-5.1%
Int. Corps	0.0%	-0.2%
Municipals	23.4%	-37.1%
Equity	9.5%	+5.9%
Real Estate	1.8%	0.0%
Total	100.0%	

Exhibit 6: Surplus Efficient Frontier with Variable Insurance Leverage

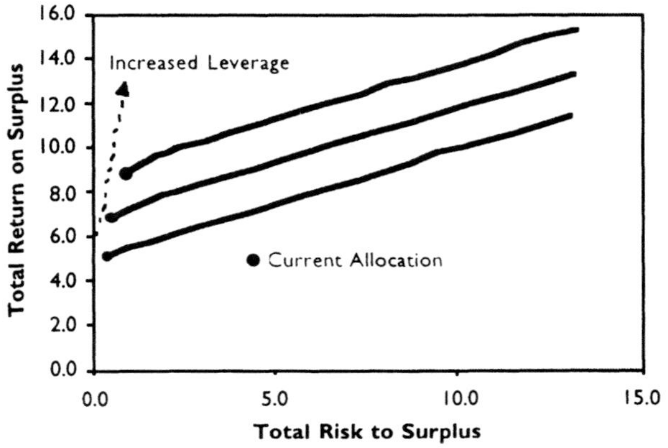

Exhibit 7: Minimum Risk Portfolio with Variable Insurance Leverage

Minimum Risk Portfolios	Current P/S	1.5 P/S	2.0 P/S
Short Bonds	64.0%	67.4%	71.1%
Interm. Treas.	33.0%	28.3%	23.3%
Int. Corps	0.0%	0.0%	0.0%
Municipals	1.2%	2.5%	3.8%
Equity	0.0%	0.0%	0.0%
Real Estate	1.8%	1.8%	1.8%
Total	100.0%	100.0%	100.0%
Return on Surplus	5.1%	6.9%	8.9%
Risk to Surplus	0.4%	0.5%	0.9%

By incorporating insurance leverage as a decision variable, the nature of efficient portfolios and risk tolerance is altered. Instead of an efficient frontier to guide insurers, they are now faced with an "efficient plane," shown in Exhibit 8, that illustrates the optimal mix of investment assets and insurance leverage.

POLICY ISSUES

Any analysis of alternative asset allocations may include the impact on a company's Risk Based Capital (RBC) or other regulatory or rating agency constraints.[13] The model can be used as a starting point for measuring the impact of asset allocation decisions on RBC through sensitivity analysis. Such analysis

---

[13] "Risk-Based Capital Requirements for Insurers," National Association of Insurance Commissioners, 1996.

entails measuring each asset allocation's marginal impact on RBC to ensure that the asset allocations fall within acceptable RBC limits.

SUMMARY

In an environment of increased competition, insurers must begin to manage their investment portfolios with greater integration between the liability and underwriting results. The insurance asset allocation model described in this chapter provides a framework for making optimal investment and capital utilization decisions. The model focuses on the company's economic surplus to measure the effect various decisions will have on the ongoing financial health of the firm.

Exhibit 8: Surplus Efficient Plane

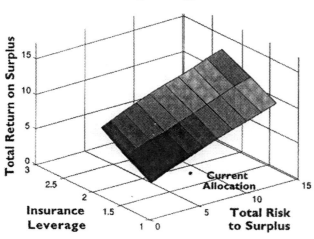

Section II:

Fixed Income Products

Chapter 5

Treasuries, Agency Debentures, Corporates, MTNs, Municipals, and Eurobonds

Frank J. Fabozzi, Ph.D., CFA
Adjunct Professor of Finance
School of Management
Yale University

INTRODUCTION

In its simplest form, a fixed income security is a financial obligation of an entity that promises to pay a specified sum of money at specified future dates. The entity that promises to make the payment is called the *issuer* of the security. Some examples of issuers are the U.S. government or a foreign government, a state or local government entity, a domestic or foreign corporation, and a supranational government such as the World Bank.

Fixed income securities fall into two general categories: debt obligations and preferred stock. In the case of a debt obligation, the issuer is called the *borrower*. The investor who purchases such a fixed income security is said to be the *lender* or *creditor*. The promised payments that the issuer agrees to make at the specified dates consist of two components: interest payments and repayment of the amount borrowed. Fixed income securities that are debt obligations include bonds, mortgage-backed securities, and asset-backed securities.

In contrast to a fixed income security that represents a debt obligation, preferred stock represents an ownership interest in a corporation. The payments that are made to the preferred stockholder include dividends and repayment of a fixed amount to retire the obligation. The dividends paid represent a distribution of the corporation's profit. Unlike investors who own a corporation's common stock, investors who own the preferred stock can realize only a contractually fixed dividend payment. Moreover, the payments that must be made to preferred stockholders have priority over the payments that a corporation pays to common stockholders. In the case of a liquidation of a corporation, preferred stockholders are given preference over common stockholders. Consequently, preferred stock is a form of equity that has characteristics similar to bonds.

Prior to the 1980s, fixed income securities were simple investment products. Holding aside default by the issuer, the investor knew how much interest would

91

be received periodically and when the amount borrowed would be repaid. Moreover, most investors purchased these securities with the intent of holding them to their maturity date. Beginning in the 1980s, the fixed income world changed. First, fixed income securities became more complex. There are features in many fixed income securities that make it difficult to determine when the principal will be repaid. For some securities it is difficult to project the amount of interest that will be received periodically. Second, the hold-to-maturity investor has been replaced by institutional investors such as insurance companies who actively trade fixed income securities.

In this chapter and the one to follow, we will review the wide range of bonds and structured products. In this chapter we look at Treasury securities, corporate bonds, medium-term notes, municipal securities, and Eurobonds. In the next chapter we focus on mortgage-backed securities and asset-backed securities.

CLASSIFICATION OF GLOBAL BOND MARKETS

While there is no uniform system for classifying global bond markets, Exhibit 1 provides a reasonable classification system. From the perspective of a given country, bond markets can be classified as either *internal* or *external*. The internal bond market is also called the *national bond market*. It can be decomposed into two parts: the domestic bond market and the foreign bond market. The *domestic bond market* is where issuers domiciled in the country issue securities and where those securities are subsequently traded.

The *foreign bond market* of a country is where the securities of issuers not domiciled in the country are sold and traded. The rules governing the issuance of foreign securities are those imposed by regulatory authorities where the security is issued. For example, bonds issued by non-U.S. corporations in the United States must comply with the regulations set forth in U.S. securities law. A non-Japanese corporation that seeks to offer bonds in Japan must comply with Japanese securities law and regulations imposed by the Japanese Ministry of Finance. Nicknames have been used to describe the various foreign bond markets. For example, the foreign bond market in the United States is called the "Yankee market." The foreign bond market in Japan is nicknamed the "Samurai market," in the United Kingdom the "Bulldog market," in the Netherlands the "Rembrandt market," and in Spain the "Matador market."

Exhibit 1: Classification of Global Bond Markets

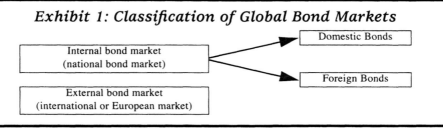

The external bond market, also called the *international bond market*, includes securities with the following distinguishing features: (1) at issuance they are offered simultaneously to investors in a number of countries, and (2) they are issued outside the jurisdiction of any single country. The external bond market is commonly referred to as the *offshore bond market*, or more popularly, the *Eurobond market* (even though this market is not limited to Europe, it began there).[1] A *global bond* is a bond that is issued and traded in both the U.S. Yankee bond market and the Eurobond market.

COUPON RATE: FIXED VERSUS FLOATING-RATE BONDS

The *coupon rate*, also called the *nominal rate*, is the interest rate that the issuer agrees to pay each year. The annual amount of the interest payment made to bondholders during the term of the bond is called the *coupon*. The coupon is determined by multiplying the coupon rate by the par value of the bond. For example, a bond with an 8% coupon rate and a par value of $1,000 will pay annual interest of $80. When describing a bond of an issuer, the coupon rate is indicated along with the maturity date. For example, the expression "6s of 12/1/2010" means a bond with a 6% coupon rate maturing on 12/1/2010.

In the United States, the usual practice is for the issuer to pay the coupon in two semiannual installments. Mortgage-backed securities and asset-backed securities typically pay interest monthly. For bonds issued in some markets outside the United States, coupon payments are made only once per year.

Zero-Coupon Bonds

Not all bonds make periodic coupon payments. Bonds that are not contracted to make periodic coupon payments are called *zero-coupon bonds*. The holder of a zero-coupon bond realizes interest by buying the bond substantially below its par value. Interest then is paid at the maturity date, with the interest being the difference between the par value and the price paid for the bond. So, for example, if an investor purchases a zero-coupon bond for 70, the interest is 30. This is the difference between the par value (100) and the price paid (70).

There is another type of bond that does not pay interest until the maturity date. This type has contractual coupon payments but those payments are accrued and distributed along with the maturity value at the maturity date. For lack of a better term, these instruments can be called *accrued coupon instruments* or *accrual securities*.

---

[1] The classification we use is by no means universally accepted. Some marker observers and compilers of statistical data on market activity refer to the external bond market as consisting of the foreign bond market and the Eurobond market.

Floating-Rate Securities

The coupon rate on a bond need not be fixed over the bond's life. *Floating-rate securities*, sometimes called *variable-rate securities*, have coupon payments that reset periodically according to some *reference rate*. The typical formula for the coupon rate at the dates when the coupon rate is reset is:

Reference rate + Index spread

The *index spread* is the additional amount that the issuer agrees to pay above the reference rate. For example, suppose that the reference rate is the 1-month London interbank offered rate (LIBOR).[2] Suppose that the index spread is 100 basis points. Then the coupon reset formula is:

1-month LIBOR + 100 basis points

So, if 1-month LIBOR on the coupon reset date is 5%, the coupon rate is reset for that period at 6% (5% plus 100 basis points).

The index spread need not be a positive value. The index spread could be subtracted from the reference rate. For example, the reference rate could be the yield on a 5-year Treasury security and the coupon rate could reset every six months based on the following coupon reset formula:

5-year Treasury yield – 90 basis points

So, if the 5-year Treasury yield is 7% on the coupon reset date, the coupon rate is 6.1% (7% minus 90 basis points).

The reference rate for most floating-rate securities is an interest rate or an interest rate index. There are some issues where this is not the case. Instead, the reference rate is some financial index such as the return on the Standard & Poor's 500 or a nonfinancial index such as the price of a commodity. Through financial engineering, issuers have been able to structure floating-rate securities with almost any reference rate. In several countries, there are government bonds whose coupon formula is tied to an inflation index. As explained later in this chapter, in 1997 the U.S. government began issuing such bonds.

Caps and Floors

A floating-rate security may have a restriction on the maximum coupon rate that will be paid at a reset date. The maximum coupon rate is called a *cap*. For example, suppose for our hypothetical floating-rate security whose coupon rate formula is 1-month LIBOR plus 100 basis points, there is a cap of 11%. If 1-month LIBOR

---

[2] LIBOR is the interest rate at which major international banks offer each other on Eurodollar certificates of deposit (CD) with given maturities. The maturities range from overnight to five years. Reference to "1-month LIBOR" means the interest rate that major international banks are offering to pay to other such banks on a CD that matures in one month.

is 10.5% at a coupon reset date, then the coupon rate formula would give a value of 11.5%. However, the cap restricts the coupon rate to 11%. Thus, for our hypothetical security, once 1-month LIBOR exceeds 10%, the coupon rate is capped at 11%.

Because a cap restricts the coupon rate from increasing, a cap is an unattractive feature for the investor. In contrast, there could be a minimum coupon rate specified for a floating-rate security. The minimum coupon rate is called a *floor*. If the coupon reset formula produces a coupon rate that is below the floor, the floor is paid instead. Thus, a floor is an attractive feature for the investor.

Inverse Floaters

Typically, the coupon reset formula on floating-rate securities is such that the coupon rate increases when the reference rate increases, and decreases when the reference rate decreases. There are issues whose coupon rate moves in the opposite direction from the change in the reference rate. Such issues are called *inverse floaters* or *reverse floaters*. A general formula for an inverse floater is:

K − L × (Reference rate)

For example, suppose that for a particular inverse floater K is 12% and L is 1. Then the coupon reset formula would be:

12% − Reference rate

Suppose that the reference rate is 1-month LIBOR, then the coupon reset formula would be

12% − 1-month LIBOR

If in some month 1-month LIBOR at the coupon reset date is 5%, the coupon rate for the period is 7%. If in the next month 1-month LIBOR declines to 4.5%, the coupon rate increases to 7.5%.

Notice that if 1-month LIBOR exceeded 12%, then the coupon reset formula would produce a negative coupon rate. To prevent this, there is a floor imposed on the coupon rate. Typically, the floor is zero. While not explicitly stated, there is a cap on the inverse floater. This occurs if 1-month LIBOR is zero. In that unlikely event, the maximum coupon rate is 12% for our hypothetical inverse floater. In general, it will be the value of K in the coupon reset formula for an inverse floater.

Suppose instead that the coupon reset formula for an inverse floater whose reference rate is 1-month LIBOR is as follows:

28% − 3 × (1-month LIBOR)

If 1-month LIBOR at a reset date is 5%, then the coupon rate for that month is 13%. If in the next month 1-month LIBOR declines to 4%, the coupon rate increases to 16%. Thus, a decline in 1-month LIBOR of 100 basis points increases the coupon rate by 300 basis points.[3] This is because the value for L in the coupon reset formula is 3. Assuming neither the cap nor the floor is reached, for each one basis point change in 1-month LIBOR the coupon rate changes by 3 basis points.

Range Notes

A *range note* is a floating-rate security whose coupon rate is equal to the reference rate as long as the reference rate is within a certain range at the reset date. If the reference rate is outside of the range, the coupon rate is zero for that period.

For example, a 3-year range note might specify that the reference rate is 1-year LIBOR and that the coupon rate resets every year. The coupon rate for the year will be 1-year LIBOR as long as 1-year LIBOR at the coupon reset date falls within the range as specified below:

	Year 1	Year 2	Year 3
Lower limit of range	4.5%	5.25%	6.00%
Upper limit of range	5.5%	6.75%	7.50%

If 1-year LIBOR is outside of the range, the coupon rate is zero. For example, if in Year 1 1-year LIBOR is 5% at the coupon reset date, the coupon rate for the year is 5%. However, if 1-year LIBOR is 6%, the coupon rate for the year is zero since 1-year LIBOR is greater than the upper limit for Year 1 of 5.5%.

Step-Up Notes

There are securities that have a coupon rate that increases over time. These securities are called *step-up notes* because the coupon rate "steps up" over time. For example, a 5-year step-up note might have a coupon rate that is 5% for the first two years and 6% for the last three years. Or, the step-up note could call for a 5% coupon rate for the first two years, 5.5% for the third and fourth years, and 6% for the fifth year. When there is only one change (or step up), as in our first example, the issue is referred to as a *single step-up note*. When there is more than one increase, as in our second example, the issue is referred to as a *multiple step-up note*.

Deferred Coupon Bonds

There are issues whose coupon payment is deferred for a specified number of years. That is, there is no coupon payment for the deferred period and then a lump sum payment at some specified date and coupon payments until maturity.

Accrued Interest

Bond issuers do not disburse coupon interest payments every day. Instead, typically in the United States coupon interest is paid every six months. In some countries, interest is paid annually. For mortgage-backed and asset-backed securities,

---

[3] A basis point is equal to 0.0001 or 0.01%. Thus, 100 basis points are equal to 1%.

interest is usually paid monthly. The coupon interest payment is made to the bondholder of record. Thus, if an investor sells a bond between coupon payments and the buyer holds it until the next coupon payment, then the entire coupon interest earned for the period will be paid to the buyer of the bond since the buyer will be the holder of record. The seller of the bond gives up the interest from the time of the last coupon payment to the time until the bond is sold. The amount of interest over this period that will be received by the buyer even though it was earned by the seller is called *accrued interest*.

In the United States and in many countries, the bond buyer must pay the bond seller the accrued interest. The amount that the buyer pays the seller is the agreed upon price for the bond plus accrued interest. This amount is called the *full price*. The agreed upon bond price without accrued interest is called the *clean price*.

A bond in which the buyer must pay the seller accrued interest is said to be trading *cum-coupon*. If the buyer forgoes the next coupon payment, the bond is said to be trading *ex-coupon*. In the United States, bonds are always traded cum coupon. There are bond markets outside the United States where bonds are traded ex-coupon for a certain period before the coupon payment date.

There are exceptions to the rule that the bond buyer must pay the bond seller accrued interest. The most important exception is when the issuer has not fulfilled its promise to make the periodic payments. In this case, the issuer is said to be in default. In such instances, the bond's price is sold without accrued interest and is said to be traded *flat*.

When calculating accrued interest, three pieces of information are needed: (1) the number of days in the accrued interest period, (2) the number of days in the coupon period, and (3) the dollar amount of the coupon payment. The number of days in the accrued interest period represents the number of days over which the investor has earned interest. Given these values, the accrued interest (AI) assuming semiannual payments is calculated as follows:

$$AI = \frac{\text{Annual dollar coupon}}{2} \times \frac{\text{Days in AI period}}{\text{Days in coupon period}}$$

For example, suppose that (1) there are 50 days in the accrued interest period, (2) there are 183 days in the coupon period, and (3) the annual coupon per $100 of par value is $8. Then the accrued interest is:

$$AI = \frac{\$8}{2} \times \frac{50}{183} = \$1.0929$$

The calculation of the number days in the accrued interest period and the number of days in the coupon period begins with the determination of three key dates: trade date, settlement date, and date of previous coupon payment. The *trade date* is the date on which the transaction is executed. The *settlement date* is the date a transaction is completed. Interest accrues from and including the date of the previous coupon payment up to but *excluding* the settlement date.

The number of days in the accrued interest period and the number of days in the coupon period may not be simply the actual number of calendar days between two dates. The reason is that there is a market convention for each type of security that specifies how to determine the number of days between two dates. These conventions are called *day count conventions*. We'll discuss these conventions when we describe the various types of bonds.

U.S. TREASURY SECURITIES[4]

U.S. Treasury securities are issued by the U.S. Department of the Treasury. These securities are backed by the full faith and credit of the U.S. government. Therefore, they are viewed as default-free securities. Interest income from Treasury securities is subject to federal income taxes but is exempt from state and local income taxes.

There are two categories of U.S. Treasury securities — discount and coupon securities. Current Treasury practice is to issue all securities with maturities of one year or less (Treasury bills) as discount securities. All securities with maturities of two years or longer are issued as coupon securities. At issuance Treasury notes have a maturity between two and ten years, and Treasury bonds at issuance have a maturity greater than ten years. Although Treasury notes are not callable, many outstanding Treasury bond issues are callable within five years of maturity. Treasury bonds issued since February 1985 are not callable. Our focus below is on Treasury notes and bonds.

Treasury coupon securities come in two forms: fixed-rate and variable-rate securities. The reference rate for the latter is the Consumer Price Index. These securities are called Treasury inflation protection securities. They are discussed in more detail below.

Treasury securities typically are issued on an auction basis according to regular cycles for securities of specific maturities. Three-month and 6-month Treasury bills are auctioned every Monday. One-year (52-week bill) Treasury bills are auctioned in the third week of every month. The Treasury regularly issues coupon securities with maturities of 2, 3, 5, 10, and 30 years.[5] Two- and 5-year notes are auctioned each month. At the beginning of the second month of each calendar quarter (February, May, August, and November), the Treasury conducts its regular refunding operations. At this time, it auctions 3-year, 10-year, and 30-year Treasury securities. Treasury inflation protection securities are issued quarterly (January, April, July, and October).

The secondary market for Treasury securities is an over-the-counter market where a group of U.S. government securities dealers provide continuous bids and offers on specific outstanding Treasuries. This secondary market is the most liquid financial market in the world.

---

[4] For a more detailed discussion of Treasury Securities and the market in which they trade, see Frank J. Fabozzi, *Treasury Securities and Derivatives* (New Hope, PA: Frank J. Fabozzi Associates, 1997).

[5] At one time, the Treasury issued 7-year notes and 20-year bonds.

In the secondary market, the most recently auctioned Treasury issues for each maturity are referred to as "on-the-run" or "current-coupon" issues. They are also referred to as the benchmark issues on bellwether issues. Issues auctioned prior to the current coupon issues typically are referred to as "off-the-run" issues; they are not as liquid as on-the-run issues. That is, the bid-ask spread is larger for off-the-run issues relative to on-the-run issues because they are not as liquid.

Treasury securities are traded prior to the time they are issued by the Treasury. This component of the Treasury secondary market is called the *when-issued market*, or "wi market." When-issued trading for both Treasury bills and Treasury coupon issues extends from the day the auction is announced until the issue day.

Treasury Inflation Protection Securities

In 1997, the U.S. Department of the Treasury issued for the first time Treasury securities that adjust for inflation. These securities are popularly referred to as *Treasury inflation protection securities* or TIPS. These securities work as follows. The coupon rate on an issue is set at a fixed rate. That rate is determined via the standard auction process. The coupon rate is called the *real rate* since it is the rate that the investor earns above the inflation rate.

The adjustment for inflation is as follows. The principal that the Treasury Department will base both the dollar amount of the coupon payment and the maturity value will be adjusted semiannually. This is called the *inflation-adjusted principal*. For example, suppose that the coupon rate for a TIPS is 3.5% and the annual inflation rate is 3%. Suppose further that an investor purchases $100,000 of par value (principal) of this issue and that the semiannual inflation rate is 1.5%. Multiplying 1.5% by the initial principal of $100,000 gives the inflation-adjusted principal of $101,500. The dollar amount of the coupon payment for the period is found by multiplying the inflation-adjusted principal times the semiannual coupon rate. In our example, it is $1,776.25 which is found by multiplying $101,500 (the inflation-adjusted principal) by 1.75% (the semiannual coupon rate). Suppose that in the subsequent semiannual period, the inflation rate is 2%. Then the inflation-adjusted principal is found by multiplying the prior inflation-adjusted principal of $101,500 by the semiannual inflation rate of 1%. The new inflation-adjusted principal would then be $102,515. The dollar amount of the coupon payment would be the semiannual coupon rate of 1.75% multiplied by the new inflation-adjusted principal of $102,515, or $1,794.01.

As can be seen, part of the adjustment for inflation comes in the coupon payment since it is based on the inflation-adjusted principal. The majority of the compensation for inflation comes in the form of the adjustment to the principal which is paid at the maturity date. However, the U.S. government has decided to tax the adjustment each year. This feature reduces the attractiveness of TIPS as investments in accounts of tax-paying entities.

Because of the possibility of disinflation (i.e., price declines), the inflation-adjusted principal at maturity may turn out to be less than the initial par value. The Treasury has structured TIPS so that they are redeemed at the greater of the inflation-adjusted principal and the initial par value.

The inflation index that the government has decided to use for the inflation adjustment. The index is the non-seasonally adjusted U.S. City Average All Items Consumer Price Index for All Urban Consumers (CPI-U). An inflation-adjusted principal must be calculated for a settlement date. The inflation-adjusted principal will be defined in terms of an *index ratio* which is the ratio of the reference CPI for the settlement date to the reference CPI for the issue date. The reference CPI will be calculated with a 3-month lag. For example, the reference CPI for May 1 will be the CPI-U reported in February. The U.S. Department of the Treasury will publish a daily index ratio for an issue each month.

Price Quotation Convention for Treasury Coupon Securities

Treasury coupon securities are quoted on a dollar price basis in price units of $\frac{1}{32}$ of 1% of par (par is taken to be $100). For example, a quote of 92-14 refers to a price of 92 and $\frac{14}{32}$. On the basis of $100,000 par value, a change in price of 1% equates to $1,000, and $\frac{1}{32}$ of 1% equates to $31.25. A plus sign following the number of 32nds means that $\frac{1}{64}$ is added to the price. For example, 92-14+ refers to a price of 92 and $\frac{29}{64}$ or 92.453125% of par value.

As explained earlier, the day count conventions for a security determine the number of days in the accrued interest period and the number of days in the coupon period. For Treasury securities, settlement is the next business day after the trade date. For Treasury coupon securities, the day count convention used is to determine the actual number of days between two dates. This is referred to as the "actual/actual" day count convention. For example, consider a Treasury coupon security whose previous coupon payment was May 15. The next coupon payment would be on November 15. Suppose this Treasury security is purchased with a settlement date of September 10. First, the number of days of accrued interest is calculated. The actual number of days between May 15 (the previous coupon date) and September 10 (the settlement date) is 118 days, as shown below:

May 15 to May 31	17 days[6]
June	30 days
July	31 days
August	31 days
September 1 to September 10	9 days[7]
	118 days

---

[6] Notice that May 15 is counted for purposes of determining the number of days in the accrued interest period.

[7] Notice that the settlement date (September 10) is not included for purposes of determining the number of days in the accrued interest period.

The number of days in the coupon period is the actual number of days between May 15 and November 15, which is 184 days. The number of days between the settlement date (September 10) and the next coupon date (November 15) is therefore 66 days (184 days – 118 days).

Stripped Treasury Securities

The U.S. Treasury does not issue zero-coupon notes or bonds. In August 1982, however, both Merrill Lynch and Salomon Brothers created synthetic zero-coupon Treasury receipts. Merrill Lynch marketed its Treasury receipts as "Treasury Income Growth Receipts" (TIGRs); Salomon Brothers marketed its as "Certificates of Accrual on Treasury Securities" (CATS).

The procedure was to purchase Treasury bonds and deposit them in a bank custody account. The dealer then issued receipts representing an ownership interest in each coupon payment on the underlying Treasury bond in the account and a receipt on the underlying Treasury bond's maturity value. This process of separating each coupon payment, as well as the principal, to sell securities backed by them is referred to as "coupon stripping." Although the receipts created from the coupon stripping process are not issued by the U.S. Treasury, the underlying bond deposited in the bank custody account is a debt obligation of the U.S. Treasury, so the cash flow from the underlying security is certain.

To illustrate the process, suppose $500 million of a Treasury bond with a 30-year maturity and a coupon rate of 6% is purchased to create zero-coupon Treasury securities. The cash flow from this Treasury bond is 60 semiannual payments of $15 million each ($500 million times 0.06 divided by 2) and the repayment of principal (corpus) of $500 million 30 years from now. This Treasury bond is deposited in a bank custody account. Receipts are then issued, each with a different single payment claim on the bank custody account. As there are 61 different payments to be made by the Treasury, a receipt representing a single payment claim on each payment is issued, which is effectively a zero-coupon bond. The amount of the maturity value for a receipt on a particular payment, whether coupon or principal, depends on the amount of the payment to be made by the U.S. Treasury on the underlying Treasury bond. In our example, 60 coupon receipts each have a maturity value of $15 million, and one receipt, the principal, has a maturity value of $500 million. The maturity dates for the receipts coincide with the corresponding payment dates by the Treasury. This is depicted in Exhibit 2.

To broaden the market and improve liquidity of these receipts, a group of primary dealers in the government market agreed to issue generic receipts that would not be directly associated with any of the participating dealers. These generic receipts are referred to as *Treasury Receipts* (TRs).

Other investment banking firms followed suit by creating their own receipts. They all are referred to as *trademark zero-coupon Treasury securities* because they are associated with a particular firm. Receipts of one firm were rarely traded by competing dealers, so the secondary market was not liquid for any one trademark security.

Exhibit 2: Creating Zero-Coupon Treasury Securities
Dealer purchases $500 million par of a 6% 30-year Treasury

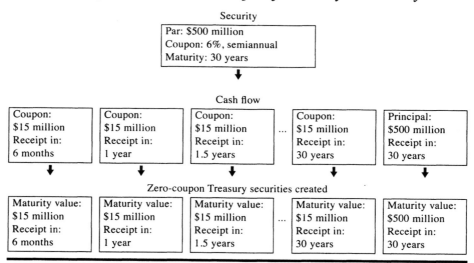

In February 1985, the U.S. Treasury announced its *Separate Trading of Registered Interest and Principal of Securities* (STRIPS) program to facilitate the stripping of Treasury securities. The zero-coupon Treasury securities created under the STRIPS program are direct obligations of the U.S. government. Creation of the STRIPS program ended the origination of trademarks and TRs.

FEDERAL AGENCY SECURITIES

The federal agency securities market can be divided into two sectors — the government sponsored enterprises securities market and the federally related institutions securities market.

Federally Related Institutions Securities

Federally related institutions are entities that are arms of the federal government that typically do not issue securities directly in the marketplace. These include: the Export-Import Bank of the United States, the Commodity Credit Corporation, the Farmers Housing Administration, the General Services Administration, the Government National Mortgage Association, the Maritime Administration, the Private Export Funding Corporation, the Rural Electrification Administration, the Rural Telephone Bank, the Small Business Administration, and the Washington Metropolitan Area Transit Authority. The Tennessee Valley Authority is a federally related institution that now issues its own securities. All federally related institutions are exempt from SEC registration. With the exception of securities of the Private Export Funding Corporation and the Tennessee Valley Authority, the securities are backed by the full faith and credit of the United States government.

Government Sponsored Enterprises Securities

Government sponsored enterprises (GSEs) are privately owned, publicly chartered entities. They were created by Congress to reduce the cost of capital for certain borrowing sectors of the economy deemed to be important enough to warrant assistance. The entities in these privileged sectors include farmers, homeowners, and students. GSEs issue securities directly in the marketplace.

There are eight GSEs. The enabling legislation dealing with a specific GSE is amended periodically. The Federal Farm Credit Bank System is responsible for the credit market in the agricultural sector of the economy. The Farm Credit Financial Association Corporation was created in 1987 to address problems in the existing Farm Credit System. Three GSEs — Federal Home Loan Bank, Federal Home Loan Mortgage Corporation, and Federal National Mortgage Association — are responsible for providing credit to the mortgage and housing sectors. The Student Loan Marketing Association provides funds to support higher education. The Financing Corporation was created in 1987 to recapitalize the Federal Savings and Loan Insurance Corporation. Because of continuing difficulties in the savings and loan association industry, the Resolution Trust Corporation was created in 1989 to liquidate or bail out insolvent institutions.

GSEs issue two types of securities: discount notes and bonds. Discount notes are short-term obligations, with maturities ranging from overnight to 360 days. Bonds are sold with maturities greater than two years. There are two types of bonds issued by federal agencies that have securitized loans. One is the standard bond which is called an *agency debenture*. The other is a mortgage-backed or asset-backed security which we will discuss in the next chapter.

With the exception of the securities issued by the Farm Credit Financial Assistance Corporation, GSE securities are not backed by the full faith and credit of the U.S. government, as is the case with Treasury securities and most federally related institutions securities. Consequently, investors purchasing securities of GSEs are exposed to credit risk.

The price quotation convention for GSE securities is the same as that for Treasury securities. That is, the bid and ask price quotations are expressed as a percentage of par plus fractional 32nds of a point. There are some GSE issues that trade with almost the same liquidity as Treasury securities. Other issues that are supported only by a few dealers trade much like off-the-run corporate bonds.

For agency debentures, the day count convention is as follows. It is assumed that every month has 30 days, that any 6-month period has 180 days, and that there are 360 days in a year. This day count convention is referred to as "30/360." For example, suppose an agency debenture is purchased with a settlement date of July 17, the previous coupon payment was on March 1, and the next coupon payment is on September 1. The number of days until the next coupon payment is 44 days as shown below:

July 17 to July 31	13 days
August	30 days
September 1	1 day
	44 days

The number of days from March 1 to July 17 is 136, which is their number of days in the accrued interest period.

CORPORATE BONDS

As the name indicates, corporate bonds are issued by corporations. Corporate bonds are classified by the type of issuer. The four general classifications used by bond information services are: (1) utilities, (2) transportations, (3) industrials, and (4) banks and finance companies. Finer breakdowns are often made to create more homogeneous groupings. For example, utilities are subdivided into electric power companies, gas distribution companies, water companies, and communication companies. Transportations are divided further into airlines, railroads, and trucking companies. Industrials are the catchall class, and the most heterogeneous of the groupings with respect to investment characteristics. Industrials include all kinds of manufacturing, merchandising, and service companies.

The promises of a corporate bond issuer and the rights of investors are set forth in great detail in a contract called a *bond indenture*. Failure to pay either the principal or interest when due constitutes legal default and court proceedings can be instituted to enforce the contract. Bondholders, as creditors, have a prior legal claim over preferred and common stockholders as to both income and assets of the corporation for the principal and interest due them.

There are two secondary corporate bond markets: the exchange market (New York Stock Exchange and American Stock Exchange) and the over-the-counter (OTC) market. Most trading takes place in the OTC market which is the market used by institutional investors.

In a typical corporate bond, there are options embedded in the issue. An embedded option is part of the structure of a bond, as opposed to a "bare option," which trades separately from any underlying security. As we describe the features of a corporate bond issue, these embedded options should be recognized since their presence, as we shall see in later chapters, affects the value of a bond and its price volatility characteristics.

Most corporate bonds are *term bonds*; that is, they run for a term of years and then become due and payable. Term bonds are often referred to as "bullet-maturity" or simply "bullet" bonds. The term may be long or short. As with Treasury securities, obligations due less than ten years from the date of issue are called notes; however, we do not make the distinction in this chapter. Term bonds may be retired by payment at final maturity or retired prior to maturity if provided for in the indenture. Some corporate bond issues are so arranged that specified principal amounts become due on specified dates. Such issues are called *serial bonds*.

The day count convention used for corporate bonds to compute accrued interest is "30/360." This is the same convention as used for agency debentures.

Security for Bonds

Either real property or personal property may be pledged to offer security beyond that of the general credit standing of the issuer. With a *mortgage bond*, the issuer has granted the bondholders a lien against the pledged assets. A lien is a legal right to sell mortgaged property to satisfy unpaid obligations to bondholders. In practice, foreclosure and sale of mortgaged property is unusual. If a default occurs, there is usually a financial reorganization of the issuer in which provision is made for settlement of the debt to bondholders. The mortgage lien is important, though, because it gives the mortgage bondholders a strong bargaining position relative to other creditors in determining the terms of a reorganization.

Some companies do not own fixed assets or other real property and so have nothing on which they can give a mortgage lien to secure bondholders. Instead, they own securities of other companies; they are holding companies and the other companies are subsidiaries. To satisfy the desire of bondholders for security, the issuer grants investors a lien on stocks, notes, bonds or whatever other kind of financial asset they own. Bonds secured by such assets are called *collateral trust bonds*.

Debenture bonds are not secured by a specific pledge of property, but that does not mean that holders have no claim on property of issuers or on their earnings. Debenture bondholders have the claim of general creditors on all assets of the issuer not pledged specifically to secure other debt. And they even have a claim on pledged assets to the extent that these assets generate proceeds in liquidation that is greater than necessary to satisfy secured creditors. *Subordinated debenture bonds* are issues that rank after secured debt, after debenture bonds, and often after some general creditors in their claim on assets and earnings.

It is important to recognize that while a superior legal status will strengthen a bondholder's chance of recovery in case of default, it will not absolutely prevent bondholders from suffering financial loss when the issuer's ability to generate cash flow adequate to pay its obligations is seriously eroded. Claims against a weak lender are often satisfied for less than par value.

Provisions for Paying off Bonds

Most corporate issues have a call provision whereby the issuer has an option to buy back all or part of the issue prior to maturity. Some issues specify that the issuer must retire a predetermined amount of the issue periodically. Various types of call provisions found in corporate bonds are discussed below.[8]

Call and Refund Provisions

An important question in negotiating the terms of a new bond issue is whether the issuer shall have the right to redeem the entire amount of bonds outstanding on a

---

[8] For a more detailed explanation of call provisions in corporate bonds, see: Richard S. Wilson and Frank J. Fabozzi, *Corporate Bonds: Structures and Analysis* (New Hope, PA: Frank J. Fabozzi Associates, 1996).

date before maturity. Issuers generally want this right because they recognize that at some time in the future the general level of interest rates may fall sufficiently below the issue's coupon rate, so redeeming the issue and replacing it with another issue with a lower coupon rate would be attractive. For the reasons discussed in Chapter 6, this right is a disadvantage to the bondholder. Thus, a call option is an embedded option granted to the issuer.

The usual practice is a provision that denies the issuer the right to redeem bonds during the first five to ten years following the date of issue with proceeds received from issuing lower-cost debt obligations ranking equal to or superior to the debt to be redeemed. This type of redemption is called *refunding*. While most long-term issues have these refunding restrictions, they may be immediately callable, in whole or in part, if the source of funds comes from other than lower interest cost money. Cash flow from operations, proceeds from a common stock sale, or funds from the sale of property are examples of such sources.

Investors often confuse refunding protection with call protection. Call protection is much more absolute in that bonds can not be redeemed *for any reason*. Refunding restrictions only provide protection against the one type of redemption mentioned above. Failure to recognize this difference has resulted in unnecessary losses for some investors.

When less than the entire issue is called, the procedure for calling the issue is specified in the indenture. The specific bonds to be called are either selected randomly or on a pro rata basis.

As a rule, corporate bonds are callable at a premium above par. Generally, the amount of the premium declines as the bond approaches maturity and often reaches par after a number of years have passed since issuance.

Sinking Fund Provision
Corporate bond indentures may require the issuer to retire a specified portion of an issue each year. This is referred to as a *sinking fund requirement*. This kind of provision for repayment of corporate debt may be designed to liquidate all of a bond issue by the maturity date, or it may be arranged to pay only a part of the total by the maturity date.

The purpose of the sinking fund provision is to reduce credit risk. Generally, the issuer may satisfy the sinking-fund requirement by either (1) making a cash payment of the face amount of the bonds to be retired to the corporate trustee who then calls the bonds for redemption using a lottery, or (2) delivering to the trustee bonds with a total face value equal to the amount that must be retired from bonds purchased in the open market. Usually, the sinking-fund call price is the par value if the bonds were originally sold at par.

Many corporate bond indentures include a provision that grants the issuer the right (i.e., option) to *accelerate* the repayment of the principal. This an another embedded option granted to the issuer since the issuer can take advantage of this provision if interest rates decline below the coupon rate. While the acceleration provision is supposedly included in an indenture to reduce the credit risk of an issuer by allowing the issuer to retire more of the scheduled amount prior to the maturity date, it effectively is a call option granted to the issuer.

Other Features

There are other features that can be included in a bond issue. These features are described below.

Convertible and Exchangeable Bonds

The conversion provision in a corporate bond issue grants the bondholder the right to convert the bond to a predetermined number of shares of common stock of the issuer. *Exchangeable bonds* grant the bondholder the right to exchange the bonds for the common stock of a firm *other* than the issuer of the bond.

Issues of Debt with Warrants

When a bond is issued, warrants may be attached as part of the offer. A *warrant* grants the holder the right to purchase a designated security at a specified price. The warrant may permit the holder to purchase the common stock of the issuer of the debt or the common stock of a firm other than the issuer's. Or, the warrant may grant the holder the right to purchase a debt obligation of the issuer.

Generally, warrants can be detached from the host bond and sold separately. The warrant can generally be exercised with cash or by exchanging the debt at par that was part of the unit offering. In the case of convertible and exchangeable bonds, only the bond may be used to exercise the investor's option to convert the bond into stock.

The warrant may permit the bondholder to buy common stock of the issuer, as does a convertible bond. However, the embedded call option in the convertible bond cannot be sold separately from the bond, while a warrant can be. Thus, the holder of a bond and a warrant is in a long position in the corporate bond of the issuer and a long position in a call option on the common stock of the issuer. The same is true of a unit of debt with warrants to buy common stock of a firm other than the issuer. The holder of a bond and a warrant in this case is in a long position in the corporate bond of the issuer and a long position in a call option on the common stock of some other firm.

Putable Bonds

A putable bond grants the bondholder the right to sell the issue back to the issuer at par value on designated dates. The advantage to the bondholder is that if interest rates rise after the issue date, thereby reducing the value of the bond, the bondholder can put the bond to the issuer for par. Thus, a putable corporate bond is a package composed of a nonputable corporate bond plus a long put option on the corporate bond. The put feature reduces the risk that the bond's price will decline below par.

Special Features in High-Yield Bonds

As explained later in this section, bonds with a quality rating below triple B are called *high-yield bonds*, or, more commonly, called *junk bonds*. There are complex bond structures in the high-yield bond area, particularly for bonds issued for LBO financing and recapitalizations producing higher debt. In an LBO or recapitalization, the heavy interest payment places severe cash flow constraints on the firm. To reduce this burden, firms involved in LBOs and recapitalizations have issued *deferred coupon structures* that permit the issuer to avoid using cash to make interest payments for a period of three to seven years. There are three types of deferred coupon structures: (1) deferred-interest bonds, (2) step-up bonds, and (3) payment-in-kind bonds.

Deferred-interest bonds are the most common type of deferred coupon structure. These bonds sell at a deep discount and do not pay interest for an initial period, typically from three to seven years. *Step-up bonds* do pay coupon interest. However, the coupon rate is low for an initial period and then increases ("steps up") to a higher coupon rate thereafter. Finally, *payment-in-kind* (PIK) bonds give the issuer an option to pay cash at a coupon payment date or give the bondholder a similar bond (i.e., a bond with the same coupon rate and a par value equal to the amount of the coupon payment that would have been paid). The period that the issuer can make this choice varies from five to ten years.

Credit Ratings

Professional money managers use various techniques to analyze information on companies and bond issues in order to estimate the ability of the issuer to live up to its future contractual obligations. This activity is known as *credit analysis*.

Some large institutional investors and most investment banking firms have their own credit analysis departments. Few individual investors and institutional bond investors, though, do their own analysis. Instead, they rely primarily on nationally recognized statistical rating organizations that perform credit analysis and issue their conclusions in the form of ratings. These organizations, commonly referred to as rating agencies, are (1) Duff and Phelps Credit Rating Co., (2) Fitch IBCA, (3) Moody's Investors Service, and (4) Standard & Poor's Corporation. The rating systems use similar symbols, as shown in Exhibit 3.

In all rating systems the term *high grade* means low credit risk, or conversely, high probability of future payments. The highest-grade bonds are designated by Moody's by the letters Aaa, and by the others as AAA. The next highest grade is Aa (Moody's) or AA; for the third grade all rating agencies use A. The next three grades are Baa (Moody's) or BBB, Ba (Moody's) or BB, and B, respectively. There are also C grades. All ratings except Moody's use plus or minus signs to provide a narrower credit quality breakdown within each class. Moody's uses 1, 2, or 3 for the same purpose. Bonds rated triple A (AAA or Aaa) are said to be *prime*; double A (AA or Aa) are of *high quality*; single A issues are called *upper medium grade*; and triple B are *medium grade*. Lower-rated bonds are said to have speculative elements or be distinctly speculative.

Bond issues that are assigned a rating in the top four categories are referred to as *investment grade bonds*. Issues that carry a rating below the top four categories are referred to as *non-investment grade bonds* or more popularly as high-yield bonds. Thus, the corporate bond market can be divided into two sectors: the investment grade and non-investment grade markets.

Occasionally the ability of an issuer to make interest and principal payments changes seriously and unexpectedly because of (1) a natural or industrial accident or some regulatory change, or (2) a takeover or corporate restructuring. These risks are referred to generically as *event risk* and will result in a downgrading of the issuer by the rating agencies.

Exhibit 3: Summary of Corporate Bond Rating Systems and Symbols

D&P	Fitch	Moody's	S&P	Summary Description
Investment Grade — High Creditworthiness				
AAA	AAA	Aaa	AAA	Gilt edge, prime, maximum safety
AA+	AA+	Aa1	AA+	
AA	AA	Aa2	AA	High-grade, high-credit quality
AA–	AA–	Aa3	AA–	
A+	A+	A1	A+	
A	A	A2	A	Upper-medium grade
A–	A–	A3	A–	
BBB+	BBB+	Baa1	BBB+	
BBB	BBB	Baa2	BBB	Lower-medium grade
BBB–	BBB–	Baa3	BBB–	
Speculative — Lower Creditworthiness				
BB+	BB+	Ba1	BB+	
BB	BB	Ba2	BB	Low grade, speculative
BB–	BB–	Ba3	BB–	
B+	B+	B1		
B	B	B2	B	Highly speculative
B–	B–	B3		
Predominantly Speculative, Substantial Risk or in Default				
	CCC+		CCC+	
CCC	CCC	Caa	CCC	Substantial risk, in poor standing
	CC	Ca	CC	May be in default, very speculative
	C	C	C	Extremely speculative
			CI	Income bonds — no interest being paid
	DDD			
DD	DD			Default
	D		D	

Bankruptcy and Creditor Rights

Corporate bonds and preferred stock are "senior" corporate securities. By senior we mean that the holder of the security has priority over the equity owners in the case of bankruptcy of a corporation. And, as we have explained, there are creditors who have priority over other creditors. Here we provide an overview of the bankruptcy process and then look at what actually happens to creditors in bankruptcies.

The Bankruptcy Process

The law governing bankruptcy in the United States is the Bankruptcy Reform Act of 1978.[9] One purpose of the act is to set forth the rules for a corporation to be either liquidated or reorganized. The *liquidation* of a corporation means that all the assets will be distributed to the holders of claims of the corporation and no corporate entity will survive. In a *reorganization*, a new corporate entity will result. Some holders of claims of the bankrupt corporation will receive cash in exchange for their claims, others may receive new securities in the corporation that results from the reorganization, and others may receive a combination of both cash and new securities in the resulting corporation.

Another purpose of the bankruptcy act is to give a corporation time to decide whether to reorganize or liquidate, and then the necessary time to formulate a plan to accomplish either a reorganization or liquidation. This is achieved because when a corporation files for bankruptcy, the act grants the corporation protection from creditors who seek to collect their claims.[10] A company that files for protection under the bankruptcy act generally becomes a "debtor-in-possession," and continues to operate its business under the supervision of the court.

The bankruptcy act is comprised of 15 chapters, each chapter covering a particular type of bankruptcy. Chapter 7 deals with the liquidation of a company; Chapter 11 deals with the reorganization of a company.

When a company is liquidated, creditors receive distributions based on the absolute priority, rule to the extent assets are available. The *absolute priority rule* is the principle that senior creditors are paid in full before junior creditors are paid anything. For secured creditors and unsecured creditors, the absolute priority rule guarantees their seniority to equity holders.

In liquidations, the absolute priority rule generally holds. In contrast, under reorganizations, there is a good body of literature that argues that strict absolute priority has not been upheld by the courts or the SEC. Studies of actual reorganizations under Chapter 11 have found that the violation of absolute prior-

---

[9] For a discussion of the Bankruptcy Reform Act of 1978 and a nontechnical description of its principal features, see Jane Tripp Howe, "Investing in Chapter 11 and Other Distressed Companies," Chapter 18 in Frank J. Fabozzi (ed.), *The Handbook of Corporate Debt Instruments* (New Hope, PA: Frank J. Fabozzi Associates, 1998).

[10] The petition for bankruptcy can be filed either by the company itself, in which case it is called a *voluntary bankruptcy*, or be filed by its creditors, in which case it is called an *involuntary bankruptcy*.

ity is the rule rather than the exception.[11] Consequently, while investors in the debt of a corporation may feel that they have priority over the equity owners and other classes of debtors, the actual outcome of a bankruptcy may be far different from what the terms of the debt agreement state.

MEDIUM-TERM NOTES

A *medium-term note* (MTN) is a debt instrument, with the unique characteristic that notes are offered continuously to investors by an agent of the issuer. Investors can select from several maturity ranges: 9 months to 1 year, more than 1 year to 18 months, more than 18 months to 2 years, and so on up to 30 years. Medium-term notes are registered with the Securities and Exchange Commission under Rule 415 (the shelf registration rule) which gives a borrower (corporation, agency, sovereign, or supranational) the maximum flexibility for issuing securities on a continuous basis.

The term "medium-term note" to describe this debt instrument is misleading. Traditionally, the term "note" or "medium-term" was used to refer to debt issues with a maturity greater than one year but less than 15 years. Certainly this is not a characteristic of MTNs since they have been sold with maturities from nine months to 30 years, and even longer. For example, in July 1993, Walt Disney Corporation issued a security with a 100-year maturity off its medium-term note shelf registration. From the perspective of the borrower, the purpose of the MTN was to fill the funding gap between commercial paper and long-term bonds. It is for this reason that they are referred to as "medium term."

Borrowers have flexibility in designing MTNs to satisfy their own needs. They can issue fixed- or floating-rate debt. The coupon payments can be denominated in U.S. dollars or in a foreign currency. In the previous section we described the various security structures. MTNs have been designed with the same features. In the next chapter we discuss asset-backed securities. There are asset-backed MTNs.

As with corporate bonds, MTNs are rated by the nationally recognized statistical rating organizations.

The Primary Market

Medium-term notes differ from bonds in the manner in which they are distributed to investors when they are initially sold. Although some investment-grade corporate bond issues are sold on a best-efforts basis, typically they are underwritten by investment bankers. MTNs have been traditionally distributed on a best-efforts

---

[11] See: Julian R. Franks and Walter N. Torous, "An Empirical Investigation of U.S. Firms in Reorganization," *Journal of Finance* (July 1989), pp. 747-769; Lawrence A. Weiss, "Bankruptcy Resolution: Direct Costs and Violation of Priority of Claims," *Journal of Financial Economics* (1990), pp. 285-314; and Frank J. Fabozzi, Jane Tripp Howe, Takashi Makabe, and Toshihide Sudo, "Recent Evidence on the Distribution Patterns in Chapter 11 Reorganizations," *Journal of Fixed Income* (Spring 1993), pp. 6-23.

basis by either an investment banking firm or other broker/dealers acting as agents. Another difference between bonds and MTNs when they are offered is that MTNs are usually sold in relatively small amounts on either a continuous or an intermittent basis, while bonds are sold in large, discrete offerings.

An entity that wants an MTN program will file a shelf registration with the SEC for the offering of securities. While the SEC registration for MTN offerings are between $100 and $1 billion, once the total is sold, the issuer can file another shelf registration. The registration will include a list of the investment banking firms, usually two to four, that the borrower has arranged to act as agents to distribute the MTNs.

The issuer then posts rates over a range of maturities: for example, nine months to one year, one year to 18 months, 18 months to two years, and annually thereafter. In an offering rate schedule an issuer will post rates as a spread over a Treasury security of comparable maturity. Rates will not be posted for maturity ranges that the issuer does not desire to sell.

The agents will then make the offering rate schedule available to their investor base interested in MTNs. An investor who is interested in the offering will contact the agent. In turn, the agent contacts the issuer to confirm the terms of the transaction. Since the maturity range in an offering rate schedule does not specify a specific maturity date, the investor can chose the final maturity subject to approval by the issuer. The minimum size that an investor can purchase an MTN offering typically ranges from $1 million to $25 million.

The rate offering schedule can be changed at any time by the issuer either in response to changing market conditions or because the issuer has raised the desired amount of funds at a given maturity. In the latter case, the issuer can either not post a rate for that maturity range or lower the rate.

Structured MTNs

At one time the typical MTN was a fixed-rate debenture that was noncallable. It is common today for issuers of MTNs to couple their offerings with transactions in the derivative markets (options, futures/forwards, swaps, caps, and floors) so as to create debt obligations with more interesting risk/return features than are available in the corporate bond market. Specifically, an issue can have a floating-rate over all or part of the life of the security and the coupon reset formula can be based on a benchmark interest rate, equity index or individual stock price, a foreign exchange rate, or a commodity index. There are MTNs with an inverse floating coupon rate. MTNs can have various embedded options included.

MTNs created when the issuer simultaneously transacts in the derivative markets are called *structured notes*. The most common derivative instrument used in creating structured notes is a swap. By using the derivative markets in combination with an offering, borrowers are able to create investment vehicles that are more customized for institutional investors to satisfy their investment objectives, but who are forbidden from using swaps for hedging. Moreover, it allows institutional investors who are restricted to investing in investment grade debt issues the opportunity to participate in other asset classes to make a market play. Hence, structured notes are sometimes referred to as "rule busters." For example, an investor who buys an MTN whose coupon rate is tied to the performance of the S&P 500 is participating in the equity market without owning common stock. If the coupon rate is tied to a foreign stock index, the investor is participating in the equity market of a foreign country without owning foreign common stock. In exchange for creating a structured note product, borrowers can reduce their funding costs.

MUNICIPAL SECURITIES

Debt obligations are issued by state and local governments and by entities that they establish. Local government units include municipalities, counties, towns and townships, school districts, and special service system districts. Included in the category of municipalities are cities, villages, boroughs, and incorporated towns that received a special state charter. Counties are geographical subdivisions of states whose functions are law enforcement, judicial administration, and construction and maintenance of roads. As with counties, towns and townships are geographical subdivisions of states and perform similar functions as counties. A special purpose service system district, or simply special district, is a political subdivision created to foster economic development or related services to a geographical area. Special districts provide public utility services (water, sewers, and drainage) and fire protection services. Public agencies or instrumentalities include authorities and commissions.

These securities are popularly referred to as *municipal securities*, despite the fact that they are also issued by states and public agencies and their instruments. There are both tax-exempt and taxable municipal securities. "Tax-exempt" means that interest on a municipal security is exempt from federal income taxation. The tax-exemption of municipal securities applies to interest income, not capital gains. The exemption may or may not extend to taxation at the state and local levels. Each state has its own rules as to how interest on municipal securities is taxed. Most municipal securities that have been issued are tax-exempt. Municipal securities are commonly referred to as *tax-exempt securities* despite the fact that there are taxable municipal securities that have been issued and are traded in the market.

Municipal securities expose investors to credit risk. The nationally recognized rating organizations rate municipal securities.

Municipal bonds are traded in the over-the-counter market supported by municipal bond dealers across the country. Markets are maintained on smaller issuers (referred to as "local credits") by regional brokerage firms, local banks, and by some of the larger Wall Street firms. Larger issuers (referred to as "general names") are supported by the larger brokerage firms and banks, many of whom have investment banking relationships with these issuers. There are brokers who serve as intermediaries in the sale of large blocks of municipal bonds among dealers and large institutional investors. In addition to these brokers and the daily offerings sent out over The Bond Buyer's "munifacts" teletype system, many dealers advertise their municipal bond offering for the retail market in what is known as *The Blue List*. This is a 100-plus-page booklet published every weekday by the Standard & Poor's Corporation that gives municipal securities offerings and prices.

As with agency debentures and corporate bonds, the day count convention used for computing accrued interest is "30/360."

Types of Municipal Securities

Municipal securities are issued for various purposes. Short-term notes typically are sold in anticipation of the receipt of funds from taxes or receipt of proceeds from the sale of a bond issue, for example. Municipalities issue long-term bonds as the principal means for financing both (1) long-term capital projects such as schools, bridges, roads, and airports, and (2) long-term budget deficits that arise from current operations.

Municipal securities are issued with one of two debt retirement structures or a combination of both. Either a bond has a *serial maturity structure* or a *term maturity structure*. A serial maturity structure requires a portion of the debt obligation to be retired each year. A term maturity structure provides for the debt obligation to be repaid on a final date.

The various provisions explained earlier for paying off a corporate issue prior to maturity — call provisions and sinking fund provisions — are also found in municipal securities. In revenue bonds there is a *catastrophe call provision* that requires the issuer to call the entire issue if the facility is destroyed.

An *official statement* describing the issue and the issuer is prepared for new offerings. Municipal securities have legal opinions which are summarized in the official statement. The importance of the legal opinion is twofold. First, bond counsel determines if the issue is indeed legally able to issue the securities. Second, bond counsel verifies that the issuer has properly prepared for the bond sale by having enacted various required ordinances, resolutions, and trust indentures and without violating any other laws and regulations.

There are basically two types of municipal security structures: tax-backed debt and revenue bonds. We describe each type below, as well as variants.

Tax-Backed Debt

Tax-backed debt obligations are instruments issued by states, counties, special districts, cities, towns, and school districts that are secured by some form of tax revenue. Tax-backed debt includes general obligation debt, appropriation-backed obligations, and debt obligations supported by public credit enhancement programs. We discuss each below.

General Obligation Debt The broadest type of tax-backed debt is *general obligation debt*. There are two types of general obligation pledges: unlimited and limited. An *unlimited tax general obligation debt* (also called an *ad valorem property tax debt*) is the stronger form of general obligation pledge because it is secured by the issuer's unlimited taxing power. The tax revenue sources include corporate and individual income taxes, sales taxes, and property taxes. Unlimited tax general obligation debt is said to be secured by the *full faith and credit of the issuer*. A limited tax general obligation debt (also called a *limited ad valorem tax debt*) is a limited tax pledge because for such debt there is a statutory limit on tax rates that the issuer may levy to service the debt.

Certain general obligation bonds are secured not only by the issuer's general taxing powers to create revenues accumulated in a general fund, but also by certain identified fees, grants, and special charges, which provide additional revenues from outside the general fund. Such bonds are known as *double-barreled* in security because of the dual nature of the revenue sources. For example, the debt obligations issued by special purpose service systems may be secured by a pledge of property taxes, a pledge of special fees/operating revenue from the service provided, or a pledge of both property taxes and special fees/operating revenues. In the last case, they are double-barreled.

Appropriation-Backed Obligations Agencies or authorities of several states have issued bonds that carry a potential state liability for making up shortfalls in the issuing entities obligation. The appropriation of funds from the state's general tax revenue must be approved by the state legislature. However, the state's pledge is not binding. Debt obligations with this nonbinding pledge of tax revenue are called *moral obligation bonds*. Because a moral obligation bond requires legislative approval to appropriate the funds, it is classified as an *appropriation-backed obligation*. The purpose of the moral obligation pledge is to enhance the credit worthiness of the issuing entity. Another type of appropriation-backed obligation is lease-backed debt.

Debt Obligations Supported by
Public Credit Enhancement Programs

While a moral obligation is a form of credit enhancement provided by a state, it is not a legally enforceable or legally binding obligation of the state. There are entities that have issued debt that carries some form of public credit enhancement that is legally enforceable. This occurs when there is a guarantee by the state or a federal agency or when there is an obligation to automatically withhold and deploy state aid to pay any defaulted debt service by the issuing entity. Typically, the latter form of public credit enhancement is used for debt obligations of a state's school systems.

Here are some examples of state credit enhancement programs. Virginia's bond guarantee program authorizes the governor to withhold state aid payments to a municipality and divert those funds to pay principal and interest to a municipality's general obligation holders in the event of a default. South Carolina's constitution requires mandatory withholding of state aid by the state treasurer if a school district is not capable of meeting its general obligation debt. Texas created the Permanent School Fund to guarantee the timely payment of principal and interest of the debt obligations of qualified school districts. The fund's income is obtained from land and mineral rights owned by the state of Texas.

Revenue Bonds

The second basic type of security structure is found in a revenue bond. Revenue bonds are issued for enterprise financings that are secured by the revenues generated by the completed projects themselves, or for general public-purpose financings in which the issuers pledge to the bondholders the tax and revenue resources that were previously part of the general fund. This latter type of revenue bond is usually created to allow issuers to raise debt outside general obligation debt limits and without voter approval.

Revenue bonds can be classified by the type of financing. These include utility revenue bonds, transportation revenue bonds, housing revenue bonds, higher education revenue bonds, health care revenue bonds, sports complex and convention center revenue bonds, seaport revenue bonds, and industrial revenue bonds. We discuss these revenue bonds below. Revenue bonds are also issued by Section 501(c)3 entities (museums and foundations).

Special Bond Structures

Some municipal securities have special security structures. These include insured bonds, bank-backed municipal bonds, and refunded bonds. We describe these three special security structures below.

Insured Bonds Insured bonds, in addition to being secured by the issuer's revenue, are also backed by insurance policies written by commercial insurance companies. Insurance on a municipal bond is an agreement by an insurance company to pay the bondholder any bond principal and/or coupon interest that is due on a stated maturity date but that has not been paid by the bond issuer. Once issued, this municipal bond insurance usually extends for the term of the bond issue, and it cannot be canceled by the insurance company.

Bank-Backed Municipal Bonds Since the 1980s, municipal obligations have been increasingly supported by various types of credit facilities provided by commercial banks. The support is in addition to the issuer's cash flow revenues. There are three basic types of bank support: letter of credit, irrevocable line of credit, and revolving line of credit.

A *letter-of-credit* is the strongest type of support available from a commercial bank. Under this arrangement, the bank is required to advance funds to the trustee if a default has occurred. An *irrevocable line of credit* is not a guarantee of the bond issue though it does provide a level of security. A *revolving line of credit* is a liquidity-type credit facility that provides a source of liquidity for payment of maturing debt in the event no other funds of the issuer are currently available. Because a bank can cancel a revolving line of credit without notice if the issuer fails to meet certain covenants, bond security depends entirely on the credit worthiness of the municipal issuer.

Refunded Bonds Although originally issued as either revenue or general obligation bonds, municipals are sometimes refunded. A refunding usually occurs when the original bonds are escrowed or collateralized by direct obligations guaranteed by the U.S. government. By this it is meant that a portfolio of securities guaranteed by the U.S. government is placed in a trust. The portfolio of securities is assembled such that the cash flows from the securities match the obligations that the issuer must pay. For example, suppose that a municipality has a 7% $100 million issue with 12 years remaining to maturity. The municipality's obligation is to make payments of $3.5 million every six months for the next 12 years and $100 million 12 years from now. If the issuer wants to refund this issue, a portfolio of U.S. government obligations can be purchased that has a cash flow of $3.5 million every six months for the next 12 years and $100 million 12 years from now.

Once this portfolio of securities whose cash flows match those of the municipality's obligation is in place, the refunded bonds are no longer secured as either general obligation or revenue bonds. The bonds are now supported by cash flows from the portfolio of securities held in an escrow fund. Such bonds, if escrowed with securities guaranteed by the U.S. government, have little, if any, credit risk. They are the safest municipal bonds available.

The escrow fund for a refunded municipal bond can be structured so that the refunded bonds are to be called at the first possible call date or a subsequent call date established in the original bond indenture. Such bonds are known as *pre-refunded municipal bonds*. While refunded bonds are usually retired at their first or subsequent call date, some are structured to match the debt obligation to the retirement date. Such bonds are known as *escrowed-to-maturity bonds*.

Municipal Derivative Securities

In recent years, a number of municipal products have been created from the basic fixed-rate municipal bonds. This has been done by splitting up cash flows of newly issued bonds as well as bonds existing in the secondary markets. These products have been created by dividing the coupon interest payments and principal payments into two or more bond classes, or *tranches*. The resulting bond classes may have far different yield and price volatility characteristics than the underlying fixed-rate municipal bond from which they were created.

The name *derivative securities* has been attributed to these bond classes because they derive their value from the underlying fixed-rate municipal bond. Much of the development in this market has paralleled that of the taxable market, specifically the mortgage-backed securities market. Two examples of municipal derivative securities are inverse floaters and municipal strip obligations. The latter are created when a municipal bond's cash flows are used to back zero-coupon instruments. The maturity value of each zero-coupon bond represents a cash flow of the underlying security. These are similar to the strips which are created in the Treasury market that we described earlier in this chapter.

EUROBONDS

At the outset of this chapter, we defined what a Eurobond is. Eurobonds can be denominated in any currency. Eurobonds are referred to by the currency in which the issuer agrees to denominate the payments. For example, U.S. dollar denominated bonds are called *Eurodollar bonds* and Japanese yen denominated bonds are called *Euroyen bonds*. The largest share of the Eurobond market is the Eurodollar bond, followed by Euroyen bonds and Eurodeutschemark bonds.

Although Eurobonds are typically registered on a national stock exchange, the most common being the Luxembourg, London, or Zurich exchanges, the bulk of all trading is in the over-the-counter market. Listing on a stock exchange is done purely to circumvent restrictions imposed on some institutional investors who are prohibited from purchasing securities that are not listed on an exchange. Some of the stronger issuers privately place issues with international institutional investors.

The Eurobond market has been characterized by new and innovative bond structures to accommodate particular needs of issuers and investors. There are, of course, the "plain vanilla," fixed-rate coupon bonds, referred to as *Euro straights*. Because they are issued on an unsecured basis, they are usually issued by high-quality entities.

Coupon payments are made annually, rather than semiannually, because of the higher cost of distributing interest to geographically dispersed bondholders. There are also zero-coupon bond issues, deferred-coupon issues, and step-up issues, all of which were described earlier.

There are issues that pay coupon interest in one currency but pay the principal in a different currency. Such issues are called *dual currency issues*. A convertible Eurobond is one that can be converted into another asset. There are bonds with attached warrants that entitle the owner to enter into another financial transaction with the issuer. Most warrants are detachable from the host bond; that is, the bondholder may detach the warrant from the bond and sell it.

There is a wide variety of floating-rate Eurobond notes. In the Eurobond market, almost all floating-rate notes are denominated in U.S. dollars with non-U.S. banks being the major issuers. The coupon rate on a Eurodollar floating-rate note is some stated margin over the London interbank offered rate (LIBOR).

Chapter 6

Mortgage-Backed Securities and Asset-Backed Securities

Frank J. Fabozzi, Ph.D., CFA
Adjunct Professor of Finance
School of Management
Yale University

INTRODUCTION

Mortgage-backed securities are securities backed by a pool of mortgage loans. While any type of mortgage loans, residential or commercial, can be used as collateral for a mortgage-backed security, most are backed by residential mortgages. Mortgage-backed securities include: (1) mortgage passthrough securities, (2) collateralized mortgage obligations, and (3) stripped mortgage-backed securities. The latter two mortgage-backed securities are referred to as *derivative mortgage-backed securities* because they are created from mortgage passthrough securities. Asset-backed securities are securities backed by other types of loans or receivables.

MORTGAGES

A *mortgage* is a loan secured by the collateral of some specified real estate property which obliges the borrower to make a predetermined series of payments. The mortgage gives the lender the right, if the borrower defaults (i.e. fails to make the contracted payments), to "foreclose" on the loan and seize the property in order to ensure that the debt is paid off. The interest rate on the mortgage loan is called the *mortgage rate* or *contract rate*. Our focus in this section is on residential mortgage loans.

When the lender makes the loan based on the credit of the borrower and on the collateral for the mortgage, the mortgage is said to be a *conventional mortgage*. The lender may require that the borrower obtain mortgage insurance to guarantee the fulfillment of the borrower's obligations. Some borrowers can qualify for mortgage insurance which is guaranteed by one of three U.S. government agencies: the Federal Housing Administration (FHA), the Veteran's Administration (VA), and the Rural Housing Service. There are also private mortgage insurers. The cost of mortgage insurance is paid by the borrowers in the form of higher mortgage payments.

There are many types of mortgage designs available in the United States. A mortgage design is a specification of the interest rate, term of the mortgage, and the manner in which the borrowed funds are repaid. Below we describe the three most popular mortgage designs: (1) the fixed-rate, level-payment, full amortized mortgage, (2) the adjustable-rate mortgage, and (3) the balloon mortgage.

Fixed-Rate, Level-Payment, Fully Amortized Mortgage

The basic idea behind the design of the fixed-rate, level-payment, fully amortized mortgage is that the borrower pays interest and repays principal in equal installments over an agreed-upon period of time, called the maturity or term of the mortgage. Thus at the end of the term, the loan has been fully amortized. The frequency of payment is typically monthly, and typically the term of a mortgage is between 15 and 30 years.

Each monthly mortgage payment for this mortgage design is due on the first of each month and consists of:

1. interest of $\frac{1}{12}$ of the fixed annual interest rate times the amount of the outstanding mortgage balance at the beginning of the previous month, and
2. a repayment of a portion of the outstanding mortgage balance (principal).

The difference between the monthly mortgage payment and the portion of the payment that represents interest equals the amount that is applied to reduce the outstanding mortgage balance. The monthly mortgage payment is designed so that after the last scheduled monthly mortgage payment is made, the amount of the outstanding mortgage balance is zero (i.e., the mortgage is fully repaid).

To illustrate this mortgage design, consider a 30-year (360-month), $100,000 mortgage with an 8.125% mortgage rate. The monthly mortgage payment would be $742.50. Exhibit 1 shows for selected months how each monthly mortgage payment is divided between interest and repayment of principal. At the beginning of month 1, the mortgage balance is $100,000, the amount of the original loan. The mortgage payment for month 1 includes interest on the $100,000 borrowed for the month. Since the interest rate is 8.125%, the monthly interest rate is 0.0067708 (0.08125 divided by 12). Interest for month 1 is therefore $677.08 ($100,000 times 0.0067708). The $65.41 difference between the monthly mortgage payment of $742.50 and the interest of $677.08 is the portion of the monthly mortgage payment that represents repayment of principal. This $65.41 in month 1 reduces the mortgage balance.

The mortgage balance at the end of month 1 (beginning of month 2) is then $99,934.59 ($100,000 minus $65.41). The interest for the second monthly mortgage payment is $676.64, the monthly interest rate (0.0066708) times the mortgage balance at the beginning of month 2 ($99,934.59). The difference between the $742.50 monthly mortgage payment and the $676.64 interest is $65.86, representing the amount of the mortgage balance paid off with that monthly mortgage payment. Notice that the last mortgage payment in month 360 is sufficient to pay off the remaining mortgage balance.

Exhibit 1: Amortization Schedule for a Level-Payment, Fixed-Rate, Fully Amortized Mortgage

Mortgage loan: $100,000   Monthly payment: $742.50
Mortgage rate: 8.125%   Term of loan: 30 years (360 months)

	Beginning of Month Mortgage Balance ($)	Mortgage Payment ($)	Scheduled Repayment ($)	Interest ($)	End of Month Mortgage Balance ($)
1	100,000.00	742.50	677.08	65.41	99,934.59
2	99,934.59	742.50	676.64	65.86	99,868.73
3	99,868.73	742.50	676.19	66.30	99,802.43
4	99,802.43	742.50	675.75	66.75	99,735.68
25	98,301.53	742.50	665.58	76.91	98,224.62
26	98,224.62	742.50	665.06	77.43	98,147.19
27	98,147.19	742.50	664.54	77.96	98,069.23
74	93,849.98	742.50	635.44	107.05	93,742.93
75	93,742.93	742.50	634.72	107.78	93,635.15
76	93,635.15	742.50	633.99	108.51	93,526.64
141	84,811.77	742.50	574.25	168.25	84,643.52
142	84,643.52	742.50	573.11	169.39	84,474.13
143	84,474.13	742.50	571.96	170.54	84,303.59
184	76,445.29	742.50	517.61	224.89	76,221.40
185	76,221.40	742.50	516.08	226.41	75,994.99
186	75,994.99	742.50	514.55	227.95	75,767.04
233	63,43.19	742.50	429.48	313.02	63,117.17
234	63,117.17	742.50	427.36	315.14	62,802.03
235	62,802.03	742.50	425.22	317.28	62,484.75
289	42,200.92	742.50	285.74	456.76	41,744.15
290	41,744.15	742.50	282.64	459.85	41,284.30
291	41,284.30	742.50	279.53	462.97	40,821.33
321	25,941.42	742.50	175.65	566.85	25,374.57
322	25,374.57	742.50	171.81	570.69	24,803.88
323	24,803.88	742.50	167.94	574.55	24,229.32
358	2,197.66	742.50	14.88	727.62	1,470.05
359	1,470.05	742.50	9.95	732.54	737.50
360	737.50	742.50	4.99	737.50	0.00

As Exhibit 1 clearly shows, *the portion of the monthly mortgage payment applied to interest declines each month and the portion applied to reducing the mortgage balance increases.* The reason for this is that as the mortgage balance is reduced with each monthly mortgage payment, the interest on the mortgage balance declines. Since the monthly mortgage payment is fixed, an increasingly larger portion of the monthly payment is applied to reduce the mortgage balance outstanding in each subsequent month.

Servicing Fee and the Cash Flows

Every mortgage loan must be serviced. Servicing of a mortgage loan involves collecting monthly payments and forwarding proceeds to owners of the loan; sending payment notices to mortgagors; reminding mortgagors when payments are overdue; maintaining records of principal balances; administering an escrow balance for real estate taxes and insurance purposes; initiating foreclosure proceedings if necessary; and, furnishing tax information to mortgagors when applicable.

The servicing fee is a portion of the mortgage rate. If the mortgage rate is 8.125% and the servicing fee is 50 basis points, then the investor receives interest of 7.625%. The interest rate that the investor receives is said to be the net interest or net coupon. The servicing fee is commonly called the *servicing spread*.

The dollar amount of the servicing fee declines over time as the mortgage amortizes. This is true for not only the mortgage design that we have just described, but for all mortgage designs.

Prepayments and Cash Flow Uncertainty

Our illustration of the cash flow from a level-payment, fixed-rate, fully amortized mortgage assumes that the homeowner does not pay off any portion of the mortgage balance prior to the scheduled due date. But homeowners do pay off all or part of their mortgage balance prior to the maturity date. A payment made in excess of the monthly mortgage payment is called a *prepayment*. A prepayment that is for a partial paydown of the mortgage balance is called a *curtailment*.

The effect of prepayments is that the amount and timing of the cash flow from a mortgage is not known with certainty. This risk is referred to as *prepayment risk*. For example, all that the investor in a $100,000, 8.125% 30-year insured mortgage knows is that as long as the loan is outstanding, interest will be received and the principal will be repaid at the scheduled date each month; then at the end of the 30 years, the investor would have received $100,000 in principal payments. What the investor does not know — the uncertainty — is for how long the loan will be outstanding, and therefore what the timing of the principal payments will be. This is true for all mortgage loans, not just level-payment, fixed-rate, fully amortized mortgages. Factors affecting prepayments will be discussed later in this chapter.

Most mortgages have no prepayment penalty. In 1996, mortgages with prepayment penalties were originated. The purpose of the penalty is to deter prepayment when interest rates decline. A prepayment penalty mortgage has the following structure. There is a period of time over which if the loan is prepaid in full or in excess of a certain amount of the outstanding balance, there is a prepayment penalty. This is referred to as the *penalty period*. During the penalty period, the borrower may prepay up to a specified amount of the outstanding balance without a penalty. The amount of the penalty is specified in terms of the number of months of interest that must be paid or a rate.

When prepayment penalty mortgages are securitized, it is important to understand that the prepayment penalty is paid to the issuer, not the investor. However, the penalty still discourages homeowners from prepaying when rates decline.

Adjustable-Rate Mortgages

As the name implies, an adjustable-rate mortgage (ARM) has an adjustable or floating coupon instead of a fixed one. The coupon adjusts periodically — monthly, semiannually or annually. Some ARMs even have coupons that adjust every three years or five years. The coupon formula for an ARM is specified in terms of an index level plus a margin. We'll discuss the common indices that are used below. The margin is typically 2% to 3%.

At origination, the mortgage usually has an initial rate for an initial period (*teaser period*) which is slightly below the rate specified by the coupon formula. This is called a *teaser rate* and makes it easier for first time home buyers to qualify for the loan. At the end of the teaser period, the loan rate is reset based on the coupon formula. Once the loan comes out of its teaser period and resets based on the coupon formula, it is said to be *fully indexed*.

To protect the homeowner from interest rate shock, there are caps or ceilings imposed on the coupon adjustment level. There are periodic caps and lifetime caps. The periodic cap limits the amount of coupon reset upward or downward from one period to another. The lifetime cap is the maximum absolute level for the coupon rate that the loan can reset to for the life of the mortgage.

Since the borrower prefers to be warned in advance of any interest rate adjustment, the coupon determination actually has to take place prior to the coupon reset. This is called the *lookback period*. For example, if the lookback period is 45 days, this means that the value for the reference rate 45 days before the anniversary date is being used to reset the coupon for the next period.

There are ARMs that can be converted into fixed-rate mortgages at the option of the borrower. These ARMS, called *convertible ARMs*, reduce the cost of refinancing. When converted, the new loan rate may be either (1) a rate determined by the lender or (2) a market-determined rate. A borrower can typically convert at any time between the first and fifth anniversary dates from the origination date.

Two categories of indices have been used in ARMs: (1) market determined rates and (2) calculated cost of funds for thrifts. The index will have an important impact on the performance of an ARM and its value. The most common market determined rates used are the 1-year, 3-year or 5-year Constant Maturity Treasury (CMT) and 3-month or 6-month London Interbank Offered Rate (LIBOR).

The cost of funds index for thrifts is calculated based on the monthly weighted average interest cost for liabilities of thrifts. The most popular is the Eleventh Federal Home Loan Bank Board District Cost of Funds Index (COFI). About 25% of ARMs are indexed to this reference rate. The Eleventh District includes the states of California, Arizona, and Nevada. The cost of funds is calculated by first computing the monthly interest expenses for all thrifts included in the Eleventh District. The interest expenses are summed and then divided by the average of the beginning and ending monthly balance. The index value is reported with a one month lag. For example, June's Eleventh District COFI is reported in July. The mortgage rate for a mortgage based on the Eleventh District COFI is usually reset based on the previous month's reported index rate. For example, if the reset date is August, the index rate reported in July will be used to set the mortgage rate. Consequently, there is a two month lag by the time the average cost of funds is reflected in the mortgage rate. This obviously is an advantage to the borrower when interest rates are rising and a disadvantage to the investor. The opposite is true when interest rates are falling.

Balloon Mortgages

In a balloon mortgage, the borrower is given long-term financing by the lender but at specified future dates the contract rate is renegotiated. Thus, the lender is providing long-term funds for what is effectively a short-term borrowing, how short depending on the frequency of the renegotiation period. Effectively it is a short-term balloon loan in which the lender agrees to provide financing for the remainder of the term of the mortgage. The balloon payment is the original amount borrowed less the amount amortized. Thus, in a balloon mortgage, the actual maturity is shorter than the stated maturity.

MORTGAGE PASSTHROUGH SECURITIES

A *mortgage passthrough security* is a security created when one or more holders of mortgages form a collection (pool) of mortgages and sell shares or participation certificates in the pool. A pool may consist of several thousand or only a few mortgages. When a mortgage is included in a pool of mortgages that is used as collateral for a mortgage passthrough security, the mortgage is said to be *securitized*.

Cash Flow Characteristics

The cash flow of a mortgage passthrough security depends on the cash flow of the underlying pool of mortgages. As we explained in the previous section, the cash flow consists of monthly mortgage payments representing interest, the scheduled repayment of principal, and any prepayments.

Payments are made to security holders each month. However, neither the amount nor the timing of the cash flow from the pool of mortgages is identical to that of the cash flow passed through to investors. The monthly cash flow for a passthrough is less than the monthly cash flow of the underlying pool of mortgages by an amount equal to servicing and other fees. The other fees are those charged by the issuer or guarantor of the passthrough for guaranteeing the issue (discussed later). The coupon rate on a passthrough, called the *passthrough coupon rate*, is less than the mortgage rate on the underlying pool of mortgages by an amount equal to the servicing and guaranteeing fees.

The timing of the cash flow is also different. The monthly mortgage payment is due from each mortgagor on the first day of each month, but there is a delay in passing through the corresponding monthly cash flow to the securityholders. The length of the delay varies by the type of passthrough security.

Not all of the mortgages that are included in a pool of mortgages that are securitized have the same mortgage rate and the same maturity. Consequently, when describing a passthrough security, a weighted average coupon rate and a weighted average maturity are determined. A *weighted average coupon rate*, or WAC, is found by weighting the mortgage rate of each mortgage loan in the pool by the amount of the mortgage outstanding. A *weighted average maturity*, or WAM, is found by weighting the remaining number of months to maturity for each mortgage loan in the pool by the amount of the outstanding mortgage balance.

Types of Mortgage Passthrough Securities

The three major types of passthrough securities are guaranteed by agencies created by Congress to increase the supply of capital to the residential mortgage market. Those agencies are the Government National Mortgage Association ("Ginnie Mae"), the Federal Home Loan Mortgage Corporation ("Freddie Mac"), and the Federal National Mortgage Association ("Fannie Mae").

While Freddie Mac and Fannie Mae are commonly referred to as "agencies" of the U.S. government, both are corporate instrumentalities of the U.S. government. That is, they are government sponsored enterprises; therefore, their guarantee does not carry the full faith and credit of the U.S. government. In contrast, Ginnie Mae is a federally related institution; it is part of the Department of Housing and Urban Development. As such, its guarantee carries the full faith and credit of the U.S. government. The securities associated with these three entities are known as *agency passthrough securities*. More than 90% of all passthrough securities are agency passthrough securities.

The balance of mortgage passthrough securities are privately issued. These securities are called *nonagency mortgage passthrough securities*. The securities are issued by thrifts, commercial banks, and private conduits. Private conduits may purchase nonconforming mortgages, pool them, and then sell passthrough securities whose collateral is the underlying pool of nonconforming mortgages. Nonagency passthrough securities are rated by the nationally recognized statistical rating organizations. Often these securities are supported by credit enhancements so that they can obtain an investment grade rating. We shall describe these securities later in this chapter.

In the secondary market, there are many seasoned issues of the same agency with the same coupon rate outstanding at any given time. Each issue is backed by a different pool of mortgages. For example, there are many seasoned pools of GNMA 8s. One issue may be backed by a pool of mortgages of only Southern California properties, while another may be backed by a pool of mortgages of only New York City homes. Others may be backed by a pool of mortgages on homes in several regions of the country. Which pool are dealers referring to when they talk about, say, GNMA 8s? They are not referring to any specific pool; rather they are referring to a "generic" security even though, as discussed later, the prepayment characteristics of passthroughs of underlying pools from different parts of the country are different.

Thus, the projected prepayment rates for passthrough securities reported by dealer firms are for generic passthroughs. A particular pool purchased may have a materially different prepayment speed from the generic benchmark.

Prepayment Conventions and Cash Flow

In order to value a passthrough security, it is necessary to project its cash flow. The difficulty is that the cash flow is unknown because of prepayments. The only way to project a cash flow is to make some assumption about the prepayment rate over the life of the underlying mortgage pool.

Estimating the cash flow from a passthrough requires making an assumption about future prepayments. Two conventions have been used as a benchmark for prepayment rates — conditional prepayment rate and Public Securities Association prepayment benchmark.

Conditional Prepayment Rate

One convention for projecting prepayments and the cash flow of a passthrough assumes that some fraction of the remaining principal in the pool is prepaid each month for the remaining term of the mortgage. The prepayment rate assumed for a pool, called the *conditional prepayment rate* (CPR), is based on the characteristics of the pool (including its historical prepayment experience) and the current and expected future economic environment.

The CPR is an annual prepayment rate. To estimate monthly prepayments, the CPR must be converted into a monthly prepayment rate, commonly referred to as the *single-monthly mortality rate* (SMM). The following formula is used to calculate the SMM for a given CPR:

$$SMM = 1 - (1 - CPR)^{1/12} \qquad (1)$$

For example, suppose that the CPR is 6%. The corresponding SMM is:

$$SMM = 1 - (1 - 0.06)^{1/12} = 1 - (0.94)^{0.08333} = 0.005143$$

An SMM of $w\%$ means that approximately $w\%$ of the remaining mortgage balance at the beginning of the month, less the scheduled principal payment, will prepay that month. That is,

Prepayment for month t = SMM × (Beginning mortgage balance for month t
– Scheduled principal payment for month t) $\qquad (2)$

For example, suppose that an investor owns a passthrough in which the remaining mortgage balance at the beginning of some month is $290 million. Assuming that the SMM is 0.5143% and the scheduled principal payment is $3 million, the estimated prepayment for the month is:

$$0.005143 \times (\$290,000,000 - \$3,000,000) = \$1,476,041$$

Exhibit 2: Graphical Depiction of 100 PSA

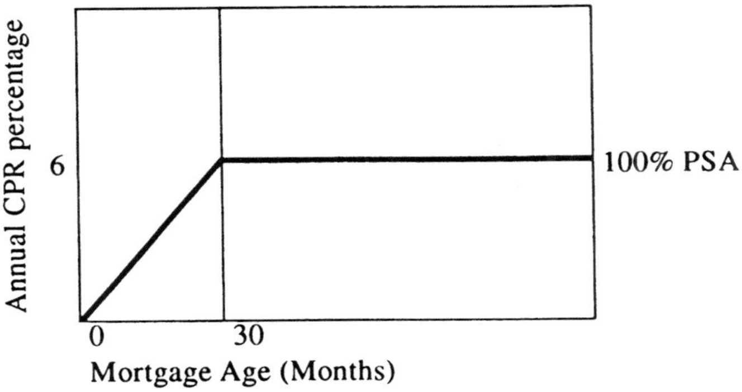

PSA Prepayment Benchmark

The Public Securities Association (PSA) prepayment benchmark is expressed as a monthly series of CPRs.[1] The PSA benchmark assumes that prepayment rates are low for newly originated mortgages and then will speed up as the mortgages become seasoned. The PSA benchmark assumes the following prepayment rates for 30-year mortgages: (1) a CPR of 0.2% for the first month, increased by 0.2% per year per month for the next 30 months when it reaches 6% per year, and (2) a 6% CPR for the remaining years.

This benchmark, referred to as "100% PSA" or simply "100 PSA," is graphically depicted in Exhibit 2. Mathematically, 100 PSA can be expressed as follows:

if $t < 30$ then CPR = 6% $(t/30)$
if $t > 30$ then CPR = 6%

where t is the number of months since the mortgages originated.

Slower or faster speeds are then referred to as some percentage of PSA. For example, 50 PSA means one-half the CPR of the PSA prepayment benchmark CPR; 150 PSA means 1.5 times the CPR of the PSA prepayment benchmark CPR; 300 PSA means three times the CPR of the prepayment benchmark CPR. A prepayment rate of 0 PSA means that no prepayments are assumed.

Illustration of Monthly Cash Flow Construction

We now show how to construct a monthly cash flow for a hypothetical passthrough given a PSA assumption. For the purpose of this illustration, the underlying mortgages for this hypothetical passthrough are assumed to be fixed-rate, level-payment, fully amortized mortgages with a weighted average coupon (WAC) rate of 8.125%. It will be assumed that the passthrough rate is 7.5% with a weighted average maturity (WAM) of 357 months.

---

[1] This benchmark is commonly referred to as a prepayment model, suggesting that it can be used to estimate prepayments. Characterization of this benchmark as a prepayment model is inappropriate. It is simply a market convention regarding the pattern of prepayments.

Exhibit 3: Monthly Cash Flow for a $400 Million Passthrough with a 7.5% Passthrough Rate, a WAC of 8.125%, and a WAM of 357 Months Assuming 100 PSA

Month	Outstanding Balance	SMM	Mortgage Payment	Net Interest	Scheduled Principal	Prepayment	Total Principal	Cash Flow
1	$400,000,000	$0.00067	$2,975,868	$2,500,000	$267,535	$267,470	$535,005	$3,035,005
2	399,464,995	0.00084	2,973,877	2,496,636	269,166	334,198	603,364	3,100,020
3	398,861,631	0.00101	2,971,387	2,492,885	270,762	400,800	671,562	3,164,447
4	398,190,069	0.00117	2,968,399	2,488,688	272,321	467,243	739,564	3,228,252
5	397,450,505	0.00134	2,964,914	2,484,066	273,843	533,493	807,335	3,291,401
6	396,643,170	0.00151	2,960,931	2,476,020	275,327	599,514	874,841	3,353,860
7	395,768,329	0.00168	2,956,453	2,473,552	276,772	665,273	942,045	3,415,597
8	394,826,284	0.00185	2,951,480	2,467,664	278,177	730,736	1,008,913	3,476,577
9	393,817,371	0.00202	2,946,013	2,461,359	279,542	795,869	1,075,410	3,536,769
10	392,741,961	0.00219	2,940,056	2,454,637	280,865	860,637	1,141,502	3,596,140
11	391,600,459	0.00236	2,933,608	2,447,503	282,147	925,008	1,207,155	3,654,658
27	364,808,016	0.00514*	2,766,461	2,280,050	296,406	1,874,688	2,171,094	4,451,144
28	362,636,921	0.00514	2,752,233	2,266,481	296,879	1,863,519	2,160,398	4,426,879
29	360,476,523	0.00514	2,738,078	2,252,978	297,351	1,852,406	2,149,758	4,402,736
30	358,326,766	0.00514	2,723,996	2,239,542	297,825	1,841,347	2,139,173	4,378,715
100	231,249,776	0.00514	1,898,682	1,445,311	332,928	1,187,608	1,520,537	2,965,848
101	229,729,239	0.00514	1,888,917	1,435,808	333,459	1,179,785	1,513,244	2,949,052
102	228,215,995	0.00514	1,879,202	1,426,350	333,990	1,172,000	1,505,990	2,932,340
103	226,710,004	0.00514	1,869,538	1,416,938	334,522	1,164,252	1,498,774	2,915,712
104	225,211,230	0.00514	1,859,923	1,407,570	335,055	1,156,541	1,491,596	2,899,166
105	223,719,634	0.00514	1,850,357	1,398,248	335,589	1,148,867	1,484,456	2,882,703
200	109,791,339	0.00514	1,133,751	686,196	390,372	562,651	953,023	1,639,219
201	108,838,316	0.00514	1,127,920	680,239	390,994	557,746	948,740	1,628,980
202	107,889,576	0.00514	1,122,119	674,310	391,617	552,863	944,480	1,618,790
203	106,945,096	0.00514	1,116,348	668,407	392,241	548,003	940,243	1,608,650
300	$32,383,611	$0.00514	$676,991	202,398	$457,727	$164,195	$621,923	$824,320
301	31,761,689	0.00514	673,510	198,511	458,457	160,993	619,449	817,960
302	31,142,239	0.00514	670,046	194,639	459,187	157,803	616,990	811,629
303	30,525,249	0.00514	666,600	190,783	459,918	154,626	614,545	805,328
352	3,034,311	0.00514	517,770	18,964	497,226	13,048	510,274	529,238
353	2,524,037	0.00514	515,107	15,775	498,018	10,420	508,437	524,213
354	2,015,600	0.00514	512,458	12,597	498,811	7,801	506,612	519,209
355	1,508,988	0.00514	509,823	9,431	499,606	5,191	504,797	514,228
356	1,004,191	0.00514	507,201	6,276	500,401	2,591	502,992	509,269
357	501,199	0.00514	504,592	3,132	501,199	0	501,199	504,331

*Since the WAM is 357 months, the underlying mortgage pool is seasoned an average of three months. Therefore, the CPR for month 27 is 6%.

Exhibit 3 shows the cash flow for selected months assuming 100 PSA. The cash flow is broken down into three components: (1) interest (based on the passthrough rate), (2) the regularly scheduled principal repayment, (3) prepayments based on 100 PSA.

Let's walk through Exhibit 3 column by column.

Column 1: This is the month.

Column 2: This column gives the outstanding mortgage balance at the beginning of the month. It is equal to the outstanding balance at the beginning of the previous month reduced by the total principal payment in the previous month.

Column 3: This column shows the SMM for 100 PSA. Two things should be noted in this column. First, for month 1, the SMM is for a passthrough that has been seasoned three months. That is, the CPR is 0.8%. This is because the WAM is 357. Second, from month 27 on, the SMM is 0.00514 which corresponds to a CPR of 6%.

Column 4: The total monthly mortgage payment is shown in this column. Notice that the total monthly mortgage payment declines over time as prepayments reduce the mortgage balance outstanding. There is a formula to determine what the monthly mortgage balance will be for each month given prepayments.[2]

Column 5: The monthly interest paid to the passthrough investor is found in this column. This value is determined by multiplying the outstanding mortgage balance at the beginning of the month by the passthrough rate of 7.5% and then dividing by 12.

Column 6: This column gives the regularly scheduled principal repayment. This is the difference between the total monthly mortgage payment [the amount shown in column (4)] and the gross coupon interest for the month. The gross coupon interest is found by multiplying 8.125% by the outstanding mortgage balance at the beginning of the month and then dividing by 12.

Column 7: The prepayment for the month is reported in this column. The prepayment is found by using equation (2). For example, in month 100, the beginning mortgage balance is $231,249,776, the scheduled principal payment is $332,928, and the SMM at 100 PSA is 0.00514301 (only 0.00514 is shown in the exhibit to save space), so the prepayment is:

$$0.00514301 \times (\$231,249,776 - \$332,928) = \$1,187,608$$

Column 8: The total principal payment, which is the sum of columns (6) and (7), is shown in this column.

Column 9: The projected monthly cash flow for this passthrough is shown in this last column. The monthly cash flow is the sum of the interest paid to the passthrough investor [column (5)] and the total principal payments for the month [column (8)].

Exhibit 4 shows selected monthly cash flows for the same passthrough assuming 165 PSA.

---

[2] The formula is presented in Chapter 19 of Frank J. Fabozzi, *Fixed Income Mathematics* (Chicago: Irwin Professional Publishing, 1997).

Exhibit 4: Monthly Cash Flow for a $400 Million Passthrough with a 7.5% Passthrough Rate, a WAC of 8.125%, and a WAM of 357 Months Assuming 165 PSA

Month	Outstanding Balance	SMM	Mortgage Payment	Net Interest	Scheduled Principal	Prepayment	Total Principal	Cash Flow
1	$400,000,000	$0.00111	$2,975,868	$2,500,000	$267,535	$442,389	$709,923	$3,209,923
2	399,290,077	0.00139	2,972,575	2,495,563	269,048	552,847	821,896	3,317,459
3	398,468,181	0.00167	2,968,456	2,490,426	270,495	663,065	933,560	3,423,986
4	397,534,624	0.00195	2,963,513	2,484,591	271,873	772,949	1,044,822	3,529,413
5	396,489,799	0.00223	2,957,747	2,478,061	273,181	882,405	1,155,586	3,633,647
6	395,334,213	0.00251	2,951,160	2,470,839	274,418	991,341	1,265,759	3,736,598
7	394,068,451	0.00279	2,943,755	2,462,928	275,583	1,099,664	1,375,246	3,838,174
8	392,693,208	0.00308	2,935,534	2,454,333	276,674	1,207,280	1,483,954	3,938,287
9	391,209,254	0.00336	2,926,503	2,445,058	277,690	1,314,099	1,591,789	4,036,847
10	389,617,464	0.00365	2,916,666	2,435,109	278,631	1,420,029	1,698,659	4,133,769
11	387,918,805	0.00393	2,906,028	2,424,493	279,494	1,524,979	1,804,473	4,228,965
27	347,334,116	0.00865 *	2,633,950	2,170,838	282,209	3,001,955	3,284,164	5,455,002
28	344,049,952	0.00865	2,611,167	2,150,312	281,662	2,973,553	3,255,215	5,405,527
29	340,794,737	0.00865	2,588,581	2,129,967	281,116	2,945,400	3,226,516	5,356,483
30	337,568,221	0.00865	2,566,190	2,109,801	280,572	2,917,496	3,198,067	5,307,869
100	170,142,350	0.00865	1,396,958	1,063,390	244,953	1,469,591	1,714,544	2,777,933
101	168,427,806	0.00865	1,384,875	1,052,674	244,478	1,454,765	1,699,243	2,751,916
102	166,728,563	0.00865	1,372,896	1,042,054	244,004	1,440,071	1,684,075	2,726,128
103	165,044,489	0.00865	1,361,020	1,031,528	243,531	1,425,508	1,669,039	2,700,567
104	163,375,450	0.00865	1,349,248	1,021,097	243,060	1,411,075	1,654,134	2,675,231
105	161,721,315	0.00865	1,337,577	1,010,758	242,589	1,396,771	1,639,359	2,650,118
200	56,746,664	0.00865	585,990	354,667	201,767	489,106	690,874	1,045,540
201	56,055,790	0.00865	580,921	350,349	201,377	483,134	684,510	1,034,859
202	55,371,280	0.00865	575,896	346,070	200,986	477,216	678,202	1,024,273
203	54,693,077	0.00865	570,915	341,832	200,597	471,353	671,950	1,013,782
300	$11,758,141	$0.00865	$245,808	$73,488	$166,196	$100,269	$266,465	$339,953
301	11,491,677	0.00865	243,682	71,823	165,874	97,967	263,841	335,664
302	11,227,836	0.00865	241,574	70,174	165,552	95,687	261,240	331,414
303	10,966,596	0.00865	239,485	68,541	165,232	93,430	258,662	327,203
352	916,910	0.00865	156,460	5,731	150,252	6,631	156,883	162,614
353	760,027	0.00865	155,107	4,750	149,961	5,277	155,238	159,988
354	604,789	0.00865	153,765	3,780	149,670	3,937	153,607	157,387
355	451,182	0.00865	152,435	2,820	149,380	2,611	151,991	154,811
356	299,191	0.00865	151,117	1,870	149,091	1,298	150,389	152,259
357	148,802	0.00865	149,809	930	148,802	0	148,802	149,732

* Since the WAM is 357 months, the underlying mortgage pool is seasoned an average of three months. Therefore the CPR for month 27 is 1.65 × 6%.

Factors Affecting Prepayment Behavior

The factors that affect prepayment behavior are: (1) prevailing mortgage rate, (2) characteristics of the underlying mortgage pool, (3) seasonal factors, and (4) general economic activity.

Prevailing Mortgage Rate

The current mortgage rate affects prepayments in three ways. First, the spread between the prevailing mortgage rate in the market and the rate paid by the homeowner affects the incentive to refinance. Second, the path of mortgage rates since the loan was originated affects prepayments through a phenomenon referred to as *refinancing burnout*. Both the spread and path of mortgage rates affect prepayments that are the product of refinancing. The third way in which the prevailing mortgage rate affects prepayments is through its effect on the affordability of housing and housing turnover. The level of mortgage rates affects housing turnover to the extent that a lower rate increases the affordability of homes.

The single most important factor affecting prepayments because of refinancing is the current level of mortgage rates relative to the borrower's contract rate. The greater the difference between the two, the greater the incentive to refinance the mortgage loan. For refinancing to make economic sense, the interest savings must be greater than the costs associated with refinancing the mortgage. These costs include legal expenses, origination fees, title insurance, and the value of the time associated with obtaining another mortgage loan. Some of these costs — such as title insurance and origination points — will vary proportionately with the amount to be financed. Other costs such as the application fee and legal expenses are typically fixed.

Historically, it has been observed that when mortgage rates fall to more than 200 basis points below the contract rate, prepayment rates increase. However, the creativity of mortgage originators in designing mortgage loans such that the refinancing costs are folded into the amount borrowed has changed the view that mortgage rates must drop dramatically below the contract rate to make refinancing economic. Moreover, mortgage originators now do an effective job of advertising to make homeowners cognizant of the economic benefits of refinancing.

The historical pattern of prepayments and economic theory suggests that it is not only the level of mortgage rates that affects prepayment behavior but also the path that mortgage rates take to get to the current level. To illustrate why, suppose the underlying contract rate for a pool of mortgage loans is 11% and that three years after origination, the prevailing mortgage rate declines to 8%. Let's consider two possible paths of the mortgage rate in getting to the 8% level. In the first path, the mortgage rate declines to 8% at the end of the first year, then rises to 13% at the end of the second year, and then falls to 8% at the end of the third year. In the second path, the mortgage rate rises to 12% at the end of the first year, continues its rise to 13% at the end of the second year, and then falls to 8% at the end of the third year.

If the mortgage rate follows the first path, those who can benefit from refinancing will more than likely take advantage of this opportunity when the mortgage rate drops to 8% in the first year. When the mortgage rate drops again to 8% at the end of the third year, the likelihood is that prepayments because of refinancing will not surge; those who can benefit by taking advantage of the refinancing opportunity will have done so already when the mortgage rate declined for the first time. This is the prepayment behavior referred to as the refinancing burnout (or simply, burnout) phenomenon.

In contrast, the expected prepayment behavior when the mortgage rate follows the second path is quite different. Prepayment rates are expected to be low in the first two years. When the mortgage rate declines to 8% in the third year, refinancing activity and therefore prepayments are expected to surge. Consequently, the burnout phenomenon is related to the path of mortgage rates.

Characteristics of the Underlying Mortgage Loans

The following characteristics of the underlying mortgage loans affect prepayments: (1) the contract rate, (2) whether the loans are FHA/VA/RHS-guaranteed or conventional, (3) the amount of seasoning, (4) the type of loan (e.g., a 30-year level payment mortgage, 5-year balloon mortgage, etc.), and (4) the geographical location of the underlying properties.

Seasonal Factors

There is a well-documented seasonal pattern in prepayments. This pattern is related to activity in the primary housing market, with home buying activity increasing in the spring, and gradually reaching a peak in the late summer. Home buying activity declines in the fall and winter. Mirroring this activity are the prepayments that result from the turnover of housing as home buyers sell their existing homes and purchase new ones. Prepayments are low in the winter months and begin to rise in the spring, reaching a peak in the summer months. However, probably because of delays in passing through prepayments, the peak may not be observed until early fall.

General Economic Activity

Economic theory would suggest that general economic activity affects prepayment behavior through its effect on housing turnover. The link is as follows: a growing economy results in a rise in personal income and in opportunities for worker migration; this increases family mobility and as a result increases housing turnover. The opposite holds for a weak economy. Some researchers suggest that prepayments can be projected by identifying and forecasting the turnover rate of the single-family housing stock.[3]

---

[3] See, for example, Joseph C. Hu, "An Alternative Prepayment Projection Based on Housing Activity," in Frank J. Fabozzi (ed.), *The Handbook of Mortgage-Backed Securities* (Chicago: Probus Publishing, 1988), pp. 639-648.

Although some modelers of prepayment behavior may incorporate macroeconomic measures of economic activity such as gross disposable product, industrial production, or housing starts, the trend has been to ignore them or limit their use to specific applications. There are two reasons why macroeconomic measures have been ignored by some modelers. First, empirical tests suggest that the inclusion of macroeconomic measures does not significantly improve the forecasting ability of a prepayment model.[4] Second, as explained later, prepayment models are based on a projection of a path for future mortgage rates. The inclusion of macroeconomic variables in a prepayment model would require the forecasting of the value of these variables over long time periods.

Macroeconomic variables, however, have been used by some researchers in prepayment models to capture the effect of housing turnover on prepayments by specifying a relationship between interest rates and housing turnover. This is the approach used in the Prudential Securities Model.[5]

Extension Risk and Contraction Risk

An investor who owns passthrough securities does not know what the cash flow will be because that depends on actual prepayments. As we noted earlier, this risk is called prepayment risk.

To understand the significance of prepayment risk, suppose an investor buys a 10% coupon Ginnie Mae at a time when mortgage rates are 10%. Let's consider what will happen to prepayments if mortgage rates decline to, say, 6%. There will be two adverse consequences. First, a basic property of fixed income securities is that the price of an option-free bond will rise. But in the case of a passthrough security, the rise in price will not be as large as that of an option-free bond because a fall in interest rates will give the borrower an incentive to prepay the loan and refinance the debt at a lower rate. This results in the same adverse consequence faced by holders of callable bonds. As in the case of those instruments, the upside price potential of a passthrough security is truncated because of prepayments. The second adverse consequence is that the cash flow must be reinvested at a lower rate. These two adverse consequences when mortgage rates decline is referred to as *contraction risk*.

Now let's look at what happens if mortgage rates rise to 15%. The price of the passthrough, like the price of any bond, will decline. But again it will decline more because the higher rates will tend to slow down the rate of prepayment, in effect increasing the amount invested at the coupon rate, which is lower than the market rate. Prepayments will slow down, because homeowners will not refinance or partially prepay their mortgages when mortgage rates are higher than the con-

---

[4] Scott F. Richard and Richard Roll, "Prepayments on Fixed-Rate Mortgage-Backed Securities," *Journal of Portfolio Management* (Spring 1989), pp. 73-79.

[5] Lakbhir S. Hayre, Kenneth Lauterbach, and Cyrus Mohebbi, "Prepayment Models and Methodologies," in Frank J. Fabozzi (ed.), *Advances and Innovations in the Bond and Mortgage Markets* (Chicago, IL: Probus Publishing, 1989), p. 338.

tract rate of 10%. Of course this is just the time when investors want prepayments to speed up so that they can reinvest the prepayments at the higher market interest rate. This adverse consequence of rising mortgage rates is called *extension risk*.

Therefore, prepayment risk encompasses contraction risk and extension risk. Prepayment risk makes passthrough securities unattractive for certain financial institutions to hold from an asset/liability perspective. Some institutional investors are concerned with extension risk and others with contraction risk when they purchase a passthrough security. This applies even for assets supporting specific types of insurance contracts. Is it possible to alter the cash flow of a passthrough so as to reduce the contraction risk and extension risk for institutional investors? This can be done, as we shall see when we describe collateralized mortgage obligations.

Average Life

The stated maturity of a mortgage passthrough security is not a useful measure. Instead, market participants calculate the *average life* of a mortgage-backed security. This is the average time to receipt of principal payments (scheduled principal payments and projected prepayments), weighted by the amount of principal expected. Mathematically, the average life is expressed as follows:

$$\text{Average life} = \sum_{t=1}^{T} \frac{t \times \text{Projected principal received at time } t}{12 \times \text{Total principal}}$$

where T is the number of months.

The average life of a passthrough depends on the PSA prepayment assumption. To see this, the average life is shown below for different prepayment speeds for the passthrough we used to illustrate the cash flow for 100 PSA and 165 PSA in Exhibits 3 and 4:

PSA Speed	50	100	165	200	300	400	500	600	700
Average life	15.11	11.66	8.76	7.68	5.63	4.44	3.68	3.16	2.78

COLLATERALIZED MORTGAGE OBLIGATIONS

As we noted, there is prepayment risk associated with investing in a mortgage passthrough security. Some institutional investors are concerned with extension risk and others with contraction risk. This problem can be mitigated by redirecting the cash flows of mortgage-related products (passthrough securities or a pool of loans) to different bond classes, called *tranches*, so as to create securities that have different exposure to prepayment risk and therefore different risk/return patterns than the mortgage-related product from which they are created.

When the cash flows of mortgage-related products are redistributed to different bond classes, the resulting securities are called *collateralized mortgage obligations* (CMO). The creation of a CMO cannot eliminate prepayment risk; it can only distribute the various forms of this risk among different classes of bondholders. The CMO's major financial innovation is that the securities created more closely satisfy the asset/ liability needs of institutional investors, thereby broadening the appeal of mortgage-backed products.

CMO Structures

There is a wide-range of CMO structures. We review these below.

Sequential-Pay Tranches

The first CMO was created in 1983 and was structured so that each class of bond would be retired sequentially. Such structures are referred to as *sequential-pay* CMOs.

To illustrate a sequential-pay CMO, we discuss FJF-01, a hypothetical deal made up to illustrate the basic features of the structure. The collateral for this hypothetical CMO is a hypothetical passthrough with a total par value of $400 million and the following characteristics: (1) the passthrough coupon rate is 7.5%, (2) the weighted average coupon (WAC) is 8.125%, and (3) the weighted average maturity (WAM) is 357 months. This is the same passthrough that we used earlier in this chapter to describe the cash flow of a passthrough based on some PSA assumption.

From this $400 million of collateral, four bond classes or tranches are created. Their characteristics are summarized in Exhibit 5. The total par value of the four tranches is equal to the par value of the collateral (i.e., the passthrough security). In this simple structure, the coupon rate is the same for each tranche and also the same as the coupon rate on the collateral. There is no reason why this must be so, and, in fact, typically the coupon rate varies by tranche.

Exhibit 5: FJF-01 — A Hypothetical 4-Tranche Sequential-Pay Structure

Tranche	Par Amount ($)	Coupon Rate (%)
A	194,500,000	7.5
B	36,000,000	7.5
C	96,500,000	7.5
D	73,000,000	7.5
Total	400,000,000	

Payment rules:

1. *For payment of periodic coupon interest:* Disburse periodic coupon interest to each tranche on the basis of the amount of principal outstanding at the beginning of the period.

2. *For disbursement of principal payments:* Disburse principal payments to tranche A until it is completely paid off. After tranche A is completely paid off, disburse principal payments to tranche B until it is completely paid off. After tranche B is completely paid off, disburse principal payments to tranche C until it is completely paid off. After tranche C is completely paid off, disburse principal payments to tranche D until it is completely paid off.

Now remember that a CMO is created by redistributing the cash flow — interest and principal — to the different tranches based on a set of payment rules. The payment rules at the bottom of Exhibit 5 describe how the cash flow from the passthrough (i.e., collateral) is to be distributed to the four tranches. There are separate rules for the payment of the coupon interest and the payment of principal, the principal being the total of the regularly scheduled principal payment and any prepayments.

While the priority rules for the disbursement of the principal payments are known, the precise amount of the principal in each period is not. This will depend on the cash flow, and therefore principal payments, of the collateral, which depends on the actual prepayment rate of the collateral. An assumed PSA speed allows the cash flow to be projected. Exhibit 6 shows the cash flow (interest, regularly scheduled principal repayment, and prepayments) assuming 165 PSA. Assuming that the collateral does prepay at 165 PSA, the cash flow available to all four tranches of FJF-01 will be precisely the cash flow shown in Exhibit 6.

To demonstrate how the priority rules for FJF-01 work, Exhibit 6 shows the cash flow for selected months assuming the collateral prepays at 165 PSA. For each tranche, the exhibit shows: (1) the balance at the end of the month, (2) the principal paid down (regularly scheduled principal repayment plus prepayments), and (3) interest. In month 1, the cash flow for the collateral consists of a principal payment of $709,923 and an interest payment of $2.5 million (0.075 times $400 million divided by 12). The interest payment is distributed to the four tranches based on the amount of the par value outstanding. So, for example, tranche A receives $1,215,625 (0.075 times $194,500,000 divided by 12) of the $2.5 million. The principal, however, is all distributed to tranche A. Therefore, the cash flow for tranche A in month 1 is $1,925,548. The principal balance at the end of month 1 for tranche A is $193,790,076 (the original principal balance of $194,500,000 less the principal payment of $709,923). No principal payment is distributed to the three other tranches because there is still a principal balance outstanding for tranche A. This will be true for months 2 through 80.

After month 81, the principal balance will be zero for tranche A. For the collateral, the cash flow in month 81 is $3,318,521, consisting of a principal payment of $2,032,196 and interest of $1,286,325. At the beginning of month 81 (end of month 80), the principal balance for tranche A is $311,926. Therefore, $311,926 of the $2,032,196 of the principal payment from the collateral will be disbursed to tranche A. After this payment is made, no additional principal payments are made to this tranche as the principal balance is zero. The remaining principal payment from the collateral, $1,720,271, is distributed to tranche B. According to the assumed prepayment speed of 165 PSA, tranche B then begins receiving principal payments in month 81.

Exhibit 6 shows that tranche B is fully paid off by month 100, when tranche C begins to receive principal payments. Tranche C is not fully paid off until month 178, at which time tranche D begins receiving the remaining principal payments. The maturity (i.e., the time until the principal is fully paid off) for these four tranches assuming 165 PSA would be 81 months for tranche A, 100 months for tranche B, 178 months for tranche C, and 357 months for tranche D.

Exhibit 6: Monthly Cash Flow for Selected Months for FJF-01 Assuming 165 PSA

	Tranche A			Tranche B		
Month	Balance ($)	Principal ($)	Interest ($)	Balance ($)	Principal ($)	Interest ($)
1	194,500,000	709,923	1,215,625	36,000,000	0	225,000
2	193,790,077	821,896	1,211,188	36,000,000	0	225,000
3	192,968,181	933,560	1,206,051	36,000,000	0	225,000
4	192,034,621	1,044,822	1,200,216	36,000,000	0	225,000
5	190,989,799	1,155,586	1,193,686	36,000,000	0	225,000
6	189,834,213	1,265,759	1,186,464	36,000,000	0	225,000
7	188,568,454	1,375,246	1,178,553	36,000,000	0	225,000
8	187,193,208	1,483,954	1,169,958	36,000,000	0	225,000
9	185,709,254	1,591,789	1,160,683	36,000,000	0	225,000
10	184,117,464	1,698,659	1,150,734	36,000,000	0	225,000
11	182,418,805	1,804,473	1,140,118	36,000,000	0	225,000
12	180,614,332	1,909,139	1,128,840	36,000,000	0	225,000
75	12,893,479	2,143,974	80,584	36,000,000	0	225,000
76	10,749,504	2,124,935	67,184	36,000,000	0	225,000
77	8,624,569	2,106,062	53,904	36,000,000	0	225,000
78	6,518,507	2,087,353	40,741	36,000,000	0	225,000
79	4,431,154	2,068,807	27,695	36,000,000	0	225,000
80	2,362,347	2,050,422	14,765	36,000,000	0	225,000
81	311,926	311,926	1,950	36,000,000	1,720,271	225,000
82	0	0	0	34,279,729	2,014,130	214,248
83	0	0	0	32,265,599	1,996,221	201,660
84	0	0	0	30,269,378	1,978,468	189,184
85	0	0	0	28,290,911	1,960,869	176,818
95	0	0	0	9,449,331	1,793,089	59,058
96	0	0	0	7,656,242	1,777,104	47,852
97	0	0	0	5,879,138	1,761,258	36,745
98	0	0	0	4,119,880	1,745,550	25,737
99	0	0	0	2,372,329	1,729,979	14,827
100	0	0	0	642,350	642,350	4,015
101	0	0	0	0	0	0
102	0	0	0	0	0	0
103	0	0	0	0	0	0
104	0	0	0	0	0	0
105	0	0	0	0	0	0

Exhibit 6 (Continued)

Month	Tranche C			Tranche D		
	Balance ($)	Principal ($)	Interest ($)	Balance ($)	Principal ($)	Interest ($)
1	96,500,000	0	603,125	73,000,000	0	456,250
2	96,500,000	0	603,125	73,000,000	0	456,250
3	96,500,000	0	603,125	73,000,000	0	456,250
4	96,500,000	0	603,125	73,000,000	0	456,250
5	96,500,000	0	603,125	73,000,000	0	456,250
6	96,500,000	0	603,125	73,000,000	0	456,250
7	96,500,000	0	603,125	73,000,000	0	456,250
8	96,500,000	0	603,125	73,000,000	0	456,250
9	96,500,000	0	603,125	73,000,000	0	456,250
10	96,500,000	0	603,125	73,000,000	0	456,250
11	96,500,000	0	603,125	73,000,000	0	456,250
12	96,500,000	0	603,125	73,000,000	0	456,250
95	96,500,000	0	603,125	73,000,000	0	456,250
96	96,500,000	0	603,125	73,000,000	0	456,250
97	96,500,000	0	603,125	73,000,000	0	456,250
98	96,500,000	0	603,125	73,000,000	0	456,250
99	96,500,000	0	603,125	73,000,000	0	456,250
100	96,500,000	1,072,194	603,125	73,000,000	0	456,250
101	95,427,806	1,699,243	596,424	73,000,000	0	456,250
102	93,728,563	1,684,075	585,804	73,000,000	0	456,250
103	92,044,489	1,669,039	575,278	73,000,000	0	456,250
104	90,375,450	1,654,134	564,847	73,000,000	0	456,250
105	88,721,315	1,639,359	554,508	73,000,000	0	456,250
175	3,260,287	869,602	20,377	73,000,000	0	456,250
176	2,390,685	861,673	14,942	73,000,000	0	456,250
177	1,529,013	853,813	9,556	73,000,000	0	456,250
178	675,199	675,199	4,220	73,000,000	170,824	456,250
179	0	0	0	72,829,176	838,300	455,182
180	0	0	0	71,990,876	830,646	449,943
181	0	0	0	71,160,230	823,058	444,751
182	0	0	0	70,337,173	815,536	439,607
183	0	0	0	69,521,637	808,081	434,510
184	0	0	0	68,713,556	800,690	429,460
185	0	0	0	67,912,866	793,365	424,455
350	0	0	0	1,235,674	160,220	7,723
351	0	0	0	1,075,454	158,544	6,722
352	0	0	0	916,910	156,883	5,731
353	0	0	0	760,027	155,238	4,750
354	0	0	0	604,789	153,607	3,780
355	0	0	0	451,182	151,991	2,820
356	0	0	0	299,191	150,389	1,870
357	0	0	0	148,802	148,802	930

Exhibit 7: Average Life for the Collateral and the Four Tranches of FJF-01 (Years)

Prepayment Speed (PSA)	Average life for				
	Collateral	Tranche A	Tranche B	Tranche C	Tranche D
50	15.11	7.48	15.98	21.02	27.24
100	11.66	4.90	10.86	15.78	24.58
165	8.76	3.48	7.49	11.19	20.27
200	7.68	3.05	6.42	9.60	18.11
300	5.63	2.32	4.64	6.81	13.36
400	4.44	1.94	3.70	5.31	10.34
500	3.68	1.69	3.12	4.38	8.35
600	3.16	1.51	2.74	3.75	6.96
700	2.78	1.38	2.47	3.30	5.95

The *principal pay down window* for a tranche is the time period between the beginning and the ending of the principal payments to that tranche. So, for example, for tranche A, the principal pay down window would be month 1 to month 81 assuming 165 PSA. For tranche B it is from month 81 to month 100. The window is also specified in terms of the length of the time from the beginning of the principal pay down window to the end of the principal pay down window. For tranche A, the window would be stated as 81 months, for tranche B 20 months. In confirmation of trades involving CMOs, the principal pay down window is specified in terms of the initial month that principal is expected to be received to the final month that principal is expected to be received.

Let's look at what has been accomplished by creating the CMO. Earlier we saw that the average life for of the passthrough is 8.76 years assuming a prepayment speed of 165 PSA. Exhibit 7 reports the average life of the collateral and the four tranches assuming different prepayment speeds. Notice that the four tranches have average lives that are both shorter and longer than the collateral thereby attracting investors who have a preference for an average life different from that of the collateral.

There is still a major problem: there is considerable variability of the average life for the tranches. We'll see how this can be tackled later on. However, there is some protection provided for each tranche against prepayment risk. This is because prioritizing the distribution of principal (i.e., establishing the payment rules for principal) effectively protects the shorter-term tranche A in this structure against extension risk. This protection must come from somewhere, so it comes from the three other tranches. Similarly, tranches C and D provide protection against extension risk for tranches A and B. At the same time, tranches C and D benefit because they are provided protection against contraction risk, the protection coming from tranches A and B.

Accrual Bonds

In FJF-01, the payment rules for interest provide for all tranches to be paid interest each month. In many sequential-pay CMO structures, at least one tranche does not receive current interest. Instead, the interest for that tranche would accrue and be added to the principal balance. Such a bond class is commonly referred to as an *accrual tranche* or a *Z bond* (because the bond is similar to a zero-coupon bond). The interest that would have been paid to the accrual bond class is then used to speed up paying down the principal balance of earlier bond classes.

To see this, consider FJF-02, a hypothetical CMO structure with the same collateral as FJF-01 and with four tranches, each with a coupon rate of 7.5%. The difference is in the last tranche, Z, which is an accrual tranche. The structure for FJF-02 is shown in Exhibit 8.

Exhibit 9 shows cash flows for selected months for tranches A and B. Let's look at month 1 and compare it to month 1 in Exhibit 6. Both cash flows are based on 165 PSA. The principal payment from the collateral is $709,923. In FJF-01, this is the principal paydown for tranche A. In FJF-02, the interest for tranche Z, $456,250, is not paid to that tranche but instead is used to pay down the principal of tranche A. So, the principal payment to tranche A in Exhibit 9 is $1,166,173, the collateral's principal payment of $709,923 plus the interest of $456,250 that was diverted from tranche Z.

The expected final maturity for tranches A, B, and C has shortened as a result of the inclusion of tranche Z. The final payout for tranche A is 64 months rather than 81 months; for tranche B it is 77 months rather than 100 months; and, for tranche C it is 112 months rather than 178 months.

The average lives for tranches A, B, and C are shorter in FJF-02 compared to FJF-01 because of the inclusion of the accrual tranche. For example, at 165 PSA, the average lives are as follows:

Structure	Tranche A	Tranche B	Tranche C
FJF-02	2.90	5.86	7.87
FJF-01	3.48	7.49	11.19

Exhibit 8: FJF-02 — A Hypothetical 4-Tranche Sequential-Pay Structure with an Accrual Bond Class

Tranche	Par Amount ($)	Coupon Rate (%)
A	194,500,000	7.5
B	36,000,000	7.5
C	96,500,000	7.5
Z (Accrual)	73,000,000	7.5
Total	400,000,000	

Payment rules:

1. *For payment of periodic coupon interest:* Disburse periodic coupon interest to tranches A, B, and C on the basis of the amount of principal outstanding at the beginning of the period. For tranche Z, accrue the interest based on the principal plus accrued interest in the previous period. The interest for tranche Z is to be paid to the earlier tranches as a principal paydown.

2. *For disbursement of principal payments:* Disburse principal payments to tranche A until it is completely paid off. After tranche A is completely paid off, disburse principal payments to tranche B until it is completely paid off. After tranche B is completely paid off, disburse principal payments to tranche C until it is completely paid off. After tranche C is completely paid off, disburse principal payments to tranche Z until the original principal balance plus accrued interest is completely paid off.

Exhibit 9: Monthly Cash Flow for Selected Months for Tranches A and B for FJF-02 Assuming 165 PSA

	Tranche A			Tranche B		
Month	Balance ($)	Principal ($)	Interest ($)	Balance ($)	Principal ($)	Interest ($)
1	194,500,000	1,166,173	1,215,625	36,000,000	0	225,000
2	193,333,827	1,280,997	1,208,336	36,000,000	0	225,000
3	192,052,829	1,395,531	1,200,330	36,000,000	0	225,000
4	190,657,298	1,509,680	1,191,608	36,000,000	0	225,000
5	189,147,619	1,623,350	1,182,173	36,000,000	0	225,000
6	187,524,269	1,736,446	1,172,027	36,000,000	0	225,000
7	185,787,823	1,848,875	1,161,174	36,000,000	0	225,000
8	183,938,947	1,960,543	1,149,618	36,000,000	0	225,000
9	181,978,404	2,071,357	1,137,365	36,000,000	0	225,000
10	179,907,047	2,181,225	1,124,419	36,000,000	0	225,000
11	177,725,822	2,290,054	1,110,786	36,000,000	0	225,000
12	175,435,768	2,397,755	1,096,474	36,000,000	0	225,000
60	15,023,406	3,109,398	93,896	36,000,000	0	225,000
61	11,914,007	3,091,812	74,463	36,000,000	0	225,000
62	8,822,195	3,074,441	55,139	36,000,000	0	225,000
63	5,747,754	3,057,282	35,923	36,000,000	0	225,000
64	2,690,472	2,690,472	16,815	36,000,000	349,863	225,000
65	0	0	0	35,650,137	3,023,598	222,813
66	0	0	0	32,626,54	3,007,069	203,916
67	0	0	0	29,619,47	2,990,748	185,122
68	0	0	0	26,628,722	2,974,633	166,430
69	0	0	0	23,654,089	2,958,722	147,838
70	0	0	0	20,695,367	2,943,014	129,346
71	0	0	0	17,752,353	2,927,508	110,952
72	0	0	0	14,824,845	2,912,203	92,655
73	0	0	0	11,912,642	2,X97,096	74,454
74	0	0	0	9,015,546	2,882,187	56,347
75	0	0	0	6,133,358	2,867,475	38,333
76	0	0	0	3,265,883	2,852,958	20,412
77	0	0	0	412,925	412,925	2,581
78	0	0	0	0	0	0
79	0	0	0	0	0	0
80	0	0	0	0	0	0

The reason for the shortening of the non-accrual tranches is that the interest that would be paid to the accrual bond is being allocated to the other tranches. Tranche Z in FJF-02 will have a longer average life than tranche D in FJF-01.

Thus, shorter-term tranches and a longer-term tranche are created by including an accrual bond. The accrual bond has appeal to investors who are concerned with reinvestment risk. Since there are no coupon payments to reinvest, reinvestment risk is eliminated until all the other tranches are paid off.

Exhibit 10: FJF-03 — A Hypothetical 5-Tranche Sequential-Pay Structure with Floater, Inverse Floater, and Accrual Bond Classes

Tranche	Par Amount ($)	Coupon Rate (%)
A	194,500,000	7.50
B	36,000,000	7.50
FL	96,500,000	1-month LIBOR + 0.50
IFL	24,125,000	28.50 − 3 × (1-month LIBOR)
Z (Accrual)	73,000,000	7.50
Total	400,000,000	

Payment rules:

1. *For payment of periodic coupon interest:* Disburse periodic coupon interest to tranches A, B, FL, and IFL on the basis of the amount of principal outstanding at the beginning of the period. For tranche Z, accrue the interest based on the principal plus accrued interest in the previous period. The interest for tranche Z is to be paid to the earlier tranches as a principal paydown. The maximum coupon rate for FL is 10% the minimum coupon rate for IFL is 0%

2. *For disbursement of principal payments:* Disburse principal payments to tranche A until it is completely paid off. After tranche A is completely paid off, disburse principal payments to tranche B until it is completely paid off. After tranche B is completely paid off, disburse principal payments to tranches FL and IFL until they are completely paid off. The principal payments between tranches FL and IFL should be made in the following way: 75% to tranche FL and 25% to tranche IFL. After tranches FL and IFI are completely paid off, disburse principal payments to tranche Z until the original principal balance plus accrued interest are completely paid off.

Floating-Rate Tranches

A floating-rate tranche can be created from a fixed-rate tranche by creating a floater and an inverse floater combination. We will illustrate the creation of a floating-rate tranche and inverse floating-rate tranche using the hypothetical CMO structure FJF-02, which is a 4-tranche sequential-pay structure with an accrual bond. We can select any of the tranches from which to create a floating-rate and inverse floating-rate tranche. In fact, we can create these two securities for more than one of the four tranches or for only a portion of one tranche.

In this case, we create a floater and an inverse floater from tranche C. The par value for this tranche is $96.5 million, and we create two tranches that have a combined par value of $96.5 million. We refer to this CMO structure with a floater and an inverse floater as FJF-03. It has five tranches, designated A, B, FL, IFL, and Z, where FL is the floating-rate tranche and IFL is the inverse floating-rate tranche. Exhibit 10 describes FJF-03. Any reference rate can be used to create a floater and the corresponding inverse floater. The reference rate for setting the coupon rate for FL and IFL in FJF-03 is 1-month LIBOR.

The amount of the par value of the floating-rate tranche will be some portion of the $96.5 million. There are an infinite number of ways to cut up the $96.5 million between the floater and inverse floater, and final partitioning will be driven by the demands of investors. In the FJF-03 structure, we made the floater from $72,375,000 or 75% of the $96.5 million. The coupon formula for the floater is 1-month LIBOR plus 50 basis points. So, for example, if LIBOR is 3.75% at the reset date, the coupon rate on the floater is 3.75% + 0.5%, or 4.25%. There is a cap on the coupon rate for the floater (discussed later).

Unlike a floating-rate note in the corporate bond market whose principal is unchanged over the life of the instrument, the floater's principal balance declines over time as principal payments are made. The principal payments to the floater are determined by the principal payments from the tranche from which the floater is created. In our CMO structure, this is tranche C.

Since the floater's par value is $72,375,000 of the $96.5 million, the balance is par value for the inverse floater. Assuming that 1-month LIBOR is the reference rate, the coupon formula for the inverse floater takes the following form:

$$K - L \times (1\text{-month LIBOR})$$

In FJF-03, K is set at 28.50% and L at 3. Thus, if 1-month LIBOR is 3.75%, the coupon rate for the month is:

$$28.50\% - 3 \times (3.75\%) = 17.25\%$$

K is the cap or maximum coupon rate for the inverse floater. In FJF-03, the cap for the inverse floater is 28.50%.

The L or multiple in the formula to determine the coupon rate for the inverse floater is called the *leverage*. The higher the leverage, the more the inverse floater's coupon rate changes for a given change in 1-month LIBOR. For example, a coupon leverage of 3 means that a 1-basis point change in 1-month LIBOR will change the coupon rate on the inverse floater by 3 basis points.

As in the case of the floater, the principal paydown of an inverse floater will be a proportionate amount of the principal paydown of tranche C.

Because 1-month LIBOR is always positive, the coupon rate paid to the floating-rate tranche cannot be negative. If there are no restrictions placed on the coupon rate for the inverse floater, however, it is possible for the coupon rate for that bond class to be negative. To prevent this, a floor, or minimum, can be placed on the coupon rate. In many structures, the floor is set at zero. Once a floor is set for the inverse floater, a cap or ceiling is imposed on the floater. In FJF-03, a floor of zero is set for the inverse floater. The floor results in a cap or maximum coupon rate for the floater of 10%.

The cap for the floater and the inverse floater, the floor for the inverse floater, the leverage, and the margin spread are not determined independently. Given four of these variables, the fifth will be determined.

Planned Amortization Class Tranches
The CMO structures discussed above attracted many institutional investors who had previously either avoided investing in mortgage-backed securities or allocated only a nominal portion of their portfolio to this sector of the bond market.

While some traditional corporate bond buyers shifted their allocation to CMOs, a majority of institutional investors remained on the sidelines, concerned about investing in an instrument they continued to perceive as posing significant prepayment risk. This concern was based on the substantial average life variability, despite the innovations designed to mitigate prepayment risk.

In 1987, several structures came to market that shared the following characteristics: if the prepayment speed is within a specified band over the collateral's life, the cash flow pattern is known. The greater predictability of the cash flow for these classes of bonds, now referred to as *planned amortization class* (PAC) bonds, occurs because there is a principal repayment schedule that must be satisfied. PAC bondholders have priority over all other classes in the CMO issue in receiving principal payments from the underlying collateral. The greater certainty of the cash flow for the PAC bonds comes at the expense of the non-PAC classes, called the *support* or *companion* bonds. It is these bonds that absorb the prepayment risk. Because PAC bonds have protection against both extension risk and contraction risk, they are said to provide *two-sided prepayment protection*.

To illustrate how to create a PAC bond, we will use as collateral the $400 million passthrough with a coupon rate of 7.5%, an 8.125% WAC, and a WAM of 357 months. The second column of Exhibit 11 shows the principal payment (regularly scheduled principal repayment plus prepayments) for selected months assuming a prepayment speed of 90 PSA, and the next column shows the principal payments for selected months assuming that the passthrough prepays at 300 PSA.

The last column of Exhibit 11 gives the minimum principal payment if the collateral speed is 90 PSA or 300 PSA for months 1 to 349. (After month 349, the outstanding principal balance will be paid off if the prepayment speed is between 90 PSA and 300 PSA.) For example, in the first month, the principal payment would be $508,169.52 if the collateral prepays at 90 PSA and $1,075,931.20 if the collateral prepays at 300 PSA. Thus, the minimum principal payment is $508,169.52, as reported in the last column of Exhibit 11. In month 103, the minimum principal payment is also the amount if the prepayment speed is 90 PSA, $1,446,761, compared to $1,458,618.04 for 300 PSA. In month 104, however, a prepayment speed of 300 PSA would produce a principal payment of $1,433,539.23, which is less than the principal payment of $1,440,825.55 assuming 90 PSA. So, $1,433,539.23 is reported in the last column of Exhibit 11. From month 104 on, the minimum principal payment is the one that would result assuming a prepayment speed of 300 PSA.

In fact, if the collateral prepays at any one speed between 90 PSA and 300 PSA over its life, the minimum principal payment would be the amount reported in the last column of Exhibit 11. For example, if we had included principal payment figures assuming a prepayment speed of 200 PSA, the minimum principal payment would not change: from month 11 through month 103, the minimum principal payment is that generated from 90 PSA, but from month 104 on, the minimum principal payment is that generated from 300 PSA.

Exhibit 11: Monthly Principal Payment for $400 Million, 7.5% Coupon Passthrough with an 8.125% WAC and a 357 WAM Assuming Prepayment Rates of 90 PSA and 300 PSA

Month	At 90% PSA ($)	At 300% PSA	Minimum Principal Payment — the PAC Schedule ($)
1	508,169.52	1,075,931.20	508,169.52
2	569,843.43	1,279,412.11	569,843.43
3	631,377.11	1,482,194.45	631,377.11
4	692,741.89	1 683,966.17	692,741.89
5	753,909.12	1,884,414.62	753,909.12
6	814,850.22	2,083,227.31	814,850.22
7	875,536.68	2,280,092.68	875,536.68
8	935,940.10	2,474,700.92	935,940.10
9	996,032.19	2,666,744.77	996,032.19
10	1,055,784.82	2,855,920.32	1,055,784.82
11	1,115,170.01	3,041,927.81	1,115,170.01
12	1,174,160.00	3,224,472.44	1,174,160.00
13	1,232,727.22	3,403,265.17	1,232,727.22
14	1,290,844.32	3,578,023.49	1,290,844.32
15	1,348,484.24	3,748,472.23	1,348,484.24
16	1,405,620.17	3,9 14,344.26	1,405,620.17
17	1,462,225.60	4,075,381.29	1,462,225.60
18	1,518,274.36	4,231,334.57	1,518,274.36
101	1,458,719.34	1,510,072.17	1,458,719.34
102	1,452,725.55	1,484,126.59	1,452,725.55
103	1,446,761.00	1,458,618.04	1,446,761.00
104	1,440,825.55	1,433,539.23	1,433,539.23
105	1,434,919.07	1,408,883.01	1,408,883.01
211	949,482.58	213,309.00	213,309.00
212	946,033.34	209,409.09	209,409.09
213	942,601.99	205,577.05	205,577.05
346	618,684.59	13,269.17	13,269.17
347	617,071.58	12,944.51	12,944.51
348	615,468.65	12,626.21	12,626.21
349	613,875.77	12,314.16	3,432.32
350	612,292.88	12,008.25	0
351	610,719.96	11,708.38	0
352	609,156.96	11,414.42	0
353	607,603.S4	11,126.28	0
354	606,060.57	10,843.85	0
355	604,527.09	10,567.02	0
356	603,003.38	10,295.70	0
357	601,489.39	10,029.78	0

Exhibit 12: FJF-04 — CMO Structure with One PAC Bond and One Support Bond

Tranche	Par amount ($)	Coupon Rate (%)
P (PAC)	243,800,000	7.5
S (Support)	156,200,000	7.5
Total	400,000,000	

Payment rules:

1. *For payment of periodic coupon interest:* Disburse periodic coupon interest to each tranche on the basis of the amount of principal outstanding at the beginning of the period.

2. *For disbursement of principal payments:* Disburse principal payments to tranche P based on its schedule of principal repayments. Tranche P has priority with respect to current and future principal payments to satisfy the schedule. Any excess principal payments in a month over the amount necessary to satisfy the schedule for tranche P are paid to tranche S. When tranche S is completely paid off, all principal payments are to be made to tranche P regardless of the schedule.

This characteristic of the collateral allows for the creation of a PAC bond, assuming that the collateral prepays over its life at a speed between 90 PSA to 300 PSA. A schedule of principal repayments that the PAC bondholders are entitled to receive before any other bond class in the CMO is specified. The monthly schedule of principal repayments is as specified in the last column of Exhibit 11, which shows the minimum principal payment. While there is no assurance that the collateral will prepay at a constant speed between these two speeds over its life, a PAC bond can be structured to assume that it will.

Exhibit 12 shows a CMO structure, FJF-04, created from the $400 million, 7.5% coupon passthrough with a WAC of 8.125% and a WAM of 357 months. There are just two tranches in this structure: a 7.5% coupon PAC bond created assuming 90 to 300 PSA with a par value of $243.8 million, and a support (non-PAC) bond with a par value of $156.2 million.

Exhibit 13 reports the average life for the PAC bond and the support bond in FJF-04 assuming various *actual* prepayment speeds. Notice that between 90 PSA and 300 PSA, the average life for the PAC bond is stable at 7.26 years. However, at slower or faster PSA speeds, the schedule is broken, and the average life changes, extending when the prepayment speed is less than 90 PSA and contracting when it is greater than 300 PSA. Even so, there is much greater variability for the average life of the support bond.

In practice, all CMO structures typically do not have just one PAC tranche. Rather, there are several PAC tranches created from the same tranche. For example, several PAC tranches that pay off in sequence can be created with a total par value equal to $243.8 million, which is the amount of the single PAC bond in FJF-04. This allows for the creation of PACs with a wide range of average lives.

For a PAC bond, the pay down window can be wide or narrow. The narrower a PAC window, the more it resembles a corporate bond with a bullet payment. PAC buyers appear to prefer tight windows, although institutional investors facing a liability schedule are generally better off with a window that more closely matches their liabilities.

Exhibit 13: Average Life for PAC Bond and Support Bond in FJF-04 Assuming Various Prepayment Speeds (Years)

Prepayment rate (PSA)	PAC Bond (P)	Support Bond (S)
0	15.97	27.26
50	9.44	24.00
90	7.26	18.56
100	7.26	18.56
150	7.26	18.56
165	7.26	11.16
200	7.26	8.38
250	7.26	5.37
300	7.26	3.13
350	6.56	2.51
400	5.92	2.17
450	5.38	1.94
500	4.93	1.77
700	3.70	1.37

Support Bonds

The support bonds are the bonds that provide prepayment protection for the PAC tranches. Consequently, support tranches expose investors to the greatest level of prepayment risk. Because of this, investors must be particularly careful in assessing the cash flow characteristics of support bonds to reduce the likelihood of adverse portfolio consequences due to prepayments.

The support bond typically is divided into different bond classes. All the bond classes we have discussed earlier are available, including sequential-pay support bond classes, floater and inverse floater support bond classes, and accrual support bond classes.

The support bond can even be partitioned to create support bond classes with a schedule of principal payments. That is, support bond classes that are PAC bonds can be created. In a structure with a PAC bond and a support bond with a PAC schedule of principal payments, the former is called a PAC I bond or Level I PAC bond and the latter a PAC II bond or Level II PAC bond. While PAC II bonds have greater prepayment protection than the support bond classes without a schedule of principal repayments, the prepayment protection is less than that provided PAC I bonds.

The support bond without a principal repayment schedule can be used to create any type of bond class. In fact, a portion of the non-PAC II support bond can be given a schedule of principal repayments. This bond class would be called a PAC III bond or a Level III PAC bond. While it provides protection against prepayments for the PAC I and PAC II bonds and is therefore subject to considerable prepayment risk, such a bond class has greater protection than the support bond class without a schedule of principal repayments.

REMICs

The issuer of a CMO wants to be sure that the trust created to pass through the interest and principal payments is not treated as a taxable entity. A provision of the Tax Reform Act of 1986, called the Real Estate Mortgage Investment Conduit (REMIC), specifies the requirements that an issuer must fulfill so that the legal entity created to issue a CMO is not taxable. Most CMOs today are created as REMICs. While it is common to hear market participants refer to a CMO as a REMIC, not all CMOs are REMICs.

STRIPPED MORTGAGE-BACKED SECURITIES

A mortgage passthrough security divides the cash flow from the underlying pool of mortgages on a pro rata basis to the securityholders. A *stripped mortgage-backed security* is created by altering that distribution of principal and interest from a pro rata distribution to an unequal distribution. The result is that the securities created will have a price/yield relationship that is different from the price/yield relationship of the underlying passthrough security.

In the most common type of stripped mortgage-backed securities all the interest is allocated to one class (called the *interest only* or *IO class*) and all the principal to the other class (called the *principal only* or *PO class*). The IO class receives no principal payments.

Principal-Only Securities

The PO security is purchased at a substantial discount from par value. The return an investor realizes depends on the speed at which prepayments are made. The faster the prepayments, the higher the investor's return. For example, suppose there is a mortgage pool consisting only of 30-year mortgages, with $400 million in principal, and that investors can purchase POs backed by this mortgage pool for $175 million. The dollar return on this investment will be $225 million. How quickly that dollar return is recovered by PO investors determines the actual return that will be realized. In the extreme case, if all homeowners in the underlying mortgage pool decide to prepay their mortgage loans immediately, PO investors will realize the $225 million immediately. At the other extreme, if all homeowners decide to remain in their homes for 30 years and make no prepayments, the $225 million will be spread out over 30 years, which would result in a lower return for PO investors.

Let's look at how the price of the PO would be expected to change as mortgage rates in the market change. When mortgage rates decline below the contract rate, prepayments are expected to speed up, accelerating payments to the PO holder. Thus, the cash flow of a PO improves (in the sense that principal repayments are received earlier). The cash flow will be discounted at a lower interest rate because the mortgage rate in the market has declined. The result is that the PO price will increase when mortgage rates decline. When mortgage rates rise above the contract rate, prepayments are expected to slow down. The cash flow deteriorates (in the sense that it takes longer to recover principal repayments). Couple this with a higher discount rate, and the price of a PO will fall when mortgage rates rise.

Interest-Only Securities

An IO has no par value. In contrast to the PO investor, the IO investor wants prepayments to be slow. The reason is that the IO investor receives interest only on the amount of the principal outstanding. When prepayments are made, less dollar interest will be received as the outstanding principal declines. In fact, if prepayments are too fast, the IO investor may not recover the amount paid for the IO even if the security is held to maturity.

Let's look at the expected price response of an IO to changes in mortgage rates. If mortgage rates decline below the contract rate, prepayments are expected to accelerate. This would result in a deterioration of the expected cash flow for an IO. While the cash flow will be discounted at a lower rate, the net effect typically is a decline in the price of an IO. If mortgage rates rise above the contract rate, the expected cash flow improves, but the cash flow is discounted at a higher interest rate. The net effect may be either a rise or fall for the IO.

Thus, we see an interesting characteristic of an IO: its price tends to move in the same direction as the change in mortgage rates (1) when mortgage rates fall below the contract rate and (2) for some range of mortgage rates above the contract rate. Both POs and IOs exhibit substantial price volatility when mortgage rates change. The greater price volatility of the IO and PO compared to the passthrough from which they were created is due to the fact that the combined price volatility of the IO and PO must be equal to the price volatility of the passthrough.

An average life for a PO can be calculated based on some prepayment assumption. However, an IO receives no principal payments, so technically an average life cannot be computed. Instead, for an IO a "cash flow average life" is computed, using the projected interest payments in the average life formula instead of principal.

NONAGENCY MORTGAGE-BACKED SECURITIES

Thus far, we looked at agency mortgage-backed securities in which the underlying mortgages are 1- to 4-single family residential mortgages. The mortgage-backed securities market includes other types of securities. These securities are called nonagency mortgage-backed securities (referred to as nonagency securities hereafter).

The underlying mortgage loans for nonagency securities can be for any type of real estate property. There are securities backed by 1- to 4-single family residential mortgages with a first lien on the mortgaged property. There are nonagency securities backed by other types of single family residential loans. These include home equity loan-backed securities and manufactured housing-loan backed securities. Commercial mortgage-backed securities are nonagency securities in which the underlying collateral is a pool of commercial mortgage loans. Commercial mortgage loans include loans for apartment buildings (multi-family housing), shopping centers, office buildings, warehouses, hotels, and nursing homes. Our focus in this section is on nonagency securities in which the underlying loans are first-lien mortgages for 1- to 4-single-family residential properties.

As with an agency mortgage-backed security, the servicer is responsible for the collection of interest and principal, which is passed along to the trustee. The servicer also handles delinquencies and foreclosures. Typically, there will be a master servicer and subservicers. The servicer plays a key role. In fact, in assessing the credit risk of a nonagency security, rating companies look carefully at the quality of the servicers.

Underlying Mortgage Loans

The underlying loans for agency securities are those that conform to the underwriting standards of the agency issuing or guaranteeing the issue. That is, only conforming loans are included in pools that are collateral for an agency mortgage-backed security. The three main underwriting standards deal with (1) the maximum loan-to-value ratio, (2) the maximum payment-to-income ratio, and (3) the maximum loan amount. A nonconforming mortgage loan is one that does not conform to the underwriting standards established by any of the agencies.

Typically, the loans for a nonagency security are nonconforming mortgage loans that fail to qualify for inclusion because the amount of the loan exceeds the limit established by the agencies. Such loans are referred to as *jumbo loans*. Jumbo loans do not necessarily have greater credit risk than conforming mortgages.

Loans that fail to qualify because of the first two underwriting standards expose the lender to greater credit risk. In general, lenders classify borrowers by credit quality. Borrowers are classified as A borrowers, B borrowers, C borrowers, and D borrowers. A borrowers are those that are viewed as having the best credit record. Such borrowers are referred to as prime borrowers. Borrowers rated below A are viewed as *subprime borrowers*. However, there is no industry-wide classification system for prime and subprime borrowers.

Differences Between Agency and Nonagency Securities

Nonagency securities can be either passthroughs or CMOs. In the agency market, CMOs are created from pools of passthrough securities. In the nonagency market, a CMO can be created from either a pool of passthroughs or unsecuritized mortgage loans. It is uncommon for nonconforming mortgage loans to be securitized as passthroughs and then the passthroughs carved up to create a CMO. Instead, in the nonagency market a CMO is typically carved out of mortgage loans that have not been securitized as passthroughs. Since a mortgage loan is commonly referred to as a whole loan, nonagency CMOs are commonly referred to as *whole-loan CMOs*.

The major differences between agency and nonagency securities have to do with guarantees, dispersion of the characteristics of the underlying collateral, servicer advances, compensating interest, and clean-up calls. We discuss each below.

Guarantees

With a nonagency security there is no explicit or implicit government guarantee of payment of interest and principal as there is with an agency security. The absence of any such guarantee means that the investor in a nonagency security is exposed to credit risk. The nationally recognized statistical rating organizations rate nonagency securities.

Dispersion of Characteristics of Underlying Collateral

While both agency and nonagency securities are backed by 1- to 4-single family residential mortgages, the underlying loans for nonagency securities will typically be more heterogeneous with respect to coupon rate and maturity of the individual loans. For example, a nonagency security might include both 15-year and 30-year mortgages in the same mortgage pool.

Servicer Advances

When there is a delinquency by the homeowner, the investor in a nonagency security may or may not be affected. This depends on whether a servicer is required to make advances. Thus, the financial capacity of the servicer to make advances is critical. Typically, a back-up servicer is used just in case the master servicer cannot meet its obligation with respect to advances. The servicer recovers advances when delinquent payments are made or the property is foreclosed and proceeds received.

There are different forms of advancing: (1) mandatory advancing, (2) optional advancing, and (3) limited advancing. The strongest form from the investor's perspective is mandatory advancing wherein failure to advance by a servicer is an event of default. However, a servicer need not advance if it can show that there is not a strong likelihood of recovery of the amount advanced when the property is ultimately disposed of. In an optional or a voluntary advancing, the servicer is not legally obligated to advance so that failure to do so is not an event of default. In a limited advancing the issuer is obligated to advance, but the amount it must advance is limited.

Compensating Interest

An additional factor to consider which is unique to nonagency securities is compensating interest. Mortgage passthroughs and CMOs pay principal and interest on a monthly basis. While homeowners may prepay their mortgage on any day throughout the month, the agencies guarantee and pay investors a full month of interest as if all the prepayments occur on the last day of the month. Unfortunately, this guarantee does not apply to nonagency securities. If a homeowner pays off a mortgage on the tenth day of the month, he will stop paying interest for the rest of the month. Because of the payment delay (for example, 25 days), the investor will receive full principal but only 10 days of interest on the 25th of the following month.

This phenomenon is known as payment interest shortfall or *compensating interest* and is handled differently by different issuers. Some issuers will pay up to only a specified amount and some will not pay at all. Actually, it the servicers who will pay any compensating interest. The servicer obtains the shortfall in interest from the servicing spread. The shortfall that will be made up to the investor may be limited to the entire servicing spread or part of the servicing spread. Thus, while an investor has protection against the loss of a full month's interest, the protection is limited.

For a nonagency security in which there is compensating interest, typically prepayments of the entire outstanding balance are covered. Curtailments (i.e., partial prepayments) are not covered.

In an agency CMO and nonagency CMO, the interest is paid to each tranche on the basis of the distribution rules for interest. In a nonagency CMO, as explained below there are tranches within credit classes. When there is a shortfall in the full month's interest, typically the shortfall is prorated among the credit classes based on the outstanding principal balance. Then, for each tranche within a credit class, the shortfall is prorated based on the interest that would be due.

In a nonagency CMO structure, the economic value of compensating interest depends on the level of prepayment and the types of CMO tranches. Generally, the faster the prepayments and the greater the coupon for the tranche, the higher the economic value of compensating interest.

Clean-Up Call Provisions

All nonagency CMO structures are issued with "clean-up" call provisions. The clean-up call provides the servicers or the residual holders (typically the issuers) the right, but not the obligation, to call all the outstanding tranches of the CMO structure when the CMO balance is paid down to a certain percentage of the original principal balance. The servicer typically finds it more costly than the servicing fee to service the CMO when the balance is paid down to a small amount. For example, suppose a $100 million CMO was originally issued with a 10% clean-up call. When the entire CMO balance is paid down to $10 million or less, the servicer can exercise the call to pay off all outstanding tranches regardless of the percentage balance of the individual tranches.

The call provision, when exercised, shortens the principal paydown window and the average life of the back-end tranches of a CMO. This provision is not unique to nonagency CMO structures. It is mandatory, however, for all nonagency CMO structures while agency CMOs may or may not have clean-up calls. Typically, Freddie Mac CMOs have 1% clean-up calls and Fannie Mae CMOs do not have clean-up calls.

Credit Enhancements

All nonagency mortgage-backed securities are credit enhanced. Credit enhancement levels are determined relative to a specific rating desired for a security by each rating company. Specifically, an investor in a triple A rated security expects to have "minimal," that is to say, virtually no chance of losing any principal due to defaults. For example, Standard & Poor's requires credit enhancement equal to four times expected losses to obtain a triple A rating.

Typically a double A or triple A rating is sought for the most senior tranche. The amount of credit enhancement necessary depends on rating agency requirements. There are two general types of credit enhancement structures: external and internal. We describe each type below.

External Credit Enhancements

External credit enhancements come in the form of third-party guarantees that provide for first loss protection against losses up to a specified level, for example, 10%. The most common forms of external credit enhancements are (1) a corporate guarantee, (2) a letter of credit, (3) pool insurance, and (4) bond insurance.

Pool insurance policies cover losses resulting from defaults and foreclosures. Policies are typically written for a dollar amount of coverage that continues in force throughout the life of the pool. However, some policies are written so that the dollar amount of coverage declines as the pool seasons as long as two conditions are met: (1) the credit performance is better than expected and (2) the rating agencies that rated the issue approve. Since only defaults and foreclosures are covered, additional insurance must be obtained to cover losses resulting from bankruptcy (i.e., court mandated modification of mortgage debt — "cramdown"), fraud arising in the origination process, and special hazards (i.e., losses resulting from events not covered by a standard homeowner's insurance policy).

Bond insurance provides the same function as in municipal bond structures. Typically, bond insurance is not used as the primary protection but to supplement other forms of credit enhancement.

A nonagency security with external credit support is subject to the credit risk of the third-party guarantor. Should the third-party guarantor be downgraded, the issue itself could be subject to downgrade even if the structure is performing as expected. This is based on the "weak link" test followed by rating agencies. According to this test, when evaluating a proposed structure, credit quality of the issue is only as good as the weakest link in credit enhancement regardless of the quality of underlying loans.

External credit enhancements do not materially alter the cash flow characteristics of a CMO structure except in the form of prepayment. In case of a default resulting in net losses within the guarantee level, investors will receive the principal amount as if a prepayment has occurred. If the net losses exceed the guarantee level, investors will have a shortfall in the cash flows.

Internal Credit Enhancements

Internal credit enhancements come in more complicated forms than external credit enhancements and may alter the cash flow characteristics of the loans even in the absence of default. The most common forms of internal credit enhancements are reserve funds and senior/subordinated structures.

Reserve Funds Reserve funds come in two forms, cash reserve funds and excess servicing spread. Cash reserve funds are straight deposits of cash generated from issuance proceeds. In this case, part of the underwriting profits from the deal are deposited into a hypothecated fund which typically invests in money market instruments. Cash reserve funds are typically used in conjunction with letters of credit or other kinds of external credit enhancements.

Excess servicing spread accounts involve the allocation of excess spread or cash into a separate reserve account after paying out the net coupon, servicing fee, and all other expenses on a monthly basis. For example, suppose that the gross weighted average coupon (gross WAC) is 7.75%, the servicing and other fees are 0.25%, and the net weighted average coupon (net WAC) is 7.25%. This means that there is excess servicing of 0.25%. The amount in the reserve account will gradually increase and can be used to pay for possible future losses.

The excess spread is analogous to the guarantee fee paid to the issuer of an agency mortgage-backed security except that this is a form of self-insurance. This form of credit enhancement relies on the assumption that defaults occur infrequently in the very early life of the loans but gradually increase in the following two to five years.

Senior/Subordinated Structure The most widely used internal credit support structure is by far the senior/subordinated structure. Today a typical structure will have a senior bond and several junior bonds. The junior bonds represent the subordinated bonds of the structure. The issuer will seek a triple A or double A rating for the senior bond. The junior bonds will have lower ratings — investment grade and non-investment grade. Typically, the most junior bond — called the *first loss piece* — will not be rated. All that has been done in this structure is credit tranching. The senior or any of the junior bonds can then be carved up to create CMO tranches.

Almost all existing senior/subordinated structures also incorporate a *shifting interest structure*. A shifting interest structure redirects prepayments disproportionally from the subordinated classes to the senior class according to a specified schedule. The rationale for the shifting interest structure is to have enough insurance outstanding to cover future losses. While the shifting interest structure is beneficial to the senior bond from a credit standpoint, it does alter the cash flow characteristics of the senior bond even in the absence of defaults.

ASSET-BACKED SECURITIES

Asset-based securities are backed by a pool of one of the following types of debt obligations: (1) installment loans, (2) leases, (3) receivables, (4) junior mortgage liens, and (5) revolving lines of credit. These securities expose investors to credit risk. The four nationally recognized statistical rating organizations rate asset-backed securities. In analyzing credit risk, the rating companies focus the credit quality of the collateral, the quality of the seller/servicer, the cash flow stress and payment structure, and the legal structure.

The credit enhancement mechanics described earlier for nonagency mortgage-backed security structures are used in asset-backed security structures. In creating an asset-backed security, issuers have drawn from the structures used in the mortgage-backed securities market. There are *passthrough* (i.e., pro rata distribution of the cash flow) and *paythrough structures*. The latter consists of multiple bond classes or tranches, just like collateralized mortgage-backed securities.

Cash Flow of Asset-Backed Securities

The collateral for an asset-backed security can be classified as either *amortizing* or *nonamortizing assets*. Amortizing assets are loans in which the borrower's periodic payment consists of scheduled principal and interest payments over the life of the loan. The standard residential mortgage loan falls into this category. Auto loans and certain types of home equity loans (specifically, closed-end home equity loans discussed later in this chapter) are amortizing assets. Any excess payment over the scheduled principal payment is a prepayment. Prepayments can be made to pay off the entire balance or a partial prepayment (a curtailment).

In contrast to amortizing assets, nonamortizing assets do not have a schedule for the periodic payments that the borrower must make. Instead, a nonamortizing asset is one in which the borrower must make a minimum periodic payment. If that payment is less than the interest on the outstanding loan balance, the shortfall is added to the outstanding loan balance. If the periodic payment is greater than the interest on the outstanding loan balance, then the difference is applied to the reduction of the outstanding loan balance. There is no schedule of principal payments (i.e., no amortization schedule) for a nonamortizing asset. Consequently, the concept of a prepayment does not apply. Credit card receivables and certain types of home equity loans described later in this chapter are examples of nonamortizing assets.

For an amortizing asset, projection of the cash flows requires projecting prepayments. One factor that may affect prepayments is the prevailing level of interest rates relative to the interest rate on the loan. In projecting prepayments it is critical to determine the extent to which borrowers take advantage of a decline in interest rates below the loan rate in order to refinance the loan.

As with nonagency mortgage-backed securities, modeling defaults for the collateral is critical in estimating the cash flows of an asset-backed security. Proceeds that are recovered in the event of a default of a loan prior to the scheduled principal repayment date of an amortizing asset represents a prepayment. Projecting prepayments for amortizing assets requires an assumption of the default rate and the recovery rate. For a nonamortizing asset, while the concept of a prepayment does not exist, a projection of defaults is still necessary to project how much will be recovered and when.

The analysis of prepayments can be performed on a pool level or a loan level. In pool-level analysis it is assumed that all loans comprising the collateral are identical. For an amortizing asset, the amortization schedule is based on the gross weighted average coupon and weighted average maturity for that single loan. Pool-level analysis is appropriate where the underlying loans are homogeneous. Loan-level analysis involves amortizing each loan (or group of homogeneous loans).

The maturity of an asset-backed security is not a meaningful parameter. Instead, the average life of the security is calculated. As with nonagency mortgage-backed securities, there is an optional clean-up call provision granted to the trustee.

Overview of the Four Major Sectors

The four largest sectors of the asset-backed securities market are securities backed by credit card receivables, auto loans, home equity loans, and manufactured housing loans. Below we provide an overview of each sector.

Auto Loan-Backed Securities

Auto loan-backed securities are issued by (1) the financial subsidiaries of auto manufacturers, (2) commercial banks, and (3) independent finance companies and small financial institutions specializing in auto loans There are auto loan-backed deals that are passthrough structures and paythrough structures. Larger deals are issued as paythroughs.

The cash flow consists of regularly scheduled monthly loan payments (interest and scheduled principal repayments) and any prepayments. Prepayments result from (1) sales and trade-ins requiring full payoff of the loan, (2) repossession and subsequent resale of the automobile, (3) loss or destruction of the vehicle, (4) payoff of the loan with cash to save on the interest cost, and (5) refinancing of the loan at a lower interest cost. Prepayments due to repossessions and subsequent resale are sensitive to the economic cycle. In recessionary economic periods, prepayments due to this factor increase. While refinancings may be a major reason for prepayments of mortgage loans, they are of minor importance for automobile loans.

Prepayments for auto loan-backed securities are measured in terms of the *absolute prepayment rate*, denoted not by APR but by ABS (probably because it was the first prepayment measure used for asset-backed securities). The ABS is the monthly prepayment expressed as a percentage of the original collateral amount. Recall that the SMM (monthly CPR) expresses prepayments based on the prior month's balance.

Credit enhancement typically is via a senior/subordinated structure. Usually there is one or more forms of additional enhancement such as cash reserves or overcollateralization. The total support is in the range of 8% to 12%.

Credit Card Receivable-Backed Securities

Credit card receivable-backed securities are backed by credit card receivables. Credit cards are originated by banks (e.g., Visa and MasterCard), retailers (e.g., JC Penney and Sears), and travel and entertainment companies (e.g., American Express). The cash flow consists of net interest, principal, and finance charges collected. Interest to security holders is paid periodically (e.g, monthly, quarterly, or semiannually). The interest may be fixed or floating.

In contrast to an auto loan-backed security, the principal repayment of a credit card receivable-backed security is not amortized. Instead, for a specified period of time, referred to as the *lockout period* or *revolving period*, the principal payments made by credit card borrowers comprising the pool are retained by the trustee and reinvested in additional receivables. The lockout period can vary from 18 months to 10 years. After the lockout period, the principal is no longer reinvested but paid to investors. This period is referred to as the *principal-amortization period* and the various types of structures are described later.

There are provisions in credit card receivable-backed securities that require earlier amortization of the principal if certain events occur. Such provisions, which are referred to as either *early amortization* or *rapid amortization*, are included to safeguard the credit quality of the issue. The only way that the cash flows can be altered is by the triggering of the early amortization provision. Early amortization is invoked if the trust is not able to generate sufficient income to cover the investor coupon and the servicing fee.

As noted earlier, the concept of prepayments does not apply to credit card receivable-backed securities since there is no amortization schedule during the lockout period. Instead, for this sector of the asset-backed securities market, participants look at the *monthly payment rate* (MPR). This measure expresses the monthly payment (which includes interest, finance charges, and any principal) of a credit card receivable portfolio as a percentage of debt outstanding in the previous month. For example, suppose a $500 million credit card receivable portfolio in January realized $50 million of payments in February. The MPR would then be 10% ($50 million divided by $500 million).

There are two reasons why the MPR is important. First, if the MPR reaches an extremely low level, there is a chance that there will be extension risk with respect to the principal payments. Second, if the MPR is very low, then there is a chance that there will not be sufficient cash flows to pay off principal. Typically, this is one of the events that could trigger early amortization of the principal.

There are three different amortization structures that have been used in credit card receivable-backed security structures: (1) passthrough structure, (2) controlled-amortization structure, and (3) bullet-payment structure. In a *passthrough structure*, the principal cash flows from the credit card accounts are paid to the security holders on a pro rata basis. In a *controlled-amortization structure*, a scheduled principal amount is established. The scheduled principal amount is sufficiently low so that the obligation can be satisfied even under certain stress scenarios. The investor is paid the lesser of the scheduled principal amount and the pro rata amount. In a *bullet-payment structure*, the investor receives the entire amount in one distribution. Since there is no assurance that the entire amount can be paid in one lump sum, the procedure is for the trustee to place principal monthly into an account that generates sufficient interest to make periodic interest payments and accumulate the principal to be repaid. The time period over which the principal is accumulated is called the accumulation period

In the earlier credit card structures, the most popular form of credit enhancement was a bank letter of credit. However, as discussed earlier in this chapter, the disadvantage of a third-party guarantee is that if the guarantor is downgraded, the structure will be downgraded regardless of how the collateral is performing. With the downgrading of banks that provided letters of credit for earlier credit card deals and the subsequent downgrading of the securities, this form of credit enhancement lost its popularity.

Today the two most popular forms of credit enhancement for credit card deals coupled with any senior/subordinated structure are the *cash collateral account* and the *collateral invested account*. Both forms of credit enhancement involve the investment of cash. In the case of the cash collateral account, funds are generally borrowed from a bank and those funds are then invested in commercial paper or other short-debt of the bank. In the collateral invested account, the funds are invested in credit card receivables within the structure rather than commercial paper or other short-term debt.

Home Equity Loan-Backed Securities

Home equity loan-backed securities are backed by home equity loans. A home equity loan (HEL) is a loan backed by residential property. Typically, the loan is a second lien on property that has already been pledged to secure a first lien. In some cases, the lien may be a third lien. In recent years, some loans have been first liens.

Home equity loans can be either closed end or open end. A closed-end HEL is structured the same way as a fully amortizing residential mortgage loan. That is, it has a fixed maturity and the payments are structured to fully amortize the loan by the maturity date. There are both fixed-rate and variable-rate closed-end HELs. Typically, variable-rate loans have a reference rate of 6-month LIBOR and have periodic caps and lifetime caps, just as with adjustable-rate mortgages discussed earlier in this chapter. The cash flow of a pool of closed-end HELs is comprised of interest, regularly scheduled principal repayments, and prepayments, just as with mortgage-backed securities. Thus, it is necessary to have a prepayment model and a default model to forecast cash flows. The prepayment speed is measured in terms of a conditional prepayment rate (CPR).

With an open-end HEL the homeowner is given a credit line and can write checks or use a credit card for up to the amount of the credit line. The amount of the credit line depends on the amount of the equity the borrower has in the property. There is a revolving period over which the homeowner can borrow funds against the line of credit. At the end of the term of the loan, the homeowner either pays off the amount borrowed in one payment or the outstanding balance is amortized.

The monthly cash flow for a home equity loan-backed security backed by closed-end HELs is the same as for mortgage-backed securities. That is, the cash flow consists of (1) net interest, (2) regularly scheduled principal payments, and

(3) prepayments Prudential Securities has developed a prepayment benchmark for closed-end, fixed-rate HELs. The benchmark reflects Prudential Securities findings that such loans season much faster than traditional single-family mortgage loans. The benchmark, referred to by Prudential Securities as the *home equity prepayment* curve (or HEP curve), assumes that the loans become seasoned after ten months (as opposed to residential mortgage loans which are assumed by the PSA prepayment benchmark to season after 30 months). The HEP curve is expressed in terms of the terminal CPR and assumes a linear increase in the CPR each month up to month 10. For example, 10% HEP means a CPR of 1% in month 1 with the CPR for each subsequent month increasing by 1% until month 10 when the CPR is 10%. An 18% HEP means a CPR of 1.8% in month 1 with the CPR for each subsequent month increasing by 1.8% until month 10 when the CPR is 18%.

In the prospectus of an offering a base case prepayment assumption is made — the initial speed and the amount of time until the collateral is expected to be seasoned. Thus, the prepayment benchmark is issue specific. Investors are now using the concept of a *prospectus prepayment curve* or PPC. This is just a multiple of the base case prepayments assumed in the prospectus. For example, in the prospectus for the Contimortgage Home Equity Loan Trust 1996-1, the base case prepayment assumption for the fixed-rate mortgages in the pool is as follows (p. 3-37):

> ... a 100% Prepayment Assumption assumes conditional prepayment rates of 4% per annum of the then outstanding principal balance of the Home Equity Loans in the Fixed Rate Group in the first month of the life of the mortgage loans and an additional 1.455% (precisely $^{16}/_{11}$%) per annum in each month thereafter until the twelfth month. Beginning in the twelfth month and in each month thereafter during the life of the mortgage loans, 100% Prepayment Assumption assumes a conditional prepayment rate of 20% per annum each month.

Therefore, if an investor analyzed the deal based on 200% PPC, this means doubling the CPRs cited in the excerpt and using 12 months for seasoning.

As with nonagency mortgage-backed securities, there are passthrough and paythrough home equity loan-backed structures. All forms of credit enhancement described earlier have been used for home equity loan-backed securities.

Manufactured Housing-Backed Securities

Manufactured housing-backed securities are backed by loans for manufactured homes. In contrast to site-built homes, manufactured homes are built at a factory and then transported to a manufactured home community or private land. These homes are more popularly referred to as mobile homes. The loan may be either a mortgage loan (for both the land and the mobile home) or a consumer retail installment loan. The typical loan for a manufactured home is 15 to 20 years. The loan repayment is structured to fully amortize the amount borrowed. Therefore, as with residential mortgage loans and HELs, the cash flow consists of net interest, regularly scheduled principal, and prepayments.

As with residential mortgage loans and HELs, prepayments on manufactured housing-backed securities are measured in terms of CPR. For manufacturing housing loans, prepayment sensitivity due to refinancing is less than it is for HELs and first lien residential mortgages. There are several reasons for this. First, the loan balances are typically small so that there is no significant dollar savings from refinancing. Second, the rate of depreciation of mobile homes may be such that in the earlier years depreciation is greater than the amount of the loan paid off. This makes it difficult to refinance the loan. Finally, typically borrowers are of lower credit quality and therefore find it difficult to obtain funds to refinance.

The payment structure is the same as with nonagency mortgage-backed securities and home equity loan-backed securities. Credit enhancements are the same as in nonagency mortgage-backed securities and home equity loan-backed securities.

Chapter 7

Interest Rate Derivatives

Frank J. Fabozzi, Ph.D., CFA
Adjunct Professor of Finance
School of Management
Yale University

INTRODUCTION

Derivative instruments are important risk control instruments in the management of insurance companies.[1] There are derivative instruments for controlling interest rate risk, equity market risk, currency risk, and commodity risk. In this chapter, we discuss interest rate derivatives. These instruments include futures/forwards, options, swaps, and caps/floors. Our focus is on their investment characteristics. In other chapters in this book, valuation and risk control strategies employing interest rate derivatives are discussed. In Chapter 26, equity derivatives and their use in equity portfolio management are covered. In the next chapter, credit risk derivatives are discussed.

INTEREST RATE FUTURES

A *futures contract* is an agreement that requires a party to the agreement either to buy or sell something at a designated future date at a predetermined price. Futures contracts are products created by exchanges. Futures contracts based on a financial instrument or a financial index are known as *financial futures*. Financial futures can be classified as (1) stock index futures, (2) interest rate futures, and (3) currency futures. Our focus in this chapter is on interest rate futures.

Mechanics of Futures Trading

A futures contract is a legal agreement between a buyer (seller) and an established exchange or its clearinghouse in which the buyer (seller) agrees to take (make) delivery of something, referred to as the *underlying*, at a specified price at the end of a designated period of time. The price at which the parties agree to transact in the future is called the *futures price*. The designated date at which the parties must transact is called the *settlement* or *delivery date*.

---

[1] The term derivative is also used to describe some types of mortgage-backed products that were described in the previous chapter. Such securities are referred to as mortgage derivatives and are not discussed in this chapter.

Liquidating a Position

Most financial futures contracts have settlement dates in the months of March, June, September, or December. This means that at a predetermined time in the contract settlement month the contract stops trading, and a price is determined by the exchange for settlement of the contract. The contract with the closest settlement date is called the *nearby futures contract*. The next futures contract is the one that settles just after the nearby futures contract. The contract farthest away in time from settlement is called the *most distant futures contract*.

A party to a futures contract has two choices on liquidation of the position. First, the position can be liquidated prior to the settlement date. For this purpose, the party must take an offsetting position in the same contract. For the buyer of a futures contract, this means selling the same number of identical futures contracts; for the seller of a futures contract, this means buying the same number of identical futures contracts.

The alternative is to wait until the settlement date. At that time the party purchasing a futures contract accepts delivery of the underlying at the agreed-upon price; the party that sells a futures contract liquidates the position by delivering the underlying at the agreed-upon price. For some interest rate futures contracts that we shall describe later, settlement is made in cash only. Such contracts are referred to as *cash settlement contracts*.

The Role of the Clearinghouse

Associated with every futures exchange is a clearinghouse, which performs several functions. One of these functions is to guarantee that the two parties to the transaction will perform.

When an investor takes a position in the futures market, the clearinghouse takes the opposite position and agrees to satisfy the terms set forth in the contract. Because of the clearinghouse, the investor need not worry about the financial strength and integrity of the party taking the opposite side of the contract. After initial execution of an order, the relationship between the two parties ends. The clearinghouse interposes itself as the buyer for every sale and the seller for every purchase. Thus investors are free to liquidate their positions without involving the other party in the original contract, and without worry that the other party may default. This is the reason why we define a futures contract as an agreement between a party and a clearinghouse associated with an exchange. Besides its guarantee function, the clearinghouse makes it simple for parties to a futures contract to unwind their positions prior to the settlement date.

Margin Requirements

When a position is first taken in a futures contract, the investor must deposit a minimum dollar amount per contract as specified by the exchange. This amount is called *initial margin* and is required as deposit for the contract. The initial margin may be in the form of an interest-bearing security such as a Treasury bill. As the price of the futures contract fluctuates, the value of the investor's equity in the position changes. At the end of each trading day, the exchange determines the settlement price for the futures contract. This price is used to mark to market the investor's position, so that any gain or loss from the position is reflected in the investor's equity account.

Maintenance margin is the minimum level (specified by the exchange) by which an investor's equity position may fall to as a result of an unfavorable price movement before the investor is required to deposit additional margin. The additional margin deposited is called *variation margin*, and it is an amount necessary to bring the equity in the account back to its initial margin level. Unlike initial margin, variation margin must be in cash, not interest-bearing instruments. Any excess margin in the account may be withdrawn by the investor. If a party to a futures contract who is required to deposit variation margin fails to do so within 24 hours, the futures position is closed out.

Although there are initial and maintenance margin requirements for buying securities on margin, the concept of margin differs for securities and futures. When securities are acquired on margin, the difference between the price of the security and the initial margin is borrowed from the broker. The security purchased serves as collateral for the loan, and the investor pays interest. For futures contracts, the initial margin, in effect, serves as "good faith" money, an indication that the investor will satisfy the obligation of the contract. Normally no money is borrowed by the investor.

Forward Contracts

A *forward contract*, just like a futures contract, is an agreement for the future delivery of something at a specified price at the end of a designated period of time. Futures contracts are standardized agreements as to the delivery date (or month) and quality of the deliverable, and are traded on organized exchanges. A forward contract differs in that it is usually non-standardized (that is, the terms of each contract are negotiated individually between buyer and seller), there is no clearinghouse, and secondary markets are often non-existent or extremely thin. Unlike a futures contract, which is an exchange-traded product, a forward contract is an over-the-counter instrument.

Futures contracts are marked to market at the end of each trading day. Consequently, futures contracts are subject to interim cash flows as additional margin may be required in the case of adverse price movements, or as cash is withdrawn in the case of favorable price movements. A forward contract may or may not be marked to market, depending on the wishes of the two parties. For a forward contract that is not marked to market, there are no interim cash flow effects because no additional margin is required.

Finally, the parties in a forward contract are exposed to credit risk because either party may default on its obligation. This risk is called *counterparty risk*. This risk is minimal in the case of futures contracts because the clearinghouse associated with the exchange guarantees the other side of the transaction. In the case of a forward contract, both parties face counterparty risk. Thus, there exists *bilateral counterparty risk*.

Other than these differences, most of what we say about futures contracts applies equally to forward contracts.

Risk and Return Characteristics of Futures Contracts

When an investor takes a position in the market by buying a futures contract, the investor is said to be in a *long position* or to be *long futures*. If, instead, the investor's opening position is the sale of a futures contract, the investor is said to be in a *short position* or to be *short futures*. The buyer of a futures contract will realize a profit if the futures price increases; the seller of a futures contract will realize a profit if the futures price decreases.

When a position is taken in a futures contract, the party need not put up the entire amount of the investment. Instead, only initial margin must be put up. Consequently, an investor can create a leveraged position by using futures.

Exchange-Traded Interest Rate Futures Contracts

Interest rate futures contracts can be classified by the maturity of their underlying security. Short-term interest rate futures contracts have an underlying security that matures in less than one year. The maturity of the underlying security of long-term futures contracts exceeds one year. Examples of the former are futures contracts in which the underlying is a 3-month Treasury bill and a 3-month Euro-dollar certificate of deposit. Examples of the latter are futures contracts in which the underlying is a Treasury coupon security and a municipal bond index. Our focus will be on futures contracts in which the underlying is a Treasury coupon security (a Treasury bond or a Treasury note). These contracts are the most widely used by insurers and other money managers of bond portfolios and we begin with the specifications of the Treasury bond futures contract.

Treasury Bond Futures

The Treasury bond futures contract is traded on the Chicago Board of Trade (CBT). The underlying instrument for a Treasury bond futures contract is a hypothetical $100,000 par value 20-year, 8% coupon bond. The futures price is quoted in terms of par being 100. Quotes are in 32nds of 1%. Thus a quote for a Treasury bond futures contract of 97-16 means 97 and $16/32$ or 97.50. So, if a buyer and seller agree on a futures price of 97-16, this means that the buyer agrees to accept delivery of the hypothetical underlying Treasury bond and pay 97.50% of par value and the seller agrees to accept 97.50% of par value. Since the par value is $100,000, the futures price that the buyer and seller agree to pay for this hypothetical Treasury bond is $97,500.

The minimum price fluctuation for the Treasury bond futures contract is a 32nd of 1%. The dollar value of a 32nd for $100,000 par value (the par value for the underlying Treasury bond) is $31.25. Thus, the minimum price fluctuation is $31.25 for this contract.

Exhibit 1: Treasury Bond Issues Acceptable for Delivery to Satisfy the June 1997 Futures Contract

Issue		Conversion
Coupon (%)	Maturity	Factor
6.625	2/15/27	0.8451
6.500	11/15/26	0.8312
6.750	8/15/26	0.8598
6.000	2/15/26	0.7767
6.875	8/15/25	0.8750
7.625	2/15/25	0.9585
7.500	11/15/24	0.9447
6.250	8/15/23	0.8097
7.125	2/15/23	0.9054
7.625	11/15/22	0.9594
7.250	8/15/22	0.9194
8.000	11/15/22	0.9998
8.125	8/15/21	1.0132
8.125	5/15/21	1.0130
7.875	2/15/21	0.9868
8.750	8/15/20	1.0783
8.750	5/15/20	1.0778
8.500	2/15/20	1.0518
8.125	8/15/19	1.0128
8.875	2/15/19	1.0891
9.000	11/15/19	1.1012
9.125	5/15/18	1.1128
8.875	8/15/17	1.0866
8.750	5/15/17	1.0736
7.500	11/15/16	0.9511
7.250	5/15/16	0.9276
9.250	2/15/16	1.1196
9.875	11/15/15	1.1781
10.625	8/15/15	1.2482
11.250	2/15/15	1.3033

We have been referring to the underlying as a hypothetical Treasury bond. The seller of a Treasury bond futures who decides to make delivery rather than liquidate his position by buying back the contract prior to the settlement date must deliver some Treasury bond. But what Treasury bond? The CBT allows the seller to deliver one of several Treasury bonds that the CBT specifies are acceptable for delivery. Exhibit 1 shows the 30 Treasury bond issues from which the seller could have selected to deliver to the buyer of the June 1997 futures contract. The CBT makes its determination of the Treasury issues that are acceptable for delivery from all outstanding Treasury issues that meet the following criteria: an issue must have at least 15 years to maturity from the date of delivery if not callable; in the case of callable bonds, the issue must not be callable for at least 15 years from the first day of the delivery month.

Conversion Factors The delivery process for the Treasury bond futures contract makes the contract interesting. At the settlement date, the seller of a futures contract (the short) is required to deliver the buyer (the long) $100,000 par value of an 8% 20-year Treasury bond. Since no such bond exists, the seller must choose from one of the acceptable deliverable Treasury bonds that the CBT has specified. Suppose the seller is entitled to deliver $100,000 of a 6% 20-year Treasury bond to settle the futures contract. The value of this bond is less than the value of an 8% 20-year bond. If the seller delivers the 6% 20-year, this would be unfair to the buyer of the futures contract who contracted to receive $100,000 of an 8% 20-year Treasury bond. Alternatively, suppose the seller delivers $100,000 of a 10% 20-year Treasury bond. The value of a 10% 20-year Treasury bond is greater than that of an 8% 20-year bond, so this would disadvantage the seller.

How can this problem be resolved? To make delivery equitable to both parties, the CBT has introduced *conversion factors* for adjusting the price of each Treasury issue that can be delivered to satisfy the Treasury bond futures contract. The conversion factor is determined by the CBT before a contract with a specific settlement date begins trading.[2] Exhibit 1 shows for each of the acceptable Treasury issues for the June 1997 futures contract the corresponding conversion factor. The conversion factor is constant throughout the life of the futures contract. The short must notify the long of the actual bond that will be delivered one day before the delivery date.

The price that the buyer must pay the seller when a Treasury bond is delivered is called the *invoice price*. The invoice price is the futures settlement price plus accrued interest on the bonds delivered. However, as just noted, the seller can deliver one of several acceptable Treasury issues and to make delivery fair to both parties, the invoice price must be adjusted based on the actual Treasury issue delivered. It is the conversion factors that are used to adjust the invoice price. The invoice price is:

Invoice price = Contract size × Futures settlement price
$$\times \text{ Conversion factor} + \text{Accrued interest on bonds delivered}$$

Suppose the Treasury June 1997 futures contract settles at 108-16 and that the issue delivered is the 11.25s of 2/15/15. The futures contract settlement price of 108-16 means 108.5% of par value or 1.085 times par value. As indicated in Exhibit 1, the conversion factor for this issue is 1.3033. Since the contract size is $100,000, the invoice price the buyer pays the seller is:

$100,000 × 1.085 × 1.3033 + Accrued interest on bonds delivered
= $141,408.05 + Accrued interest on bonds delivered

Cheapest-to-Deliver Issue In selecting the issue to be delivered, the short will select from among all of the deliverable issues the one that is cheapest to deliver. This issue is referred to as the *cheapest-to-deliver issue*; it plays a key role in the

---

[2] The conversion factor is based on the price that a deliverable bond would sell for at the beginning of the delivery month if it were to yield 8%.

pricing of this futures contract. The cheapest to deliver issue is determined by participants in the market as follows. For each of the acceptable Treasury issues from which the seller can select, the seller calculates the return that can be earned by buying that issue and delivering it at the settlement date. Note that the seller can calculate the return since he knows the price of the Treasury issue now and the futures price that will be received when he delivers the issue. The calculated return is called the *implied repo rate*. The cheapest-to-deliver issue is then the one issue among all acceptable Treasury issues with the highest implied repo rate since it is the issue that would give the seller of the futures contract the highest return by buying and then delivering the issue. This is depicted in Exhibit 2.

Other Delivery Options In addition to the choice of which acceptable Treasury issue to deliver — sometimes referred to as the *quality option* or *swap option* — the short has two more options granted under CBT delivery guidelines. The short is permitted to decide when in the delivery month delivery actually will take place. This is called the *timing option*. The other option is the right of the short to give notice of intent to deliver up to 8:00 P.M. Chicago time after the closing of the exchange (3:15 P.M. Chicago time) on the date when the futures settlement price has been fixed. This option is referred to as the *wild card option*. The quality option, the timing option, and the wild card option (in sum referred to as the *delivery options*), mean that the long position can never be sure which Treasury bond will be delivered or when it will be delivered. The delivery options are summarized in Exhibit 3.

Exhibit 2: Determination of Cheapest-to-Deliver Issue Based on the Implied Repo Rate

Buy this issue	Deliver this issue at futures price	Calculate return (implied repo rate)
Acceptable Treasury issue #1	Deliver issue #1	Implied repo rate #1
Acceptable Treasury issue #2	Deliver issue #2	Implied repo rate #2
Acceptable Treasury issue #3	Deliver issue #3	Implied repo rate #3
.	.	.
Acceptable Treasury issue #N	Deliver issue #N	Implied repo rate #N

Note: Cheapest to deliver is the issue that produces maximum implied repo rate.

Exhibit 3: Delivery Options Granted to the Short (Seller) of a CBT Treasury Bond Futures Contract

Delivery option	Description
Quality or swap option	Choice of which acceptable Treasury issue to deliver
Timing option	Choice of when in delivery month to deliver
Wild card option	Choice to deliver after the closing price of the futures contract is determined

Treasury Note Futures

There are three Treasury note futures contracts: 10-year, 5-year, and 2-year. All three contracts are modeled after the Treasury bond futures contract and are traded on the CBT. The underlying instrument for the 10-year Treasury note futures contract is a hypothetical $100,000 par value 10-year 8% Treasury note. There are several acceptable Treasury issues that may be delivered by the short. An issue is acceptable if the maturity is not less than 6.5 years and not greater than 10 years from the first day of the delivery month. The delivery options granted to the short position and the minimum price fluctuation are the same as for the Treasury bond futures contract.

For the 5-year Treasury note futures contract, the underlying is $100,000 par value of a U.S. Treasury note that satisfies the following conditions: (1) an original maturity of not more than five years and three months, (2) a remaining maturity no greater then five years and three months, and (3) a remaining maturity not less than four years and three months. The minimum price fluctuation for this contract is a 64th of 1%. The dollar value of a 64th for a $100,000 par value is $15.625 and is therefore the minimum price fluctuation.

The underlying for the 2-year Treasury note futures contract is $200,000 par value of a U.S. Treasury note with a remaining maturity of not more than two years and not less than one year and nine months. Moreover, the original maturity of the note delivered to satisfy the 2-year futures cannot be more than five years and two months. The minimum price fluctuation for this contract is a 128th of 1%. The dollar value of a 128th for a $200,000 par value is $15.625 and is therefore the minimum price fluctuation.

INTEREST RATE OPTIONS

An *option* is a contract in which the writer of the option grants the buyer of the option the right, but not the obligation, to purchase from or sell to the writer something at a specified price within a specified period of time (or at a specified date). The *writer*, also referred to as the *seller*, grants this right to the buyer in exchange for a certain sum of money, which is called the *option price* or *option premium*. The price at which the underlying for the contract may be bought or sold is called the *exercise* or *strike price*. The date after which an option is void is called the *expiration date*. Our focus is on options where the "something" underlying the option is an interest rate instrument or an interest rate.

When an option grants the buyer the right to purchase the designated instrument from the writer (seller), it is referred to as a *call option*, or *call*. When the option buyer has the right to sell the designated instrument to the writer, the option is called a *put option*, or *put*.

An option is also categorized according to when the option buyer may exercise the option. There are options that may be exercised at any time up to and including the expiration date. Such an option is referred to as an *American option*. There are options that may be exercised only at the expiration date. An option with this feature is called a *European option*. An option that can be exercised prior to maturity but only on designated dates is called a *modified American*, *Bermuda*, or *Atlantic option*.

The maximum amount that an option buyer can lose is the option price. The maximum profit that the option writer can realize is the option price. The option buyer has substantial upside return potential, while the option writer has substantial downside risk. We'll investigate the risk/reward relationship for option positions later.

Differences Between Options and Futures Contracts

Unlike in a futures contract, one party to an option contract is not obligated to transact. Specifically, the option buyer has the right, but not the obligation, to transact. The option writer does have the obligation to perform if the option buyer decides to exercise the option. In the case of a futures contract, both buyer and seller are obligated to perform. Of course, a futures buyer does not pay the seller to accept the obligation, while an option buyer pays the option seller an option price.

Consequently, the risk/reward characteristics of the two contracts are also different. In the case of a futures contract, the buyer of the contract realizes a dollar-for-dollar gain when the price of the futures contract increases and suffers a dollar-for-dollar loss when the price of the futures contract drops. The opposite occurs for the seller of a futures contract. Options do not provide this symmetric risk/reward relationship. The most that the buyer of an option can lose is the option price. While the buyer of an option retains all the potential benefits, the gain is always reduced by the amount of the option price. The maximum profit that the writer may realize is the option price; this is offset against substantial downside risk.

Both parties to a futures contract are required to post margin. There are no margin requirements for the buyer of an option once the option price has been paid in full. Because the option price is the maximum amount that the investor can lose, no matter how adverse the price movement of the underlying asset, there is no need for margin. Because the writer of an option has agreed to accept all of the risk (and none of the reward) of the position in the underlying asset, the writer is generally required to put up the option price received as margin. In addition, as price changes occur that adversely affect the writer's position, the writer is required to deposit additional margin (with some exceptions) as the position is marked to market.

Exhibit 4: Comparison of Profit and Loss Profile for a Long Call Position and a Long Asset Position

Price of Asset XYZ at Expiration Date	Net Profit/Loss for		Price of Asset XYZ at Expiration Date	Net Profit/Loss for	
	Long Call*	Short Asset XYZ		Long Call*	Short Asset XYZ
$150	$47	$50	100	−3	0
140	37	40	99	−3	−1
130	27	30	98	−3	−2
120	17	20	97	−3	−3
115	12	15	96	−3	−4
114	11	14	95	−3	−5
113	10	13	94	−3	−6
112	9	12	93	−3	−7
111	8	11	92	−3	−8
110	7	10	91	−3	−9
109	6	9	90	−3	−10
108	5	8	89	−3	−11
107	4	7	88	−3	−12
106	3	6	87	−3	−13
105	2	5	86	−3	−14
104	1	4	85	−3	−15
103	0	3	80	−3	−20
102	−1	2	70	−3	−30
101	−2	1	60	−3	−40

* Price at expiration = $100 − $3, Maximum loss = $3

Risk and Return Characteristics of Options

Here we illustrate the risk and return characteristics of the four basic option positions — buying a call option, selling a call option, buying a put option, and selling a put option. The illustrations *assume that each option position is held to the expiration date and not exercised early.* Also, to simplify the illustrations, we ignore transaction costs.

Buying Call Options

The purchase of a call option creates a financial position referred to as a *long call position.* To illustrate this position, assume that there is a call option on Asset XYZ that expires in one month and has a strike price of $100. The option price is $3. Suppose that the current price of Asset XYZ is $100. At the expiration date the profit or loss for the investor who purchases this call option is shown in the second column of Exhibit 4. The maximum loss is the option price and there is substantial upside potential.

It is worthwhile to compare the profit and loss profile of the call option buyer to taking a long position in one unit of Asset XYZ. The payoff from the position depends on Asset XYZ's price at the expiration date. Exhibit 4 compares the long call strategy and the long position in Asset XYZ. This comparison clearly demonstrates the way in which an option can change the risk/return profile for investors. An investor who takes a long position in Asset XYZ realizes a profit of $1 for every $1 increase in Asset XYZ's price. As Asset XYZ's price falls, however, the investor loses dollar-for-dollar. If the price drops by more than $3, the long position in Asset XYZ results in a loss of more than $3. The long call strategy, in contrast, limits the loss to only the option price of $3 but retains the upside potential, which will be $3 less than for the long position in Asset XYZ.

We can also use this hypothetical call option to demonstrate the speculative appeal of options. Suppose an investor has strong expectations that Asset XYZ's price will rise in one month. At an option price of $3, the speculator can purchase 33.33 call options for each $100 invested. If Asset XYZ's price rises, the investor realizes the price appreciation associated with 33.33 units of Asset XYZ, while with the same $100, the investor could buy only one unit of Asset XYZ selling at $100, realizing the appreciation associated with one unit if Asset XYZ's price increases. Now, suppose that in one month the price of Asset XYZ rises to $120. The long call position will result in a profit of $566.50 [($20 × 33.33) − $100] or a return of 566.5% on the $100 investment in the call option. The long position in Asset XYZ results in a profit of $20, for only a 20% return on $100.

It is this greater leverage that attracts investors to options when they wish to speculate on price movements. There are drawbacks of leverage, however. Suppose that Asset XYZ's price is unchanged at $100 at the expiration date. The long call position results in this case in a loss of the entire investment of $100, while the long position in Asset XYZ produces neither a gain nor a loss.

Writing (Selling) Call Options

The writer of a call option is said to be in a *short call position*. To illustrate the option seller's (writer's) position, we use the same call option we used to illustrate buying a call option. The profit and loss profile of the short call position (that is, the position of the call option writer) is the mirror image of the profit and loss profile of the long call position (the position of the call option buyer). That is, the profit of the short call position for any given price for Asset XYZ at the expiration date is the same as the loss of the long call position. Consequently, the maximum profit that the short call position can produce is the option price. The maximum loss is not limited because it is the highest price reached by Asset XYZ on or before the expiration date, less the option price; this price can be indefinitely high. In fact, for an option in which the underlying is a fixed-income security assuming that interest rates cannot be negative, the maximum price is simply the sum of all the coupon payments and the principal.

Buying Put Options

The buying of a put option creates a financial position referred to as a *long put position*. To illustrate this position, we assume a hypothetical put option on one unit of Asset XYZ with one month to maturity and a strike price of $100. Assume the put option is selling for $2. The current price of Asset XYZ is $100. The profit or loss for this position at the expiration date depends on the market price of Asset XYZ. The profit and loss profile for the long put position is shown in the second column of Exhibit 5.

As with all long option positions, the loss is limited to the option price. The profit potential, however, is substantial: the theoretical maximum profit is generated if Asset XYZ's price falls to zero. Contrast this profit potential with that of the buyer of a call option. If Asset XYZ is common stock, the theoretical maximum profit for a call buyer cannot be determined beforehand because it depends on the highest price that can be reached for the stock before or at the option expiration date. If Asset XYZ is a bond, its maximum price is the sum of the total coupon payments plus the principal.

To see how an option alters the risk/return profile for an investor, we again compare it to a position in Asset XYZ. The long put position is compared to taking a short position in Asset XYZ because this is the position that would realize a profit if the price of the asset falls. Suppose an investor sells Asset XYZ short for $100. Exhibit 5 compares the profit and loss profile for the long put position and short position in Asset XYZ.

While the investor who takes a short position in Asset XYZ faces all the downside risk as well as the upside potential, the long put position limits the downside risk to the option price while still maintaining upside potential (reduced only by an amount equal to the option price).

Exhibit 5: Comparison of Profit and Loss Profile for a Long Put Position and a Short Asset Position

Price of Asset XYZ at Expiration Date	Net Profit/Loss for		Price of Asset XYZ at Expiration Date	Net Profit/Loss for	
	Long Put ($)*	Short Asset XYZ ($)**		Long Put ($)*	Short Asset XYZ ($)**
150	-2	-50	91	7	9
140	-2	-40	90	8	10
130	-2	-30	89	9	11
120	-2	-20	88	10	12
115	-2	-15	87	11	13
110	-2	-10	86	12	14
105	-2	-5	85	13	15
100	-2	0	84	14	16
99	-1	1	83	15	17
98	0	2	82	16	18
97	1	3	81	17	19
96	2	4	80	18	20
95	3	5	75	23	25
94	4	6	70	28	30
93	5	7	65	33	35
92	6	8	60	38	40

* $100 – Price at expiration – $2, Maximum loss = $2
** $100 – Price at expiration

Writing (Selling) Put Options

Writing a put option creates a financial position referred to as a *short put position*. The profit and loss profile for a short put option is the mirror image of the long put option. The maximum profit from this position is the option price. The theoretical maximum loss can be substantial should the price of the underlying asset fall; at the outside, if the price were to fall all the way to zero, the loss would be as large as the strike price less the option price.

To summarize, buying calls or selling puts allows the investor to gain if the price of the underlying asset rises. Selling calls and buying puts allows the investor to gain if the price of the underlying asset falls.

Considering the Time Value of Money

Our illustrations of the four option positions do not address the time value of money. Specifically, the buyer of an option must pay the seller the option price at the time the option is purchased. Thus, the buyer must finance the purchase price of the option or, assuming the purchase price does not have to be borrowed, the buyer loses the income that can be earned by investing the amount of the option price until the option is sold or exercised. In contrast, assuming that the seller does not have to use the option price received as margin for the short position or can use an interest-earning asset as security, the seller has the opportunity to earn income from the proceeds of the option sale.

The time value of money changes the profit/loss profile of the option positions we have discussed. The break-even price for the buyer and the seller of an option will not be the same as in our illustrations. The break-even price for the underlying asset at the expiration date is higher for the buyer of the option; for the seller, it is lower.

Our comparisons of an option position with a position in the underlying instrument also ignore the time value of money. We have not considered the fact that the underlying asset may generate interim cash flows (dividends in the case of common stock, interest in the case of bonds). The buyer of a call option is not entitled to any interim cash flows generated by the underlying asset. The buyer of the underlying asset, however, would receive any interim cash flows and would have the opportunity to reinvest them. A complete comparison of the position of the long call option position and the long position in the underlying asset must take into account the additional dollars from reinvesting any interim cash flows.

Exchange-Traded versus OTC Options

Options, like other financial instruments, may be traded either on an organized exchange or in the over-the-counter market. An exchange that wants to create an options contract must obtain approval from regulators. Exchange-traded options have three advantages. First, the strike price and expiration date of the contract are standardized. Second, as in the case of futures contracts, the direct link between buyer and seller is severed after the order is executed because of the interchangeability of exchange-traded options. The clearinghouse associated with the exchange where the option trades performs the same function in the options market that it does in the futures market. Finally, transaction costs are lower for exchange-traded options than for OTC options.

The higher cost of an OTC option reflects the cost of customizing the option for the many situations where an institutional investor needs to have a tailor-made option because the standardized exchange-traded option does not satisfy its investment objectives. Investment banking firms and commercial banks act as principals as well as brokers in the OTC options market. While an OTC option is less liquid than an exchange-traded option, this is typically not of concern to an institutional investor — most institutional investors who use OTC options as part of an asset/liability strategy intend to hold them to expiration.

Exchange-traded interest rate options can be written on a fixed income security or an interest rate futures contract. The former options are called *options on physicals*. For reasons to be explained later, options on interest rate futures have been far more popular than options on physicals. However, portfolio managers have made increasingly greater use of over-the-counter options. Exhibit 6 summarizes the types of options.

Exchange-Traded Futures Options
There are futures options on all the interest rate futures contracts mentioned earlier in this chapter. An option on a futures contract, commonly referred to as a *futures option*, gives the buyer the right to buy from or sell to the writer a designated futures contract at the strike price at any time during the life of the option. If the futures option is a call option, the buyer has the right to purchase one designated futures contract at the strike price. That is, the buyer has the right to acquire a long futures position in the underlying futures contract. If the buyer exercises the call option, the writer acquires a corresponding short position in the futures contract.

A put option on a futures contract grants the buyer the right to sell one designated futures contract to the writer at the strike price. That is, the option buyer has the right to acquire a short position in the designated futures contract. If the put option is exercised, the writer acquires a corresponding long position in the designated futures contract.

As the parties to the futures option will realize a position in a futures contract when the option is exercised, the question is: what will the futures price be? That is, at what futures price will the long be required to pay for the instrument underlying the futures contract, and at what futures price will the short be required to sell the instrument underlying the futures contract?

Exhibit 6: Exchange-Traded and OTC Options

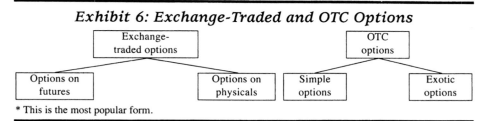

* This is the most popular form.

Upon exercise, the futures price for the futures contract will be set equal to the strike price. The position of the two parties is then immediately marked-to-market in terms of the then-current futures price. Thus, the futures position of the two parties will be at the prevailing futures price. At the same time, the option buyer will receive from the option seller the economic benefit from exercising. In the case of a call futures option, the option writer must pay the difference between the current futures price and the strike price to the buyer of the option. In the case of a put futures option, the option writer must pay the option buyer the difference between the strike price and the current futures price.

For example, suppose an investor buys a call option on some futures contract in which the strike price is 85. Assume also that the futures price is 95 and that the buyer exercises the call option. Upon exercise, the call buyer is given a long position in the futures contract at 85 and the call writer is assigned the corresponding short position in the futures contract at 85. The futures positions of the buyer and the writer are immediately marked-to-market by the exchange. Because the prevailing futures price is 95 and the strike price is 85, the long futures position (the position of the call buyer) realizes a gain of 10, while the short futures position (the position of the call writer) realizes a loss of 10. The call writer pays the exchange 10 and the call buyer receives from the exchange 10. The call buyer, who now has a long futures position at 95, can either liquidate the futures position at 95 or maintain a long futures position. If the former course of action is taken, the call buyer sells a futures contract at the prevailing futures price of 95. There is no gain or loss from liquidating the position. Overall, the call buyer realizes a gain of 10. The call buyer who elects to hold the long futures position will face the same risk and reward of holding such a position, but still realizes a gain of 10 from the exercise of the call option.

Suppose instead that the futures option is a put rather than a call, and the current futures price is 60 rather than 95. Then if the buyer of this put option exercises it, the buyer would have a short position in the futures contract at 85; the option writer would have a long position in the futures contract at 85. The exchange then marks the position to market at the then-current futures price of 60, resulting in a gain to the put buyer of 25 and a loss to the put writer of the same amount. The put buyer who now has a short futures position at 60 can either liquidate the short futures position by buying a futures contract at the prevailing futures price of 60 or maintain the short futures position. In either case the put buyer realizes a gain of 25 from exercising the put option.

There are no margin requirements for the buyer of a futures option once the option price has been paid in full. Because the option price is the maximum amount that the buyer can lose, regardless of how adverse the price movement of the underlying instrument, there is no need for margin.

Because the writer (seller) of a futures option has agreed to accept all of the risk (and none of the reward) of the position in the underlying instrument, the writer (seller) is required to deposit not only the margin required on the interest rate futures contract position but also (with certain exceptions) the option price that is received from writing the option. In addition, as prices adversely affect the writer's position, the writer would be required to deposit variation margin as it is marked to market.

The price of a futures option is quoted in 64ths of 1% of par value. For example, a price of 24 means $24/64$ of 1% of par value. Since the par value of a Treasury bond futures contract is $100,000, an option price of 24 means: $[(24/64)/100] \times \$100,000 = \$375$. In general, the price of a futures option quoted at Q is equal to:

$$\text{Option price} = \left[\frac{Q/64}{100}\right] \times \$100,000$$

There are three reasons why futures options on fixed income securities have largely supplanted options on physicals as the options vehicle of choice for institutional investors who want to use exchange-traded options. First, unlike options on fixed income securities, options on Treasury coupon futures do not require payments for accrued interest to be made. Consequently, when a futures option is exercised, the call buyer and the put writer need not compensate the other party for accrued interest. Second, futures options are believed to be "cleaner" instruments because of the reduced likelihood of delivery squeezes. Market participants who must deliver an instrument are concerned that at the time of delivery the instrument to be delivered will be in short supply, resulting in a higher price to acquire the instrument. As the deliverable supply of futures contracts is more than adequate for futures options currently traded, there is no concern about a delivery squeeze. Finally, in order to price any option, it is imperative to know at all times the price of the underlying instrument. In the bond market, current prices are not as easily available as price information on the futures contract. The reason is that as bonds trade in the over-the-counter market there is no reporting system with recent price information. Thus, an investor who wanted to purchase an option on a Treasury bond would have to call several dealer firms to obtain a price. In contrast, futures contracts are traded on an exchange and, as a result, price information is reported.

Over-the-Counter Options

Institutional investors who want to purchase an option on a specific Treasury security or a Ginnie Mae passthrough can do so on an over-the-counter basis. There are government and mortgage-backed securities dealers who make a market in options on specific securities. Over-the-counter options, also called *dealer options*, usually are purchased by institutional investors who want to hedge the risk associated with a specific security. For example, a thrift may be interested in hedging its position in a specific mortgage passthrough security. Typically, the maturity of the option coincides with the time period over which the buyer of the option wants to hedge, so the buyer is not concerned with the option's liquidity.

As explained earlier with forward contracts, in the absence of a clearing-house the parties to any over-the-counter contract are exposed to counterparty risk. In the case of forward contracts where both parties are obligated to perform, both parties face counterparty risk. In contrast, in the case of an option, once the option buyer pays the option price, it has satisfied its obligation. It is only the seller that must perform if the option is exercised. Thus, the option buyer is exposed to counterparty risk — the risk that the option seller will fail to perform.

OTC options can be customized in any manner sought by an institutional investor. Basically, if a dealer can reasonably hedge the risk associated with the opposite side of the option sought, it will create the option desired by a customer. OTC options are not limited to European or American type. An option can be cre-ated in which the option can be exercised at several specified dates as well as the expiration date. Such options are referred to as *modified American options*, *Ber-muda options*, and *Atlantic options*.

Exotic Options The more complex OTC options created are called *exotic options*. Here are just two types of such exotic options: alternative options and outperfor-mance options. An *alternative option*, also called an *either-or option*, has a payoff which is the best independent payoff of two distinct assets. For example, suppose that a manager buys an alternative call option with the following terms:

1. the underlying asset is one unit of Bond M or one unit of Bond N
2. the strike price for Bond M is $80
3. the strike price for Bond N is $110
4. the expiration date is three months from now
5. the option can only be exercised three months from now (that is, it is a European option)

At the expiration date, the manager can decide to buy from the writer of this option *either* one unit of Bond M at $80 or one unit of Bond N at $110. The manager will buy the bond with the larger payoff. So, for example, if the prices of Bonds M and N at the expiration date are $84 and $140, respectively, then the payoff would be $4 if the manager elects to exercise to buy Bond M but $30 if he elects to exercise to buy Bond N. Thus, the manager will exercise to buy Bond N. If the price for either bond at the expiration date is below the strike price, the manager will let the option expire worthless.

An *outperformance option* is an option whose payoff is based on the rel-ative payoff of two assets at the expiration date. For example, consider the follow-ing outperformance call option purchased by a manager:

1. Portfolio A consists of long-term Treasury bonds with a market value of $40 million
2. Portfolio B consists of mortgage passthrough securities with a market value of $40 million

3. the expiration date is six months from now and is a European option
4. the strike is equal to:
   market value of Portfolio B – market value of Portfolio A

At the expiration date, if the market value of Portfolio A is greater than the market value of Portfolio B, then there is no value to this option and it will expire worthless. The option will be exercised if the market value of Portfolio B exceeds the market value of Portfolio A at the expiration date.

INTEREST RATE SWAPS

In an interest rate swap, two parties agree to exchange periodic interest payments. The dollar amount of the interest payments exchanged is based on some predetermined dollar principal, which is called the *notional principal*. The dollar amount each counterparty pays to the other is the agreed-upon periodic interest rate times the notional principal. The only dollars that are exchanged between the parties are the interest payments, not the notional principal. In the most common type of swap, one party agrees to pay the other party fixed interest payments at designated dates for the life of the contract. This party is referred to as the *fixed-rate payer*. The other party, who agrees to make interest rate payments that float with some reference rate, is referred to as the *floating-rate payer*.

The reference rates that have been used for the floating rate in an interest rate swap are those on various money market instruments: Treasury bills, the London interbank offered rate, commercial paper, bankers acceptances, certificates of deposit, the federal funds rate, and the prime rate. The most common is the London interbank offered rate (LIBOR). LIBOR is the rate at which prime banks offer to pay on Eurodollar deposits available to other prime banks for a given maturity. Basically, it is viewed as the global cost of bank borrowing. There is not just one rate but a rate for different maturities. For example, there is a 1-month LIBOR, 3-month LIBOR, 6-month LIBOR, etc.

To illustrate an interest rate swap, suppose that for the next five years party X agrees to pay party Y 10% per year, while party Y agrees to pay party X 6-month LIBOR (the reference rate). Party X is a fixed-rate payer/floating-rate receiver, while party Y is a floating-rate payer/fixed-rate receiver. Assume that the notional principal is $50 million, and that payments are exchanged every six months for the next five years. This means that every six months, party X (the fixed-rate payer/floating-rate receiver) will pay party Y $2.5 million (10% times $50 million divided by 2). The amount that party Y (the floating-rate payer/fixed-rate receiver) will pay party X will be 6-month LIBOR times $50 million divided by 2. If 6-month LIBOR is 7%, party Y will pay party X $1.75 million (7% times $50 million divided by 2). Note that we divide by two because one-half year's interest is being paid.

The convention that has evolved for quoting swaps levels is that a swap dealer sets the floating rate equal to the reference rate and then quotes the fixed rate that will apply. The fixed rate is some spread above the Treasury yield curve with the same term to maturity as the swap.

Entering Into a Swap and Counterparty Risk

Interest rate swaps are over-the-counter instruments. This means that they are not traded on an exchange. An institutional investor wishing to enter into a swap transaction can do so through either a securities firm or a commercial bank that transacts in swaps.[3] These entities can do one of the following. First, they can arrange or broker a swap between two parties that want to enter into an interest rate swap. In this case, the securities firm or commercial bank is acting in a brokerage capacity. The broker is not a party to the swap.

The second way in which a securities firm or commercial bank can get an institutional investor into a swap position is by taking the other side of the swap. This means that the securities firm or the commercial bank is a dealer rather than a broker in the transaction. Acting as a dealer, the securities firm or the commercial bank must hedge its swap position in the same way that it hedges its position in other securities that it holds. Also it means that the dealer (which we refer to as a swap dealer) is the counterparty to the transaction. Merrill Lynch, for example, is a swap dealer. If an institutional investor entered into a swap with Merrill Lynch, the institutional investor will look to Merrill Lynch to satisfy the obligations of the swap; similarly, Merrill Lynch looks to the institutional investor to fulfill its obligations as set forth in the swap. Today, most swaps are transacted using a swap dealer.

The risks that the two parties take on when they enter into a swap is that the other party will fail to fulfill its obligations as set forth in the swap agreement. That is, each party faces default risk and therefore there is bilateral counterparty risk. Because of counterparty risk, not all securities firms and commercial banks can be swap dealers. Several securities firms have established subsidiaries that are separately capitalized so that they have triple-A credit ratings, permitting them to enter into swap transactions as dealers.

Risk/Return Characteristics of an Interest Rate Swap

The value of an interest rate swap will fluctuate with market interest rates. To see how, let's consider our hypothetical swap. Suppose that interest rates change immediately after parties X and Y enter into the swap. First, consider what would happen if the market demanded that in any 5-year swap the fixed-rate payer must pay 11% in order to receive 6-month LIBOR. If party X (the fixed-rate payer) wants to sell its position to party A, then party A will benefit by having to pay only 10% (the origi-

---

[3] Don't get confused here about the role of commercial banks. A bank can use a swap in its asset/liability management. Or, a bank can transact (buy and sell) swaps to clients to generate fee income. It is in the latter sense that we are discussing the role of a commercial bank in the swap market here.

nal swap rate agreed upon) rather than 11% (the current swap rate) to receive 6-month LIBOR. Party X will want compensation for this benefit. Consequently, the value of party X's position has increased. Thus, if interest rates increase, the fixed-rate payer will realize a profit and the floating-rate payer will realize a loss.

Next, consider what would happen if interest rates decline to, say, 6%. Now a 5-year swap would require a new fixed-rate payer to pay 6% rather than 10% to receive 6-month LIBOR. If party X wants to sell its position to party B, the latter would demand compensation to take over the position. In other words, if interest rates decline, the fixed-rate payer will realize a loss, while the floating-rate payer will realize a profit.

Interpreting a Swap Position

There are two ways that a swap position can be interpreted: (1) a package of forward/futures contracts, and (2) a package of cash flows from buying and selling cash market instruments.

Package of Forward Contracts

Contrast the position of the counterparties in an interest rate swap summarized above to the position of the long and short interest rate futures (forward) contract discussed in the previous chapter. The long futures position gains if interest rates decline and loses if interest rates rise — this is similar to the risk/return profile for a floating-rate payer. The risk/return profile for a fixed-rate payer is similar to that of the short futures position: a gain if interest rates increase and a loss if interest rates decrease. By taking a closer look at the interest rate swap we can understand why the risk/return relationships are similar.

Consider party X's position in our previous swap illustration. Party X has agreed to pay 10% and receive 6-month LIBOR. More specifically, assuming a $50 million notional principal, X has agreed to buy a commodity called "6-month LIBOR" for $2.5 million. This is effectively a 6-month forward contract where X agrees to pay $2.5 million in exchange for delivery of 6-month LIBOR. If interest rates increase to 11%, the price of that commodity (6-month LIBOR) is higher, resulting in a gain for the fixed-rate payer, who is effectively long a 6-month forward contract on 6-month LIBOR. The floating-rate payer is effectively short a 6-month forward contract on 6-month LIBOR. There is therefore an implicit forward contract corresponding to each exchange date.

Now we can see why there is a similarity between the risk/return relationship for an interest rate swap and a forward contract. If interest rates increase to, say, 11%, the price of that commodity (6-month LIBOR) increases to $2.75 million (11% times $50 million divided by 2). The long forward position (the fixed-rate payer) gains, and the short forward position (the floating-rate payer) loses. If interest rates decline to, say, 9%, the price of our commodity decreases to $2.25 million (9% times $50 million divided by 2). The short forward position (the floating-rate payer) gains, and the long forward position (the fixed-rate payer) loses.

Consequently, interest rate swaps can be viewed as a package of more basic interest rate derivatives, such as forwards. The pricing of an interest rate swap will then depend on the price of a package of forward contracts with the same settlement dates in which the underlying for the forward contract is the same reference rate. This is the fundamental principle in valuing swaps.

While an interest rate swap may be nothing more than a package of forward contracts, it is not a redundant contract for several reasons. First, maturities for forward or futures contracts do not extend out as far as those of an interest rate swap; an interest rate swap with a term of 15 years or longer can be obtained. Second, an interest rate swap is a more transactionally efficient instrument. By this we mean that in one transaction an entity can effectively establish a payoff equivalent to a package of forward contracts. The forward contracts would each have to be negotiated separately. Third, the interest rate swap market has grown in liquidity since its establishment in 1981; interest rate swaps now provide more liquidity than forward contracts, particularly long-dated (i.e., long-term) forward contracts.

Package of Cash Market Instruments

To understand why a swap can also be interpreted as a package of cash market instruments, consider an investor who enters into the transaction below:

- buy a $50 million par of a 5-year floating-rate bond that pays 6-month LIBOR every six months
- finance the purchase by borrowing $50 million for five years on terms requiring 10% annual interest rate paid every six months

The cash flows for this transaction are set forth in Exhibit 7. The second column of the exhibit shows the cash flow from purchasing the 5-year floating-rate bond. There is a $50 million cash outlay and then ten cash inflows. The amount of the cash inflows is uncertain because they depend on future LIBOR. The next column shows the cash flow from borrowing $50 million on a fixed-rate basis. The last column shows the net cash flow from the entire transaction. As the last column indicates, there is no initial cash flow (no cash inflow or cash outlay). In all ten 6-month periods, the net position results in a cash inflow of LIBOR and a cash outlay of $2.5 million. This net position, however, is identical to the position of a fixed-rate payer/floating-rate receiver.

It can be seen from the net cash flow in Exhibit 7 that a fixed-rate payer has a cash market position that is equivalent to a long position in a floating-rate bond and a short position in a fixed-rate bond — the short position being the equivalent of borrowing by issuing a fixed-rate bond.

What about the position of a floating-rate payer? It can be easily demonstrated that the position of a floating-rate payer is equivalent to purchasing a fixed-rate bond and financing that purchase at a floating rate, where the floating rate is the reference rate for the swap. That is, the position of a floating-rate payer is equivalent to a long position in a fixed-rate bond and a short position in a floating-rate bond.

Exhibit 7: Cash Flow for the Purchase of a 5-Year Floating-Rate Bond Financed by Borrowing on a Fixed-Rate Basis

Transaction:

- Purchase for $50 million a 5-year floating-rate bond:
    floating rate = LIBOR, semiannual pay
- Borrow $50 million for five years:
    fixed rate = 10%, semiannual payments

Six Month Period	Cash Flow (In Millions of Dollars) From:		
	Floating-Rate Bond*	Borrowing Cost	Net
0	−$50	+$50.0	$0
1	+(LIBOR$_1$/2) × 50	−2.5	+(LIBOR$_1$/2) × 50 − 2.5
2	+(LIBOR$_2$/2) × 50	−2.5	+(LIBOR$_2$/2) × 50 − 2.5
3	+(LIBOR$_3$/2) × 50	−2.5	+(LIBOR$_3$/2) × 50 − 2.5
4	+(LIBOR$_4$/2) × 50	−2.5	+(LIBOR$_4$/2) × 50 − 2.5
5	+(LIBOR$_5$/2) × 50	−2.5	+(LIBOR$_5$/2) × 50 − 2.5
6	+(LIBOR$_6$/2) × 50	−2.5	+(LIBOR$_6$/2) × 50 − 2.5
7	+(LIBOR$_7$/2) × 50	−2.5	+(LIBOR$_7$/2) × 50 − 2.5
8	+(LIBOR$_8$/2) × 50	−2.5	+(LIBOR$_8$/2) × 50 − 2.5
9	+(LIBOR$_9$/2) × 50	−2.5	+(LIBOR$_9$/2) × 50 − 2.5
10	+(LIBOR$_{10}$/2) × 50 + 50	−52.5	+(LIBOR$_{10}$/2) × 50 − 2.5

* The subscript for LIBOR indicates the 6-month LIBOR as per the terms of the floating-rate bond at time t.

INTEREST RATE AGREEMENTS (CAPS AND FLOORS)

An *interest rate agreement* is an agreement between two parties whereby one party for an upfront premium agrees to compensate the other at specific time periods if the reference rate is different from a predetermined level. When one party agrees to pay the other when the reference rate exceeds a predetermined level, the agreement is referred to as an *interest rate cap* or *ceiling*. The agreement is referred to as an *interest rate floor* when one party agrees to pay the other when the reference rate falls below a predetermined level. The predetermined level is called the *strike rate*.

The terms of an interest rate agreement include:

1. The reference rate
2. The strike rate that sets the ceiling or floor
3. The length of the agreement
4. The frequency of settlement
5. The notional principal

For example, suppose that C buys an interest rate cap from D with terms as follows:

1. The reference rate is 3-month LIBOR.
2. The strike rate is 6%.

3. The agreement is for four years.
4. Settlement is every three months.
5. The notional principal is $20 million.

Under this agreement, every three months for the next four years, D will pay C whenever 3-month LIBOR exceeds 6% at a settlement date. (Actually the payment is made arrears.). The payment will equal the dollar value of the difference between 3-month LIBOR and 6% times the notional principal divided by 4. For example, if three months from now 3-month LIBOR on a settlement date is 8%, then D will pay C 2% (8% minus 6%) times $20 million divided by 4, or $100,000. If 3-month LIBOR is 6% or less, D does not have to pay anything to C.

In the case of an interest rate floor, assume the same terms as the interest rate cap we just illustrated. In this case, if 3-month LIBOR is 8%, C receives nothing from D, but if 3-month LIBOR is less than 6%, D compensates C for the difference. For example, if 3-month LIBOR is 5%, D will pay C $50,000 (6% minus 5% times $20 million divided by 4).

Interest rate caps and floors can be combined to create an *interest rate collar*. This is done by buying an interest rate cap and selling an interest rate floor.

Risk/Return Characteristic

In an interest rate agreement, the buyer pays an upfront fee which represents the maximum amount that the buyer can lose and the maximum amount that the seller (writer) can gain. The only party that is required to perform is the seller of the interest rate agreement. The buyer of an interest rate cap benefits if the reference rate rises above the strike rate because the seller must compensate the buyer. The buyer of an interest rate floor benefits if the reference rate falls below the strike rate, because the seller must compensate the buyer.

To better understand interest rate caps and interest rate floors, we can look at them as in essence equivalent to a package of interest rate options. Since the buyer benefits if the interest rate rises above the strike rate, an interest rate cap is similar to purchasing a package of call options on the reference rate; the seller of an interest rate cap has effectively sold a package of these options. The buyer of an interest rate floor benefits from a decline in the reference rate below the strike rate. Therefore, the buyer of an interest rate floor has effectively bought a package of put options on the reference rate from the seller. An interest rate collar is equivalent to buying a package of call options and selling a package of put options. Once again, a complex contract can be seen to be a package of basic contracts, options in the case of interest rate agreements.

The seller of an interest cap or floor does not face counterparty risk once the buyer pays the fee. In contrast, the buyer faces counterparty risk. Thus, as with options, there is unilateral counterparty risk.

Chapter 8

Credit Derivatives

Mark J. P. Anson, Ph.D., CFA, CPA
Portfolio Manager
OppenheimerFunds, Inc.

INTRODUCTION

Credit derivatives are financial instruments which are designed to transfer the credit exposure of an underlying asset or issuer between two or more parties. They are individually negotiated financial contracts which may take the form of options, swaps, forwards, or credit-linked notes where the payoffs are linked to, or derived from, the credit characteristics of a referenced asset or issuer. With credit derivatives, a portfolio manager can either acquire or hedge credit risk.

Many asset managers have portfolios which are very sensitive to changes in the spread between riskless and risky assets and credit derivatives are an efficient way to hedge this exposure. Conversely, other asset managers may use credit derivatives to target specific exposures as a way to enhance portfolio returns. In each case, the ability to transfer credit risk and return provides a new tool for portfolio mangers to improve performance.

We begin this chapter with a short discussion on the importance of credit risk. We then review the four main types of credit derivatives: credit options, credit forwards, credit swaps, and credit-linked notes. We describe their structure and consider their practical applications. Lastly, we discuss some important risks associated with the use of these new derivatives.

WHY CREDIT RISK IS IMPORTANT

A fixed income debt instrument represents a basket of risks. There is the risk from changes in interest rates (duration and convexity risk), the risk that the issuer will refinance the debt issue (call risk), and the risk of defaults, downgrades, and widening credit spreads (credit risk). The total return from a fixed income investment such as a corporate bond is the compensation for assuming all of these risks. Depending upon the rating on the underlying debt instrument, the return from credit risk can be a significant part of a bond's total return.

However, the default rate on credit risky bonds can be quite high. Estimates of the default rates for high-yield bonds range from 3.17% to 6.25%.[1] Credit derivatives, therefore, appeal to portfolio managers who invest in high-yield or "junk" bonds, real estate, or other credit dependent assets. The possibility of default is a significant risk for portfolio managers, and one that can be effectively hedged by shifting the credit exposure.

In addition to default risk for junk investments, there is the risk of downgrades for investment-grade bonds and the risk of increased credit spreads. Downgrade risk occurs when a nationally recognized statistical rating organization such Standard & Poors, Moody's Investment Services, Duff & Phelps, or Fitch's reduces its outstanding credit rating for an issuer based on an evaluation of that issuer's current earning power versus its capacity to pay its fixed income obligations as they become due. For instance, through the first six months of 1997, 83 corporate bond issues representing $14.7 billion were downgraded at least one rating category.[2]

Credit spread risk is the risk that the interest rate spread for a risky bond over a riskless bond will increase after the risky bond has been purchased. For instance, in the United States, corporate bonds are typically priced at a spread to comparable U.S. Treasury bonds. Should this spread widen after purchase of the corporate bond, the portfolio manager would suffer a diminution of the portfolio's value. Credit spreads can widen based on macroeconomic events such as volatility in the financial markets.

As an example, in October of 1997, a rapid decline in Asian stock markets spilled over into the U.S. stock markets causing a significant decline in equities.[3] The turbulence in the financial markets, both domestically and worldwide, resulted in a "flight to safety" of investment capital. In other words, investors sought safer havens of investment to avoid further losses and volatility. This flight to safety resulted in a significant increase in credit spreads of corporate bonds to U.S. Treasuries.

For instance, at June 30, 1997, corporate bonds rated BB by Standard & Poors were trading at an average spread over U.S. Treasuries of 215 basis points.[4] However, by October 31, 1997, this spread had increased to 319 basis points. For a $1,000 market value BB-rated corporate bond with a duration of 5, this resulted in a loss of value of about $52.50 per bond.

In their simplest form, credit derivatives may be nothing more than the purchase of credit protection. The ability to isolate credit risk and manage it independently of underlying bond positions is the key benefit of credit derivatives.

---

[1] See Edward Altman, "Measuring Corporate Bond Mortality and Performance," *Journal of Finance* (June 1991), pp. 909-922; and Gabriella Petrucci, *High-Yield Review — First-Half 1997*, Salomon Brothers Corporate Bond Research (August 1997).

[2] See Peter Acciavatti and Robert Manowitz, *1997 High Yield Semi-Annual Review* (New York: Chase Securities Inc., 1997), p. A-83.

[3] For instance, the Dow Jones Industrial Average suffered a one day decline of value of 554 points on October 27, 1997.

[4] See Chase Securities Inc., "High-Yield Research Weekly Update," Chase High-Yield Research (November 4, 1997), p. 43.

Prior to the introduction of credit derivatives, the only way to manage credit exposure was to buy and sell the underlying assets. Because of transaction costs and tax issues this was an inefficient way to hedge or gain exposure.

Credit derivatives, therefore, represent a natural extension of the financial markets to unbundle the risk and return buckets associated with a particular financial asset, such as credit risk. They offer an important method for investment managers to hedge their exposure to credit risk because they permit the transfer of the exposure from one party to another. Credit derivatives allow for an efficient exchange of credit exposure in return for credit protection.

However, credit risk is not all one-sided. There are a number of reasons why a seller of credit protection may be willing to assume the credit risk of an underlying financial asset or issuer. For instance, in 1997 there were more credit rating upgrades than downgrades. Through the first half of 1997 a total $23.2 billion of corporate bonds were upgraded compared to a total of $14.7 billion that were downgraded.[5] One reason for the net credit rating upgrades was a strong stock market which encouraged public offerings of stock by credit risky companies. A large portion of these equity financings were used to reduce outstanding costly debt, resulting in improved balance sheets and credit ratings for the issuers. A second reason for the net upgrades was a strong economy which contributed to superior operating results for domestic corporations. Consequently, asset managers had ample opportunity in 1997 to target specific credit risks which benefited from a ratings upgrade.

In addition to credit upgrades, there are other financial events which have a positive effect on credit risky bonds. Mergers and acquisitions, for instance, are a frequent occurrence in the high yield market. Even though a credit risky issuer may have a low debt rating, it may have valuable technology worth acquiring. High yield issuers tend to be small to mid-cap companies with viable products but nascent cash flows. Consequently, they make attractive takeover candidates for financially mature companies.

Lastly, with a strong economy, banks have been willing to provide term loans to high yield companies at more attractive rates than the bond markets. Consequently, it has been advantageous for credit risky companies to redeem their high-yield bonds and replace the bonds with a lower cost term loan. The resulting premium for redemption of high-yield bonds is a positive credit event which enhances portfolio returns.

CREDIT OPTIONS

Credit options are different from standard debt options because while the latter is designed to protect against market risk (i.e. interest rate risk), credit options are constructed to protect against credit risk. Thus, the purpose of credit options is to price credit risk independently of market risk. Credit options may be written on

---

[5] See Acciavatti and Manowitz, pp. A-79 to A-83.

an underlying asset or on a spread over a referenced riskless asset. These two type of options — one triggered by a decline in the value of an asset and one triggered by the change in the asset's spread over a comparable risk-free rate — have different payout structures.[6]

Credit Options Written on an Underlying Asset

In its simplest form, a credit option can be a binary option. With a binary credit option, the option seller will pay out a fixed sum if and when a default event occurs with respect to a referenced credit (e.g. the underlying issuer is unable to pay its obligations as they become due). Therefore, a binary option represents two states of the world: default or no default. It is the clearest example of credit protection. At maturity of the option, if the referenced credit has defaulted the option holder receives a predetermined payout. If there is no default at maturity of the option, the option buyer receives nothing and forgoes the option premium. A binary credit option could also be triggered by a ratings downgrade.

A European binary credit option pays out a fixed sum only at maturity if the referenced credit is in default. An American binary option can be exercised at any time during its life. Consequently, if an American binary credit option is in the money (a default event has occurred), it will be exercised immediately because delaying exercise will reduce the present value of the fixed payment.

Exhibit 1 presents a binary credit option where the payout is dependent upon whether the referenced credit is in default. The strike price of the option can be set to a minimum net worth of the underlying issuer below which default is probable. For instance, if the firm value of the referenced credit (assets – liabilities) falls to $100 million, then the option will pay 20 cents on every dollar of bond outstanding, or $200 for each $1,000 face value bond. In practice, high-yield bonds trade considerably below their face value and defaulted bonds generally trade at 40 to 50 cents on the dollar. Consequently, the payout to the credit option does not need to cover the full face value of the bond to protect the portfolio manager.

Mathematically, the payoff to a binary put option is stated as:

$$P(V(t);\$100{,}000{,}000) = \begin{cases} \$200 \text{ if } V(t) < \$100{,}000{,}000 \\ 0 \text{ if } V(t) \geq \$100{,}000{,}000 \end{cases} \tag{1}$$

where

$100,000,000 = the strike price set equal to a minimum firm value
$V(t)$ = the value of the firm at maturity t of the option
$200 = a fixed payment if firm value declines below $100,000,000

---

[6] Note that credit options are different from options on credit risky assets. In the latter case, these options are on the outright asset, but the asset is subject to credit risk, i.e., the issuer may default on the security. Conversely, credit options recognize the possibility of default and construct the payoff on the option to be a function of the decline in asset value due to default. For a thorough analysis of options on credit risky assets, see Robert Jarrow and Stuart Turnbull, "Pricing Derivatives on Financial Assets Subject to Credit Risk," *Journal of Finance* (March 1995) pp. 53-85.

Exhibit 1: Binary Credit Option

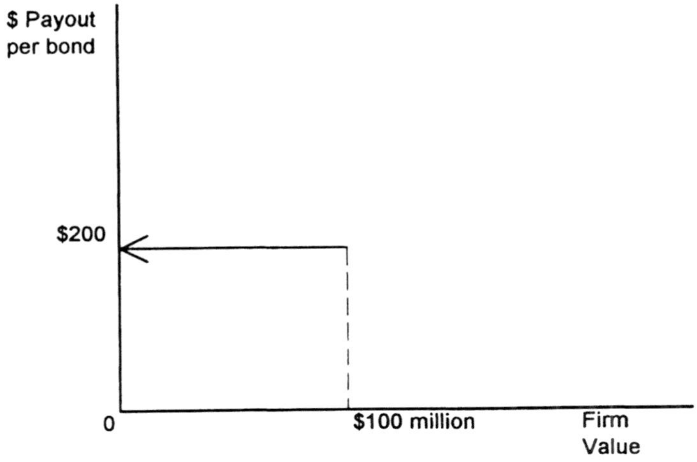

Equation (1) demonstrates the payoff for a put option. The option pays a fixed sum of $200 per bond if the value of the referenced credit declines below a minimum value ($100 million), and nothing if the value of the referenced credit at maturity of the option is above the strike price.

An alternative to binary options is an option where the option writer agrees to compensate the option buyer for a decline in the value of a financial asset below a specified strike price. This type of option is also a put option — it is in-the-money only when the value of the underlying asset declines below the strike price. In practice, these types of credit options are usually specified in terms of the acceptable default spread of the bond in question. That is, upon exercise of the credit option, the payoff is determined by subtracting the market price of the bond from the strike price, where the strike price is determined by taking the present value of the bond's cash flows discounted at the risk-free rate plus the strike credit spread over the remaining life of the outstanding bond.

Mathematically, this is determined by the following formula:

$$P[D(t); K] = \text{Max } [0, K - D(t)] \tag{2}$$

where

K	=	$F[\exp-(r + \text{spread})(T - t)]$
$D(t)$	=	the market value of a financial asset at time t, the maturity of the option
F	=	the face value of a zero-coupon debt instrument
r	=	the riskless rate
spread	=	the specified (strike) credit spread over the riskless rate

Exhibit 2: Credit Put Option on BB Rated Debt Issue

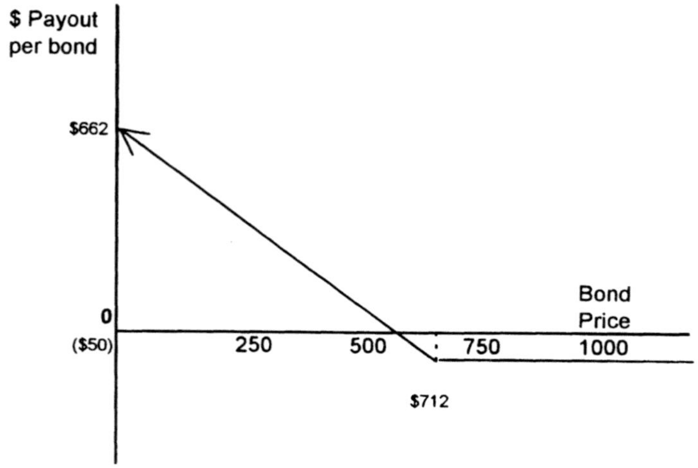

T	= the maturity of the bond
t	= the time to maturity of the option
exp	= the exponential power of e

Continuing with our example of BB rated bonds, the credit spread of 215 basis points in June 1997 was the lowest spread in several years. It would not be unreasonable for an investor to expect the credit spread to widen back to an historical average in excess of 300 basis points, resulting in a decline in value of BB rated bonds. To protect against this anticipated decline in value, a portfolio manager could purchase a credit put option.

Assume that the portfolio manager purchases a $1,000 face value zero-coupon BB bond, with five years to maturity, in June at a credit spread which is 215 basis points to comparable U.S. Treasury bonds. However, to protect against a widening of the credit spread with respect to these bonds, the portfolio manager also purchases a one year credit option for $50 whose strike is established at a credit spread of 225 basis points. In June 1997, comparable U.S. Treasury bonds were trading at a rate of 6.25%. Using equation (2), the strike of the credit option is then set equal to $1,000[exp–(6.25% + 2.25%)(5 – 1)] = $712. If the high-yield bond trades below this value, then the portfolio manager receives the difference between $712 and the market value of the bond. This example is demonstrated in Exhibit 2.

Valuing credit options in the form of equation (2) implicitly assumes constant market risk, i.e., that interest rate volatility is not essential. In other words, credit options are dependent upon the value of the firm's assets and not that of interest rates. If the option has a relatively short maturity, the simplifying assumption that interest rates are constant is not crucial to the valuation of the option, but for longer duration options, the assumption that interest rates remain constant may be unrealistic. However, empirical evidence indicates that high-yield bonds are less sensitive to interest rate changes than high-grade bonds and are more sensitive to changes in firm value than high-grade bonds.[7]

Equation (2) expresses the strike price of a credit option on a zero-coupon bond. If we can accurately estimate the value of the underlying referenced credit, the probability of default can be estimated with increasing confidence as the maturity of the bond draws near. As a result, default does not come as a random surprise. However, unlike zero-coupon bonds, coupon-paying bonds can default prior to their maturity at any coupon date and any credit risk derivative on a coupon-paying bond must price each potential default date.

A simple solution for credit options on a coupon-paying bond, is to adjust the strike price of the credit option based on all cash flows paid over the life of the bond. Thus, the strike price K must be the sum of a series of the type expressed in equation (2) where F, the face value of the bond, is replaced by the future cash flow (either a coupon payment or maturity value of the bond) and time T is the payment date of the bond cash flow.

On a general note, it can be observed that credit put options will be a decreasing function of firm value. As the value of the firm increases, the credit rating on the outstanding debt is also expected to increase and the value of the put option decreases. In fact, the credit option becomes almost worthless when firm value is high enough because the outstanding debt becomes almost credit risk free. However, credit put options are increasing in the volatility of firm value for two reasons. As the volatility of the firm assets increases, the value of outstanding bonds decreases and the value of the put option increases. Additionally, an increase in volatility has the same value enhancing impact in option pricing models as higher volatility has on the value of a put option on the firm's common stock.[8]

Credit derivatives may be used to exploit inefficiencies in the market when there is imperfect correlation between stock prices and interest rates. For instance, when interest rates and stock prices are negatively correlated, corporate debt values may be higher than when the correlation is positive. Credit spreads in the market may not correctly reflect the correlations between stocks and the term

---

[7] See B. Cornell and K. Green, "The Investment Performance of Low Grade Bond Funds," *Journal of Finance* (March 1991), pp. 29-48.

[8] In practice, the pricing of credit options is quite complicated and beyond the scope of this discussion. For instance, one author has developed a model for credit options that incorporates firm value as an underlying stochastic variable as well as random strike prices. See Sanjiv R. Das, "Credit Risk Derivatives," *Journal of Derivatives* (Spring 1995), pp. 7-23. Another paper uses mean reverting credit spreads and interest rates to determine the value of credit spread options. See Francis A. Longstaff and Eduardo S. Schwartz, "Valuing Credit Derivatives," *Journal of Fixed Income* (June 1995), pp.6-12. Still another author values credit derivatives as barrier options. See Yiannos A. Pierides, "Valuation of Credit Risk Derivatives," Chapter 13 in Frank J. Fabozzi (ed.), *The Handbook of Fixed Income Options* (Burr Ridge, IL: Irwin Professional Publishing, 1996). For a complete discussion and comparison of these pricing models see Mark J. P. Anson, "Risks and Rewards of Credit Derivatives," OppenheimerFunds working paper (1997).

structure of interest rates. As a result, investors may hold a portfolio of corporate bonds and credit derivatives, which may cost less than equivalent riskless debt yet offer the same risk and return characteristics.

Credit options may also be used in conjunction with other derivative transactions. For instance, with respect to over-the-counter derivatives such as swaps and off-exchange options, downgrade provisions in the derivative documentation can protect a derivative buyer from credit risk. However, the buyer must be able to establish a downgrade trigger at some point before the counterparty is in the throes of financial distress. Additionally, the downgrade trigger provision terminates the transaction; a credit option hedges the credit exposure but does not automatically truncate the transaction cash flows.

Credit Spread Options

The second type of credit option is a call option on the level of the credit spread over a referenced benchmark such as U.S. Treasury securities. If the credit spread widens, the referenced asset will decline in value. This type of credit option is structured so that the option is in-the-money when the credit spread exceeds the specified spread level. The payoff is determined by taking the difference in the credit spreads multiplied by a specified notional amount and by a risk factor. In a mathematical format, the payoff at maturity of the option may be specified as:

$$C[\text{spread}(t); K] = (\text{spread} - K) \times \text{notional amount} \times \text{risk factor} \qquad (3)$$

where

$\text{spread}(t)$ = the spread for the financial asset over the riskless rate at the maturity of the option at time t

K = the specified strike spread for the financial asset over the riskless rate

The notional amount is a contractually specified dollar amount. The "risk factor" is based on the interest rate sensitivity of the unsecured debt and represents the dollar value of a 1 basis point change in the credit spread.[9]

An example may clarify. Consider the 30-year Treasury bond trading at a yield of 6.25% and the unsecured debt of Company A trading at a spread to U.S. Treasuries of 2.5%. If the portfolio manager believes that the unsecured debt of Company A is overvalued, she can purchase a credit spread option on the debt of Company A, struck at a spread of 250 basis points. This is the same as the portfolio manager expressing the view that the price of the referenced asset is inflated at its current market spread, and that she expects this spread to widen above 250 basis points.

Assume the portfolio manager purchases a $20 million notional at-the-money-call option on the credit spread between the debt of Company A and U.S.

---

[9] The risk factor is determined by the standard measures of duration and convexity.

Treasuries. The tenor of the option is one year, the premium costs 125 basis points, and the risk factor for the unsecured debt is 6.25. At maturity, the portfolio manager will receive the following payout: (change in credit spread) × (notional amount) × (risk factor). If the credit spread widens to 300 basis points at maturity of the option, the portfolio manager will earn: (0.005 × $20,000,000 × 6.25) – $250,000 = $375,000. This is demonstrated in Exhibit 3.

Credit spreads can be reviewed from either a macroeconomic or microeconomic analysis. Under a macroeconomic view, a slowdown in the economy can lead to a flight of capital to more secure investments such as U.S. Treasury securities, resulting in wider credit spreads across all securities. Under a microeconomic analysis, a buyer of a credit option can express the view that the credit quality of the underlying referenced issuer will decline due to poor operating performance. In either scenario, the price of the referenced asset "cheapens" relative to U.S. Treasury securities.

Alternatively, credit spread options may be used as income enhancement tools. The portfolio manager may believe that the credit spread for Company A will not exceed 300 basis points. To monetize this view, she can sell a put option on the credit spread with the strike set at 300 basis points. Additionally, the portfolio manager can agree to physically settle the option. In effect, the portfolio manager has agreed to buy the debt of Company A at a spread to U.S. Treasuries of 300 basis points — her targeted purchase price — and she can use the premium received from the sale of the credit option to finance the purchase price should the put be exercised.

Exhibit 3: Credit Call Option Credit Spread Option Struck at 250 Basis Points

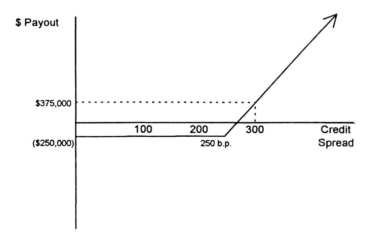

Furthermore, by selling a put option on a credit spread an investor can capitalize on a higher credit spread volatility than on a sale of the yield volatility for the same bond.[10] Higher spread volatility is the result of the less than perfect correlation between the referenced debt and the comparable Treasury bond. Therefore, an investor can receive a higher put premium by selling richer spread volatility than by selling a put on the underlying debt.

Credit spread options are relative value options. Their value is not derived from the absolute price change of the underlying referenced asset, but rather from the price change of the referenced asset relative to U.S. Treasury securities. By purchasing a call option on the credit spread between the referenced asset and U.S. Treasuries, the option is in the money only if the price of the referenced asset declines more than the prices of U.S. Treasury securities (i.e. the credit spread widens).

Credit spread options are therefore underperformance options. Similar to outperformance options where the payoff is contingent on the relative outperformance of one referenced asset over a second referenced asset, the payoff of a credit spread call option is contingent upon the relative underperformance of a referenced asset compared to U.S. Treasury securities.

Credit spread options are not designed to protect against market risk such as interest rate spikes where both the Treasury security and the referenced asset decline in value at the same time. Instead, credit options are another form of insurance against a credit decline in the referenced asset or issuer. This strategy can be used to protect the value of an existing portfolio position should its spread relative to U.S. Treasuries increase. However, this type of option will not protect against an absolute decline in value of the referenced asset if the value of U.S. Treasury securities also decline.

Credit spread options may also be used by corporate treasurers to hedge the credit risk embedded in future borrowing requirements. Typically, the spread paid by corporations based on different rating levels compared to U.S. Treasury securities tends to widen during periods of economic downturns. Credit call options on the spread over U.S. Treasuries can protect against an overall rise in the risk premiums for different rating levels. The payoff from the option can be used to offset the increased funding costs.

CREDIT FORWARDS

Credit forward contracts, like credit options, are an essential building block in the derivatives market. They may be contracted either on bond values or on credit spreads. They can be used by corporations that wish to lock in their funding costs, or by portfolio managers who wish to purchase credit exposure. In particular, corporations can purchase credit derivatives referenced to their own debt to hedge their cost of capital.

---

[10] See Bjorn Flesaker, Lane Hughston, Laurence Schreiber, and Lloyd Sprung, "Taking All the Credit," *Risk* (September 1994), pp. 104-108.

Continuing with our example of BB rated bonds, consider a corporate treasurer who, in June 1997, is concerned that over the next six months his firm's borrowing cost will increase beyond the current BB rated credit spread of 215 basis points. Macroeconomic events such as the turmoil that occurred in the worldwide financial markets in October 1997 could (and, in fact, did) widen credit spreads for BB rated debt. Alternatively, the treasurer may expect poor future operating performance for his firm, which may increase the company's credit spread above the average spread of 215 basis points.

To hedge this risk, the treasurer can purchase a 6-month credit spread forward contract at a spread of 215 basis points. If the credit spread for the company's debt widens above 215 basis points, the treasurer will receive a positive payment. However, if the credit spread declines below 215 basis points, the treasurer must make a payment to the credit forward seller.

The exact payment amount at maturity of the credit forward is determined by the following equation:

$$\text{[credit spread at maturity − contracted credit spread]} \times \text{duration} \times \text{notional value} \tag{4}$$

where the credit spread at maturity is the observable market spread at maturity of the credit forward; the contracted credit spread is the spread established at the outset of the forward agreement; the duration is the duration of the referenced credit asset; and notional value is the dollar amount of economic exposure.

Assume that, in fact, the credit spread on the company's BB rated debt increases to 300 basis points over a comparable U.S. Treasury security by December 1997, that the duration of the bonds to be issued is 5, and the amount to be financed is $50 million. At maturity of the credit forward contract, the treasurer will receive:

$$[3\% - 2.15\%] \times 5 \times \$50,000,000 = \$2,125,000$$

However, if the credit spread declined to 200 basis points at maturity of the credit forward, the treasurer must pay:

$$[2.0\% - 2.15\%] \times 5 \times \$50,000,000 = -\$375,000$$

Exhibit 4 demonstrates the payout for a credit forward.

This example of credit forwards highlights an essential difference between all forward and option contracts. The purchaser of a forward contract receives the upside appreciation of the underlying asset, but also shares in its depreciation. In the example above, the treasurer is required to make a payment to the credit forward seller if the credit spread declines in value. In the unlikely event that the credit spread narrowed to zero, the maximum the treasurer would have to pay is $5,375,000. In contrast, the purchase of an option allows the investor to profit from his position, but limits his downside loss to the option premium paid.

Exhibit 4: Credit Forward

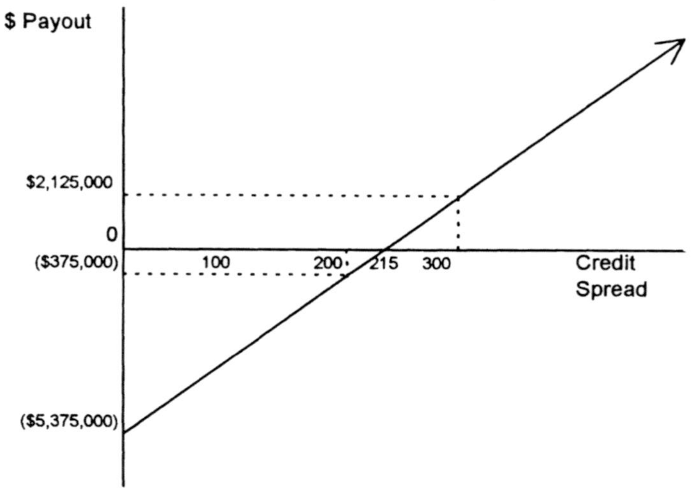

In addition to hedging financing costs, credit forwards are a useful tool to forecast future default premiums. By constructing zero-coupon yield curves for corporate bonds and Treasury securities and subtracting these curves to obtain their difference, it is possible to derive a zero-credit spread curve. From the zero-credit curve it is then a simple matter to derive forward credit spreads.[11]

Deriving forward credit spreads has two important implications. First, these derived spreads represent the market's unbiased expectation regarding future credit spreads. Consequently, they reflect the credit market's best guess as to future default probabilities. Second, implied forward credit spreads can be compared to current market spreads for possible arbitrage opportunities. In fact, existing credit spreads should be priced close to the implied forward credit spreads to limit such arbitrage opportunities. A large discrepancy between implied and existing spreads would reflect a fundamental mispricing of credit risk, and offer an opportunity to profit from credit exposure.

CREDIT SWAPS

Credit swaps come in two flavors: credit default swaps and total return swaps. Credit default swaps are used to shift credit exposure to a credit protection seller. They have a similar economic effect to credit options discussed above. Total return credit swaps are a way to increase an investor's exposure to credit risk and the returns commensurate with that risk.

---

[11] For a demonstration of this process, see Charles Smithson and Hal Holappa, "Credit Derivatives," *Risk* (December 1995), pp. 38-39.

Exhibit 5: Credit Default Swap

Credit Default Swaps

A credit default swap is similar to a credit option in that its primary purpose is to hedge the credit exposure to a referenced asset or issuer. In this sense, credit default swaps operate much like a standby letter of credit. A credit default swap is the simplest form of credit insurance among all credit derivatives.

There are two main types of credit default swaps. In the first type, the credit protection buyer pays a fee to the credit protection seller in return for the right to receive a payment conditional upon the default of a referenced credit. The referenced credit can be a single asset, such as a commercial loan, or a basket of assets, such as a junk bond portfolio. The credit protection buyer continues to receive the total return on the referenced asset. However, should this total return be negative, i.e., the referenced basket of assets has declined in value (either through defaults or downgrades), the total return receiver will receive a payment from the credit protection seller. This type of swap is presented in Exhibit 5.

Mechanically, the contractual documentation for a one period credit default swap will identify the referenced asset, its initial value (V_0), the time to maturity of the swap (T), and a referenced payment rate (R). The payment R may be a single bullet payment or can be a floating-rate benchmarked to LIBOR. At maturity, if the value of the asset has declined, the credit protection buyer receives a payment of $V_0 - V_T$ from the credit protection seller and pays the referenced payment rate R. If the value of the referenced asset has increased in value, the credit protection buyer receives the value $V_T - V_0$ from the underlying asset and pays R. In this simple one period example, the credit default swap acts very much like a credit put option described above. However, for multi-period transactions, there are two differences between a credit default swap and a put option.

First, the credit protection buyer can pay for the protection premium over several settlement dates, t_1 through time T instead of paying an option premium up front. Second, the credit protection buyer can receive payments $V_{t_2} - V_{t_1}$ at intermediate settlement dates where $t_2 \le T$ and $0 \le t_1 < t_2$. Therefore, if the value of the referenced asset continues to deteriorate, the credit protection buyer may receive several payments.

Alternatively, the credit protection buyer can pay the total return on a referenced asset to the credit protection seller in return for receiving a periodic payment. The credit protection buyer keeps the referenced asset on its balance sheet but receives a known payment on the scheduled payment dates for the referenced asset. In return, it pays to the credit protection seller on each cash flow date the total return from the referenced asset. Additionally, depending on how the swap agreement is structured, the credit protection buyer may be reimbursed for the decline in value of the referenced credit. This credit default swap is presented in Exhibit 6.

Default swaps usually contain a minimum threshold or materiality clause requiring that the decline in the referenced credit be significant and confirmed by an objective source. This can be as simple as a credit downgrade by a nationally recognized statistical rating organization or a percentage decline in market value of the asset. Additionally, the payment by the credit protection seller can be set to incorporate a recovery rate on the referenced asset. This value may be determined by the market price of the defaulted asset several months after the actual default.

Large banks are the natural dealers for credit default swaps because it is consistent with their letter of credit business. On the one hand, banks may sell credit default swaps as a natural extension of their credit protection business. Alternatively, a bank may use a credit swap to hedge its exposure to a referenced credit who is a customer of the bank. In this way the bank can limit its exposure to the client without physically transferring the client's loans off its balance sheet. Therefore the bank can protect its exposure without disturbing its relationship with its client.

The methods used to determine the amount of the payment obligated of the credit protection seller under the swap agreement can vary greatly. For instance, a credit default swap can specify at contract date the exact amount of payment that will be made by the swap seller should the referenced credit party default. Conversely, the default swap can be structured so that the amount of the swap payment by the seller is determined after the default event. Under these circumstances, the amount payable by the swap seller is determined based upon the observed prices of similar debt obligations of the borrower in the bond market. Lastly, the swap can be documented much like a credit put option where the amount to be paid by the credit protection seller is an established strike price less the current market value of the referenced asset.

Total Return Credit Swap

A total return credit swap is different from a credit default swap in that the latter is used to hedge a credit exposure while the former is used to increase credit exposure. A total return credit swap transfers all of the economic exposure of a reference asset or a referenced basket of assets to the credit swap purchaser. A total return credit swap includes all cash flows that flow from the referenced assets as well as the capital appreciation or depreciation of those assets. In return for receiving this exposure to an underlying asset, the credit swap purchaser pays a floating rate plus any depreciation of the referenced asset to the credit swap seller.

Exhibit 6: Credit Default Swap

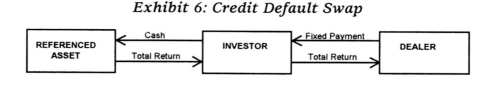

Exhibit 7: Total Return Credit Swaps

If the total return payer owns the underlying referenced assets, it has transferred its economic exposure to the total return receiver. Effectively then, the total return payer has a neutral position which typically will earn LIBOR plus a spread. However, the total return payer has only transferred the economic exposure to the total return receiver; it has not transferred the actual assets. The total return payer must continue to fund the underlying assets at its marginal cost of borrowing or at the opportunity cost of investing elsewhere the capital tied up by the referenced assets.

The underlying asset basket may be composed of any type of referenced credit to which the total return receiver wishes to become exposed. This may include loan participation interests, junk bonds, accounts receivables, or other high-yielding debt. It is usually the case that the total return receiver chooses the exact credit risks to be incorporated into the referenced asset basket.

The total return payer may not initially own the referenced assets before the swap is transacted. Instead, after the swap is negotiated, the total return payer will purchase the referenced assets to hedge its obligations to pay the total return to the total return receiver. In order to purchase the referenced assets, the total return payer must borrow capital. This borrowing cost is factored into the floating rate that the total return receiver must pay to the swap seller. Exhibit 7 diagrams how a total return credit swap works.

In some cases, a total return credit swap is may be transacted through a special purpose entity such as a corporation or a trust. Some counterparties, such as mutual funds, often have restrictions on the type of transactions they may enter. For instance, a mutual fund may be limited by the terms of its prospectus from transacting in swaps. Additionally, under the Internal Revenue Code, income from swap contracts is generally not considered "good income" for tax purposes.[12]

In these circumstances, a trust or a corporation is established as a conduit between the mutual fund and the total return payer where the trust or corporation enters into the credit swap with the total return payer and passes through the credit swap payments to the mutual fund. The trust/corporation accomplishes the pass through by selling private securities to the mutual fund which incorporate the swap payments paid to the trust.[13] Exhibit 8 demonstrates this pass through structure.

---

[12] See Internal Revenue Code, 1986 Code — Subchapter M, Sec. 851(b)(2) (Chicago, IL: Commerce Clearing House, 1993).

[13] These private securities are typically in the form of Securities and Exchange Commission (SEC) Rule 144A securities which are not required to be registered with the SEC but which may be sold only to Qualified Institutional Buyers. See SEC Release No. 33-6862, CCH par. 84,523, April 30, 1990, amended in SEC Release No. 33-6963, CCH par. 85,052, effective October 28, 1992. Additionally, a third-party investor usually invests in the special purpose vehicle (SPV) as an equity investor. This prevents the SPV from being consolidated on the balance sheet of the mutual fund.

Exhibit 8: Leveraged Credit Swap

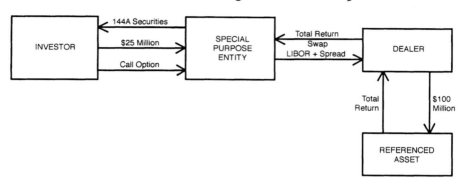

There are several benefits in purchasing a total return credit swap as opposed to purchasing the referenced assets themselves. First, the total return receiver does not have to finance the purchase of the referenced assets itself. Instead, it pays a fee to the total return payer in return for receiving the total return on the referenced assets. In effect, the total return receiver has rented the balance sheet of the total return payer: the referenced assets remain on the balance sheet of the total return payer, but the total return receiver receives the economic exposure to the referenced assets as if they were on its balance sheet.

Second, the total return receiver can achieve the same economic exposure in one swap transaction that would otherwise take several cash market transactions to achieve. In this way a total return swap is much more efficient than the cash market. For example, if a total return receiver wanted to gain exposure to the commercial loan market, it could purchase loan participation interests through various loan syndications. However, it would take several syndication transactions to achieve the same economic exposure that a total return credit swap can offer in one transaction. Furthermore, a total return credit swap can offer a diversified basket of referenced assets.

Third, the total return receiver can take advantage of the natural expertise of the total return payer. Large money-center banks are natural dealers in the total return credit swap market. Their core business is the credit analysis of customers and the lending of money. To the extent the total return receiver is not as experienced in credit analysis as a large money-center bank, it can rely on the bank's expertise to choose appropriate credit risks for the underlying basket of referenced assets.

Fourth, a total return swap can incorporate leverage. Leverage is the ability to achieve a greater economic exposure than capital invested. With a total return credit swap, a total return swap receiver can specify a leverage percentage (e.g., 400%) to increase its exposure to a referenced basket of assets. For instance, a total return payer can contract to receive the total return on a reference basket of

$100 million loan syndication interests, while putting up only $25 million as collateral. In effect, the total return receiver has a leverage factor of 4: it has invested $25 million to receive an economic exposure worth $100 million. However, in order to protect the total return payer, leveraged swaps typically have an embedded call option to unwind the swap before the invested capital is depleted. Exhibit 8 demonstrates the use of swap leverage through a special purpose vehicle.

CREDIT LINKED NOTES

Credit linked notes are hybrid instruments which combine the elements of a debt instrument with either an embedded credit option or credit swap. They are cash market instruments but represent a synthetic high-yield bond, loan participation interest, or credit investment. Credit linked notes may have a maturity of anywhere from three months to several years, with 1 to 3 years being the most likely term of credit exposure. These notes are often issued as 144A private securities and may be issued through special purpose vehicles such as those described above for total return credit swaps. Like credit options, forwards, and swaps, credit linked notes allow an investor to take a tailored view towards credit risk.

Credit linked notes may contain embedded options, embedded forward contracts, or both. Credit linked notes with embedded options can effect a credit view of the investor with respect to declining or improving credit spreads of an underlying referenced credit. For example, an investor may be willing to sell a put option on a credit spread in return for a higher coupon payment on the credit linked note. Under normal market conditions, an investor might expect to receive a coupon of 7% on a "plain vanilla" medium term note. However, if the investor believes that the credit spread on an underlying referenced asset is priced fairly, he can monetize this view by selling a binary put option against the spread and receiving the put premium in the form of a higher coupon paid on the note.

This is demonstrated in Exhibit 9 where the investor buys a note and simultaneously sells to the issuer of the note a binary put option on the credit rating of a referenced BBB creditor and receives 50 basis points of premium. The notional amount of the option is the same as the face value of the note ($10,000,000), and the binary payout is set at 190 basis points — the difference between the BBB and BB average credit spreads.[14] If the BBB rating does not deteriorate, the option will expire out of the money and the option premium will provide incremental coupon income up to 7.50%. However, if the credit rating on the referenced creditor declines to BB, then the short put will expire in the money and the note buyer will receive a lower coupon payment 5.1%.

Credit linked notes with an embedded call option have the advantage of principal protection. At maturity of the note, the noteholder is promised at least a

---

[14] This was the actual credit spread between BBB and BB rated bonds in early November 1997.

return of his principal, or face value, of the note with a chance for additional appreciation if the credit option matures in the money. Credit linked notes with embedded forwards, however, do not have the advantage of principal protection. Depending on the ending value of the embedded credit forward, the noteholder may receive more or less than the face value of the credit note. Credit notes linked to forward contracts, therefore, entail greater risk to the noteholder than credit notes linked to option contracts. The tradeoff for the greater risk is usually in the form of a higher coupon payment.

In practice, the cost of a credit linked note to the investor (in terms of lower coupon payments) can be quite high. Unlike the more common equity linked note, for example, where there is a large options and futures market for equity indices, there is no exchange traded market for credit options. Without a deep, liquid market for credit options, the issuer of the credit linked note may not be able to effectively hedge the credit exposure embedded in the note. The only way for the issuer to accurately hedge its short credit exposure is to buy the underlying referenced asset at its financing cost. This financing cost, in turn, is passed on to the investor in terms of a lower coupon payment.

Just like total return swaps, credit linked notes may contain leverage which can enhance return, but only at the increased risk of loss of principal to the noteholders. For instance, a credit linked note with a leverage factor of 2 will increase in value by 2 basis points for every 1 basis point decline in value of the referenced credit spread. However, if the referenced credit spread increased by 1 basis point by the maturity of the note, the credit investor would receive back only 99.98 of its invested principal.

Exhibit 9: Credit Linked Note with a Short Binary Put Option

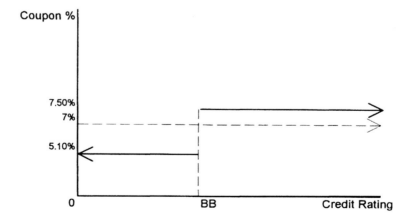

Exhibit 10: Credit Linked Note with an Embedded Forward, an Embedded Short Credit Call, and an Embedded Long Credit Put

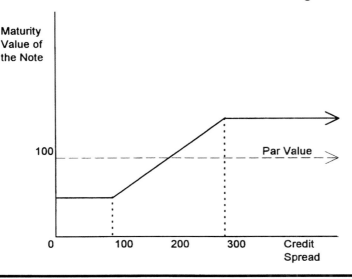

Credit linked notes can become quite complicated, combining both embedded options and embedded forwards. Consider the credit linked note in Exhibit 10 which is short a call option on a referenced credit spread struck at 300 basis points, long a put option on the credit spread struck at 100 basis points, and long a credit spread forward contract priced at a current spread of 200 basis points. If the referenced credit spread remains at 200 basis, the investor will receive the par value of the note at maturity. If the credit spread widens, the credit investor will receive at maturity a payment in excess of the par value. However, the appreciation of the note is capped at a credit spread of 300 basis points by the short credit call option. Conversely, if the referenced credit spread narrows, the principal value of the note returned at maturity will decline. The depreciation of the note is stopped by the long credit put option at a credit spread of 100 basis points.

In Exhibit 10, the long protective credit put option can be financed by the sale of the credit call option. Some upside potential is sacrificed to pay for downside protection. Between the credit spread range of 100 and 300 basis points, the principal value of the note is allowed to fluctuate.

RISKS OF CREDIT DERIVATIVES

The recent history of losses associated with derivative instruments have highlighted their risky nature. Significant losses at Barings, Plc., Orange County, Gibson Greetings, Procter & Gamble, Pier 1 Imports, Daiwa Bank in New York, the

Wisconsin Investment Board, and the Sumitomo Corporation have ushered in a new age of risk consciousness.[15] Although derivatives are essential tools for income enhancement and hedging exposure, there are many risks associated with their use. Below, we highlight those risks most pertinent to credit derivatives.

Credit Risk

Credit risk is defined as the risk to cash flows as a result of an obligor's failure to honor its commitments under a transaction or contractual agreement. Although credit derivatives are designed to effectively hedge the credit risk of a referenced asset, another type of credit risk is introduced through their use: counterparty credit risk. Credit derivatives are not exchange traded; they are transacted in the over-the-counter financial markets as privately negotiated contracts between two parties. Consequently, a purchaser of a credit derivative assumes the credit risk of the seller's performance under the contractual agreement documenting the credit derivative.

Conversely, for the seller of the credit derivative, the primary credit risk is that of the referenced asset. That is, the seller of the credit derivative will be required to make a payment when the credit quality of the referenced asset has deteriorated. The credit derivative seller bears the credit risk of the referenced asset just as if that asset were on its balance sheet instead of the balance sheet of the credit derivative purchaser. However, with respect to a total return credit swap, because the total return may be positive or negative, both the total return receiver and the total return payer have exposure to the referenced asset or issuer.

For the credit derivative purchaser, the credit risk is the same as that for swaps, forwards and other over-the-counter derivative contracts. Therefore, the same type of credit analysis applies as to that of a swap counterparty. Before purchasing a credit derivative, a buyer of credit protection should evaluate the financial condition of the seller of the credit derivative. Additionally, during the term of the credit derivative, the purchaser should continually monitor the financial condition of its counterparty.

For the credit protection buyer to incur a loss, both the referenced asset must suffer a credit deterioration and the credit derivative seller must fail to honor its obligations under the credit derivative agreement. Therefore, the credit derivative purchaser should consider the joint probability distribution of a referenced asset and counterparty default. The best way to minimize this joint probability is

---

[15] See, "Top Managers at Barings Face Fresh Criticism," *The Financial Times Limited* (July 20, 1996), p. 4; "Orange County Seeks Protective Order Vacating Depositions," *Derivatives Litigation Reporter* (April 22, 1996), p. 12; "Gibson Files Lawsuit over Derivatives," *The New York Times* (September 13, 1994), sec. D, p.1; "Procter & Gamble Reaches Accord with Bankers Trust," *Los Angeles Times* (May 10, 1996), part D, p.2; Pier 1 Shareholders Fault Board for $20M Derivatives Loss," *Derivatives Litigation Reporter* (May 27, 1996), p.3; "Lack of Care Costs Funds; Wisconsin Audit Cites 'Excessive Risk' in Derivatives Losses," *Pensions & Investments* (July 24, 1995), p. 32; "Daiwa Debacle Shows Flaws in High-Voltage Finance," *Asahi News Service* (September 29, 1995); "How Copper Lost its Luster for Sumitomo," *The New York Times* (June 15, 1996), p. 31.

to seek sellers of credit protection whose business operations have a low correlation with the potential default cycle of the referenced asset.

For instance, consider an insurance company that wishes to hedge the credit risk associated with a high-yield bond issued by Company Y, an industrial producer of heavy machinery whose bonds are currently rated BB. The seller of the credit derivative is a large money center bank with a large commercial loan department. Under the analysis discussed above, the insurance company should consider the operating cycle of Company Y as compared to that of the bank to determine whether a significant deterioration of Company Y's performance would occur at the same time as a downturn in the bank's performance. Unless the bank has a significant loan portfolio concentrated in the same heavy machinery industry as Company Y, it is unlikely that there is a high correlation between the bank's performance and that of Company Y. Even so, after the purchase of the credit derivative from the bank, the insurance company should continue to monitor the bank's performance for any signs of deterioration in its operations separate and distinct from those of Company Y.

Documentation Risk

Credit derivatives are a relatively new form of financial derivative instrument. Unlike swaps, forwards, and stock options, uniform documentation for credit derivatives does not exist. Although, the International Swap Dealers Association (ISDA) has established standardized documentation which is used by the financial industry to document financial swaps, it has not developed contracts for credit derivatives.[16] Consequently, two dealers offering similar credit derivative transactions, may present different documentation. To the extent that total rate of return swaps and default swaps resemble other swap transactions, ISDA documentation may suffice. However, other credit derivatives such as credit options are typically subject to the individual documentation of the option seller.

For credit linked notes and default swaps, the criteria for default and the manner of calculating cash flows after a default are key issues to define. Without standardized contract forms, each term and definition of the credit derivative must be individually negotiated. Not only is this time consuming and expensive, it can be risky if the contractual terms are not well understood by both parties. Legal counsel for a credit protection buyer must play an integral role before a credit derivative is purchased.

For instance, when conducting a credit swap through a special purpose vehicle such as a trust, the following documentation will need to be negotiated: the trust document, the master swap agreement and supplementary schedule, swap confirmations, a note indenture, and a private placement memorandum. Negotiating these documents is time consuming as well as legally intensive, and considerable expense may be incurred by inside and outside legal counsel.

---

[16] ISDA is currently working on documentation for credit swaps within a Master Schedule. However, standard language is still being developed.

To the extent possible, a buyer of credit derivatives should strive to have the contractual terms consistent across all counterparties. Given the relative newness of these type of derivatives, the best way to ensure consistency is to develop a standard contract form in-house by the credit protection buyer. This will provide a starting point when negotiating the terms of the credit derivative with the dealer community, and subject the buyer less to the individuality of dealer contract forms.

Pricing Risk

Pricing risk is common to all derivative transactions, including credit derivatives. As the derivative markets have matured, the mathematical models used to price derivatives have become more complex. These models are increasingly dependent upon sophisticated assumptions regarding underlying economic parameters. Consequently, the prices of credit derivatives are very sensitive to the assumptions of the models.

Consider, for instance, the pricing of a credit default swap. The credit protection seller receives the total return on a referenced basket of assets in return for paying to the credit protection buyer a floating-interest rate which is reset quarterly. To determine the present value of the credit swap, it is necessary to forecast the forward value of the quarterly credit payments, discount the individual forward values back to the present, and then take the summation of the present values.

However, the large and infrequent nature of credit payments required under a credit swap makes it difficult to accurately forecast the future payment amounts. Furthermore, the credit payments are dependent on a credit downgrade or default, which are discrete events as opposed to a risk neutral appreciation of value under standard forward pricing models.

Pricing models for credit options may involve stochastic strike prices, path dependent barrier options, mean reverting random credit spreads, or compound option modeling. Which model to choose depends on the structure of the transaction and the assumptions of the credit protection buyer and seller. If the term of the option is short and interest rates are assumed to be relatively constant, stochastic strike prices may not be necessary. Alternatively, if the referenced asset has a single coupon payment over the term of the option, path dependent pricing may not be needed. Further, if mean reverting credit spreads are used, their correlation with the term structure must be determined. Finally, compound option pricing is only practical with European options — those exercisable at maturity.[17]

Given the relative immaturity of the credit derivative market, price discovery is one of the key issues facing credit derivatives. The complexity of the option models discussed above indicates that very sophisticated proprietary models must be used to properly value credit derivatives. However, until consistent valuation technology is developed, credit derivative purchasers must rely on the pricing of the credit dealer. The lack of uniform technology makes the pricing of credit derivatives less transparent and increases the pricing risk.

---

[17] For a more detailed discussion on pricing credit derivatives, see the bibliography provided in footnote 8.

The complexity of pricing credit derivatives is compounded by the difficulty in hedging such transactions. Consider a default swap where the seller of the credit default swap will most likely make infrequent, but large, payments. The lack of continuity in payments, and the large, random cash outflows are in direct contrast to other financial derivatives, such as forwards and options, which have a continuous pricing function. The lack of a continuous pricing function makes it difficult to find an effective hedge which will match both the infrequent nature, and the size, of the cash outflows which the seller of the default swap must make under the credit derivative agreement. Yet a well developed derivative market depends on the ability to offset the risk of the derivative instruments. Without this hedging ability, a risk neutral position cannot be established which is a fundamental element in determining derivative prices.

Liquidity Risk

Currently, there are no exchange traded credit derivatives. Instead, they are traded over-the- counter as customized transactions designed to hedge or expose a specific risk for the credit derivative buyer. The very nature of this customization makes credit derivatives illiquid. Credit derivatives will not suit all parties in the financial market and therefore a party to a tailored credit derivative contract may be unable to obtain a "fair value" should he wish to exit his position before maturity.

Furthermore, with a relatively new market for credit derivatives, the dealer market for transacting in these instruments is still thin. Consequently, participants in this market may find it difficult to price transactions and to hedge cash flow exposures in an efficient manner. As a result, credit derivative participants may find themselves more vulnerable to a higher volatility of cash flows than other more developed derivative instruments. This is all the more compounded by the lack of an exchange traded product.

Lack of marketability, or liquidity risk, is hard to quantify. One way to manage this risk would be to take a "haircut" from the model or quoted price of the credit derivative. This haircutted price would incorporate the cost to the credit derivative seller to liquidate the credit derivative (or to repurchase it from the credit derivative buyer) before its maturity, as well as the cost of unwinding the seller's hedge position for the derivative instrument. Consequently, a "fair exit price" may be a more accurate reflection of the true market value of the credit derivative rather than a theoretical or model value.

Regulatory Risk

With the relative youth of credit derivatives, regulators have not had time to formulate policies with respect to these instruments. Currently, banking regulations require a bank that hedges a loan via a credit swap to reserve capital against both the loan and the swap contract, rather than netting the two positions. However, bank regulators are beginning to address the issue of capital requirements for credit derivatives.

For instance, the Office of the Comptroller of the Currency (OCC) recently noted that national banks must ensure that credit derivatives are incorporated into their risk-based capital computations.[18] However, over the near term, the OCC has decided that risk-based capital calculations for credit derivatives will be determined on a case-by-case basis through a review of the specific characteristics of each transaction. Absent further guidance, it is up to the banks to determine whether the credit derivative resembles more, for instance, a standby letter of credit or an interest rate linked instrument in computing their capital requirements. There is a risk that inconsistent capital treatment for these derivatives may result in over exposed financial institutions with insufficient capital to cover potential defaults.

A similar lack of guidance exists with respect to risk-based capital requirements for federally chartered banks. According to the Federal Reserve Board of Governors, if a bank provides an unrestricted credit derivative to protect an entity from a credit default of a referenced asset or issuer, the bank must take a full capital charge based on the creditworthiness of the referenced asset or issuer.[19] However, if the bank provides a restrictive credit derivative such that the transfer of credit risk to the bank is limited, then the bank is directed to hold only "appropriate capital" while it is exposed to the credit risk of the referenced asset. What capital allocation constitutes an appropriate amount is left to the bank's discretion.

CONCLUSION

Credit derivatives are a relatively new addition to the financial markets. They provide an additional filter by which portfolio managers may isolate, price, and trade the fundamental credit risk associated with a fixed income investment. Consequently, credit derivatives offer an efficient way to gain, or hedge, exposure to the credit markets through options, forwards, swaps or credit linked notes. However, credit derivatives are not without risks. The relative infancy of the market raises issues of pricing, liquidity, documentation, and regulation. Until these transactions become more uniform, participants in the high-yield and credit markets should use proper risk due diligence before entering into a credit derivative transaction.

---

[18] See, Comptroller of the Currency, Release OCC NR 96-84, August 12, 1996.
[19] See, Board of Governors of the Federal Reserve System, Division of Banking Supervision and Regulation, SR 96-17, August 12, 1996.

Chapter 9

Catastrophe-Linked Securities

Sunita Ganapati
Associate
Lehman Brothers

Mark Retik
Associate
Lehman Brothers

Paul Puleo
Senior Vice President
Lehman Brothers

Beth Starr
Senior Vice President
Lehman Brothers

INTRODUCTION

Catastrophe-linked securities (CLS), an emerging class of structured insurance risk products, offer returns that are linked to the occurrence of catastrophic events such as earthquakes and hurricanes. These securities can provide investors with diversification from corporate and asset-backed securities at comparable or wider spreads. Issued through special-purpose vehicles, these securities offer an opportunity to participate directly in catastrophe risk without having to assume the operational risks inherent in securities issued by property and casualty insurance and reinsurance companies that underwrite this risk. Investing in "pure" catastrophe risk can also improve the risk/return profile of a diversified portfolio of assets because this risk is generally uncorrelated with the systematic risks present in other securities markets.

   An outgrowth of the need for additional reinsurance capacity following Hurricane Andrew (1992) and the Northridge Earthquake (1994), which in combination produced $29 billion in industrywide insured losses,[1] CLS provide insurers with a new form of reinsurance protection. In exchange for a reinsurance premium (i.e., interest on the securities), investors assume financial exposure to the risk that a catastrophe will strike and will generate insured losses above a certain

---

[1] A.M. Best.

level. If such a catastrophe occurs, CLS investors would receive a reduced yield and/or lose part or all of their principal, and the insurer would receive a reinsurance claim payment. By transferring catastrophe risks to the capital markets in this manner, insurance companies are supplementing their use of traditional reinsurance and internal loss management mechanisms to reduce volatility in their financial statements and preserve overall liquidity.

As the CLS market develops, we believe that spreads will tighten considerably, similar to the way corporate high yield spreads have responded as that market has matured. Tightening will result as liquidity increases in the market and CLS investors become increasingly sophisticated at valuing catastrophe risk.

In this chapter, we discuss catastrophes and the role that reinsurance has traditionally played in mitigating catastrophic losses. We describe developments in the capital markets that have led to catastrophe risk securitization and outline typical CLS structures. We then discuss the use of simulation models to conduct CLS analysis and consider related rating agency approaches. Finally, we provide a framework for assessing relative valuation and offer our outlook for this emerging asset class.

CATASTROPHE RISK MANAGEMENT

Economic Impact of Catastrophes

Catastrophes are low probability natural events that cause widespread property damage; they include earthquakes, hurricanes, hailstorms, and floods. (Appendix A provides a description of earthquakes and hurricanes, the two types of catastrophes that have historically caused the most insured losses.) Though the timing of a catastrophe is inherently unpredictable, the insurance industry uses sophisticated mathematical models to estimate the probability of occurrence of an event and expected losses.

Insured losses from catastrophes have been increasing since 1970 (see Exhibit 1), coinciding with population migration toward high-risk coastal regions during the same period. From 1970 to 1990, population in the Pacific and South Atlantic coastal states increased by 51% and 45%, respectively, far more than the countrywide increase of 24% over the same period.[2] This population shift has increased the demand for insured dwellings in these areas and consequently has increased the potential for insured loss.

After Hurricane Andrew in 1992, the insurance industry took various measures to counter increased exposure to losses. Major U.S. personal lines insurers attempted to reduce their risk concentration by limiting issuance of new policies in high risk areas. Additional measures included increases in policy premiums and deductibles. Insurers also sought to hedge their balance sheets and earnings against catastrophes by increasing coverage from traditional reinsurance and exploring other financial alternatives, particularly for low probability, high severity events.

---

[2] *Statistical Abstract of the U.S.*, 1992, National Data Book.

Exhibit 1: Industrywide Insured Issues, 1970-1996

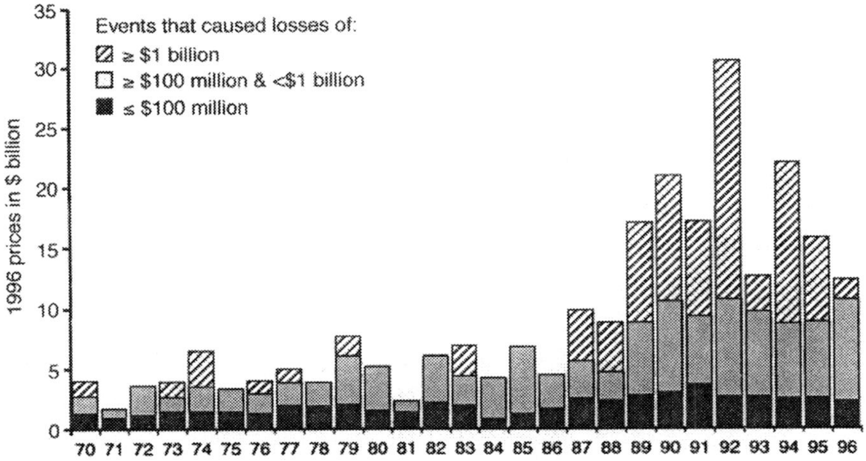

Source: Swiss Re, sigma no. 3/1997.

Exhibit 2: Key Reinsurance Terms

Excess-of-loss contracts cover against losses over an *attachment point*, up to a predetermined limit. For example, a reinsurance contract with an attachment point of $100 million and a limit of $150 million covers the insurance company for the first $50 million of losses in excess of $100 million.

Quota-share or pro-rata contracts provide coverage against a predetermined percent of catastrophic losses. Under this type of agreement, the reinsurer assumes a percentage of the insurance company's premiums and losses.

Retention is the amount of losses for which the primary insurer is responsible — $100 million in the preceding example.

Exposure is the amount ceded to the reinsurer — $50 million in the preceding example.

Rate-on-line is the premium paid by the insurer to purchase reinsurance as a percentage of the exposure.

Traditional Reinsurance

Reinsurance gives an insurer the ability to transfer risk with the primary purpose of either smoothing its income stream or protecting its balance sheet. Catastrophe management is an essential component of a reinsurance program for large property insurers. Risk can be transferred in one of two ways — excess-of-loss reinsurance and quota-share or pro rata reinsurance. Exhibit 2 provides a summary of key reinsurance terms. Catastrophe reinsurance is typically written on an excess-of-loss basis.

Exhibit 3: Paragon Catastrophe Price Index, 1984-July 1996

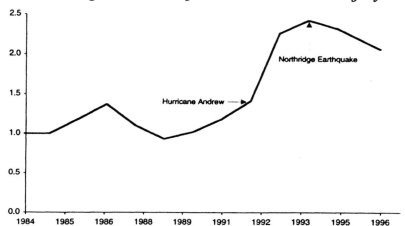

Note: The Paragon Catastrophe Price Index reflects reinsurance premiums of 300 companies and includes an estimated 60% of insurance industry premiums.

After Hurricane Andrew, reinsurance companies changed the structure of contracts by raising their attachment points, and capping their aggregate exposures, thus reducing the overall amount of coverage provided. At the same time, insurers were seeking increased reinsurance coverage. This raised reinsurance pricing above historical levels in the early 1990s as shown by the Paragon Catastrophe Price Index (see Exhibit 3). However, reinsurance premiums have been falling since 1994 with the additional capacity injected by Bermuda reinsurers (see Appendix B for a discussion of Bermuda reinsurers) and the re-entry of Lloyd's syndicates into the reinsurance market. Further, no single catastrophe has caused extraordinary losses (such as Hurricane Andrew or the Northridge earthquake) since 1994. However, initial indications are that reinsurance capacity today is still inadequate to meet potential losses from large catastrophes; the shortfall in reinsurance is estimated at $30-$50 billion for an event that causes $60-$80 billion[3] in insured losses. As a result, many insurance companies need to supplement the capacity of the current reinsurance market with the capacity potentially available in the capital markets (the estimated size of the fixed income markets is $10 trillion[4]).

Catastrophe Risk Layers

Catastrophe risk can be viewed as composed of layers of risk from events with decreasing probability of occurrence and increasing magnitude of losses. Sophisticated modeling efforts have shown that catastrophic events occur in random intervals of time and less severe catastrophes occur with more frequency. Risk

---

[3] Lehman Brothers estimate.

[4] Estimate based on market value of the Lehman Brothers Global Family of Indices.

management of catastrophe losses varies from one insurer to another. Exhibit 4 shows a probability distribution of insured losses and the sources of risk capital that an insurer may use to manage its catastrophe exposure.

Catastrophes resulting in gross insured losses of less than 5% of a major property insurer's statutory surplus, occur frequently and are assumed to be part of the normal course of business. Losses from these events are absorbed by an insurer's operating cash flow, policyholders' surplus, or "working layer" reinsurance program. Events that cause losses between 5% and 10% of surplus are generally covered by purchasing traditional reinsurance contracts.

As insurers have increased use of advanced catastrophe modeling to predict losses, they have tended to purchase coverage equal to their probable loss under a severe loss scenario or, at a minimum, for losses in excess of 10% of their capital. However, large insurers find that protecting their balance sheet against an infrequent but large catastrophe is currently priced too high due to lack of capacity in the reinsurance industry for covering this type of risk. Hence, insurers are seeking capital market solutions to bridge this gap in capacity and to create a more efficient risk transfer mechanism.

RECENT CAPITAL MARKETS DEVELOPMENTS

As insurers explore alternative solutions for gaining additional reinsurance coverage, they have participated in several creative capital market developments including government initiatives, exchange-traded derivatives, and CLS.

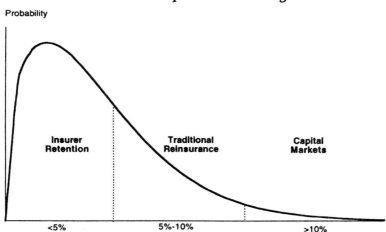

Exhibit 4: An Illustration of
Insurer Catastrophe Risk Management

Government Initiatives

In response to reduced property insurance availability after Hurricane Andrew, the U.S. and state governments created various funds to provide additional capacity in the event of a catastrophe. These include the Florida Hurricane Catastrophe Fund, the California Earthquake Authority, the Hawaii Hurricane Relief Fund, and others. These funds are set up to access the capital markets immediately after an event to provide additional funding either directly to homeowners or to insurance companies.

The California Earthquake Authority (CEA) is the largest of these funds, providing up to $12.5 billion of support to insurers in California. The program was designed to include a combination of letter of credit facilities, reinsurance policies directly from reinsurers, and the capital markets. In 1996 the CEA attempted to issue a catastrophe-linked security similar to the structure described in more detail below for an additional $1.5 billion of coverage in excess of $7 billion. Because of the high pricing of that issue relative to prevailing reinsurance rates, Berkshire Hathaway's reinsurance subsidiary purchased the entire transaction.

The Florida Hurricane Catastrophe Fund provides reinsurance capacity to all primary insurers writing homeowner policies in Florida. The fund collects annual premiums from these insurers and holds these payments for future claims. The fund intends to meet any additional capacity requirements following an event by raising capital in the fixed income markets. A bond issue after a substantial hurricane would be paid entirely by assessing surcharges on the primary insurers in Florida.

The Hawaii Hurricane Relief Fund took yet another approach. Because its funding needs are smaller than those of other states, it relies on a letter of credit syndicated through various commercial banks. This fund assesses homeowners directly, instead of assessing primary insurers as in Florida, and uses the assessments to repay any future draws on the letter of credit.

These special funds are expected to provide incremental capacity to the property-casualty industry and potentially bridge part of the gap in reinsurance supply.

Exchange-Traded Options and Swap Contracts

The introduction of exchange-traded catastrophe risk contracts in 1995 marked the entry of insurance risk products into the capital markets. Derivative contracts are offered on the Chicago Board of Trade (CBOT), Catex, and Bermuda Commodities Exchange. A description of the contracts appears in Appendix C.

These developments are meaningful steps in achieving incremental risk transfer for reinsurance, but the exchanges have so far met with limited success. Although trading volumes at the CBOT have grown over the last year, the total value of catastrophe exposure that has been hedged since the beginning of 1996 is estimated at only $40 million.[5] Trading on the Catex has been thin and the Bermuda

---

[5] Chicago Board of Trade.

Commodities Exchange was launched in November 1997. Lack of liquidity in the market, relatively small transaction size, and concerns about basis risk[6] have deterred insurance companies and potential investors from entering the market. These exchanges could develop into reasonable ways to supplement reinsurance if investors outside the insurance and reinsurance industry begin to participate.

Securitization of Catastrophe Risk

Securitizing insurance risk is the transfer or sale in the form of an investment security, of part of the underwriting risks associated with a group of insurance policies. Insurance companies expect that securitizing insurance risk will play a significant role in meeting the shortage in reinsurance capacity. Investing in CLS is akin to issuing a reinsurance contract where the investor covers the insurer for a fixed amount of losses over a specified value (the attachment point or trigger). Several issues of catastrophe-linked securities have been marketed in 1997, and approximately six issues have been placed in the private markets.

As with any new capital market product, structures are still evolving. The transactions that have been placed have had varying structures and have covered catastrophe and other types of insurance risk. Exhibit 5 provides a list of transactions.

STRUCTURE OF CATASTROPHE-LINKED SECURITIES

Catastrophe-linked securities are issued for an expected maturity with the payment of coupon and retirement of principal dependent on occurrence of a catastrophic event with losses greater than a specified trigger during a defined risk or loss-occurrence period. As in other asset-backed transactions, the issuer sets up a special purpose vehicle (SPV) that is bankruptcy remote. The vehicle is generally set up offshore for regulatory and tax reasons and issues securities that carry the risk of catastrophe losses over a specified level. It then issues a back-to-back reinsurance contract to the insurer, thus providing the reinsurance protection.

Exhibit 5: Transactions as of February 1998

Issuer/Sponsor	Deal Size	Securitized Risks
USAA Residential Re	$477 million	U.S. eastern seaboard hurricane risk
Hannover Re	$125 million	Various U.S., European, Japanese, Australian, and Canadian perils
Swiss Re	$137 million	California earthquake risk
Winterthur	$290 million	Weather-related automobile claims in Switzerland
St. Paul Re	$70 million	Various insurance risks in revolving facility

---

[6] Basis risk is the risk of exposure differences between the value of losses estimated by the underlying index such as the Property Claims Services index and the value of loss claims from the insurer's book of policies.

The security, like reinsurance, can be structured as a quota-share or an excess-of-loss issue. In the quota-share structure, the issuer shares with investors a fixed percentage of losses over the attachment point. A recently placed issue by Hannover Re was structured so that the risk of losses and ultimate returns on the company's entire portfolio over a predefined level was shared proportionately by investors and the issuer. In an excess-of-loss structure, investors absorb losses over the attachment point for the total amount of the issue (equivalent to exposure amount in a reinsurance contract). Such a structure was used in the USAA Residential Re transaction. By issuing a security with an excess-of-loss structure and retaining a portion of the security, issuers can also create hybrid structures.

The underlying catastrophe can either be one type of event, such as earthquakes as in the CEA deal, or a mix of events, as in the Hannover Re deal, which involved seven types of risk. Risks can be spread across geographic region, type of event, or underlying property type (residential, commercial, industrial, etc.). Only events that occur prior to the end of the specified loss occurrence period and result in losses in excess of the attachment point are considered loss events for the securities. Underlying losses in any specific transaction can be based either on the insurer's book of policies or on a basket of risks as measured, for example, by the PCS index.[7]

The SPV invests cash raised from the issue in high quality, liquid, fixed income instruments (typically U.S. Treasuries or AAA rated securities). This short-term portfolio is used to cover losses from events or to repay investors on maturity of the bond, and to provide a minimum rate of return (e.g., LIBOR, Treasury bill). The contract is structured like a cash-collateralized reinsurance contract, and unlike traditional reinsurance contracts, does not carry any credit risk of the reinsurer. The coupon on the CLS includes a spread over the minimum rate earned by the short-term portfolio. The insurer pays the spread to the SPV, which passes through the total coupon payment to investors (see Exhibit 6).

The maturity of the security is based on the period during which a loss event can occur, called the risk period (or the loss occurrence period), and the time for computation of losses, called the *development period*. The development period may be up to one year, during which time the company receives final claims, surveys its policyholders' properties and determines total damage claims. Typically, loss estimates 2 to 3 months after the catastrophe give an indication of whether losses from the event have exceeded the trigger. However, the actual amount of losses is determined after the development period (i.e., after final claims are received). The CLS may be structured with a fixed maturity after the end of the specified loss occurrence period that includes an estimated development period, or may have a scheduled maturity date that can be extended for a maximum period equal to the development period, thus exposing investors to some extension risk.

---

[7] The PCS index is described in Appendix C.

Exhibit 6: Illustrative CLS Structure

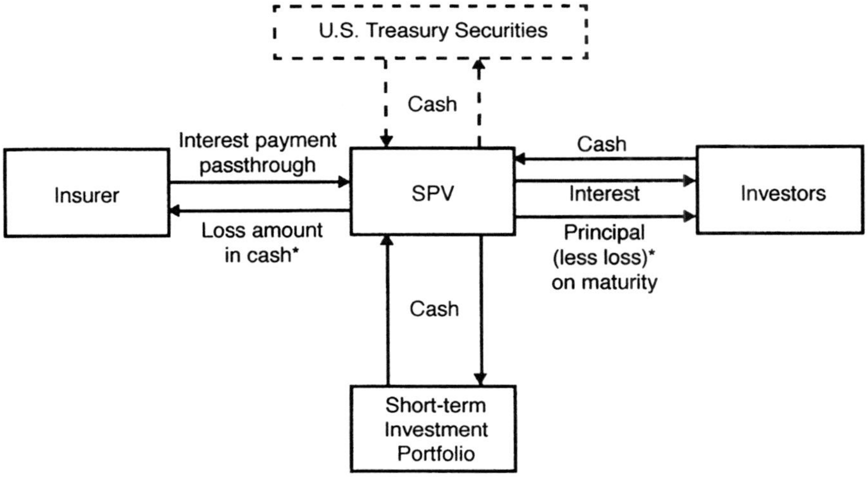

* In case of loss trigger.

To attract a wider investor base, some structures provide protection of principal, with only coupon at risk. This is accomplished by establishing a structural feature (as detailed in the dashed box in Exhibit 6) which provides the investor with U.S. Treasury STRIPS with a par value equal to the principal value of the CLS, upon occurrence of a qualifying catastrophe. The USAA Residential Re transaction included such a principal-protected structure. Since principal for these securities is backed by U.S. Treasuries, these securities will generally be rated higher than CLS with principal at risk. Nevertheless, investors face the risk of earning little or no yield for the remaining period of the STRIPS. A related structure which has been considered involves swapping U.S. Treasury securities held by the SPV for surplus notes or equity of the insurer upon occurrence of a qualifying catastrophe.

SIMULATION MODELING OF CATASTROPHE-LINKED SECURITIES

Evaluating principal-at-risk catastrophe-linked securities is conceptually similar to evaluating other fixed income securities with a material risk of default, such as corporates or subordinated ABS. Estimating the performance of a particular security requires assessing the likelihood of default, and the loss of principal and interest associated with such a default. Default risk on a corporate bond is assessed by examining historical corporate default probabilities, industry- and issuer-specific credit considerations, and the security's relative position in the issuer's capital structure. Default risk on most asset-backed securities (such as those backed by credit card receivables, auto loans, etc.) is based on an actuarial analysis of a large pool of receivables.

Default on a catastrophe-linked security, on the other hand, is generally triggered by a catastrophe of sufficient magnitude to cause a specified level of losses on insured properties. To assess the default risk, it is necessary to estimate the likelihood and intensity of catastrophic events, the susceptibility of insured properties to the effects of these events, the insurance policies in effect, and the specific terms of the transaction. Each factor contributes uniquely to the default risk of the security.

Over the past decade, specialized catastrophe models have been developed to assist insurance and reinsurance companies and intermediaries in analyzing catastrophe exposures and in pricing insurance policies.[8] Virtually all reinsurers rely on one or more of these models to guide underwriting decisions.[9] In recent years, these models have been refined to assist in evaluating the prospect for default on catastrophe-linked securities. Since historical information on hurricanes and earthquakes alone is insufficient to estimate the current catastrophe loss potential (based on the relative infrequency of these events), these models use an alternative approach based on sophisticated simulation techniques. This approach simulates catastrophic events in terms of their constituent meteorological or seismic characteristics and determines the impact of these events on insured properties. Engineering and actuarial analyses are then used to estimate the level of catastrophe-related losses — expressed as a probability distribution — on each individual insured property for a given period of time. Running a large number of simulations ensures that the probability distribution of catastrophe losses will converge to a stable, representative distribution and therefore produce statistically robust results.

Modeling companies employ various methodologies to estimate catastrophe loss distributions, and techniques to estimate hurricanes are distinct from those used for earthquakes. However, a common set of elements is incorporated in all the models. Exhibit 7 shows how the parts of a catastrophe model fit together. We describe each part, discuss the resulting catastrophe loss distribution, and explore how these tools can assist investors in making prudent investment decisions.

Catastrophe Likelihood Model

The likelihood that a catastrophe will strike during the term of the catastrophe-linked security will directly affect the ultimate probability of security default (if a catastrophe does not occur then principal and interest will be fully preserved). The first step in the catastrophe model is to predict the likelihood of zero, one, or more catastrophes occurring in a given year. Historical data on catastrophe frequency, coupled with statistical smoothing techniques, are used to select an appropriate probability distribution and estimate its parameters. Most modeling companies use either Poisson or negative binomial distributions to estimate hurricane frequency. Exhibit 8 shows a sample distribution of annual hurricane occurrences for all categories of hurricane severity.

---

[8] Some of the specialized catastrophe modeling firms include Applied Insurance Research, Equecat, Impact Forecasting, Risk Management Solutions, and Tillinghast/Towers Perrin.

[9] One important implication of the widespread use of catastrophe models is that pricing of the debt and equity securities issued by insurers and reinsurers implicitly reflects the results of these models.

Exhibit 7: Catastrophe Model Schematic

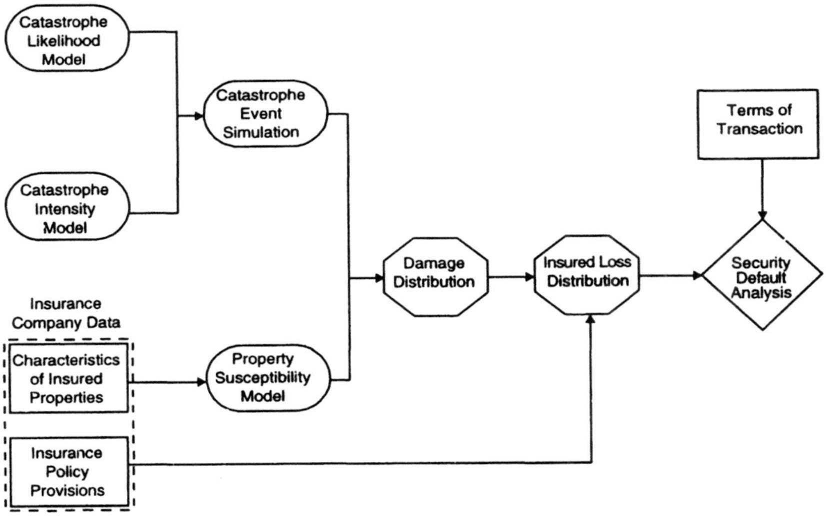

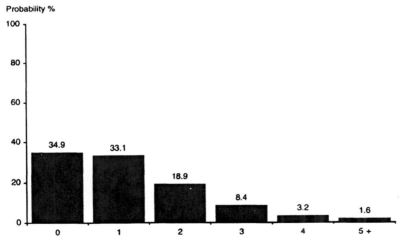

Exhibit 8: Sample Probability Distribution of Annual Number of Hurricane Occurrences
All Hurricane Strength Categories

Note: This distribution of annual hurricane occurrences is depicted using a negative binomial distribution (with parameters s= 5 and p = 0.81).

Catastrophe Intensity Model

The catastrophe intensity model predicts an event's potential for damage. Similar to catastrophe likelihood, catastrophe intensity is estimated using a probabilistic approach. The model uses separate probability distributions for location of initial catastrophe strike, movement following initial strike, dispersion, length of time until dissipation, and level of severity at each location. These probability distributions explicitly account for virtually all potential catastrophe scenarios, setting parameters using complete historical seismic and meteorological data provided by the U.S. National Weather Service, National Hurricane Center, U.S. Geological Survey, and other industry groups. This simulation-driven technique generates "weighted average" probability distributions for each salient catastrophe attribute and, collectively, produces a robust, comprehensive catastrophe profile.

For hurricanes, the attributes estimated in the intensity model include landfall location, central pressure along path, radius of maximum winds, forward velocity along path, track angle, maximum over-water wind speed, and adjustments due to surface friction. Severity at any point along the hurricane's path is generally measured in terms of central pressure or, equivalently, wind speed. These measures can be translated into escalating category values 1 through 5 on the Saffir-Simpson hurricane intensity scale, the meteorological industry standard (see Appendix A).

In earthquake intensity models, the key attributes affecting intensity include regional seismicity, regional geology, attenuation of seismic energy, local soil conditions, and potential hazards including landslide, liquefaction, and fire. Quake intensity at each site is rated 1 to 12 on the Modified Mercalli Intensity scale (see Appendix A).

Catastrophe Event Simulation

Catastrophe likelihood and intensity profiles in combination fully characterize annual catastrophic event activity. Melding the output from the likelihood and intensity models permits a complete catastrophe event simulation. Typically, at least several thousand years of catastrophic event activity are simulated to enhance the statistical significance of results.

Property Susceptibility Model

The specific residential and commercial properties covered by CLS have varying levels of susceptibility to catastrophe. To the extent that properties are more resilient, catastrophe-related damages will be mitigated. Damages will also be lessened if properties are located at sufficient distances from catastrophe-prone areas. The property-specific attributes determine vulnerability. In the property susceptibility model, insurance company data on the attributes of insured properties are combined with engineering analysis to define relationships between catastrophe severity and damage for insured properties. Key to the robustness of the property susceptibility model is the calculation of separate damage ratios for each insured property covered by the transaction. These relationships are typically expressed as a damage ratio, which is the percentage of the property value that is damaged for a given level of catastrophe intensity. This analysis is necessarily conducted separately for each construction class (e.g., wood frame, masonry, etc.) and for different building code specifications.

Damage Distribution

The results from the catastrophe event simulation and property susceptibility models are then linked to produce a probability distribution of annual catastrophe-related damages. This distribution represents the probability that, given the annual frequency and intensity of catastrophes and the vulnerability of properties to catastrophe-related events, damages on a particular property will equal a certain amount over the course of one year.

Insured Loss Distribution

Once the damage distribution has been computed, the insurance policy provisions in place on each property covered under the transaction are then superimposed to determine a distribution of insured losses. Insured losses on a property are almost always less than total damages on the property due to policy requirements that limit claim payments in the event of a catastrophe. Policy deductibles and depreciated cost provisions are two examples of such limitations. Properties carrying full replacement cost policy riders, on the other hand, will have insured loss distributions that more closely approach their associated damage distributions. Individual insured loss distributions on each property are then summed to arrive at an aggregate insured loss distribution on the whole block of insured properties.

Security Default Analysis

Investors can use the aggregate insured loss distribution in conjunction with the specific terms of the transaction to ascertain the probability of default on the catastrophe-linked security in question. For transactions structured as excess-of-loss reinsurance arrangements, the annual probability of security default will equal the annual probability that insured losses exceed the attachment point. This number — frequently referred to as the annual probability of exceedance — is the area under the insured loss distribution curve to the right of the attachment point value (see Exhibit 9). This statistic can be compared to default probabilities on other securities to draw conclusions on relative creditworthiness.

The insured loss distribution can be used to derive other statistics that are helpful to investors. Examples are the expected annual losses, expected recovery rate, maximum likelihood amount of annual losses, 99% confidence interval of annual losses, and number of years on average between which losses of a certain magnitude are expected to occur (the so-called return period). This information can assist investors in assessing the risk associated with particular catastrophe-linked securities.

Exhibit 9: Sample Probability of Default on an Excess-of-Loss Catastrophe-Linked Security

Probability

Prob[Security Default] = Prob[Annual Insured Losses > X]

Attachment Point

Annual Insured Losses   X

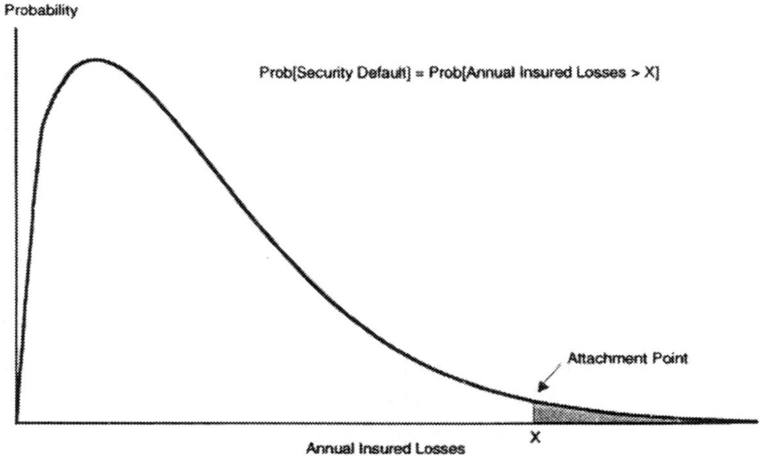

RATING AGENCY CONSIDERATIONS

The four major rating agencies have all developed criteria for rating catastrophe-linked securities and are furnishing ratings on transactions. At present, the methodology used by each agency is similar — though each is being continually refined, reflecting the relative newness and prospect for growth of this asset class.[10] The approaches used to rate principal-at-risk and principal-protected catastrophe-linked securities are different.

Principal-at-Risk Securities

The agencies rate principal-at-risk catastrophe-linked securities to reflect loss and timing risks to both principal and interest. Because this approach is also used to rate corporate credits and ABS structures, it is possible to draw conclusions on relative creditworthiness between these securities and catastrophe-linked securities based on ratings.

In analyzing principal-at-risk securities, the rating agencies consider structural and insurance risks. The structural analysis is essentially the same as the analysis used to rate any structured security, and is identical to the approach

---

[10] This section is based on discussions with analysts at S&P and Moody's, along with publications on catastrophe-linked security rating approaches from S&P ("Behind the Ratings — Structured Finance Alternative to Reinsurance," *Standard & Poor's CreditWeek*, November 13, 1996), Fitch (Structured Finance and Catastrophic Risk, *Fitch Financial Institutions Special Report*, February 3, 1997), and DCR (*DCR's Approach to Rating Catastrophe Bonds*, Duff & Phelps Credit Rating Co., January 1997).

used to rate principal-protected catastrophe-linked securities (discussed below). This analysis focuses on the transaction's legal structure, the quality of collateral, the bankruptcy-remote status of the SPV issuer, the flow of funds, and the market, counterparty and legal risks inherent in the transaction.

Although structural risk is an important element in the rating methodology, the key risk that the rating agencies analyze is insurance risk. Principal-at-risk catastrophe-linked securities are subject to the risk that insured losses on properties related to the specific transaction will exceed some attachment point (for an excess-of-loss type of reinsurance structure, for example).

The rating agencies rely on the results of simulation-driven catastrophe models to assign their ratings. However, the agencies first validate the analytic integrity of the model and test the quality of the insurance company data used by the model.

These "stress tests" are conducted through a due diligence process. This process typically involves assessing the appropriateness of the probability distributions employed by the model to simulate catastrophe frequency and intensity. Both the underlying density functions and parameters are considered. Occasionally, a rating agency will request a modification of the probability distribution to generate more conservative results (e.g., it might ask to recalculate the insured loss distribution using twice the assumed catastrophe frequency).

In addition, property damage vulnerability relationships are examined. Vulnerability functions are considered for each property characteristic (e.g., construction type, elevation, building usage, etc.) using engineering and actuarial analysis. In all cases, consistency with published industry and academic literature is tested. Some rating agencies retain the services of outside meteorological or seismic experts to assist in evaluating the model.

The insurance company data used by the model are reviewed by the rating agencies for accuracy. These data include both the book of insured properties and the policy provisions in place on each property. Conservative adjustments are made to account for incomplete data in each case.

Finally, certain indirect factors are sometimes also accounted for in the rating analysis. These include demand surge (the effect of a catastrophe on local equilibrium prices for building materials and wages), growth and change of mix in the insured book of business over the course of the security's term, and the insurance company's claims handling and loss management/settlement procedures.

Principal-Protected Securities

The approach used to rate principal-protected catastrophe-linked securities is consistent with the approach for other structured securities that offer principal protection. The rating agencies traditionally provide ratings for certain structured securities that reflect the loss and timing risks associated with default on principal only. That is, the risk that interest is not paid on a timely basis is not explicitly taken into account in the rating.[11] As a result, the approach that rating agencies are taking on principal-protected catastrophe-linked securities is to rate only the principal component. The rating assigned will reflect the quality of the underlying collateral that is providing the principal protection. For this reason, structures supported by U.S. Treasuries or STRIPS are expected be rated AAA. On the other hand, if the issuing insurer's surplus notes are providing the principal protection, then the structure is expected to be assigned the rating on the surplus notes. This is consistent with the rating agencies' "look-through" approach to rating all principal-protected structured transactions.

RELATIVE VALUE

Framework for Pricing

Catastrophe-linked securities are expected to trade at a significant spread over Treasuries. This spread has two components: the base spread and the risk premium. The base spread reflects the minimum spread an investor should require on CLS to break even relative to an investment in comparable maturity risk-free assets (i.e., U.S. Treasuries). This component accounts for the expected loss of principal and interest on CLS. The second component, the risk premium, represents compensation for the uncertainty of estimated losses on CLS and the fact that it is a new asset class. Another way of viewing the risk premium is as the additional return investors should receive for researching the catastrophe risk associated with these securities (in the same way as investors are compensated for research on other ABS).

The CLS base spread can be computed, using the insured loss distribution for the transaction, as the annual probability of exceedance (as defined above) multiplied by one minus the expected recovery rate. The recovery rate on CLS reflects the percentage of principal recovered in the event of default. This rate will depend on the magnitude of insured losses from the catastrophe and can range from 0% (insured losses exceed total value of issued securities) to 100% (insured losses less than or equal to attachment point). The CLS risk premium can then be calculated as the offered spread on the security minus the base spread.

Spreads on corporate bonds can be similarly decomposed. The base spread on a corporate reflects the probability of default times one minus the expected recovery rate, and the risk premium is the offered spread in excess of the base spread. Exhibit 10 shows corporate 1-year default rates and indicative spreads. The default rates reflect historical corporate defaults between 1970-1996 based on a recent Moody's study, and can serve as an estimate of the future probability of corporate defaults. Recovery rates on corporate bonds are estimated by Moody's at 40% of par on average. Together these can serve as the basis for comparison with expected losses on CLS.

---

[11] One exception is Standard & Poor's convention of providing an "r" suffix on ratings of certain securities to reflect yield volatility.

Exhibit 10: Default Rates and Indicative Spreads of Corporate Bonds

Rating	One-Year Defaults 1970-1996*	Expected Loss (% of par)**	Indicative Spreads to Treasury (bp)*** 5/15/97
Aaa	0.00%	0.00%	20
Aa	0.03	0.02	21
A	0.01	0.01	27
Baa	0.12	0.07	42
Ba	1.36	0.82	135
B	7.27	4.36	300

* *Historical Default Rates of Corporate Bond Issuers, 1920-1996*, Moody's Investors Service, January 1997.
** Assumes 40% recovery rate
*** 2-year spreads used as proxy for 1-year spreads.

Comparing spreads and expected losses on CLS with similarly rated corporates can provide an indication of relative value. CLS relative value versus corporate bonds with the same rating can be assessed in one of two ways. In the first case the base spread on the CLS can equal the base spread on the corporate (i.e., the expected loss on the two securities is the same), yet the risk premium is higher on the CLS. For example, if a Ba rated CLS has a base spread of 82 bp (annual probability of exceedance of 1.36% multiplied by one minus expected recovery rate of 40%) and is offered at a spread greater than 135 bp (the indicative spread of a corporate bond with the same probability of default and expected recovery rate), then the CLS offers relative value.

The second case where a CLS offers relative value is when the offered spread on the two securities are equal but the expected loss on the CLS is less than that of the corporate bond (as a result of either a lower probability of default or a higher recovery rate or both). In our example, if the CLS and corporate are both offered at a spread of 135 bp but the expected loss on the CLS is less than 0.82%, then the CLS offers relative value.

Spread Outlook

We expect that current CLS issues will be priced more attractively than future issues, since investors are likely to demand a premium for the lower liquidity associated with a new product. Additionally, some insurance companies may be willing to pay an initial premium over reinsurance rates to develop new sources of reinsurance capital, in the expectation that a long-term, stable alternative could potentially improve the efficiency in the market. Spreads are likely to narrow as understanding of the underlying risk grows, liquidity increases, and investor acceptance broadens. A parallel is distinguishable in the corporate market. Exhibit 11 illustrates that, although the corporate market is cyclical, there has been a long-term tightening of spreads as appetite for high yield corporate bonds has grown and the risk is better understood.

Exhibit 11: High Yield Corporate Spreads by Credit Quality, 1987-April 30, 1997

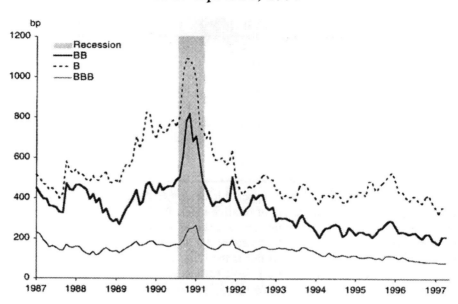

An additional consideration is that for an issue affected by underlying seasonal events (floods, hurricanes, hailstorms, etc.) that has a maturity date occurring after the season, there is a strong possibility that spreads will tighten if no trigger event occurs before the end of the season. This tightening should reflect the substantially reduced probability of default on the securities.

An Uncorrelated Asset Class

CLS offer investors the unique opportunity to invest exclusively in catastrophe risk and may provide potential diversification benefits. Although investors can invest in catastrophe risks by buying insurance and/or reinsurance company equity and debt, these investments are not a perfect substitute for the pure catastrophe exposure inherent in CLS. First, CLS do not carry the idiosyncratic[12] risks associated with an investment in securities of an insurance or reinsurance company. CLS also allow investors to avoid principal-agent risks (such as the risk that equity-holders may have incentives to restructure the debt or increase the overall riskiness of the company, to the disadvantage of bondholders) inherent in a corporate security.

Second, the occurrence and magnitude of natural hazards are expected to be uncorrelated with movements in the stock and bond markets. On the other

---

[12] Idiosyncratic or nonsystematic risk is the diversifiable risk of a security.

hand, insurance and reinsurance company securities do involve a significant portion of systematic risk. A recent study by Canter, Cole, and Sandor[13] shows that a portfolio of ten prominent catastrophe reinsurance companies has a strong positive correlation (beta of 0.83) with stock market movements. As a result, buying reinsurance company equity does not bring significant diversification benefits. In this respect, CLS offer better diversification opportunities since they are expected to have near zero betas. The correlation between the yearly percentage change in the S&P 500 index and the yearly percentage change in the PCS index over the period 1976-1996 is statistically insignificant (see Exhibit 12).

Modern portfolio theory states that an uncorrelated asset would be an attractive addition to a well diversified portfolio even at a required rate of return that is equal to the risk free rate of return. If CLS offer returns in excess of the risk-free rate (Treasury bill rate) and do not exhibit systematic risk, then investing in these securities can improve overall portfolio performance on a risk-adjusted basis. Investors who purchase CLS can potentially receive an attractive expected return and improve the diversification of their current portfolio.

Exhibit 12: Correlation of PCS Index and S&P 500 Index

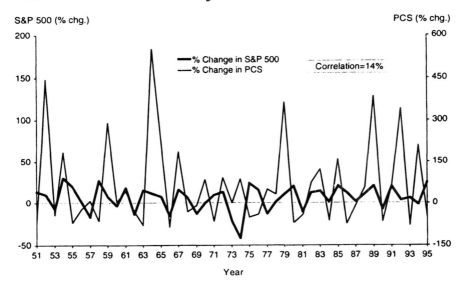

Source: CBOT

---

[13] Michael S. Canter, Joseph B. Cole, and Richard L. Sandor, "Insurance Derivatives: A new asset class for the capital markets and a new hedging tool for the insurance industry," *Journal of Derivatives* (Winter 1996), pp. 89-104.

A study by Froot, Murphy, Stern, and Usher[14] based on pricing and claims on actual catastrophe reinsurance contracts brokered by the reinsurance intermediary, Guy Carpenter & Company Inc., draws three valuable conclusions. First, the correlation of catastrophe risk with stocks and bonds is statistically indistinguishable from zero. Second, assuming that returns on reinsurance contracts provide a reasonable proxy for expected returns on CLS, the study shows that investment in such a portfolio of catastrophe reinsurance contracts from 1970-1994 would have generated returns 200 bp above the Treasury bill rate. Third, adding the portfolio of reinsurance contracts improves the efficiency of a diversified portfolio. Using a base portfolio of 70% domestic assets (70% stocks, 30% bonds) and 30% foreign assets (70% stocks, 30% bonds), the study shows that the "reward to risk ratio"[15] grows from 26% to 30% as the addition of catastrophe risk goes from 5% to 25%. Even though the past is no guarantee for future results, historical data provide strong evidence that catastrophe-linked securities offer portfolio opportunities to investors.

OTHER CONSIDERATIONS

In evaluating CLS, in addition to conducting a thorough relative value analysis, it is important for investors to examine several transaction-specific criteria, including these:

- *Insurer Coparticipation:* In CLS, since insurers could potentially take action that affects the value of the transaction (e.g., increase risk profile of policies, reduce deductibles, improperly adjudicate claims, etc.) risk of moral hazard exists. One method of mitigating this risk is to structure quota-share transactions, where the insurer shares losses proportionately with investors. An excess-of-loss structure lowers the risk to the extent that losses from lower layers are absorbed by the insurer's own capital. Hybrid structures may also be used to achieve insurer coparticipation objectives.
- *Quality of Insurer:* Catastrophe-linked securities isolate the underlying catastrophe risk from credit risk of the insurer. Nevertheless, the quality of the insurer is important since it determines the company's ability to implement pricing changes, collect accurate policy level data, and influence the quality of the underlying pool of policies.
- *Diversification of Underlying Events:* To the extent that occurrences of one catastrophic event is independent of another event, a pool of underlying

---

[14] Kenneth Froot, Brian Murphy, Aaron Stern, and Stephen Usher, "The Emerging Asset Class: Insurance Risk," *Guy Carpenter & Company Inc.'s Review of Catastrophes Exposures and the Capital Markets*, July 1995.

[15] Measured as the realized return minus the risk-free return divided by the standard deviation of the portfolio return.

policies that is diversified across regions or types of events (earthquakes, hurricanes, floods, etc.) or index-based (using the PCS Index, for example) may be less risky than one without this diversification.

* *Quality of the Modeling Company:* The security is priced and rated based on the probability of default, which in turn depends on probability of exceedance as calculated by the modeling company. It is therefore important for the company to be well-regarded in the industry.

OUTLOOK

We think that the CLS market is likely to develop within the context of a general trend toward securitization of insurance risk. Innovative investment choices will be introduced that will enable investors to buy insurance risk products tailored to their particular risk/return preferences. Securitization of life insurance risks (e.g., mortality, lapsation, etc.) and other property risks (e.g., space satellite launches, pipelines, etc.) will likely follow. Investors will be able to choose from securities subject to one risk (e.g., California earthquake), a diversified pool of risks (e.g., Japan earthquake and Florida hurricane), and/or risks measured by a recognized industry index. Multiyear structures will also be introduced, and OTC insurance derivatives will supplement the use of cash instruments in these securitizations.

We believe that the market for CLS will grow significantly in the years ahead, driven by the fundamental need of the insurance industry to create additional catastrophe reinsurance capacity and investor desire to achieve uncorrelated excess returns relative to comparably rated corporate and ABS investments. As the market matures and investors become more comfortable assuming catastrophe risk, spreads on these securities will likely tighten. Based on the existing gap in reinsurance capacity required to cover a $60 billion industrywide catastrophe, we believe that annual CLS issuance could reach $40 billion.

APPENDIX A
A DESCRIPTION OF HURRICANES AND EARTHQUAKES

Earthquakes[1]

Earthquakes are vibrations, sometimes violent, of the earth's surface caused by abrupt releases of energy in the earth's crust. They occur along preexisting fault lines, or zones of fracture in the earth's crust composed of crushed rock between blocks of rock that form naturally weak areas. When stress in the earth's outer layer builds up, it causes rocks on either side of the fault line to move relative to each other. This results in a sudden slippage, which releases energy in waves that travels through the rocks and produces shaking. Hazards that may result include landslide, liquefaction (solid soil liquefying), and fire.

The United States Geological Survey uses a 12-level scale known as the Modified Mercalli Intensity (MMI) scale to identify the intensity of quakes (i.e., their surface-level effects). Lower values on the MMI scale are derived from human and structural response to shaking, while higher intensities are based on permanent ground distortion. Though the Richter scale is a widely used measure of earthquake intensity, all the catastrophe models are based on the Mercalli intensity scale.

Earthquakes occur primarily in three zones of the earth. The largest earthquake belt, along which roughly 81% of the world's largest earthquakes occur, is known as the circum-Pacific seismic belt. As its name suggests, the belt runs around the rim of the Pacific Ocean, from Chile north to Alaska, west to Japan, and south to New Zealand. The second largest belt, which accounts for about 17% of the world's largest earthquakes, is known as the Alpide. It extends from Java to Sumatra, through the Himalayas and the Mediterranean, and out into the Atlantic. The third prominent belt follows the submerged mid-Atlantic Ridge. Within the United States, the largest earthquake belt runs from north to south in California where the Pacific and North American techtonic plates meet. The boundary between the plates is the San Andreas fault, an 800-mile-long fault system that extends to depths of at least 10 miles. This system, which produces thousands of small earthquakes every year, was responsible for the San Francisco earthquake of 1906 that caused landscape offsets up to 21 feet and registered intensities as high as 11 on the MMI, as well as the Northridge earthquake.

Hurricanes[2]

Hurricanes are part of a family of weather systems known as "tropical cyclones." A hurricane begins as a disorganized storm system that forms over warm, tropical waters. If and when the storm system becomes more organized, it is classified as a "tropical depression" and given a number by the National Hurricane Center. If the winds in a tropical depression grow in intensity to 40 mph, it is reclassified as a

---

[1] Source: U.S. Geological Survey; National Earthquake Information Center

[2] Source: U.S. Department of Commerce, National Oceanic and Atmospheric Administration.

"tropical storm" and given a name. When the winds in the storm reach 74 mph, the storm is upgraded to hurricane status.

The winds of a hurricane are structured around a central "eye," which is an area free of clouds and relatively calm. A band of strong winds and precipitation, known as the maximum radius of winds, develops outside the eye of the storm. As these winds wrap around the eye in a counterclockwise motion, air flow moves toward the center of the storm. Energy in the form of moist air and vapor is released as the air flow spirals upward, widening the difference between the pressure at the hurricane's center and its perimeter — the central pressure difference. An increasing central pressure difference increases the maximum wind speed, which ultimately determines the storm's potential to inflict damage.

Hurricane intensity is measured on the Saffir-Simpson scale on the basis of sustained wind speed (see Exhibit A-1).

All Atlantic and Gulf coastal areas are subject to hurricanes or tropical storms. For the U.S., the peak hurricane threat exists from mid-August to late October, although the official hurricane season extends from June 1 through November 30.

Exhibit A-1: Saffir-Simpson Scale for Hurricane Intensity

Saffir-Simpson Category	Sustained Wind Speed (mph)	% of Occurrences since 1900*	Examples (States Affected)
1	74-95	2.6%	1988: Florence (LA); Charley (NC)
2	96-110	41.0	1985: Kate (FL); 1991: Bob (RI)
3	111-130	35.9	1983: Alicia (TX); 1993: Emily (NC)
4	131-155	17.9	1989: Hugo (SC); 1992: Andrew (FL)
5	155 +	2.6	1935: Labor Day Hurricane (FL); 1969: Camille (LA/MS)

* Source: Applied Insurance Research.

APPENDIX B
CATASTROPHES AND THE BERMUDA MARKET

Raising more private or public equity capital is one alternative to expand resources available to cover catastrophe risk. Primarily in response to Hurricane Andrew, the island of Bermuda has flourished into an accepted insurance market. Investment banks, commercial banks, hedge funds, insurers, and reinsurers all sought to capitalize on the returns available in the catastrophe reinsurance market. By the middle of 1994, roughly $4 billion of new capital was available in Bermuda for catastrophe reinsurance. Shortly thereafter, Bermuda's insurance regulatory climate became more structured, adding legitimacy to a budding insurance market. With a wealth of capital, Bermuda is now a recognized force in the reinsurance market. Several companies have rapidly captured market share (28% of world insurance premiums) and recently contributed $700 million to the California Earthquake Authority in reinsurance contracts. The return that these insurers has earned have been exceptional. As a group, the eight reinsurers earned a 51.9% gross margin and 22% return on equity in 1995 (see Exhibit B-1). The companies have made such superior returns that their invested capital rose to $5 billion in 1995. Many of these companies are using excess capital to buy back stock or to diversify product lines.

But the Bermuda market does not possess the capacity to meet all the catastrophe demands of the U.S. market's major personal lines insurers in high risk regions. One concern is that the balance sheets of the Bermuda reinsurers have not been put through the necessary stress of a massive natural event (the last one was the 1994 Northridge earthquake, which occurred before many of these companies were set up), and hence their ability to withstand such an event is still undetermined.

Exhibit B-1: Bermuda Reinsurers

Reinsurance Company	Invested Capital ($ mill.)*	Return on Equity (1995)**
Centre Cat	312	15.5%
Global Capital Re	425	22.0
International P/C Re	309	19.0
LaSalle Re	200	19.2
Mid Ocean Re	700	20.5
Partner Re	950	19.1
Renaissance Re	240	44.0
Tempest Re	500	15.1
Total	3,636	22.0

* Institutional Investor
** Standard & Poor's, *Bermuda Catastrophe Reinsurance Market Report*, February 1997.

APPENDIX C
EXCHANGE TRADED DERIVATIVE CONTRACTS

The Chicago Board of Trade has offered since 1992 a catastrophe futures contract based on an index provided by the Insurance Services Office (ISO). This contract was not popular because the ISO index was based only on losses of the top 25 companies and hence was not considered reliable in predicting catastrophe losses. In 1995, the CBOT began offering option contracts with underlying indices computed by Property Claims Services' (PCS); these indices have gradually become the industry accepted standards. Contracts trade based on each of the PCS indices (see Exhibit C-1).

The PCS indices are based on surveys of insurance companies and their estimates of claims after the occurrence of an event. The losses can occur during a risk period (quarterly or annually depending on the seasonality of the catastrophe), at the beginning of which the index is set to zero. Each point on the index translates to a $100 million loss. The loss data are collected during a loss development period that can extend from six to twelve months. Contracts trade in the risk and development period of the index.

At the CBOT, investors can buy and sell standardized call/put option contracts, where the underlying index is a PCS Catastrophe Index. A buyer can purchase either a small-cap option with strike of 0-195 (aggregate losses up to $20 billion) or a large-cap contract with strike of 200-495 (losses of $20-$50 billion). By simultaneously buying call options with a lower strike and selling calls with a higher strike, a buyer can synthetically create an excess-of-loss reinsurance contract. On expiration, the buyer of an in-the-money call option receives the difference between the final index value and the strike, multiplied by $200. The settlement is in cash and is limited by the loss cap of 195 or 495. The buyer of the contract pays a premium that is quoted as points per spread contract, which is similar to the rate on line in a reinsurance contract.

Catex Swaps

Another recently introduced mechanism for diversifying catastrophe risk is provided by the Catex exchanges in New Jersey and Bermuda, set up in late 1996. The exchange in New Jersey is restricted to insurers, reinsurers, and self-insurers, whereas the Bermuda exchange allows for nontraditional investors, such as hedge funds and investment banks. Through the exchange, subscribers can swap catastrophe risk exposures over a nationwide computer system. An insurer can diversify its exposure to catastrophes by exchanging a basket of its own risks for a different basket of risks. For example, if an insurance company determines that its portfolio has an over-concentration of risk in Florida hurricanes, it can enter into an agreement with another market participant to swap California earthquake risk for its Florida risk. Inasmuch as Catex swaps help insurers diversify their balance sheets, the swaps reduce the need for capital, thus indirectly adding to the risk capacity in the industry.

Exhibit C-1: PCS Indices

National
Eastern
Northeastern
Southeastern
Midwestern
Western

Section III:

Valuation

Chapter 10

Interest Rate Models

Oren Cheyette, Ph.D.
Manager, Fixed Income Research
BARRA, Inc.

INTRODUCTION

An interest rate model is a probabilistic description of the future evolution of interest rates. Based on today's information, future interest rates are uncertain: an interest rate model is a characterization of that uncertainty. Quantitative analysis of securities with rate dependent cash flows requires application of such a model in order to find the present value of the uncertainty. Since virtually all financial instruments other than default- and option-free bonds have interest rate sensitive cash flows, this matters to most fixed-income portfolio managers and actuaries, as well as to traders and users of interest rate derivatives.

For financial instrument valuation and risk estimation one wants to use only models that are arbitrage free and matched to the currently observed term structure of interest rates. "Arbitrage free" means just that if one values the same cash flows in two different ways, one should get the same result. For example, a 10-year bond putable at par by the holder in 5 years can also be viewed as a 5-year bond with an option of the holder to extend the maturity for another 5 years. An arbitrage-free model will produce the same value for the structure viewed either way. This is also known as the *law of one price*. The term structure matching condition means that when a default-free straight bond is valued according to the model, the result should be the same as if the bond's cash flows are simply discounted according to the current default-free term structure. A model that fails to satisfy either of these conditions cannot be trusted for general problems, though it may be usable in some limited context.

For equity derivatives, lognormality of prices (leading to the Black-Scholes formula for calls and puts) is the standard starting point for option calculations. In the fixed-income market, unfortunately, there is no equally natural and simple assumption. Wall Street dealers routinely use a multiplicity of models based on widely varying assumptions in different markets. For example, an options desk most likely uses a version of the Black formula to value interest rate caps and floors. This use assumes a lognormal distribution of bond prices (since, e.g., a caplet is a put on a 3-month discount bond), which in turn implies a normal distribution of interest rates. A few feet away, the mortgage desk may use a lognormal interest rate model to evaluate their

237

passthrough and CMO effective durations. And on the next floor, actuaries may use variants of both types of models to analyze their annuities and insurance policies.

It may seem that one's major concern in choosing an interest rate model should be the accuracy with which it represents the empirical volatility of the term structure of rates, and its ability to fit market prices of vanilla derivatives such as at-the-money caps and swaptions. These are clearly important criteria, but they are not decisive. The first criterion is hard to pin down, depending strongly on what historical period one chooses to examine. The second criterion is easy to satisfy for most commonly used models, by the simple (though unappealing) expedient of permitting predicted future volatility to be time dependent. So, while important, this concern doesn't really do much to narrow the choices.

A critical issue in selecting an interest rate model is, instead, ease of application. For some models it is difficult or impossible to provide efficient valuation algorithms for all financial instruments of interest to a typical investor. Given that one would like to analyze all financial instruments using the same underlying assumptions, this is a significant problem. At the same time, one would prefer not to stray too far from economic reasonableness — such as by using the Black-Scholes formula to value callable bonds. These considerations lead to a fairly narrow menu of choices among the known interest rate models.

The organization of this chapter is as follows. In the next section I provide a (brief) discussion of the principles of valuation algorithms. This will give a context for many of the points made in the third section, which provides an overview of the various characteristics that differentiate interest rate models. Finally, in the fourth section I describe the empirical evidence on interest rate dynamics and provide a quantitative comparison of a family of models that closely match those in common use. I have tried to emphasize those issues that are primarily of interest for application of the models in practical settings. There is little point in having the theoretically ideal model if it can't actually be implemented as part of a valuation algorithm.

VALUATION

Valuation algorithms for rate dependent contingent claims are usually based on a risk neutral formula, which states that the present value of an uncertain cash flow at time T is given by the average over all interest rate scenarios of the scenario cash flow divided by the scenario value at time T of a money market investment of \$1 today.[1] More formally, the value of a security is given by the expectation (average) over interest rate scenarios

$$P = E\left[\sum_i \frac{C_i}{M_i}\right] \tag{1}$$

---

[1] The money market account is the *numeraire*.

where C_i is the security's cash flows and M_i is the money market account value at time t_i in each scenario, calculated by assuming continual reinvestment at the prevailing short rate.

The probability weights used in the average are chosen so that the expected rate of return on any security over the next instant is the same, namely the short rate. These are the so-called "risk neutral" probability weights: they would be the true weights if investors were indifferent to bearing interest rate risk. In that case, investors would demand no excess return relative to a (riskless) money market account in order to hold risky positions — hence equation (1).

It is important to emphasize that the valuation formula is not dependent on any *assumption* of risk neutrality. Financial instruments are valued by equation (1) *as if* the market were indifferent to interest rate risk *and* the correct discount factor for a future cash flow were the inverse of the money market return. Both statements are false for the real world, but the errors are offsetting: a valuation formula based on probabilities implying a nonzero market price of interest rate risk and the corresponding scenario discount factors would give the same value.

There are two approaches to computing the average in equation (1): by direct brute force evaluation, or indirectly by solving a related differential equation. The brute force method is usually called the Monte Carlo method. It consists of generating a large number of possible interest rate scenarios based on the interest rate model, computing the cash flows and money market values in each one, and averaging. Properly speaking, only path generation based on random numbers is a Monte Carlo method. There are other scenario methods — e.g., complete sampling of a tree — that do not depend on the use of random numbers. Given sufficient computer resources, the scenario method can tackle essentially any type of financial instrument.[2]

A variety of schemes are known for choosing scenario sample paths efficiently, but none of them are even remotely as fast and accurate as the second technique. In certain cases (discussed in more detail in the next section) the average in equation (1) obeys a partial differential equation — like the one derived by Black and Scholes for equity options — for which there exist fast and accurate numerical solution methods, or in special cases even analytical solutions. This happens only for interest rate models of a particular type, and then only for certain security types, such as caps, floors, swaptions, and options on bonds. For securities such as mortgage passthroughs, CMOs, index amortizing swaps, and for some insurance policies and annuities, simulation methods are the only alternative.

MODEL TAXONOMY

The last two decades have seen the development of a tremendous profusion of models for valuation of interest rate sensitive financial instruments. In order to

---

[2] This is true even for American options. For a review see P. Boyle, M. Broadie, and P. Glasserman, "Monte Carlo Methods for Security Pricing," working paper, 1995, to appear in the *Journal of Economic Dynamics and Control*.

better understand these models, it is helpful to recognize a number of features that characterize and distinguish them. These are features of particular relevance to practitioners wishing to implement valuation algorithms, as they render some models completely unsuitable for certain types of financial instruments.[3] The following subsections enumerate some of the major dimensions of variation among the different models.

One- versus Multi-Factor

In many cases, the value of an interest rate contingent claim depends, effectively, on the prices of many underlying assets. For example, while the payoff of a caplet depends only on the reset date value of a zero coupon bond maturing at the payment date (valued based on, say, 3-month LIBOR), the payoff to an option on a coupon bond depends on the exercise date values of all of the bond's remaining interest and principal payments. Valuation of such an option is in principle an inherently multi-dimensional problem.

Fortunately, in practice these values are highly correlated. The degree of correlation can be quantified by examining the covariance matrix of changes in spot rates of different maturities. A principal component analysis of the covariance matrix decomposes the motion of the spot curve into independent (uncorrelated) components. The largest principal component describes a common shift of all interest rates in the same direction. The next leading components are a twist, with short rates moving one way and long rates the other, and a "butterfly" motion, with short and long rates moving one way, and intermediate rates the other. Based on analysis of weekly data from the Federal Reserve H15 series of benchmark Treasury yields from 1983 through 1995, the shift component accounts for 84% of the total variance of spot rates, while twist and butterfly account for 11% and 4%, leaving about 1% for all remaining principal components.

The shift factor alone explains a large fraction of the overall movement of spot rates. As a result, valuation can be reduced to a one factor problem in many instances with little loss of accuracy. Only securities whose payoffs are primarily sensitive to the shape of the spot curve rather than its overall level (such as dual index floaters, which depend on the difference between a long and a short rate) will not be modeled well with this approach.

In principle it is straightforward to move from a one-factor model to a multi-factor one. In practice, though, implementations of multi-factor valuation models can be complicated and slow, and require estimation of many more volatility and correlation parameters than are needed for one-factor models, so there may be some benefit to using a one-factor model when possible. The remainder of this chapter will focus on one-factor models.[4]

---

[3] There is, unfortunately, a version of Murphy's law applicable to interest rate models, which states that the computational tractability of a model is inversely proportional to its economic realism.

[4] For an exposition of two-factor models, see D.F. Babbel and C.B. Merrill, *Valuation of Interest Sensitive Financial Instruments* (New Hope, PA: Frank J. Fabozzi Associates and Society of Actuaries, 1996).

Exogenous versus Endogenous Term Structure

The first interest rate models were not constructed so as to fit an arbitrary initial term structure. Instead, with a view towards analytical simplicity, the Vasicek[5] and Cox-Ingersoll-Ross[6] (CIR) models contain a few constant parameters that define an endogenously specified term structure. That is, the initial spot curve is given by an analytical formula in terms of the model parameters. These are sometimes also called "equilibrium" models, as they posit yield curves derived from an assumption of economic equilibrium based on a given market price of risk and other parameters governing collective expectations.

For *dynamically* reasonable choices of the parameters — values that give plausible long-run interest rate distributions and option prices — the term structures achievable in these models have far too little curvature to accurately represent typical empirical spot rate curves. This is because the mean reversion parameter, governing the rate at which the short rate reverts towards the long-run mean, also governs the volatility of long-term rates relative to the volatility of the short rate — the "term structure of volatility." To achieve the observed level of long-rate volatility (or to price options on long-term securities well) requires that there be relatively little mean reversion, but this implies low curvature yield curves. This problem can be partially solved by moving to a multi-factor framework — but at a significant cost as discussed earlier. These models are therefore not particularly useful as the basis for valuation algorithms — they simply have too few degrees of freedom to faithfully represent real markets.

To be used for valuation, a model must be "calibrated" to the initial spot rate curve. That is, the model structure must accommodate an exogenously determined spot rate curve, typically given by fitting to bond prices, or sometimes to futures prices and swap rates. All models in common use are of this type.

There is a "trick" invented by Dybvig that converts an endogenous model to a calibrated exogenous one.[7] The trick can be viewed as splitting the nominal interest rate into two parts: the stochastic part modeled endogenously, and a non-stochastic drift term, which compensates for the mismatch of the endogenous term structure and the observed one. (BARRA uses this technique to modify the CIR model to match the observed term structure in its fixed income analytics.) The price of this method is that the volatility function is no longer a simple function of the nominal interest rate, because the nominal rate is not the one that governs the level of volatility.

---

[5] O. Vasicek, "An Equilibrium Characterization of the Term Structure," *Journal of Financial Economics* (November 1977).

[6] J.C. Cox, J.E. Ingersoll Jr., and S.A. Ross, "A Theory of the Term Structure of Interest Rates," *Econometrica* (March 1985).

[7] P. Dybvig, "Bond and Bond Option Pricing Based on the Current Term Structure," in M. A. H. Dempster and S. Pliska (eds.), *Mathematics of Derivative Securities* (Cambridge, U.K.: Cambridge University Press, 1997).

Short Rate versus Yield Curve

The risk neutral valuation formula requires that one know the sequence of short rates for each scenario, so an interest rate model must provide this information. For this reason, many interest rate models are simply models of the stochastic evolution of the short rate. A second reason for the desirability of such models is that they have the *Markov property*, meaning that the evolution of the short rate at each instant depends only on its current value — not on how it got there. The practical signifi-cance of this is that, as alluded to in the previous section, the valuation problem for many types of financial instruments can be reduced to solving a partial differential equation, for which there exist efficient analytical and numerical techniques. To be amenable to this calculation technique, a financial instrument's cash flow at time t must depend only on the state of affairs at that time, not on how the evolution occurred prior to t or it must be equivalent to a portfolio of such securities (for example, a callable bond is a position long a straight bond and short a call option).

Short-rate models have two parts. One specifies the average rate of change ("drift") of the short rate at each instant; the other specifies the instanta-neous volatility of the short rate. The conventional notation for this is

$$dr(t) = \mu(r,t)dt + \sigma(r,t)dz(t) \tag{2}$$

The left-hand side of this equation is the change in the short rate over the next instant. The first term on the right is the drift multiplied by the size of the time step. The second is the volatility multiplied by a normally distributed random increment. For most models, the drift component must be determined through a numerical technique to match the initial spot rate curve, while for a small number of models there exists an analytical relationship. In general, there exists a no-arbi-trage relationship linking the initial forward rate curve, the volatility $\sigma(r,t)$, the market price of interest rate risk, and the drift term $\mu(r,t)$. However, since typi-cally one must solve for the drift numerically, this relationship plays no role in model construction. Differences between models arise from different depen-dences of the drift and volatility terms on the short rate.

For financial instruments whose cash flows don't depend on the interest rate history, the expectation formula (1) for present value obeys the Feynman-Kac equation

$$\frac{1}{2}\sigma^2 P_{rr} + (\mu - \lambda)P_r + P_t - rP + c = 0 \tag{3}$$

where, for example, P_r denotes the partial derivative of P with respect to r, c is the payment rate of the financial instrument, and λ, which can be time and rate depen-dent, is the market price of interest rate risk.

The terms in this equation can be understood as follows. In the absence of uncertainty ($\sigma = 0$), the equation involves four terms. The last three assert that the value of the security increases at the risk-free rate (rP), and decreases by the amount of any payments (c). The term $(\mu - \lambda)P_r$ accounts for change in value due to the change in the term structure with time, as rates move up the forward curve. In the absence of uncertainty it is easy to express $(\mu - \lambda)$ in terms of the initial forward rates. In the presence of uncertainty this term depends on the volatility as well, and we also have the first term, which is the main source of the complexity of valuation models.

The Vasicek and CIR models are models of the short rate. Both have the same form for the drift term, namely a tendency for the short rate to rise when it is below the long-term mean, and fall when it is above. That is, the short-rate drift has the form $\mu = \kappa(\theta - r)$, where r is the short rate and κ and θ are the mean reversion and long-term rate constants. The two models differ in the rate dependence of the volatility: it is constant (when expressed as points per year) in the Vasicek model, and proportional to the square root of the short rate in the CIR model.

The Dybvig-adjusted Vasicek model is the mean reverting generalization of the Ho-Lee model,[8] also known as the mean reverting Gaussian (MRG) model or the Hull-White model.[9] The MRG model has particularly simple analytical expressions for values of many assets — in particular, bonds and European options on bonds. Like the original Vasicek model, it permits the occurrence of negative interest rates with positive probability. However, for typical initial spot curves and volatility parameters, the probability of negative rates is quite small.

Other popular models of this type are the Black-Derman-Toy[10] (BDT) and Black-Karasinski[11] (BK) models, in which the volatility is proportional to the short rate, so that the ratio of volatility to rate level is constant. For these models, unlike the MRG and Dybvig-adjusted CIR models, the drift term is not simple. These models require numerical fitting to the initial interest rate and volatility term structures. The drift term is therefore not known analytically. In the BDT model, the short-rate volatility is also linked to the mean reversion strength (which is also generally time dependent) in such a way that — in the usual situation where long rates are less volatile than the short rate — the short-rate volatility decreases in the future. This feature is undesirable: one doesn't want to link the observation that the long end of the curve has relatively low volatility to a forecast that in the future the short rate will become less volatile. This problem motivated the development of the BK model in which mean reversion and volatility are delinked.

All of these models are explicit models of the short rate alone. It happens that in the Vasicek and CIR models (with or without the Dybvig adjustment) it is possible to express the entire forward curve as a function of the current short rate through fairly simple analytical formulas. This is not possible in the BDT and BK models, or

[8] T.S.Y. Ho and S.B. Lee, "Term Structure Movements and Pricing Interest Rate Contingent Claims," *Journal of Finance* (December 1986); and, J. Hull and A. White, "Pricing Interest Rate Derivative Securities," *The Review of Financial Studies*, 3:4 (1990).

[9] This model was also derived in F. Jamshidian, "The One-Factor Gaussian Interest Rate Model: Theory and Implementation," Merrill Lynch working paper, 1988.

[10] F. Black, E. Derman and W. Toy, "A One Factor Model of Interest Rates and its Application to Treasury Bond Options," *Financial Analysts Journal* (January/February 1990).

[11] F. Black and P. Karasinski, "Bond and Option Prices when Short Rates are Lognormal," *Financial Analysts Journal* (July/August 1992).

generally in other models of short-rate dynamics, other than by highly inefficient numerical techniques. Indeed, it is possible to show that the only short-rate models consistent with an arbitrary initial term structure for which one can find the whole forward curve analytically are in a class that includes the MRG and Dybvig-adjusted CIR models as special cases, namely where the short-rate volatility has the form[12]

$$\sigma(r, t) = \sqrt{\sigma_1(t) + \sigma_2(t)r}.$$

While valuation of certain assets (e.g., callable bonds) does not require knowledge of longer rates, there are broad asset classes that do. For example, mortgage prepayment models are typically driven off a long-term Treasury par yield, such as the 10-year rate. Therefore a generic short-rate model such as BDT or BK is unsuitable if one seeks to analyze a variety of assets in a common interest rate framework.

An alternative approach to interest rate modeling is to specify the dynamics of the entire term structure. The volatility of the term structure is then given by some specified function, which most generally could be a function of time, maturity, and spot rates. A special case of this approach (in a discrete time framework) is the Ho-Lee model mentioned earlier, for which the term structure of volatility is a parallel shift of the spot rate curve, whose magnitude is independent of time and the level of rates. A completely general continuous time, multi-factor framework for constructing such models was given by Heath, Jarrow and Morton (HJM).[13]

It is sometimes said that all interest rate models are HJM models. This is technically true: in principle, every arbitrage-free model of the term structure can be described in their framework. In practice, however, it is impossible to do this analytically for most short-rate Markov models. The only ones for which it is possible are those in the MRG-CIR family described earlier. The BDT and BK models, for instance, cannot be translated to the HJM framework other than by impracticable numerical means. To put a model in HJM form, one must know the term structure of volatility at all times, and this is generally not possible for short-rate Markov models.

If feasible, the HJM approach is clearly very attractive, since one knows now not just the short rate but also all longer rates as well. In addition, HJM models are very "natural," in the sense that the basic inputs to the model are the initial term structure of interest rates and a term structure of interest rate volatility for each independent motion of the yield curve.

The reason for the qualification in the last paragraph is that a generic HJM model requires keeping track of a potentially enormous amount of information. The HJM framework imposes no structure other than the requirement of no-arbitrage on the dynamics of the term structure. Each forward rate of fixed maturity evolves separately, so that one must keep track of each one separately. Since there are an infinite number of distinct forward rates, this can be difficult. This

---

[12] A. Jeffrey, "Single Factor Heath-Jarrow-Morton Term Structure Models Based on Markov Spot Interest Rate Dynamics," *Journal of Financial and Quantitative Analysis*, 30:4 (December 1995).

[13] D. Heath, R. Jarrow, and A. Morton, "Bond Pricing and the Term Structure of Interest Rates: A New Methodology for Contingent Claims Valuation," *Econometrica*, 60:1 (January 1992).

difficulty occurs even in a one factor HJM model, for which there is only one source of random movement of the term structure. A general HJM model does not have the Markov property that leads to valuation formulas expressed as solutions to partial differential equations. This makes it impossible to accurately value interest rate options without using huge amounts of computer time, since one is forced to use simulation methods.

In practice a simulation algorithm breaks the evolution of the term structure up into discrete time steps, so one need keep track of and simulate only forward rates for the finite set of simulation times. Still, this can be a large number (e.g., 360 or more for a mortgage passthrough), and this computational burden, combined with the inefficiency of simulation methods has prevented general HJM models from coming into more widespread use.

Some applications require simulation methods because the assets' structures (e.g., mortgage-backed securities) are not compatible with differential equation methods. For applications where one is solely interested in modeling such assets, there exists a class of HJM models that significantly simplify the forward rate calculations.[14] The simplest version of such models, the "two state Markov model," permits an arbitrary dependence of short-rate volatility on both time and the level of interest rates, while the ratio of forward-rate volatility to short-rate volatility is solely a function of term. That is, the volatility of $f(t,T)$, the term T forward rate at time t takes the form

$$\sigma_f(r, t, T) = \sigma(r, t)e^{-\int_t^T k(u)du} \tag{4}$$

where $\sigma(r,t) = \sigma_f(r,t,t)$ is the short-rate volatility and $k(t)$ determines the mean reversion rate or equivalently, the rate of decrease of forward rate volatility with term. The evolution of all forward rates in this model can be described in terms of two state variables: the short rate (or any other forward or spot rate), and the slope of the forward curve at the origin. The second variable can be expressed in terms of the total variance experienced by a forward rate of fixed maturity by the time it has become the short rate. The stochastic evolution equations for the two state variables can be written as

$$d\tilde{r}(t) = (V(t) - k(t)\tilde{r})dt + \sigma(r, t)dz(t)$$

$$V_t(t) = \sigma^2(r, t) - 2k(t)V(t) \tag{5}$$

---

[14] O. Cheyette, "Term Structure Dynamics and Mortgage Valuation," *Journal of Fixed Income* (March 1992). The two state Markov model was also described in P. Ritchken and L. Sankarasubramanian, "Volatility Structure of Forward Rates and the Dynamics of the Term Structure," *Mathematical Finance*, 5(1) (1995), pp. 55-72.

where $\tilde{r}(t) \equiv r(t) - f(0, t)$ is the deviation of the short rate from the initial forward rate curve. The state variable $V(t)$ has initial value $V(0)=0$; its evolution equation is non-stochastic and can be integrated to give

$$V(t) = \int_0^t \sigma_f^2(r, s, t)ds = \int_0^t \sigma^2(r, s)e^{-2\int_s^t k(u)du} ds \tag{6}$$

In terms of these state variables, the forward curve is given by

$$f(t, T) = f(0, T) + \phi(t, T)\left(\tilde{r} + V(t)\int_t^T \phi(t, s)ds\right) \tag{7}$$

where

$$\phi(t, T) = \sigma_f(r, t, T)/\sigma_f(r, t, t) = e^{-\int_t^T k(s)ds}$$

is a deterministic function.

Instead of having to keep track of hundreds of forward rates, one need only model the evolution of the two state variables. Path independent asset prices also obey a partial differential equation in this model, so it appears possible at least in principle to use more efficient numerical methods. The equation, analogous to equation (3), is

$$\frac{1}{2}\sigma^2 P_{\tilde{r}\tilde{r}} + (V - k\tilde{r})P_{\tilde{r}} + (\sigma^2 - 2kV)P_V + P_t - rP + c = 0. \tag{8}$$

Unlike equation (3), for which one must use the equation itself applied to bonds to solve for the coefficient $\mu-\lambda$, here the coefficient functions are all known in terms of the initial data: the short-rate volatility and the initial forward curve. This simplification has come at the price of adding a dimension, as we now have to contend also with a term involving the first derivative with respect to V, and so the equation is much more difficult to solve efficiently by standard techniques.

In the special case where $\sigma(r,t)$ is independent of r, this model is the MRG model mentioned earlier. In this case, V is a deterministic function of t, so the P_V term disappears from equation (8), leaving a two dimensional equation that has analytical solutions for European options on bonds, and straightforward numerical techniques for valuing American bond options. Since bond prices are lognormally distributed in this model, it should be no surprise that the formula for options on pure discount bounds (PDB's) looks much like the Black-Scholes formula. The value of a call with strike price K, exercise date t on a PDB maturing at time T is given by

$$C = P(T)N(h_1) - KP(t)N(h_2), \tag{9}$$

where

$$h_1 = \frac{k}{(1 - e^{-k(T-t)})\sqrt{V(t)}} \ln \frac{P(T)}{KP(t)} + \frac{\sqrt{V(t)}(1 - e^{-k(T-t)})}{2k},$$

$$h_2 = h_1 - \frac{\sqrt{V(t)}(1 - e^{-k(T-t)})}{k},$$

$N(x)$ is the Gaussian distribution, and $P(t)$ and $P(T)$ are prices of PDB's maturing at t and T. (The put value can be obtained by put-call parity.) Options on coupon bonds can be valued by adding up a portfolio of options on PDBs, one for each coupon or principal payment after the exercise date, with strike prices such that they are all at-the-money at the same value of the short rate. The Dybvig-adjusted CIR model has similar formulas for bond options, involving the non-central χ^2 distribution instead of the Gaussian one.

If $\sigma(r,t)$ depends on r, the model becomes similar to some other standard models. For example, $\sigma(r,t)=a\sqrt{r}$ has the same rate dependence as the CIR model, while choosing $\sigma(r,t)=br$ gives a model similar to BK, though in each case the drift and term structure of volatility are different.

Unless one has some short- or long-term view on trends in short-rate volatility, it is most natural to choose $\sigma(r,t)$ to be time independent, and similarly $k(u)$ to be constant. This is equivalent to saying that the shape of the volatility term structure — though not necessarily its magnitude — should be constant over time. (Otherwise, as in the BDT model, one is imposing an undesirable linkage between today's shape of the forward rate volatility curve and future volatility curves.) In that case, the term structure of forward-rate volatility is exponentially decreasing with maturity, and the integrals in equations (6) and (7) can be computed, giving for the forward curve

$$f(t, T) = f(0, T) + e^{-k(T-t)}\left(\tilde{r} + V(t)\frac{1 - e^{-k(T-t)}}{k}\right). \qquad (10)$$

Finally, if the volatility is assumed rate independent as well, the integral expression for $V(t)$ can be evaluated to give

$$V(t) = \sigma^2 \frac{1 - e^{-2kt}}{2k}, \qquad (11)$$

and we obtain the forward curves of the MRG model.

Empirically, neither the historical volatility nor the implied volatility falls off so neatly. Instead, volatility typically increases with term out to between 1 and 3 years, then drops off. The two state Markov model cannot accommodate this behavior, except by imposing a forecast of increasing then decreasing short-rate volatility, or a short run of negative mean reversion. There is, however, an extension of the model that permits modeling of humped or other more complicated volatility curves, at the cost of introducing additional state variables.[15] With five state variables, for example, it is possible to model the dominant volatility term structure of the U.S. Treasury spot curve very accurately.

Recently, a model of bond price dynamics was devised[16] that does not fit the dichotomy of this section, for the simple reason that it is not a model of interest rates, but is instead a model of discount factors (PDB prices). Rather than using a valuation formula based on risk-neutral rate movements and a money-market numeraire, the model is based on another probability distribution and numeraire with many nice properties. The developers of the model call their approach the "positive interest" framework, since it has the attractive feature that all models in the framework have positive interest rates at all times. In addition, the interest rate process is guaranteed not to explode. Like the HJM approach, this model is really a framework for constructing specific models, as it imposes no structure other than that dictated by the requirements of arbitrage freedom, calibration, and positivity of rates. Unfortunately, the only published model based on this approach (the "rational lognormal model"[17]) suffers from some fairly serious financial defects.[18] First, interest rates are bounded below at a level that approaches the forward rate curve, so floors with strikes below the bound are valued at zero, as are long calls on bonds with low but nonzero coupons. Second, the short-rate volatility decreases over time and eventually approaches zero. So, while the model provides closed form solutions for many types of derivatives, its defects seem to render it unusable.

EMPIRICAL AND NUMERICAL CONSIDERATIONS

Given the profusion of models, it is reasonable to ask whether there are empirical or other considerations that can help motivate a choice of one model for applications. One might take the view that one should use whichever model is most convenient for the particular problem at hand — e.g., BDT or BK for bonds with embedded options, Black model for caps and floors, a two state Markov model for mortgages, and a ten state, two factor Markov-HJM model for dual index amortizing floaters. The obvious problem with this approach is that it can't be used to find hedging relationships or relative value between financial instruments valued according to the different models. I take as a given, then, that we seek models that can be used effectively for valuation of most types of financial instruments with minimum compromise of financial reasonableness. The choice will likely depend

---

[15] O. Cheyette, "Markov Representation of the HJM Model," working paper, 1995.

[16] B. Flesaker and L. P. Hughston, "Positive Interest," *Risk Magazine* (January 1996) and "Dynamic Models for Yield Curve Evolution," working paper (January 1996).

[17] Ibid.

[18] O. Cheyette and L. Goldberg, unpublished note, and L. Goldberg, "Volatility of the Short Rate in the Rational Lognormal Model," *Finance and Stochastics* 2 (1998), p. 199.

on how many and what kinds of assets one needs to value. A trader of vanilla options may be less concerned about cross-market consistency issues than a manager of portfolios of callable bonds and mortgage-backed securities.

The major empirical consideration — and one that has produced a large amount of inconclusive research — is the assumed dependence of volatility on the level of interest rates. Different researchers have reported various evidence that volatility is best explained (1) as a power of the short rate[19] ($\sigma \propto r\gamma$) — with γ so large that models with this volatility have rates running off to infinity with high probability ("explosions"), (2) by a GARCH model with very long (possibly infinite) persistence,[20] (3) by some combination of GARCH with a power law dependence on rates,[21] (4) by none of the above.[22] All of this work has been in the context of short-rate Markov models.

Here I will present some fairly straightforward evidence in favor of choice (4) based on analysis of movements of the whole term structure of spot rates, rather than just short rates, from U.S. Treasury yields over the period 1977 to early 1996.

The result is that the market appears to be well described by "eras" with very different rate dependences of volatility, possibly coinciding with periods of different Federal Reserve policies. Since all the models in common use have a power law dependence of volatility on rates, I attempted to determine the best fit to the exponent (γ) relating the two. My purpose here is not so much to provide another entrant in this already crowded field, but rather to suggest that there may be no simple answer to the empirical question. No model with constant parameters seems to do a very good job. A surprising result, given the degree to which the market for interest rate derivatives has exploded and the widespread use of lognormal models, is that the period since 1987 is best modeled by a nearly *normal* model of interest rate volatility.

The data used in the analysis consisted of spot rate curves derived from the Federal Reserve H15 series of weekly average benchmark yields. The benchmark yields are given as semiannually compounded yields of hypothetical par bonds with fixed maturities ranging from 3 months to 30 years, derived by interpolation from actively traded issues. The data cover the period from early 1977, when a 30-year bond was first issued, through March of 1996. The spot curves are represented as continuous, piecewise linear functions, constructed by a root finding procedure to exactly match the given yields, assumed to be yields of par bonds. (This is similar to the conventional bootstrapping method.) The two data points surrounding the 1987 crash were excluded: the short and intermediate markets moved by around ten standard deviations during the crash, and this extreme event would have had a significant skewing effect on the analysis.

---

[19] K.C. Chan, G.A. Karolyi, F.A. Longstaff, and A.B. Sanders, "An Empirical Comparson of Alternative Models of the Short Rate," *Journal of Finance* 47:3 (1992).

[20] See R.J. Brenner, R.H. Harjes, and K.F. Kroner, "Another Look at Alternative Models of the Short-Term Interest Rate," University of Arizona working paper (1993), and references therein.

[21] Ibid.

[22] Y.Aït-Sahalia, "Testing Continuous Time Models of the Spot Interest Rate," *Review of Financial Studies*, 9:2 (1996).

Exhibit 1: Parameter Estimates for the Two State Markov Model with Power Law Volatility over Various Sample Periods*

Sample Period	Exponent (γ)	Mean Reversion (k)	Comments
3/1/77 - 3/29/96	1.04 ± 0.07	0.054 ± 0.007	Full data set
3/1/77 - 1/1/87	1.6 ± 0.10	0.10 ± 0.020	Pre-Greenspan
3/1/77 - 1/1/83	1.72 ± 0.15	0.22 ± 0.040	"Monetarist"policy
1/1/83 - 3/29/96	0.45 ± 0.07	0.019 ± 0.005	Post high-rate period
1/1/87 - 3/29/96	0.19 ± 0.09	0.016 ± 0.004	Greenspan

* The uncertainties are one standard deviation estimates based on bootstrap Monte Carlo resampling.

A parsimonious representation of the spot curve dynamics is given by the two state Markov model with constant mean reversion k and volatility that is time independent and proportional to a power of the short rate: $\sigma(r) = \beta r\gamma$. In this case, the term structure of spot rate volatility, given by integrating equation (4), is

$$\sigma(r_t)v(T) = \beta r_t^\gamma \frac{1 - e^{-kT}}{kT} \qquad (12)$$

where T is the maturity and r_t is the time t short rate. The time t weekly change in the spot rate curve is then given by the change due to the passage of time ("rolling up the forward curve") plus a random change of the form $v(T)x_t$, where for each t, x_t, is an independent normal random variable with distribution $N(\mu, \sigma(r_t)\sqrt{52})$. (The systematic drift μ of x_t, over time was assumed to be independent of time and the rate level.) The parameters β, γ, and k are estimated as follows. First, using an initial guess for γ, k is estimated by a maximum likelihood fit of the maturity dependence of $v(T)$ to the spot curve changes. Then, using this value of k, another maximum likelihood fit is applied to fit the variance of x_t to the power law model of $\sigma(r_t)$. The procedure is then iterated to improve the estimates of k and γ, but it turns out that the best fit value of k is quite insensitive to the value of γ, and vice versa.

One advantage of looking at the entire term structure is that we avoid modeling just idiosyncratic behavior of the short end, e.g., that it is largely determined by the Federal Reserve. An additional feature of this analysis is proper accounting for the effect of the "arbitrage-free drift" — namely, the systematic change of interest rates due purely to the shape of the forward curve at the start of each period. Prior analyses have typically involved fitting to endogenous short-rate models with constant parameters not calibrated to each period's term structure. The present approach mitigates a fundamental problem of prior research in the context of one-factor models, namely that interest rate dynamics are poorly described by a single factor. By re-initializing the drift parameters at the start of each sample period and studying the volatility of changes to a well-defined term structure factor, the effects of additional factors are excluded from the analysis.

The results for the different time periods are shown in Exhibit 1. (The exhibit doesn't include the best fit values of β, which are not relevant to the empirical issue at hand.) The error estimates reported in the exhibit are derived by a bootstrap Monte Carlo procedure that constructs artificial data sets by random sampling of the original set with replacement and applies the same analysis to them.[23] It is apparent that the different subperiods are well described by very different exponents and mean reversion. The different periods were chosen to include or exclude the monetarist policy "experiment" under Volcker of the late 1970s and early 1980s, and also to sample just the Greenspan era. For the period since 1987, the best fit exponent of 0.19 is significantly different from zero at the 95% confidence level, but not at the 99% level. However, the best fit value is well below the threshold of 0.5 required to guarantee positivity of interest rates, with 99% confidence. There appears to be weak sensitivity of volatility to the rate level, but much less than is implied by a number of models in widespread use — in particular, BDT, BK, and CIR.

The estimates for the mean reversion parameter k can be understood through the connection of mean reversion to the term structure of volatility. Large values of k imply large fluctuations in short rates compared to long rates, since longer rates reflect the expectation that changes in short rates will not persist forever. The early 1980s saw just such a phenomenon, with the yield curve becoming very steeply inverted for a brief period. Since then, the volatility of the short rate (in absolute terms of points per year) has been only slightly higher than that of long-term rates.

Exhibit 2 gives a graphical representation of the data. There is clear evidence that the simple power law model is not a good fit and that the data display regime shifts. The exhibit shows the volatility of the factor in equation (12) using the value of k appropriate to the period January 1987-March 1996 (the "Greenspan era"). The vertical coordinate of each dot represents the volatility of the factor over a 52-week period; the horizontal coordinate shows the 3-month spot rate (a proxy for the short rate) at the start of the 52-week period. (Note that the maximum likelihood estimation is not based on the data points shown, but on the individual weekly changes.) The dots are broken into two sets: the x's are for start dates prior to January 1987, the diamonds for later dates. Divided in this way, the data suggest fairly strongly that volatility has been nearly independent of interest rates since 1987 — a time during which the short rate has ranged from around 3% to over 9%.

From an empirical perspective, then, no simple choice of model works well. Among the simple models of volatility, the MRG model most closely matches the recent behavior of U.S. Treasury term structure.

There is an issue of financial plausibility here, as well as an empirical one. Some models permit interest rates to become negative, which is undesirable, though how big a problem this is isn't obvious. The class of simple models that provably have positive interest rates without suffering from explosions and match the initial term structure is quite small. The BDT and BK models satisfy these conditions, but don't provide information about future yield curves as needed for the mortgage problem. The Dybvig-adjusted CIR model also satisfies the conditions, but is somewhat hard to work with. There is a lognormal HJM model that avoids negative rates, but it is analytically intractable and suffers from explosions.[24] The lognormal version of the two state Markov model also suffers from

---

[23] B.J. Efron and R.J. Tibshirani, *An Introduction to the Bootstrap* (New York: Chapman & Hall, 1993).

[24] Heath, Jarrow, and Morton, *op. cit.*

explosions, though, as with the lognormal HJM model, these can be eliminated by capping the volatility at some large value. The rational lognormal model has positive rates without explosions, but unreasonable long-term volatility.

It is therefore worth asking whether the empirical question is important. It might turn out to be unimportant in the sense that, properly compared, models that differ only in their assumed dependence of volatility on rates actually give similar answers for option values.

The trick in comparing models is to be sure that the comparisons are truly "apples to apples," by matching term structures of volatility. It is easy to imagine getting different results valuing the same option using the MRG, CIR, and BK models, even though the initial volatilities are set equal — not because of different assumptions about the dependence of volatility on rates, but because the long-term volatilities are different in the three models even when the short-rate volatilities are the same. There are a number of published papers claiming to demonstrate dramatic differences between models, but which actually demonstrate just that the models have been calibrated differently.[25]

Exhibit 2: 52 Week Volatility of Term Structure Changes Plotted Against the 3-Month Spot Rate at the Start of the Period

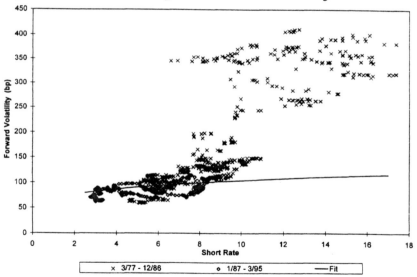

The x's are periods starting 3/77 through 12/86. The diamonds are periods starting 1/87 through 3/95. The data points are based on the best fit k for the period 1/87-3/96, as described in the text. The solid curve shows the best fit to a power law model. The best fit parameters are β=91 bp, γ=0.19. (This is *not* a fit to the points shown here, which are provided solely to give a visual feel for the data.)

---

[25] For a recent example, see M. Uhrig and U. Walter, "A New Numerical Approach to Fitting the Initial Yield Curve," *Journal of Fixed Income* (March 1996).

The two state Markov framework provides a convenient means to compare different choices for the dependence of volatility on rates while holding the initial term structure of volatility fixed. Choosing different forms for $\sigma(r)$ while setting k to a constant in expression (4) gives exactly this comparison. We can value options using these different assumptions and compare time values. (Intrinsic value — the value of the option when the volatility is zero — is of course the same in all models.) To be precise, we set $\sigma(r, t)=\sigma_0(r/r_0)\gamma$, where σ_0 is the initial annualized volatility of the short rate in absolute terms (e.g., 100 bp/year) and r_0 is the initial short rate. Choosing the exponent $\gamma=\{0, 0.5, 1\}$ then gives the MRG model, a square root volatility model (not CIR), and a lognormal model (not BK), respectively.

The results can be summarized by saying that a derivatives trader probably cares about the choice of exponent γ, but a fixed-income portfolio manager probably doesn't. The reason is that the differences in time value are small, except when the time value itself is small — for deep in- or out-of-the-money options. A derivatives trader may be required to price a deep out-of-the-money option, and would get very different results across models, having calibrated them using at-the-money options. A portfolio manager, on the other hand, has option positions embedded in bonds, mortgage-backed securities, etc., whose time value is a small fraction of total portfolio value. So differences that show up only for deep in- or out-of-the-money options are of little consequence. Moreover, a deep out-of-the-money option has small option delta, so small differences in valuation have little effect on measures of portfolio interest rate risk. An in-the-money option can be viewed as a position in the underlying asset plus an out-of-the-money option, so the same reasoning applies.

Exhibit 3 shows the results of one such comparison for a 5-year quarterly pay cap, with a flat initial term structure and modestly decreasing term structure of volatility. The time value for all three values of γ peaks at the same value for an at-the-money cap. Caps with higher strike rates have the largest time value in the lognormal model, because the volatility is increasing for rate moves in the direction that make them valuable. Understanding the behavior for lower strike caps requires using put-call parity: an in-the-money cap can be viewed as paying fixed in a rate swap and owning a floor. The swap has no time value, and the floor has only time value (since it is out-of-the money). The floor's time value is greatest for the MRG model, because it gives the largest volatility for rate moves in the direction that make it valuable. In each case, the square root model gives values intermediate between the MRG and lognormal models, for obvious reasons. At the extremes, 250 bp in or out of the money, time values differ by as much as a factor of 2 between the MRG and lognormal models. At these extremes, though, the time value is only a tenth of its value for the at-the-money cap.

If the initial term structure is not flat, the model differences can be larger. For example, if the term structure is positively sloped, then the model prices match up for an in-the-money rather than at-the-money cap. Using the same parameters as for Exhibit 3, but using the actual Treasury term structure as of 5/13/96 instead of a flat 7% curve, the time values differ at the peak by about 20% — about half a point — between the MRG and lognormal models. Interestingly, as shown in Exhibit 4, even though the time values can be rather different, the option deltas are rather close for the three models. (The deltas are even closer in the flat term structure case.) In this example, if a 9.5% cap were embedded in a floating-rate note priced around par, the effective duration attributable to the cap according to the lognormal model would be 0.49 year, while according to the MRG model it would be 0.17 year. The difference shrinks as the rate gets closer to the cap. This ⅓ year difference isn't trivial, but it's also not large compared to the effect of other modeling assumptions, such as the overall level of volatility or, if mortgages are involved, prepayment expectations.

These are just two numerical examples, but it is easy to see how different variations would affect these results. An inverted term structure would make the MRG model time value largest at the peak and the lognormal model value the smallest. Holding σ_0 constant, higher initial interest rates would yield smaller valuation differences across models since there would be less variation of volatility around the mean. Larger values of the mean reversion k would also produce smaller differences between models, since the short-rate distribution would be tighter around the mean.

Exhibit 3: Time Values for Five Year Quarterly Pay Caps for Gaussian, Square Root and Lognormal Two State Markov Models with Identical Initial Term Structure of Volatility and a 7% Flat Initial Yield Curve*

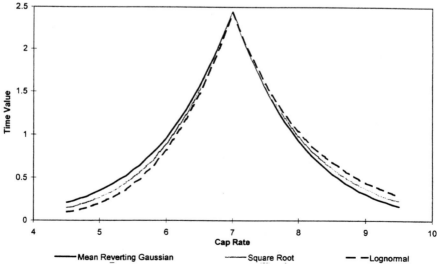

* The model parameters (described in the text) are σ_0=100 bp/yr., k=0.02/yr., equivalent to an initial short-rate volatility of 14.8%, and a 10-year yield volatility of 13.6%.

*Exhibit 4: Sensitivity of Cap Value to Change in Rate Level as a Function of Cap Rate**

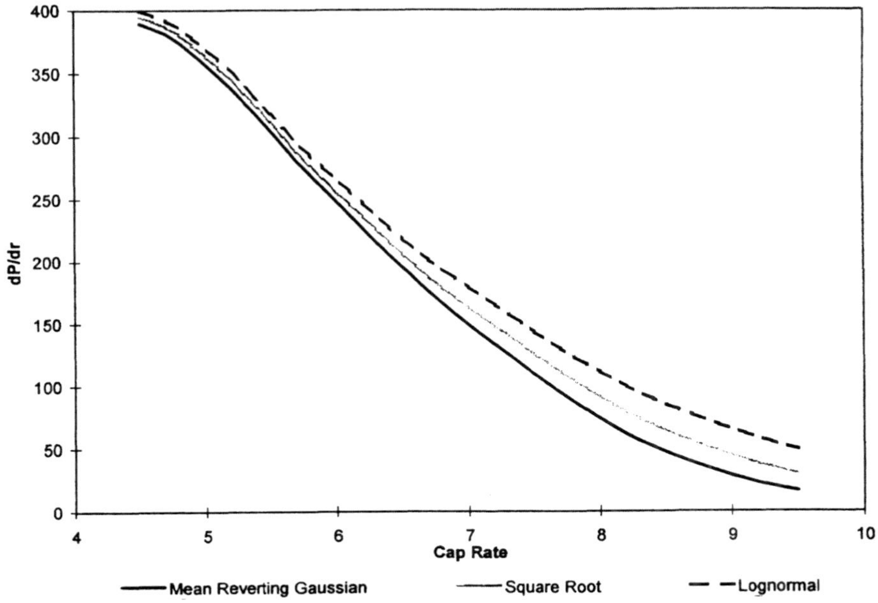
400
350
300
250
200
150
100
50
0
dP/dr
4
5
6
7
8
9
10
Cap Rate
Mean Reverting Gaussian
Square Root
Lognormal

* The cap structure and model parameters are the same as used for Exhibit 3, except that the initial term structure is the (positively sloped) U.S. Treasury curve as of 5/13/96. The short rate volatility is 19.9% and the ten year yield volatility is 14.9%.

Finally, there is the question raised earlier as to whether one should be concerned about the possibility of negative interest rates in some models. From a practical standpoint, this is an issue only if it leads to a significant contribution to pricing from negative rates. One simple way to test this is to look at pricing of a call struck at par for a zero coupon bond. Exhibit 5 shows such a test for the MRG model. For reasonable parameter choices (here taken to be σ_0=100 bp/year, k = 0.02/year, or 20% volatility of a 5% short rate), the call values are quite modest, especially compared to those of a call on a par bond, which gives a feel for the time value of at-the-money options over the same period. The worst case is a call on the longest maturity zero coupon bond which, with a flat 5% yield curve, is priced at 0.60. This is just 5% of the value of a par call on a 30-year par bond. Using the actual May 1996 yield curve, all the option values — other than on the 30-year zero — are negligible. For the 30-year zero the call is worth just 1% of the value of the call on a 30-year par bond. In October 1993, the U.S. Treasury market had the lowest short rate since 1963, and the lowest 10-year rate since 1967. Using that yield curve as a worst case, the zero coupon bond call values are only very slightly higher than the May 1996 values, and still effectively negligible for practical purposes.

Exhibit 5: Valuation of a Continuous Par Call on Zero Coupon and Par Bonds of Various Maturities in the MRG Model

Model parameters are:

$$\sigma_0 \ = \ 100 \text{ bp/year}$$
$$k \ = \ 0.02/\text{year}$$

The value of the call on the zero coupon bond should be zero in every case, assuming non-negative interest rates.

Term	5% Flat Curve		7% Flat Curve		5/96 US Tsy Yields		10/93 US Tsy Yields	
	Zero Cpn	Par Bond	Zero Cpn	Par Bond	Zero Cpn	Par Bond	Zero Cpn	Par Bond
3 Year	<0.01	0.96	<0.01	0.93	<0.01	0.65	<0.01	0.62
5	<0.01	1.93	<0.01	1.83	<0.01	1.43	<0.01	1.27
10	0.06	4.54	<0.01	4.07	<0.01	3.47	0.02	3.06
30	0.60	11.55	0.10	8.85	0.08	7.86	0.09	7.26

Again, it is easy to see how these results change with different assumptions. An inverted curve makes negative rates likelier, so increases the value of a par call on a zero coupon bond. (On the other hand, inverted curves at low interest rate levels are rare.) Conversely, a positive slope to the curve makes negative rates less likely, decreasing the call value. Holding σ_0 constant, lower interest rates produce larger call values. Increasing k produces smaller call values. The only circumstances that are really problematic for the MRG model are flat or inverted yield curves at very low rate levels, with relatively high volatility.

CONCLUSIONS

For portfolio analysis applications, the mean reverting Gaussian model has much to recommend it. For this model, it is easy to implement valuation algorithms for both path independent financial instruments such as bond options, and path dependent financial instruments such as CMOs and annuities. It is one of the simplest models in which it is possible to follow the evolution of the entire yield curve (à la HJM), making it especially useful for valuing assets like mortgage-backed securities whose cash flows depend on longer term rates. The oft raised bogeyman of negative interest rates proves to have little consequence for option pricing, since negative rates occur with very low probability for reasonable values of the model parameters and initial term structure.

Option values are somewhat (though not very) sensitive to the assumed dependence of volatility on the level of rates. The empirical evidence on this relationship is far from clear, with the data (at least in the United States) showing evidence of eras, possibly associated with central bank policy. The numerical evidence shows that, for a sloped term structure, different power law relationships give modestly different at-the-money option time values, and larger relative differences for deep in- or out-of-the-money options. These differences are unlikely to be significant to fixed-income portfolio managers, but are probably a concern for derivatives traders.

Chapter 11

The Four Faces of an Interest Rate Model

Peter Fitton
Director of R&D
Neuristics Corporation

James F. McNatt, CFA
Principal
The Eager Street Group, Inc.

INTRODUCTION

Models of the term structure of interest rates are becoming increasingly important in the practice of finance and actuarial science. However, practitioner understanding of these models has not always kept pace with the breadth of their application. In particular, misinterpretation of the proper uses of a particular model can lead to significant errors. In this chapter, we attempt to clear up some of the most commonly misconstrued aspects of interest rate models: the choice between an arbitrage-free or equilibrium model, and the choice between risk neutral or realistic parameterizations of a model. These two dimensions define four classes of model forms, each of which has its own proper use.

Much of the confusion has arisen from overuse and misuse of the term "arbitrage-free." Virtually all finance practitioners believe that market participants quickly take advantage of any opportunities for risk-free arbitrage among financial assets, so that these opportunities do not exist for long; thus, the term "arbitrage-free" sounds as if it would be a good characteristic for any model to have. Simply based on these positive connotations, it almost seems hard to believe that anyone would not want their model to be arbitrage-free. Briefly, in the world of finance this expression has the associations of motherhood and apple pie.

Unfortunately, this has led some users (and even builders) of interest rate models to link uncritically the expression "arbitrage-free" with the adjective "good." One objective of this chapter is to show that arbitrage-free models are not

The authors would like to thank David Becker of Lincoln National Life for asking the questions that motivated this chapter, and for the many helpful comments that were applied herein. Any remaining errors are the authors' alone.

appropriate for all purposes. Further, we show that just because a model uses the arbitrage-free approach does not mean that it is necessarily good, even for the purposes for which arbitrage-free models are appropriately used.

Another common confusion ensues from implicitly equating the terms "arbitrage-free" and "risk neutral." This arises partly from the fact that, in the academic and practitioner literature, there have been very few papers which have applied the arbitrage-free technique to a model that was not in risk neutral form. We explain the reason for this below. The natural result is that the terms have sometimes been used interchangeably. In addition, since quantitative risk management is a relatively new concept to the finance community, most well-known papers have focused only on the application of interest rate models to simple valuation and hedging problems. These have not required either the realistic or equilibrium approaches to modeling. This lack of published work has led to a mistaken belief that an arbitrage-free, risk neutral model is the only valid kind of term structure model. In this chapter, we intend to dispel that notion.

CATEGORIZATION OF APPROACHES TO TERM STRUCTURE MODELING

Arbitrage-Free Modeling

Arbitrage-free models take certain market prices as given, and adjust model parameters in order to fit the prices exactly. Despite being called "term structure" models, they do not in reality attempt to emulate the dynamics of the term structure. Instead, they assume some computationally convenient, but essentially arbitrary, random process underlying the yield curve, and then add time dependent constants to the drift (mean) and volatility (standard deviation) of the process until all market prices are matched. To achieve this exact fit, they require at least one parameter for every market price used as an input to the model.

For valuation, it is possible to produce reasonable current prices for many assets without having a realistic term structure model, by using arbitrage-free models for interpolation among existing prices. To this end, the trading models used by most dealers in the over-the-counter derivatives market employ enormous numbers of time dependent parameters. These achieve an exact fit to prices of assets in particular classes, without regard to any differences between the behaviors of the models and the actual behavior of the term structure over time. Placed in terms of a physical analogy, the distinction here is between creating a robot based on a photograph of an animal, and creating a robot based on multiple observations of the animal through time. While the robot produced using only the photograph may *look* like the animal, only the robot built based on behavioral observations will *act* like the animal. An arbitrage-free model is like the former robot, constructed with reference to only a single point in time; that is, a snapshot of the fixed-income marketplace.

As an example of an arbitrage-free model, at *RISK Magazine's* "Advanced Mathematics for Derivatives" conference in New York on October 26 and 27, 1995, Merrill Lynch's Greg Merchant presented a linear normal model that used time dependent drifts, volatilities, and correlations to reproduce prices in the Eurodollar, cap, and swaption markets, respectively. It is important to realize that an arbitrage-free model such as this one is just an interpolation system, which reads prices off some complicated hyper-surface that passes through each of the points at which prices are known.

Equilibrium Modeling

In contrast to arbitrage-free models, equilibrium term structure models are truly models of the term structure process. Rather than interpolating among prices at one particular point in time, they attempt to capture the behaviors of the term structure over time. An equilibrium model employs a statistical approach, assuming that market prices are observed with some statistical error, so that the term structure must be *estimated*, rather than taken as given. Equilibrium models do not exactly match market prices at the time of estimation, because they use a small set of state variables (fundamental components of the interest rate process) to describe the term structure. Extant equilibrium models do not contain time dependent parameters; instead they contain a small number of statistically estimated constant parameters, drawn from the historical time series of the yield curve.

Risk Neutral Probabilities:
The Derivative Pricing Probability Measure

When we create a model for pricing interest rate derivatives, the "underlying" is not the price of a traded security, as it would be in a model for equity options. Instead, we specify a random process for the instantaneous, risk-free spot interest rate, the rate payable on an investment in default-free government bonds for a very short period of time. For convenience, we call this interest rate "the short rate." Financial analysts have chosen to create models around the short rate because it is the only truly riskless interest rate in financial markets. An investment in default-free bonds for any non-instantaneous period of time carries *market risk*, the chance that the short rate will rise during the term of the investment, leading to a decline in the investment's value.

As with any risky investment, an investor in bonds subject to market risk expects to earn a risk-free return (that is, the return from continuously investing at the short rate, whatever that may be) plus a risk premium, which could increase or decrease as the term of the investment increases. Thus, the spot rate for a particular term is composed of the return expected under the random process for the short rate up to the end of that term, plus a *term premium*, an additional return to compensate the investor for the interest rate risk of the investment. The term premium offered in the market depends on the aggregate risk preference of market participants, taking into account their natural preferences for securities that conform to their investment (term) needs.

Let r_t be the short rate at time t. Let $D(t, T)$ be the price, at time t, of a discount bond paying one dollar at time T. Let $s(t, T)$ be the spot rate at time t for the term $(T-t)$. Finally, let $\phi(T-t)$ be the term premium (expressed as an annual excess rate of return) required by investors for a term of $(T-t)$. All rates are continuously compounded. We can then write,

$$D(t, T) = \frac{1}{e^{s(t, T) \times (T - t)}} = \frac{1}{e^{\phi(T - t) \times (T - t)}} E\left[\frac{1}{e^{\int_t^T r_s ds}}\right] \tag{1}$$

The second term in the two-term expression above is a discount factor that reflects the expected return from investing continuously at the short rate for the term $(T-t)$. The first term is the additional discount factor that accounts for the return premium that investors require to compensate them for the market risk of investing for a term of $(T-t)$. The use of an integral in the expression for the expected short rate discount factor is necessary because the short rate is continuously changing over the bond's term.

From this description and formula, it may seem necessary to know the term premium for every possible term, in addition to knowing the random process for the short rate, in order to value a default-free discount bond. This is not the case, however. As in the pricing of a forward contract or option on a stock, we can use the mathematical sleight-of-hand known as *risk neutral valuation* to find the relative value of a security that is derivative of the short rate.

The principle of risk neutral valuation as it applies to bonds and other interest rate derivatives is that, regardless of how risk averse investors are, we can identify a set of spot rates that values discount bonds correctly relative to the rest of the market. We do not have to identify separately the term premium embedded in each spot rate in order to use it to discount future cash flows. This fact can be used to make the valuation of all interest rate derivatives easier by *risk adjusting* the term structure model; that is, by changing the probability distribution of the short rate so that the spot rate of every term is, under the new model, equal to the expected return from investing at the short rate over the same term. This is accomplished by redefining the model so that, instead of being a random process for the short rate, it is a random process for the short rate plus a function of the term premium. If we specify the process for r_t^* in such a way that

$$r_s^* = r_s + \phi(s - t) + \phi'(s - t) \times (s - t) \tag{2}$$

at every future point in time s (accomplished by adjusting the rate of increase of r_t upward) then we can write,

$$D(t, T) = \frac{1}{e^{s(t, T) \times (T - t)}} = E\left[\frac{1}{e^{\int_t^T (r_s + \phi(T - t)) ds}}\right] = E\left[\frac{1}{e^{\int_t^T r_s^* ds}}\right] \tag{3}$$

By transforming the short rate process in this manner, we have created a process for a random variable which, when used to discount a certain future cash flow, gives an expected present value equal to the present value obtained by discounting that cash flow at the appropriate spot rate. It is important to note that this random variable is no longer the short rate, but something artificial that we might refer to as the *risk adjusted short rate*.[1]

The resulting *risk neutral model* might be construed as a model for the true behavior of the short rate in an imaginary world of risk neutral market participants, where there is no extra expected return to compensate investors for the extra price risk in bonds of longer maturity. This impression, while accurate, is not very informative. The important aspect of the risk neutral model is that the term premia, whatever their values, that exist in the marketplace are embedded in the interest rate process itself, so that the expected discounted value of a cash flow at the risk adjusted short rate is equal to the discounted value of the cash flow at the spot rate.[2]

The value of the *risk neutral probability measure* is that, under this parameterization, an interest-sensitive instrument's price can be estimated by averaging the present values of its cash flows, discounted at the short term interest rates along each path of the short rate under which those cash flows occur. In contrast, valuing assets under the model before it was risk adjusted would require a more complicated discounting procedure which applied additional discount factors to the short rate paths to compensate for market risk; however, the price obtained under both approaches would be the same. For this reason, we use randomly generated scenarios from risk neutral interest rate models for pricing.

To sum up, there is nothing magical about risk neutrality. There are any number of changes of variables we could make to a short rate process that would retain the structure of the model, but have a different (but equivalent) probability distribution for the new variable. We could change the measure to represent imaginary worlds in which market participants were risk seeking (negative term pre-

---

[1] This is not the way that risk neutrality is usually presented. Typically, writers have focused on the stochastic calculus, using Girsanov's Theorem to justify a change of probability measure to an *equivalent* (i.e., an event has zero probability under one measure if and only if it has zero probability under the other measure) *martingale measure*. This complexity and terminology can obscure the simple intuition that we are making a change of variables in order to restate the problem in a more easily solvable form. For this approach to explaining risk neutral valuation, see G. Courtadon, "The Pricing of Options on Default-free Bonds," *Journal of Financial and Quantitative Analysis* (March 1982), pp. 301-29, or J. Harrison and S. Pliska, "Martingales and Stochastic Integrals in the Theory of Continuous Trading," *Stochastic Processes and their Applications* (1981), pp. 215-260.

[2] Note that this is *not* the same as the expectations hypothesis of the term structure, which holds that the term structure's shape is determined solely by the market's expectations about future rates. The expectations hypothesis is a theory of the real term structure process, whereas the risk neutral approach is an analytical convenience which takes no position about the truth or falsity of any term structure theory. For a brief, cogent discussion of the expectations hypothesis in contrast to risk neutral pricing, see Don Chance, "Theories of the Term Structure: Part I," *Essays in Derivatives* (New Hope, PA: Frank J. Fabozzi Associates, 1998).

mia), or more risk averse than in the real world; regardless, as long as we structured the discounting procedure properly we would always determine the same model price for an interest rate derivative. The specific change of variables that produces a risk neutral model simply makes the algebra easier than the others, because one can ignore risk preferences.

Realistic Probabilities: The Estimated Market Probability Measure

We have described why risk neutral interest rate scenarios are preferred for pricing bonds and interest rate derivatives. However, it is important to note that risk neutral scenarios are not appropriate for all purposes. For example, for scenario-based evaluation of portfolio strategies, realistic simulation is needed. And a computerized system for stress testing asset/liability strategies under adverse movements in interest rates is to actuaries what a wind tunnel is to aerospace engineers. The relevance of the information provided by the testing depends completely on the realism of the simulated environment. Stated differently, the test environment must be like the real environment; if not, the test results are not useful.

The realistic term structure process desired for this kind of stress testing must be distinguished from the risk neutral term structure process used for pricing. The risk neutral process generates scenarios in which all term premia are zero. This process lacks realism; in the real world, term premia are clearly not zero, as evidenced by the fact that the implied spot curve from Treasuries has been upward sloping 85% of the time in the 1955-94 period.[3] This predominantly upward slope reflects an expected return premium for bonds of longer maturity, although approximately 15% of the time some other configuration of buyer preferences can be inferred; for example, an inverted curve suggests that buyers demand an increasing premium for decreasing the term of their positions.

Thus, the user of an interest rate model must be careful. When generating scenarios for reserve adequacy testing, where the purpose is to examine the effect on a company's balance sheet of changes in the real (risk averse) world, he must not use the scenarios from a risk neutral interest rate model.

WHEN DO I USE EACH OF THE MODELING APPROACHES?

The two dimensions, risk neutral versus realistic and arbitrage-free versus equilibrium, define four classes of modeling approaches. Each has its appropriate use.

---

[3] This fact is one of the many useful observations about the realistic term structure process appearing in David Becker, *Stylized Historical Facts Regarding Treasury Interest Rates from 1955 to 1994* (Fort Wayne, IN: Technical report, Lincoln National Life, 1995). See also David Becker, "The Frequency of Inversions of the Yield Curve, and Historical Data on the Volatility and Level of Interest Rates," *Risks and Rewards* (October 1991), pp. 3-5.

Risk Neutral and Arbitrage-Free

The risk neutral and arbitrage-free model is the most familiar form of an interest rate model for most analysts. The model has been risk adjusted to use for pricing interest rate derivatives, and its parameters have been interpolated from a set of current market prices rather than being statistically estimated from historical data. It is appropriately used for current pricing when the set of market prices is complete and reliable.

It is worth noting that, just because two models are each both risk neutral and arbitrage-free, we cannot conclude that they will give the same price for a particular interest rate derivative. Two arbitrage-free models will produce the same prices only for the instruments in a subset common to both sets of input data. The form of the model, and particularly the number of random factors underlying the term structure process, can make a large difference to valuations of the other instruments.

When the market data are sparse, the behavior of the model becomes important. For example, the value of a Bermudan or American swaption depends on the correlations among rates of different maturities. The swaption market is not liquid, nor are its prices widely disseminated, so there is no way to estimate a "term structure of correlations" that would allow a simple arbitrage-free model to interpolate reasonable swaption prices. In this case, a multi-factor model which captures the nature of correlations among rates of different maturities, including the way that those correlations are influenced by the shape of the term structure, will perform better for pricing swaptions than will a one-factor model. Models with good statistical fit to historical correlation series are needed for Bermudan or American options on floating-rate notes, caps, and floors for the same reason. Model behavior is also important for long-dated caps and floors, where there is a lack of reliable data for estimating the "term structure of volatilities" beyond the 5-year tenor.

Risk Neutral and Equilibrium

There are a number of sources of "error" in quotations of the market prices of bonds, so that the discount rates that exactly match a set of price quotations may contain bond-specific effects, corrupting the pricing of other instruments. These sources, defined as any effects on a bond's market price apart from the discount rates applying to all market instruments, include differences in liquidity, differential tax effects, bid-ask spreads (the bid-ask spread defines a range of possible market prices, implying a range of possible discount rates), quotation stickiness, timeliness of data, the human element of the data collection and reporting process, and market imperfections.

Since arbitrage-free models accept all input prices as given, without reference to their reasonability or comparability to other prices in the input data, they impound in the pricing model any bond-specific effects. In contrast, equilibrium models capture the global behavior of the term structure over time, so security-specific effects are treated in the appropriate way, as noise. For this reason, risk neutral equilibrium models can have an advantage over arbitrage-free models in that equilibrium models are not overly sensitive to outliers. Also, for current pricing (as distinguished from horizon pricing, described below), equilibrium models can be estimated from historical data when current market prices are sparse. Thus, a risk neutral and equilibrium model can be used for pricing when the current market prices are unreliable or unavailable.

For most standard instruments, circumstances rarely prevail such that the current market prices needed for estimating an arbitrage-free model are not available. However, such circumstances always prevail for horizon pricing, where the analyst calculates a price for an instrument in some assumed future state of the market. Since arbitrage-free models require a full set of market prices as input, arbitrage-free models are useless for horizon pricing, the future prices being unknown. Thus, the horizon prices obtained under the different values of the state variables in an equilibrium model provide an analytical capability that arbitrage-free models lack.

USING MODELS OF BORROWER BEHAVIOR WITH A RISK NEUTRAL INTEREST RATE MODEL

Often, an interest rate model is not enough to determine the value of a fixed income security or interest rate derivative. To value mortgage-backed securities or collateralized mortgage obligations, one also needs a prepayment model. To value bonds or interest rate derivatives with significant credit risk, one needs a model of default and recovery. To value interest-sensitive annuities and insurance liabilities, one needs models of lapse and other policyholder behaviors. In all of these behavioral models, the levels of certain interest rates are important explanatory variates, meaning that, for example, the prepayment speeds in a CMO valuation system are driven primarily by the interest rate scenarios.

Common practice has been to estimate parameters for prepayment, default, and lapse models using regression on historical data about interest rates and other variables. Then, in the valuation process, the analyst uses the interest rates from a set of risk neutral scenarios to derive estimates for the rates of prepayment, default, or lapse along those scenarios. This borrower behavior information is combined with the interest rates to produce cash flows and, ultimately, prices. Unfortunately, this practice leads to highly misleading results.

The primary problem here is that the regressions have been estimated using historical data, reflecting the *real* probability distributions of borrower behavior, and then used with scenarios from a risk neutral model, with an *artificial* probability distribution. The risk neutral model is not a process for the short rate; rather, it is a process for the risk adjusted short rate. Since the real world is risk averse, the risk adjusted short rate usually has an expected value much higher than the market's forecast of the short rate; the extra premium for interest rate risk permits one to value optionable default-free bonds by reference to the forward rate curve.

The same procedure can be applied to corporate bonds. Corporate bonds are exposed to default risk in addition to interest rate risk. One may construct a behavioral model of failure to pay based on historical data about default rates and recovery, perhaps using bond ratings as explanatory variates in addition to interest rates. One can then attempt to compute the present value of a corporate bond by finding the expected value of the discounted cash flows from the two models in combination: a risk neutral model of the Treasury curve, and a realistic model of default behavior as a function of interest rates and other variables. Because the cash flows of the bond, adjusted for default, will be less than the cash flows for a default-free bond, the model will price the corporate bond at a positive spread over the Treasury curve.

This spread will almost certainly be substantially too low in comparison to the corporate's market price. The reason for this is that, just as investors demand a return premium for interest rate risk, they demand an additional return for default risk. The application of an econometrically estimated model of default to pricing has ignored the default risk premium encapsulated in the prices of corporate bonds. Market practice has evolved a simple solution to this; one adjusts the default model to fit (statistically, in the equilibrium case; exactly, in the arbitrage-free case) the current prices of active corporates in the appropriate rating class. By using the market prices of active corporates to imbed the default risk premium in the model, the analyst is really applying the principle of risk neutral valuation to the default rate. The combined model of risk adjusted interest rates and risk adjusted default rates now discounts using the corporate bond spot rate curve instead of the Treasury spot curve.

The same technique of risk neutralizing a model by embedding information about risk premia derived from current market prices, can be applied to prepayment models as well. The results of a prepayment model can be risk adjusted by examining the prices of active mortgage backed securities. Unfortunately, one can only guess at the appropriate expected return premium for insurance policy lapse risk or mortality risk. Nevertheless, these quantities should be used to "risk neutralize" these models of behavior to the extent practical. The integrity of risk neutral valuation depends on risk adjusting all variables modeled; otherwise, model prices will be consistently overstated.

A final note can be made in this regard about option adjusted spread (OAS). OAS can be understood in this context as a crude method to risk adjust the pricing system to reflect all risk factors not explicitly modeled.

Realistic and Arbitrage-Free

A realistic, arbitrage-free model starts by exactly matching the term structure of interest rates implied by a set of market prices on an initial date, then evolves that curve into the future according to the realistic probability measure. This form of a model is useful for producing scenarios for evaluation of hedges or portfolio strategies, where it is important that the initial curve in each scenario exactly matches current market prices. The difficulty with such an approach lies in the estimation; realistic, arbitrage-free models are affected by *confounding*, where it is impossible to discriminate between model misspecification error and the term premia. Since the model parameters have been set to match market prices exactly, without regard to historical behavior, too few degrees of freedom remain to estimate both the term premia and an error term. Unless the model perfectly describes the true term structure process (that is, the time dependent parameters make the residual pricing error zero at all past and future dates, not just on the date of estimation), the term premia cannot be determined. The result is that realistic, arbitrage-free models are not of practical use.

Realistic and Equilibrium

Since the arbitrage-free form of a realistic model is not available, the equilibrium form must be used for stress testing, Value at Risk (VAR) calculations, reserve and asset adequacy testing, and other uses of realistic scenarios.

Some analysts express concern that, because the *predicted* initial curve under the equilibrium model does not perfectly match observed market prices, then the results of scenario testing will be invalid. However, the use of an equilibrium form does not require that the predictions be used instead of the current market prices as the first point in a scenario. The scenarios can contain the observed curve at the initial date and the conditional predictions at future dates. This does not introduce inconsistency, because the equilibrium model is a statistical model of term structure behavior; by taking this approach we explicitly recognize that its predictions will deviate from observed values by some error. In contrast, the use of an arbitrage-free, realistic model implicitly assumes that the model used for the term structure process is absolutely correct.

Summary of the Four Faces

Exhibit 1 summarizes the uses of the four faces of an interest rate model. Exhibit 2 shows the mathematical form of a commonly used interest rate model, disseminated by Black and Karasinski,[4] under each of the modeling approaches and probability measures. In each equation, u is the natural logarithm of the short rate.

Exhibit 1: When to Use Each of the Model Types

Model Classification	Risk Neutral	Realistic
Arbitrage-free	• Current pricing, where input data (market prices) are reliable	• Unusable, since term premium cannot be reliably estimated
Equilibrium	• Current pricing, where inputs (market prices) are unreliable or unavailable • Horizon pricing	• Stress testing • Reserve and asset adequacy testing

[4] Fischer Black and Piotr Karasinski, "Bond and Option Pricing when Short Rates are Lognormal," *Financial Analysts Journal* (July-August 1991), pp. 52-59.

Exhibit 2: Four Forms of the Black-Karasinski Model

Model Classification	Risk Neutral	Realistic
Arbitrage-free	$du = \kappa(t)\,(\theta(t) - u)\,dt + \sigma(t)\,dz$ • u_0 and $\theta(t)$ matched to bond prices • $\kappa(t)$ and $\sigma(t)$ matched to cap or option prices	$du = \kappa(t)\,(\theta(t) - \lambda(u,t) - u)\,dt + \sigma(t)\,dz$ • u_0 and $\theta(t)$ matched to bond prices • $\kappa(t)$ and $\sigma(t)$ matched to cap or option prices • $\lambda(u,t)$ cannot be reliably estimated
Equilibrium	$du = \kappa(\theta - u)\,dt + \sigma\,dz$ • u_0 statistically fit to bond prices • κ, θ, σ historically estimated	$du = \kappa(\theta - \lambda(u) - u)\,dt + \sigma\,dz$ • u_0 statistically fit to bond prices • $\kappa, \theta, \sigma, \lambda(u)$ historically estimated

In the above models, σ is the instantaneous volatility of the short rate process, κ is the rate of mean reversion, θ is the mean level to which the natural logarithm of the short rate is reverting, and λ represents the term premium demanded by the market for holding bonds of longer maturity. The value of the state variable u at the time of estimation is represented by u_0.

The realistic model forms can be distinguished from the risk neutral forms by the presence of the term premium function λ. The difference between the arbitrage-free forms and the equilibrium forms can be discerned in that the parameters of the arbitrage-free forms are functions of time.

Chapter 12

Valuing Path-Dependent Securities: Some Numerical Examples

C. Douglas Howard, Ph.D.
Assistant Professor of Mathematics
Baruch College, CUNY

INTRODUCTION

Lattice-based valuation techniques are today commonly used to value a host of financial instruments. The procedure typically involves modeling the random behavior of a relevant market observable (often called the "factor"). If the application involved valuing a stock option, for example, the factor would be the underlying stock price. To value a collateralized mortgage obligation (CMO), some proxy for the general level of interest rates would be more relevant. The underlying lattice usually represents a discrete version of a continuous stochastic process that the factor is presumed to follow over time. With some securities, the stock option for example, the procedure is quite straightforward. With other securities, however, the methodology becomes quite cumbersome. The CMO is an extreme example of this latter category.

A major source of complexity arises from "path dependence." This occurs when knowing the value $F(t^*)$ of the factor at some time $t^*>0$ (our convention is that time 0 corresponds to today) does not provide sufficient information to calculate the cash flow generated by the security at time t^*. Rather, in the case of path dependence, the time t^* cash flow also depends in some manner on $F(t)$ for all or some of $0 \le t < t^*$, i.e., how the value of F got to $F(t^*)$ is important.

Consider again a stock option, a European call to be precise. Path dependence is not present in this example. Let $F(t)$ denote the underlying stock price at time t. Suppose the option is exercisable at time T at a strike of K. At any time prior to T, a European option generates no cash flow regardless of what happens to F, thus exhibiting path independence for times $t^*<T$. At time T, the cash flow generated is given by max $(0, F(T) - K)$ — how F got to $F(T)$ is again irrelevant. Note that path dependence *does not* mean simply that the security's cash flow depends

---

Research for this chapter was supported by Andrew Kalotay Associates, Inc. The author thanks Lee Bittengle for surveying the literature on this topic.

on the factor's path. Indeed, the stock option's time T payoff depends on the path of the underlying stock — but *only* through the underlying's value at time T.

A CMO, on the other hand, is heavily path-dependent. Among many other things, we must certainly know the amount of the underlying mortgage pool still outstanding at time $t*$ to calculate the time $t*$ cash flow of the CMO. This, unfortunately, is a function of the prepayment experience from time 0 to time $t*$ which, in turn, is a function of the path of interest rates over this entire period — not just the rate environment at time $t*$.

In this chapter we examine closely two fixed-income securities exhibiting intermediate degrees of path dependence. The first, an indexed amortizing note (IAN), is simply a bond that makes principal payments prior to its stated maturity that are a prescribed function of the prevailing level of interest rates: principal payments are structured to accelerate in low rate environments. As with the much more complicated CMO, path dependence arises because the amount of the IAN outstanding at any point in time (and hence the IAN's cash flow at that time) depends on prior interest rates. The second example, an interest rate derivative, is a periodic cap on a short-term rate. Specifically we study a floating-rate note (FRN) with the feature that its coupon rate, which adjusts yearly, is permitted to increase only a limited amount from one year to the next. If market rates decrease from one year to the next, the FRN's coupon rate decreases accordingly unaffected by the periodic cap. Periodic caps are commonly found embedded along with a host of other option-like features in adjustable-rate mortgages. In this chapter, a one-factor model is used because it is simpler to illustrate the concept of path-dependent securities and their valuation. The principles also apply when a two-factor model is used, where payments are tied to one factor (and its evolution) and valuation is performed using the short-rate factor.

This chapter is organized as follows. In the next section we review the basic methodology of lattice-based arbitrage-free pricing, first abstractly and then with a concrete example. We outline the difference between recursive and Monte Carlo (path sampling) methodologies. This section also develops the notation we use in subsequent sections. Following this, we value a simple IAN first via Monte Carlo and then, with the introduction of a necessary non-stochastic "state" variable, via a recursive procedure. In the last section we subject the periodic cap to the same analysis and discuss some numerical procedures that make problems of this sort more tractable. In this second example a different state variable is called for.

In this chapter, a one-factor model (i.e., a model with one stochastic variable) is used because it is simpler to illustrate the concept of path-dependent securities and their valuation. In some applications, two or more factors may be needed to determine a security's cash flow. The principles illustrated here work equally well in this setting. Note that, for purposes of discounting, the short-term interest rate must always be one of the factors present.

To the author's knowledge, recursive techniques using coupled non-stochastic state variables first appeared in practice in the late 1980's to value sinking fund bonds[1] whose complicated package of embedded options exhibit substantial

---

[1] Salomon Brothers Inc. developed such a model.

path-dependence. Hull and White[2] describe the use of this procedure in a different context. Prior to the advent of the state variable technique, less efficient Monte Carlo procedures were commonly used to value path-dependent securities.[3]

ARBITRAGE-FREE PRICING

The Single-Period Case

Consider the following single-period setup. At some future time $\Delta t > 0$, m different "states of the world" are possible. We label these possible outcomes $1, 2, ...,$ m. For the moment we leave the notion of what exactly a state of the world is as an abstraction. However, let's suppose that this notion contains sufficient information to know the payoff of any security C at time Δt once the outcome is specified. We denote these state-dependent (future) payoffs by $C(1), C(2), ..., C(m)$ and we presume there is no cash flow prior, nor subsequent, to time Δt . Let $aC + bC'$ denote the security that pays $aC(j)+bC'(j)$ in state j (i.e., $aC+bC'$ is a portfolio comprising a units of security C and b units of security C'). Any reasonable method $V(\cdot)$ of ascribing value to securities based on these future payoffs should satisfy:

$$V(aC + bC') = aV(C) + bV(C') \tag{1}$$

$$\text{if } C(j) > 0 \text{ for } 1 \le j \le m \text{ then } V(C) > 0 \tag{2}$$

Condition (1) says that a portfolio may be valued by summing the values of its constituent securities weighted by amounts held in the portfolio, while condition (2) is the "arbitrage-free" condition that any security generating positive payoff in every future outcome has positive value today. One can show that any such $V(\cdot)$ must be of the form:

$$V(C) = e^{-r\Delta t}(p_1 C(1) + p_2 C(2) + ... + p_m C(m)) \tag{3}$$

where $p_1, p_2, ..., p_m$ satisfy

$$\text{each } p_j \ge 0 \text{ and } \sum_{j=1}^{m} p_j = 1 \tag{4}$$

Note, in particular, that the p_j behave like probabilities (they are referred to as *arbitrage probabilities*). For any security C, this calculation represents the expected payoff of C at time Δt discounted back to today at the continuously compounding annual risk-free rate r.

---

[2] See J. Hull and A. White, "Efficient Procedures for Valuing European and American Path-Dependent Options," *Journal of Derivatives* (Fall 1993), pp. 21-31. For other numerical examples and a good list of further references, see Chapter 18 in J. Hull, *Options, Futures, and Other Derivatives* (Englewood Cliffs, NJ: Prentice Hall, 1997).

[3] See, for example, W.C. Hunter and D.W. Stowe, "Path-Dependent Options: Valuation and Applications," *Economic Review*, Federal Reserve Bank of Atlanta, 77:2 (1992), pp. 29-34.

The Multi-Period Case

Most securities generate a sequence of cash flow over time — not just one future payoff. The single-period model generalizes to accommodate this fact. Suppose our security C generates cash flow at a sequence of times $0 = t < t_1 < t_2 < ... < t_n = T$. Between the t_i and after T there is no possibility of cash flow. At the i-th period there are $m(i)$ possible states of the world which, again, we label $1, 2, ..., m(i)$. When $i=0$, of course, there is only one state so $m(0)=1$. We assume that the description of the states at period i contains any information necessary to calculate the state-dependent period i cash flow $CF_i(j)$ for each state $1 \le j \le m(i)$. In the multi-period model, an "outcome" corresponds to a sequence of states

$$\omega = (j_1, ..., j_n) \text{ where } 1 \le j_i \le m(i)$$

representing how the world unfolds over time. We let Ω represent the space of all such outcomes.

We shall refer to a pair (i,j), where i is a time period $(0 \le i < n)$ and j is a state $(1 \le j \le m(i))$, as a "node." Assume that at each node there resides a single-period arbitrage-free pricing (AFP) model specified by the node-dependent risk-free rate r_{ij} and arbitrage probabilities $p_i(j \to j')$ for each j' with $1 \le j' \le m(i + 1)$. This latter expression represents the probability of a transition from state j in period i to state j' in period $i+1$.

Suppose that at time t_i we are in state j. The aggregate payoff of C one period forward (at time t_{i+1}) comes from two sources: (1) the cash flow $CF_{i+1}(j')$ generated by C at time t_{i+1} (which depends on the period $i+1$ state j'); and (2) the value, which we denote $V_{i+1}(j')$, assigned at node $(i+1,j')$ to the *subsequent* cash flow that C may generate at times $t_{i+2}, ..., t_n$. Using equation (3), we deduce that we must have

$$V_i(j) = e^{-r_{ij}(t_{i+1} - t_i)} \sum_{j' = 1}^{m(i + 1)} p_i(j \to j')[CF_{i + 1}(j') + V_{i + 1}(j')] \tag{5}$$

if our model is to satisfy conditions (1) and (2) at each node. Since we know the state dependent cash flow $CF_{i+1}(j')$, this procedure makes sense if we know the $V_{i+1}(j')$'s. But we know that $V_n(j') = 0$ for $1 \le j' \le m(n)$: this is merely the statement that there *is no* cash flow subsequent to time t_n. This allows us to apply equation (5) when $i=n-1$ to calculate the $V_{n-1}(j)$'s. But then we can apply equation (5) to $i=n-2$ and so forth, backwards (recursively) through the lattice, until we have calculated $V_0(1)$. But $V_0(1)$ represents the value today of all future cash flow — precisely what we are interested in.

A Simple Example

We make this concrete with a simple example. In the subsequent sections, we will expand upon this same example for purposes of valuing the IAN and periodic cap. Suppose each $t_i = i$ (so cash flow can occur only annually) and consider the lattice shown in Exhibit 1. The arbitrage probabilities are prescribed as follows:

Exhibit 1: State-Dependent 1-Year Risk-Free Rate

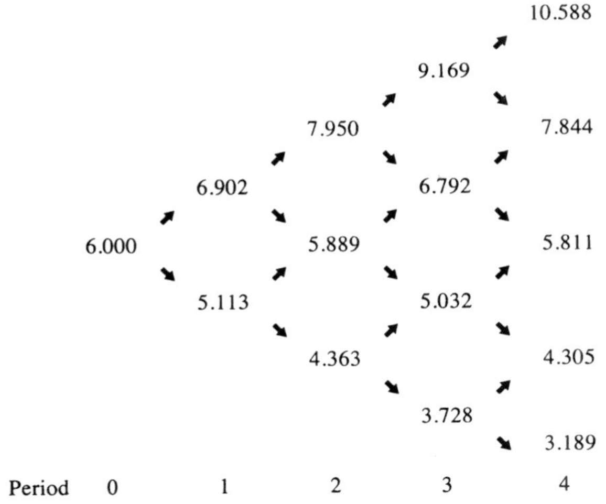

```
                                                        10.588
                                                      ↗
                                            9.169
                                          ↗       ↘
                               7.950                  7.844
                             ↗       ↘              ↗
                    6.902                  6.792
                  ↗       ↘              ↗       ↘
         6.000                  5.889                  5.811
              ↘              ↗       ↘              ↗
                    5.113                  5.032
                          ↘              ↗       ↘
                               4.363                  4.305
                                     ↘              ↗
                                          3.728
                                                ↘
                                                    ↘   3.189

Period   0          1          2          3          4
```

$$p_i(j \to j') = \begin{cases} 0.5 & \text{if } j' = j \text{ or } j' = j+1 \\ 0 & \text{otherwise} \end{cases}$$

and only those transitions with positive probability are shown in Exhibit 1. The numbers at each node correspond to the r_{ij} stated as rates compounded *annually* so as to correspond, for convenience, to the time increments. With the r_{ij} quoted in this manner and noting that $t_{i+1} - t_i = 1$, equation (5) must be rewritten as

$$V_i(j) = \frac{1}{1+r_{ij}} \sum_{j'=1}^{m(i+1)} p_i(j \to j')[CF_{i+1}(j') + V_{i+1}(j')] \tag{6}$$

and setting into this the values for our arbitrage probabilities yields

$$V_i(j) = \frac{1}{1+r_{ij}}[0.5(CF_{i+1}(j) + V_{i+1}(j))$$
$$+ 0.5(CF_{i+1}(j+1) + V_{i+1}(j+1))] \tag{7}$$

We use this setup to value a (risk-free) bond that pays $6 in years 1, 2, and 3, and $106 in year 4 irrespective of the states in those periods. Exhibit 2 shows the values of $C_i(j)$ and $V_i(j)$ that equation (7) produces in this setting. For example, letting $\langle 6.902 \rangle$ denote the state (in period 1) in which the 1-year rate is 6.902%, the calculation of $V_1(\langle 6.902 \rangle)$ is

$$V_1(\langle 6.902 \rangle) = \frac{1}{1.06902}[0.5(6.0 + 100.190) + 0.5(6.0 + 96.505)] = 97.610$$

Exhibit 2: State-Dependent $C_i(\cdot)$ and $V_i(\cdot)$ for the 3-Year Note

Period 0	Period 1	Period 2	Period 3	Period 4
				106.000 0.000
			6.000 97.097	
		6.000 96.505		106.000 0.000
	6.000 97.610		6.000 99.258	
		6.000 100.190		106.000 0.000
100.000				
	6.000 102.390		6.000 100.922	
		6.000 103.060		106.000 0.000
			6.000 102.190	
				106.000 0.000

We note that this bond is valued today at 100.0. In fact, the four bonds paying a 6% annual coupon maturing in 1, 2, 3, and 4 years are all valued at 100.0. This lattice was *constructed* to explain a flat 6% term structure. One can also confirm that the local volatility of the 1-year rate is 15% throughout the lattice (e.g., ½ log(6.902/5.113) = 0.15).

There is another algorithm that arrives at the 100.0 value of the 4 year 6% bond. Specifically: (1) calculate the period-by-period cash flow corresponding to each of the (sixteen) 4 year paths through the lattice; (2) discount each of those flows back to today using the earlier path-dependent r_{ij} to arrive at a "path-dependent present value" $PV(\omega)$; (3) calculate the expected PV over the sixteen paths ω. We represent a path ω by a sequence of +'s and –'s depending on whether at each juncture we move up or down, respectively. Then, for this 4 year 6% bond, we have, for example:

$$PV(+ + + +) = 106.0/1.09169/1.0795/1.06902/1.06$$
$$+ \ 6.0/1.0795/1.06902/1.06$$
$$+ \ 6.0/1.06902/1.06$$
$$+ \ 6.0/1.06$$
$$= 95.237$$

Note also that $PV(+ + + -) = 95.237$ also. This is because neither the year 4 cash flow nor the discounting process depend on the year 4 interest rate. This holds in this case for all paths ω: $PV(\omega)$ is independent of the last + or – step. Notationally, we write this as $PV(+ + + \pm) = 95.237$. Calculating an expected value over the eight equally likely pairs of paths $(+ + + \pm)$, $(+ + - \pm)$, $(+ - + \pm)$, $(+ - - \pm)$, $(- + + \pm)$, $(- + - \pm)$, $(- - + \pm)$, and $(- - - \pm)$ (respectively) gives:

$$V_0(1) = (95.237+97.004+98.678+100.064$$
$$+100.261+101.671+102.997+104.088) \, / \, 8 \qquad (8)$$
$$= 100.000$$

This procedure works for general securities in the setting of equation (6). In fact, letting

$$p(\omega) = \prod_{i=0}^{n-1} p_i(j_i \rightarrow j_{i+1})$$

denote the probability of observing the path $\omega = (j_1, ...,j_n)$, (where $j_0=1$ — today's state) we have in general that

$$V_0(1) = \sum_{\omega \in \Omega} PV(\omega)p(\omega) = \sum_{\omega \in \Omega} \left[\sum_{i=1}^{n} CF_i(j_i)d_i(\omega) \right] p(\omega) \qquad (9)$$

where

$$d_i(\omega) = \prod_{k=0}^{i-1} \frac{1}{1+r_{kj_k}}$$

is the path-dependent discount factor that discounts a period i cash flow to today. (Equation (9) can be proved by induction on the length of the lattice and partitioning Ω on the value of j_1.)

We refer to equation (9) as the Monte Carlo approach. This is somewhat of a misnomer since equation (9) samples *every* path ω through the lattice and calculates the average of $PV(\omega)$ weighted by the probability of observing each path ω. In practice, the scale of the problem will be much larger and there will be too many paths through the lattice to perform an exhaustive sampling. Usually, therefore, Monte Carlo simulation involves *estimating* $V_0(1)$ by randomly sampling paths through the lattice in a manner such that the probability of selecting any particular path ω is precisely $p(\omega)$. In general (and depending on the variance of $PV(\omega)$ across paths), accurate estimates require a large number of sample paths making the method computationally inefficient.

INDEXED AMORTIZING NOTES

Presently we apply these two approaches to the IAN — our first example of a path-dependent security. The stochastic factor is the one year risk-free rate, which follows the stochastic process in the previous example (Exhibit 1). Recall that this means 6% is a market yield for risk-free bonds maturing in 1, 2, 3, and 4 years. The security is a 4-year IAN paying interest annually at a fixed rate of 6% per year. Regardless of what happens to interest rates, there is no principal payment the first year (the "lock-out" period). In years two and three, the amount of principal paid depends on the level of the 1-year rate via the "amortization schedule": if the 1-year rate is below 5%, 75% of the remaining balance is repaid; if the rate is between 5% and 6%, 50% of the balance is repaid; if the rate exceeds 6%, there is no principal payment. If a principal payment made in accordance with this formula brings the outstanding balance below 20% of the amount originally issued (which we take to be 100.0), the entire bond is retired immediately (the "clean-up" provision). At maturity in year 4 any remaining principal is amortized. Instruments with these qualitative features are quite common, both as stand-alone notes and, more frequently, as the fixed-pay side of interest rate swaps. We observe that the amortization schedule accelerates principal payment in low rate environments and thus behaves like a partial par call. We expect, therefore, that this note will be valued below 100.0 since a note with the same coupon but no principal acceleration is valued at 100.0.

Valuation Via Monte Carlo

First we value the IAN via Monte Carlo, where it is again feasible to sample every path and calculate exactly the expected value of $PV(\omega)$. Again, we describe paths by a sequence of + or − signs, so, for example $\omega = (- - - -)$ corresponds to the following progression of the 1-year yield:

year 1		year 2		year 3		year 4
6.000%	→	5.113%	→	4.363%	→	3.728%	→	3.189%

producing the following sequence of principal payments:

year 1	year 2	year 3	year 4
0.0	75.0	25.0	0.0

This particular path illustrates the lock-out period (year 1: there is no amortization even though 5.113 < 6.0), the amortization schedule (year 2: the payment is 75.0 because 4.363 < 5.0), and the clean-up provision (year 3: the payment *would be* 0.75 × 25.0 but this would leave only 6.25 outstanding which is less than the clean-up provision). When interest payments on the outstanding principal are added, the following sequence of cash flow results:

year 1	year 2	year 3	year 4
6.0	81.0	26.5	0.0

The resulting PV is calculated as

$$PV(- - - -) = 26.5/1.04363/1.05113/1.06$$
$$+ 81.0/1.05113/1.06$$
$$+ 6.0/1.06$$
$$= 101.148$$

Exhibit 3: Path-by-Path Analysis of the IAN

ω	Year 1	Year 2	Year 3	Year 4	PV(ω)
(+ + + +)	6.000	6.000	6.000	106.000	95.237
(+ + + −)	6.000	6.000	6.000	106.000	95.237
(+ + − +)	6.000	6.000	6.000	106.000	97.004
(+ + − −)	6.000	6.000	6.000	106.000	97.004
(+ − + +)	6.000	56.000	3.000	53.000	98.941
(+ − + −)	6.000	56.000	3.000	53.000	98.941
(+ − − +)	6.000	56.000	28.000	26.500	99.442
(+ − − −)	6.000	56.000	28.000	26.500	99.442
(− + + +)	6.000	56.000	3.000	53.000	100.528
(− + + −)	6.000	56.000	3.000	53.000	100.528
(− + − +)	6.000	56.000	28.000	26.500	101.038
(− + − −)	6.000	56.000	28.000	26.500	101.038
(− − + +)	6.000	81.000	26.500	0.000	101.148
(− − + −)	6.000	81.000	26.500	0.000	101.148
(− − − +)	6.000	81.000	26.500	0.000	101.148
(− − − −)	6.000	81.000	26.500	0.000	101.148

Repeating this exercise for each of the 16 paths through the lattice yields the table of cash flow and *PV* shown in Exhibit 3. Since each path through this lattice has equal probability, we may calculate the expected value of $PV(\omega)$ by simply averaging the final column in this table. This yields 99.311. Any recursive procedure, of course, must agree with this calculation of value.

The path dependence of the IAN can be observed in this table. For example, consider the paths (+ + − −), (+ − + −), (− + − +), and (− − + +). In each case, the state in year 4 corresponds to a 1-year rate of 5.811%, i.e., each of these paths ends up in state ⟨5.811⟩. However, the year 4 cash flow corresponding to these paths is 106.0, 53.0, 26.5, and 0.0, respectively. Hence the cash flow in year 4 cannot be deduced from the state in year 4 — it is influenced also by how one gets to that state.

Recursive Valuation

To value the IAN recursively, we partition the interest rate states (like ⟨5.811⟩) by further specifying how much of the IAN is outstanding *before* the principal payment of that year. The state ⟨5.811⟩, for example, is partitioned into ⟨5.811, 100⟩, ⟨5.811, 50⟩, ⟨5.811, 25⟩, and ⟨5.811, 0⟩. This additional variable, whose values partition the state as specified by the value of the stochastic variable, is referred to as a non-stochastic state variable and its range of attainable values is referred to as the state space. (It is easy in this example to verify that the state space is {0, 25, 50, 100}, i.e., at all times one of these amounts must be outstanding. More about this later.) Notice that some states, ⟨3.189, 100⟩ for example, are impossible to reach. This phenomenon will not make our calculations incorrect, it just means that we will do some unnecessary calculations.

Once the time t 1-year rate and amount outstanding (prior to current-period amortization) are *both* specified as, say, $\langle r, P \rangle$, the time t cash flow can easily be calculated: the interest component is just $0.06P$; the principal component is deduced from the value of P, the lock-out period, the amortization table, and the clean-up provision by the formula

$$\text{time } t \text{ principal payment} = \begin{cases} 0 & \text{if } t = 1 \\ 0.75P & \text{if } t = 2 \text{ or } 3, r < 5\%, \text{ and } 0.25P > 20 \\ 0.5P & \text{if } t = 2 \text{ or } 3, 5\% \leq r < 6\%, \text{ and } 0.5P > 20 \\ 0 & \text{if } t = 2 \text{ or } 3, \text{ and } r \geq 6\% \\ P & \text{otherwise} \end{cases}$$

and the state-dependent cash flow is the sum of interest and principal. We begin our recursive calculations at the end of the lattice, just as we do when there is no path dependence. Exhibit 4 shows for periods 1 through 4 the cash flow $CF_i(\langle r, P \rangle)$ calculated as just described (and shown as principal and interest combined) as well as the value of subsequent cash flow $V_i(\langle r, P \rangle)$ (shown just below the cash flow) for each combination of r and P.

We reiterate that $V_4(\langle r, P \rangle) = 0$ for all r and P since there is no cash flow after year 4. Since the IAN matures in period 4, the cash flow is simply the sum of the amount outstanding and interest on that amount — a calculation that is independent of the 1-year rate at period 4. For example, the period 4 cash flow corresponding to state $\langle 4.305, 25 \rangle$ is $25.0 + 1.5 = 26.5$.

The situation is more complicated in period 3. Here the amortization schedule and the amount outstanding interact to determine the cash flow. Consider, for example, the calculations corresponding to state $\langle 5.032, 50 \rangle$. The interest payment of 3 is calculated as 0.06×50.0. Also, since $5.0 \leq 5.032 < 6.0$, 50% of the outstanding amount is prepaid in period 3. This principal payment of 25.0 leaves 25.0 still outstanding — an amount which exceeds the clean-up provision. The state $\langle 5.032, 50 \rangle$ cash flow is therefore $25.0 + 3.0 = 28.0$. Next we calculate $V_3(\langle 5.032, 50 \rangle)$. From a rate of 5.032% in year 3, the stochastic interest rate process moves to either 4.305% or 5.811% in year 4 — each possibility with probability ½ (see Exhibit 1). Since 50.0 of principal was outstanding (before the period 3 payment) and 25.0 is paid off in period 3, the amount outstanding changes to 25.0. Thus, from state $\langle 5.032, 50 \rangle$ in period 3, one moves to either $\langle 4.305, 25 \rangle$ or $\langle 5.811, 25 \rangle$ in year 4 with each possibility having probability ½. We therefore have, using equation (6) and the period 4 results in Exhibit 4,

$$V_3(\langle 5.032, 50 \rangle) = \frac{1}{1.05032}[0.5(26.5 + 0.0) + 0.5(26.5 + 0.0)] = 25.230$$

Compare this with the analogous calculations for state $\langle 5.032, 25 \rangle$ in period 3. The interest cash flow is $0.06 \times 25.0 = 1.5$. The principal payment specified by the amortization schedule is again 50% of the amount outstanding which results in a payment of $12.5 = 0.5 \times 25.0$. This would leave only 12.5 remaining outstanding, however, so the clean-up provision requires that the entire amount of 25.0 be retired leaving nothing outstanding. Thus, from state $\langle 5.032, 25 \rangle$ in period 3, one moves to either $\langle 4.305, 0 \rangle$ or $\langle 5.811, 0 \rangle$ in period 4, with probability ½. Hence

$$V_3(\langle 5.032, 25 \rangle) = \frac{1}{1.05032}[0.5(0.0 + 0.0) + 0.5(0.0 + 0.0)] = 0.0$$

The calculations in period 2 are analogous. For example, in state $\langle 5.889, 100 \rangle$, the principal payment is 50.0 generating a cash flow of 6.0+50.0=56.0 and leaving 50.0 remaining outstanding. Hence one moves from state $\langle 5.889, 100 \rangle$ in period 2 to either $\langle 5.032, 50 \rangle$ or $\langle 6.792, 50 \rangle$ in period 3, each with equal likelihood. Thus

$$V_2(\langle 5.889, 100 \rangle) = \frac{1}{1.05889}[0.5(28.0 + 25.230) + 0.5(3.0 + 49.629)]$$

$$= 49.986$$

Exhibit 4: $CF_i(\cdot)$ and $V_i(\cdot)$ for the IAN

| | | Amount Outstanding | | | |
		0	25	50	100
Period 1	6.902%	0.000	1.500	3.000	6.000
		0.000	24.381	48.732	97.515
	5.113	0.000	1.500	3.000	6.000
		0.000	25.211	50.393	101.024
Period 2	7.950	0.000	1.500	3.000	6.000
		0.000	24.127	48.253	96.506
	5.889	0.000	26.500	28.000	56.000
		0.000	0.000	24.939	49.986
	4.363	0.000	26.500	53.000	81.000
		0.000	0.000	0.000	25.392
Period 3	9.169	0.000	1.500	3.000	6.000
		0.000	24.274	48.549	97.097
	6.792	0.000	1.500	3.000	6.000
		0.000	24.815	49.629	99.258
	5.032	0.000	26.500	28.000	56.000
		0.000	0.000	25.230	50.461
	3.728	0.000	26.500	53.000	81.000
		0.000	0.000	0.000	25.548
Period 4	10.588	0.000	26.500	53.000	106.000
		0.000	0.000	0.000	0.000
	7.844	0.000	26.500	53.000	106.000
		0.000	0.000	0.000	0.000
	5.811	0.000	26.500	53.000	106.000
		0.000	0.000	0.000	0.000
	4.305	0.000	26.500	53.000	106.000
		0.000	0.000	0.000	0.000
	3.189	0.000	26.500	53.000	106.000
		0.000	0.000	0.000	0.000

Similarly, in period 1, one moves from state $\langle 5.113,100 \rangle$ to either $\langle 4.363,100 \rangle$ or $\langle 5.889,100 \rangle$ in period 2, each with equal likelihood. Thus, $CF_1(\langle 5.113,100 \rangle) = 0.06 \times 100.0$ (plus 0 principal) and

$$V_1(\langle 5.113, 100 \rangle) = \frac{1}{1.05113}[0.5(81.0 + 25.392) + 0.5(56.0 + 49.986)]$$

$$= 101.024$$

Finally, at time 0 (not shown in Exhibit 4), there is only today's state $\langle 6.000, 100 \rangle$ to calculate. From this state we move to either $\langle 5.113,100 \rangle$ or $\langle 6.902,100 \rangle$, each with probability ½. We therefore have

$$V_0(1) = V_0(\langle 6.000, 100 \rangle) = \frac{1}{1.06}[0.5(6.0 + 101.024) + 0.5(6.0 + 97.515)]$$

$$= 99.311$$

This agrees, as required, with the result obtained via the Monte Carlo analysis.

Selecting the Necessary State Space

As we previously observed, only the amounts in the list {0,25,50,100} can be outstanding at any point in time. This is because the IAN starts with 100.0 outstanding and this list is closed under the rules of principal amortization (the amortization schedule and the clean-up provision). (For example, if we amortize 50% of 50.0 we get 25.0 outstanding, another number in the list.) In general, it may not be so easy to construct an exhaustive list of possible states or, commonly, the list of possible states may be very large. A very effective numerical procedure is to partition the range of the state space (in this case, the range is from 0 to 100 outstanding) into a manageable number of "buckets," for example: 0, 20-30, 30-40,..., 90-100. Sometimes a surprisingly small number of buckets can lead to a very good approximation of the precise answer. We illustrate this technique with the periodic cap in the next section.

Notice also that not all the states in each period can be reached. For example, in periods 1 and 2 only those states with 100.0 outstanding are reached. This is because the lock-out provision prevents any amortization until year 2. Thus, even in year 2, the amount outstanding prior to that year's amortization must be 100.0. In Exhibit 4 we have highlighted the region of each period's state space that is actually reachable.

From the standpoint of computational efficiency, it may be better to first pass *forward* through the lattice to determine which states are actually reachable. Then, during the recursive process described above, it is only necessary to calculate the CF_i and V_i values for those states that are flagged as reachable in the first pass. In our IAN example, this would result in substantial savings. On the other hand, in some situations, this forward pass may take more time than it saves. It may be better to compromise and avoid only some of the unused state space by (non-time-consuming) ad hoc reasoning. In the case of the IAN, for example, the unnecessary states in periods 1 and 2 could be avoided simply by recognizing the effects of the lock-out provision. The best computational strategy will certainly depend on the application.

PERIODIC CAPS

In this final section we subject a floating-rate note with an embedded periodic cap to similar analyses. We illustrate with this application both the bucketing and forward pass numerical procedures described above. Specifically, consider a 4-year FRN that, for ease of exposition, pays interest annually. Its initial rate of interest is 6% — today's 1-year risk-free rate. Each year, the note's rate of interest resets to the new 1-year risk-free rate subject to the constraint that the rate is not permitted to increase (a very strong periodic cap!). In year 4, the note makes a final interest rate payment (of at most 6% due to the periodic cap) and returns the original principal (which we again take to be 100.0). We study this instrument in the same yield environment as before: a flat 6% term structure with a 15% volatility. Exhibit 1 again represents the underlying interest rate process.

Valuation via Monte Carlo

Consider again the interest rate path $\omega = (- - - -)$ through the lattice in Exhibit 1:

	year 1	year 2	year 3	year 4
6.000% →	5.113% →	4.363% →	3.728% →	3.189%

Since the 1-year yield decreases steadily along this path, the periodic cap has no impact. The capped FRN behaves just as an uncapped FRN producing the following sequence of cash flow:

year 1	year 2	year 3	year 4
6.000	5.113	4.363	103.728

resulting in the *PV* calculation:

$$\begin{aligned} PV(- - - -) &= 103.728/1.03728/1.04363/1.05113/1.06 \\ &+ 4.363/1.04363/1.05113/1.06 \\ &+ 5.113/1.05113/1.06 \\ &+ 6.0/1.06 \\ &= 100.000 \end{aligned}$$

It is not surprising that for this choice of ω we have a path-dependent present value of exactly 100.000 since the security is always paying a rate of interest equal to the discount rate.

In the scenario corresponding to $\omega = (+ + + +)$, which unfolds as follows:

	year 1	year 2	year 3	year 4
6.000% →	6.902% →	7.950% →	9.169% →	10.588%

Exhibit 5: Path-by-Path Analysis of the Capped FRN

ω	Year 1	Year 2	Year 3	Year 4	PV(ω)
(+ + + +)	6.000	6.000	6.000	106.000	95.237
(+ + + −)	6.000	6.000	6.000	106.000	95.237
(+ + − +)	6.000	6.000	6.000	106.000	97.004
(+ + − −)	6.000	6.000	6.000	106.000	97.004
(+ − + +)	6.000	6.000	5.889	105.889	98.499
(+ − + −)	6.000	6.000	5.889	105.889	98.499
(+ − − +)	6.000	6.000	5.889	105.032	99.204
(+ − − −)	6.000	6.000	5.889	105.032	99.204
(− + + +)	6.000	5.113	5.113	105.113	98.010
(− + + −)	6.000	5.113	5.113	105.113	98.010
(− + − +)	6.000	5.113	5.113	105.032	99.342
(− + − −)	6.000	5.113	5.113	105.032	99.342
(− − + +)	6.000	5.113	4.363	104.363	99.452
(− − + −)	6.000	5.113	4.363	104.363	99.452
(− − − +)	6.000	5.113	4.363	103.728	100.000
(− − − −)	6.000	5.113	4.363	103.728	100.000

the situation is very different. In each year, the periodic cap is binding, preventing the interest rate from increasing. The resulting sequence of cash flow is therefore:

year 1	year 2	year 3	year 4
6.000	6.000	6.000	106.000

which produces the result $PV(\omega) = 95.237$.

Exhibit 5 shows the same analysis for all 16 paths through the lattice. Since the paths are all equally likely, the arithmetic average of the path-dependent present values yields the value of the capped FRN. This number is 98.343. Noting that the value of the uncapped FRN is 100.000 (this follows since, in every path, the uncapped FRN is always paying an interest rate equal to the discount rate), we deduce that the value of the periodic cap (to the issuer) is 100.000 − 98.343 = 1.657. As with the IAN, this is an exact calculation representing an exhaustive sampling of the 16 paths through the lattice. In practice, of course, an exhaustive sampling would be impossible and valuing a periodic cap with this approach would require true Monte Carlo path sampling.

Exhibit 5 reveals the path-dependent nature of the capped FRN. In particular, the six paths that end in year 4 at the interest rate state ⟨5.881⟩ (i.e., paths with two +'s and two −'s) produce five different cash flow amounts corresponding to that state. Notice also that the periodic cap behaves very differently from a straight cap at 6% (see, for example, the path $\omega = (− + − +)$).

Recursive Valuation

Finally, we use a recursive procedure to value the capped FRN and hence the periodic cap itself. In this example, the non-stochastic state variable that we couple with the stochastic process governing the 1-year risk-free rate is simply the current interest rate that the capped FRN is paying, a number which we call C. At any period a state is denoted by $\langle r, C \rangle$, where C takes on values in

$$C = \{3.728, 4.363, 5.032, 5.113, 5.889, 6.000\}$$

and r is the state-dependent 1-year risk-free rate. We remark that only in year 4 are all six possibilities for C attainable. In our simple example, C is quickly obtained from a glance at Exhibit 5. As previously mentioned, in general it may be impractical to explicitly calculate the state space or its size may render the calculations intractable. A numerical shortcut is necessary.

Bucketing and the Forward Pass
We illustrate the bucketing procedure described above by crudely *assuming* that C takes on one of the four values in

$$\hat{C} = \{3.000, 4.000, 5.000, 6.000\}$$

a numerical simplification that will result in obtaining only an approximate solution. (We think of these numbers as buckets into which intermediate values are placed.) In period 4, for example, r assumes one of five possible values each of which is partitioned by the four states of C, yielding 20 states of the world.

Exhibit 6 shows the forward pass analysis that is used to flag the subset of states in each period that are actually reachable. The period 0 analysis is straightforward. Referring to today's state simply as $\langle 6.000 \rangle$ (today's value of r), the value of r moves from 6.000 to either 5.113 or 6.902 (refer again to Exhibit 1) and in either case the period 1 value of C will be 6.000 (the capped FRN's initial interest rate). Hence only the states $\langle 5.113, 6.000 \rangle$ and $\langle 6.902, 6.000 \rangle$ are reachable in period 1. The period 1 analysis illustrates a ramification of the bucketing approximation. From state $\langle 5.113, 6.000 \rangle$ the value of r moves to either 4.363 or 5.889. The value of C, however, should change to 5.113 (because the FRN is permitted to reset downward) which is a number not present in $\hat{C}$. Numerically, we will interpolate between what happens when C=5.000 and C=6.000 in period 2. Therefore, to calculate values in state $\langle 5.113, 6.000 \rangle$ in period 1 we must have already calculated values in states $\langle 4.363, 5.000 \rangle$, $\langle 4.363, 6.000 \rangle$, $\langle 5.889, 5.000 \rangle$, and $\langle 5.889, 6.000 \rangle$ in period 2. We therefore flag these four states as reachable. From state $\langle 6.902, 6.000 \rangle$ in period 1, in contrast, the value of C is not permitted to reset upward to 6.902 and only states $\langle 5.889, 6.000 \rangle$ and $\langle 7.950, 6.000 \rangle$ are reachable in period 2. We collect the (five) states in period 2 that it is possible to reach from the reachable states in period 1 and repeat the analysis at each of these states. Moving forward period-by-period confirms that we need only calculate values for the portion of the state space in Exhibit 7 where numbers are displayed.

The Recursive Valuation Pass
Finally, we move backward through the lattice calculating the relevant values of $CF_i(\cdot)$ and $V_i(\cdot)$ (see Exhibit 7 — calculations start at the bottom).

Exhibit 6: State Transitions for the Capped FRN

Period	From	To
Today	⟨6.000⟩	⟨5.113, 6.000⟩, ⟨6.902, 6.000⟩
1	⟨5.113, 6.000⟩	⟨4.363, 5.000⟩, ⟨4.363, 6.000⟩, ⟨5.889, 5.000⟩, ⟨5.889, 6.000⟩
	⟨6.902, 6.000⟩	⟨5.889, 6.000⟩, ⟨7.950, 6.000⟩
2	⟨4.363, 5.000⟩	⟨3.728, 4.000⟩, ⟨3.728, 5.000⟩, ⟨5.032, 4.000⟩, ⟨5.032, 5.000⟩
	⟨4.363, 6.000⟩	⟨3.728, 4.000⟩, ⟨3.728, 5.000⟩, ⟨5.032, 4.000⟩, ⟨5.032, 5.000⟩
	⟨5.889, 5.000⟩	⟨5.032, 5.000⟩, ⟨6.792, 5.000⟩
	⟨5.889, 6.000⟩	⟨5.032, 5.000⟩, ⟨5.032, 6.000⟩, ⟨6.792, 5.000⟩, ⟨6.792, 6.000⟩
	⟨7.950, 6.000⟩	⟨6.792, 6.000⟩, ⟨9.169, 6.000⟩
3	⟨3.728, 4.000⟩	⟨3.189, 3.000⟩, ⟨3.189, 4.000⟩, ⟨4.305, 3.000⟩, ⟨4.305, 4.000⟩
	⟨3.728, 5.000⟩	⟨3.189, 3.000⟩, ⟨3.189, 4.000⟩, ⟨4.305, 3.000⟩, ⟨4.305, 4.000⟩
	⟨5.032, 4.000⟩	⟨4.305, 4.000⟩, ⟨5.811, 4.000⟩
	⟨5.032, 5.000⟩	⟨4.305, 5.000⟩, ⟨5.811, 5.000⟩
	⟨5.032, 6.000⟩	⟨4.305, 5.000⟩, ⟨4.305, 6.000⟩, ⟨5.811, 5.000⟩, ⟨5.811, 6.000⟩
	⟨6.792, 5.000⟩	⟨5.811, 5.000⟩, ⟨7.844, 5.000⟩
	⟨6.792, 6.000⟩	⟨5.811, 6.000⟩, ⟨7.844, 6.000⟩
	⟨9.169, 6.000⟩	⟨7.844, 6.000⟩, ⟨10.588, 6.000⟩

Exhibit 7: CF_i(·) and V_i(·) for the Capped FRN

		Current Coupon Rate			
		3.000	4.000	5.000	6.000
Period 1	6.902%				6.000
					97.334
	5.113				6.000
					99.139
Period 2	7.950				6.000
					96.505
	5.889			5.000	6.000
				98.354	99.599
	4.363			5.000	6.000
				99.695	99.695
Period 3	9.169				6.000
					97.097
	6.792			5.000	6.000
				98.322	99.258
	5.032		4.000	5.000	6.000
			99.017	99.970	100.000
	3.728		4.000	5.000	
			100.000	100.000	
Period 4	10.588				106.000
					0.000
	7.844			105.000	106.000
				0.000	0.000
	5.811		104.000	105.000	106.000
			0.000	0.000	0.000
	4.305	103.000	104.000	105.000	106.000
		0.000	0.000	0.000	0.000
	3.189	103.000	104.000		
		0.000	0.000		

In period 4 (at maturity), $V_4(\cdot)=0$ as usual. The cash flow at maturity is just 100.000 (the return of principal) plus C (the current interest rate that the FRN is paying). This produces the period 4 results. For example: $CF_4(\langle 7.844, 5.000 \rangle) = 100.0 + 5.0 = 105.0$. In periods 1 through 3, $CF_i(\langle r, C \rangle)=C$ since the FRN repays principal only at maturity.

We verify three calculations of $V_i(\cdot)$. First, from state $\langle 5.032, 5.000 \rangle$ in period 3, the value of r moves to either 4.305 or 5.811 with equal likelihood. The value of C does not change in this case since $5.032 > 5.000$. So from state $\langle 5.032, 5.000 \rangle$ in period 3, we branch to either $\langle 4.305, 5.000 \rangle$ or $\langle 5.811, 5.000 \rangle$ in period 4 with equal likelihood and we have

$$V_3(\langle 5.032, 5.000 \rangle) = \frac{1}{1.05032}[0.5(CF_4(\langle 4.305, 5.000 \rangle) + V_4(\langle 4.305, 5.000 \rangle))$$

$$+ 0.5(CF_4(\langle 5.881, 5.000 \rangle) + V_4(\langle 5.881, 5.000 \rangle))]$$

$$= \frac{1}{1.05032}[0.5(105.000 + 0.0) + 0.5(105.000 + 0.0)]$$

$$= 99.970$$

Next, from state $\langle 4.363, 5.000 \rangle$ in period 2, the value of r moves to either 3.728 or 5.032, each with probability $\frac{1}{2}$. The value of C should change to 4.363 since $4.363 < 5.000$, but this number is not in $\hat{C}$. If it *were*, we would calculate

$$V_2(\langle 4.363, 5.000 \rangle) = \frac{1}{1.04363}[0.5(CF_3(\langle 3.728, 4.363 \rangle) + V_3(\langle 3.728, 4.363 \rangle))$$

$$+ 0.5(CF_3(\langle 5.032, 4.363 \rangle) + V_3(\langle 5.032, 4.363 \rangle))] \quad (10)$$

However, we have calculated neither $V_3(\langle 3.728, 4.363 \rangle)$ nor $V_3(\langle 5.032, 4.363 \rangle)$ nor the corresponding values for $CF_3(\langle \cdot, 4.363 \rangle)$, so we estimate them by interpolating between values that we have calculated. In particular,

$$V_3(\langle 3.728, 4.363 \rangle) \approx 0.637 V_3(\langle 3.728, 4.000 \rangle) + 0.363 V_3(\langle 3.728, 5.000 \rangle)$$

$$= 100.000$$

and

$$V_3(\langle 5.032, 4.363 \rangle) \approx 0.637 V_3(\langle 5.032, 4.000 \rangle) + 0.363 V_3(\langle 5.032, 5.000 \rangle)$$

$$= 99.363$$

while both interpolated values for $CF_3(\langle \cdot, 4.363 \rangle)$ are, not surprisingly, 4.363. Setting these estimates into equation (10) gives $V_2(\langle 4.363, 5.000 \rangle) = 99.695$.

Finally, today's value of the capped FRN is calculated from the period 1 values by

$$V_0(\langle 6.000 \rangle) = \frac{1}{1.06}[0.5(6.0 + 99.139) + 0.5(6.0 + 97.334)] = 98.336$$

which puts the value of the periodic cap at $100.000 - 98.336 = 1.664$. As predicted, this is not in precise agreement with the exhaustive path-by-path analysis that produced the value of 98.343 for the capped FRN and 1.657 for the periodic cap. This is because we bucketed the state space of C into the four quantities in $\hat{C}$. By increasing the number of states (using more, and smaller, buckets), the degree of error is reduced. For example, when we take

$$\hat{C} = \{3.000, 3.500, 4.000, 4.500, 5.000, 5.500, 6.000\}$$

the recursive process yields 98.341 (1.659 for the periodic cap).

CONCLUSION

We have worked through two simple numerical examples that illustrate how non-stochastic state variables may be coupled with a stochastic interest rate process to value path-dependent fixed-income securities using recursive techniques. In our 4-period examples, of course, this technique offers little, if any, improvement over exhaustive path sampling. In more realistic settings, however, recursion is generally much more efficient than Monte Carlo path sampling.

Path dependence occurs in many forms and with varying degrees of complexity. Sometimes it is necessary to couple more than one state variable to the stochastic process. Consider, for example, a hybrid of the IAN and capped FRN. Such a note would pay down principal in accordance with a rate sensitive amortization schedule, while paying a rate of interest that resets periodically but that is permitted to increase only a limited amount with each reset. Generalizing the notation of our previous sections, a state would be described as $\langle r, P, C \rangle$ where r is the stochastic risk-free rate, P is the amount of the note currently outstanding, and C is its current coupon rate.

Chapter 13

Problems Encountered in Valuing Interest Rate Derivatives

Yiannos A. Pierides, Ph.D.
Assistant Professor of Finance
Department of Public and Business Administration
University of Cyprus

INTRODUCTION

In this chapter we describe the procedure involved in valuing any interest rate derivative. We then apply this valuation procedure to two interest rate derivatives, one plain vanilla and the other exotic, in order to explain some of the practical problems involved.

STATE OF THE ART VALUATION OF INTEREST RATE DERIVATIVES

The pricing of any interest rate derivative involves the following three stage procedure:

Stage 1: Adopt an assumption about the evolution (or probability distribution) of the short-term interest rate.
Stage 2: Specify the payoff to the derivative at its maturity.
Stage 3: Calculate the price of the derivative as its discounted expected payoff.

Below we describe the three stages.

Stage 1: Adopt an Assumption about the Evolution of the Short-Term Interest Rate

The first stage is perhaps the most crucial one in the whole procedure. Several researchers have proposed different assumptions. The pioneering ones are Vasicek,[1] Cox, Ingersoll, and Ross[2] (henceforth CIR), and Hull and White[3]

---

[1] Oldrich Vasicek, "An Equilibrium Characterization of the Term Structure," *Journal of Financial Economics* Vol. 5 (1977), pp. 177-188.

[2] John Cox, Jonathan Ingersoll, and Stephen Ross, "A Theory of the Term Structure of Interest Rates," *Econometrica* Vol. 53, No. 2 (1985), pp 385-407.

[3] John Hull and Alan White, "Pricing Interest Rate Derivatives," *Review of Financial Studies* Vol. 3, No. 4 (1990), pp. 573-592.

(henceforth HW). The interest rate stochastic process proposed by each researcher is shown below:

Model	Stochastic Process
Vasicek	$dr(t) = (a + br(t))dt + \sigma dW(t)$
CIR	$dr(t) = \kappa(\theta - r(t))dt + \sigma(r(t))^{0.5}\, dW(t)$
HW	$dr(t) = (\theta(t) + a(t)(b - r(t)))dt + \sigma(t)\, dW(t)$

The Vasicek model assumes that the interest rate follows an Ornstein-Uhlenbeck process: a, b and σ are the parametetrs of the process and $W(t)$ is a standard Brownian motion under a probability measure P. This is a Gaussian process which leads to relatively simple closed form solutions for the price of Treasury bonds and for the price of plain vanilla options on such bonds. Its main drawbacks are (1) it implies that the interest rate may become negative and (2) it implies that the volatility of the interest rate is independent of the level of the interest rate.

CIR proposed a stochastic process for the interest rate that does not suffer from the drawbacks of the Vasicek process. As in the case of the Vasicek process κ, θ, and σ are the parametetrs of the process and $W(t)$ is a standard Brownian motion under a probability measure P. This process became known as the *square root process* because it implies that the volatility of the interest rate is not independent of the interest rate; instead it is proportional to the square root of the interest rate. Also, the interest rate cannot become negative. CIR showed that this process leads to closed form solutions for the price of Treasury bonds and for the price of plain vanilla options on such bonds

HW point out that a major drawback of both the Vasicek model and the CIR model is that they are not consistent with any initial term structure of interest rates and interest rate volatilities that are observed in the market. In other words, these models do not imply a perfect fit to the initial term structure of interest rates and interest rate volatilities that are observed in the market.

HW proposed an extension to the Vasicek process that provides a perfect fit to the initial term structure of interest rates and interest rate volatilities that are observed in the market. The process became known as the *extended Vasicek or Hull and White (HW) process*. In this process $a(t)$, $\theta(t)$, b and $\sigma(t)$ are the parametetrs of the process and $W(t)$ is a standard Brownian motion under a probability measure P. Note that unlike the Vasicek and CIR processes, three of the four parameters of this process are time dependent and this enables one to estimate these parameters in a way that provides a perfect fit to the initial term structure of interest rates and interest rate volatilities that are observed in the market. Unfortunately, the HW process suffers from the same drawback as the Vasicek process, namely that the interest rate can become negative. HW showed that this process leads to closed form solutions for the price of Treasury bonds and for the price of plain vanilla options on such bonds.

Stage 2: Specify the Payoff to the Interest Rate Derivative

Consider a call option on the interest rate with exercise price y and maturity T. The payoff at maturity will be MAX $(r(T) - y, 0)$. This derivative is an example of a non-path dependent derivative. The reason is that the payoff at maturity depends only on the interest rate at maturity and not on the path that the interest rate followed to reach its terminal value at maturity.

Similarly, consider a call option on the price of a zero-coupon Treasury bond (of maturity TB) with exercise price X and maturity T. The payoff at maturity will be MAX $(P(T, TB) - X, 0)$, where $P(T, TB)$ is the bond price at T. This qualifies as an interest rate derivative because the bond price depends on the interest rate. Also, it is a non-path dependent derivative because the payoff at maturity depends only on the interest rate at maturity (which in turn determines the bond price at maturity) and not on the path that the interest rate followed during the option's life.

Let us now give an example of a path dependent derivative. A European lookback put option on a zero-coupon Treasury bond has all the features of a regular European put except that the exercise price equals the maximum bond price during the option's life. In other words, the owner of this lookback option is entitled to sell at the option's maturity the underlying Treasury bond for a price equal to the maximum price at which this bond traded during the option's life. It follows that the payoff to this option at its maturity will be equal to the difference between the maximum bond price during the option's life and the bond price at maturity .

This lookback put is path dependent because the payoff at maturity depends not only on the bond price at maturity (as in the case of a regular put) but also on the path that the bond price followed during the option's life. The reason is that it is this path of bond prices that determines the maximum bond price during the option's life. Of course, the path of bond prices will depend on the path of interest rates during the option's life.

Such a derivative is traded (over the counter) since there is substantial demand for it. The reason is that it enables investors to achieve perfect market timing (i.e., sell at the highest price). This derivative is called "lookback" because at its maturity, its payoff can only be determined by "looking back in time" to determine the maximum bond price during the option's life.

Stage 3: Calculate the Derivative Price as the Discounted Expectation of its Payoff

Harrison and Kreps[4] and Huang[5] show that any interest rate derivative can be priced using a no-arbitrage methodology, given an appropriate assumption about the evolution of the interest rate. Using this methodology, the correct derivative

---

[4] Michael Harrison and David Kreps, "Martingales and Arbitrage in Multiperiod Securities Markets," *Journal of Economic Theory*, 1979.

[5] Chi-Fu Huang, "The Term Structure of Interest Rates and the Pricing of Interest Rate Sensitive Securities," working paper, Sloan School, M.I.T., 1991.

price is equal to the discounted expectation of its payoff under a particular proba-bility measure. This will be analysed further in the sections that follow.

Depending on the derivative we are pricing, it may or may not be possi-ble to derive a closed form formula for its price. To calculate a price we must cal-culate a discounted expected value of the payoff to the derivative at its maturity. In general, the more complicated this payoff is the less likely it is that we can get a closed form formula. For example, in the case of path dependent derivatives it is usually impossible to get a closed form formula. In such cases, we calculate the discounted expected value of the payoff using Monte Carlo simulation of the interest rate stochastic process.

VALUATION OF A EUROPEAN CALL OPTION ON A ZERO-COUPON TREASURY BOND

We will now apply the three stage methodology to the valuation of two interest rate derivatives. One derivative is a European call option on the price of a zero-coupon Treasury bond and the other a European lookback put option on a zero coupon Treasury bond. We will price both derivatives using the CIR and HW sto-chastic processes for the interest rate in Stage 1. The Vasicek process is not used because it is a special case of the HW process.

Applying the CIR Model

Recall that CIR assume that the short-term interest rate $r(t)$ follows a square root process i.e.,

$$dr = k(\theta - r)dt + \sigma\sqrt{r}dw$$

k = intensity of mean reversion
θ = long-run mean of interest rate
σ = volatility of r
w = standard Brownian motion under a probability measure P.

Consider any interest rate derivative paying a random payoff $x(\tau)$ at time $\tau > 0$. To avoid the existence of arbitrage opportunities, its (normalized) price can be calculated as the conditional expectation of the (normalized) payoff under an equivalent martingale probability measure. In particular, let

$x(t)$ = price at t of security paying random payoff $x(\tau)$ at $\tau > t$
$B(t)$ = price process for the instantaneously riskless asset that is used as the numeraire i.e.,

$$B(t) = \exp\left(\int_0^t r(s)ds\right)$$

$w^*(t)$ = standard Brownian motion under a measure Q equivalent to P, where

$$w^*(t) = w(t) + \int_0^t \frac{\lambda}{\sigma}\sqrt{r(s)}ds \;; \lambda \text{ is a scalar.}$$

Substituting for $w(t)$ in the interest rate process we get the risk-adjusted interest rate process

$$dr = (k\theta - (k + \lambda)r)dt + \sigma\sqrt{r}dw^* \tag{1}$$

Then, if E^* denotes expectation under the risk-adjusted interest rate process.

$$\frac{x(t)}{B(t)} = E^*\left[\frac{x(\tau)}{B(\tau)}\right] \tag{2}$$

Since a zero-coupon Treasury bond of maturity TB pays \$1.00 with certainty at TB, its price at t, denoted $P(t, TB)$, is given by

$$\frac{P(t, TB)}{B(t)} = E^*\left[\frac{1}{B(TB)}\right] \Rightarrow P(t, TB) = E^*\left[\exp\left(-\int_t^{TB} r(s)ds\right)\right] \tag{3}$$

CIR show that

$$P(t, TB) = A(t, TB) \exp(-r(t)G(t, TB)) \tag{4}$$

$$A(t, TB) = \left[\frac{2\gamma\exp\left[(b + \gamma)\dfrac{TB - t}{2}\right]}{(\gamma + b)(\exp(\gamma(TB - t)) - 1) + 2\gamma}\right]^{\frac{2c}{\sigma^2}} \tag{5}$$

$$G(t, TB) = \frac{2(\exp(\gamma(TB - t)) - 1)}{(\gamma + b)(\exp(\gamma(TB - t)) - 1) + 2\gamma} \tag{6}$$

$$b = k + \lambda \;; c = k\theta; \gamma = \sqrt{b^2 + 2\sigma^2}$$

Consider now a European call option on a Treasury bond of maturity TB. The current time is t and the option has maturity T (with $TB > T > t$) and exercise price X. Let $C(t)$ be the option price at time t. Then, using equation (2),

$$\frac{C(t)}{B(t)} = E^*\left[\frac{\text{MAX}(P(T, TB) - X, 0)}{B(T)}\right] \tag{7}$$

CIR provide the following closed form formula for $C(t)$:

$$C(t) = P(t, TB)\chi^2\left(2r^*(\varphi + \psi + G(T, TB)), \frac{4c}{\sigma^2}, \frac{2\varphi^2 re^{\gamma(T - t)}}{(\varphi + \psi + G(T, TB))}\right)$$

$$- XP(t, T)\chi^2[2r^*(\varphi + \psi), 4c/\sigma^2, 2\varphi^2 re^{\gamma(T - t)}/(\varphi + \psi)] \tag{8}$$

where

χ^2 = the non-central chi-square distribution function

φ = $2\gamma / (\sigma^2 (e\gamma^{(T-t)} - 1))$

ψ = $(b+\gamma) / \sigma^2$

r^* = $\log (A(T, TB) / X) / G(T,TB)$

We now apply this formula to a specific example. To do this we must first specify the parameters of the CIR process. It is assumed that these parameters are those estimated by Chan, Karolyi, Longstaff, and Sanders (henceforth CKLS).[6] These parameter estimates are:

$$\kappa\theta = 0.0189, \kappa + \lambda = 0.2339, \sigma = 0.0085 \tag{9}$$

Consider a European call on a zero-coupon Treasury with $T = 3$ years and $TB = 6$ years. The bond has a face value of 100, and the exercise price of the option is presumed to be equal to the current bond price. Exhibit 1 gives the option price for different initial interest rates and bond prices.

Applying the HW Model

We now consider the pricing of the identical call option under the HW model and compare the prices obtained with those of Exhibit 1 for the CIR model.

HW assume that the short-term interest rate $r(t)$ follows a process that is described by the stochastic differential equation

$$dr = [\theta(t) + \alpha(t)(b - r)]dt + \sigma(t)dw(t) \tag{10}$$

$\theta(t)$ = time dependent drift

$\alpha(t)$ = time dependent reversion rate

b = long-term level of interest rate

$\sigma(t)$ = time dependent volatility

$w(t)$ = standard Brownian motion under measure P.

As in the case of the CIR model, the (normalized) price of any security paying a random interest dependent payoff $x(\tau)$ at $\tau > 0$ is calculated as the conditional expectation of the (normalized) payoff under an equivalent martingale measure. Let $x(t)$ and $B(t)$ be defined as in the case of the CIR model, and define:

$w^{**}(t)$ = standard Brownian motion under a measure Q equivalent to P,

where

$$w^{**}(t) = w(t) + \int_0^t \lambda(s)ds \; ; \lambda(s) = \text{bounded function of time.}$$

---

[6] K. Chan, G. Karolyi, F. Longstaff, and A. Sanders, "An Empirical Comparison of Alternative Models of the Short Term Interest Rate," *Journal of Finance* (1992), pp. 1209-1227.

Exhibit 1: Bond and Call Prices Using the CIR Model

r(0)	Bond Price	Call Price
0.20	42.62	16.66
0.19	43.98	16.62
0.18	45.39	16.54
0.17	46.84	16.42
0.16	48.35	16.27
0.15	49.91	16.08
0.14	51.50	15.84
0.13	53.15	15.55
0.12	54.86	15.22
0.11	56.61	14.81
0.10	58.43	14.35
0.09	60.30	13.83
0.08	62.24	13.23
0.07	64.23	12.56
0.06	66.29	11.82
0.05	68.42	10.98
0.04	70.61	10.06
0.03	72.88	9.04
0.02	75.22	7.91
0.01	77.62	6.69

Using the equation for $w^{**}(t)$ to substitute for $w(t)$ in the interest rate process, we get

$$dr = (\phi(t) - \alpha(t)r)dt + \sigma(t)dw^{**}$$

$$\phi(t) = \theta(t) + \alpha(t)b - \lambda(t)\sigma(t)$$

(11)

This is the risk-adjusted HW interest rate process. Then,

$$\frac{x(t)}{B(t)} = E^{**}\left[\frac{x(\tau)}{B(\tau)}\right]$$

(12)

where E^{**} denotes expectation under the risk adjusted HW interest rate process.

Since a zero-coupon Treasury bond of maturity TB pays \$1.00 with certainty at TB,

$$\frac{P(t, TB)}{B(t)} = E^{**}\left[\frac{1}{B(TB)}\right] \Rightarrow P(t, TB) = E^{**}\left[\exp\left(-\int_t^{TB} r(s)ds\right)\right]$$

(13)

HW provide a closed form solution for $P(t, TB)$ of the form

$$P(t, TB) = A(t, TB) \exp[-r(t)G(t, TB)]$$

(14)

where $A(t, TB)$ and $G(t, TB)$ are given by

$$G(t, TB) = \frac{G(0, TB) - G(0, t)}{\partial G(0, t)/\partial t}$$

$$F(t, TB) = \log A(t, TB)$$

$$F(t, TB) = F(0, TB) - F(0, t) - G(t, TB)\frac{\partial F(0, t)}{\partial t}$$

$$- \frac{1}{2}\left[G(t, TB)\frac{\partial G(0, t)}{\partial t} \right]^2 \int_0^t \left[\frac{\sigma(\tau)}{\partial G(0, \tau)/\partial \tau} \right]^2 d\tau$$

Furthermore, HW show that $\phi(t)$ and $\alpha(t)$ are related to $A(0, t)$ and $G(0, t)$ through the following equations:

$$\alpha(t) = -\frac{\partial^2 G(0, t)/\partial t^2}{\partial G(0, t)/\partial t} \tag{15}$$

$$\phi(t) = -\alpha(t)\frac{\partial F(0, t)}{\partial t} - \frac{\partial^2 F(0, t)}{\partial t^2} + \left[\frac{\partial G(0, t)}{\partial t}\right]^2 \int_0^t \left[\frac{\sigma(\tau)}{\partial G(0, \tau)/\partial \tau}\right]^2 d\tau \tag{16}$$

Consider now a European call option on a Treasury bond of maturity TB. The current time is t and the option has maturity T (with $TB > T > t$) and exercise price X. Let $C(t)$ be the option price at time t. Then, using equation (12),

$$\frac{C(t)}{B(t)} = E^{**}\left[\frac{MAX(P(T, TB) - X,0)}{B(T)}\right] \tag{17}$$

HW provide the following closed form solution:

$$C(t) = P(t,TB)N(h) - XP(t,T) N(h - \sigma_p) \tag{18}$$

where

$N(\ ) =$ the cumulative normal distribution function

$h = (\sigma_p/2) + (1/\sigma_p) \log[P(t,TB)/(X P(t,T))]$

$$\sigma_p^2 = [G(0, TB) - G(0, T)]^2 \int_t^T \left[\frac{\sigma(\tau)}{\partial G(0, \tau)/\partial \tau}\right]^2 d\tau$$

HW argue that the price of an interest rate derivative is insensitive to the assumption made about the evolution of the interest rate in stage 1 as long as one very important condition is met. This condition states that as long as the parameters of the stochastic process are estimated in such a way that this stochastic process is consistent with the current term structure of bond yields the choice of stochastic process does not affect that much the prices obtained. From now on, we will refer to this condition as the *consistency condition*.

To demonstrate this, HW assume that the correct yield curve is the one given by the CIR process and figure out a way of estimating the parameters of the HW process assuming that the CIR yield curve is the correct one. Thus, they obtain two stochastic processes whose estimated parameters are consistent with

$$PMAX(P(0, TB), M(0), 0, T) = E^{**}\left[\frac{M(T)}{B(T)}\right] - P(0, TB)$$

$$= E^{**}\left[M(T)\left(\exp\left(-\int_0^T r(s)ds\right)\right)\right] - P(0, TB) \tag{27}$$

As in the case of the CIR model, no closed form solution exists to this valuation problem because of the path dependent nature of the option. For this reason, we calculate the price using Monte Carlo simulation.

The simulation is carried out in exactly the same way as for the CIR process. The only thing that changes is the use of the risk-adjusted interest rate process

$$r_{t_i} = r_{t_{i-1}} + (\phi(t_{i-1}) - \alpha(t_{i-1})r_{t_{i-1}})(t_i - t_{i-1}) + \sigma\sqrt{r(0)}\sqrt{t_i - t_{i-1}}\tilde{\varepsilon} \tag{28}$$

The parameters of the HW process are estimated by assuming that the CIR term structure is the correct one with parameters estimated by CKLS. This implies that the consistency condition is satisfied and enables us to compare CIR and HW prices using Exhibit 4.

Exhibit 4: Comparison of Bond and Lookback Prices for Different Initial Interest Rates Using CIR and HW Models

r(0)	Bond Price	Lookback Price(CIR)	Lookback Price (HW)
0.20	42.62	0.4420	0.7493
0.19	43.98	0.4595	0.7651
0.18	45.39	0.4778	0.7803
0.17	46.84	0.4968	0.7946
0.16	48.35	0.5166	0.8077
0.15	49.91	0.5371	0.8194
0.14	51.50	0.5582	0.8291
0.13	53.15	0.5800	0.8364
0.12	54.86	0.6027	0.8409
0.11	56.61	0.6264	0.8419
0.10	58.43	0.6511	0.8385
0.09	60.30	0.6766	0.8293
0.08	62.24	0.7028	0.8131
0.07	64.23	0.7300	0.7877
0.06	66.29	0.7583	0.7504
0.05	68.42	0.7875	0.6974
0.04	70.61	0.8173	0.6236
0.03	72.88	0.8475	0.5217
0.02	75.22	0.8774	0.3821
0.01	77.62	0.9056	0.1971

There are two striking features of Exhibit 4: (1) the magnitude of the differences in the price given by each stochastic process and (2) for some initial interest rates one model gives a higher price whereas for other initial interest rates it is the other model that gives a higher price. For example, note that for an initial interest rate of 0.01 (1%) the price given by the CIR model exceeds the price given by the HW model by a multiple of four. Alternatively, for an initial interest rate of 0.2 (20%) the price given by the HW model exceeds that given by the CIR model by a multiple of approximately two. These results are very different from the results of HW and indicate that even if the consistency condition is met, different stochastic processes can give very different prices for complex interest rate derivatives. We now turn to an explanation of these price differences.

Explanation of Price Differences

The HW model gives higher lookback put prices than the CIR model for interest rates above or very close to the long-run mean of the interest rate process, which was estimated by CKLS to be 0.08. However, for interest rates below 0.07, the HW model gives lower lookback put prices.

To explain these results, consider the benefit and cost of exercising this option at maturity. The benefit is the maximum bond price over the option's life, and the cost is the bond price at maturity. The option will always be in the money at maturity.

For comparison purposes, let us take the CIR model as the base case and investigate how the benefit and cost of exercising the option at maturity change under the HW model. Since we are comparing the current (i.e., time 0) prices under the two models, we should examine the present value of the benefit and the present value of the cost of exercising the option at maturity. The present value of the cost of exercising is the same in both models: it is the current price of the bond with maturity $TB = 6$ which is the same in both models. As a result, the differences in the current option prices arise because of differences in the present value of the benefit.

To investigate how the present value of the benefit might differ in the two models, let us examine the nature of the stochastic process for the interest rate in the two models. We begin by considering the drift term. Both the CIR and HW interest rate processes are mean reverting. The long-run mean estimated by CKLS is 0.08. This means that whenever the interest rate is below (above) 0.08, the drift term will tend to increase (decrease) it. Furthermore, the volatility terms in the two models are different. The volatility of the interest rate in CIR at time t is $\sigma\sqrt{r(t-1)}$ whereas the volatility term in HW at all t is $\sigma\sqrt{r(0)}$. The reason for this is that we fit the HW model in such a way that its initial (i.e., time 0) interest rate volatility is the same as in the CIR model. A direct consequence of this is that for a given initial interest rate, the volatility term implies a higher probability of a lower interest rate in the HW model and a higher probability of a higher interest rate in the CIR model.

The key to understanding why the HW model gives higher (lower) look-back put prices when the interest rate is above (below) its long-run mean is to realize that a low interest rate in either the CIR or the HW model is much more useful in establishing a high maximum bond price over the option's life if it occurs late during the option's life. The reason for this is that for a given interest rate, bond prices in both models increase with the passage of time.

Consider the case where $r = 0.01$ (i.e., the interest rate is substantially below its long-run mean of 0.08). Early in the option's life, the HW model will be more likely to give a lower interest rate than the CIR model. However, for the reason given in the previous paragraph, this will not be very useful in establishing a high maximum bond price over the option's life.

Furthermore, note that the drift term will tend to increase the interest rate in both models over time; as a result, by the time the option has been outstanding for, say, 80% of its life, the interest rate will be, on average, much higher in both models. The crucial thing to realize is that at that time, the volatility of the interest rate will be much higher in the CIR model — recall that time t volatility in CIR is given by $\sigma\sqrt{r(t-1)}$, whereas, volatility in HW at all t is $\sigma\sqrt{0.01}$. A direct consequence of this is that towards the end of the option's life the higher volatility in CIR will imply a higher probability of a lower interest rate in CIR (compared to HW). As explained in the previous section, a low interest rate will be much more useful in establishing a high maximum bond price over the option's life if it occurs late in the option's life. Since we established that the HW (CIR) model will imply a higher probability of a lower interest rate early (late) in the option's life, the probability of a higher maximum bond price is higher in the CIR model and, therefore, the option's benefit is higher in the CIR model. This explains why the CIR model gives higher lookback put prices for an interest rate of 0.01. Similar considerations apply for interest rates in the 0.02 to 0.06 range (i.e., for interest rates below the long-run mean). The CIR model gives higher lookback put prices in these cases too.

Let us now consider the case where $r = 0.20$. Early in the option's life, the HW model will imply a higher probability of a lower interest rate. As explained above, this will not be very useful in establishing a high maximum bond price over the option's life. The important thing to realize is that, unlike the case where $r = 0.01$, the HW model will also imply a higher probability of a lower interest rate late in the option's life. On average, the interest rate will reach a much lower level by the time the option has been outstanding for, say, 80% of its life. At that time, the volatility of the interest rate will be much higher in the HW model. (Recall that volatility at time t is $\sigma\sqrt{r(t-1)}$ in the CIR model and $\sigma\sqrt{0.2}$ in the HW model.) Hence, towards the end of the option's life, the higher volatility in the HW model will imply a higher probability of a lower interest rate (compared to the CIR model). The HW model will therefore imply a higher probability of a lower interest rate both early and late in the option's life; as a result, the probability of a higher maximum bond price over the option's life and therefore the option's benefit is higher for the HW model. This explains why the HW model gives a higher price for a lookback put option when $r = 0.20$. Similar considerations apply for interest rates in the 0.08 to 0.19 range, i.e., for interest rates above the long-run mean. The HW model gives higher lookback put prices in these cases too.

CONCLUSION

This chapter has presented a methodology that can be used to value any interest rate derivative. This methodology was applied to the valuation of two derivatives, one plain vanilla (a call on the bond price) and the other exotic (a lookback put on the bond price). In the case of the plain vanilla derivative, it was shown that its price is insensitive to the modeler's choice of stochastic process for the short-term interest rate as long as a consistency condition is met. However, in the case of the exotic derivative, the price is very sensitive to the modeler's choice of stochastic process for the short-term interest rate even if the consistency condition is met.

Where does this leave us? The problem is that there is widespread disagreement as to which stochastic process provides a better fit to market data (for example, see CKLS). Part of the problem is that the empirical results are very sensitive to the period from which the market data is drawn and to the choice of econometric methodology. It therefore appears that different researchers will, in general, disagree on the price they obtain for complex interest rate derivatives because each researcher will prefer to use a different stochastic process for the short-term interest rate. One can only hope that advances in econometric methodology will permit the development of a consensus on the correct stochastic process in the not too distant future.

Chapter 14

Speeding Up the Valuation Process

Faye S. Albert, FSA
President
Albert Associates

Graham Lord, Ph.D., FSA
President
Lord Consulting

Irwin T. Vanderhoof, Ph.D, FSA
Clinical Professor of Finance and Insurance
Stern School of Business
New York University

INTRODUCTION

Cash flows whose size and/or timing are related to current interest rates, or their evolution over time, are known as interest-sensitive cash flows. As has been pointed out in other chapters of this book, most insurance liabilities and assets feature cash flows that, in some way, are interest sensitive. To estimate the value of instruments exhibiting such cash flows, analysts have turned to a family of methods designed specifically for that purpose. These methods include Monte Carlo simulations, interest rate lattices, finite differences, closed-form solutions, and sparse grids.[1]

Other than utilizing closed-form solutions, these methods are often cumbersome and time consuming. Unfortunately, closed-form solutions do not exist for many valuation models, and where they are available, they generally are not suited for the valuation of cash flows that are path dependent — i.e., that depend on the evolution of interest rates. For financial instruments exhibiting this kind of interest rate sensitivity, Monte Carlo methods are typically employed.

---

[1] See D. Babbel and C. Merrill, "Economic Valuation Models for Insurers," *North American Actuarial Journal*, forthcoming in 1999, for a description of these various approaches.

In this chapter, we present an outline of recently developed sampling techniques designed to reduce the computational time and increase the accuracy of Monte Carlo-type valuation exercises. We describe "low discrepancy sequences" that can be used to speed up the valuation process, and compare this process with traditional Monte Carlo methods.

MONTE CARLO METHODS

Why Use Them?

Most analysts now agree that some sort of option adjusted pricing and scenario testing is a highly desirable part of the valuation of complex assets and liabilities and the entire asset/liability modeling process. Unfortunately, analysis of the complex options, explicit or embedded, in both assets and liabilities often requires the use of Monte Carlo calculations.

The Monte Carlo method is often necessary when there are no explicit formulas for these functions, and because the use of product rules for numerical integration leads to intractable calculations if the number of dimensions is large. Monte Carlo methods avoid the problem by changing the approach to one of sampling. Choose a certain number of points, each with as many coordinates as there are variables in the problem. These points are chosen from "supposed" to be random distributions that relate to the probability of occurrence of corresponding values of the variables. Then the average of the resulting values associated with these points is calculated. No value is produced that represents a maximum possible error, just a value for the average error. That level of average error decreases in proportion to the square root of the number of points, independent of the number of dimensions in the problem. The standard deviation of the result is inversely proportional to the square root of the number of points used in the calculation. This overcomes the "curse of dimensionality."

Other Problems Exist

The crude Monte Carlo process is based on the idea that we can create a series of random numbers, say between 0 and 1, which can then be input to some inverse function (that is, inverse of a cumulative distribution function), that will translate this series into a distribution of the actual variable we are interested in. Random numbers between 0 and 1 can be translated into interest rates, or stock market prices, or almost anything else. Everything then depends upon the random numbers being random and the whole process being the desired statistical sampling.

With every solution come new problems. Random numbers present their own problems. First there is the problem of bias. Random numbers are not normally produced by truly random processes. Usually the desire is not for random processes, but rather for something that seems random, but is reproducible so that answers can be checked when there is a change in the parameters. For this reason deterministic processes have been used, like squaring a number and then taking the middle digits of the result. The resulting numbers are often called "pseudo-random numbers." But whether a physical or numerical process is used, some kind of bias is likely. (In numerical processes the start is usually the choice of some "seed" which is where the bias begins.) If there is a bias in the values from 0 to 1, then there will be a bias in the translated result and in the outcome. Unless we can check the results against a known closed form answer, the amount of the bias is essentially unknowable because the series may never converge to the exact right answer. The only way to insure against this is to average the values from several different processes.

A second problem with the use of random numbers is that the convergence can be slow. To reduce the standard deviation in the average of all the calculated values (which we use as our expected value) by a factor of 10, we must increase the number of points by a factor of 100. This may not seem too bad when we go from 100 to 10,000 points, but the next step, to 1 million points is a killer.

A third problem is also related to the increasing number of points required for any specific level of accuracy in the final distribution of results. The problem is, "How many points will we need if we want to make statements about the probability of occurrence of some event in the future?" As an example take the value at risk" form of statement. "I can say with 99% certainty that there is less than a 5% chance that we will lose more than $5,000,000 over the next year because of interest rate fluctuations." How many points are necessary for that calculation? Probably too many to be practical.

ADDITIONAL RESEARCH

Modifications to Address the Monte Carlo Problems

Considerable efforts have been focused on the first and second problems. Ilya Sobol refers to the "infamous RANDU" generator for random numbers supplied with the IBM 360 and extensively used in Russia. The Monte Carlo calculations converged — but to the wrong answers. There have been considerable improvements, but the problem still exists. A recent article in *Science* referred to a problem in physics in which bias was detected in one of the high dimensions of a series of points. When we get down to exploring a partial linear dependence between the values in three or more dimensions, the solution becomes more difficult than the problem.

Much effort has also been spent on increasing the speed of convergence. The approaches most frequently referred to on Wall Street are various "variance reduction" techniques, which have been around about as long as Monte Carlo itself. An example is the use of antithetic variables. This technique attempts to replace the stated problem with a pair of problems that have the same expected value as the original problem, but that vary in opposite directions, so that the expected value of the combination is the same as the expected value of the original problem, but the variance of the combination of the two has a lower variance than the original problem.

While these techniques will speed the convergence, they do so as their name implies — they reduce the variance of the results. This means that they improve convergence by reducing the amount of information concerning the remaining shape of the distribution of results. Another drawback to these techniques is that each new problem may require developing a new set of equations for their solution. Nevertheless, these techniques are regularly and often satisfactorily used for problems in finance as well as in the physical sciences.

Quasi-Random Numbers

Based upon the work of Roth[2] and others, a different kind of approach was developed by Traub and Wozniakowski,[3] Papegeorgiou and Traub,[4] and Paskov.[5] Papers by Traub and Wozniakowski established that instead of using random points, a set of points carefully chosen according to number theoretic criteria would work better for the kind of integration process that has traditionally used Monte Carlo techniques. This number can be called a "quasi-random" number. At the suggestion of Irwin T. Vanderhoof and under Traub's direction, Paskov established that the use of special points allows the quick convergence of the values of tranches of a collateralized mortgage obligation (CMO). Other studies have supported this conclusion. The current work of Traub and Papegeorgiou is a continuation of these studies for other financial instruments such as options, and the like. An attempt is also being made to apply the techniques to solutions of problems in physics.

The basic intuition behind these special points is simple. Imagine a 1" × 1" square marked out on a piece of paper. Now pepper the square with ink dots. Now mark off all possible different square sub-regions of the unit square. (This is better done with number theoretic methods than by hand.) For each of these different regions we can compute the area and can see the number of dots included. The distribution of dots that minimizes the difference between the percentage of dots in each region and the area of that region for all possible regions is a low discrepancy sequence. For this to be true, in some sense, each point must be using up a similar area in the square. If the square is a probability space, then each point must represent a region of equal probability area.

For a one-dimensional problem the solution is the mid-point rule. However, as the number of dimensions increases, the complexity of calculating these low discrepancy sequences becomes formidable. Once they are calculated, though, they can be reused indefinitely; they don't wear out. In theory these low discrepancy sequences should outperform random numbers for low dimensions, but not necessarily for larger numbers of dimensions. Let's see how they work out.

---

[2] K. F. Roth, "On Irregularities of Distribution," *Mathematica* I (1954), pp. 73-79; and, "On Irregularities of Distribution," *Acta Arithmetica* IV, 37 (1980), pp. 67-75.

[3] J.F. Traub and H. Wozniakowski, "Theory and Applications of Information-Based Complexity," SFI Studies in the Science of Complexity Lectures, III, Addison-Wesley, 1991; and J.F. Traub and H. Wozniakowski, "Breaking Intractability," *Scientific American*, 170: 1, 1994, pp.102-07.

[4] A. Papageorgiou and J.F. Traub, "New Results on Deterministic Pricing of Financial Derivatives," Presented at Mathematical Problems in Finance, Institute for Advanced Study, Princeton, N.J., April 15, 1996.

[5] Spassimir Paskov, "Analysis of Multivariate Problems with applications to Finance." Unpublished doctoral dissertation accepted in the Graduate School of Arts and Sciences of Columbia University, 1994.

Exhibit 1: Comparison of Actual to Estimate

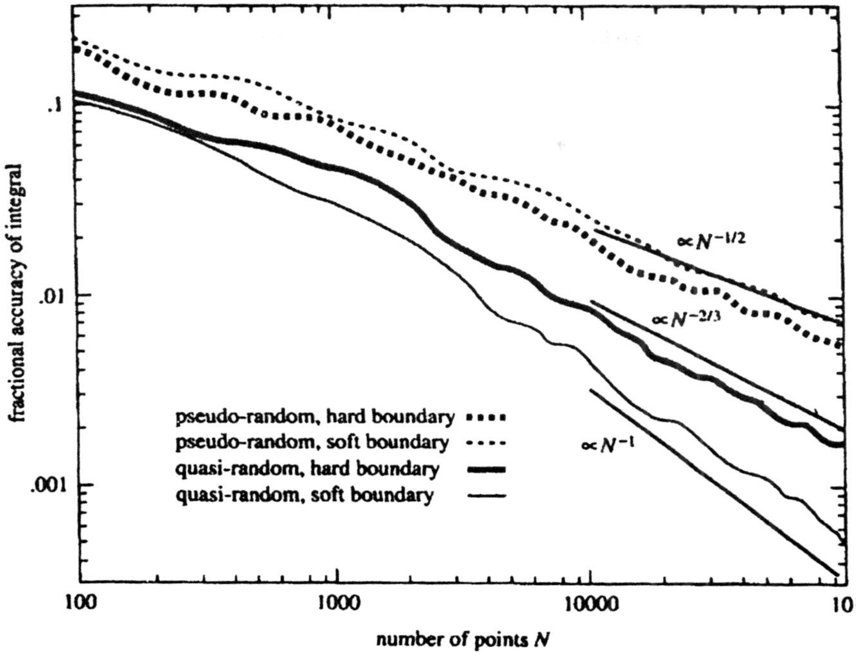

In a series of tests, including the Paskov studies on a CMO, low discrepancy sequences were found to speed convergence by a factor of at least 10 compared to random numbers; and low discrepancy sequences answers do not seem to be subject to a bias. They also outperform variance reduction techniques and again produce unbiased answers. Other investigators have found the same results. In particular, the studies done by Traub and Papegeorgiou found that in valuing the residual tranche of a CMO, when 10^{-4} accuracy was required, low discrepancy sequences beat out random numbers by a factor of 500.

Example Comparing Estimate to Actual

An easy non-financial example of this discussion can be shown by estimating the value of three-dimensional functions, defined on a torus, for which the answer is known. Exhibit 1 shows the Monte Carlo random number based results converge as $n^{-\frac{1}{2}}$, while low discrepancy sequences results converge as n^{-1}. The difference becomes immense with increasing n, a point to which we shall return. The low discrepancy sequences accuracy is better than would be predicted by theory.

Exhibit 2: Comparison of Investment Strategies for SPDAs Using Low Discrepancy Sequences

	Number of Scenarios									
	999		200		100		50		25	
Percentile	Long	Med.	Long	Med.	Long	Med.	Long	Med.	Long	Med.
95%	188.6	133.2	184.6	132.3	181.1	131.4	191.4	135.5	195.4	134.9
90%	177.1	125.0	175.1	124.5	169.6	126.5	173.2	131.2	182.0	131.8
85%	166.8	120.6	166.7	119.6	154.7	118.1	166.4	120.7	168.1	128.6
75%	146.2	111.3	150.2	111.0	141.3	106.8	146.4	110.4	152.6	108.5
Med	103.3	89.1	103.5	91.1	107.1	89.1	107.2	85.7	87.4	83.8
25%	45.3	62.2	41.4	60.7	53.3	67.9	37.4	59.5	25.8	52.9
15%	6.0	45.2	4.1	50.5	21.3	52.0	13.9	51.7	9.6	47.0
10%	−21.1	31.4	−7.8	34.9	4.6	41.3	−106.1	−19.6	−67.3	1.0
5%	−62.7	14.7	−48.9	16.7	−118.0	−19.9	−138.3	−31.7	−131.7	−27.3
Cond. Mean	111.6	87.5	108.1	87.1	107.2	90.3	109.1	93.0	101.7	89.9
Std. Dev.	53.1	31.5	55.9	31.2	50.0	26.4	55.9	27.5	64.2	30.5
Ruin Prob.	13.3%	3.9%	12%	3.5%	10%	7%	12%	12%	12%	12%

Test of Low Discrepancy Sequences

All of this has been a prelude to a specific test. The authors of this study have believed that low discrepancy sequences should not only converge more rapidly but could preserve the shape of the probability distribution. If this is generally true, it should be true for a specific asset/liability modeling situation. How does it work in practice? To answer this question, Dan Vesper of ARM Financial Group used Tillinghast Actuarial Software (TAS) to conduct an asset/liability modeling test on an actual block of business.

The sets of interest rate scenarios were those we generated using low discrepancy sequence disturbances. The block of business involves 12,000 single premium deferred annuities (SPDAs) issued 1986-1996, and the contracts had 1-, 3-, and 5-year initial guarantees. Surrender charges grade to zero in five to seven years; crediting rates are based on portfolio earned rates; and lapses depend on a competitor rate defined as the spread from medium-term Treasury rates.

The interest rate process starts with the March 31, 1996 term structure. Using disturbances chosen from the low discrepancy sequences technology, those rates are modified each quarter by the effect of two correlated log normal distributions, one medium and one short. Since two independent rates are estimated for the next quarter for each of 40 quarters, 80 dimensions are considered. There are various limitations on the movement of interest rates that prevent what is commonly perceived to be aberrant scenarios from emerging.

Exhibit 2 shows results, as measured by the ending market value of surplus, of both a long and medium-term investment strategy. The 200 scenarios were a subset of the original 999. The 100 scenarios were the first 100 of the original 999. The 50 scenarios were the first 50 of the original 999, and so forth.

The results must be viewed as remarkable. There is no significant information lost in going from 999 to 200 scenarios. As we reduce the number of scenarios to 100, 50, and 25, we do lose progressively more information about the shape of the probability distribution. However, usable results are available, even with such small samples; the qualitative difference between a long and a medium term investment strategy is preserved. On the basis of this example it would seem that tests of investment or crediting rate strategies using as few as 25 runs might produce usable results.

We are again faced with the anomaly that results are still better than theoretically predicted. There is little difference in results for 999 scenarios compared with 50 scenarios. The medians do not greatly change. The conditional means (conditional, because negative values are not used in the calculation) are quite stable. Even the calculated conditional standard deviations are stable. Of course it is true that the medium investment strategy is designed to minimize the variance across scenarios. But what about the similar result that shows up with the longer term strategy? We know that part of the reason for these striking results is in the nature of the function being evaluated, but much of the reason for the goodness of the answer is still unknown.

CONCLUSION

The conclusion from all the studies to date is that using low discrepancy sequences in financial studies should be seriously investigated. The results converge rapidly with no known bias and preserve the shape of the probability distribution. We are all concerned about the number of scenarios required to get reasonable results. Low discrepancy sequences technology seems to provide a way for getting usable results with a limited number of scenarios. As a consequence the number of calculations falls within practical limits. If we solve this, we can get to worrying about the real problem of how good our assumptions are.

Section IV:

Measuring and Controlling Interest Rate Risk

Chapter 15

Fixed Income Risk

Ronald N. Kahn, Ph.D.
Director of Research
BARRA, Inc.

INTRODUCTION

Risk analysis has been central to investing since at least the 1950s, when Harry Markowitz showed mathematically exactly how diversification reduced risk.[1] Since then, risk analysis has developed into a very powerful tool relied upon by institutional investors. If expected return is the protagonist in the drama of fixed income portfolio management, then risk is the antagonist.

This chapter will discuss definitions of risk, describe some key characteristics of risk, present approaches to modeling risk, and discuss risk model uses. The important lessons are:

- The standard deviation of return is the best overall definition of risk.
- Risks don't add.
- Duration measures exposure to risk, rather than risk.
- Institutional investors care more about active than total risk.
- Risk models identify the important sources of risk: interest rates, spreads, prepayment factors, volatility, and currencies.
- Risk model uses include current portfolio risk analysis, portfolio construction and rebalancing, and past portfolio performance analysis.

We start with our definition of risk.

DEFINING RISK

All definitions of risk arise fundamentally from the probability distribution of possible returns. This distribution describes the probability that the return will be between 1% and 1.01%, the probability of returns between 1.01% and 1.02%, etc. The return in question can describe a bond or a portfolio, a total return or return relative to a benchmark.

---

[1] H.M. Markowitz, "Portfolio Selection: Efficient Diversification of Investment," *Cowles Foundation Monograph 16* (New Haven CT: Yale University Press, 1959).

The distribution of returns describes probabilities of all possible outcomes. As such, it is complicated and full of detail. It can answer all questions about returns and probabilities. It can be a forecast, or a summary of realized returns.

Unfortunately the distribution of returns is too complicated and detailed in its entirety. Hence all definitions of risk attempt to capture in a single number the essentials of risk more fully described in the complete distribution. Each definition of risk will have at least some shortcomings, due to this simplification. Different definitions may also have shortcomings based on difficulties of accurate forecasting. Let's discuss some possible risk definitions in turn.

The *standard deviation* measures the spread of the distribution about its mean. Investors commonly refer to the standard deviation as the *volatility*. The *variance* is the square of the standard deviation. If returns are normally distributed, then two-thirds of them fall within one standard deviation of the mean. As the standard deviation decreases, the band within which most returns will fall narrows. The standard deviation measures the uncertainty of the returns.

Standard deviation was Harry Markowitz' definition of risk, and it has been the standard in the institutional investment community ever since. It will be our definition of risk. Standard deviation is a very well understood and unambiguous statistic. It is particularly applicable to existing tools for building portfolios. Standard deviations tend to be relatively stable over time (especially compared to mean returns and other moments of the distribution), and econometricians have developed very powerful tools for accurately forecasting standard deviations.

Critics of the standard deviation point out that it measures the possibility of returns both above and below the mean. Most investors would define risk based on small or negative returns (though short sellers have the opposite view). This has generated an alternative risk measure: *semivariance*, or *downside risk*.

Semivariance is defined in analogy to variance, based on deviations from the mean, but using only returns below the mean. If the returns are symmetric, i.e. the return is equally likely to be x percent above or x percent below the mean, then the semivariance is just exactly one-half the variance. Analysts differ in defining *downside risk*. One approach defines downside risk as the square root of the semivariance, in analogy to the relation between standard deviation and variance.

Downside risk clearly answers the critics of standard deviation, by focusing entirely on the undesirable returns. However, there are several problems with downside risk. First, its definition is not as unambiguous as standard deviation or variance, nor are its statistical properties as well known, so it isn't an ideal choice for a universal risk definition. We need a definition which managers, plan sponsors, and beneficiaries can all use.

Second, it is computationally challenging for large portfolio construction problems. In fact, while we can aggregate individual bond standard deviations into a portfolio standard deviation, for other measures of risk we must rely much more on simple historical extrapolation of portfolio return patterns.

Third, to the extent that investment returns are reasonably symmetric, most definitions of downside risk are simply proportional to standard deviation or variance and so contain no additional information. To the extent that investment returns may not be symmetric, there are problems forecasting downside risk. Return asymmetries are not stable over time, and so are very difficult to forecast. Realized downside risk may not be a good forecast of future downside risk. Moreover, we estimate downside risk with only half of the data, losing statistical accuracy.

Shortfall probability is another risk definition, and perhaps one closely related to intuition for what risk is. The shortfall probability is the probability that the return will lie below some target amount. Shortfall probability has the advantage of closely corresponding to an intuitive definition of risk. However, it faces the same problems as downside risk: ambiguity, poor statistical understanding, difficulty of forecasting, and dependence on individual investor preferences.

Forecasting is a particularly thorny problem, and it's accentuated the lower the shortfall target. At the extreme, probability forecasts for very large shortfalls are influenced by perhaps only 1 or 2 observations.

Value at risk is similar to shortfall probability. Where shortfall probability takes a target return and calculates the probability of returns falling below that, value at risk takes a target probability, e.g. the 1% or 5% lowest returns, and converts that probability to an associated return. Value at risk is closely related to shortfall probability, and shares the same advantages and disadvantages.

Where does the normal distribution fit into this discussion of risk statistics? The normal distribution is a standard assumption in academic investment research and is a standard distribution throughout statistics. It is completely defined by its mean and standard deviation. Much research has shown that investment returns do not exactly follow normal distributions, but instead have wider distributions, i.e. the probability of extreme events is larger for real investments than a normal distribution would imply.

The above five risk definitions all attempt to capture the risk inherent in the "true" return distribution. An alternative approach could assume that returns are normally distributed. Then the mean and standard deviation immediately fix the other statistics: downside risk, semivariance, shortfall probability, and value at risk. Such an approach might robustly forecast quantities of most interest to individual investors, using the most accurate calculations and a few reasonable assumptions. Many currently popular estimates of value at risk use exactly this approach.

Faced with these possibilities, we choose the standard deviation as our definition of risk. It is well understood, unambiguous, and accurately forecastable. And, by assuming normal distributions, we can translate standard deviation into value at risk numbers, for example.

DURATION IS NOT RISK

What about duration, the traditional measure of fixed income risk? There are two problems using duration as risk. First, duration isn't directly connected to the distribution of returns. Duration measures exposure to risk, rather than risk. Second, duration measures only one source of risk: parallel interest rate moves.

For a bond of price P, the duration D measures the return per unit parallel interest rate move Δs:

$$D = -\frac{1}{P} \cdot \frac{\Delta P}{\Delta s} \tag{1}$$

So duration relates bond returns to parallel interest rate moves:

$$r = \frac{\Delta P}{P} = -D \cdot \Delta s \tag{2}$$

Assuming stable duration, bond risk relates to interest rate risk as:

$$STD\{r\} = D \cdot STD\{\Delta s\} \tag{3}$$

If interest rate moves have an annual volatility of 1%, then a 5-year duration bond should exhibit an annual volatility of 5%, based on interest rate risk. Duration measures a bond's exposure to interest rate (parallel shift) volatility.

BASIC RISK MATH

The standard deviation has some interesting and important characteristics. Representing means as μ, standard deviations as σ, and portfolio holdings as h, we know that:

$$\mu\{h_1 \cdot r_1 + h_2 \cdot r_2\} = h_1 \cdot \mu_1 + h_2 \cdot \mu_2 \tag{4}$$

We call this the *portfolio property*. According to equation (4), the portfolio's mean return is the weighted average of the mean returns of its constituents.

The standard deviation does not have the portfolio property. In particular:

$$\sigma^2\{h_1 \cdot r_1 + h_2 \cdot r_2\} = h_1^2 \cdot \sigma_1^2 + h_2^2 \cdot \sigma_2^2 + 2 \cdot h_1 \cdot h_2 \cdot \sigma_1 \cdot \sigma_2 \cdot \rho_{12} \tag{5}$$

where ρ_{12} is the correlation between r_1 and r_2, and $\sigma_{12} = \sigma_1 \cdot \sigma_2 \cdot \rho_{12}$ is the covariance between r_1 and r_2. Then, because correlations must range between -1 and 1:

$$\sigma\{h_1 \cdot r_1 + h_2 \cdot r_2\} \leq h_1 \cdot \sigma_1 + h_2 \cdot \sigma_2 \tag{6}$$

with the equality above holding only if the two returns are perfectly correlated ($\rho_{12}=1$). For risk, the whole is less than the sum of its parts. This is the key to portfolio diversification.

For further insight into this, the risk of an equal weighted portfolio of N bonds, where every bond has risk σ and all bonds have pairwise correlation ρ, is:

$$\sigma_P = \sigma \cdot \sqrt{\frac{1 + \rho \cdot (N-1)}{N}} \tag{7}$$

As the correlation drops to zero this becomes:

$$\sigma_P = \frac{\sigma}{\sqrt{N}} \tag{8}$$

the key to lowering risk is holding many bonds. In the limit that the portfolio contains a very large number of correlated bonds, this becomes:

$$\sigma_P \Rightarrow \sigma \cdot \sqrt{\rho} . \tag{9}$$

This provides a lower bound on risk, even for portfolios containing many bonds.

The Covariance Matrix

In the general case, portfolios contain many bonds of differing volatilities and correlations. Equation (5) then generalizes to:

$$\sigma^2 \{ h_1 \cdot r_1 + h_2 \cdot r_2 + \ldots + h_N \cdot r_N \}$$
$$= h_1^2 \cdot \sigma_1^2 + h_2^2 \cdot \sigma_2^2 + \ldots + h_N^2 \cdot \sigma_N^2 + 2 \cdot h_1 \cdot h_2 \cdot \sigma_1 \cdot \sigma_2 \cdot \rho_{12} + \ldots \tag{10}$$

For large portfolios, this calculation involves quite a number of terms. We can simplify this notationally by introducing the covariance matrix $\mathbf{V}$ which contains all the variances and covariances:

$$\mathbf{V} = \begin{bmatrix} \sigma_1^2 & \sigma_{12} & \cdots & \\ \vdots & \sigma_2^2 & & \\ & & \ddots & \\ & & & \sigma_N^2 \end{bmatrix} \tag{11}$$

and then

$$\sigma_P^2 = \mathbf{h}_P^T \cdot \mathbf{V} \cdot \mathbf{h}_P , \tag{12}$$

where $\mathbf{h}_P$ is an N-vector containing all the portfolio holdings. Equation (12) has the advantage of notational simplicity, though understanding portfolio risk still involves the calculation in equation (10).

Annualizing Risk

We can use equation (10) to annualize risk. The annual return to a bond is the sum of 12 monthly bond returns:

$$r_A = r_J + r_F + \ldots + r_D \tag{13}$$

$$\sigma_A^2 = \sigma_J^2 + \sigma_F^2 + \ldots + \sigma_D^2 + \text{covariance terms} \tag{14}$$

Now we will make two generally valid assumptions. First, we will assume stationarity. The return variance is the same each month. Second we will assume that returns are uncorrelated across time, i.e., all the covariance terms in equation (14) are zero. These assumptions mean that:

$$\sigma_A^2 = 12 \cdot \sigma_{monthly}^2 \tag{15}$$

and more generally variance grows with the length of the return horizon. This allows us to measure risk over different horizons, but report it in consistent units.

Active Risk

Investment managers care about relative risk even more than total risk. If an investment manager is being compared to a performance benchmark then the difference in return between his portfolio's return r_P and the benchmark's return r_B is of crucial importance. The difference is called the *active return*, r_A. The *active risk*, ψ_A, is defined as the standard deviation of active return;

$$\psi_P = STD\{r_A\} = STD\{r_P - r_B\} \tag{16}$$

We sometimes call this active risk the "tracking error" of the portfolio, since it describes how well the portfolio can track the benchmark.

HISTORICAL RISK

The key ingredient for calculating portfolio risk is the covariance matrix. A risk model's job is estimating that covariance matrix. The most obvious approach is to use historical variances and covariances. This procedure is neither robust nor reasonable.

Data from T periods is used to estimate the N by N covariance matrix. But the N by N covariance matrix contains $N(N+1)/2$ independent numbers (all the variances and covariances). Each of the T observations includes N numbers (the set of N returns that period), and each variance and covariance requires at least 2 numbers for estimation. Unless $NT \geq 2N(N+1)/2$, or unless $T > N$, there will be active positions that will appear riskless.

So the historical approach requires $T > N$. For a monthly historical covariance matrix of just 500 bonds, this would require over 40 years of data, a severe problem since most bond maturities are less than 40 years. And, even when T is greater than N, this historical procedure still has several problems:

- Historical risk cannot deal with the changing maturity of bonds. Over the course of a year, each bond's risk will change as its maturity shortens.
- Circumventing the $T > N$ restriction requires short time periods, one day or one week, while the forecast horizon of the manager is generally one quarter or one year.

- Sample bias will lead to some gross misestimates of covariance. A 500 asset covariance matrix contains 125,250 independent numbers. If 5% of these are poor estimates, we have 6,262 poor estimates.

The reader will note limited enthusiasm for historical models of risk. We now turn to more structured models of risk.

STRUCTURAL RISK MODELS

In the previous section, we considered historical risk and found it wanting. In this section we look at structural multifactor risk models and trumpet their virtues.[2]

The multiple factor risk model is based on the notion that the return of a bond can be explained by a collection of common factors plus an idiosyncratic element that pertains to that particular bond. We can think of the common factors as forces that affect a group of bonds, for example interest rate or corporate spread movements. Below, we discuss possible types of factors in detail.

By identifying important factors we can reduce the size of the problem. Instead of dealing with 6,000 bonds (and 18,003,000 independent variances and covariances), we deal with approximately 50 factors. The bonds change, the factors do not. The situation is much simpler when we focus on the smaller number of factors and allow the bonds to change their exposures to those factors.

A structural risk model begins by analyzing returns according to a simple linear structure comprised of four components: the bond's exposures to the factors, the excess returns, the attributed factor returns, and the specific returns. The structure is

$$r_n = \sum_k X_{n,k}(t) \cdot f_k(t) + u_n(t) \tag{17}$$

where:

$X_{n,k}(t)$ is the *exposure* of asset n to factor k. This exposure is known at time t. Exposures are frequently called *factor loadings*.

$r_n(t)$ is the *excess return* (return above the risk free return) on bond n during the period from time t to time $t + 1$.

$f_k(t)$ is the *factor return* to factor k during the period from time t to time $t + 1$.

---

[2] For references see Richard C. Grinold and Ronald N. Kahn, *Active Portfolio Management* (Chicago: Probus Publishing, 1995, Chapter 3); Richard C. Grinold and Ronald N. Kahn, "Multiple Factor Models for Portfolio Risk," in John W. Peavy III, (ed), *A Practitioner's Guide to Factor Models* (Charlottesville, VA: AIMR, 1994); Ronald N. Kahn, "Fixed Income Risk Modeling," Chapter 34 in Frank J. Fabozzi, (ed), *The Handbook of Fixed Income Securities*, Fourth Edition (Homewood IL: Business One Irwin, 1995); Ronald N. Kahn, "Fixed Income Risk Modeling in the 1990's," *Journal of Portfolio Management* (Fall, 1995), pp. 94-101; and Andrew Rudd and Henry K. Clasing Jr. *Modern Portfolio Theory*, (Orinda, CA: Andrew Rudd, 1988), Chapters 2 and 3.

$u_n(t)$ is bond n's *specific return* during the period from time t to time $t + 1$. This is the return that cannot be explained by the factors. It is sometimes called the *idiosyncratic return*, the return not explained by the model. However, the risk model will account for specific risk. Thus our risk predictions will explicitly consider the risk of u_n.

We have been very careful to define the time structure in the model. The exposures are known at time t: the beginning of the period. The asset returns, factor returns, and specific returns span the period from time t to time $t + 1$. In the rest of this chapter, we will suppress the explicit time variables.

We do not require causality in this model structure. The factors may or may not be the basic driving forces for security returns. They are, however, dimensions along which to analyze risk.

We will now assume that the specific returns are not correlated with the factor returns, and are not correlated with each other. With these assumptions and the return structure of equation (17), the risk structure is:

$$V_{n,m} = \sum_{k1,k2} X_{n,k1} \cdot F_{k1,k1} \cdot X_{m,k2} + \Delta_{n,m} \tag{18}$$

where:

$V_{n,m}$ is the covariance of asset n with asset m. If $n = m$, this gives the variance of asset n.

$X_{n,k1}$ is the exposure of asset n to factor $k1$, as defined above.

$F_{k1,k2}$ is the covariance of factor $k1$ with factor $k2$. If $k1 = k2$, this gives the variance of factor $k1$.

$\Delta_{n,m}$ is the specific covariance of asset n with asset m. We assume that all specific risk correlations are zero, so this term is zero unless $n = m$. In that case, this gives the specific variance of asset n.

FIXED INCOME FACTORS

So much for the framework, what are the important factors? In researching this question, we must keep in mind the diversity of fixed income instruments: from Treasury bonds to corporate bonds to mortgages and CMOs; and from fixed coupons to floating-rate notes.

The important factors in the market include interest rates, yield spreads, prepayments, volatilities, and currencies for global bonds.

We have extensively analyzed interest rate risk movements and identified the three most important factors as interest rate shift, twist, and butterfly movements. The most important spread movements include movements in sector spreads and movements in quality spreads. These sources of fixed income risk are well known and fairly well understood.

Prepayment risk concerns the risk of unexpected prepayments. This is a type of model risk and is not well understood. Most models include forecasts of prepayments along interest rate paths. Models then price mortgage-dependent cash flows based on these forecasts. But adjusting mortgage cash flows based on a prepayment model helps to estimate interest rate risk, not prepayment risk. *As defined here, prepayment risk is the risk that the prepayment model is wrong.*

Actually, prepayment risk is somewhat more general than this. A model which correctly predicts prepayments may not match market expectations. And it is market expectations which drive mortgage prices. The prepayment model defines the dimensions of the problem. The volatility along each dimension arises both from forecasting errors and changes in market expectations.

What are these dimensions of the prepayment model? To begin with, the models do not fit all observed prepayments exactly. And so for any particular generic passthrough we expect its prepayments to deviate randomly from the model forecasts. Fortunately these deviations should have mean zero, and so will average out over time and over the different passthroughs in the portfolio.

More critical and systematic sources of prepayment risk involve unexpected changes in model parameters governing baseline (discount mortgage) prepayments, rate dependent prepayments, and burnout. All of these can be significant sources of prepayment risk.

Volatility risk is the risk of unexpected changes in volatility. We use option models to analyze fixed income instruments, and input estimated term structures of volatility. But the option analysis usually extends only to estimating interest rate risk; that is, option-adjusted durations. But what if short- or long-rate volatility is unexpectedly high? How will that affect the portfolio? This is analogous to an option trader's vega risk.

Exposures

The straightforward way to calculate the exposures $X_{n,j}$ in equations (17) and (18), given a model of instrument pricing, is to "shock" the model successively along each dimension of risk and re-value the instruments. For interest rate factors this corresponds to shocking the term structure, re-valuing, and calculating the returns generated by that shock. For unexpected prepayments, this corresponds to shocking the prepayment model, re-valuing the instruments, and calculating the returns generated.

To mitigate problems of instability, we should define our shocks based on realistic expectations of their possible size. For interest rate risk, this approach to estimating exposures is very different from the traditional duration approach. It is not only more meaningful, it is more flexible: it handles negative duration IOs as easily as Treasury bonds.

FACTOR COVARIANCE

Given these exposures, we must also estimate the variances and covariances of the fixed income factors. Here we can use historical analysis, on this significantly reduced set of data. We can also use more sophisticated approaches, including weighting more recent observations more heavily, and scaling the factor covariance matrix **F** up or down based on nonlinear volatility forecasts[3] for overall market volatility.

EXAMPLES

To understand this approach to risk modeling in more detail, we will now apply it to the set of sample instruments shown in Exhibit 1. These include a non-callable Treasury bond, callable and putable corporate bonds, a corporate floating-rate note, a passthrough mortgage, and a PO and IO. The specific analysis date is August 31, 1993, though as you will see, the general pattern of results is typically valid.

To compare magnitudes of risk, we will convert exposures to every risk factor to an equivalent annual movement. (We can impose this definition of the exposures X, as long as we consistently define the covariance matrix **F**.) So, for example, we will interpret the term structure shift exposures as the returns generated by a one-standard-deviation (annual) shift up in interest rates, and the baseline prepayment exposures as the returns generated by a one-standard-deviation (annual) shift up in baseline prepayment rates. For the purposes of this chapter, we will ignore the subtleties of how best to calculate such exposures: based on positive or negative shocks, multiple shocks, and so on.

Let's start with interest rate risk. Exhibit 2 shows monthly shift, twist, and butterfly shapes. For this example we have defined these factors using principal components analysis, but we also could have used more intuitive shapes: a parallel shift, linear twist, and others. Exhibit 3 shows the exposures of the sample instruments to each of these shapes — the X's — scaled to an annual positive movement. So most of the shift exposures are negative because a rise in rates negatively affects returns for most bonds. The IO has a positive exposure because of its negative duration.

Exhibit 1: Term Structure Exposure Examples
Sample Instruments

			Price	Duration
U.S. Treasury	11.875% of November 2003		148.60	6.52
Caterpillar	6.000% of May 2007	(Callable)	93.25	7.45
Dow	8.550% of October 2009	(Putable)	119.34	7.81
Citicorp	8.910% of May 1995	(Floater)	106.84	0.18
GNMA	8.000% issued 1992		104.33	3.49
GNMA	8.000% issued 1992	PO	67.77	18.44
GNMA	8.000% issued 1992	IO	36.56	−24.20

---

[3] For references on nonlinear volatility forecasts, see Tim Bollerslev, Ray Y. Chou, Narayan Jayaraman, and Kenneth F. Kroner, "ARCH Modeling in Finance: A Selective Review of the Theory and Empirical Evidence, with Suggestions for Future Research," *Journal of Econometrics*, Vol. 52 (1992), pp. 5-59; and Robert F. Engle, "Autoregressive Conditional Heteroskedasticity with Estimates of the Variance of U.K. Inflation," *Econometrica*, Vol. 50 (1982), pp. 987-1008.

Exhibit 2: U.S. Shift/Twist/Butterfly Shapes

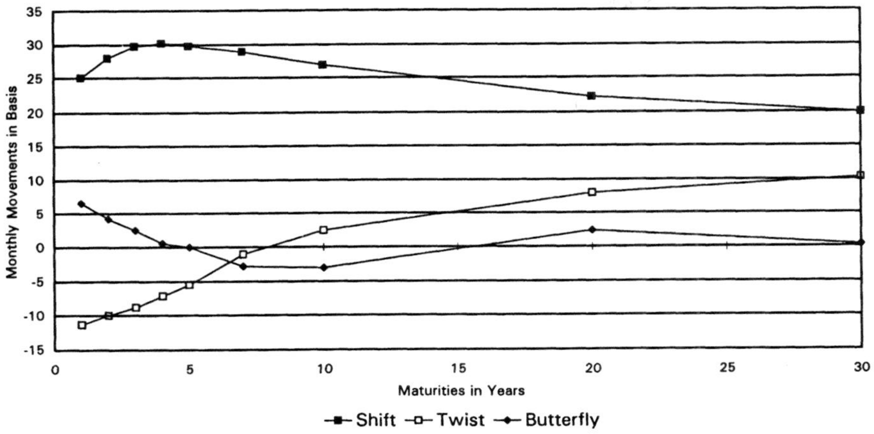

-■- Shift -□- Twist -◆- Butterfly

Exhibit 3: Term Structure Exposure Examples

Security	Shift	Twist	Butterfly
Treasury	-7.16%	0.39%	0.61%
Callable Corp.	-8.48%	-0.24%	0.61%
Putable Corp.	-7.86%	-0.27%	0.05%
Corp. Floater	-0.24%	0.10%	-0.04%
GNMA	-4.43%	0.28%	-0.31%
PO	-23.15%	3.12%	3.67%
IO	30.28%	-5.02%	-7.69%

For each instrument, the shift is the dominant source of interest rate risk. However we cannot ignore the twist and butterfly risk in many circumstances. Active risk relative to a benchmark, for example, will depend on active exposures. For most institutional portfolios, active durations (and similarly active shift exposures) will be near zero. Also note that the twist and butterfly exposures of the IO are comparable in magnitude to the shift exposure of the long bonds.

Next consider spread risk: the risk that yield spreads could widen or tighten, independent of any moves in interest rates. Exhibit 4 shows yield spread risk exposures for the sample instruments based on a widening spread shock.

Spread risk depends on yield spread volatility and the duration of the instrument. For almost all these examples, spread risk is smaller in magnitude than interest rate shift risk, but comparable or even larger than twist or butterfly risk. Especially for some corporate bonds, it can be the dominant source of active risk (assuming an active shift risk exposure near zero).

Exhibit 4: Yield Spread Risk Exposures

Instrument	Spread Risk Exposure
Treasury Bond	−1.15%
Callable Corp.	−3.21%
Putable Corp.	−3.27%
Corp. Floater	−1.20%
GNMA	−1.45%
PO	−7.67%
IO	10.06%

Exhibit 5: Prepayment Risk Movements

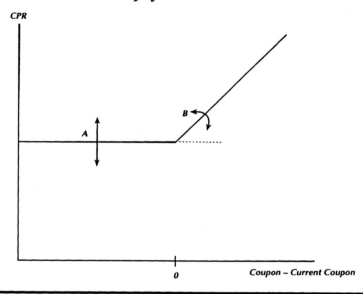

For this example corporate floating-rate note, spread risk dominates interest rate risk. For floaters, the coupon reset mitigates interest rate risk but not default risk. For purposes of interest rate risk, the floater effective maturity is the next reset date. But for spread risk, the relevant cash flows extend all the way out to the true maturity.

Now consider two sources of prepayment risk shown schematically in Exhibit 5, which shows a generic prepayment model with the forecast conditional prepayment rate (CPR) a function of the difference between the mortgage coupon and the current coupon. The movement A denotes baseline prepayment risk and the movement B denotes rate-dependent prepayment risk. Exhibit 6 shows sample instrument exposures to these risk factors. First note that the Treasury bond and the corporate bonds are not exposed to this prepayment risk. If we shock the pre-payment model while holding all other parameters fixed, the prices of these bonds will not change. This does not mean that we expect no change in interest rates correlated with a change in prepayments. We account for such effects in the factor covariance matrix, not the factor exposures.

Exhibit 6 also shows that the IO exposure to baseline prepayment risk is comparable to its exposure to interest rate shift risk. If we combine this IO with a Treasury strip to create a zero duration portfolio, we would still be exposed to very significant risks.

In contrast to the IO and PO, the passthrough mortgage has relatively low exposures to prepayment risk. This is because the passthrough is only at a slight premium, so prepayments have only a small impact on price.

To account for volatility risk we can look for shocks to short-rate volatility and/or long-rate volatility. For consistency with our option model, we will parametrize volatility shocks as volatility shifts, where short- and long-rate volatilities move in parallel; and volatility twists, where long-rate volatility moves relative to a fixed short-rate volatility.

Exhibit 7 shows volatility risk exposures for the sample instruments. Since the Treasury bond is noncallable, its volatility risk is zero. Since the floater resets to par at the next reset date no matter what the volatility, its volatility risk is zero. Once again, volatility risk is highest for the IO. Volatility risk in general is smaller in magnitude than other risk sources, but it still may be hard to ignore in some circumstances. For active risk, assuming shift risk exposure near zero, volatility risk is comparable in magnitude to twist and butterfly risk for the callable corporate bonds.

Exhibit 6: Prepayment Exposure Examples

Security	Baseline	Rate Dependent
Treasury	0.00%	0.00%
Callable Corp.	0.00%	0.00%
Putable Corp.	0.00%	0.00%
Corp. Floater	0.00%	0.00%
GNMA	-0.04%	-0.52%
PO	12.14%	4.72%
IO	-22.58%	-10.20%

Exhibit 7: Volatility Exposure Examples

Security	Volatility Shift	Volatility Twist
Treasury	0.00%	0.00%
Callable Corp.	-0.22%	-0.32%
Putable Corp.	0.23%	0.39%
Corp. Floater	0.00%	0.00%
GNMA	-0.20%	-0.25%
PO	0.81%	0.45%
IO	-2.08%	-1.54%

Exhibit 8: Annual Risk Forecasts

Security	Total Annual Risk Forecast
Treasury	7.29%
Callable Corp.	9.10%
Putable Corp.	8.54%
Corp. Floater	1.27%
GNMA	4.71%
PO	26.84%
IO	41.41%

Risk Analysis

We have completed the exercise of calculating each sample instrument's exposures to the risk factors. The exposures of a portfolio of these assets would be just the portfolio-weighted average of the instrument exposures.

To complete the analysis of risk, we must combine these exposures with the covariance matrix F, according to equation (18). Only when we combine our risk exposures with the covariance matrix can we see our overall risk.

Equation (18) also includes a contribution from each instrument's specific risk. This risk is idiosyncratic to each instrument and independent of the risk factors.

When we combine these effects, we find the total risk forecasts for the sample instruments listed in Exhibit 8.

The risk rankings aren't surprising — IO's and PO's are riskier than Treasuries, corporates, and straight passthrough mortgages on August 31, 1993 and most other days as well. But the magnitudes of the differences are impressive, and the sources of these differences, as we have observed, are insightful. Significant contributions to IO and PO risk arise from prepayment risks not traditionally analyzed. No combination of Treasuries can hedge out these significant risk factors.

THE USES OF A RISK MODEL

Having now covered in detail the structure of a fixed income risk model, what are its investment applications? Broadly speaking, there are three. They involve the present, the future, and the past. We will describe them in turn, mainly focusing on uses concerning present risk.

The Present: Current Portfolio Risk Analysis

The multiple factor risk model analyzes current portfolio risk. It measures overall risk. More significantly it decomposes that risk in several ways. This decomposition of risk identifies the important sources of risk in the portfolio and links those sources with aspirations for active return.

One way to divide the risk is to look at risk relative to a benchmark and identify the active risk. Another way to divide the risk is between the model risk and the specific risk. The risk model can also perform marginal analysis: what assets are most and least diversifying in the portfolio, at the margin?

Risk analysis is important for both *passive management* and *active management*. Passive managers attempt to match the returns to a particular benchmark. Passive managers run index funds. But, depending on the benchmark, the manager's portfolio may not include all the bonds in the benchmark, possibly due to the prohibitive transactions costs for holding the thousands of assets in a broad benchmark. Current portfolio risk analysis can tell a passive manager the risk of his portfolio relative to his benchmark. This is his active risk, or *tracking error*. It is the volatility of the difference in return between the portfolio and the benchmark. Passive managers want minimum tracking error.

Active managers attempt to outperform their benchmarks. Their goal is not to track the benchmark as closely as possible. Still, risk analysis is important in active management, to focus active strategies. Active managers want to take on risk only along those dimensions they believe they can outperform.

By suitably decomposing current portfolio risk, active managers can better understand the positioning of their portfolios. Risk analysis can tell active managers not only what their active risk is, but why and how to change it. Risk analysis can classify active bets into inherent bets, intentional bets, and incidental bets:

Inherent: An active manager who is trying to outperform a benchmark will have to bear the benchmark risk. This risk is a constant part of the task that is not under the portfolio manager's control.

Intentional: An active portfolio manager has identified bonds that will do well and bonds that will do poorly. The manager should expect that these bonds will appear as important marginal sources of active risk. This is welcome news; it tells the portfolio manager that he has taken active positions that are consistent with his beliefs.

Incidental: These are unintentional side effects of the manager's active position. The manager has inadvertently created an active position on some factor that is a significant contributor to marginal active risk. Incidental bets often arise through incremental portfolio management, where a sequence of decisions, each plausible in isolation, leads to an accumulated incidental risk.

The Future

A risk model helps design future portfolios. Risk is one of the important design parameters in portfolio construction, which trades off expected return and risk.

The Past

A risk model helps to evaluate the past performance of the portfolio. The risk model offers a decomposition of active return and allows for an attribution of risk to each category of return. Thus the risks undertaken by the manager will be clear, as well as the outcomes from taking those active positions. This allows the manager to determine which active bets have been rewarded and which have been penalized.

SUMMARY

Portfolio management centers on the trade-off between expected returns and risk. This chapter has focused on risk. We have quantified risk as the standard deviation of annual returns, though by assuming normal distributions we could report standard deviations as value at risk numbers. Institutional portfolio managers care mainly about active risk. Risk models, and structural risk models in particular, can provide insightful analysis by decomposing risk into total and active risk; and by identifying inherent, intentional, and incidental bets. Accurate risk models include all important sources of risk, especially interest rates, spread movements, prepayment and volatility risk, and currency risk. Risk models can analyze the present risks and bets in a portfolio, forecast future risk as part of the portfolio construction process, and analyze past risks to facilitate performance analysis.

TECHNICAL APPENDIX:
MARGINAL CONTRIBUTIONS TO RISK

The risk model in matrix notation is written as

$$\mathbf{r} = \mathbf{X} \cdot \mathbf{f} + \mathbf{u}, \qquad\qquad\qquad\qquad \text{(A-1)}$$

where $\mathbf{r}$ is an N vector of excess returns, $\mathbf{X}$ is an N by K matrix of factor exposures, $\mathbf{f}$ is a K vector of factor returns, and $\mathbf{u}$ is an N vector of specific returns.

We assume that the specific returns $\mathbf{u}$ are uncorrelated with the factor returns $\mathbf{f}$, and that the covariance of specific return u_n with specific return u_m is zero, if $m \neq n$. With these assumptions we can express the N by N covariance matrix $\mathbf{V}$ of bond returns as

$$\mathbf{V} = \mathbf{X} \cdot \mathbf{F} \cdot \mathbf{X}^T + \Delta, \qquad\qquad\qquad\qquad \text{(A-2)}$$

where $\mathbf{F}$ is the K by K covariance matrix of the factor returns and Δ is the N by N diagonal matrix of specific variance.

Marginal Contributions

Although total allocation of risk is difficult, we can examine the marginal effects of a change in the portfolio. This type of sensitivity analysis allows us to see what factors and assets have the largest impact on risk. The marginal impact on risk is measured by the partial derivative of the risk with respect to the asset holding.

We can compute these marginal contributions for total risk and active risk. The N vector of marginal contributions to total risk is:

$$\mathbf{MCTR} = \frac{\partial \sigma_P}{\partial \mathbf{h}_P^T} = \frac{\mathbf{V} \cdot \mathbf{h}_P}{\sigma_P}. \qquad\qquad\qquad\qquad \text{(A-3)}$$

The $\mathbf{MCTR}(n)$ is the partial derivative of σ_P with respect to $\mathbf{h}_P(n)$. We can think of it as the change in portfolio risk given a 1% increase in the holding of asset n, financed by decreasing the cash account by 1%.

The marginal contribution to active risk is given by

$$\mathbf{MCAR} = \frac{\partial \psi_P}{\partial \mathbf{h}_{PA}^T} = \frac{\mathbf{V} \cdot \mathbf{h}_{PA}}{\psi_P}, \qquad\qquad\qquad\qquad \text{(A-4)}$$

where $\mathbf{h}_{PA}$ measures the active portfolio holdings.

Using equations (A-3) and (A-4), and the definitions of total and active risk, we can also show that:

$$\mathbf{h}_P^T \cdot \mathbf{MCTR} = \sigma_P \qquad\qquad\qquad\qquad \text{(A-5)}$$

$$\mathbf{h}_{PA}^{T} \cdot \mathbf{MCAR} = \psi_{P}.$$

(A-6)

This means that we could, for example, interpret $\mathbf{h}_{PA}(n) \cdot \mathbf{MCAR}(n)$ as asset n's contribution to active risk.

Chapter 16

Term Structure Factor Models

Robert C. Kuberek
Vice President and Principal
Wilshire Associates Incorporated

INTRODUCTION

Quantitative models of risk provide portfolio managers with valuable tools in the construction and maintenance of investment portfolios that meet specific performance objectives. Fixed income portfolio management is especially amenable to quantitative risk modeling because so much structure is present in the pricing of fixed income securities and because the returns of investment grade fixed income securities are so highly correlated with one another. Factor models provide a particularly powerful technique for modeling fixed income portfolio risk. Moreover, because the main sources of risk (and correlation) in the returns of investment grade fixed income portfolios relate to the shape and position of the yield curve, *term structure* factor models represent the most important of these models.

The purpose of this chapter is to review some of the leading approaches to term structure factor modeling. However, to understand how term structure factor models work and how they fit into the risk management landscape it is useful first to define this important class of risk models and to put their development in historical perspective. This is the objective of the next section. Succeeding sections discuss the application of factor models to risk management, identify the major types of term structure factor models, describe leading examples of each type of term structure model, and discuss the advantages and disadvantages of each.

FACTOR MODELS DEFINED AND HISTORICAL BACKGROUND

Whether risk is measured in terms of standard deviation of return, standard deviation of tracking error relative to a benchmark, value-at risk or probability of underperforming some target, a useful first step in building a factor model is to develop a quantitative description of returns that relates returns meaningfully to other quantities and that has statistical moments that can be estimated easily and reliably. One of the simplest descriptions of return that meets these requirements is the market model for common stocks.[1] In this model, asset returns are generated by the process

---

[1] The market model follows from the assumption that stock returns are multi-variate normal. See Eugene F. Fama, *Foundations of Finance* (New York: Basic Books, 1976).

$$\tilde{R}_i = a_i + b_i\tilde{R}_m + \tilde{e}_i \qquad (1)$$

where

R_i = the total return of asset i

R_m = the total return of the market portfolio

e_i = a random error term that is uncorrelated with the market return

and the tilde ($\sim$) denotes a random variable.

If it is further assumed that the residual error terms in equation (1) are uncorrelated *across* assets after taking out the influence of the single index return R_m, then this model is an example of a simple "factor" model where the single factor is the return of the market portfolio. It is also a *linear* factor model because it is linear in the factor return R_m. The particular description of the return-generating process in (1) is closely identified with the Capital Asset Pricing Model (CAPM) of William Sharpe[2] and John Lintner.[3]

Another well-known example of a linear factor model for risky assets underlies the Arbitrage Pricing Theory (the APT) of Stephen Ross.[4] This type of return model, which is very general, assumes that it is not possible to completely eliminate the correlations of residuals across assets with a single index. In this more general model, returns are generated by the following process:

$$\tilde{r}_i = a_i + b_{i1}\tilde{f}_1 + b_{i2}\tilde{f}_2 + \ldots + b_{ik}\tilde{f}_k + \tilde{e}_i \qquad (2)$$

where

r_i = the excess return of asset i over the risk-free rate

f_j = the return to risk factor j

e_i = a mean-zero random residual error term that is uncorrelated with the factor returns and uncorrelated across assets

In the APT model, excess returns are generated by a linear process which is the sum of a risk premium a, a set of random factor effects bf, and a random, asset-specific residual. Examples of factors include index returns, unexpected changes in GNP, changes in corporate bond yield spreads, beta, and the ratio of earnings to price. It often simplifies matters further to assume that the factor returns and the residuals are normally distributed.

---

[2] William F. Sharpe, "Capital Asset Prices: A Theory of Market Equilibrium under Conditions of Risk," *Journal of Finance* (September 1964), pp. 425-442.

[3] John Lintner, "The Valuation of Risk Assets and the Selection of Risk Investments in Stock Portfolios and Capital Budgets," *Review of Economics and Statistics* (February 1965), pp. 13-37.

[4] Stephen A. Ross, "The Arbitrage Theory of Capital Asset Pricing," *Journal of Economic Theory* (December 1976), pp. 341-360.

USING FACTOR MODELS TO MEASURE RISK

The moments of a linear factor model are the means, variances and covariances of the factor returns, and the variances of the residuals (one for each asset).[5] The usefulness and power of factor models in risk management lie in the fact that once the values of the moments are determined together with the exposures of the risky assets to the factors, it becomes possible to compute portfolio risk using any one of a number of definitions.

For example, suppose that the k factors f in equation (2) have $k \times k$ covariance matrix Ψ. Furthermore, suppose that a particular portfolio holds n ($>k$) assets with the $n \times 1$ weight vector x. The portfolio excess return can be written in matrix form as

$$\tilde{r}_p = x'a + x'B\tilde{f} + x'\tilde{e} \tag{3}$$

where B is an $n \times k$ matrix of exposures in which the ith row consists of the b's in equation (2).

Equation (3) gives the portfolio return for a portfolio of assets whose returns are generated by equation (2). The first term in equation (3) is the average risk premium in the portfolio, which is a weighted average of the risk premiums of the individual holdings. The second term is the part of the return that is explained by the k common factors f, and the third term is the aggregate residual return, the unexpected return or noise in the portfolio return that is not explained by the risk factors.

The variance, or total risk, of the portfolio return then is

$$\text{var}(\tilde{r}_p) = x'B\Psi B'x + x'Dx \tag{4}$$

where D is an $n \times n$ diagonal matrix whose non-zero elements are the variances of the residuals in equation (2).[6] Decomposition of return variance in this way has important computational benefits. By reducing the size of the non-diagonal covariance matrix from $n \times n$ to $k \times k$, for example, portfolio optimization can be performed using significantly less cpu time and computer memory.[7]

---

[5] Factor models have moments and parameters. Moments are the means, variances and covariances of the factor returns. Parameters are used in defining and measuring the factors. For example, the *variance* of a factor is a moment, while the *weights* of the stocks in the index that represents the factor are parameters. The number of moments (means, variances and covariances) in a factor model is a function of the number of factors. The number of parameters in the model, on the other hand, depends on the specification of the model.

[6] The decomposition of return variance in this manner is traceable to William F. Sharpe, "A Simplified Model for Portfolio Analysis," *Management Science* (January 1963), pp. 277-293.

[7] In their original paper, which studied single and multiple index portfolios in portfolio selection, Kalman J. Cohen and Jerry A. Pogue ("An Empirical Evaluation of Alternative Portfolio Selection Models," *Journal of Business* 40 (1967), pp. 166-193), reported that a single optimization involving only 150 securities required 90 minutes of processing time on an IBM 7090 computer using the full $n \times n$ covariance matrix. While computers presumably have gotten faster in the years since Cohen and Pogue did their work, the relative advantage of equation (4) in computational time surely remains.

Equation (4) decomposes portfolio risk into two components. The first component represents the contribution to total risk from the exposures to the common risk factors while the second represents the contribution from residuals. The contributions to return variance can be separated in this way because of the assumption in equation (2) that the factor returns are uncorrelated with the residual returns. Moreover, the residual variance matrix $\mathbf{D}$ has the especially simple diagonal form because of the assumption in equation (2) that the residuals are uncorrelated *across* assets. An important feature of this measure of risk is that the second term, the residual variance, tends to shrink with the number of assets in the portfolio. Thus, portfolio managers can diversify away the residual risk in their portfolios but not the systematic, factor risk.

Furthermore, since equation (3) applies to any portfolio, including a benchmark portfolio, the variance of the tracking error of a portfolio relative to a benchmark can be written as

$$\text{var}(\tilde{r}_p - \tilde{r}_b) = [x_p - x_b]'\mathbf{B}\Psi\mathbf{B}'[x_p - x_b] + [x_p - x_b]'\mathbf{D}[x_p - x_b] \qquad (5)$$

where the weighting vectors x are now subscripted to denote whether they relate to the portfolio or to the benchmark. The reader will notice that in equation (5) the variance of the tracking error goes to zero as the weight differences from the benchmark go to zero — if one holds the index, the tracking error variance is zero.

TYPES OF FACTOR MODELS

In terms of equation (2), factor models can be categorized according to how the factor exposures and factor returns are measured. In this regard, it is customary to classify factor models as macroeconomic, statistical or fundamental.

Macroeconomic Factor Models

In macroeconomic factor models, the factor returns in equation (2) represent unexpected changes in quantities that are observable. Quantities that are commonly employed as macroeconomic factors include the returns of specified indexes of common stocks, such as capital goods or materials and services indexes, as well as unexpected changes in measures of aggregate economic activity, such as industrial production, personal income or employment. Since the factor returns are directly observable, the moments of the factor model (the means, variances, and covariances of the factor returns) can be estimated directly from the *time series* of factor returns. Assets are differentiated by their exposures to these variables, which are the b's in equation (2). These exposures can be estimated by regressing time series of individual stock returns (or of portfolios of similar stocks) on the observed factor returns, using equation (2), with the stock returns as the dependent variable and the observed factor returns f as the independent variables. Examples of macroeconomic factor models include the single and multiple index models of Cohen and Pogue[8] and the APT model of Chen, Roll, and Ross.[9]

Macroeconomic factor models have the great advantage that because the factors are observable, they are easy to relate to the performance of individual stocks in an intuitive way. One can imagine (whether it is true or not), for example, that airline stocks would tend to do well in an economic upturn, while drug stocks might be relatively insensitive to general economic conditions. A disadvantage of this approach is that with only a small number of factors it may be difficult to eliminate correlation of residuals across assets. A second disadvantage of this type of factor model is that it may be difficult to measure either the exposures of the assets to the macroeconomic variables or the returns to these variables using data of arbitrary frequency. For example, one could identify a factor with the Federal Reserve's Industrial Production index, but this statistic is published only monthly, making it impossible to estimate and use the model in this form with daily returns data.

Statistical Factor Models

The second traditional type of factor model is the statistical model. In this type of model a statistical procedure, such as factor analysis or principal components analysis, is used both to identify the factors and to measure the factor returns. In principal components analysis, for example, a factor model is constructed using a multivariate time series of individual stock returns. The covariance (or correlation) matrix of stock returns is factored by identifying some small number of linear combinations (the principal components) of stock returns that account for most of the return variance in the sample. Thus the factor returns end up being linear combinations of individual stock returns and the factor exposures are the multiple regression coefficients of individual stock returns with these principal components.[10]

An advantage of this method relative to pure macroeconomic factor models is that one can remove as much of the correlation in residuals as one likes by including as many principal components as desired, all the way up to the number of stocks (or stock portfolios) in the original sample. A second advantage relative to macroeconomic factor models is that returns are the only inputs and thus frequency is not an issue: the model can be estimated with any frequency for which the individual stock returns are available.

A disadvantage of the statistical approach is that the factors are not observable in the sense that one cannot make measurements of the factor returns independently of the stock returns themselves and in the sense that the factors do not always correspond to quantities that can be related easily to stock returns.

---

[8] Cohen and Pogue, "An Empirical Evaluation of Alternative Portfolio Selection Models."

[9] Nai-Fu Chen, Richard Roll, and Stephen A. Ross, "Economic Forces and the Stock Market," *Journal of Business* (1986), pp. 383-404.

[10] For an early application of this approach, see Benjamin King, "Market and Industry Factors in Stock Price Behavior," *Journal of Business* 39 (1966), pp. 139-190.

A disadvantage of both the pure macroeconomic factor models (when the factor returns are observed and the exposures are estimated) and the statistical approaches is that the exposure of a given stock to a factor can, and probably does, change over time as the company's business mix and capital structure change. Because of their reliance on *time series* estimates of factor exposure, neither of these approaches handles this problem gracefully. A related disadvantage of both pure macroeconomic factor models and statistical factor models is that new securities are difficult to fit in a portfolio because there is no history with which to estimate the exposures.

Fundamental Factor Models

The fundamental approach combines some of the advantages of macroeconomic factor models and statistical factor models while avoiding certain of their difficulties.[11] The fundamental approach identifies the factors with a stock's exposures to a set of attributes, which can include the stock's beta, its ratio of earnings-to price (e/p), its economic sector (e.g., capital goods), and its industry classification (e.g., automotive). In this type of factor model the factor exposures are the exposures to the economic variables, the actual (or normalized) values of the fundamentals (e.g., the actual e/p ratio) and, in the case of a classification factor, simply a dummy variable that has a value of one if the stock falls into the category or zero otherwise. Factor returns are not observed directly but are inferred by regressing *cross-sections* of stock returns against their exposures to the set of factors.[12]

An important advantage of the fundamental approach relative to the macroeconomic and statistical approaches is that as the exposure of a stock to a given factor changes over time, these exposure changes can be tracked immediately so that measures of portfolio risk correctly reflect the current condition of the portfolio's underlying assets. By the same token it is easy to include new securities in a portfolio because no history is required to estimate their factor exposures.

TYPES OF TERM STRUCTURE FACTOR MODELS

The general framework of equation (2) can be applied to fixed income securities easily. However, for investment grade fixed income securities, the main sources of risk relate to the level and shape of the yield curve. Thus, the appropriate factor models are term structure factor models, where the factors in equation (2) are defined specifically to explain the returns of default free bonds, such as Treasuries or stripped Treasuries, and thus describe changes in yield curve level and shape.[13]

---

[11] Examples of this approach include, Eugene F. Fama and James MacBeth, "Risk, Return and Equilibrium: Empirical Tests," *Journal of Political Economy* (1973), pp. 607-636, and Eugene F. Fama and Kenneth R. French, "The Cross-Section of Expected Stock Returns," *Journal of Finance* (June 1992), pp. 427-465.

[12] In this case the beta, if it is included as a factor, is estimated or modeled using *a prior* time series.

[13] For non-Treasury securities additional factors can be important in determining portfolio risk. See, for example, Robert C. Kuberek, "Common Factors in Bond Portfolio Returns," Wilshire Associates Incorporated (1989).

An important feature of term structure factor models is that, because the factors mainly explain the risk of yield changes, in each model there is a characteristic yield curve shift associated with each factor. Still, as will be seen, each of the models described here bears a resemblance to one or another of the common stock models already described. Along these lines, term structure factor models can be classified in four types, as follows:

1. arbitrage models
2. principal components models
3. spot rate models
4. functional models

Term structure factor models that use equilibrium or arbitrage methods, especially Cox, Ingersoll, and Ross[14] and Richard[15] are analogous to macroeconomic factor models for common stocks. These models work by postulating dynamics for a set of observable state variables that are assumed to underlie interest rates and deriving (in the case of equilibrium models) or assuming (in the case of arbitrage models) some equilibrium condition for expected returns, then *deriving* the term structure.[16] Examples of state variables underlying these models include the short-term nominal interest rate, the short-term "real" rate of interest, the rate of inflation, and the unexpected component of the change in the Consumer Price Index. A unique feature of the equilibrium/arbitrage approach, relative to other types of term structure factor models, is that the equilibrium/arbitrage approach produces term structure factor models that are rigorously consistent with security valuation. In other words, these models provide both bond prices and dynamics.

Term structure factor models based on principal components or factor analysis, such as Gultekin and Rogalski[17] and Litterman and Scheinkman,[18] are

---

[14] John C. Cox, Jonathan E. Ingersoll, and Stephen A. Ross, "A Theory of the Term Structure of Interest Rates," Working Paper (August 1978) and John C. Cox, Jonathan E. Ingersoll, and Stephen A. Ross, "A Theory of the Term Structure of Interest Rates," *Econometrica* (1985), pp. 385-407.

[15] Scott F. Richard, "An Arbitrage Model of the Term Structure of Interest Rates," *Journal of Financial Economics* (1978), pp.33-57.

[16] In distinguishing the arbitrage approach from their own equilibrium approach, Cox, Ingersoll, and Ross write, "An alternative to the equilibrium approach taken here is based purely on arbitrage considerations. Here is a brief summary of this argument. Assume that all uncertainty is described by some set of state variables. If there are no pure arbitrage opportunities in the economy, then there exists a (not necessarily unique) set of state-space prices which support current contingent claim values... By assuming that the state variables follow an *exogenously* specified diffusion process, one obtains a valuation equation of the same general form as [CIR (1978) eq.] (25). However, the resulting equation contains *undetermined* coefficients which depend on both preferences and production opportunities and *can be identified only in a general equilibrium setting*" (italics supplied). Notwithstanding this criticism, however, as Richard and others have shown, arbitrage models are powerful, easy to develop, and, providing one is willing and has the means to solve them numerically, reasonably practical.

[17] N. Bulent Gultekin and Richard J. Rogalski, "Government Bond Returns, Measurement of Interest Rate Risk and the Arbitrage Pricing Theory," *Journal of Finance* (1985), pp. 43-61.

[18] Robert Litterman and José Scheinkman, "Common Factors Affecting Bond Returns," *Journal of Fixed Income* (June 1991), pp. 54-61.

analogous to the statistical factor models for common stocks described previously. In this type of model, factor analysis or principal components analysis is used to identify the factors underlying the returns of bonds of different maturities or, almost equivalently, to identify the factors underlying the movements of yields at different maturities. As with the common stock return models, the factor returns typically are linear combinations of the returns of zero-coupon bonds and the factor exposures are the multiple regression coefficients of individual bond returns with these principal components.

Two other approaches, spot rate models and polynomial models, bear some resemblance to fundamental models for common stocks in that the factors are most naturally identified with different measures of exposure. Spot rate models identify the term structure factors directly with the durations of zero-coupon bonds at specified points along the term structure. An important example of this type of model is J. P. Morgan's RiskMetrics™ model,[19] which identifies factors with the durations of zero coupon bonds at ten points along the yield curve, 3-months, 1-year, 2 years, 3-years, 5-years, 7-years, 10-years, 15-years, 20-years, and 30 years. Duration for coupon bonds can be calculated either directly from the cash flows, if the cash flows are well defined, using so-called cash-flow mapping techniques, or with the aid of a yield-curve-based valuation model (e.g., an option-adjusted-spread, or OAS, model), in the case of bonds with embedded options and payment contingencies.[20] The RiskMetrics™ model and approach are in wide use in a variety of risk management applications, but especially in applications focusing on value-at-risk.

Functional models, for example Kuberek[21] and Willner,[22] seek to represent yield curve risk using approximating functions that are based on, or related to, polynomials. These models fit smooth curves to actual yield curve movements, where the fitted shifts represent a composite of a basic set of yield curve shift components, reflecting, for example, change in yield curve level, change in slope, and change in curvature. Factors are identified with the durations of zero-coupon Treasuries with respect to these pre-specified shift components. Superficially, the basic yield curve shift components resemble principal components shifts, but are generated not by a historical data sample but by some underlying mathematical reasoning.

---

[19] For a comprehensive description of this approach, see "RiskMetrics — Technical Document," J.P. Morgan/Reuters, 1996.

[20] See, for example, Robert C. Kuberek and Prescott C. Cogswell, "On the Pricing of Interest Rate Contingent Claims in a Binomial Lattice," Wilshire Associates Incorporated (May 1990). These term-structure-based OAS models are prerequisite for measuring exposures to term-structure factors for any but the simplest fixed income securities. The general approach is to fit the model to the quoted price of a bond by iterating on a spread over the initial term structure, then numerically to compute the factor exposure by shifting the starting term structure and re-calculating the model value of the bond at the same spread.

[21] Robert C. Kuberek, "An Approximate Factor Model for U.S. Treasuries," *Proceedings of the Seminar on the Analysis of Security Prices* (November 1990), The University of Chicago Center for Research in Securities Prices, pp. 71-106.

[22] Ram Willner, "A New Tool for Portfolio Managers: Level, Slope and Curvature Durations," *Journal of Fixed Income* (June 1996), pp. 48-59.

In fact, as will be seen, all of the term structure factor models described here can be represented as a form of equation (2). Moreover, all of the term structure factor models described here share the property that the factor returns in the model represent the amounts and direction of each characteristic yield curve shift allowed in the model, and the exposures, the b's in equation (2), are the durations of the bonds with respect to these yield curve shifts. From this perspective, a useful way to distinguish the models is in the number of characteristic yield curve movements that each model implies and in the forms of these characteristic yield curve movements.

The remainder of this chapter will explore a leading example of each of the four term structure factor models described above. The examples that will be used are (1) for arbitrage models, the one-factor equilibrium term structure model of Cox, Ingersoll, and Ross; (2) for principal components models, Litterman and Scheinkman; (3) for spot rate models, J. P. Morgan's RiskMetrics™ model; and, (4) for functional models, Kuberek. To facilitate the comparison of the different models, each of the models is recast to describe yield curve risk at the same 12 points along the yield curve — 9 months, 1 year, 1.5 years, 2 years, 3 years, 4 years, 5 years, 7 years, 10 years, 15 years, 20 years, and 30 years.

ARBITRAGE MODELS

The Cox, Ingersoll, and Ross equilibrium term structure model (CIR) is developed fully within the context of a single-good production economy with stochastic production possibilities and uncertain technological change. However, the model can be developed using arbitrage arguments, providing that the specification of the equilibrium condition for expected bond returns is consistent with their general equilibrium formulation.[23]

Assume that there is one factor, which is represented by the short-term interest rate r. Further, assume that this rate evolves according to the process

$$dr = \kappa(\mu - r)dt + \sigma\sqrt{r}dz \qquad (6)$$

where

μ = long-term average value of the short-term interest rate r

κ = rate of reversion of the short-term interest rate r toward its long-term average value

$\sigma r^{1/2}$ = standard deviation of unexpected changes in the short-term interest rate

dz = a standard Brownian motion

---

[23] The CIR model is constructed for an economy where money does not play a role and therefore the short-term interest rate in the model is a "real" rate. Nevertheless, by convention the one-factor CIR model is applied to the nominal term structure, where the short-term rate in the model is regarded as a nominal rate.

Equation (6) says that the change in the short-term interest rate r over the period dt is the sum of two components, a drift component, which represents the expected reversion of the short-term rate toward the mean, and a surprise term that reflects unexpected changes in interest rates. This description of interest rate dynamics has several important properties. These include mean reversion, volatility of interest rates that increases with the level of interest rates, and the fact that the future behavior of the interest rate depends only on it current value and not on the history of its movements.

If the price $P(r,T)$ of a zero-coupon bond paying \$1 in T years depends only on the short-term interest rate r and the maturity T, it follows from Ito's lemma[24] that the return over a period dt of a zero-coupon bond with maturity T is

$$\tilde{r}_T = \left\{ (P_r/P)k(\mu-r) + P_t/P + \frac{1}{2}(P_{rr}/P)\sigma^2 r - r \right\} dt + (P_r/P)\sigma\sqrt{r}dz \qquad (7)$$

The first term on the right hand side of equation (7) is the expected excess return of the T-year maturity zero-coupon bond. It consists of four components. The first is that part of the return due to the expected movement of the short-term rate r toward its long-term average value μ. The second component is due to accretion toward par. The third component is that part of the expected return that is due to convexity. The fourth component is the current value of the short-term rate, subtracted to obtain the expected excess return.

The second term on the right hand side of equation (7) is the effect of the unexpected component of the change in the short-term interest rate.

If it is assumed that the expected excess return of the T-year zero-coupon bond in equilibrium is proportional to the bond's "duration" with respect to the short-term interest rate by a risk premium λr, that represents the price of interest rate risk per unit of duration, then equation (7) becomes

$$\tilde{r}_T = (P_r/P)\lambda rdt + (P_r/P)\sigma\sqrt{r}dz \qquad (8)$$

Equation (8) says that the excess return on a zero coupon bond of maturity T is the sum of two components, a risk premium that is proportional to the product of the bond's duration with respect to r and the risk premium λr, and a surprise that is the product of the bond's duration and the unexpected change in the interest rate r.

Careful inspection of equation (8) shows that it has exactly the form of equation (2) where

$$a = (P_r/P)\lambda rdt \qquad (9a)$$

and

---

[24] For a discussion of the application of Ito's lemma to the pricing of bonds, see S. Fischer, "The Demand for Index Bonds," *Journal of Political Economy* (1975), pp. 509-534.

$$b = (P_r/P) \tag{9b}$$

Under these conditions CIR provide a closed-form expression for the duration P_r/P of a zero-coupon bond maturity T. This is given by the following formula:

$$\frac{P_r(r, T)}{P} = -\frac{2(e^{\gamma T} - 1)}{(\gamma + k + \lambda)(e^{\gamma T} - 1) + 2\gamma} \tag{10}$$

where

$$\gamma = \sqrt{(\kappa + \lambda)^2 + 2\sigma^2}$$

The CIR model produces a single characteristic yield shift as illustrated in Exhibit 1. The shift, which resembles a twist at the short end of the curve, describes yield curve behavior when yield changes are perfectly correlated and when short-term yields tend to move more than long-term yields. This tendency for short-term interest rates to be more volatile than long rates is a result of the mean reversion in the short rate assumed for the model and described in equation (6). For example, suppose that the values of the parameters in equation (10) for this example are as follows: $\kappa = 0.1$, $\lambda = -0.04$ (a negative value corresponds to a positive term premium), and $\sigma = 0.03578$. These parameter values are consistent with a 10-year mean reversion time, a term premium of 20 basis points per year of duration, and an annual standard deviation of short-term interest rate changes of 80 basis points. Given these values for the parameters, if the short rate increases by 100 basis points, the 30-year zero-coupon rate will increase by only just over 20 basis points.

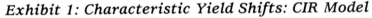

Exhibit 1: Characteristic Yield Shifts: CIR Model

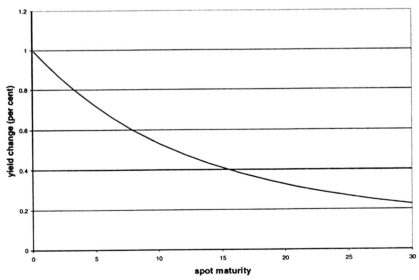

Exhibit 2: Bond Durations: CIR Model

Time to Maturity	b_1
0.75	-0.71
1.00	-0.93
1.50	-1.35
2.00	-1.74
3.00	-2.45
4.00	-3.05
5.00	-3.58
7.00	-4.43
10.00	-5.32
15.00	-6.16
20.00	-6.56
30.00	-6.84

As can be seen in Exhibit 2, for this combination of parameter values the CIR durations of zero-coupon bonds do not increase as rapidly as their ordinary durations, which are just the times-to-maturity of the bonds. This is a reflection of the tendency for long rates to rise by less than short rates, when short rates rise, and for long rates to fall by less than short rates, when short rates fall. Thus, CIR durations suggest that ordinary durations overstate the risk of long maturity bonds relative to short maturity bonds.

The CIR model has several advantages over other approaches. First, it is rigorously consistent with the valuation of fixed income securities. In other words, the model produces both prices and returns. A second advantage is that the model is defined continuously in maturity: exposures can be calculated for zero-coupon bonds of any maturity without recourse to approximation or interpolation. A third advantage, which has already been mentioned, is that the moments — the mean and variance of the (single) factor return — can be estimated directly by observing the time series of factor returns, in this case the time series of changes in the short-term interest rate.

A disadvantage of this model is that it allows only one type of yield curve shift and is thus very limited in the variety of actual yield curve behaviors that it can describe. This is not a shortcoming of the general approach, however. CIR also present a two-factor model, with uncertain short-term interest rates and uncertain inflation, within the context of their general equilibrium model, and Richard and others have proposed other two-factor and multi-factor models based on arbitrage arguments. However, for the variety of interest rate dynamics that have known solutions like equation (10), the models tend to have a large number of parameters and very complicated forms.

A second minor disadvantage of the one-factor CIR model as a factor model is evident from inspection of equation (8), namely, that the coefficients in the factor model depend on the level of interest rates. This dependence of the coefficients on the level of interest rates is plausible on the grounds that it is consistent with the presumption that interest rates tend to be more volatile when interest rate levels are higher. However, it means that this model cannot be implemented by regressing cross sections of bond returns on their durations, then averaging over time to obtain the moments, without first normalizing the exposures for the level of interest rates.

PRINCIPAL COMPONENTS MODELS

A second major category of term structure factor models is based on principal components analysis. In this approach, the returns of zero coupon bonds of different maturities are factor analyzed to extract a (hopefully small) set of characteristic yield curve shifts, defined at discreet maturities, that together explain a large proportion of the total variance of returns in the sample. The factors are thus the amounts and direction of each type of characteristic yield curve shift that combine to explain the returns of a cross-section of bond returns for a given performance period. Gultekin and Rogalski use this technique on coupon Treasuries, while Litterman and Scheinkman use the method to factor analyze the returns of Treasury implied zero-coupon bonds.[25] Because the use of implied zeros is more consistent with generalizations of equation (2) for any bond, the focus here will be on the approach of Litterman and Scheinkman (LS).

To illustrate the LS model, suppose that returns are available for implied zeros at twelve maturities, as follows: 9 months, 1 year, 1.5 years, 2 years, 3 years, 4 years, 5 years, 7 years, 10 years, 15 years, 20 years, and 30 years. With principal components one can specify any number of factors up to the number of securities in the data sample — in this case 12. Typically, a number is chosen such that most of the variance in the sample is explained by the factors selected. For the example here, the first three principal components typically explain more than 98% of the variance in the data sample, so three is chosen as the number of factors. The characteristic yield curve shifts that correspond to the first three yield curve factors are shown in Exhibit 3.

The first yield curve factor is the relatively flat curve near the top of Exhibit 3. This corresponds to a yield shift that is roughly, but not exactly, uniform. The second shift is a pivoting shift for which short rates fall and long rates rise. This shift is almost uniform for maturities greater than 15 years. The third shift is a change in curvature, with short rates rising, intermediate rates falling and long rates rising. Actual yield curve shifts are represented as composites of these three characteristic yield shifts. The principal components procedure works

---

[25] Implied zero-coupon bonds, or implied zeros, are hypothetical bonds that are priced using discount factors that are consistent with the discount factors that the market uses to price actual coupon Treasuries. While these bond prices cannot be observed directly, their existence is somewhat validated by the possibility of creating them synthetically by constructing hedge portfolio of coupon Treasuries. Also, a closely related security, the Treasury strip, does actually exist. The reason for using implied zeros in preference to actual Treasury strips to build a factor model is the availability of more history for backtesting: Treasury strips did not exist before the early 1980s, whereas Treasury prices are widely available back to 1974 and implied zero curves are available back even further.

in such a way that the factors are uncorrelated in the data sample that was used to generate them. This uncorrelatedness of the factors is a consequence of the property of principal components referred to as orthogonality.

The exposures or "durations" of the implied zeros with respect to each of these factors, the b's in equation (2) are shown in Exhibit 4. As with the analogous common stock models, factor returns are produced by the principal components procedure itself but, alternatively, can be estimated by regressing the returns of cross-sections of zero-coupon bonds on the durations implied by the characteristic yield shifts that are produced by the principal components analysis (Exhibit 4). The durations are scaled to the characteristic yield shifts themselves, so that, for example, one unit of return for the second factor corresponds to a yield shift of 0.38% at 30 years. Thus, to obtain the return of the 5-year zero coupon bond resulting from one half unit of return for the second factor, assuming the factor returns for the other factors are zero for a given period, it is only necessary to multiply the duration (−0.20) by the factor return (0.50) to get −0.10%. In practice, the realized factor returns will all be non-zero, but then the effects are computed in the same way for each factor and the results added together to get the total excess return predicted for that security, as in equation (2).[26]

Exhibit 3: Characteristic Yield Curve Shifts: Principal Components Model

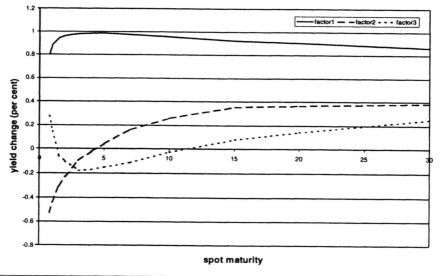

spot maturity

---

[26] The scaling of principal components models is pretty arbitrary. Thus, for example, the model here could have been scaled so that the characteristic yield shift of the second factor was 1.00% at 30 years instead of 0.38% (see Exhibit 2). In this case the duration of the 30-year bond with respect to the second factor would have had to have been scaled up accordingly. The content and explanatory power of the complete factor model would remain the same, however. In particular, the returns predicted for a bond, given its exposures and given the realized factor returns estimated for the performance period, would be identical.

Exhibit 4: Bond Durations: Principal Components Model

Time to Maturity	b_1	b_2	b_3
0.75	-0.60	0.40	-0.21
1.00	-0.88	0.44	-0.14
1.50	-1.41	0.46	0.08
2.00	-1.93	0.46	0.20
3.00	-2.93	0.29	0.53
4.00	-3.93	0.10	0.67
5.00	-4.92	-0.20	0.75
7.00	-6.83	-1.13	0.77
10.00	-9.56	-2.60	0.24
15.00	-13.84	-5.33	-1.17
20.00	-18.10	-7.35	-2.81
30.00	-25.89	-11.58	-7.51

An advantage of the principal components approach in term structure factor modeling is that the actual data provide guidance in defining the factors. A disadvantage of the principal components model, which is inherent in the approach, is the large number of parameters required. In the example here with three principal components, 36 parameters are required. These are the parameters required to describe the characteristic yield curve shift for each of the three factors at each of 12 maturities. A second disadvantage is that the exact definition of the factors, and therefore of the exposures, depends on the data sample used to extract the principal components. As experience is accumulated, the data change and the definition of the factors, and thus the durations of bonds, change.

A third disadvantage of this approach is that the model is not defined continuously on maturity. Thus, to calculate factor exposures for bonds with maturity or cash flow dates different from the maturities of the zeros used to define the factors, some interpolation of the characteristic yield curve shifts must be performed. The larger the number of maturities used to define the factors, the less interpolation is needed, but the more parameters are required. Of course, there is no guarantee that once the factors are defined, using a particular historical data sample, the factor returns still will be uncorrelated out of sample.

SPOT RATE MODELS

Spot rate models identify factors with the durations of zero-coupon bonds at each of a number of points along the yield curve. The factors thus can be interpreted as changes in the yields of these hypothetical zero-coupon bonds. Moreover, any number of yield curve points can be used to define the model, so the portfolio manager has wide latitude in defining the model to suit the specific application. Spot rate models have the least content in terms of economic assumptions and, correspondingly, the fewest parameters.

One of the leading examples of spot rate models is J. P. Morgan's Risk-Metrics™ model.[27] This model defines ten points along the yield curve and provides the variance-covariance matrix, the Ψ in equation (4), of spot rate changes for 13 countries including the United States. The RiskMetrics™ model is widely applied in measuring value-at-risk. The portfolio's "value-at-risk" is the largest *dollar* loss (or loss in terms of some other reference currency) that a portfolio will suffer "ordinarily." For example, if a portfolio will lose not more than $100, 95% of the time, then the value at-risk is said to be $100. Value-at-risk can be computed from equation (4), as follows:

$$\text{Value-at-Risk} = 1.65 \, (\text{Portfolio Value}) \, [\text{var}(r_p)]^{\frac{1}{2}}$$

As with all the term structure factor models described here, however, spot rate models can be estimated in at least two ways. The time series of factor returns can be estimated by measuring the yield changes at each yield curve point in the model, as with a macroeconomic factor model for common stocks. Alternatively, one may calculate the durations of the bonds with respect to the spot rate changes and regress bond returns cross-sectionally on these durations to create a time-series of factor returns. Typically, the second method is more direct because, by using this method, the yield curve itself does not need to be estimated.

Exhibit 5 shows the characteristic yield curve shifts for the first four spot rate factors in the 12-factor formulation. As the exhibit makes clear, the characteristic yield curve movements of spot rate models have a very extreme appearance. A yield change is either zero, off a given yield curve point, or 100 basis points, on the yield curve point. Yield changes are interpolated between adjacent points. In other words, if one of the bond's cash flows falls between the stipulated yield curve points, that cash flow has *some* duration with respect to both the adjacent points. Spot rate factors can be scaled, as in the example here, so that the duration of a zero-coupon bond to a given spot rate change is just equal to that bond's time to maturity.

Exhibit 6 shows durations for the first four factors in the 12-factor spot rate model. A feature of spot rate models is that because of the way the models are defined, the spot rate durations of a bond, if scaled this way, add up approximately to the ordinary duration of the bond.

A major advantage of spot rate models over principal components models is that fewer parameters are required. Where principal components models imply that spot rate changes at various maturities can combine only in the ways implied by the principal components, in spot rate models spot rate changes can combine in any way that is possible using the number of spot rates in the model. Like arbitrage models and unlike principal components models, the factors in spot rate models are not required to be orthogonal.

---

[27] For a discussion this approach as compared with the principal components approach, see Bennett W. Golub and Leo M. Tilman, "Measuring Yield Curve Risk Using Principal Components Analysis, Value at Risk and Key Rate Durations," *Journal of Portfolio Management* (Summer 1997), pp. 72 84.

Exhibit 5: Characteristic Yield Shifts: Spot Rate Model

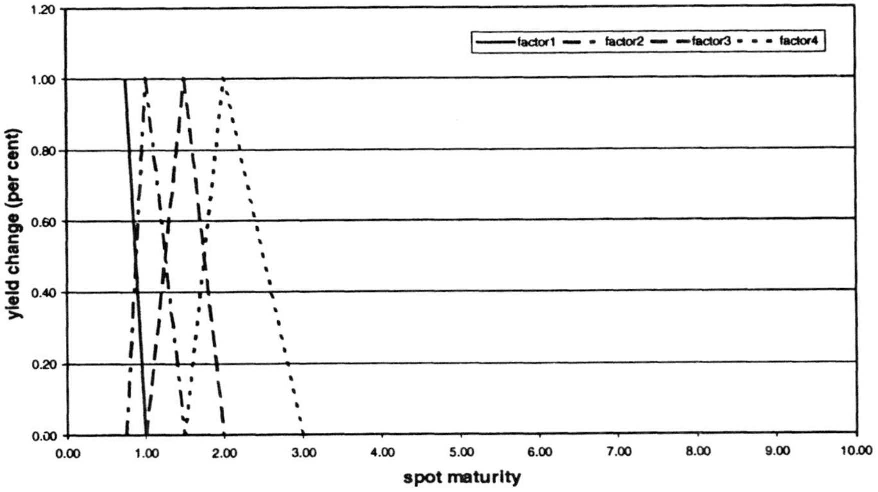

Exhibit 6: Bond Durations: Spot Rate Model

Time to Maturity	b_1	b_2	b_3	b_4
0.75	-0.75	0.00	0.00	0.00
1.00	0.00	-1.00	0.00	0.00
1.50	0.00	0.00	-1.50	0.00
2.00	0.00	0.00	0.00	-2.00
3.00	0.00	0.00	0.00	0.00
4.00	0.00	0.00	0.00	0.00
5.00	0.00	0.00	0.00	0.00
7.00	0.00	0.00	0.00	0.00
10.00	0.00	0.00	0.00	0.00
15.00	0.00	0.00	0.00	0.00
20.00	0.00	0.00	0.00	0.00
30.00	0.00	0.00	0.00	0.00

A disadvantage of the spot rate approach is the fact that the characteristic yield curve shifts in the spot rate model, as illustrated in Exhibit 3, do not correspond with yield curve movements that actually take place. Nor are the characteristic yield curve shifts defined continuously on maturity. Thus, as with principal components models, some interpolation of yield changes is required to apply the model to bonds with cash flows (or yield curve exposures) at times other than the points defined in the model.

A third disadvantage of spot rate models is the fact that a large number of factors are required to model yield curve risk accurately. To use an example, suppose that one wanted to reproduce with spot rate changes the characteristic yield curve movements of a principal components model as described in Exhibit 3. To accomplish this it would be necessary to combine 12 spot rate shifts in the appropriate proportions to recover the information in just one principal components shift. As a consequence, portfolio managers need to use a large number of durations to manage interest rate risk effectively using this approach.

FUNCTIONAL MODELS

Functional models combine the advantages of arbitrage models, continuity and consistency with equilibrium pricing, with the parsimony of principal components models. Functional models assume that zero-coupon yield changes are defined continuously in maturity, for example with a shift function $f(T)$:

$$f(T) = \Delta y(T) \tag{11}$$

where $\Delta y(T)$ is the change in the zero-coupon yield at maturity T. Then, a Taylor series or some other approximating function can be applied to the function $f(T)$, retaining the number of terms that are sufficient to describe actual yield curve movements adequately. Durations are computed from the approximating function directly. For example, the yield shift function $f(T)$ can be approximated by a Taylor series, as follows:

$$f(T) = c_0 + c_1 T + c_2 T^2 + \ldots \tag{12}$$

The factors are identified with the resulting durations, which can be derived easily from equation (12).

Chambers, Carleton, and McEnally employ this idea to devolop risk measures for use in immunization and hedging, but do not explore the implications of this approach for developing term structure factor models.[28] Similarly, Nelson and Siegel use exponentials to fit yield levels at the short end of the yield curve, but do not extend their approach to the long end of the curve, except to test extrapolations of the model as fitted to Treasury bills, nor to the identification of a factor model.[29]

Kuberek uses the functionals that are proposed by Nelson and Siegel, to model the short-end of the forward rate curve, for the purpose of approximating the shift function given by equation (11) for zero-coupon yields. This three-factor model has the following form:

$$f(T) \approx c_0 + c_1 e^{-T/q} + c_2 (T/q) e^{1-T/q} \tag{13}$$

---

[28] D. R. Chambers, W. T. Carleton, and R. W. McEnally, "Immunizing Default free Bond Portfolios with a Duration Vector," *Journal of Financial and Quantitative Analysis* (1988), pp. 89-104. See also, D. R. Chambers and W. T. Carleton, "A More General Duration Approach," Unpublished Manuscript (1981).
[29] Charles R. Nelson and Andrew F. Siegel, "A Parsimonious Modeling of Yield Curves," *Journal of Business* (October 1987), pp. 473-489.

where q is a parameter.[30] The model given by equation (13) resembles equation (12) except that the second and third terms contain an exponential decay. This exponential form has the benefit that, in contrast to equation (12), changes in yield curve level and shape will not become unbounded in maturity.

With this formulation, the zero-coupon bond durations, the b's in equation (2), take the very simple form

$$b_{ij} = w_j(T_i)T_i \tag{14}$$

where

$$w_1 = -1$$
$$w_2 = -Te^{-T/q}$$
$$w_3 = -T^2/qe^{1-T/q}$$

and where the b_{ij} are the exposures of the ith zero-coupon bond to the jth factor.

Thus, the first factor in this three-factor model represents the effect of a precisely uniform change in the level of interest rates, the second factor represents the effect of a change in slope of the yield curve, and the third factor represents the effect of a change in curvature of the yield curve. Factor returns can be estimated by regressing cross-sections of zero-coupon bond returns on these durations.

Exhibit 7 shows these characteristic yield curve movements for the three-factor functional model in equation (13). In this exponential form the characteristic yield shifts represent changes in level (factor 1), slope (factor 2), and curvature (factor 3). The model is specified so that changes in slope affect short rates more than long rates. This is consistent with the behavior of the yield curve at certain times, where short rates are more volatile than long rates. To reproduce yield curve movements where long rates change by more than short rates, factors 1 and 2 can be combined. For example, an upward shift of one unit of factor 2 (100 basis points at the short end) combined with a downward shift of one unit of factor 1 (100 basis points uniformly) produces a flattening of 100 basis points at the long end, with short rates unchanged. Additional complexity in yield curve movements, including various combinations of change in slope and curvature, can be achieved by including factor 3.

The zero-coupon bond durations are given in Exhibit 8. As can be seen, the durations at various maturities with respect to the first factor are equivalent to the ordinary (effective) duration of the bonds. The durations with respect to the second factor, which represents a change in slope, increase in magnitude with maturity to seven years, then decrease. The third factor's durations increase in magnitude to 14 years, then decrease.

---

[30] The value of the single parameters q, which represents the location of the maximum in the third shift component and simultaneously determines the rate of decay in the second, can be chosen in any convenient way. Kuberek ("An Approximate Factor Model for U.S. Treasuries") uses the value of q that maximizes the ability of the three-factor model to describe a wide variety of yield curve shifts under diffuse priors.

Exhibit 7: Characteristic Yield Curve Shifts: Functional Model

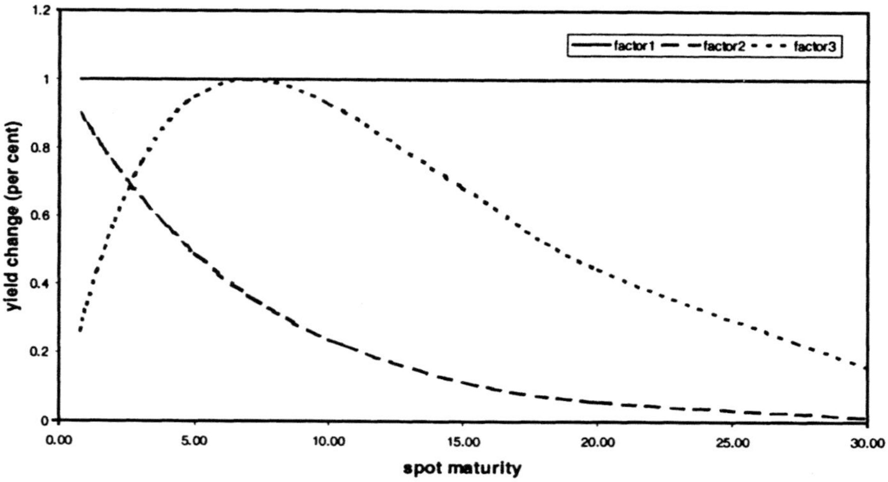

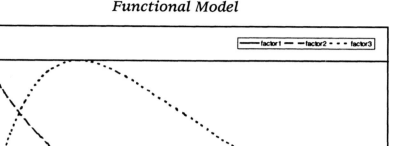

Exhibit 8: Bond Durations: Functional Model

Time to Maturity	b_1	b_2	b_3
0.75	−0.75	−0.67	−0.20
1.00	−1.00	−0.87	−0.34
1.50	−1.50	−1.21	−0.71
2.00	−2.00	−1.50	−1.17
3.00	−3.00	−1.95	−2.28
4.00	−4.00	−2.26	−3.51
5.00	−5.00	−2.45	−4.75
7.00	−7.00	−2.58	−7.00
10.00	−10.00	−2.40	−9.31
15.00	−15.00	−1.76	−10.25
20.00	−20.00	−1.15	−8.92
30.00	−30.00	−0.41	−4.81

The model described here, which is based on approximating functions, has several significant advantages. Most usefully, ordinary (effective) duration, as conventionally defined, is the first factor. Second, unlike the principal components models and spot rate models, the model is inherently consistent with rigorous equilibrium or arbitrage term structure models that imply yield changes that are continuous in maturity, including the CIR model already described. Third, it has only one parameter (and it has no more *moments* than any other three-factor model). Finally, the yield shifts implied by this model correspond with yield curve movements that portfolio managers can easily imagine occurring, namely, changes in level, slope, and curvature.

Because of the particularly simple form of equation (14), the durations of coupon bonds also have a very simple form, as follows:

$$b_j = \sum_h w_j(T_h)s_h T_h / \sum_h s_h \tag{15}$$

where s_h is the present value of the hth cash flow and where the w's are as given in equation (14). Equation (15) is simply the formula for ordinary duration, with an added weighting term $w(T)$. For the first factor, w has a value of unity for all maturities T equation (14), so the associated duration is simply the ordinary (effective) duration. More generally, bond durations in this model are calculated in the same way as ordinary (effective) duration, except that cash flows are weighted differently to reflect the differential exposure to various alternative yield curve shifts.

Like the arbitrage and spot rate models, the factors in functional models are not required to be orthogonal. However, if uncorrelatedness of factor returns is desired, the three factors in equation (14) can easily be rotated to have this property, for example, by estimating the factor returns and extracting the principal components.

CONCLUSION

Term structure factor models can be classified in one of four categories: arbitrage models, principal components models, spot rate models, and functional models. Examples of these reviewed here are the models of Cox, Ingersoll and Ross (arbitrage), Litterman and Scheinkman (principal components), J. P. Morgan's Risk-Metrics™ (spot rate), and Kuberek (functional). Each approach resembles, in some important way, one or another of the traditional types of factor models for common stocks, macroeconomic, statistical, and fundamental.

As with common stock models, the approaches to term structure factor models reviewed here differ primarily in the identification of the factors and in how the factor exposures and factor returns are measured. Arbitrage models assume some underlying set of state variables, then derive the term structure and its dynamics. Principal components models extract factor returns from the excess returns of zero-coupon bonds at specified maturities using statistical techniques. Spot rate models associate factors with yield changes at every point (of a specified set) along the yield curve, and functional models use pre-specified yield curve shifts to fit actual yield curve movements, where the shift components are motivated by equilibrium considerations.

At the extremes, the one-factor model of Cox, Ingersoll, and Ross is most rigorously consistent with equilibrium pricing, but is also the most restrictive in describing actual yield curve movements, while spot rate models are most descriptive, but have the most factors (and thus, the most durations) of any approach. Principal components and functional models find a middle ground, compromising between the structure and rigorousness of arbitrage models, with few factors, and the explanatory power of spot rate models, with many. Principal components models have the advantage that actual data guide in the identification of the factors, but suffer from the defect that the durations are sample dependent. Functional models have the advantage that the factors can be pre specified in a manner that is convenient to the portfolio manager, for example by defining the factors in such a way that ordinary duration, as conventionally defined, is the first factor.

An important common feature of the models reviewed here relates to the fact that each one associates factors with characteristic yield curve movements. Specifically, factor exposures can be estimated in these models by subjecting a bond to each of the characteristic yield shifts, using a term-structure-based valuation model, or OAS model, to see how much return results. Indeed, the application of term structure factor models crucially depends on the availability and usability of these ancillary valuation models.

The power and usefulness of term structure factor models lie in their application to risk management. Once the moments of the model are determined together with the exposures of the portfolio to each of the factors, it becomes possible to measure portfolio risk in any number of ways, including return variance, tracking error relative to a benchmark, and value-at-risk. By further assuming that the factor returns are normally distributed, it becomes possible to characterize the distribution of portfolio return fully, regardless of its composition.

Chapter 17

Effective and Ineffective Duration Measures for Life Insurers

David F. Babbel, Ph.D.
Professor of Insurance and Finance
The Wharton School
University of Pennsylvania

INTRODUCTION

One of the insurance industry's most useful applications of duration analysis is in asset/liability management (ALM). In such applications, a balance is sought between the duration of assets and liabilities so that the volatility of economic surplus is contained to desirable levels. Surplus duration is measured as:

$$D_S = (D_A - D_L)\frac{A}{S} + D_L$$

where:

D_S = duration of economic surplus
D_A = duration of assets
D_L = duration of liabilities
A = market value of assets
S = economic surplus = $A - L$ where L denotes present value of liabilities

This equation appears to be very simple, but looks can be deceiving. It implies that if asset and liability durations are matched, surplus duration will converge to the same level as liability duration. Moreover, in cases where economic surplus is positive, if the duration of assets is shorter than that of liabilities by a sufficient amount, the firm can achieve a surplus duration of zero. If care is taken to ensure that convexities are also well matched, this can result in a minimal exposure to interest rate risk. Such low exposure to interest rate risk has been rewarded by the stock market.[1] The equation also implies that a proper balance between asset and liability durations becomes more crucial as leverage, $A \div S$, is increased.

---

[1] See Kim B. Staking and David F. Babbel, "The Relation between Capital Structure, Interest Rate Sensitivity, and Market Value in the Property-Liability Insurance Industry," *Journal of Risk and Insurance* (December 1995), and Kim B. Staking and David F. Babbel, "Insurer Surplus Duration and Market Value Revisited," *Journal of Risk and Insurance* (March 1998).

But all is not as simple as it would appear. First, there is the issue of proper measurement of the market value of assets, some of which may not be particularly liquid. Even more painstaking is the estimation of the present value of insurance liabilities, most of which feature interest-sensitive cash flows and therefore elicit sophisticated valuation technology.[2] Economic surplus is then derived as the difference between these two items. But will it include liquidation value? going concern value? default put option value?[3]

Once these questions have been resolved, there is the challenge of estimating the durations of assets and liabilities. There are numerous definitions of duration, and several ways to estimate it. Some measures attempt to take into account basis risk between short-term and long-term interest rates, while others assume parallel shifts in the term structure of interest.[4] Some take into account credit risk, while others assume implicitly that interest rates relating to all creditworthiness levels move in lock step.[5] Some take into account currency movements and liquidity differences, while others ignore these factors. But the main way in which these duration measures differ is in whether they accommodate properly the interest rate sensitivity of the cash flows. In this chapter, we focus on that issue and show how important it can be to a life insurer.

TRADITIONAL AND MODERN APPROACHES TO DURATION MEASUREMENT

Duration measurement has a long history, dating back to 60 years ago when Macaulay[6] and Hicks[7] introduced the concepts. Today, this tradition is embodied in the use of what is known as "modified duration." We will not rehearse the formula or its derivation here, as it is available in virtually any investment management textbook. Suffice it to say that modified duration, as well as the original Macaulay measure, remain in popular use even today.

One of the problems with using such duration measures for insurers is that most insurance cash flows are not fixed. Many are somehow related to interest rate levels or historic interest rate movements. Indeed, with most assets and liabilities of a typical life insurer, this is the case. Under these circumstances, use of the traditional duration measures will be highly misleading, and they should be replaced with what are known as "effective duration" measures.

---

[2] For a thorough presentation of this technology, see David F. Babbel and Craig B. Merrill, *Valuation of Interest-Sensitive Financial Instruments* (New Hope, PA: Frank J. Fabozzi Associates, 1996).

[3] Such questions are beyond the scope of this chapter, but are addressed in Chapter 2.

[4] See David F. Babbel, "Duration and the Term Structure of Interest Rate Volatility," *Innovations in Bond Portfolio Analysis: Duration and Immunization* (New York: JAI Press, 1983).

[5] See David F. Babbel, Craig B. Merrill, and William H. Panning, "Default Risk and the Effective Duration of Bonds," *Financial Analysts Journal* (January/February 1997).

[6] F. R. Macaulay, *Some Theoretical Problems Suggested by the Movements of Interest Rates, Bond Yields, and Stock Prices in the United States Since 1856* (New York: Columbia University Press, 1938).

[7] J. R. Hicks, *Value and Capital* (Oxford: Clarendon Press, 1939).

Effective duration measures are based on stochastic interest rate valuation models. Because most stochastic interest rate processes do not have closed form solutions for duration, numerical procedures are usually employed to estimate duration. Perhaps the most conventional approach to measuring duration is a numerical procedure where three valuations are performed, with each valuation performed by an interest rate lattice (or simulation paths) being positioned at a different level of interest rates. An initial valuation is performed using a tree that is calibrated to current interest rates. Then each short rate in the entire tree is increased by 50 basis points and a new valuation is performed.[8] Again, each short rate is reduced by 50 basis points from the initial tree levels, and a third valuation is performed. Finally, the percentage change in price is scaled by the change in interest rates, which in this case amounts to 100 basis points, resulting in a measure of effective duration.

There are variations on this theme that are sometimes used. In one approach, the near-term short rates undergo full adjustment, while the short rates furthest away undergo only partial adjustment, or even no adjustment at all. This variation is intended to capture better what is considered to be a plausible mean-reverting interest rate process. Interest rate simulations, as opposed to and even in conjunction with multinomial interest rate lattices, are sometimes used to estimate the three values needed for computing duration. These variations help the analyst to capture cash flows that are sensitive to interest rate histories as well as interest rate levels.

Another approach that is often used is to perform a single valuation using an interest rate lattice. At each node in the lattice a value is implicit. Thus, by comparing the value at the initial node with the value at an adjacent node, and taking into account the movement in interest rates between nodes, a measure of duration can be calculated. This approach has two advantages. First, it requires no additional work, as the values are already implicit at the nodes. Second, it is consistent with the stochastic interest rate process assumed. In other words, interest rates are simply following along one of their potential paths and not departing from the assumptions. The drawback is that the measure of duration produced is incorporating a time dimension that strains the conventional concept of duration (which denotes the change in price for an instantaneous change in interest rates). Yet if the nodes are spaced closely together in time, the distortion is minimal, and furthermore, it may even be a better measure of price sensitivity to interest rate moves, which indeed do occur over time. We are not so concerned with what is orthodox here, but rather with what is useful. All of these approaches based on numerical solutions to stochastic interest rate processes are useful to the practitioner of ALM. Moreover, they are far better than employing one of the traditional duration formulas which make no attempt to account for any interest rate sensitivity in the cash flows of the assets or liabilities.

---

[8] Some practitioners use a 1 basis point, or even a ½ basis point shift as an alternative to a 50 basis point shift. When this is done, the percentage change in price must be scaled to take into account the change in interest rates used in order to get an appropriate measure of duration.

Exhibit 1: Sample Duration Measures

	Effective	Modified
Single Premium Deferred Annuities:		
With Interest Guarantee	2.3	7.9
No Interest Guarantee	0.4	4.2
Term Life Insurance	2.9	9.5
Traditional Whole Life Insurance	4.3	15.9
Universal Life	3.2	16.4

DURATIONS OF INSURANCE LIABILITIES

For many financial instruments, traditional duration measures produce durations that are close to those generated by effective duration measures. This is true for many government notes, bonds, and non-callable corporate notes and bonds. As credit quality is reduced, and call or prepayment options are introduced, the traditional measures diverge more from the effective measures. When cash flows are tied to some index, the divergence can be quite large. But for insurance liabilities, the durations produced by the alternative approaches are typically far apart. Using one measure as a rough approximation of the other is simply foolhardy.

In Exhibit 1 we show some durations calculated for generic, seasoned insurance policies using standard mortality tables and lapse assumptions in a moderate interest rate environment. The effective durations were computed using a popular software package based on stochastic interest rates, and the modified durations were computed based on projected static cash flows and interest rates. The levels shown in the exhibit are not that important and should not be relied on as estimates for a given firm, because they can be highly sensitive to details of the policy provisions and will change depending on an individual insurer's lapse, mortality, and morbidity experience, in conjunction with the economic environment under which the durations are measured. But what *is* important in Exhibit 1 are the substantial differences between the effective and "ineffective" (i.e., traditional) duration measures.

What we have witnessed in consulting with numerous insurers is that while duration measures are typically employed in ALM, different measures are often used for assets versus liabilities. Some insurers use modified durations for assets and effective durations for liabilities, while others do just the opposite, depending on the software they have available. Some, in an effort to achieve consistency, use modified durations both for assets and liabilities. While use of inconsistently defined durations is clearly harmful, consistency in and of itself is not the solution, as it is possible to be consistently wrong! As previously noted, traditional durations can serve as rough approximations for effective durations for some asset categories, but this is not the case for insurance liabilities (with the possible exceptions of immediate life annuities and GICs, not shown). And because life insurance liabilities are replete with so many options and provisions that make their cash flow patterns sensitive to interest rate levels and histories, modified durations should be eschewed by all insurers.

To illustrate the potential danger of using modified durations for assessing the interest rate sensitivity of insurance liabilities, consider the following hypothetical situation. Suppose that modified durations are used by an insurer with equal amounts of value tied up in each of the five categories of policies shown in Exhibit 1. The weighted average modified duration of liabilities would be 10.8 years. Next, suppose the insurer has attempted to minimize its surplus duration by purchasing assets with an aggregate (effective) duration of 10.3 years. Assume the insurer is operating with assets of 100 and liabilities of 95, giving a surplus of 5. Then surplus duration is given as:

$$D_S = (10.3 - 10.8)\frac{100}{5} + 10.8 = 0.8 \text{ years}$$

The problem with this calculation for surplus duration is that it has nothing to do with the interest rate exposure of surplus because the liabilities duration number does not indicate the interest rate risk of the liabilities. The liabilities actually will manifest a level of interest rate exposure that can be computed by averaging the effective duration measures. The weighted average is 2.6 years. Therefore, the true interest rate exposure of surplus, as measured by surplus duration, is not 0.8 but 156.6! In other words, the equity value of the firm will be almost 200 times more volatile than that implied by the above equation. A mere 7 basis points increase in the general level of interest rates could lead to the loss of a firm's entire economic surplus.

$$D_S = (10.3 - 2.6)\frac{100}{5} + 2.6 = 156.6 \text{ years}$$

Employing modified duration measures on both sides of the balance sheet does nothing to solve this problem. It simply leads to balancing something that needs no balancing. Indeed, the very act of attempting to balance asset and liability modified durations can lead to a much more reckless interest rate exposure than if the problem is entirely ignored!

CONCLUDING REMARKS

We conclude that when estimating and attempting to manage the interest rate exposure of the insurance firm, it is essential to measure correctly the exposure of the assets and liabilities, using a consistent methodology. The methodology must be capable of taking into account any interest rate sensitivities in the asset and liability cash flows, and must be keyed to the same reference rates of interest. Only then can the firm calculate its surplus exposure, intelligently manage it, and keep it within desirable bounds.

Chapter 18

Yield Curve Risk Management

Robert R. Reitano, Ph.D., F.S.A.
Vice President
John Hancock Mutual Life Insurance Company

INTRODUCTION

Yield curve risk management pertains to the general discipline of controlling the sensitivity of a portfolio of fixed-income securities to changes in one or more interest rates or yield curves. In general, the purpose for wanting control can be defensive or offensive, strategic or tactical, but in virtually all such cases, the sensitivity of the given portfolio is being controlled relative to the sensitivity of a second "target" fixed-income portfolio. For example, in asset/liability management, one controls the sensitivity of assets relative to fixed-income liabilities. In total-return fixed income management, one typically controls the sensitivity of the asset portfolio relative to a fixed-income benchmark index which defines the performance objective of the portfolio. Finally, in fixed-income market-neutral portfolios, one manages the sensitivities of a long portfolio of fixed-income assets relative to a short portfolio of fixed-income derivatives, such as interest rate futures contracts.

Defensive yield curve risk management means controlling interest rate sensitivity with the primary objective of protecting against losses relative to the target portfolio; in contrast, the primary objective of offensive or opportunistic management is to capitalize on perceived opportunities for gains. Defensive risk management can be strategic or tactical. A strategic implementation involves risk management in light of longer term models of the behavior of interest rates, while a tactical implementation is in response to shorter term expectations for such behavior. Offensive risk management is by definition tactical.[1] Asset/liability management and market-neutral portfolio management tend to be primarily strategic and defensive but with perhaps a tactical leaning, while total-return management tends to be strongly tactical but with perhaps a defensive leaning. Exceptions are not rare.

---

[1] One documented example of a strategic offensive management approach pertains to portfolios at the very short (under 1 year) end of the yield curve, where longer portfolios enjoy a "liquidity premium" relative to shorter portfolios. See for example, Robin Grieves, and Alan J. Marcos, "Riding the Yield Curve: Reprise," *Journal of Portfolio Management* (Summer 1992), pp. 67-76.

The author dedicates this chapter to his mathematics advisor and mentor, Professor Alberto P. Calderón, on the occasion of his 75th birthday.

Independent of the objective of the yield curve risk management program, the first fundamental problem is one of quantifying the interest rate sensitivities of a given fixed-income portfolio. The next fundamental problem is either one of developing defensive risk management strategies from a longer term model of yield curve movements, or developing opportunistic tactics to capitalize on shorter term expectations. The last fundamental problem relates to the development of yield curve models, both strategic and tactical.

The purpose of this chapter is to provide a detailed survey of various approaches to the problem of quantifying interest rate sensitivity, emphasizing both the theoretical merits and practical shortcomings, and to discuss the implications of these approaches for defensive and opportunistic portfolio management. As for models of yield curve movements, useful strategic approaches will be outlined. Tactical models of yield curve expectations will not be surveyed because practitioners are silent both on the methodologies utilized, and especially on all but selective reports of the efficacy of such models.

SINGLE FACTOR YIELD CURVE MODELS[2]

Mathematical Framework

A single factor model is a model for which all of the uncertainty in the future movement of all interest rates is reduced to uncertainty about a single factor, which is typically thought of as a statistical entity, i.e., random variable. There are many such models, as will be seen, because there are many reasonable ways in which this unique factor can be specified. We suspend for now the question of whether or not *any* one factor is sufficient, and simply note that given the assumption of adequacy, many possibilities for a factor can be evaluated. Moreover, independent of any such adequacy assumption, it seems reasonable to expect that there must be a "best" such factor, which might in fact work very well.

Given this factor, which we denote as i even though in some models this variable may not be an interest rate in the usual sense, we can now model the price of the security or portfolio of interest as a function of this variable, $P(i)$, and inquire into the sensitivity of price to changes in this variable. Luckily for portfolio managers, Leibnitz and Newton developed calculus centuries earlier, so this inquiry has a fruitful conclusion. Specifically, it is well known that:

$$P(j) = P(i) + P'(i)(j-i) + 0.5P''(i)(j-i)^2 + \ldots \tag{1}$$

where $P'(i)$ and $P''(i)$ denote the first and second derivatives of $P(i)$, respectively.

Equation (1), which is recognizable to math aficionados as a Taylor series expansion, states that by knowing the value of a function and its derivatives at a

---

[2] For more technical details on these models and their properties, and additional historical references, see Robert R. Reitano, "Multivariate Duration Analysis," *Transactions of the Society of Actuaries*, XLIII (1991), pp. 335-91.

point i, it is possible to determine the exact value of the function at a point j. While this equation is not valid for all functions in theory, it is valid for the fixed-income price functions encountered in practice. Besides providing an identity for the exact value of $P(j)$, equation (1) also provides a basis for approximating $P(j)$: simply stop after the first two or three terms. Just how well a given number of terms works depends on the security and the size of the "shift" implied by the factor shift, $j-i$. In general, the approximation of any given security will deteriorate as $j-i$ increases, while for a given value of $j-i$, a given approximation will deteriorate for securities which are more "exotic;" i.e., contain more embedded optionality.

For finance applications, equation (1) is always restated by factoring out $P(i)$; that way, the units of the derivative terms are relative, so for a given security they are independent of the dollar amount held. Special notation and terminology for these "relative" derivatives have evolved, so that rewritten in the common finance fashion, and omitting terms beyond the second derivative, equation (1) becomes:

$$P(j) \approx P(i)[1 - D(i)(j-i) + 0.5C(i)(j-i)^2] \tag{2}$$

The "duration," $D(i)$ or D for short, has picked up a mysterious negative sign compared to equation (1), but this is because duration is defined as a negative derivative to be more compatible with the "Macaulay duration"[3] which was developed earlier and outside a calculus context. While apparent by comparison, the definitions of duration and convexity are:

$$D(i) = -\frac{P'(i)}{P(i)}; \; C(i) = \frac{P''(i)}{P(i)} \tag{3}$$

Of course, in finance as in any application of mathematics, derivatives must often be approximated since there may be no simple closed formula for the function of interest which allows an exact differentiation. In these cases, derivatives can be approximated by:

$$P'(i) \approx \frac{P(i + \Delta i) - P(i - \Delta i)}{2\Delta i} \tag{4}$$

$$P''(i) \approx \frac{P(i + \Delta i) - 2P(i) + P(i - \Delta i)}{(\Delta i)^2} \tag{4b}$$

In equation (4a), the so-called "central difference" formula is given. An alternative method, though typically biased because of the price function's convexity, is the forward difference formula which uses $P(i)$ in the numerator, instead of $P(i-\Delta i)$, and Δi in the denominator. For any approximation application, there is no useful rule of thumb as to how small Δi must be to give a good numerical approximation. Perhaps using trial and error, the objective is to determine a value so that the approximation produced "stabilizes," and changes little if smaller values are used.

---

[3] Frederick R. Macaulay, *Some Theoretical Problems Suggested by the Movements of Interest Rates, Bond Yields, and Stock Prices in the United States Since 1856* (New York: Columbia University Press, 1938).

This is not as inefficient as it seems, as once the necessary tolerance is calibrated for a given asset class, it tends to remain stable so further testing is unnecessary.

Equation (3) has as a simple consequence the fact that duration and convexity have the "portfolio" property. That is, given the durations or convexities of a collection of securities, the corresponding measure of the portfolio is easily calculated as a weighted average of the individual measures, with weights equal to the "relative" prices of the securities, and where relative price is the ratio of security price to portfolio price. Specifically:

$$D^P = \frac{\sum P_j D^{P_j}}{\sum P_j}; \quad C^P = \frac{\sum P_j C^{P_j}}{\sum P_j}$$

These identities have numerous applications. For example, one can calculate measures for surplus given values for assets and liabilities; embedded option characteristics can be determined from those of a security with options and its "optionless" counterpart; portfolio effects of a given trade can be predicted, and, desired effects at the portfolio level can readily be translated to the trade required; etc.

Yield to Maturity Approach

The simplest and most natural one factor model is based on the yield to maturity (YTM) of a security. This value, of course, equals the unique interest rate i, so that the present value of the cash flows equals the price, $P(i)$. That is: $P(i)=\Sigma c_t v^{mt}$, where c_t equals the time t cash flow (t is usually denominated in yearly time increments, by convention), and $v=(1+i)^{-1}$ for annual YTMs, $v=(1+0.5i)^{-1}$ for semi-annual YTMs, and $v=(1+i/m)^{-1}$ in general. Equation (3) now produces the familiar:

$$D = \frac{\sum tc_t v^{mt+1}}{P}; \quad C = \frac{\sum t(t+1/m)c_t v^{mt+2}}{P} \tag{5}$$

The Macaulay duration of a security, D^M, equals: D/v. While not actually derived within a calculus context, nor as a result of a pursuit of a measure of price sensitivity, it was soon realized that D^M provided such a measure as long as it was first multiplied by v. Macaulay duration remains popular despite this numerical shortcoming because it has the intuitive interpretation as a weighted-average-time-to-receipt of the cash flows: $D^M=\Sigma tw_t$, where $w_t=c_t v^{mt}/P$. Consequently, for a zero-coupon bond, D^M equals the maturity. Interpreting the weights as probabilities, since they sum to one (though need not be all positive), D^M equals the average or "expected" value of t, $E[t]$. Extending the analogy, if we define the Macaulay convexity, C^M, as C/v^2, this measure equals $E[t^2]+E[t]/m$, which can in turn be expressed in terms of the variance of t, and hence has the intuitive appeal as a measure of cash flow dispersion.

Unfortunately, besides the minor inconvenience of having to scale the Macaulay measures to use for an approximation formula given by equation (2), these measures have limited use in securities with embedded options where the basic formulas make little sense. In addition, when the durations of such securities are calculated in terms of equations (3) and (4), and converted into the Macaulay counterpart, the value often defies interpretation in terms of measures of t and implied cash flows. For example, interest-only strips (IOs) have negative durations, and principal-only strips (POs) have duration values far in excess of the time to receipt of the last cash flow. Nonetheless, Macaulay advocates persist and often refer to D and C in equation (3) as "modified" duration and convexity to avoid confusion.

Beyond the Macaulay shortcomings, the YTM one factor formulation itself suffers a fatal flaw. That is, YTMs of fixed cash-flow securities cannot satisfy *any* one factor relationship, except under the most restrictive model for the shape and movement of the term structure of interest rates (i.e., the "yield curve"). This restrictive model is that the yield curve is flat, and can only move in parallel.

For example,[4] the assumption that all YTMs move by equal amounts readily implies this conclusion. However, this result leaves open the possibility that YTMs may satisfy a more complicated one factor relationship. That is, perhaps there is a function, $Y(i,y)$, where $Y(0,y)=y$, or today's YTMs, so that as the factor i changes, each y-value changes according to $Y(i,y)$. For the above classical result, it was assumed that $Y(i,y)=y+i$. As it turns out, even the general one factor model requires the yield curve to be flat and move only in parallel.

Even more generally, it can be shown that the above conclusion also extends to general multi-factor models. That is, if $Y(\mathbf{i},y)$ is a given model with $Y(\mathbf{0},y)=y$, and $\mathbf{i}$ denotes the factor vector, it turns out that the YTM shift model, $y \rightarrow Y(\mathbf{i},y)$, can never be consistent if the yield curve is not flat. The proof of this result is technical and tedious, and beyond the scope of this chapter.

Consequently, even though YTMs are a natural factor framework for single security analysis, they provide a hopeless dead end for portfolio analysis and management. This is because to perform portfolio analysis, one must be able to calculate the one factor sensitivity of the total portfolio from the sensitivities of the individual securities. To do that, one needs in essence a model which specifies how the individual YTMs move as a collective. But as was noted, no such model can in general exist.

Other Single Factor Models

The problem with YTM is that it summarizes too much information; many cash flow structures can have the same YTM. Therefore, based on virtually any example of how the underlying term structure moves, these initially equal YTMs will move to different values. In fact, this observation underlies the proofs of the results noted above. But within this observation of the problem with YTMs lies an alternative potential solution to the single factor problem: simply model the movement of the term structure of interest rates directly as a one factor model.

---

[4] See Jonathan E. Ingersoll, Jr., Jeffrey Skelton, and Roman L. Weil, "Duration Forty Years Later," *Journal of Financial and Quantitative Analysis* (November 1978), pp. 627-650.

The price and price sensitivity of all assets can then be related to today's yield curve and the single factor proposed for its movement.

Of course, there are any number of ways of doing this. First off, one must choose the initial term structure. The most common models are the "par bond" curve, and "spot rate" models, typically denominated in semi-annual equivalent units, although a forward rate model is equally serviceable. The obvious starting points for these models are the "on-the-run" Treasury bond and Treasury strip (i.e., zero coupon bond) curves. Typically, various levels of "quality spreads" are added to these "risk-free" rates to allow the market pricing of securities with default risk.

The next step is to define the manner in which these underlying term structures move, assuming a single factor format. Many models have evolved,[5] among them:

Parallel (Additive) Shift:	$i_t \rightarrow i_t + i$
Multiplicative Shift:	$i_t \rightarrow i_t (1+i)$
Lognormal Shift:	$i_t \rightarrow i_t e^i$
Log-Additive Shift:	$i_t \rightarrow i_t + i \ln(1+\alpha t)/\alpha t$
Directional Shift:	$i_t \rightarrow i_t + n_t i$

where in each of the above specifications, i_t denotes the initial (pre-shift) value of the term structure utilized at maturity t, i denotes the single factor, α is a parameter, and n_t a maturity-specific shift parameter. The first such model introduced was the additive shift by Fisher and Weil, then multiplicative by Bierwag and Kaufman, log-additive by Khang, who also devised a log-multiplicative model, and directional by Reitano.[6] Of course, many other specifications have been studied as well.

While not initially obvious, the directional shift model is the most general specification possible for the purpose of defining a duration measure. To see this, consider the specification: $Y(i, i_t)$, where $Y(0, i_t) = i_t$. It is easy to check using equation (3) that this specification gives the same duration value as the directional model with $n_t = \partial_1 Y(0, i_t)$, where ∂_i denotes differentiation with respect to i.

Using any single factor specification, it is not difficult to prove the following identity [compare to equation (2)]:

$$P(j) = P(i) \exp\left[-\int_i^j D(s)ds\right] \qquad (6)$$

In contrast to equation (2), this identity states that the price on factor value j is completely determined by the price on factor value i and the duration values at all

---

[5] In addition to the references in footnotes 2 and 3, see G. O. Bierwag, *Duration Analysis* (Cambridge, MA: Ballinger Publishing, 1987), and the references therein.

[6] Lawrence Fisher and Roman L. Weil, "Coping with the Risk of Interest Rate Fluctuations: Returns to Bondholders from Naive and Optimal Strategies," *Journal of Business* (October 1971), pp. 408-31; G.O. Bierwag and George Kaufman, "Coping with the Risk of Interest Rate Fluctuations: A Note," *Journal of Business* (July 1977); Chulson Khang, "Bond Immunization when Short-Term Interest Rates Fluctuate More Than Long-Term Rates," University of Oregon Working Paper (1977); Reitano, "Multivariate Duration Analysis."

factor values between i and j. On the surface, it indicates that all higher order derivatives of the price function are irrelevant, and to control price, one only needs to control duration. While this observation is formally valid, it does not carry with it the practical significance one might expect for yield curve management. In short, one cannot manage duration with the precision required by equation (6) without also managing convexity.

While this will also be discussed below in the context of time dynamics, it is easy to understand this point in the current context. To determine the "manageability" of duration, we need to understand the sensitivity of duration to changes in the factor. Applying equation (1) to the function $D(i)$, we get:

$$D(j) \approx D(i) + [D^2(i) - C(i)](j - i) \tag{7}$$

Consequently, even for the smallest of factor shifts, $j-i$, the change in duration will reflect the magnitude of convexity relative to duration squared.

When convexity is relatively large, duration will decrease with increases in the factor; for example, noncallable bonds and insurance and annuity contracts with long embedded put options have this property. When convexity is relatively small or negative, duration will increase with increases in the factor; for example, callable bonds, mortgage-backed securities, and collateralized mortgage obligations have this property. Finally, when convexity equals duration squared, such as is nearly true for zero coupon bonds, duration is relatively insensitive to factor changes.

Equation (6) also provides a new approximation basis for price sensitivity, which in many situations is superior to the approximation basis derived above in equation (2) for a given "order" in terms of $j-i$. For example, the first order approximation:

$$P(j) \approx P(i) \exp[-D(i)(j - i)] \tag{8}$$

is often superior to the first order approximation implied by equation (2). In addition, these two approximations can often be used together to provide upper and lower bounds for the exact value of $P(j)$.

Beyond the formal mathematics underlying equations (6) and (8), a relatively simple and intuitive explanation can be given. Imagine dividing the factor shift interval, $[i,j]$, into a large number of subintervals, $[t_j,t_{j+1}]$, and on each, approximating the relative change, $P(t_{j+1})/P(t_j)$, by $1-D(t_j)\Delta t$ reflecting equation (2). Of course, the total relative change, $P(j)/P(i)$, is just the product of the subinterval changes. As can be shown, if all the intermediate duration values used are exact, equation (6) is produced in the limit, whereas setting all to $D(i)$ produces equation (8). Approximating the intermediate durations based on equation (7) provides the second order exponential approximation.

Single Factor Yield Curve Management

The opportunistic, i.e., tactical, implications of any one factor model are quite obvious. Given an expectation for the "sign" of the factor change, i.e., positive or negative, one simply trades to the maximum feasible value of duration of the opposite sign. For example, a negative shift expectation motivates a maximum positive duration, as is easily seen from any of the above approximations. Convexity can be ignored for this purpose since in any one factor model, $j-i$ will quite small so the duration effects on price will overwhelm the convexity effects; that is, $j-i$ will be very large compared to $(j-i)^2$. Of course, this aggressive strategy carries the risk that if the realized factor shift has the opposite sign, large losses are possible.

When less certain of the sign of the factor shift, tactical management becomes more subtle. For example, given a likely range for the shift, say: -0.01 to 0.02, a probability distribution, say rectangular, and a personal utility function for wealth, $u(w)$, one would seek a duration value which maximized one's expected utility, $E[u(P(j))]$, which is approximated by: $P(i)E[u(1-D(i)(j-i))]$. Equating the first derivative with respect to D to zero, one must solve: $E[(j-i)u'(1-D(j-i))]=0$, for $D=D(i)$. If the solution exists, it is easy to see that this must be an expected utility maximizing duration value when the manager is risk averse (i.e., $u''(w)<0$). This analysis could be further refined by considering the duration-income relationship over the period modeled.

In defensive yield curve management, one seeks to find conditions which will minimize factor exposure of the managed portfolio relative to a target portfolio. As noted above, asset/liability and market-neutral portfolio management are examples of this, but so is active management of a fixed-income portfolio to match a benchmark index. In each such case, one can create an "objective" portfolio equal to a long portfolio of assets and a short position in the target portfolio. In market-neutral strategies, this objective portfolio is actively managed on both the long and short (i.e., futures, for example) positions, where in general active management only occurs in the long position.

For example, in ALM the objective portfolio is surplus, $S(i)$, and the objective price function is given by: $S(i)=A(i)-L(i)$. Using equation (2), although this result can be derived more formally, it seems apparent that to minimize surplus sensitivity to factor changes, one must have $D^S(i)=0$, since otherwise one will have first order exposure to "unfavorable" shifts. Furthermore, once this is done, one can in theory make surplus favorably exposed to all factor shifts by making $C^S(i)>0$. Using equation (3) to convert these conditions to conditions on assets and liabilities, we get:

$$D^A = \frac{L}{A}D^L; \quad C^A > \frac{L}{A}C^L \tag{9}$$

While one must assume that $S(i)\neq0$ to derive these "immunization" conditions, they remain valid if $S=0$.

The conditions in equation (9) can be interpreted in two ways. First, consistent with equation (2), the equivalent conditions $D^S=0$ and $C^S>0$, create a surplus function which has the graph of an upright parabola with equation:

$$S(j) \approx S(i)[1 + C^S(j-i)^2] \tag{10}$$

where this statement is approximately correct with error magnitude: $(j-i)^3$, which is usually quite small.

Secondly, using equation (7), these conditions assure that the duration of surplus will always have the "right" sign. That is, with error magnitude $(j-i)^2$:

$$D^S(j) \approx -C^S(i)(j-i) \tag{11}$$

so duration will become positive for negative factor shifts, and conversely. That this is a favorable factor sensitivity for surplus duration stems from the identity in equation (6), since this in turn assures that the exponent of "exp" will be positive, and surplus will always grow.

One of the troubling implications of equation (10) is that perhaps immunization works too well; we have now created a portfolio which is instantaneously riskless, and with real opportunities for a profit due to a change in the factor value. This is, in theory, the holy grail of finance, but in practice, it is usually an indication that a mistake has been made. But has one? Does equation (10) really imply a risk-free arbitrage? On close examination, the answer is an unambiguous not necessarily.

First, the real world is not constrained by our single factor representation of it. If the term structure shifts in a way that is outside that anticipated by the model used, this immunization equation is no longer valid. Second, even if the real world were constrained by our model, what does "instantaneously" immunized really mean? If it means we are immunized against instantaneous factor shifts, what is that? Does anything really happen "instantaneously," without the passage of any time? Of course not! Even within the realm of our single factor world, every shift in the factor corresponds to some shift in time, which the above analysis ignores. This time dynamic will be addressed below, but for now, suffice it to note that equation (10) does not imply the possibility of untold riches.

The above development centered on the objective of immunizing today's surplus value, but can readily be applied to market-neutral portfolios, with $L(i)$ denoting the short portfolio, and to actively managed indexed portfolios, with $L(i)$ denoting the benchmark index. In the surplus context, one may also be interested in immunizing other objective functions, such as the surplus ratio: $S(i)/A(i)$, or the time T forward value of surplus: $S(i)/Z_T(i)$, where $Z_T(i)$ denotes the price of a T-period zero-coupon bond.[7] In these cases, analogous conditions to those in equation (9) can be developed (see equation (34) in the multi-factor development below).

Single (and Multi-)Factor Yield Curve Management Failure

Unfortunately, single and multi-factor yield curve management can fail, and at times fail seriously. Fortunately, these failures are always explainable; indeed, they are predictable. Specifically, it is always the case that such failures are traceable to the failure of one or more of the assumptions required in the development

---

[7] See Robert R. Reitano, "Multivariate Immunization Theory," *Transactions of the Society of Actuaries* XLIII(1991), pp. 392-438 for more details on these objective functions.

of the management strategy. While we illustrate this in the context of single factor models, the validity of these comments in the more general case will be obvious.

As a simple example, it is implicit in the above development that prices, and the associated durations and convexities, are calculated accurately, properly, and consistently. The need for accuracy is self evident. As an example of an improper calculation, consider the pricing of a callable bond or MBS as the present value of noncallable or best-guess callable cash flows at a given spread to Treasuries. Such a spread can always be found, of course, so that today's price is accurately reproduced. However, such a valuation scheme will provide erroneous durations because it ignores the sensitivity of cash flows to changes in the factor. More subtly, even for option-adjusted valuations, it is important that the prepayment model utilized be calibrated as closely as feasible to that underlying traded prices.

Inconsistent calculations occur primarily due to inconsistencies in the manner in which the term structure and shift factor are specified. For example, a yield curve can be specified in par bond, spot, or forward rates; in continuous, semi-annual, monthly, etc., nominal units; and as a credit quality specific curve, Treasuries plus credit spreads, or Treasuries plus option-adjusted spreads. Besides consistency between all valuation yield curves, it is equally important that the shift factor be consistently modeled in terms of both the parameters above, and the manner in which the factor is applied. For example, any multiplicative factor model will provide one set of price sensitivities if applied to the Treasury curve underlying the credit-adjusted valuation curves, and a different set if applied directly to the credit-adjusted curves.

Consistency problems also occur when using stochastic yield curve generators for price valuations. In theory, the exact price is produced only when an infeasible number of "yield curve paths" is generated, where each path is usually generated by first generating a binomial "bit string" of 0s and 1s. To utilize such systems, one typically samples several hundred to several thousand such bit strings, and uses the resulting price as an approximation to the theoretically correct result. The consistency problem occurs in the application of equation (3) which requires three such price estimates. If three sets of bit strings are generated, the resulting D and C values will reflect both price sensitivities and the errors in the estimated prices. To avoid this inconsistency, it is better to generate only one set, and use it for all three valuations.

The major challenge today in achieving correct calculations from practitioner-developed pricing systems stems from the complexity of the finance theory, computer programs, and data manipulations required. For vendor-developed software, assuming correct calculations, the primary challenge is producing valuations which are consistent with the results of practitioner-developed and other vendor supplied systems. In general, when working with more than one system it is better to calculate all price sensitivities directly using equation (4) than use vendor supplied sensitivities, since one can then control consistency through the term structure specifications.

Beyond inaccurate, improper and inconsistent valuations, failure of a yield curve management strategy can also be due to unanticipated higher order effects, model risk, and most importantly, what has been called factor risk or stochastic process risk.

A *higher order effect* means the effect of the first term of the Taylor series in equation (1) that is ignored. For example, it is not uncommon to only partially implement the immunization conditions of equation (9) by balancing durations, but ignoring convexities. This strategy is typically justified by the commitment to rebalance duration frequently, and the belief that this will imply that rebalancing will occur only after small shifts, for which the convexity implications are minor. Unfortunately, the yield curve can occasionally move quickly and significantly, and generate substantial losses.

As a simple example, consider duration balancing mortgage-backed securities and single premium deferred annuities using equation (9). The convexities of these portfolios violate the immunizing condition since as is obvious, MBSs lengthen when rates rises due to the short call option, and SPDAs shorten due to the long put (i.e., surrender) option. Consequently, the duration of surplus moves in exactly the wrong direction — positive for rate increases and conversely. For small shifts, this "tracking" error may seem minor, but large losses have been realized in periods of large shifts.

Model risk means using the wrong pricing model. The simplest example is the improper valuation of a callable bond discussed above. More common examples include using a different option pricing model (i.e., different yield curve dynamics) or most seriously, a different option election behavior function than those used underlying traded prices. The behavior function risk is by far the most serious since it is standard practice to assume, say, that the mortgagors underlying MBSs are relatively inefficient in the election of their call (i.e., refinancing) options. Unfortunately, these assumptions are regularly updated as experience emerges, with major updates not uncommon. In essence, immunization fails because the sensitivity of the prepayment model to a change in factor values was not modeled for the calculated D and C values from equation (3).

Finally, and perhaps most obvious, is *stochastic process risk*. This is the risk that the yield curve shift experienced is inconsistent with the factor assumed.[8] For example, one may immunize against parallel shifts, but experience a steepening shift.

While using a multi-factor model mitigates stochastic process risk more or less, depending on the number and quality of the factors used, the other causes

---

[8] For theoretical estimates and illustrations of this risk, see Robert R. Reitano, "Nonparallel Yield Curve Shifts and Durational Leverage," *Journal of Portfolio Management* (Summer 1990), pp. 62-7; Robert R. Reitano, "Nonparallel Yield Curve Shifts and Spread Leverage," *Journal of Portfolio Management* (Spring 1991), pp. 82-7; Robert R. Reitano, "Nonparallel Yield Curve Shifts and Convexity," *Transactions of the Society of Actuaries*, XLIV (1992), pp. 479-507; Robert R. Reitano, "Nonparallel Yield Curve Shifts and Immunization," *Journal of Portfolio Management* (Spring 1992), pp. 36-43. See also: G.O. Bierwag, G.C. Kaufman, and A. Toevs, "Bond Portfolio Immunization and Stochastic Process Risk," *Journal of Bank Research* (Winter 1983) for the first formal analysis of this risk.

of management failure discussed above apply equally well in these more general models, and will not be repeated below.

Single Factor Yield Curve Management:
The Time Dynamic

The above discussion ignored the fact that a price function modeled as $P(i)$ can only represent the price sensitivities of a portfolio to an immediate shift in interest rates; that is, to a shift which occurs before the passage of time has a material effect on the portfolio and its price sensitivities. Such shifts are also called *instantaneous shifts*. In reality, price would be better modeled as an explicit function of time, as would the factor value, that is, $P=P(t,i(t))$.

To this end, we use the methods of Ito stochastic calculus.[9] To begin with, we need a model for the evolution of the factor $i(t)$ in time, where this factor will also be denoted i_t. A tremendously important and general model is that of an Ito process, whereby the "instantaneous" change in i_t, denoted di_t, satisfies:

$$di_t = \mu(t, i_t)dt + \sigma(t, i_t)dz_t \tag{12}$$

where z_t denotes Brownian motion. This "differential" expression is shorthand for the notion that i_T, or the value of the factor at time T, is a random variable that is a stochastic integral, and that i_T is given by:

$$i_T = i_0 + \int_0^T \mu(t, i_t)dt + \int_0^T \sigma(t, i_t)dz_t \tag{13}$$

One of the critical contributions of Ito was introducing the manner in which the integrals in equation (13) could be interpreted, and determining properties of the functions μ and σ that were sufficient to make these integrals, and functions of these integrals, well defined in that context.

For our purpose, it is sufficient to think of equation (12) as describing how i_t changes in a very short time increment. Specifically, this equation can be interpreted as stating that $i_{t+\Delta_t} - i_t$, or Δi_t for short, is approximately normally distributed with mean (i.e., expectation) and variance given by:

$$E(\Delta i_t) \approx \mu(t, i_t)\Delta t; \ \text{Var}(\Delta i_t) \approx \sigma(t, i_t)^2 \Delta t \tag{14}$$

where the approximations are good to the order of $(\Delta t)^2$. Because of equation (14), $\mu(t,i_t)$ is generally referred to as the "drift" coefficient, and $\sigma(t,i_t)$ as the "diffusion coefficient."

Returning to the subject of primary interest, if the factor i_t is assumed to follow the Ito process defined in equation (12), what can be said about a function of that process; or more specifically, what can be said about $P(t,i_t)$?

---

[9] See John C. Hull, *Options, Futures and Other Derivative Securities* (Englewood Cliffs, New Jersey: Prentice Hall, 1993), second edition.

Another critically important contribution of Ito, which has come to be known as Ito's Lemma, answers this question. It states that if P is a fairly smooth function (i.e., twice differentiable with continuous second derivatives), then P_t $\equiv P(t, i_t)$ is also a stochastic integral with drift and diffusion coefficients definable in terms of the coefficients in equation (12) and the derivatives of P. Applying this result and dividing the Ito expression for dP_t by P_t produces:

$$\frac{dP_t}{P_t} = \left(\frac{\partial_t P_t}{P_t} - D_t \mu_t + \frac{1}{2} C_t \sigma_t^2\right) dt - D_t \sigma_t dz_t \tag{15}$$

where D_t, C_t, μ_t, and σ_t denote $D(t, i_t)$, etc., and ∂_t denotes differentiation with respect to t.

While initially imposing, equation (15) has a relatively simply interpretation in terms of single factor yield curve management. Before discussing this, let's first look at what equation (15) reduces to for the simply example of a T-period zero-coupon bond, and where i_t denotes the $(T-t)$-period spot rate at time t. For this example, $P(t, i_t) \equiv \exp[-(T-t)i_t]$, and a calculation produces:

$$\frac{dP_t}{P_t} = \left(i_t - (T-t)\mu_t + \frac{1}{2}(T-t)^2 \sigma_t^2\right) dt - (T-t)\sigma_t dz_t \tag{16}$$

These equations state that the relative price change (i.e., dP_t / P_t) has three components of drift at time t. The first component reflects the relative time-derivative, also known as the security's earnings rate, which for time zero is just the $(T-t)$-period spot rate at that time. The second drift component is the "expected" factor gain or loss reflecting the security's duration at that time and the expected change in the factor, and is reminiscent of equation (2). The third component is perhaps unexpected based on the earlier analysis which ignored time drift, and represents the "expected" factor gain or loss reflecting half the security's convexity and the variance of the factor. The surprise is that in these equations, convexity is first order in time as is duration, in contrast to the implication of equation (2), where convexity was a second-order adjustment in factor units. That such a convexity adjustment is appropriate can be inferred by treating j in equation (2) as a random variable and taking expectations. The convexity term then is multiplied by $\sigma^2 + \mu^2$ instead of just σ^2 as in equation (15), but this is a start. Just what happens to the μ^2 term, not to mention all the other terms of the Taylor series, must remain a mystery for now, with a resolution contained in the theory of stochastic calculus.

The diffusion coefficient in equations (15) and (16) is no surprise. Specifically, these terms state, due to the interpretation in equation (14), that the standard deviation of a portfolio equals the standard deviation of the factor times the duration of the portfolio. That is, duration acts like a lever when $|D| > 1$, and like a buffer when $|D| < 1$, in translating factor volatility into portfolio volatility. Of course, $|D|$ denotes the absolute value of D.

While providing an elegant and complete framework for representing the time dynamic of a portfolio, equation (15) does not generally alter the conclusions developed earlier using the naive, time-static model. For example, applying this equation to the surplus function $S_t = S(t, i_t)$, it becomes clear that the conditions of equation (9), that $D^S = 0$ and $C^S > 0$, are again necessary. These immunization conditions then force dS_t / S_t to have only the earnings rate and convexity drift terms, and *no* stochastic term; but only for an instant! At any time $t + \Delta t$, the D^S and C^S values change (see below) and immunization is certainly lost because the stochastic term in equation (15) depends on D^S. That is, having $D^S = 0$ and $C^S > 0$ initially does not protect surplus even a moment later as in the static model, where these conditions assured that D^S would move in the right direction relative to the factor move. Here, as soon as D^S strays away from 0, immunization is lost due to the diffusion term in equation (15).

So how can we be sure that duration will immediately drift away from zero? The answer can be found in a second application of Ito's Lemma, this time to $D_t \equiv D(t, i_t)$, the duration of surplus, to get:

$$dD_t = (\partial_t D_t + (D_t^2 - C_t)\mu_t + 0.5[D_t(D_t^2 - C_t) - \partial_i C_t]\sigma_t^2)dt$$

$$+ (D_t^2 - C_t)\sigma_t dz_t \qquad (17)$$

While the drift term in equation (17) is complicated, it need not concern us for the question at hand. Looking to the diffusion coefficient, at time zero this term is equal to $-C_0\sigma_0$, which is strictly negative by the immunization condition and the assumption that the factor is not deterministic (i.e., $\sigma_t > 0$). Consequently, even though initially zero, the duration of surplus will immediately change in an unpredictable way due to the non-zero diffusion coefficient, and hence, the immunization property will be immediately lost.

While the above derivation and conclusion was based on the simple model in equation (12), with only one Brownian motion term, dz_t, it holds equally well if it is assumed that the single factor, i_t, depends on several such terms, $dz_t^{(k)}$, $k = 1, 2, ..., n$. Moreover, with still more effort and advanced Ito calculus, this conclusion holds for the general vector valued Ito process, $d\mathbf{i}_t$, where $\mathbf{i}_t$ denotes the vector of factors in the multi-factor model discussed below, and each depends on the collection of Brownian motions above; i.e., on the vector valued Brownian motion, $d\mathbf{z}_t$.

Of course, this does not imply that immunization is not effective in managing yield curve risk. It simply implies that immunization does not create the risk-free arbitrage implied by equation (10), above, or in the multi-factor counterpart in equation (32) below.

Is There a "Best" Single Factor Model?

Before exiting the realm of single factor models, it makes sense to at least consider the question: Is there a best factor to use when you are using only one factor? Before answering this, it makes sense to first contemplate in what way do we mean "best." Of course, the best single factor model is the one which exactly predicts the "nature" of the yield curve shift which occurs over the period of interest. For example, during a period of parallel shifts, one can hardly do better than the

Fisher-Weil model. Unfortunely, since such predictions seem to be impossible to make with confidence, we abandon this notion of "best."

At the other extreme, what if we not only did not possess perfect foresight, but we had no knowledge at all? That is, what if it were the case that any yield curve shift that was possible was equally likely and that historical data were of no value in determining shifts to come. In a sense, yield curve shifts were just a random walk limited only to the extent that shifts which allowed riskless arbitrage were "banned." In such a world, it is hard to imagine by what paradigm we could evaluate whether a given single factor model was best.

Consequently, we pose the question and propose an answer within the framework of an informational "middle-ground," as it were, whereby we assume that we have good information on the "necessary" structure of yield curve moves, but that past experience suggests that there are random components in these moves which preclude perfect predictions. That is, using a sample of historical shifts and the assumption that future shifts will be selected from the same statistical "urn," we pose the question: Is there a single shift, which when used to underlie a single factor model, will provide the best predictor of yield curves to come? This model of shifts is also called a "stationary" model, in the sense that all of the statistics of the series are assumed to be fixed in time.

We now investigate an answer to this question under the additional assumption that sequential shifts have no autocorrelation structure and can be assumed to be independent. The approach to be taken is known as the *method of principal components*.[10] To begin, assume that we are given a collection of historical yield curve shifts: $\{Y_j\}$, where each shift is a vector: $Y=(y_1, y_2, ..., y_m)$, of changes at selected points on the term structure. Our goal is to find a vector, P, so that its multiples approximate the original shifts as closely as possible. We use multiples of P because in the context of a single factor model, P represents the "shape" of the term structure shift, while the multiples equal values of the factor modeled.

One method for simultaneously approximating all shifts is the method of principal components, which seeks to minimize the sum of the squared-lengths of the residual terms: $\sum |Y_j - a_j P|^2$, where the multiples, a_j, are chosen optimally, and $|P|^2$ denotes the length of P squared, $|P|^2=\sum p_j^2$. It is sometimes convenient to express this value in the notation of the dot or inner product of vectors $|P|^2=P\cdot P$, where in general this product is defined as $X\cdot Y=\sum x_j y_j$, and will also be denoted: (X,Y). In order to simplify the interpretation of results later, it is standard practice to first normalize the yield curve shifts to have a mean of zero. That is, we seek to approximate $\{Y_j'\}=\{Y_j - E[Y_j]\}$ with multiples of P, where $E[Y_j]$ denotes the mean or average shift vector.

---

[10] For the traditional derivation of this approach, see Henri Theil, *Principles of Economics* (New York: John Wiley & Sons, 1971), and, Samuel S. Wilks, *Mathematical Statistics* (New York: John Wiley & Sons, 1962). For an application of this method in the multi-factor context to yield curve management, see Robert Litterman and Jose Scheinkman, "Common Factors Affecting Bond Returns," *The Journal of Fixed Income* (June 1991), pp. 54-61.

As it turns out, given any value of P it is straightforward to de.ermine the optimal values for the multiples of P; specifically, $a_j = (P, Y_j')/ |P|^2$, which geometrically represents the "projection" of Y_j' onto P. This can be readily derived by defining $f(a) = \sum |Y_j - E[Y_j] - a_j P|^2$, with $a = (a_1, \ldots, a_n)$, and setting the partial derivatives equal to zero. This derivation is simplified by rewriting the terms in the summation as inner products $|X|^2 = (X, X)$, and rewriting each term as $|Y_j'|^2 - 2a_j(Y_j', P) + a_j^2 |P|^2$. That this value of a identifies a minimum of $f(a)$ follows from the positive definiteness of the (diagonal) matrix of second derivatives. Below, we assume that P is a unit vector, i.e., $|P| = 1$, to simplify this expression for a_j.

The problem of identifying the "best" single factor model now becomes:

$$\text{Minimize: } \sum |Y_j' - (Y_j', P) P|^2 \qquad (18)$$

over all unit vectors, P. Unfortunately, methods of calculus quickly produce a mess here because unlike the search for the a_j, setting these partial derivatives to zero produces difficult nonlinear equations. We need a trick!

Rewriting the terms in the summation in equation (18) as inner products, and rearranging, we get:

$$\text{Minimize: } \sum |Y_j'|^2 - \sum (Y_j', P)^2 \qquad (19)$$

which is equivalent to maximizing the second summation since the first is independent of P. This second summation can be rewritten as a matrix product $P^T V P$, where V is $n-1$ times the variance/covariance matrix of the sample $\{Y_j\}$, justifying the normalization of the sample above; P^T is the row vector transpose of the column vector P; and n is the sample size. Since this matrix has the special property of positive semi-definiteness (which is in fact usually the stronger condition of positive definiteness in practice), finding the maximum of this "quadratic form" is easy. Specifically, it is well-known[11] that this expression is maximized when $P = E_1$, the unit "eigenvector" or "characteristic vector" of V associated with the largest (eigen)characteristic value, e_1.

As an aside, let's recall some linear algebra. First, an eigenvector of a matrix, V, is a vector, E, so that $VE = eV$ for some constant, e. That is, multiplying by the matrix just "stretches" the vector if $e > 1$, "compresses" the vector if $0 < e < 1$, and zeros it out if $e = 0$. If e is negative, matrix multiplication first "flips" the vector $180°$, then stretches or compresses. In general, e can also be a complex number. Because V is a symmetric matrix, $V = V^T$, it is well known that all eigenvalues are real, and that there exists a complete set of orthogonal (i.e., $(E_i, E_j) = 0$ for $i \neq j$) eigenvectors. Because V is also positive semi-definite, i.e., $E^T V E \geq 0$, for all E, the eigenvalues satisfy: $e_j \geq 0$. Finally, for the typical case of V positive definite, i.e., $E^T V E = 0$ only when $E = 0$, the eigenvalues are strictly positive.

---

[11] See any linear algebra textbook that discusses quadratic forms: for example, Gilbert Strang, *Linear Algebra and Its Applications* (New York: Academic Press, 1976).

Now that we have **P**, just how good is it? Returning to equation (19), the "total variation" of the original sample $\sum |Y_j'|^2$ equals $\sum e_j$, where $e_2, \ldots, e_m$, denote the remaining characteristic values of **V** in descending order (all are non-negative because **V** is positive semi-definite). This assertion follows from the observation that both equal the "trace," or sum of the main diagonal components, of **V**. In addition, the second term in equation (19) is easily seen to equal e_1, since it can be rewritten as $E_1^T V E_1 = e_1 |E_1|^2$, and E_1 has unit length. Consequently, the total variation of the sample *net* of the first principal component is $\sum e_j - e_1$, for a relative reduction of $e_1 / \sum e_j$, which is often 60-80%.

As for the "shape" of E_1, what can be said? As noted by an associate,[12] since **V** is a "positive" matrix, i.e., all components are positive, it must be the case by the Perron-Frobenius Theorem that all of the components of E_1 are also positive. Of course, that does not imply that this is a parallel shift, but only that it is a yield curve shift for which all points move in the same direction. In practice,[13] however, the first principal component looks somewhat linear, but decreases from the short to long maturities; that is, short rates have a tendency to move more than long rates.

MULTI-FACTOR YIELD CURVE MODELS

Mathematical Framework

As expected, it is relatively straightforward to generalize the mathematics underlying single factor model risk analysis to its multi-factor counterpart since once again, only calculus is required. Given a collection of factors, $i_1, i_2, \ldots, i_m$, assumed to capture the statistical drivers of yield curve movements, and which will often be denoted as a vector, $\mathbf{i} = (i_1, i_2, \ldots, i_m)$, it is natural to model the price of a security or portfolio as a function of these factors $P(\mathbf{i})$. Generalizing the single factor case, there is a multivariate version of the Taylor series expansion which gives the value of the price function on $\mathbf{j}$, $P(\mathbf{j})$, in terms of the value of the price function and its various derivatives on $\mathbf{i}$. Specifically:

$$P(\mathbf{j}) = P(\mathbf{i}) + \sum \partial_k P(\mathbf{i})(j_k - i_k) + 0.5 \sum\sum \partial_{kl} P(\mathbf{i})(j_k - i_k)(j_l - i_l) + \ldots\ldots \quad (20)$$

where ∂_k and ∂_{kl} denote first and second order partial derivatives.

Restating equation (20) analogously to equation (2), one identifies natural generalizations of the notions of duration and convexity in this multi-factor framework:[14]

---

[12] Benjamin Wurzburger, personal communication. See Marvin Marcus and Henryk Minc, *A Survey of Matrix Theory and Matrix Inequalities* (New York: Dover Publications, 1992), for properties of positive matrices.

[13] See Litterman and Scheinkman, "Common Factors Affecting Bond Returns."

[14] See Reitano "Multivariate Duration Analysis" for a more complete treatment of risk analysis based on multi-factor (i.e., multivariate) models.

$$P(\mathbf{j}) \approx P(\mathbf{i})[1 - \sum D_k(\mathbf{i}) \, (j_k - i_k) + 0.5 \sum\sum C_{kl}(\mathbf{i}) \, (j_k - i_k)(j_l - i_l)] \qquad (21)$$
$$= P(\mathbf{i})[1 - \mathbf{D}(\mathbf{i}) \cdot \Delta\mathbf{i} + 0.5\Delta\mathbf{i}^T \mathbf{C}(\mathbf{i})\Delta\mathbf{i}]$$

where $\Delta\mathbf{i} = \mathbf{j} - \mathbf{i}$. In equation (21), the first approximation is in terms of "partial" durations, $D_k(\mathbf{i})$, and "partial" convexities, $C_{kl}(\mathbf{i})$, while the second uses the more compact vector and matrix notation of the "total duration vector," $\mathbf{D}(\mathbf{i}) \equiv (D_1(\mathbf{i}),....,$ $D_m(\mathbf{i}))$, and "total convexity matrix," $\mathbf{C}(\mathbf{i}) \equiv (C_{kl}(\mathbf{i}))$, where:

$$D_k(\mathbf{i}) = -\partial_k P(\mathbf{i}) \, / \, P(\mathbf{i}), \qquad C_{kl}(\mathbf{i}) = \partial_{kl} P(\mathbf{i}) \, / \, P(\mathbf{i}) \qquad (22)$$

$\mathbf{C}$ is a "symmetric" matrix, i.e., $C_{kl} = C_{lk}$, reflecting a well-known analogous property of second-order partial derivatives.

Just as for the single factor model and equation (4), equation (22) has as a consequence that all of the above duration and convexity measures enjoy the portfolio property, in that the corresponding measure for a portfolio equals the price-, or market-value-weighted average of the component security measures.

Analogous to equation (4), it is also the case that partial durations and convexities can be approximated by finite difference methods. For example:

$$\partial_k P(\mathbf{i}) \approx [P(\mathbf{i} + \Delta i \mathbf{E}_k) - P(\mathbf{i} - \Delta i \mathbf{E}_k)] \, / \, [2\Delta i] \qquad (23)$$

$$\partial_{kl} P(\mathbf{i}) \approx [P(\mathbf{i} + \Delta i(\mathbf{E}_j + \mathbf{E}_k)) - P(\mathbf{i} + \Delta i(\mathbf{E}_l - \mathbf{E}_k)) - P(\mathbf{i} + \Delta i(\mathbf{E}_k - \mathbf{E}_l))$$
$$+ P(\mathbf{i} - \Delta i(\mathbf{E}_k + \mathbf{E}_l))] \, / \, [2\Delta i]^2 \qquad (23b)$$

where $\mathbf{E}_k$ is a vector with all 0's except for the kth component, which is a 1. Although these equations at first seem imposing, they are easily programmed and simply require calculated prices on the original term structure, $\mathbf{i}$, as well as on a host of term structures where one or two of the factors is shifted up or down by a "small" amount.

In all, given m factors, equation (23a) requires $2m$ calculated prices in addition to the price on the original term structure, or only m additional prices if the "forward" difference approach is taken. Equation (23b) requires a good deal more effort, requiring in addition to the prices used in equation (23a), a total of $2(m^2 - m)$ additional valuations.

Analogous to equation (6), there is an identity for multi-factor models which relates the price on $\mathbf{j}$, $P(\mathbf{j})$, to the price on $\mathbf{i}$, and values of the total duration vector "between" $\mathbf{j}$ and $\mathbf{i}$. To this end, let $\gamma(t)$ denote a parametrization of term structures so that $\gamma(0) = \mathbf{i}$, and $\gamma(1) = \mathbf{j}$. For example, a simple linear shift could be defined as $\gamma(t) = \mathbf{i} + (\mathbf{j} - \mathbf{i})t$. The identity is then:

$$P(\mathbf{j}) = P(\mathbf{i})\exp(-\smallint\mathbf{D}(\gamma(t)) \cdot \gamma'(t)dt) \qquad (24)$$

where the integral is taken over [0,1], and $\gamma'(t)$ denotes the derivative of this vector valued function, which in the case of the above simple example is $\gamma'(t) = \Delta\mathbf{i}$.

This identity gives rise to an alternative approximation approach, similar to equation (8), which in its first order version replaces the integral with $D(i) \cdot \gamma'(0)$, in general, or with $D(i) \cdot \Delta i$ in the linear case.

Multi-Factor Models

With the first general single factor term structure model introduced in 1971 by Fisher and Weil, multi-factor models have been investigated since 1976.[15] The first such model was:

$$\textit{Mixed Additive-Multiplicative Shift:}\quad i_t \rightarrow (1 + i)i_t + j$$
$$i \rightarrow (1 + i)i + j\mathbf{M}$$

where i and j denote the two factors, and i_t denotes the term structure at maturity t. Letting $\mathbf{i}$ denote the term structure in vector notation, and $\mathbf{M}$ the vector with all 1's, this multi-factor model can also be represented as in the second expression above, where the various operations are by convention to be interpreted component by component.

Another model, generalizing the directional model earlier, is the:

$$\textit{Multi-Directional Model:}\quad \mathbf{i} \rightarrow \mathbf{i} + \sum j_k \mathbf{N}_k$$

where $\{\mathbf{N}_k\}$ are a collection of fixed vectors, and the various j_k are the factors. One implementation of this model is derived from a principal component analysis, whereby the various direction vectors used represent some or all of the principal components of term structure movements (see below).

Another example of this model is the key (spot) rate model of Ho.[16] Here, $\mathbf{i}$ denotes the risk-free term structure of 360 monthly spot rates from 1 month to 30 years, derived from a procedure which reflects the prices of all traded Treasuries, subject to various smoothness criteria. From this vector, "key" rates are selected at maturities: 1, 2, 3, 5, 7, 10, 20, and 30 years, and each rate has associated with it a "pyramid" direction vector defined to be 1 at the key rate maturity, 0 at maturities equal to or greater than the next key rate, and maturities equal to or smaller than the prior key rate, and with all other values linearly interpolated. Consequently, the collection $\{\mathbf{N}_k\}$ so defined forms a "partition of unity" in that $\sum \mathbf{N}_k = \mathbf{M}$, the parallel shift vector of all 1's.

Another convenient parametrization of the term structure was introduced by Reitano as part of the first general study of these models, and called the "yield

---

[15] See G.O.Bierwag, "Measures of Duration," University of Oregon, working paper, 1976. Other historical references can be found in Bierwag, *Duration Analysis*. See also D.R.Chambers, W.T. Carleton, and R.W. McEnally, "Immunizing Default-Free Bond Portfolios With a Duration Vector," *Journal of Financial and Quantitative Analysis* (March 1988), pp. 89-104; T.S.Y. Ho, *Strategic Fixed Income Management* (Homewood, Ill.: Dow Jones-Irwin, 1990); T.S.Y. Ho, "Key Rate Durations: Measures of Interest Rate Risks," *Journal of Fixed Income* (September 1992), pp.29-44; and the various papers by Reitano referred to in this chapter.

[16] See Ho, "Key Rate Durations: Measures of Interest Rate Risks."

curve driver" model.[17] Here, **i** denotes the term structure of "on the run" treasury bond yields, at maturities 0.25, 0.5, 1, 2, 3, 5, 7, 10, 20, and 30 years, with other maturities developed using interpolation by spline or other methods, and the entire term structure is then converted to spot rates for valuations in the usual way. Consequently, these ten or so yields form the "drivers" of the valuation process. The shift model is then:

Yield Curve Driver Model: $\mathbf{i} \rightarrow \mathbf{i} + \Delta\mathbf{i}$

where $\Delta\mathbf{i}$ denotes the vector of factors of yield curve driver shifts $\Delta\mathbf{i}=(\Delta\mathbf{i}_1, \Delta\mathbf{i}_2, \ldots, \Delta\mathbf{i}_m)$. Of course, the yield curve driver model can be implemented with an arbitrary number of yield curve drivers, and within any term structure basis.

Relationships Between Single and Multi-Factor Models

Once a multi-factor model is developed, it is only natural to investigate its properties relative to single factor, and other multi-factor models. For instance, assume that partial durations and convexities have been calculated as in equation (22). Next, fix a direction vector, **N**, denominated in components consistent with the multi-factor model, which specifies the fixed relationship assumed to hold between the various factor movements. For instance, the original factors could be based on yield curve drivers, key rates, or a multi-factor directional model. What then is the relationship between the duration and convexity in the single factor directional model, called "directional" durations and convexities, and the "partials" of the multi-factor model?

As proved elsewhere,[18] denoting by D_N and C_N the directional duration and directional convexity calculated as in equation (3) using the directional shift model:

$$D_N = \mathbf{D} \cdot \mathbf{N} \qquad C_N = \mathbf{N}^T \mathbf{C} \mathbf{N} \qquad (25)$$

where **D** and **C** denote the total duration vector and total convexity matrix of the multi-factor model as defined in equations (22) and (23). That is, the directional duration and convexity of the single factor model is easily calculated by:

$$D_N = \sum D_j n_j \qquad C_N = \sum\sum C_{jk} n_j n_k \qquad (25b)$$

where $\mathbf{N}=(n_1, n_2, \ldots, n_m)$.

A simple consequence of equation (25) follows when **N** is set equal to the parallel shift vector, **M**, which has all its components equal to 1. Specifically, the resultant duration and convexity is equal to the sum of the "partials:"

$$D = \sum D_j \qquad C = \sum\sum C_{jk} \qquad (26)$$

---

[17] See Reitano, "Multivariate Duration Analysis."
[18] See Reitano, "Multivariate Duration Analysis."

Equations (25) and (26) are identities between exactly calculated durations and convexities (i.e., identities between the underlying derivatives). Consequently, for durations and convexities approximated using the finite difference equations (4) and (23), these identities will hold only approximately. Similarly, for measures calculated using yield curve scenario sampling techniques, the resultant values will only approximately satisfy these identities, even when the binary bit strings are controlled as discussed above. To be certain that the resulting "errors" are the result of such approximations, and not calculation errors, it is important to "stress test" calculations by decreasing the finite difference interval, increasing the sample size, and verifying that the convergence assured by the theory is observed.

It is also important that equation (26) not be too hastily applied in anticipation that the "traditional" duration and convexity measures of Fisher-Weil will be produced from any multi-factor model. This equation simply states that if the individual factors of a multi-factor model are assumed to move "in parallel," that the sum of the partials will reproduce the results of the single factor model where this assumption is modeled explicitly. A few examples will clarify this point.

For the yield curve driver model, the individual factors are defined as the respective shifts of the various yield curve drivers: $\Delta \mathbf{i} = (\Delta i_1, \Delta i_2, \ldots, \Delta i_m)$. The associated parallel shift model reflects the assumption that each shift component, Δi_j, is equal to i, say. Is this model now equivalent to the Fisher-Weil parallel shift model where each point of the term structure is shifted in parallel? A little thought reveals that this will be the case only if the interpolation algorithm used converts parallel shifts of the yield curve drivers to parallel shifts of all the interpolated points of the term structure. Linear interpolation has this property, of course. On the other hand, if the Fisher-Weil parallel shift model is "defined" in terms of the yield curve drivers, the resulting duration and convexity will satisfy equation (26), independent of the interpolation method used.

As another example, consider the multi-factor directional model, where the shift is given by $\sum j_k \mathbf{N}_k$, and where the $\{j_k\}$ are the factors. Assume next that these factors are modeled to move in parallel; that is, where each j_k equals a given single factor, i. By construction, this single factor model will now be a single factor directional model, where shifts are modeled as $(\sum \mathbf{N}_k)i$. Is this parallel shift model that of Fisher-Weil? Only when the sum of the direction vectors equals $\mathbf{M}$, the vector of all 1's. An example of when this condition holds is the key rate model, as noted above. However, it is clear from this construction that any multi-factor directional model for which the direction vectors form a "partition of unity," $\sum \mathbf{N}_k = \mathbf{M}$, will enjoy the property that the partial durations and convexities will sum to the corresponding traditional values.

Equation (25) can be generalized to relate the total duration vectors and total convexity matrices of two multi-factor models for which the factors are functionally related. For simplicity, we assume here that this functional relationship is linear. Specifically, consider the above multi-factor directional model with shift $\sum j_k \mathbf{N}_k$, and where $\{j_k\}$ are interpreted as the factors, denoted $\mathbf{j}$ for short, and $\{\mathbf{N}_k\}$

are interpreted as fixed. Consider next the general multi-factor model whereby each point of the term structure is modeled as a separate factor, and parametrized in terms of the term structure vector $\mathbf{i}$. What is the relationship between the total duration vectors of the two models? Letting $\mathbf{N}$ denote the matrix with the $\{\mathbf{N}_j\}$ as columns, we have in matrix notation ($\mathbf{D}$ is interpreted as a row matrix):

$$\mathbf{D}(\mathbf{j}) = \mathbf{D}(\mathbf{i})\mathbf{N} \quad \mathbf{C}(\mathbf{j}) = \mathbf{N}^T\mathbf{C}(\mathbf{i})\mathbf{N} \tag{27}$$

Equation (27) provides a more formal way of justifying the observations above regarding "parallel" shift relationships. By equation (25), the parallel shift duration in $\mathbf{j}$-space is equal to $\mathbf{D}(\mathbf{j})\bullet\mathbf{M}$, which can also be expressed in matrix notation as $\mathbf{D}(\mathbf{j})\mathbf{M}$, where $\mathbf{M}=(1,1,.....,1)$. Is this equal to the parallel shift duration in $\mathbf{i}$-space? Using equation (27), we see that $\mathbf{D}(\mathbf{j})\mathbf{M}=\mathbf{D}(\mathbf{i})\mathbf{N}\mathbf{M}$, so the answer is in the affirmative if and only if $\mathbf{N}\mathbf{M}=\mathbf{M}$, which is equivalent to $\sum\mathbf{N}_k=\mathbf{M}$; i.e., $\{\mathbf{N}_k\}$ form a partition of unity. The careful reader will note that in the above argument, the symbol $\mathbf{M}$ was used with dimension equal to that of $\mathbf{j}$-space, as well as $\mathbf{i}$-space. The transition occurred in the equation $\mathbf{N}\mathbf{M}=\mathbf{M}$, in which the $\mathbf{M}$ on the left had dimension equal to the number of columns of $\mathbf{N}$ (i.e., the number of the $\mathbf{N}_k$, or j_k), while the $\mathbf{M}$ on the right had dimension equal to the number of rows of $\mathbf{N}$ (i.e., the dimension of the $\mathbf{N}_k$, or $\mathbf{i}$).

Is There a "Best" Multi-Factor Model?

Without a great deal of thought, the obvious answer to the above question is: Yes, the model with the number of "independent" factors equal to the number of yields on the term structure being modeled. For instance, if the term structure is modeled as a vector in 360-space, describing monthly spot rates from 1-month to 30 years, one such multi-factor model is the general yield curve driver model: $\mathbf{i}\rightarrow\mathbf{i}+\Delta\mathbf{i}$, where the shift vector describes the component by component moves along the curve. Alternatively, one could use any multi-factor directional model with 360 linearly independent direction vectors. This generalizes the above general yield curve driver model which is equivalent to a multi-factor directional model with $\mathbf{N}_k=(0,..,1,0,...0)$, with 1 in the kth component.

For the yield curve driver model described earlier, with 10 or so yields identified on a par bond curve and the rest interpolated, again it makes little difference whether one parametrizes factors as described, or in terms of a multi-factor directional model with 10 linearly independent direction vectors. While one parametrization may be more convenient to work with than the other, they will be equivalent in terms of their ability to capture all feasible shifts in the given model.

It is also clear that adding linearly dependent direction vectors to a multi-factor model in no way improves the model's descriptive ability or analytic power. More factors are only better if they are independent factors.

Returning to the title of this section, the real question is: Is there a "best" multi-factor model when the number of factors is "small," i.e., small relative to the number of parameters in the term structure model? In the single factor case discussed above, this distinction did not need to be made because all term structure models have at least one parameter, so of necessity, single factor models are relatively "sparse" in their descriptive ability. However, as was shown above, one single factor model was indeed "best" in terms of capturing the largest share of the movement in historical yield curve shifts.

Specifically, if $\{Y_j'\}$ represents a collection of historical yield curve shifts, denominated in units compatible with the term structure model used, and normalized to have mean 0, we saw that the "best" direction vector to use to approximate this collection was E_1, the unit eigenvector of the variance/covariance matrix of these shifts, V, associated with the largest eigenvalue, e_1. In that development, the Y_j were assumed to have dimension m, so we next consider the generalization of this result to multi-factor models with less than m factors. In actuality, the two factor development provides the template and will be seen to be easily generalized.

To this end, we seek a direction vector, P, so that for optimally chosen $\{b_j\}$, the following is minimized: $\sum |Y_j' - a_j E_1 - b_j P|^2$, where as noted earlier, $a_j = (E_1, Y_j')$. Not surprisingly, the same derivation shows that the optimizing b_j equals: $(P, Y_j' - a_j E_1)/|P|^2$. Before proceeding, let's simplify this expression by requiring P to also be a unit vector, and "orthogonal" to E_1, i.e., $(P, E_1) = 0$. Then, mirroring the formula for a_j, we have: $b_j = (P, Y_j')$.

Another neat consequence of this orthogonality assumption is that the objective function to be minimized reduces to:

$$\text{Minimize: } \sum |Y_j'|^2 - \sum (Y_j', E_1)^2 - \sum (Y_j', P)^2 \tag{28}$$

because $|X|^2 = (X, X)$, and all the mixed terms in E_1 and P disappear. Comparing equation (28) to equation (19), a clear pattern emerges in the problem to be solved. Specifically, the problem is to *maximize* the last term, $\sum (Y_j', P)^2$, which equals $P^T V P$, subject to $|P| = 1$, and $(P, E_1) = 0$.

As expected, the solution to this problem is well known to be E_2, the eigenvector of V associated with the second largest eigenvalue, e_2. Using these first two principal components, E_1 and E_2, in a 2-factor directional model explains $(e_1 + e_2)/\sum e_j$ of the total variation of the sample, which is often 80% to 90%.

Generalizing the above derivation, it is apparent that the "best" n-factor directional model uses the first n eigenvectors of V, corresponding to the largest eigenvalues, which need not be distinct. That is, a single eigenvalue can have multiple eigenvectors in theory. In that case, it is irrelevant in which order they are used once the given eigenvalue is brought into the model. This n-factor directional model then explains $\sum' e_j / \sum e_j$, where the sum in the numerator includes only the first n eigenvalues, and each summation includes eigenvalues up to their multiplicity (i.e., number of eigenvectors used).

Multi-Factor Yield Curve Management I

Once a multi-factor model is in place, how do we evaluate and reduce the strategic or tactical risk implied by the portfolio's durational profile, or, how do we evaluate and enhance the tactical opportunities?

To begin with, recall equation (21) which provides an approximation to the value of price on multi-factor value $\mathbf{j}\equiv\mathbf{i}+\Delta\mathbf{i}$, $P(\mathbf{j})$, based on the value of price, durations and convexities on $\mathbf{i}$: $P(\mathbf{i})$, $\mathbf{D}(\mathbf{i})$, and $C(\mathbf{i})$; and on $\Delta\mathbf{i}$. Using only the durational term, the expression $P(\mathbf{i}+\Delta\mathbf{i})/P(\mathbf{i})$ can be approximated by $R(\Delta\mathbf{i})$:

$$R(\Delta\mathbf{i}) = (1 - \mathbf{D}(\mathbf{i})\cdot\Delta\mathbf{i}) \qquad (29)$$

Recalling the well known Cauchy-Schwarz inequality, that: $|\mathbf{X}\cdot\mathbf{Y}|\leq|\mathbf{X}||\mathbf{Y}|$, we have that the absolute variation of this price ratio from 1 is bounded by:

$$|R(\Delta\mathbf{i}) - 1| = |-\mathbf{D}(\mathbf{i})\cdot\Delta\mathbf{i}| \leq |\mathbf{D}(\mathbf{i})|\,|\Delta\mathbf{i}| \qquad (30)$$

Taking risk assessment first, equation (30) provides an upper bound to risk based on the total duration vector and an estimate of the maximum shift possible. For the yield curve driver model, $|\mathbf{D}(\mathbf{i})|$ is equal to the square root of the sum of the partial durations squared:

$$\sqrt{\Sigma D_j^2}$$

by definition, and an estimate of $|\Delta\mathbf{i}|$ can be made by an analysis of historical yield curve data denominated in the same units as the yield curve driver basis.

Within a multi-factor directional model, such as the key rate model, $|\mathbf{D}(\mathbf{i})|$ again reflects the partial durations under this model, which in turn are directional durations to the direction vectors. For example, if the model used is: $\Delta\mathbf{i}=\sum j_k\mathbf{E}_k$, with $\{\mathbf{E}_k\}$ defined from a principal component analysis, each partial duration to j_k, $D_k(\mathbf{i})$, is in fact a directional duration with respect to $\mathbf{E}_k$, $D_E(\mathbf{i})$, which in turn is equal to, by equation (27), $\mathbf{D}(\mathbf{i})\cdot\mathbf{E}_k$, where here $\mathbf{D}(\mathbf{i})$ equals the total duration vector with respect to the yield curve driver model underlying the principal components. The estimate here for $|\Delta\mathbf{i}|$ is again based on historical data, but recognizing that for this multi-factor directional model, $\Delta\mathbf{i}$ is defined in terms of the coefficients of the principal components in the yield curve expansions. That is, since each historical yield curve can be expanded $\mathbf{Y}_k=\sum(\mathbf{Y}_k,\mathbf{E}_j)\mathbf{E}_j$, we have $\Delta\mathbf{Y}_k\equiv\mathbf{Y}_{k+1}-\mathbf{Y}_k=\sum(\Delta\mathbf{Y}_k,\mathbf{E}_j)\mathbf{E}_j$, and the components of the parameter vector in equation (30), $\Delta\mathbf{i}$, are the $(\Delta\mathbf{Y}, \mathbf{E}_j)$ terms and hence:

$$|\Delta\mathbf{i}| = \sqrt{[\Sigma(\Delta\mathbf{Y},\mathbf{E}_j)^2]}$$

for each shift, $\Delta\mathbf{Y}$.

Opportunistically, equation (30) can be utilized by investigating the relationship between $\mathbf{D}(\mathbf{i})$ and $\Delta\mathbf{i}$ that assures the most favorable result. Besides providing an inequality for a dot product, the Cauchy-Schwarz derivation identifies the relationship between the two vectors which assures that the largest or smallest value is in fact obtained. Specifically, it turns out that the maximum value of a dot product is obtained when $\mathbf{X}$ equals a positive multiple of $\mathbf{Y}$, denoted $\mathbf{X}\sim\mathbf{Y}$, while the minimum value is obtained when $\mathbf{X}$ is a negative multiple, $\mathbf{X}\approx-\mathbf{Y}$.

Consequently, referring to equation (30), to take a maximum opportunistic position on an anticipated factor shift $\Delta\mathbf{i}$, one needs to trade to achieve a total duration vector, $\mathbf{D(i)}$, so that $-\mathbf{D(i)}$ is positively proportional to this anticipated shift; i.e., $\mathbf{D(i)}$ must be positively proportional to $-\Delta\mathbf{i}$. Hence, one wants negative durational exposure to positive anticipated factor shifts and conversely, and the more one anticipates the factor to move, the more durational exposure is sought. This generalizes the one factor opportunistic tactic in a natural way.

However, there are infinitely many vectors positively proportional to $-\Delta\mathbf{i}$, so which should be targeted? Again, the answer is analogous to the single factor case where it was clear that for negative shifts, maximize $D(\mathbf{i})$, and conversely. Here, "larger" multiples are better than smaller multiples since this strategy magnifies the effect. Specifically, if $\mathbf{D(i)}=-a\Delta\mathbf{i}$, where a is assumed to be positive, then by equation (30), $|R(\Delta\mathbf{i})-1|=a|\Delta\mathbf{i}|^2$, so the larger a is the better.

When making an explicit assumption about $\Delta\mathbf{i}$ is deemed imprudent, but one wishes to take advantage of beliefs about the probable range of such factor shifts, as in the single factor model, a utility based analysis is possible. To this end, assume that the likely behavior of $\Delta\mathbf{i}$ can be modeled in terms of a probability distribution, however crude, and that a utility function, $u(w)$, has been selected. Consider the expected utility objective function to be maximized: $f(\mathbf{D})=E[u(1-\mathbf{D}\bullet\Delta\mathbf{i})]$. Equating the partial derivatives with respect to the various D_j to zero, the following system of equations is produced:

$$E[\Delta i_j\, u'(1 - \mathbf{D}\bullet\Delta\mathbf{i})] = 0$$

It is easy to see that any solution, $\mathbf{D}$, to this system is a utility maximizing total duration vector for a risk averse investor, because the matrix of second degree partial derivatives $(E[\Delta i_j\Delta i_k u''(1-\mathbf{D}\bullet\Delta\mathbf{i})])$ is positive definite.

To see this, let $\mathbf{X}$ be any vector and consider the matrix product: $\mathbf{X}^T\mathbf{AX}$, where $\mathbf{A}$ is this second derivative matrix. Using properties of expectations, we get: $\mathbf{X}^T\mathbf{AX}=E[(\sum\Delta i_k x_k)^2 u''(1-\mathbf{D}\bullet\Delta\mathbf{i})]$, which is positive unless the entire probability mass of $\Delta\mathbf{i}$ is concentrated on a hyperplane. In that case, there is an $\mathbf{X}$ so that $\sum\Delta i_k x_k=0$ for all $\Delta\mathbf{i}$. Of course, in this case, the number of factors can in fact be reduced by 1, and the process repeated.

We next return to a risk assessment perspective, and investigate theoretical risk "elimination" with an immunization strategy. As in the case for single factor models, we in reality eliminate risk only to factor shifts encompassed by the given model, since we can not escape stochastic process risk unless the model is full dimensional (i.e., the same dimension as the number of points on the term structure). However, even in that case, protection is compromised once the time dynamics of the portfolio are taken into consideration.

To this end, consider equation (21). In order to eliminate the risk to all factor shifts encompassed by the model, it is evident that as in the single factor case, we must have $\mathbf{D(i)}=\mathbf{0}$. In actuality, it is only necessary that $\mathbf{D(i)}\bullet\Delta\mathbf{i}=0$ for all feasible factor shifts, $\Delta\mathbf{i}$. However, this equation implies that $\mathbf{D(i)}=\mathbf{0}$, except in the case when all feasible shifts belong to a hyperplane of the factor space. In that case, the number of factors in the model can be reduced to the point where $\mathbf{D}(i)=0$ is the conclusion. This vector equation is equivalent to $D_j(i)=0$ for all j. When the model is a multi-factor directional model, these equations are equivalent to having the directional durations with respect to the model's directions all zero; i.e., $D_E(j)=D(j) \cdot E=0$ for all $\mathbf{E}$ in the model. This result follows from equation (27), where here, $\mathbf{D}(j)$ denotes the total duration vector on the yield curve driver model underlying the directional model.

Besides the durational constraint, immunization theory also recognizes the potential for gains and losses from the convexity term, and seeks to make them only gains. Again referring to equation (21), we seek to have: $\Delta i^T C(i)\Delta i \geq 0$, for all Δi. That is, we seek to have the total convexity matrix positive semi-definite, although the purists might require positive definiteness: $\Delta i^T C(i)\Delta i > 0$, except if $\Delta i = 0$. In the multi-factor directional model, this condition on the convexity matrix in units of direction factors, i, can also be translated to a condition on the convexity matrix in units of the yield curve driver model underlying the directional model, using equation (27).

Let $\mathbf{j}$ denote the yield curve driver units, $\mathbf{j}=\sum i_k \mathbf{N}_k = \mathbf{N}i$, where $\mathbf{N}$ denotes the matrix with the $\mathbf{N}_k$ as columns. Then

$$\Delta i^T C(i)\Delta i = \Delta i^T N^T C(j)N\Delta i = (N\Delta i)^T C(j)N\Delta i$$

so the conclusion is that $C(j)$, the convexity matrix in yield curve driver units, must be positive (semi-)definite on the space generated by the collection of direction vectors used. For example, if the direction vectors used are from a principal component analysis, $\{\mathbf{E}_j\}$, the yield curve driver convexity matrix must have this property on all yield curve shifts generated by these components.

Combining the above results, immunization criteria for a general multi-factor model can be easily stated in terms of the price function of interest, $P(i)$. When applied, the general equation (21) becomes the multi-factor counterpart to equation (10):

$$P(j) \approx P(i)(1 + 0.5\Delta i^T C(i)\Delta i) \tag{31}$$

where $C(i)$ is at least positive semi-definite, so it is always the case that $P(j) \geq P(i)$.

However, as noted above, this price function typically represents a net portfolio such as surplus, a market-neutral account, or an asset portfolio net of a notional index portfolio, so it is more relevant to state these criteria in terms of these underlying price functions. To do this, we need to recall that as a consequence of equation (22), total duration vectors and convexity matrices enjoy the portfolio property. That is, if $\{P_k(i)\}$ are a collection of non-zero price functions with duration vectors, $\{\mathbf{D}_k(i)\}$, and convexity matrices, $\{C_k(i)\}$, then if $P(i)=\sum P_k(i)$ is non-zero:

$$\mathbf{D}(i) = \sum w_k \mathbf{D}_k(i) \qquad C(i) = \sum w_k C_k(i) \tag{32}$$

where $w_k = P_k(i)/P(i)$.

Using equation (32) applied to a surplus portfolio, $S(i)=A(i)-L(i)$, we obtain the following conditions for immunization against yield curve shifts implied by the multi-factor model used:

$$\mathbf{D}^A(i) = [L(i)/A(i)]\mathbf{D}^L(i) \quad A(i)\mathbf{C}^A(i) - L(i)\mathbf{C}^L(i) \gg 0 \tag{33}$$

where $\mathbf{X} \gg 0$ denotes that $\mathbf{X}$ is a positive definite matrix.

The conditions of equation (33) provide protection for the current value of surplus against "instantaneous" shifts in the factors. One can also develop conditions which protect the value of the surplus ratio, $(A(i)/L(i))/A(i)$, which turn out to be identical to those in equation (33) *except* that the values of assets and liabilities are omitted.[19] Another strategy, with applications to surplus as well as to other portfolios discussed above, is the strategy of immunizing the *forward* value of surplus against instantaneous shifts.

To make this notion precise, let $Z_k(i)$ denote the value of a k-period, zero-coupon bond with maturity value $1, where as always, this value reflects the term structure implied by the factor value, i. If $P(i)$ denotes the price function for a given portfolio, define the forward price function, denoted $P_k(i)$, by:

$$P_k(i) = P(i)/Z_k(i)$$

Intuitively, $P_k(i)$ represents the value of the portfolio at time k that can be locked-in today by selling the portfolio and buying the zero. Strictly stated, this value is locked-in only if the zero is risk-free, but we assume that this poses no valuation problems and that the necessary term structure is also driven by the multi-factor model used.

Immunization criteria for $P_k(i)$ are:

$$\mathbf{D}^A(i) = [L(i)\mathbf{D}^L(i) + S(i)\mathbf{D}^Z(i)]/A(i)$$

$$A(i)\mathbf{C}^A(i) - L(i)\mathbf{C}^L(i) - S(i)\mathbf{C}^Z(i) \gg 0 \tag{34}$$

where $\mathbf{D}^Z$ and $\mathbf{C}^Z$ denote the duration vector and convexity matrix of $Z_k(i)$. Note that the conditions in equation (34) reduce to those in (33) when $k=0$, as expected. Note also that the conditions in equation (34) are equivalent to the requirement that surplus have the same durational structure, and more convexity (i.e., in the sense of positive definiteness), than the k-period zero-coupon bond.

When either equation (33) or equation (34) is utilized in equation (31), it appears that we have constructed conditions which assure a risk-free arbitrage for surplus, on the one hand, or the forward value of surplus, on the other. However, in the same way that this conclusion was overstated in the one factor case using equations (9) and (10), it is again overstated here, and for the same reason. The

---

[19] See Reitano, "Multivariate Immunization Theory" for more details on all the immunization models discussed.

reason is that the multi-factor immunization conditions were developed without regard for the time dynamics of the portfolio in question. It was explicitly assumed that the portfolio's characteristics did not change as the factor shifted, so as before, the above immunization conditions can only be said to provide protection against "instantaneous" factor shifts.

In the more realistic model which explicitly recognizes the time dynamic, what was modeled as $P(\mathbf{i})$ above, would be modeled as $P(t, \mathbf{i}_t)$, where $\mathbf{i}_t$ denoted the dependence of the factor vector on time. As in the one factor case, when $\mathbf{i}_t$ is assumed to follow a multi-factor Ito process, one discovers that the immunization condition on the duration structure can only hold instantaneously, due to the diffusion coefficients, and hence no risk-free arbitrage is created.

Multi-Factor Yield Curve Management II[20]

Once an immunization theory has been developed within a multi-factor context and implemented, two fundamental truisms are discovered: (1) the more factors that are used, the more restrictive the conditions become until virtual cash-matching is required; and, (2) the less factors that are used, the more likely immunization will fail because the model is too sparse to capture the true variability of term structure shifts.

While initially discouraging, these truisms compel a rethinking of the underlying framework for immunization theory. The classical goal of immunization theory is the virtual elimination of downside risk, but in practice, it is only to a subset of feasible shifts that the portfolio is protected. Worse yet, the typical approach completely ignores the potential for loss from shifts outside the model used. As an alternative, rather than seek complete protection from some shifts and have unknown protection from others, perhaps it would be better to have a strategy which provided a minimal amount of risk from all shifts.

The search for such a strategy lead to the development of the theory of "stochastic immunization." Its goal is to minimize the "risk," as yet to be defined, of the relative price function $P(\mathbf{i}+\Delta\mathbf{i})/P(\mathbf{i})$, which is approximated by the linear function, $R(\Delta\mathbf{i})$, defined in equation (29). More generally, its goal is to minimize risk subject to various constraints and objectives of interest.

To develop a measure of risk, first note that since $\Delta\mathbf{i}$ is fundamentally a stochastic variable, it makes sense to follow Markowitz,[21] and consider the variance of $R(\Delta\mathbf{i})$. As it turns out:

$$\mathrm{Var}[R(\Delta\mathbf{i})] = \mathbf{D}(\mathbf{i})\mathbf{K}\mathbf{D}(\mathbf{i})^T$$

where $\mathbf{K}$ denotes the variance/covariance matrix of the factor change vector, $\Delta\mathbf{i}$ (recall that above, $\mathbf{V}$ denoted $n-1$ times the variance/covariance matrix; i.e., $\mathbf{V}=(n-1)\mathbf{K}$). For

---

[20] For details on the approach developed here, see Robert R. Reitano, "Multivariate Stochastic Immunization," *Transactions of the Society of Actuaries*, XLV (1993), pp. 425-484 and, "Non-Parallel Yield Curve Shifts and Stochastic Immunization," *Journal of Portfolio Management* (Winter 1996), pp. 71-78.

[21] Harry Markowitz, *Portfolio Selection: Efficient Diversification of Investments* (New York: John Wiley & Sons, 1959).

simplicity, Δi will be referred to as if its components were in fact changes in the term structure at designated maturities, although the model applies equally well in the general multi-factor case. Recall also that $D(i)$ is by convention treated as a row matrix, and hence the placement of the transpose symbol above.

Variance is an important measure to minimize because its value determines the likelihood that the random variable under consideration can assume relatively large values. For instance, when normally distributed, only 32% of the distribution is more than one standard deviation away (recall S.D.$=\sqrt{\text{Var}}$), only 5% more than 2 S.D.'s, 0.2% more than 3 S.D.'s, etc. While Ito calculus assumes that factors are "locally" normal, i.e., over infinitesimal time increments, we cannot assume the same for Δi or $R(\Delta i)$ over finite time interval shifts. So what does variance imply in the general case?

An important result, known as Chebyshev's Inequality, provides the answer in the general case. Specifically, it states that for any constant $a>0$, the distribution of $R(\Delta i)$ satisfies:

$$Pr(\{\Delta i: |R(\Delta i) - E[R(\Delta i)]|^2 \geq a\}) \leq \text{Var}[R(\Delta i)]/a$$

That is, the probability that the random variable, $R(\Delta i)$, is far from its expected value depends on the variance. Setting $a=n^2\text{Var}[R(\Delta i)]$, and rearranging, we get:

$$Pr(\{\Delta i: |R(\Delta i) - E[R(\Delta i)]| \geq n(\text{S.D.})\}) \leq n^{-2}$$

which is much weaker than in the normal case. For example, the probability that the random variable is at least 3 S.D.'s away from its mean is no more than about 11% in general, compared with 0.2% for the normal.

Because of this relatively weak general upper bound, and the importance of limiting the likelihood of "outlier" values of $R(\Delta i)$, another risk measure of interest follows from equation (30), which can be restated:

$$|R(\Delta i) - E[R(\Delta i)]| \leq |D(i)| \, |\Delta i - E[\Delta i]|$$

That is, the difference between the approximate relative price ratio, $R(\Delta i)$, and its expected value, $E[R(\Delta i)]$, is bounded above by the length of the duration vector, $D(i)$, and the length of the yield curve shift less its mean. Because that last term can be assumed to be bounded, $|D(i)|$, or equivalently, $|D(i)|^2$, can be viewed as a risk proxy in that by making it small, outliers in the distribution of $R(\Delta i)$ can be limited, not only in probability as is assured by Chebyshev, but completely.

Both risk proxies above, $\text{Var}[R(\Delta i)]$ and $|D(i)|^2$, can be weighted and combined into a general risk proxy which provides the user with the option of giving these measures the relative weights desired. Specifically, for a general weighting parameter, w, we define a risk measure, $RM(w)$, by:

$$RM(w) = w\text{Var}[R(\Delta i)] + (1 - w)|D(i)|^2$$

where we assume $0 \le w \le 1$. As it turns out, $RM(w)$ can also be written as a quadratic form in $\mathbf{D}$, similar to the above expression for variance. That is, defining $\mathbf{K}_w \equiv w\mathbf{K} + (1 - w)\mathbf{I}$, we have:

$$RM(w) = \mathbf{D}\mathbf{K}_w\mathbf{D}^T \qquad (35)$$

As noted above, $\mathbf{K}$ is at least positive *semi*-definite in theory, although in practice, it will be positive definite for appropriate factor parametrizations. In any case, $\mathbf{K}_w$ is positive definite for $w<1$, so we assume that $\mathbf{K}_I=\mathbf{K}$ also has this property. On a practical note, while the theory only requires $0 \le w \le 1$, in practice, w must be relatively close to 1. This is due to the fact that the units of $\mathbf{K}$ are of the order of magnitude of 10^{-5} or so, depending on the length of the period underlying Δi, while the units of $\mathbf{I}$ are magnitude 1. Hence, unless w is close to 1 to offset this unit disparity, the risk minimization problem will effectively reduce to the minimization of $|\mathbf{D}(i)|^2$.

Because $\mathbf{K}_w$ is positive definite, as noted above, it is completely trivial to minimize $RM(w)$ for any w. That is, the minimum of $RM(w)$ is 0, and this value is obtained if and only if $\mathbf{D}=\mathbf{0}$, by definition. This conclusion is equivalent to that which is obtained by applying the traditional notion of immunization to this multi-factor setting. We have not yet obtained anything of value using this new immunization paradigm.

The payoff for this model is the ability of the portfolio manager to incorporate a host of constraints and strategic objectives into the minimization problem. One such objective relates to the targeting of the term structure shift (i.e., factor shift) return, $E[R(\Delta i)]$. An easy calculation shows that since $R(\Delta i)=1-\mathbf{D}\cdot\Delta i$:

$$E[R(\Delta i)] = 1 - \mathbf{D}\cdot E[\Delta i]$$

where $E[\Delta i]$ is the expected yield curve (i.e., factor) vector shift. Consequently, one can target $E[R(\Delta i)]=r$, using the constraint: $\mathbf{D}\cdot E[\Delta i]=1-r$.

In practice, this objective can be used strategically or tactically. In the former case, one selects $E[\Delta i]$ based on an analysis of historical data; in the latter case, $E[\Delta i]$ represents a personal view of short-term expectations on which one seeks to take a position. Admittedly, the strategic approach has limited applicability because historical values of $E[\Delta i]$ are so dependent on the period analyzed. Consequently, the selection of a value often involves a process which is fundamentally tactical in nature. As a final point, the strategic choice $E[\Delta i]=\mathbf{0}$, adds nothing to the problem and can be omitted because this assumption in no way constrains the solution, $\mathbf{D}$, sought.

Another constraint of interest is the targeting of one or more directional durations. That is, based on a principal component or other analysis, or tactically selected direction vectors, one may want to target directional duration values $D_N=\mathbf{D}\cdot\mathbf{N}$, for various values of $\mathbf{N}$. For example, choosing $\mathbf{N}=\mathbf{M}\equiv(1,1,..,1)$, allows the targeting of the parallel factor shift duration measure.

In practice, the direction vectors selected and the values of the directional durations targeted will reflect the application in hand. For example, if surplus is the object portfolio underlying the price function, one might simply target traditional duration to 0 or a small value consistent with the traditional theory. More generally, one could limit the directional duration exposures to one or several of the principal component directions. A similar approach might be taken with a market neutral portfolio, or a portfolio actively managed against an index fund where one creates an objective portfolio equal to a long position in the active portfolio and a short position in the index. Alternatively, this last application can be handled by targeting the various directional durations of the actively managed portfolio to those of the index fund.

A final constraint of interest is one which reflects the assets available for trading from the initial total durational structure to that identified as the solution to the constrained risk minimization problem. This asset collection is important since the fewer securities it contains, the less likely one will be able to achieve the desired outcome without specifically providing for the implied limitations. For example, if one can only trade 5-year and 10-year bonds, it is apparent that the portfolio's 20-year partial duration can not be changed. Hence, when developing the constrained minimization problem, it is important to have some constraint so that the solution does not require a change in this value.

In general, it turns out that the asset trading set imposes constraints by defining direction vectors for which the directional durations of the portfolio can not be changed. That is, it defines a collection $\{N_j\}$, so that the solution to the problem, D, must satisfy $D \cdot N_j = D(i) \cdot N_j$, where $D(i)$ denotes the original portfolio total duration vector. As expected, when the asset trading set is sufficiently large, the above set of vectors is empty, implying that the duration of the portfolio can be changed in any direction.

To determine the constraining direction vectors implied by the given asset trading set, first note that any trade in the portfolio must be "cash neutral;" that is, the totality of purchases must equal the totality of sales. While one may initially reject this notion with the counterexample of a portfolio with excessive cash, a moment of thought reveals that cash neutrality is again obeyed since the purchases must be funded by the sale of short-term securities, such as commercial paper, or the "sale" of cash holdings in a STIF (i.e., short term investment fund) account. In any case, these "cash" positions are part of the initial portfolio value, and this value does not change after a trade; i.e., trades are always cash neutral.

Next, assume that there are n assets available, with total duration vectors $\{D_k(i)\}$. Form the matrix, A, with $n-1$ columns equal to: D_1-D_n, ..., $D_{n-1}-D_n$. It is irrelevant which asset is chosen as the nth; while the matrix A will look different, the same constraints result in the end. Finally, determine a "basis" for the null space of A^T. That is, determine any collection of independent vectors that span the vector space of solutions to $A^T N = 0$. This can be accomplished with available software, or with more effort, by reducing this system of equations to upper triangular form. The number of such solutions is called the nullity of A^T, and denoted $v(A^T)$, or v for short.

The collection of null space vectors: $N_1, N_2,..., N_v$ then represent the directions in which the directional duration of the portfolio can not be changed by trading the given assets. That is, this collection of tradable assets requires the following constraints on the risk minimization problem: $D•N_j=D(i)•N_j$, for $j=1, 2,....,v$.

In summary, note that every constraint or strategic objective above could be represented by a linear equation for the total duration vector of the form $D•N=r$, for some vector N and value r. Collecting all such constraint vectors as columns of a matrix, B, and the associated values into a vector, r, all such constraint equations can be compactly expressed as $DB=r^T$. Consequently, the constrained risk minimization problem of "stochastic immunization" can be expressed:

$$\text{Minimize: } DK_wD^T, \text{ subject to: } DB = r^T \tag{36}$$

Before presenting a solution to equation (36) which requires conditions on B, let's pause to understand why conditions are needed. First off, no limitation has yet been placed on the number of restrictions allowed in the equation $DB=r^T$. Even on an intuitive level this seems problematic since if there are too many constraints, there will likely be no solutions; i.e., we will have an empty constraint set. For example, in 2 dimensions if $D=(x,y)$, the three constraints: $2x+2y=4$, $2x+3y=4$, and $2x+3y=8$, have no solution, as is easily verified. In general, the number of constraints must be no greater than the dimension of D, or m. But is that enough to assure a "consistent" constraint set?

In general the answer is no. Returning to the above example of three equations, any one gives a consistent constraint set of a straight line, as do equations 1 and 2 together, or, 1 and 3, in each case giving a constraint set of a single point. But equations 2 and 3 produce an empty set! In this case the problem is that the constraint direction vectors agree, equalling $(2,3)$, but the constraint values do not, producing an empty intersection. Geometrically, the constraint lines are parallel. If the constraint values also agreed, the constraints would be redundant, and only one needed.

In m dimensions, the constraint set will always be problem free if the set of direction vectors, i.e., the columns of B, are linearly independent. Automatically, this condition assures that the number of such constraints is less than the dimension of D, but also, that inconsistent and redundant constraints illustrated above are avoided.

Assuming that B has linearly independent columns, i.e., that the constraint direction vectors have this property, the solution to equation (36), D_o, is unique and given by:

$$D_o^T = K_w^{-1}B(B^TK_w^{-1}B)^{-1}r \tag{37}$$

Further, the value of the risk measure for this total duration vector, $RM_o(w)= D_oK_wD_o^T$, is given by:

$$RM_o(w) = r^T(B^TK_w^{-1}B)^{-1}r \tag{38}$$

While equations (36) and (37) appear imposing because of the needed matrix manipulations, they are easily evaluated using popular computer software.

Equation (38) can be interpreted as defining an "efficient frontier" in (Risk, $\mathbf{r}$)-space, reflecting the constraint direction vectors assumed in $\mathbf{B}$. Specifically, if $\mathbf{D}'$ is any total duration vector satisfying $\mathbf{DB}=\mathbf{r}^T$, then $RM(w) \geq RM_o(w)$. It is not difficult to show that the "shape" of this frontier is a paraboloid in (Risk, $\mathbf{r}$)-space.

For example, if $\mathbf{B}$ has only one column equal to $\mathbf{M}=(1, 1, \ldots, 1)$, then $\mathbf{DB}=\mathbf{r}^T$ reduces to: $D=r$, where D denotes the traditional parallel factor shift duration measure. Equation (38) then reduces to $RM_o(w)=cr^2$, where $c=(\mathbf{M}^T\mathbf{K}_w{}^{-1}\mathbf{M})^{-1}=1/\sum\sum(\mathbf{K}^{-1})_{jk}$, and $(\mathbf{K}^{-1})_{jk}$ denotes the jk^{th} element of $\mathbf{K}^{-1}$. Clearly, this efficient frontier is a parabola in (Risk, r)-space.

Once $\mathbf{D}_o$ has been calculated from equation (38), the final problem is to develop the trade that will convert the current total duration vector, $\mathbf{D(i)}=\mathbf{D}$, into the optimum total duration vector, $\mathbf{D}_o$. To this end, let $\mathbf{a}=(a_1, a_2, \ldots, a_n)$ denote the "trade vector," with a_j corresponding to the amount traded of the jth asset, which as before is assumed to have total duration vector, $\mathbf{D}_j$. By convention, we will interpret $a_j > 0$ as denoting a purchase, and $a_j < 0$ a sale (of course, $a_j = 0$ means "no trade").

If $P(\mathbf{i})=P$ denotes the value of the portfolio pre-trade, then by equation (32), the total duration vector after a trade, $\mathbf{D}'$, is given by: $\mathbf{D}'=[P\mathbf{D}+\sum a_j\mathbf{D}_j]/P$, since all trades are cash neutral (i.e., $\sum a_j = 0$). Of course, the goal of the trade it to make $\mathbf{D}'=\mathbf{D}_o$. Equating expressions, and substituting: $a_n=-\sum a_j$, where $j<n$, we get:

$$\mathbf{Aa}' = P[\mathbf{D}_o - \mathbf{D}]^T \tag{39}$$

where $\mathbf{A}$ is the matrix used above in connection with the asset trading set constraints (i.e., with columns equal to $\mathbf{D}_j-\mathbf{D}_n, j=1, 2, \ldots, n-1$), $\mathbf{a}'$ is the "truncated" trade vector: $\mathbf{a}'=(a_1, \ldots, a_{n-1})$, and a_n is implicitly defined by the condition of cash neutrality.

Equation (39) will always be solvable with a sufficient number of assets (i.e., large enough so that $\mathbf{A}$ has "rank" equal to m, the dimension of $\mathbf{D}$), or with fewer assets if constraints are imposed in equation (36) as discussed above. Being solvable, of course, does not mean "uniquely solvable." In general, there will be an infinite number of solutions from which to chose based on criteria outside the scope of the problem so far.

As is well known, if the solution of equation (39) is not unique, then there exists vectors $\mathbf{a}_j', j=0, 1, \ldots v$, so that $\mathbf{a}_o'$ is an arbitrary solution to this equation, and the other $\mathbf{a}_j'$ span the null space of $\mathbf{A}$: $\{a'|\mathbf{Aa}'=0\}$. It should be noted that here, $v=v(\mathbf{A})$ denotes the "nullity" of $\mathbf{A}$, in contrast to the discussion on asset trading set constraints where this standard notation denoted the nullity of $\mathbf{A}^T$. Consequently, any solution of equation (39) can be expressed as $\mathbf{a}'=\mathbf{a}_o'+\sum b_j\mathbf{a}_j'$.

Once this standard expression is derived, the actual implemented solution can be required to satisfy additional constraints on current yield, average quality, amount traded, etc. Many such constraints will in themselves require the solution to a minimization/maximization problem, which can usually be solved with standard techniques.

For example, one might chose to minimize the amount traded to limit bid/asked trading costs. Using linear programming software, the problem is to: Minimize $\sum |a_j'|$, summing j from 1 to n, where $\mathbf{a}'=(a_1', \ldots, a_{n-1}')$ solves: $\mathbf{a}'=\mathbf{a}_o'+\sum b_j\mathbf{a}_j'$, and a_n' is defined as: $-\sum a_j'$, for cash neutrality. In the absence of such software, one could solve a related problem analytically: Minimize $\sum |a_j'|^2$, subject to the same constraints. Note that a_n' can be written as: $-\mathbf{a}'\cdot\mathbf{M}$, where $\mathbf{M}=(1,1,\ldots,1)$ as before. Consequently, $\sum |a_j'|^2=\mathbf{a}'\cdot\mathbf{a}'+[\mathbf{a}'\cdot\mathbf{M}]^2$.

Additional Considerations for Multi-Factor Models

Throughout the above development, the intuitive framework for the multi-factor representations was the term structure. That is, it was intuitively assumed that the factors utilized were in one way or another, directly related to the dependence of yield on maturity. This yield could be defined on a par bond, spot, or forward basis, and be denominated in semi-annual or any nominal basis. In general then, the multiple factors related either to movements in these yields directly, as in the general yield curve driver model, or were related indirectly by assuming certain "structural" relationships in the factor movements, as in the general multi-factor directional model.

However, these multi-factor models have much wider applicability. For instance, even in the realm of a term structure, there is not a unique structure but many such structures. Risk-free yields represent the most obvious example of a term structure because of the "real time" availability of traded yields. But at every credit quality another structure exists, although generally less observable across all maturities in real time. Even different sectors of the fixed-income markets often trade at different yields for a fixed given credit quality and maturity, sometimes due to factors such as liquidity and optionality, but equally often not apparently related to any such analytic variable.

Fortunately, such sector differentials are usually relatively small, so it is not unrealistic to ignore them in a strategic model, the goal of which is to develop yield curve management strategies, even though it would be foolhardy to ignore such differentials in a tactical model, the goal of which is to develop cheap/rich insights. Consequently, for a realistic model of "term structure" movements, one needs not only the term structure of risk free rates, but also the term structure of risk spreads for the various credit qualities. Within such a multi-factor model, one could also evaluate "credit spread" durations and partial durations,[22] and evaluate the risks of immunization strategies to shifts among the various spreads. For example, multi-term structure shifts which widen quality spreads would be expected to adversely affect the real value of surplus if assets were of a lower quality than liabilities, although simple single-term structure models would not identify this risk because such models implicitly assume that all spreads move in lock-step.

---

[22] See Reitano, "Nonparallel Yield Curve Shifts and Spread Leverage," for more details on the multi-factor framework. See also Martin L. Liebowitz, William S. Krasker and Ardavan Nozari, "Spread Duration: A New Tool for Bond Portfolio Management," *Journal of Portfolio Management* (Spring 1990).

Naturally, the more general and realistic multi-term structure model can be accommodated in a multi-factor framework by defining i to not only reflect risk-free term structure parameters, but also the term structure parameters for credit spreads at the various qualities. While the resulting multi-factor models will have more dimensions than simple single-term structure models, the various risk analyses and immunization strategies are as easily implemented using computer routines.

One real difficulty, however, is the development of statistical assumptions needed for principal component analyses, or for stochastic immunization discussed above, or any application which requires the variance/covariance matrix of the factor vector. For risk-free statistics, of course, this analysis is relatively easy due to the volumes of data on historical Treasury yield curves which are readily available. For credit spreads, available data must first be "scrubbed" for consistency, and oftentimes holes filled in the series. Even then, spread statistics tend to be more stylistic than risk-free statistics, although still of potential value.

Another extension of the multi-factor framework, but this time beyond the term structure of yields, is to the parameter "yield volatility," or in the more general case, the "volatility term structure." Because of the prevalence of embedded options in fixed-income securities, including liabilities, and because of the dependence of the value of such options on volatility, it is only natural to explicitly model this dependency and seek to manage it, either strategically or tactically.

Recognizing such parameters explicitly as part of the multi-factor structure provides continuity between option management via the "Greeks"(i.e., gamma and delta), and general yield curve management via the notions of "volatility duration" and "volatility convexity." In fact, these latter measures are more convenient in practice for embedded options because they represent measures of the sensitivity of price to changes in the factor directly, in contrast to the "Greeks" which provide option price sensitivities to changes in the underlying security's price, which in turn must be converted to a factor basis. Moreover, even though mathematically equivalent, the volatility duration/convexity analytics are oftentimes far easier to use because in many applications, embedded options can not be easily defined as options on a simple, well-defined underlying security, for which the "Greeks" are easily calculated.

For example, even a callable bond's embedded option has a complicated security underlying it; namely, the callable bond itself. While one can formally perform the decomposition of the embedded option into gamma, etc., it is far more efficient to simply calculate the volatility duration of the bond directly; or better yet, the volatility partial durations.

Chapter 19

Hedging Corporate Securities with Treasury and Derivative Instruments

Shrikant Ramamurthy
Senior Vice President
Fixed-Income Research
Prudential Securities Incorporated

INTRODUCTION

The corporate bond market has grown significantly in the 1990s, with total debt outstanding rising from $1.4 trillion in 1990 to $2.1 trillion at the end of September 1997.[1] The variety of fixed-rate products that are issued by corporations has also expanded to include not only bullet bonds, but also amortizing and option-embedded bonds. With this type of growth and product diversity in the market, corporate bond portfolios and dealer inventories of corporate products have also increased significantly.

Since corporate securities, like other fixed income securities, exhibit price volatility on a daily basis, hedging price volatility has become more important in this expanding market. The price of a corporate bond is affected by many factors, including movements in interest rates, changing credit spreads, and changing values of any embedded options. Hedging strategies offer a mechanism to minimize the price volatility of corporate securities to many of these factors. Hedging strategies are of importance to many market participants, such as underwriters and dealers whose goal is to provide liquidity, portfolio managers who are trying to either shorten duration or protect positions from potential losses, and corporate treasurers who want to lock in rates prior to refinancing or issuing new debt.

This chapter provides an introduction to hedging corporate securities, both bullet and option-embedded securities, using Treasury securities, futures contracts

---

[1] Outstanding debt statistics are from the Bond Market Association.

and/or interest rate swaps.[2] Each of these hedging instruments provides an alternative mechanism to hedge the price risk of a corporate bond and each has its own distinct advantages and disadvantages in terms of cost and suitability. Treasury securities are generally the most common hedge instruments but, as we shall see, futures and swaps may be more appropriate instruments for many hedging applications.

The starting point of this chapter is a discussion of the mechanics and goals of a hedging strategy. Hedging strategies are then developed using the dollar-value-of-a-basis-point (DVBP) approach. The DVBP approach is applied using Treasuries and other derivative instruments. Examples of constructing and evaluating hedge strategies for bullet bonds and option-embedded corporate bonds are included. As will be demonstrated, DVBP-based hedging strategies are flexible and applicable to many different types of securities; however, ultimately, any hedging strategy has its limits in providing absolute price protection.

THE MECHANICS OF HEDGING

The goal of any hedging strategy is to minimize price volatility. Corporate bond prices are generally affected by movements in interest rates, changes in credit risk, changes in the price of credit risk, optionality, financing costs, supply, liquidity, event risk, perception of future growth, inflation, earnings, etc. Since movements in interest rates are the primary source of price volatility, this chapter will deal primarily with hedging interest rate risk. We will also discuss spread risk and techniques to mitigate the credit risk inherent in corporate securities. Many corporate securities contain embedded call or put options, or optional sinking fund provisions. These embedded options, in any form, affect pricing, and we will discuss how these risks can be mitigated.

A successful hedging strategy for a specific bond position or portfolio has several components that can be broken down as follows:

- identify the sources of price volatility
- determine the amount of price volatility that is acceptable
- find the appropriate hedge instrument
- determine the optimal position in the hedge instrument
- analyze the cost and effectiveness of the hedge strategy

---

[2] For more information on the basics of hedging fixed-income securities, see Shrikant Ramamurthy, "The Basics of Cash Market Hedging," Chapter 10 in Frank J. Fabozzi (ed.), *Perspectives on Interest Rate Risk Management for Money Managers and Traders* (New Hope, PA: Frank J. Fabozzi Associates, 1998). For more information on hedging with interest rate swaps, see Shrikant Ramamurthy, "Hedging Fixed-Income Securities with Interest-Rate Swaps," Chapter 11 in *Perspectives on Interest Rate Risk Management for Money Managers and Traders*. For more information on hedging in the asset/liability context, see Anand K. Bhattacharya, Edward Fitzgerald, and Shrikant Ramamurthy, "Risk Management in an Asset/Liability Framework," Chapter 8 in Frank J. Fabozzi and Atsuo Konishi (eds.), *The Handbook of Asset/Liability Management*, (Chicago, IL: Probus Publishing, 1996).

Identifying the Sources of Price Risk

The first step in hedging a security is determining the factors that contribute to its price fluctuations. Typically for corporate securities, changes in interest rates and credit spreads are the primary factors that affect prices. For example, a short-term corporate bond's price changes as short-term interest rates change, or as perceptions of the issuer's credit quality changes. On a long-term corporate bond, prices change as long-term rates change or as long-term corporate credit spreads change.

For an option-embedded corporate bond, interest rates affect not only the bond component of the security, but also the option component. For example, a callable bond can be decomposed into a bullet bond position with the same maturity and a short position in a call option. That is,

$$\text{Callable Bond} = \text{Bullet Bond (to Maturity date)} - \text{Call option} \tag{1}$$

A put bond can be decomposed into a bullet bond of the same maturity and a long put option position on the underlying bullet bond. That is,

$$\text{Put Bond} = \text{Bullet Bond (to Maturity date)} + \text{Put option} \tag{2}$$

For option-embedded bonds, interest rates affect both the value of the bullet bond and the option. For a callable bond, as rates rise, the value of the bullet bond falls; however, the value of the option also falls, dampening the decrease in the value of the callable bond. Similarly, when rates decline, the increase in the value of a callable bond is dampened by an increase in the value of the embedded call option. For put bonds, as rates rise, the value of the bullet bond falls; however, the value of the put option increases, which dampens the decrease in the value of the put bond. When hedging option-embedded corporate securities, the effects of interest rate movements on optionality need to be explicitly accounted. For option-embedded bonds, the shape of the yield curve and movements in volatility also affect the value of the embedded option.

Once the sources of price risk have been identified, the next step is to determine the amount of price protection that is required from a hedge strategy. A perfect hedge will theoretically (but never practically) eliminate all price risk and, in effect, lock in the future price of a security under any scenario. Of course, in this circumstance, any price appreciation potential is also eliminated. The elimination of all risk eliminates all the potential return as well. The goal of a hedge strategy may instead be to eliminate some, but not all, price uncertainty in order to achieve some incremental return. A hedge alters the risk/return profile of a portfolio and, by adjusting the amount invested in the hedge instrument, an appropriate risk/return profile can be derived and maintained.

Determining the Appropriate Hedge Position

Once the sources of price risk and the amount of risk to be hedged have been determined, the next steps are to find appropriate hedge instruments and to determine the appropriate investment in the hedge instruments. The appropriate position in the hedge instrument is a function of the dollar-value-of-a-basis-point (DVBP) of both the security to be hedged and the hedge instrument.

The DVBP of a security is the security's price change for a 1 basis point change in interest rates. In other words, DVBP expresses a security's dollar sensitivity to interest rates. For a bullet bond with no embedded options, DVBP is a function of the duration and price of the security, and is given by,

$$DVBP = \frac{\text{Par amount} \times (\text{Price} + \text{Accrued}) \times \text{Modified duration}}{1,000,000} \tag{3}$$

Since the price movement for a bond is different for an increase or a decrease in interest rates due to the bond's convexity, the DVBP is effectively an average price change for a 1 basis point change in interest rates. Exhibit 1 shows the DVBP calculation for a $1 million position in a non-callable bond, in this case a 10-year corporate bond issued by Citicorp.

The implicit assumption in equation (3) is that the modified duration of a security accurately describes a security's percentage price change for a 1% change in interest rates and that interest rate movements and yield movements on the corporate security are simultaneous and identical. This typically is not true for option-embedded bonds and for bonds priced off two benchmark securities. For option-embedded bonds, the modified duration does not describe the price movement of the security as interest rates change. Also, movements in option-embedded bond yields are not identical to movements in interest rates. Generally, for a callable bond, yield movements are smaller than interest rate movements. If rates move 10 basis points, yields on callable bonds will move less than 10 basis points because of the changing value of the call option. Also, for a corporate bond priced off two benchmarks, say the average of the 5- and 10-year Treasury notes, the corporate bond's yield will change by only half a basis point for every basis point move in the 10-year Treasury.

Exhibit 1: DVBP Computation for $1 Million Par Amount of 10-Year Citicorp Notes

Issuer	Coupon (%)	Maturity (Yrs.)	Price ($)	Accrued ($)	Yield (%)	Spread (BPs)	Mod. Dur.
Citicorp	7.20	6/15/07	104.882	0.34	6.50	+75	6.837

$$DVBP = \frac{\text{Dollar par amount} \times (\text{Price} + \text{Accrued}) \times \text{Modified Duration}}{1,000,000}$$

$$= \frac{1,000,000 \times (104.882 + 0.34) \times 6.837}{1,000,000}$$

$$= \$719.40$$

* Price information as of 12/29/97.

Exhibit 2: DVBP Computation for $1 Million Par Amount of 10-Year Callable FNMA Notes

Issuer	Coupon (%)	Maturity (Yrs.)	Call Date (Yrs.)	Price ($)	Yield (%)	Spread (BPs)	OAS (BPs)
FNMA	6.65	1/19/07	1/19/00	99.78	6.68	+93	25

Constant-OAS Prices			
Yield Curve Shift	Price	Yield (%)	Spread (BPs)
Up 25 BPs	98.595	6.85	+85
Down 25 BPS	100.916	6.52	+102

$$DVBP = \frac{\text{Dollar par amount} \times \text{Change in Constant-OAS Price}}{\text{Yield-Curve Shift} \times 100}$$

$$= \frac{1,000,000 \times (100.916 - 98.595)}{50 \times 100}$$

$$= \$464.20$$

* Price information as of 12/20/97. Note: OASs computed at 14% volatility.

For option-embedded bonds and for any bond in general, including bullet bonds, the DVBP of a security is a function of the explicit price movements of the security to changes in interest rates. In its general form, DVBP can be defined as,

$$DVBP = \frac{\text{Dollar par amount} \times (\text{Change in constant-OAS price})}{\text{Yield curve shift in bps} \times 100} \tag{4}$$

In the above formulation, the DVBP explicitly accounts for the change in the value of a security due to the changing values of any embedded options. The price changes in equation (4) must be determined either from a theoretical model or empirically. Generally, when a model is used to generate prices under different rate scenarios, a constant-OAS pricing assumption is used, although any assumption can be used. For example, callable premiums currently trade at wider OASs than callable discounts. This market reality can be readily accounted for in the DVBP computation by using the appropriate OASs in computing the respective scenario prices.

Typically, the DVBP for option-embedded bonds is computed assuming parallel interest rate shifts occurring in increments of 10 to 25 basis points. Exhibit 2 shows the computation of the DVBP of a 10-year FNMA issue that is callable after three years. Notice in the example that, as interest rates move 25 basis points, the yield on the FNMA callable changes by less than 25 basis points.

The Hedge Ratio

Once the DVBP of the security to be hedged has been determined, the next step is to find an appropriate hedge instrument and to determine the appropriate position in the hedge instrument. The hedge ratio describes the appropriate position in a hedge instrument and is a function of the DVBP of both the security being hedged and the hedge instrument. The position in the hedge instrument is determined such that the change in the market value of the hedge instrument is equal to the change in the market value of the position being hedged for a given change in rates. A hedge is implemented by taking an opposite position in the hedge instrument. Mathematically the hedge ratio is given by,

$$\text{Hedge ratio} = \frac{\text{DVBP of security to be hedged}}{\text{DVBP of hedge instrument}} \qquad (5)$$

Typically the hedge ratio is computed using the DVBP for a $1 million par amount of the underlying security. If many units of a security are to be hedged, multiplying the hedge ratio by the number of units to be hedged will determine the position needed in the hedge instrument.

CHOOSING A HEDGE INSTRUMENT

For hedging corporate securities, many different types of hedge instruments can be utilized, including cash market securities, like Treasury notes, and other instruments, like futures contracts and interest rate swaps. In the following sections we discuss the hedging implications of using these instruments.

Cash Market Securities

The most common instruments used for hedging in the cash market are Treasury securities. Since most corporate securities are priced off Treasury securities, using similar Treasuries as hedge instruments provides ideal protection against interest rate risk. Also, Treasury securities have no credit risk and are extremely liquid. From a hedge implementation standpoint, using Treasuries is fairly simple. The DVBP of a bullet Treasury is given by equation (3) and the hedge ratio is given by equation (5).

There can be disadvantages to using Treasuries as hedge instruments. First, many corporate bonds are priced off on-the-run Treasury securities that may be on "special." For example, the 10-year Treasury note currently is on special. When a security is on special, it is in short supply and is expensive to borrow in the repo markets. As a result, the financing income that can be earned from a short position is greatly reduced, which increases the cost of hedging.

Another disadvantage is that Treasury securities are on-balance-sheet items, unlike futures contracts and swaps, which, for some market participants, may have capital structure implications. A third negative with using Treasury securities to hedge is that they only provide protection against interest rate risk and no protection against spread risk. In spite of these limitations, Treasuries are the most common hedge instruments, especially for hedging individual positions.

Futures Instruments

Treasury futures contracts are available on 2-, 5-, and 10-year notes, as well as on the long bond. These contracts are actively traded and are widely used for hedging. The contracts are based on hypothetical 8% coupon bearing instruments maturing in 2, 5, 10, and 20 years. The bond, 10- and 5-year note contracts are the most liquid futures contracts.

Treasury futures contracts contain several timing and delivery options that complicate scenario pricing and DVBP computations. Treasury futures contracts require physical delivery at maturity. The seller has the right to deliver any one of many securities during a designated time period. As a result, a Treasury futures contract will track the one cash security that is cheapest to deliver (CTD) against the contract. As rates change, however, the CTD security also may change. Generally, low duration issues tend to be CTD when rates are low and high duration issues tend to be CTD when rates are high. A futures contract tends to lose duration in a rallying market and gain duration in a bear market, making the contract a negatively convex security.

The DVBP of a futures contract needs to be computed using a model that explicitly accounts for the changing values of the options embedded in the futures contract. As a quick and simple approximation, the DVBP of the CTD security (after adjusting for the conversion factor) is sometimes used to represent the DVBP of a futures contract. This approximation is more appropriate when the CTD security is unlikely to change, even for large moves in rates, as is currently the case for the 10- and 30-year futures contracts.

Hedging with futures has several advantages/disadvantages relative to hedging with cash instruments. One advantage is that, because a futures contract typically tracks an off-the-run Treasury issue,[3] the sometimes prohibitive cost of shorting on-the-run Treasuries that are on special is reduced. Furthermore, a futures contract enables a hedger to participate in the off-the-run market, using a more liquid instrument than off-the-run Treasuries. This is especially useful when hedging corporates that are priced to off-the-run Treasuries.

The major disadvantage of using a futures contract versus a Treasury security is basis risk. Basis risk, in the context of hedging with futures, refers to the scenario in which movements in futures prices do not correspond to movements in cash prices. A futures contract's price movements are largely related to price movements in the Treasury security that is the cheapest to deliver into the futures contract. Typically, the CTD security is not an on-the-run Treasury security. Thus, when hedging a security that is priced to an on-the-run Treasury with a futures contract, there is risk that movements in futures prices will not fully hedge price movements in the security that is being hedged. Currently, the CTD issue for the 10-year futures contract is the Treasury 7.875% coupon of 11/04, a 7-year security. To the extent that 7- and 10-year Treasury rates do not move in unison, hedging a 10-year corporate bond with 10-year futures contracts will be less effective.

Generally speaking, futures contracts are used in hedging bond portfolios rather than individual positions. Futures are most useful when exposure to a cer-

---

[3] At the time of this writing, the CTD security on the March 1998 bond contract is the Treasury 11.25s of 2/15 and the CTD on the 10-year futures contract is the 7.875s of 11/04.

tain part of the curve, and not specifically to a particular Treasury, is required. Futures are used to hedge individual positions when liquidity is required, or if there are balance sheet or cost considerations associated with using Treasuries.

Interest Rate Swaps

To understand how interest rate swaps can be used as hedge instruments, it is useful to characterize swaps in an alternative fashion. An interest rate swap is a contractual agreement between two parties to exchange fixed and floating cash flows periodically. In a generic interest rate swap, one party agrees to pay a floating interest rate (typically based off LIBOR), while the counterparty agrees to pay a fixed rate of interest for a specified period of time, where the interest cash flows are computed off some notional amount.

The exchange of fixed and floating cash flows in a swap is equivalent to the cash flows from a long position in a fixed-rate bond, and a short position in a floating-rate bond. As a result, a swap can alternatively be viewed as a long position in a fixed-rate bond that is 100% financed at short-term interest rates, like term repurchase (repo) rates or LIBOR rates. The coupon cash flows on this portfolio replicate the cash flows on the swap, and the par amount that is received at maturity from the fixed-rate bond repays the borrowing used to finance the purchase of the fixed-rate bond. Essentially, a swap in the hedging context can be viewed as a financed fixed-rate bond.

Swaps are priced on a spread basis relative to Treasuries like most corporate securities. As a result, swaps can serve as an alternate hedging instrument to Treasury securities and futures contracts. Interest rate swaps have many advantages over Treasuries. First, interest rate swaps are off the balance sheet. Second, when an off-the-run maturity needs to be hedged, or when the hedge instrument is a Treasury security that is on special, a swap can be a less expensive hedging instrument. Swaps can be structured for any maturity, and are not constrained by any supply issues. Currently there are over $5 trillion in notional amount of U.S. dollar swaps outstanding. Third, since swaps are priced off Treasury securities, swaps provide the same protection from interest rate risk as Treasury securities. In addition, to the extent that swap spreads (the spreads between swap rates and similar maturity Treasuries) are correlated with corporate spreads, interest rate swaps will provide additional price protection over Treasuries.

Interest rate swaps have advantages over interest rate futures contracts in the context of hedging fixed income securities. Swaps are available for any maturity; however, exchange-traded futures contracts[4] have limited maturities. Also, hedging with futures contracts, as discussed earlier, exposes the hedged portfolio to basis risk.

The disadvantage of using swaps as hedge instruments is lack of liquidity. Bid/offer spreads in the swap market can amount to a few basis points in yield and

---

[4] Our discussion on futures is limited to the 2-year, 5-year, 10-year and bond futures contracts and do not include Eurodollar futures contracts. Eurodollar futures are a proxy for interest rate swaps and can be used to synthetically create swap positions.

swaps are not readily tradeable instruments. Usually, an interest rate swap agreement cannot be traded to another party without the prior approval of the original counterparty to the swap. As a result, swaps at times are not traded and are instead liquidated at their market value when a party to the swap wants to cancel the swap arrangement.

In general, interest rate swaps are useful in managing the overall interest rate risk of a portfolio and are less useful in managing the interest rate risk of an individual position. Also, swap spreads are correlated with generic corporate bond spreads but not with specific corporate credit spreads. Thus, swaps will be more effective in providing a hedge against portfolio credit risk.

The mechanics of hedging with swaps are similar to that of using any other instrument, except care must be taken in computing and understanding the DVBP of a swap. The DVBP of a swap can be shown to be equal to,[5]

$$DVBP \text{ (Swap)} = DVBP \text{ (Fixed-rate bond)} - DVBP \text{ (Floating-rate bond)} \quad (6)$$

In general, the DVBP of a swap is approximately equal to the DVBP of a fixed-rate bond with maturity spanning from the next reset date to the maturity date of the swap. The DVBP of a 5-year swap is similar to the DVBP of a 4.75-year fixed-rate bond; the DVBP of a 2.25-year swap is similar to the DVBP of a 2-year fixed-rate bond.

Although the DVBP of a swap is similar to that of a slightly shorter fixed-rate bond, it will change differently over time than the DVBP of a fixed-rate bond. This is very important to note in the hedging context. The DVBP of a swap just prior to a reset date will be identical to the DVBP of a fixed-rate bond because the DVBP of the floater at this time is zero. However, just after the reset date, the floater will have a DVBP that is similar to the DVBP of a fixed-rate bond that matures on the next reset date. As a result, the DVBP on a swap will immediately decline by the DVBP of the floater just after the reset date. Between reset periods, the DVBP of the swap will not change much as both the DVBP of the fixed-rate bond and that of the floater will decline in similar fashion. This is very different from the DVBP of a fixed-rate bond, which declines steadily over time.

Exhibit 3 graphically displays over time the DVBP for a 2-year swap and a fixed-rate bond. The DVBP of the fixed-rate bond declines as a function of time, while the DVBP of the swap declines in a jump fashion around the quarterly reset date of the floating rate on the swap. The DVBP of the swap between reset dates is relatively stable and actually increases incrementally as the next reset date approaches. This is because the DVBP of a floating-rate note declines slightly faster than the DVBP of a fixed-rate note during these time periods.[6]

---

[5] For more information on the pricing and interest rate sensitivity of interest rate swaps, see David Audley, Richard Chin, and Shrikant Ramamurthy, "The Interest-Rate Swap Market: Valuation, Applications and Perspectives," *Fixed- Income Research*, Prudential Securities Incorporated, April 1994.

[6] The modified duration and DVBP of a bond is a concave monotonic function of maturity (i.e., the duration and DVBP increase at a decreasing rate as a function of maturity). As a result, the DVBP of a floating-rate bond, which behaves essentially like a short dated fixed-rate bond, decreases faster over time than the DVBP of a long dated fixed-rate bond.

Exhibit 3: DVBP of a 2-Year Swap and Fixed-Rate Bond over Time

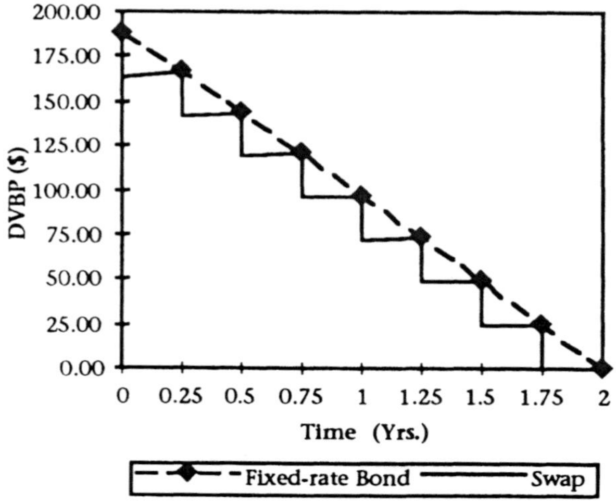

HEDGING APPLICATIONS

In this section, we apply the hedging concepts discussed herein to hedge a bullet corporate security and a callable corporate security. Treasuries, futures contracts, and swaps are each used as hedge instruments, although, only one of these instruments will be most appropriate in an actual application.

Bullet-Bond Hedge

Exhibit 4 displays a hedge for the Citicorp 7.20s of 6/07. For a long $10 million position in Citicorp notes, either $9.67 million in Treasury notes or $10.11 million in swaps need to be shorted as a hedge. If futures contracts are used, the hedge would utilize 123 10-year futures contracts, where each futures contract requires the delivery of $100,000 par amount of eligible Treasury notes. These hedge ratios are a function of the respective DVBPs of the individual instruments, and equation (5).

As can be seen from Exhibit 4, all three hedge instruments provide protection against interest rate risk. If rates move 50 basis points, the unhedged Citicorp notes can gain or lose more than $350,000. If the Citicorp position is hedged with Treasuries or swaps, the price variation of the portfolio is minimized to under $1,100 in a 50 basis point range for rates. If futures are used, the hedged position actually gains $1,000 to $2,000 in scenarios where rates rise or fall by 50 basis points.

Exhibit 4: Hedging a Corporate Bullet Bond

Objective: Hedge $10 million of Citicorp 7.20s of 6/07.

Issuer	Coupon (%)	Maturity	Price ($)	Yield (%)	Spread (BPs)	DVBP ($)	Hedge Ratio
Citicorp	7.20	6/15/07	104.882	6.50	+75	719.40	—
Hedge Instruments							
10-Yr. Treasuries	6.125	8/15/07	102-22+	5.75	—	743.70	0.967
10-Yr. Futures	—	3/20/98	112-05	—	—	58.60	12.300
10-Yr. Swap	—	1/02/08	0.00	—	+48	711.60	1.011

	Change in Portfolio Value	
	Rates Decrease 50 BPs	Rates Increase 50 BPs
Unhedged Portfolio	367,500	-352,200
Hedge w/ Treasuries	340	-907
Hedge w/ Futures	960	2,040
Hedge w/ Swaps	-807	-1,079

* Price information as of 12/29/97.

While the hedges in Exhibit 4 clearly limit price movements in the Citicorp hedged position, none of the hedges are "perfect" hedges. This is so for several reasons. First, the hedge ratios that are used have been rounded and are not exact. Second, the prices on 10-year Treasuries and futures have been rounded to the nearest 64th to reflect trading convention. A third reason that the hedges are not perfect is because of the effect that convexity has on DVBP.

A non-callable bond's price will change more for a given decrease in interest rates than for the same magnitude increase in rates due to its positive convexity. Since the DVBP of a bond is computed using the average price change for a 1 basis point change in interest rates, the hedge ratio will never be the exact ratio needed (although it will be very close) for a given realization of interest rate change. If there is a strong opinion about the general direction of future interest rate movements, then the hedge ratio could be adjusted appropriately for the given directionality in interest rates, and a more efficient hedge could be constructed. Generally, however, for modest interest rate movements, this convexity effect is not large.

The futures based hedge in Exhibit 4 is the best hedge for two reasons. Generally, because a futures contract provides the seller the right to deliver any one of several bonds into the contract, a futures contract has negatively convex price characteristics; that is, futures tend to lose duration in market rallies and gain duration when interest rates rise. This is an advantage in the hedging context where futures contracts are sold as hedge instruments. A second reason that futures contracts look attractive in hedging the Citicorp notes is because the analysis of the hedge does not account for any basis risk. If the 7- to 10-year part of the Treasury yield curve steepened or flattened, the futures hedge in Exhibit 4 would be far less successful in hedging interest rate risk than the other instruments.

Spread Risk

One important assumption that has been made in the hedging analysis thus far is that credit spreads remain constant. This may not be the case. The pricing spread associated with any security can change as interest rates change or as the perceived credit risk of the issuer changes. Other event-related risk can also affect the pricing spread. A good case in point is the sell-off in the corporate market due to the turmoil in Asia in late 1997/earlier 1998.

Yield spread risk that is due to event risk is difficult to hedge. However, general sector risks may be hedged to an extent if they are properly anticipated. Upcoming problems in particular sectors can sometimes be anticipated by examining trends in the economy or interest rates, or by anticipating the effects of upcoming changes in regulations, political structure, etc. In these scenarios, and in situations in which portfolio managers wish to maintain holdings in corporate securities, the effect of widening spreads may be mitigated by buying put options on a sector index, by shorting a basket of stocks in the sector or by taking a position in any portfolio that will be similarly affected by such changes. These positions would be in addition to any positions used to hedge interest rate risk.

Yield spread risk due to changing interest rates may be mitigated if there is a known correlation between the direction and magnitude of interest rate moves and spread changes. If spreads widen when the market rallies and spreads tighten when the market sells off, then the price volatility associated with these spread changes can be reduced by shorting fewer Treasury securities than the number given by the hedge ratio.

Among all the interest rate hedge instruments available, interest rate swaps probably provide the best protection against spread risk. Generally, swap spreads move in the same direction as corporate spreads, although the degree and timing of movements are not always symmetric. To the extent that a corporate portfolio's spread is positively correlated with swap spreads, swaps will provide protection against spread risk and be more effective hedging instruments than futures or Treasury notes.

In general, the effects of yield spread changes can be accommodated into a hedging strategy. However, in the short run, pricing spreads are generally not volatile, and the risks that yield spreads will change dramatically may not be an overriding factor in the hedging context.

Hedging Option-Embedded Bonds

Option-embedded bonds, such as callable bonds or put bonds, can be hedged using basically the same approach as that for bullet bonds. Since yield spreads on option-embedded bonds change as interest rates change due to the changing value of the embedded option, the DVBP on an option-embedded bond needs to explicitly account for these changes. A constant-OAS approach to determining the DVBP for an option-embedded bond is one approach that explicitly accounts for the changing value of any embedded options. A non-constant OAS assumption can also be utilized in computing DVBP if such an assumption better reflects the expected trading characteristics of a security.

Exhibit 5 displays a hedge for FNMA 6.65s of 1/07 that are callable from 1/00. The DVBP of the FNMA callable is $464.20 per $1 million par amount, and the DVBP is the average price change for a 1 basis point change in interest rates. For $10 million FNMA callables, a hedge can be constructed by either shorting $6.24 million 10-year Treasuries or by shorting $6.52 million notional amount of 10-year swaps. If futures contracts are used, 79 contracts are required. Notice that for the FNMA callable, each of the hedge ratios are much smaller than the hedge ratios used for hedging the Citicorp bullet bonds in the earlier example. Callable bonds have lower durations than similar maturity bullet bonds because of the embedded short call option position, which results in callable bonds having less price sensitivity and smaller hedge ratios than bullet bonds.

If the FNMA callable is not hedged, the position can vary in value substantially for a 50 basis point move in rates. If rates rise by 50 basis points, the position will decline in value by $352,000. If rates decline by 50 basis points, it will gain in value by $221,600. If the position is hedged using either Treasury notes, futures contracts or swaps, the variation in portfolio value for a 50 basis point move in rates is reduced to approximately $15,000. The best performing hedge instrument is the futures contract, again because of the small amount of negative convexity in the futures contract. The futures contract, like the FNMA callable, loses duration in a rallying market and gains duration when rates rise, which provides for a more effective hedge. The futures contract does not provide a perfect hedge because the FNMA callable is more negatively convex than the 10-year futures contract.

Exhibit 5: Hedging an Agency Callable Bond

Objective: Hedge $10 million of FNMA 6.65s of 1/07.

Issuer	Coupon (%)	Maturity	Call Date	Price ($)	Yield (%)	Spread (BPs)	DVBP ($)	Hedge Ratio
FNMA	6.65	1/19/07	1/19/00	99.78	6.68	+93	464.20	—
Hedge Instruments								
10-Yr. Treasuries	6.125	8/15/07	—	102-22+	5.75	—	743.70	0.624
10-Yr. Futures	—	3/20/98	—	112-05	—	—	58.60	7.900
10-Yr. Swap	—	1/02/98	—	0.00	—	+48	711.60	0.652

	Change in Portfolio Value	
	Rates Decrease 50 BPs	Rates Increase 50 BPs
Unhedged Portfolio	221,600	−352,200
Hedge w/ Treasuries	−15,325	−14,612
Hedge w/ Futures	−13,820	−13,780
Hedge w/ Swaps	−15,924	−14,860

* Prices as of 12/29/97.

Hedging Considerations for Option-Embedded Notes

In general, for any option-embedded security, including corporate callable notes, the hedge ratio will change as interest rates change. For example, as the market rallies and continues to rally, callable spreads will continue widening and the hedge ratio for a callable note will decline. If rates rise, then the hedge ratio will increase.

The hedge ratio using Treasury notes, swaps or even futures contracts at current levels, is not static because callable notes are negatively convex instruments, while Treasuries and swaps are positively convex instruments and futures are less negatively convex instruments.[7] As rates rally, Treasury prices rise at a faster rate than callable bond prices and the position in the hedge instrument consequently needs to be reduced. For example, if rates rally 25 basis points, the hedge needs to reduced by buying back some of the short position in the hedging instrument. If this adjustment is not made, then the hedge will not provide absolute price protection and, in fact, may over- or under-hedge a position. The hedges in Exhibit 5 are not perfect hedges because the hedges were constructed for 25 basis point movements in rates, but were evaluated assuming that rates moved by 50 basis points without any adjustment to the hedge positions.

An alternative way to hedge option-embedded notes is to use bullets like Treasuries or swaps to hedge just the bullet component and to use options to hedge the option component. This type of hedge will not need to be monitored as frequently and the hedge ratio will be less volatile as like securities are being hedged with like securities. An alternative to this approach is to use callable swaps. A callable swap is a swap in which one party has the right to terminate the swap prior to maturity. Since a callable swap has an embedded long position in a call position, this may be a more natural and efficient way to hedge a callable security that has a short position in a call option. However, for hedging an option-embedded security for short time horizons like a week or a month, the use of options or callable swaps in a hedging strategy can be expensive given the reduced liquidity in these markets. Typically, individual option-embedded bonds are hedged using just Treasuries or futures, with the hedge ratio adjusted periodically for interest rate movements.

A second consideration in the hedging analysis presented here is the assumption of constant OAS in determining the DVBP and associated hedge ratio. The use of a constant OAS assumption in this chapter was made more for simplicity. OASs are not constant in the marketplace and may change as rates change. For example, in the federal agency debt market, OASs for similar-duration premiums are much wider than for discounts. This market dynamic can be explicitly accounted for in the DVBP approach by using different OASs to compute the scenario prices in equation (5). Also, the use of an empirical hedge ratio, where historical data are used to compute a hedge ratio, would implicitly account for

---

[7] At current levels, the optionality in most financial futures contracts is limited.

changing OASs in different environments.[8] However, to the extent that history may not be a gauge for the future trading characteristics of a security, an empirical hedge ratio may be less useful.

Another consideration to keep in mind is that any option-embedded bond's price is dependent on factors other than just credit risk and changes in the yield of the pricing instrument. These factors include the shape of the curve and volatility. As volatility increases, callable spreads widen and put bond spreads tighten to reflect the higher cost of the embedded option.[9] The hedging analysis presented in this chapter does not hedge this volatility risk. Effectively, the hedging example for the FNMA callable maintains a short position in volatility. If volatility rises in our example, the callable bond's price will decline with no change in the value of the hedge instruments. If volatility risk is of concern, the use of options is necessary in any hedging strategy. If changes in volatility can be anticipated as interest rates move, then this can be accounted for by under or over utilizing a hedge. In this type of application, the DVBP of a security would be computed using scenario-based volatility levels to compute scenario prices.

The shape of the curve is also an important determinant of callable spreads. The hedge ratios described in this chapter are based on parallel interest rate movements and do not account for the effects of a change in the shape of curve. Generally, as the curve flattens, callable spreads widen, and if the curve steepens callable spreads tighten.[10] For example, spreads on a 10-year maturity bond callable after three years (10/NC-3Y) will widen if 3-year yields rise and 10-year yields remain unchanged. Ten-year hedging instruments will not provide any price protection when 10/NC-3Y prices fall in this environment.

To hedge yield curve risk for option-embedded securities, it is best to use multiple hedge instruments from all the parts of the curve that affect the pricing of the security being hedged. In the case of the 10/NC-3Y, both 3-year and 10-year instruments would be appropriate. The hedge ratio relative to the 3-year part of the curve can be computed by using a DVBP for the 10/NC-3Y that is computed by assuming that only Treasury yields three years and in change, while the rest of the yield curve remains unchanged. Similarly, the hedge ratio relative to the 10-year part of the curve can be computed by using the DVBP of the 10/NC-3Y that is computed by assuming that Treasury yields three years and in do not change, while yields on the longer end of the curve change. This type of strategy

---

[8] As an alternative to model determined hedge ratios (also known as theoretical hedge ratios), hedge ratios can also be empirically determined. Empirical hedge ratios are typically determined by regressing recent price changes on the security to be hedged on price changes of the hedging instruments.

[9] Callable spreads can widen 3 to 8 basis points for a 100 basis point increase in volatility. For more information on the effects of the volatility on callable spreads, see Shrikant Ramamurthy, "Federal Agency Debt," *Spread Talk*, Fixed-Income Research, Prudential Securities Incorporated, February 21, 1997.

[10] Callable spreads can widen two to five basis points for every ten basis points of curve flattening. For more information on the effects of the shape of the curve on callable spreads, see Shrikant Ramamurthy, "Federal Agency Debt," *Spread Talk*, Fixed-Income Research, Prudential Securities Incorporated, March 21, 1997.

would provide hedge exposure to multiple parts of the curve and would be effective for both parallel and non-parallel yield curve shifts.

Typically, for individual bond positions, yield curve risk is generally not accounted for in a hedging strategy. Instead, the pricing benchmark is used as a hedging instrument and the hedge ratio is adjusted to account for a particular view on the future shape of the yield curve. As in the case of hedging spread, OAS or volatility risk, this is more art than science. In the final analysis, the DVBP that is used to compute a hedge ratio needs to reflect the anticipated price behavior of a security (incorporating any views on spreads, curve, and volatility) and, to that extent, should reflect both theory and market reality. These combined approaches should work together to produce a more effective hedge.

SUMMARY

Hedging price volatility is a very important function in the fixed income marketplace. This chapter has provided an introduction to hedging corporate bullet and callable securities using Treasury notes, futures contracts, and interest rate swaps. The basic procedure for constructing a hedge starts by correctly identifying the sources of price risk including the effects of interest rates, the curve, volatility, and spread movements. A hedge is constructed by taking an opposite position in a hedge instrument with similar price sensitivity to the security to be hedged.

The appropriate position in the hedge instrument is a function of the DVBP of both the security being hedged and the hedge instrument. The DVBP of any security is effectively an average price change for a 1 basis point change in rates and should incorporate any spread/OAS changes that are anticipated in different rate environments. In the context of the above framework, DVBP is a very flexible tool and also can incorporate other factors that may be important in the hedge strategy. Once a hedge is constructed and implemented, it needs to be monitored over time. The DVBP of a security, the hedge vehicle, and the hedge ratio will change over time and as interest rates change. An effective hedge strategy should reflect this dynamic behavior to the highest extent possible and may need to be adjusted periodically.

Among the hedge instruments generally used in hedging applications, Treasuries are the most common for obvious reasons. Treasury notes are very liquid and, since most corporate notes are benchmarked off Treasury notes, Treasuries provide the best price protection against interest rate risk. Futures contracts are also desirable hedge instruments because they are very liquid and are off-balance-sheet instruments. In addition, the negative convexity embedded in a futures contract has positive implications in the hedging context. The biggest negative in using futures contracts for hedging corporate securities is the exposure to basis risk, which reflects the risk that price movements in the futures position may not reflect price movements in the underlying security that is being hedged. This typically happens when the curve steepens or flattens.

Interest rate swaps are also off-balance-sheet instruments and, given their customized nature, offer tremendous flexibility as hedge instruments. To the extent that swap spreads are correlated with corporate spreads, swaps often can reduce spread risk in addition to hedging interest rate risk. When Treasuries are on special, swaps and futures have the added advantage of being cheaper hedge instruments. The disadvantage to using swaps is that they are less liquid than Treasuries or futures. Therefore, swaps may be more appropriate for longer-term hedging applications. Also, given that swap spreads are correlated to generic corporate spreads and not to individual credit spreads, swaps are more appropriate for hedging corporate portfolios rather than individual positions.

Chapter 20

Valuation and Portfolio Risk Management with Mortgage-Backed Securities

Stavros A. Zenios, Ph.D.
Professor of Management Science
University of Cyprus

INTRODUCTION

Mortgage-backed securities (MBS) are complex and difficult to value because they embody features of both bonds and options. The homeowner's ability to *prepay* outstanding principal represents a call option on the underlying mortgage. For any specific mortgage within a pool, it is uncertain whether this call option will be exercised and, if so, when. Many factors outside the charactestics of the pool can also affect the option's value. These include the level, structure and history of interest rates, the market's perception of future interest rates, and total and disposable consumer income. Adding to the complexity has been the constant stream of innovative new derivative securities based on MBS, the risk and return characteristics of which may bear little resemblance to the original security.

Valuation of a MBS involves relating possible future paths of interest rates to the cash flows generated by the security. The valuation should take into account both principal and interest payments, as well as the possibility of prepayment of the mortgage (i.e., exercise of the underlying call option). The analysis is carried out using simulations, which generate paths of interest rates, usually in monthly intervals for a period of 30 years until maturity of the underlying mortgage loans.

The general framework of the valuation analysis has three phases.

Phase I. Generate arbitrage free interest rate scenarios consistent with the prevailing term structure of interest rates.

Phase II. Generate cash flows for each interest rate scenario. This requires a model that can project the prepayment activity of homeowners under a host of economic conditions.

Phase III. Use the cash flows and the short-term interest rates along each path to compute expected net present value of the cash flows (i.e., the *price*), and the usual derivatives (i.e., *duration* and *convexity*) or to compute an *option-adjusted premium* over the Treasury yield curve.

Phase III can be easily extended to calculate *holding-period returns*. This analysis projects the return of the MBS under a range of economic scenarios for a target holding period. Armed with the wealth of information about the pool's behavior generated in Phase III we can then address issues of portfolio management for large protfolios of MBS.

In this chapter we discuss both valuation and portfolio risk management techniques. We assume throughout that readers are familiar with the calculations required to estimate the principal and interest payment of an MBS. Cash flow calculations for a given prepayment are also assumed known.

VALUATION TECHNIQUES

Pricing

A fair price for a fixed-income security can be obtained as the expected discounted value of its cash flows, with discounting done at the risk-free rate.[1] The pricing model is based on Monte Carlo simulation of the term-structure which is used to generate paths of risk-free rates.[2] The security cash flows for each path are then generated and the present value of these discounted cash flows can be computed and averaged, thus estimating the fair market value of the projected cash flow streams. This is, in turn, the fair price for the security.

To make this idea precise we need to hypothesize first a model of the term structure of interest rates. We use here a binomial lattice model[3] such as the one illustrated in Exhibit 1. The lattice discretizes the time horizon from 0 to T into, say, monthly steps and it assumes that the short-term rates at each step can move to one of two possible states (UP or DOWN). All possible states of the binomial lattice can be described using a series of *base* rates $\{r_{0t}, t=0,1,..., T\}$, and *volatilities* $\{k_t, t=0,1, ..., T\}$. The short-term rate at any state σ of the binomial lattice at some point t is then given by

$$r_t^\sigma = r_t^0 (k_t)^\sigma$$

---

[1] See John C. Cox, Jr. Jonathan E. Ingersoll, and Stephen A. Ross, "A Theory of the Term Structure of Interest Rates," *Econometrica* (March 1985), pp. 385-407.

[2] The use of Monte Carlo simulations for options pricing was pioneered by P. Boyle, "Options: A Monte Carlo Approach," *Journal of Financial Economics* (May 1977), pp. 323-338. See J.M. Hutchinson and S.A. Zenios, "Financial Simulations on a Massively Parallel Connection Machine," *International Journal of Supercomputer Applications* (1991), Vol. 5, pp. 27-45, for its application to the pricing of mortgage securities.

[3] See F. Black, E. Derman, and W. Toy, "A One-Factor Model of Interest Rates and its Application to Treasury Bond Options," *Financial Analysts Journal* (Jan./Feb. 1990), pp. 33-39.

Exhibit 1: A Binomial Lattice of Interest Rates

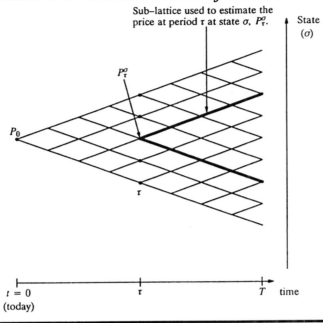

The base rate and volatility parameters of the model are calibrated using market data. In particular, for the model we have assumed (i.e., Black-Derman-Toy) we need as input the term structure of interest rates ($\{r_t\}$, $t=1,2,...,T$) and the term structure of interest rate volatilities.

Let S_0 denote a set of interest rate scenarios that emanate from the current, zero, state of the binomial lattice. Let also r_t^s be the short-term discount rate at time period t associated with scenario $s \in S_0$, and C_{jt}^s be the cash flow generated by security j at period t, under the given scenario. A fair price for the security is given by

$$P_{j0} = \frac{1}{|S_0|} \sum_{s=1}^{|S_0|} \sum_{t=1}^{T} \frac{C_{jt}^s}{\prod_{i=1}^{t}(1 + r_i^s)} \tag{1}$$

This is the fundamental pricing equation that provides the basis for more advanced valuation tools developed later. We point out that this equation can be easily extended to price the security at some future time period τ, conditioned on the state of the lattice at that period. (See equation (3) below and the discussion that follows.)

It is also worth noting the computational complexity of this equation. The number of paths emanating from the origin of a binomial lattice is 2^T, which is an extremely large number even for moderate time horizons T. While for simple securities, such as straight bonds, we can simply compute discounted cash flows at the vertices of the lattice (and there are only $T^2/2$ vertices), for MBS we need to examine paths of interest rates. This is so because the cash flows generated by a MBS depend not only on the current level of interest rates but also on the path that interest rates followed from the origination of the MBS until the present. This *path-dependence* is a result of the prepayment activity of the MBS. Hence, we cannot avoid working with paths of interest rates obtained from the binomial lattice. We hasten to add, however, that it is possible to work only with a small sample of paths using techniques from statistical sampling. The use of high-performance computers and networks of workstations also speeds up substantially the computations[4] and such pricing calculations are now performed routinely by institutions dealing with MBS.

Option-Adjusted Premia

Most fixed-income securities cannot be priced using the riskless discount rates implied by the Treasury yield curve, as we did in equation (1). In particular, the price of the security has to reflect the credit, liquidity, default, and prepayment risks associated with this instrument. In order to value the risks associated with a fixed-income instrument we compute an *option-adjusted premium* (OAP).[5] The OAP analysis estimates the multiplicative adjustment factor for the Treasury rates that will equate today's (observed) market price with the "fair" price obtained by computing the expected present value of the cash flows. The discrepancy between the market price and the theoretical price is due to the various risks that are present in most fixed-income securities, but are not present in the Treasury market. Hence, this analysis will price the risks.

The OAP for a given security, denoted by ρ_j, is estimated based on the current market price, P_{j0}. In particular, it is the solution of the following nonlinear equation in ρ_j

$$P_{j0} = \frac{1}{|S_0|} \sum_{s=1}^{|S_0|} \sum_{t=1}^{T} \frac{C_{jt}^s}{\prod_{i=1}^{t}(1 + \rho_j r_i^s)} \tag{2}$$

Now, however, we have what appears at first glance to be a gap in our analysis: in order to price the security we need the option-adjusted premium, while the option-adjusted premium is calculated using the market price of the security. Indeed, it is impossible to price a security unless we know the risks associated with it. However, for securities as complex as MBS we need to resort to market information to determine the appropriate risk premium. The typical remedy in

---

[4] See L.D. Cagan, N.S. Carriero, and S.A. Zenios, "Computer Network Approach to Pricing Mortgage-Backed Securities," *Financial Analysts Journal* (March/April 1993), pp. 55-62.

[5] See D.F. Babbel and S.A. Zenios, "Pitfalls in the Analysis of Option-Adjusted Spreads," *Financial Analysts Journal* (July/August 1992), pp. 65-69, or Y. Ben-Dov, L. Hayre, and V. Pica, "Mortgage Valuation Models at Prudential Securities," *Interfaces*, 22 (1992), pp. 55-71.

completing the gap of our analysis is to use market prices for actively traded MBS to determine the OAP for a broad family of similar MBS, and then use this premium to price new securities, or securities with similar risk characteristics. Furthermore, differences in the OAP values of similar securities are used as indicators for identifying mispriced securities.

Once we have priced the various risks associated with the security we can proceed to price the security at some future time period, τ, conditional on the state σ of the lattice. Assuming a set $S\sigma$ of interest rate scenarios emanating from the state σ at period τ, the option-adjusted price of the security, $P_{j\tau}^{\sigma}$, can be calculated using a simple modification of equation (2) as:

$$P_{j\tau}^{\sigma} = \frac{1}{|S_0|} \sum_{s=1}^{|S_0|} \sum_{t=1}^{T} \frac{c_{jt}^{s}}{\prod_{i=\tau}^{t}(1 + \rho_j r_i^s)} \tag{3}$$

We point out that the price $P_{j\tau}^{\sigma}$ does not depend only on the state σ but also on the history of interest rates from $t = 0$ to $t = \tau$ that pass through this state.[6] We could now sample paths from $t = 0$ that pass through state σ at $t = \tau$. Let $S_{0,\sigma}$ denote the set of such paths, and let $P_{j\tau}^{s(\sigma)}$, $s(\sigma) \in S_{0,\sigma}$, be the price of the security at state σ obtained by applying equation (3), conditioned on the fact that interest rate scenarios s in $S\sigma$ originate from scenarios $s(\sigma)$ in $S_{0,\sigma}$. Then the expected price of the security at σ is given by

$$P_{j\tau}^{\sigma} = \frac{1}{|S_{0,\sigma}|} \sum_{s(\sigma) \in S_{0,\sigma}} P_{j\tau}^{s(\sigma)} \tag{4}$$

However, as we will see later, the path-dependent prices $P_{j\tau}^{s(\sigma)}$ provide useful information in the calculation of scenarios of holding period returns. The price computed using equation (4) is of little use in practice.

Duration and Convexity

The next step in the valuation analysis is to estimate the sensitivity of the computed prices to changes in the term structure. *Duration* and *convexity* are commonly used to measure the first and second derivative of the price of a security with respect to changes of the term structure of interest rates.

In order to capture the complex dependency of the cash flows of a fixed-income security to changes in the term structure we resort to the Monte Carlo

---

[6] In particular, the cash flows generated by a MBS at periods after τ will depend on the economic environment experienced prior to τ. For example, if the security has experienced periods of high prepayments then subsequent changes of interest rates will have less impact on the generated cash flows. Although the short-term rates prior to τ do not appear explicitly in the pricing equations, the economic activity prior to τ is used in the estimation of the cash flows c_{jt}^{s} for $t \geq \tau$

simulation procedure described next. Using Monte Carlo simulations to calculate option-adjusted duration and convexity involves the following steps:

Step 0: Initialize the stochastic process of interest rates, based on the current term structure, and use it to compute the option-adjusted premium ρ_j implied by the current market prices P_{j0} (equation (2)).

Step 1: Shift the term structure by -50 basis points, and recalibrate the stochastic process of interest rates.

Step 2: Sample interest rate paths $\{r_t^{-s}\}$ from the stochastic process calibrated in Step 1, and use the security cash flow projection model to compute option-adjusted prices:

$$P_j^- = \frac{1}{|S_0|} \sum_{s=1}^{|S_0|} \sum_{t=1}^{T} \frac{C_{jt}^s}{\prod_{i=1}^{t} (1 + \rho_j r_i^{-s})} \tag{5}$$

Step 3: Shift the term structure by $+50$ basis points, and recalibrate the stochastic process of interest rates.

Step 4: Sample interest rate paths $\{r_t^{+s}\}$ from the stochastic process calibrated in Step 3, and use the security cash flow projection model to compute option-adjusted prices:

$$P_j^+ = \frac{1}{|S_0|} \sum_{s=1}^{|S_0|} \sum_{t=1}^{T} \frac{C_{jt}^s}{\prod_{i=1}^{t} (1 + \rho_j r_i^{+s})} \tag{6}$$

Step 5: The *option-adjusted duration* of the security is given by

$$\Delta_j = \frac{P_j^+ - P_j^-}{100} \tag{7}$$

and the *option-adjusted convexity* by

$$\Gamma_j = \frac{P_j^+ - 2P_{j0} + P_j^-}{50^2} \tag{8}$$

Holding Period Returns

We now extend the valuation tools further, and estimate scenarios of returns of the MBS during a target holding period. These scenarios are, once more, generated using Monte Carlo simulation and they incorporate all available information about prepayment activity, option-adjusted premia, and interest rates.

The rate of return of a security j during the holding period τ is determined by the price of the security at the end of the holding period and the accrued value of any cash flows generated by the security. For a MBS we need to estimate the accrued value of principal, interest, and prepayments during the holding period, and price the unpaid balance of the security at the end of the holding period. To this end we rely again on a procedure for generating scenarios of the term structure, and on the model that predicts the prepayment activity for each scenario. For a given interest rate scenario s, the rate of return of security j is given by

$$R_{j\tau}^s = \frac{F_{j\tau}^s + V_{j\tau}^s}{P_{j0}} \tag{9}$$

where

$F_{j\tau}^s$ is the accrued value of the cash flows generated by the security, reinvested at the short-term rates under scenario s.

$V_{j\tau}^s$ is the value of unpaid balance at the end of the holding period, conditioned on scenario s. This is given by

$$V_{j\tau}^s = B_{j\tau}^s P_{j\tau}^s$$

where $B_{j\tau}^s$ is the unpaid balance of the mortgage security and $P_{j\tau}^s$ is the price, per unit face value, of the security. Both quantities are computed at the end of the holding period, and are conditioned on the scenario s. The estimation of security prices at the end of a holding period, given a scenario s, has been discussed above, see equation (3) and the discussion that follows.

P_{j0} denotes the current market price of the security.

Exhibit 2 illustrates the distribution of prices of a typical MBS during different time horizons. Note that for shorter time horizons the distribution is highly asymmetric, a result of the embedded prepayment option. As the holding period approaches the maturity of the security then the prepayment option is, for all practical purposes, worthless and the prices are symmetric. Furthermore, the average price of the security converges to par, as it should towards its maturity.

PORTFOLIO RISK MANAGEMENT TECHNIQUES

Having mastered the techniques for the valuation of MBS we can now address the problem of managing the risk of a portfolio of such securities. We will see how the valuation models developed in the previous section (i.e., the models for estimating duration, convexity, option-adjusted premia, and holding period returns) can be incorporated in a hierarchy of portfolio risk management models. These models capture increasingly more complex aspects of the portfolio manager's problem.

Exhibit 2: Distribution of the Estimated Prices of a MBS at Different Points in Time Obtained Using Monte Carlo Simulations

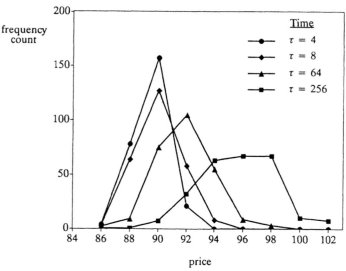

We loosely define the portfolio manager's problem as follows:

Construct a portfolio of mortgage securities whose performance measures will remain invariant under a wide range of uncertain scenarios.

For now we leave unspecified what we mean by *performance measures* and the precise nature of uncertainty. The key idea is to decide what goals we want our portfolio to achieve, specify measures that indicate that the goals are achieved, and make sure that these goals are still met when the economic environment changes. The three models we introduce in the next section allow the portfolio managers to specify increasingly more complex goals, and ensure that these goals are met for a broad set of scenarios.

Example Applications

The precise goals of the portfolio manager depend on the underlying application. We describe here three practical applications where one needs to deal with MBS and their inherent uncertainties:

Indexation: Passive portfolio managers would like to build a portfolio of fixed-income securities that will track a prespecified index. For example, Lehman Brothers and Salomon Brothers publish a monthly mortgage index that is (presumably) indicative of the overall state of this segment of fixed-income markets. Investors who wish to invest in mortgages may be satisfied if their portfolio closely tracks the index. The performance measure of such a portfolio is the difference in return between the portfolio and the index. This difference has to be very small for all changes in the index caused by interest rate movements and by variations in prepayment activity.

Liability Payback: Insurance and pension fund companies are typically heavily exposed to MBS. These instruments are considered as an investment for paying back a variety of the liabilities of these institutions. The goal of the portfolio manager is to construct a portfolio of MBS that will pay the future stream of liabilities. Uncertainty here appears once more in the form of interest rate changes and changes in the timing of payments from the MBS. Furthermore, the timing of the liability stream may also be subject to uncertain variations: For example, the timing of payments to holders of single premium deferred annuities may change as annuitants exercise the option to lapse.

Debt Issuance: Government agencies, like Fannie Mae and Freddie Mac, fund the purchase of fixed-income assets (typically mortgages) by issuing debt. The problem of a portfolio manager is to decide which type of debt — maturity, yield, call-option — to issue in order to fund the purchase of a specific set of assets. Of course, there is no reason to assume that the assets have been pre-specified: the model may choose an appropriate asset mix from a large universe of available MBS or other fixed-income securities. The timings of both assets and liabilities may be uncertain in this application. The goal of the portfolio manager is to ensure that the payments against the issued debt will be met from the available assets, irrespectively of the timing of cash flows and fluctuations in interest rates.

Classification of Portfolio Management Models

We first start with a general classification of portfolio management models. We assume that a portfolio of MBS (the *assets*) are bought in order to fund some future obligation (the *liability*). Hence, the portfolio problem we are dealing with is the classical asset/liability management model, with MBS as assets.

The asset/liability management models we develop in the next section can be classified as: (1) static, (2) single-period, stochastic, and (3) multiperiod, dynamic, and stochastic. It is important to understand how the models address increasingly more complex aspects of the asset/liability management problem. Only then can the portfolio manager decide which model may be more appropriate for the application at hand. Of course, this decision has to be weighted against the increasing complexity — both conceptual and computational — of the models.

Static models hedge against small changes from the current state of the world. For example, a term structure is input to the model which matches assets and liabilities under this structure. Conditions are then imposed to guarantee that if the term structure deviates somewhat from the assumed value, the assets and liabilities will move in the same direction and by equal amounts. This is the fundamental principle behind *portfolio immunization.*[7]

Single-period, stochastic models do not permit the specification of a stochastic process that describes changes of the economic environment from its current status. However, modern finance abounds with theories that describe interest rates, and other volatile factors, using stochastic processes. Stochastic differential calculus is often used to price interest-rate contingencies. For complex instruments analysts resort to Monte Carlo simulations as we have seen in previous sections. A stochastic asset/liability model describes the *distribution* of returns of both assets and liabilities in the volatile environment, and ensures that movements of both sides of the balance sheet are highly correlated. This idea is not new: Markowitz pioneered the notion of risk management for equities via the use of correlations in his seminal paper.[8] However, for the fixed-income world this approach has only recently received attention.[9] The implementation of this strategy requires the generation of scenarios of holding period returns, as explained earlier.

The single-period stochastic model outlined above is *myopic.* That is, it builds a portfolio that will have a well behaved distribution of error (error = asset return – liability return) under the specified stochastic process. However, it does not account for the fact that the portfolio manager is likely to rebalance the portfolio once some surplus is realized. Furthermore, as the stochastic process evolves across time different portfolios may be more appropriate for capturing the correlations of assets and liabilities. The single-period model may recommend a conservative strategy, while a more aggressive approach would be justified once we explicitly recognize the manager's ability to rebalance the portfolio.

What is needed is a model that explicitly captures both the stochastic nature of the problem, but also the fact that the portfolio is managed in a dynamic, multi-period context. Mathematical models under the general term of *stochastic programming with recourse* provide the framework for dealing with this broad problem. Stochastic programming has a history almost as long as *linear program-*

---

[7] See P.E. Christensen and F.J. Fabozzi, "Bond Immunization: An Asset Liability Optimization Strategy," in F.J. Fabozzi and I.M. Pollack (editors) *The Handbook of Fixed Income Securities* (Dow Jones Irwin, 1987), for a discussion of the finance-theoretic principles behind immunization. See H. Dahl, A. Meeraus, and S.A. Zenios, "Some Financial Optimization Models: I. Risk Management," Chapter 1 in S.A. Zenios (ed.), *Financial Optimization* (Cambridge University Press, 1993), for operational models.

[8] H. Markowitz, "Portfolio Selection," *Journal of Finance,* 7 (1952), pp. 77-91.

[9] The framework for the diversification of fixed-income portfolios was developed by J.M. Mulvey and S.A. Zenios, "Capturing the Correlations of Fixed-Income Instruments," *Management Science,* 40 (1994), pp. 1329-1342. For an application to MBS by Fannie Mae see M.R. Holmer, "The Asset/Liability Management System at Fannie Mae," *Interfaces,* 24 (1994), pp. 3-21.

ming.[10] However, it was not until the early 1970s[11] that its significance for portfolio management was realized. With the recent advances in high-performance computing this approach has been receiving renewed interest from the academic literature.[12] We are also aware of work in several industrial settings for the deployment of such models in practice.

We continue now with a mathematical description of a model from each class. The formulations are general since our goal is to describe the key components of the models. In order to operationalize each model for the applications mentioned earlier additional specifications are needed. We do not completely specify the details, as those will only distract from the general principles we want to convey.

The following notation is generic to all models. Additional information will be defined as needed later. The universe of MBS is indexed by a set J and the market price of each security $j \in J$ is denoted by P_{j0}. The stream of liabilities is denoted by L_t, where $t = 0,1,...,T$, denotes a time index. Given is also a term structure, specified by a set of forward rates $\{r_t\}$, $t = 1,2,..., T$. The problem of the portfolio manager is to decide the holdings of each security x_j in a portfolio that will match the assets with the target liability stream.

For the stochastic models we also need to specify a set of scenarios S. The scenarios can be very general: they can represent a series of term structures drawn from some stochastic process of interest rates, or they can represent levels of prepayment activity for the mortgage securities, or they can represent levels of the liability stream, and so on. Whenever a model parameter is super-scripted by an index $s \in S$ it is understood that the value of the parameter is scenario dependent. In this respect, we will use C_{jt}^s to denote the cash flow generated by security $j \in J$ (per unit face value), and r_t^s to denote the discount rate at period $t = 1,..., T$, under scenario $s \in S$.

A Static Model: Duration Matching

Given the term structure, a stream of projected cash flows for the fixed-income security, and a stream of liabilities we can build a *dedicated* portfolio. That is, a portfolio of least cost — or maximum yield — of MBS that will match the stream of liabilities. Let C_{jt} denote the cash flow generated by security j at period t. This

---

[10] See G. B. Dantzig, "Linear Programming under Uncertainty," *Management Science*, 1 (1955), pp. 197-206, and R. J. B. Wets, "Stochastic Programs with Fixed Resources: the Equivalent Deterministic Problem," *SIAM Review*, 16 (1974), pp. 309-339.

[11] S.P. Bradley and D.B. Crane, "A Dynamic Model for Bond Portfolio Management," *Management Science* (October 1972), pp. 139-151.

[12] B. Golub, M. Holmer, R. McKendall, L. Pohlman, and S.A. Zenios, "Stochastic Programming Models for Money Management," *European Journal of Operational Research*, 85 (1995), pp. 282-296; R.S. Hiller and J. Eckstein, "Stochastic Dedication: Designing Fixed Income Portfolios Using Massively Parallel Benders Decomposition," *Management Science*, 39 (1994), pp. 1422-1438; J.M. Mulvey and H. Vladimirou, "Stochastic Network Optimization Models for Investment Planning," *Annals of Operations Research*, 20 (1989), pp. 187-217; and, S.A. Zenios, "Massively Parallel Computations for Financial Modeling under Uncertainty," in J. Mesirov (ed.) *Very Large Scale Computing in the 21st Century* (Philadelphia, PA, 1991), pp. 273-294.

stream is projected conditional on the current term structure. Consider now the following optimization model:

$$\text{Minimize}_{x} \sum_{j \in J} P_{j0} x_j \tag{10}$$

$$\text{s.t.} \sum_{j \in J} \left(\sum_{t=1}^{T} \frac{C_{jt}}{\prod_{\tau=1}^{t}(1+r_{\tau})} \right) x_j \geq \sum_{t=1}^{T} \frac{L_t}{\prod_{\tau=1}^{t}(1+r_{\tau})} \tag{11}$$

$$x_j \geq 0 \tag{12}$$

This model will choose the least-cost portfolio, with the property that the present value of the portfolio cash flows will be at least equal to the present value of the liabilities. If the timing and magnitude of assets and liabilities does not change, and neither do the discount factors, then it is easy to see that the portfolio will ensure timely payments against the liabilities. (It is assumed in this model that unlimited borrowing is allowed, at all time periods, at the prevailing discount rate $r\tau$. The model can be modified to eliminate borrowing, or permit limited borrowing at a spread over the rate $r\tau$.)

To account for the stochasticity of the security's cash flow, and the changes of the term structure, the model can be extended to match the sensitivities of both assets and liabilities to such stochasticity. As discussed earlier, the duration of a security measures the sensitivity of its price to small parallel shifts to the term structure. Hence, we extend the model to develop an *immunized* portfolio which will match both present values and durations of assets and liabilities. If Δ_l is the liability duration we can obtain an immunized portfolio by solving the following linear program:

$$\text{Minimize}_{x} \sum_{j \in J} P_{j0} x_j \tag{13}$$

$$\text{s.t.} \sum_{j \in J} \left(\sum_{t=1}^{T} \frac{C_{jt}}{\prod_{\tau=1}^{t}(1+r_{\tau})} \right) x_j \geq \sum_{t=1}^{T} \frac{L_t}{\prod_{\tau=1}^{t}(1+r_{\tau})} \tag{14}$$

$$\sum_{j \in J} \Delta_j x_j = \Delta_l \tag{15}$$

$$x_j \geq 0 \tag{16}$$

The model could be extended further to match the convexities of assets and liabilities. Matching higher derivatives is also possible. At the limit the derivative matched portfolio will be identical to a cash flow matched portfolio.

A Stochastic Model: Capturing Correlations

Portfolios of fixed-income securities have traditionally been managed using the simple concepts of duration and convexity matching of the previous section. With the increased volatility of the term structure, following monetary deregulation in the late 1970s, this approach became overly simplistic. The difficulty is further exacerbated with the constant stream of innovations in this market. In this respect the tradition of models based on diversification, that started with Markowitz's seminal work, has much to offer to the managers of fixed-income portfolios.[13]

In this section we introduce a stochastic model for managing portfolios of MBS. The model explicitly recognizes the volatility of MBS prices, and the correlation of prices in a portfolio, and develops the tradeoffs between return and volatility. The optimization model we adopt is based on the *mean-absolute deviation* (MAD) framework.[14] A MAD model is suitable for the fixed-income securities with embedded options since they exhibit highly asymmetric distributions of return.

One of the challenges in applying the MAD model — or any other risk-return model for that matter — to fixed-income securities is that instruments with a fixed term to maturity are vanishing. Furthermore, the payout function of several kinds of fixed-income securities is path-dependent. Hence, at any point in time we have only one observation of price variations. Therefore, we cannot resort to the statistical analysis of historical data in order to capture the volatility and correlation of returns. Hence, we need to resort to Monte Carlo simulation of the short-term risk-free rates in order to obtain holding period returns of the fixed-income security during the target holding period. Such a Monte Carlo simulation procedure was developed in previous sections (see, for example, equation (9)) and the discussion that follows. For now we assume that a random vector of holding period returns has been generated for each security.

Let $(R_j)_{j \in J}$ denote this vector random variable and let $\overline{R}_j = E(R_j)$ denote its expected value. (For simplicity we have dropped the subscript τ that denotes the dependence of the return on the holding period τ.) Let also $x = (x_j)_{j \in J}$ denote the composition of the portfolio that contains a liability with return ρ. The return of the portfolio is $R = \Sigma_{j \in J} R_j x_j + \rho$. The mean-absolute deviation of return of this portfolio is defined by:

$$w(R) = E\{|R - E(R)|\} \tag{17}$$

where $E(.)$ denotes expectation.

Assume now that a sample of the random variables R_j is available. That is, R_j takes the value R_j^s for some scenario $s \in S$, and we assume for simplicity that all scenarios in S are equiprobable. Then, an unbiased estimate for the mean-absolute deviation of return of the portfolio is:

---

[13] See Mulvey and Zenios, "Capturing the Correlations of Fixed-Income Instruments."

[14] See H. Konno and H. Yamazaki, "Mean-Absolute Deviation Portfolio Optimization Model and its Applications to Tokyo Stock Market," *Management Science*, 37 (1991), pp. 519-531.

$$w(R) = E\{|R - E(R)|\} \tag{18}$$

$$= E\left\{\left|\sum_{j \in J} (R_j - \bar{R}_j) x_j\right|\right\} \tag{19}$$

$$= \frac{1}{|S| + |J|} \sum_{s \in S} \left|\sum_{j \in J} (R_j^s - \bar{R}_j) x_j\right| \tag{20}$$

The MAD model is written as:

Minimize $w(R)$ $\qquad$ (21)

s.t. $\displaystyle\sum_{j \in J} \bar{R}_j x_j \geq \rho$ $\qquad$ (22)

$\displaystyle\sum_{j \in J} x_j = 1$ $\qquad$ (23)

$0 \leq x_j \leq u_j$, for all $j \in J$ $\qquad$ (24)

This model can be reformulated into a linear programming problem. (We use the standard reformulation for minimizing absolute values. The minimand |x| is replaced by y, where y is constrained as $y \geq x$ and $y \geq -x$.) In doing so it is also possible to differentially penalize the upside from the downside deviation of the portfolio return from its mean. Let μ_d and μ_u denote penalty parameters for the downside and upside errors respectively. Then the MAD model can be written as the following linear program:

Minimize $\displaystyle\frac{1}{|S| + |J|} \sum_{s \in S} y^s$ $\qquad$ (25)

s.t. $\displaystyle y^s + \mu_d \sum_{j \in J} (R_j^s - \bar{R}_j) x_j \geq 0$, for all $s \in S$ $\qquad$ (26)

$\displaystyle y^s + \mu_u \sum_{j \in J} (R_j^s - \bar{R}_j) x_j \geq 0$, for all $s \in S$ $\qquad$ (27)

$\displaystyle\sum_{j \in J} \bar{R}_j x_j \geq \rho$ $\qquad$ (28)

$\displaystyle\sum_{j \in J} x_j \geq 1$ $\qquad$ (29)

$0 \leq x_j \leq u_j$, for all $j \in J$ $\qquad$ (30)

A Multiperiod, Dynamic Model: Stochastic Optimization

We extend now the stochastic model of the previous section to a setting with multiple time priods. The multiperiod, stochastic model captures the dynamics of the following situation:

A portfolio manager must make investment decisions facing an uncertain future. After these *first-stage* decisions are made, a realization of the uncertain future is observed, and the manager determines an optimal *second-stage* (or, recourse) decision. The objective is to maximize the expected utility of final wealth.

The first-stage decision deals with the purchase of a portfolio of fixed-income securities. Uncertainty in this decision making framework is reflected in the level of interest rates, and the cash flows that will be obtained from the portfolio. The second-stage decision deals with borrowing (lending) decisions when the fixed-income cash flows lag (lead) the target liabilities. Decisions to rebalance the portfolio at some future time period(s), by purchasing or selling securities, are also included in the second stage.

This model is substantially more flexible than the previous two models in that it explicitly allows for portfolio rebalancing at future time periods, as more information about the uncertain scenarios becomes available. Transaction costs can, therefore, also be incorporated. Furthermore, by explicitly representing the scenarios in the constraints we can include scenarios not only of interest rates but also of prepayments, spreads, risk premia and the like. The detailed mathematical program for the multiperiod stochastic programming model is defined in the appendix.

PORTFOLIO RISK MANAGEMENT APPLICATIONS

We now illustrate the application of the models developed in this chapter to two specific real-world settings. We first show how MBS can be included in an immunized portfolio to fund a liability stream. Furthermore, we use this application to illustrate that stochastic models, even single-period ones, have superior performance than static models, such as immunization. The second application summarizes results from a successful implementation of the stochastic portfolio management ideas to track the Salomon Brothers index of MBS.

Immunization of an Insurance Liability Stream

We apply the MAD model for funding a liability stream obtained from a major insurance corporation. Using the term structure of April 26, 1991, we calculated the following descriptors of the liability:

Term	100 months
Present value	$166,163,900.00
Modified duration	4.1792 years

Using the portfolio immunization models we built a portfolio that was duration and convexity matched against the liabilities. The portfolio was built from a universe of both MBS and U.S. Treasury securities. Different levels of exposure to the mortgage market were imposed on an ad hoc basis. We list below the percentage savings realized when the liability is funded using a portfolio of MBS and Treasuries, over the cost of funding the liabilities using only the risk-free rate.

Cost of portfolio using Treasuries only	$166,163,861.00
(Savings)	0.00%
Cost of portfolio using up to 25% MBS	$152,993,690.00
(Savings)	7.92%
Cost of portfolio using up to 50% MBS	$142,529,529.00
(Savings)	16.58%
Cost of portfolio using up to 100% MBS	$137,489,656.00
(Savings)	21.07%
Cost of mixed U.S.Treasury-MBS portfolio	$136,124,130.00
(Savings)	22.07%

While it is clear from this example that using MBS in an integrated asset/liability management system produces substantial gains, the savings summarized above will not be necessarily realized in practice. They will be realized only if the term structure shifts in parallel and in small levels from that of April 26, 1991.

To assess the return of the portfolio under different economic conditions we conducted a Monte Carlo simulation of the returns of the immunized portfolio over the holding period. The results are reported in Exhibit 3. The 100% MBS portfolio produced expected returns of 10.469% with a standard deviation of these returns 0.406. The mixed portfolio of U.S. Treasuries and MBS has a slightly reduced expected return of 10.448%, but substantially reduced standard deviation of 0.293.

We also developed a MAD portfolio for funding the insurance liability. The efficient frontier is shown in Exhibit 4. On the same figure we show the results of the simulation of the immunized portfolio. First, we observe from this figure that substantial rates of return can be realized with relatively little risk. Second, we observe that the portfolio obtained using standard immunization techniques lies below the efficient frontier. These results illustrate the superiority of the MAD model in managing portfolios of complex instruments, like MBS, as opposed to traditional fixed-income management tools. Exhibit 3 summarizes the expected return and standard deviation of both immunized and MAD portfolios.

Exhibit 3: Performance of Immunized and MAD Portfolios

Model	100% MBS portfolio		Mixed Portfolio	
	Exp. return	Std. dev.	Exp. return	Std. dev.
Immunized	10.469	0.406	10.448	0.293
MAD (equal risk)	10.783	0.405	10.692	0.293
MAD (equal return)	10.469	0.234	10.448	0.206

Exhibit 4: Efficient Frontier of the Mean Absolute Deviation Portfolio of MBS and the Return-Variance Profile of the Immunized Portfolio

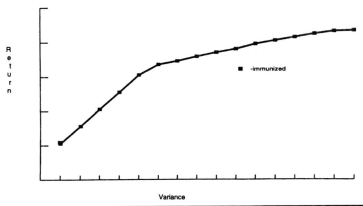

Tracking a Mortgage Index

One of the first successful applications of stochastic portfolio optimization models for fixed-income securities was to the management of the MBS portfolio of a major insurance corporation.[15] A MAD model was developed to track the Salomon Index of mortgage-backed securities. The index consists of a representative of all traded fixed-rate, passthrough securities, issued by FNMA, GNMA and FHLMC. The index is a sanitized image of the mortgage market: for example, cash flows generated by the mortgage pools are assumed to be reinvested in the index itself. There are also holdings in very small pools, and actual investments in such pools may be impossible due to liquidity difficulties. Finally, the composition of the index is changing from month to month without incurring any transaction costs. Since the MBS compromise approximately one-third of broad-based bond indexes, creating a *tradeable* portfolio that closely tracks the index is of great interest to investors.

The model estimates holding period returns of all securities in the index, and builds a portfolio that minimizes the mean-absolute deviation of the returns of the portfolio from the expected return of the index. Upside and downside risks are penalized differentially, with no penalty on upside risk and infinite penalty on downside risk. (Downside risk is realized when the portfolio underperforms the index by an amount that exceeds a small acceptable margin, set to be −5bp in monthly returns.)

The indexation model was tested over the period January 1989 to December 1991. During this period the index realized an annual return of 13.96%. In back-testing the model we used the following methodology: at the beginning of each month a binomial lattice was calibrated based on the term structure of that day. The lattice was used to estimate holding period returns, and the MAD model

[15] See K.J. Worzel, C.Vassiadou-Zeniou, and S.A. Zenios, "Integrated Simulation and Optimization Models for Tracking Fixed-Income Indices," *Operations Research*, 42 (1994), pp. 223-233.

was used to select a portfolio. The performance of the portfolio was recorded at the end of the month, based on observed market prices, and the process was repeated. Transaction costs of ⅔₂bp were charged, and cash flows from the mortgage pools were reinvested at the 1-month Treasury rate. The initial portfolio (January 1989) was selected using the method outlined above, but no transaction costs were paid.

During the testing period the portfolio realized an annual return of 14.18%, +22bp over the index return. The portfolio never underperformed the index by more than −3.6bp in monthly return, while the outperformance was more substantial (Exhibit 5). The standard deviation of the index return over the test period was 0.155, while the portfolio return had a standard deviation of 0.158. The portfolio would typically consist of approximately 25 securities, none of which accounted for more than 12% of the total portfolio.

Exhibit 5: Return of a $100M Investment in the Salomon Brothers Mortgage Index and Tracking Error of the Indexed Portfolio (January 1989 - December 1991)

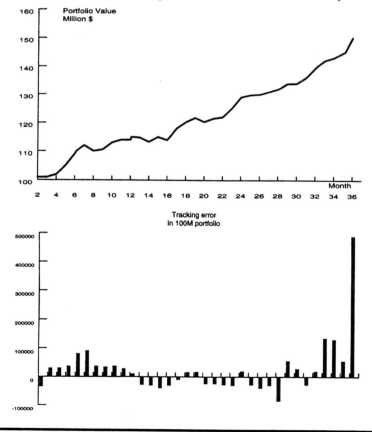

APPENDIX: STOCHASTIC PROGRAMMING PORTFOLIO FORMULATION

We give in this appendix a detailed mathematical formulation of the stochastic programming model for multiperiod, dynamic portfolio management as introduced in previous sections. We will be using the following notation. The parameters of the model are:

T = discretization of the planning horizon, $T = \{1, 2, 3, ..., \overline{T}\}$, and T_0 = $\{0, 1, 2, 3, ..., \overline{T}\}$. $\overline{T}$ denotes the end of the planning horizon.

b_j = initial holdings (in face value) of instrument $j \in J$, and b_0 initial holdings in a risk-free asset (e.g., cash).

r_t^s = 1-year forward interest rate at time period $t \in T_0$ under scenario $s \in S$.

spr = spread between the lending and borrowing rates.

pf_{jt}^s = cash flow generated from instrument $j \in J$ at time period $t \in T$ under scenario $s \in S$, expressed as a percentage of face value. It includes principal and interest payments of the fixed-income security, as well as cash flows generated due to defaults, prepayments, lapse, exercise of the embedded call option, etc.

ξ_{jt}^s = price per unit of face value of security $j \in J$ sold at period t under scenario s. The cost of the transaction is subtracted from the actual price to obtain this coefficient. The price at $t = 0$ is independent of the scenario and denoted by ξ_{j0}.

ζ_{jt}^s = price per unit of face value of security $j \in J$ purchased at period t under scenario s. The cost of the transaction is added to the actual price to obtain this coefficient. The price at $t = 0$ in independent of the scenario, and is denoted by ζ_{j0}.

L_t = liability due at time period $t \in T$. It is assumed here to be independent of the realized scenario, although this assumption can be easily relaxed.

The model variables are:

x_j = first stage variable, denoting the face value of instrument $j \in J$ purchased at the beginning of the planning horizon (i.e., at $t = 0$).

x_{jt}^s = second stage variable, denoting the face value of instrument $j \in J$ purchased at time period t under scenario s.

y_j = first stage variable, denoting the face value of instrument $j \in J$ sold at the beginning of the planning horizon, (i.e., at $t = 0$).

y_{jt}^s = second stage variable, denoting the face value of instrument $j \in J$ sold at time period t under scenario s (i.e., at $t = 0$).

z_{jt}^s = second stage variable denoting the face value of instrument $j \in J$ in the portfolio at time period $t \in T$, under scenario s. z_{j0} denotes the starting composition of the portfolio, after first-stage decisions have been made, and is independent of the scenarios.

w_{jt}^s = second stage accounting variable indicating the cash flow generated by security j at time period t under scenario s.

y_t^{-s} = second stage recourse variable indicating the amount owed at time period $t+1$ due to borrowing decisions made at period t under scenario s.

y_t^{+s} = second stage recourse variable indicating the surplus invested in the risk asset at time period t.

$U(WT^s)$ = the utility of terminal wealth realized under scenario s. Appropriate choices of utility functions are, for example, the isoelastic utility $1/\gamma(WT^s)\gamma$.

The model can now be formulated as follows:

Maximize $\dfrac{1}{|S|} \sum_{s \in S} U(WT^s)$

s.t. $z_{j0} + y_j - \dfrac{x_j}{\xi_{j0}} = b_j, \quad j \in J$

$$y_0^{+s} + \sum_{j \in J} x_j - \sum_{j \in J} (1 - \xi_j) y_j - \frac{1}{(1 + r_0^s + spr)} y_0^{-s} = b_0, \quad s \in S$$

$$z_{jt-1}^s + x_{jt}^s - w_{jt}^s - z_{jt}^s - y_{jt}^s = 0, \quad t \in T, \ j \in J, \ s \in S$$

$$w_{jt}^s - pf_{jt}^s z_{jt-1}^s = 0, \quad t \in T, \ j \in J, \ s \in S$$

$$\xi_{jt}^s y_{jt}^s + \sum_{j \in J} w_{jt}^s - \frac{x_{jt}^s}{\xi_{jt}} + (1 + r_{t-1}^s) y_{t-1}^{+s} - y_{t-1}^{-s}$$

$$+ \frac{1}{(1 + r_t^s + spr)} y_t^{-s} - y_t^{+s} = L_t, \quad t \in T, \ s \in S$$

$$WT^s = \sum_{j \in J} z_{j\bar{T}}^s \xi_{j\bar{T}}^s - y_{\bar{T}-1}^{-s}$$

The first constraint of this mathematical program reflects first stage decisions, and is deterministic. Subsequent constraints depend on the realized scenario, as well as the first stage decisions. The terminal wealth WT^s is computed by accumulating the total surplus net any outstanding debt at the end of the planning horizon and liquidating any securities that remain in the portfolio.

Chapter 21

Hedging Mortgage Passthrough Securities

Kenneth B. Dunn, Ph.D.
Portfolio Manager
Miller Anderson & Sherrerd, LLP

Roberto M. Sella
Portfolio Manager
Miller Anderson & Sherrerd, LLP

INTRODUCTION

With the exception of the Treasury market, the mortgage passthrough market is the most liquid bond market in the United States. Mortgage-backed securities (MBSs) make up about 30% of broad bond-market indices. Because mortgage securities often outperform government securities *with the same interest-rate risk*, they can be used to generate excess returns in client portfolios when the yield advantage of mortgages is attractive.

To execute this strategy successfully, the prepayment risk of mortgages must be managed carefully; when interest rates decline, most homeowners exercise their option to prepay their mortgages,[1] and, as a result, the duration of a mortgage portfolio (its price sensitivity to changes in interest rates) decreases. In other words, when interest rates decline, prepayments cause the value of a mortgage portfolio to increase less than that of a Treasury portfolio with the same initial duration. For this reason, many consider mortgages to be market-directional investments that should be avoided when one expects interest rates to decline. This perception is exacerbated by the common practice of comparing the returns of the mortgage index with the returns of the government and corporate indices *without adjusting for differences in duration*. Because the mortgage index typically has less duration than either the corporate or government index, it generally has better relative performance when interest rates rise than when interest rates fall.

We do not believe that mortgages, when properly managed, are market-directional investments. Proper management begins with separating mortgage valua-

---

[1] One can think of holding a mortgage passthrough security as equivalent to owning a fixed-rate bond and selling a prepayment option to the homeowner.

tion decisions from decisions concerning the appropriate interest-rate sensitivity of the portfolio. In turn, this separation of the value decision from the duration decision hinges critically on proper hedging. Without proper hedging to offset the changes in mortgage durations caused by interest rate movements, the portfolio's duration would drift adversely from its target. In other words, the portfolio would be shorter than desired when interest rates decline and longer than desired when interest rates rise.

Proper hedging requires understanding the principal risks of MBSs. In the next section, we provide a brief description of these risks. We then review how interest rates change over time, explain why our proprietary calculation of interest-rate risk is a better measure than duration for hedging mortgages, and describe our method of hedging mortgages with Treasuries and options. We conclude by showing how our hedging method is applied to a current-coupon mortgage and a "cuspy"-coupon mortgage.

MORTGAGE SECURITY RISKS

There are five principal risks in mortgage securities: spread, interest-rate, prepayment, volatility, and model risk. The yield of a mortgage security — the cumulative reward for bearing all five of these risks — has two components: the yield on equal interest-rate risk Treasury securities plus a spread. This spread is itself the sum of the option cost, which is the expected cost of bearing prepayment risk, and the option-adjusted spread (OAS), which is the risk premium for bearing the remaining risks, including model risk.

Spread Risk

We invest in mortgage securities when their spreads versus Treasuries are large enough to compensate for the risk surrounding the homeowner's prepayment option. Because the OAS can be thought of as the risk premium for holding mortgages, we do not hedge this risk. If we hedge against spread widening, we also give up the benefit from spread narrowing. Instead, we seek to capture the OAS over time, increasing the allocation to mortgages when yield spreads are wide and reducing these investments when yield spreads are narrow.

To calculate the OAS for any mortgage security, we use a prepayment model that assigns an expected prepayment rate every month — implying an expected cash flow — for a given interest-rate path. We then discount these expected cash flows at U.S. Treasury rates to obtain their present value. This process is repeated for a large number of interest-rate paths. Finally, we calculate the average present value of the cash flows across all paths. Typically, the average present value across all paths is not equal to the price of the security. However, we can search for a unique "spread" (in basis points) that, when added to the U.S. Treasury rates, equates the average present value to the price of the security. This spread is called the OAS.

Historical comparisons are of only limited use for making judgments about current OAS levels relative to the past, because option-adjusted spreads depend on their underlying prepayment models. As a model changes, so does the OAS for a given MBS. Over the past few years, prepayment models have changed significantly, making comparisons to historical OASs tenuous. We augment OAS analysis with other tools to help us identify periods when mortgage spreads are attractive, attempting to avoid periods when spread widening will erase the yield advantage over Treasuries with the same interest-rate risk. The risk that the OAS may change, or spread risk, is managed by investing heavily in mortgages only when the initial OAS is large.

Interest-Rate Risk

The interest-rate risk of a mortgage security corresponds to the interest-rate risk of comparable Treasury securities; this risk can be hedged directly by selling a package of Treasury notes or interest-rate futures. Once we have hedged the interest-rate risk of a mortgage security, we are left with the Treasury bill return plus a spread over Treasuries. We cannot capture all of this spread because some of it is needed to cover the cost of the homeowner's prepayment option.

Prepayment Risk

When interest rates decline, homeowners have an economic incentive to prepay their existing mortgages by refinancing at a lower rate. As a result, the average lives (or durations) of mortgage securities vary as interest rates change: they extend as rates rise and shorten as rates fall. Therefore, the percentage increase in price of an MBS for successive 25 basis point declines in yield becomes smaller and smaller. Conversely, the percentage decline in price becomes greater as interest rates rise. This effect, which is known as negative convexity, can be significant — particularly for mortgage securities that concentrate prepayment risk such as interest-only strips.

When interest rates change we must offset the change in mortgage durations in order to keep the overall interest-rate risk of the portfolio at its desired target. Neglecting to do so would leave the portfolio with less interest-rate risk than desired after interest rates decline and more risk than desired after rates increase. We adjust for changes in mortgage durations — or equivalently, manage negative convexity — either by buying options[2] or by hedging dynamically. Hedging dynamically requires lengthening duration — buying futures — after prices have risen, and shortening duration — selling futures — after prices have fallen. Whether we employ this "buy high/sell low" dynamic strategy, or buy options, we are bearing the cost associated with managing negative convexity, foregoing part of the spread over Treasuries.

---

[2] A viable alternative to buying options is buying mortgage derivatives with positive convexity, such as principal-only strips.

Volatility Risk

Like other options, the homeowner's prepayment option is more valuable when future interest-rate volatility is expected to be high than when it is expected to be low.[3] Because the yield spread adjusts to compensate the investor for selling the prepayment option to the homeowner, spreads tend to widen when expected volatility increases and narrow when volatility declines.

We manage volatility risk by choosing whether to buy options or to hedge dynamically. When the volatility implied in option prices is high and we believe that future realized volatility will be lower than implied, we hedge dynamically. When implied volatility is low and we believe that actual future volatility will be higher than implied, we hedge the mortgage position by purchasing options.[4] Because implied volatilities have tended to exceed subsequent realized volatility, we have generally hedged dynamically to a greater extent than we have hedged through the use of options.

Model Risk

Mortgage prepayment models generate cash flows for a given set of interest-rate paths. But what happens when the models are wrong? In the rally of 1993, premium mortgages prepaid at much faster rates than predicted by most prepayment models in use at that time. Investors who had purchased interest-only strips (IOs) backed by premium mortgages, and had relied on the prepayment predictions of those mortgage models, sustained losses. It is important to note that prior to the rally, the OAS on IOs seemed attractive on a historical basis. However, the *model* OAS assumed a prepayment rate of 40% per annum for premium mortgages; the actual prepayment rate for premium mortgages was as high as 60%, causing the *realized* OAS to be negative. Current models, having been calibrated to the 1993 experience, predict much faster prepayments than those used in 1993. Although *we do not know the magnitude of model error going forward*, we can measure sensitivity to model error by increasing the prepayment rate assumed by the model for securities that are hurt by prepayments.

Over time it has become cheaper to refinance mortgages as technological improvements have reduced the costs associated with refinancing. We expect this type of prepayment innovation to continue in the years ahead. Models calibrated to past behavior will understate the impact of innovation. Therefore, when we evaluate securities that are vulnerable to this type of risk, we carefully consider the likelihood and the effect of prepayment innovation in determining the size of our investments. Although we cannot hedge model risk explicitly, we can measure it and manage it by keeping our portfolios' exposure to this risk in line with that of the broad indices.

---

[3] Higher interest-rate volatility increases the likelihood of lower rates in the future, making the option to refinance more valuable.

[4] Any bond option can be "replicated" dynamically by a portfolio of bonds and cash. If future volatility turns out to be less (greater) than that initially implied in option prices, the replicating portfolio will have cost less (more) than buying the option.

Exhibit 1: Yield Curve Shifts: Changes in the Overall Level of Interest Rates

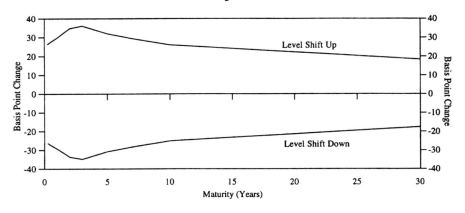

Source: Miller Anderson & Sherrerd, LLP

HOW INTEREST RATES CHANGE OVER TIME

To hedge mortgage securities effectively, we need to understand how interest rates change over time. Scott Richard and Benjamin Gord[5] introduced the concept of "interest-rate sensitivity" (IRS) used by Miller Anderson & Sherrerd and discussed why it is a better measure of interest-rate risk than modified or effective duration. Very briefly, duration measures of interest-rate risk assume that the yield curve moves up or down by the same amount at every maturity. Empirically, we have found that yield-curve changes are not parallel. Rather, when the level of interest rates changes, 2-year yields move about twice as much as 30-year yields, which is why the yield curve typically steepens in a bond market rally and flattens in a selloff. (Theoretical studies support the finding that long-term interest rates are less volatile than short-term interest rates.) This pattern implies that duration overstates the interest-rate risk of longer-term bonds and understates the risk of shorter-term bonds. This "level" effect is shown in Exhibit 1. Empirically, we have also found that the yield curve sometimes reshapes without a meaningful change in the overall level of interest rates. We call this second factor a "twist" (Exhibit 2). Together, these two factors explain about 96% of past yield-curve reshapings.

---

[5] Scott F. Richard and Benjamin J. Gord, "Measuring and Managing Interest-Rate Risk," Chapter 2 in Frank J. Fabozzi (ed.), *Managing Fixed Income Portfolios* (New Hope, PA: Frank J. Fabozzi Associates, 1997).

Exhibit 2: Yield-Curve Twists: Flattening and Steepening

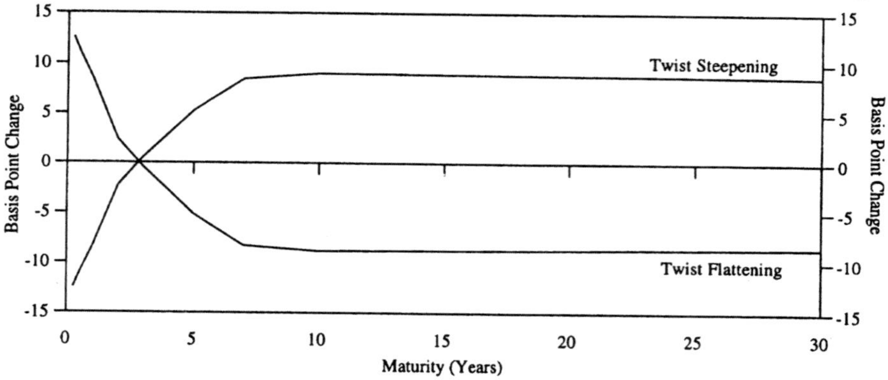

Source: Miller Anderson & Sherrerd, LLP

HEDGING METHOD

With an understanding of how the yield curve changes over time — and the effect of these changes on the homeowner's prepayment option — we can estimate how mortgage prices will change as interest rates change. Since two factors (the "level" and "twist" factors discussed above) have accounted for most of the cha ges in the yield curve, two Treasury notes (typically the 2-year and 10-year) can hedge virtually all of the interest-rate risk in mortgage investments.

To hedge mortgage securities, we begin by expressing a particular security in terms of an equivalent position in U.S. Treasuries (or equivalent futures contracts). We identify this equivalent position by picking a package of 2-year and 10-year Treasuries that — on average — has the same price performance as the MBS under the "level" and "twist" yield-curve scenarios.[6] For hedging purposes, the direction of the change — up or down in the case of the "level" factor, flattening or steepening in the case of the "twist" factor — is not known. Assuming that either direction is equally likely, we calculate the "average" price changes of the MBS, the 2-year note, and the 10-year note for both the "level" and "twist" scenarios. In this way we calculate the unique quantities of 2-year and 10-year notes that will simultaneously hedge the mortgage's price response to both "level" and "twist" scenarios.[7] This combination is the appropriate hedge for typical yield-curve shifts and therefore defines the interest-rate sensitivity of the mortgage in terms of 2-year and 10-year notes.

[6] We hold option-adjusted spreads constant and assume immediate yield-curve shifts when calculating horizon prices.

[7] We solve for the amount of 2-year ($H2$) and 10-year ($H10$) futures that have the same average price performance as the mortgage, assuming both level and twist movements in the yield curve. The 2-bond hedge in Exhibit 4 was determined by solving the following two equations:

Level: $H2 \times (0.62) + H10 \times (1.69) = 1.22$
Twist: $H2 \times (0.01) + H10 \times (0.55) = 0.25$

Exhibit 3: Mortgage Price/Yield Curve

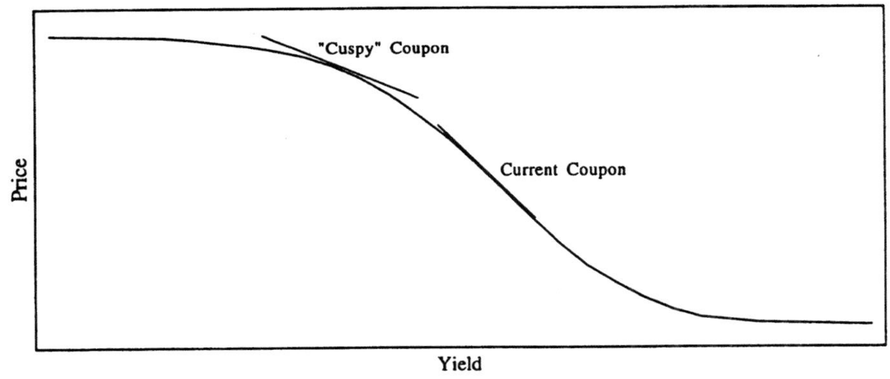

Source: Miller Anderson & Sherrerd, LLP

The equivalent position in Treasuries will not exactly match the price performance of the MBS in the different yield-curve scenarios. This hedging error is a measure of the negative convexity[8] of the security. We choose to manage this negative convexity either by dynamically buying and selling U.S. Treasuries to adjust the hedges as interest rates change or by buying options. We base this choice on the implied volatility of option prices and on our own forecast of future realized volatility.

In many cases, the "average" price change is a good approximation of how the security's price will change for a small movement in interest rates. (See the line labeled Current Coupon in Exhibit 3.) However, some securities are very sensitive to small movements in interest rates. For example, a mortgage whose coupon is 100 basis points higher than the current coupon (often referred to as a "cuspy"-coupon mortgage) could be prepaid slowly if rates rise by 25 basis points but very quickly if rates fall by 25 basis points. Small changes in interest rates have large effects on prepayments for such securities and hence on their prices.

In this case, averaging the price changes is not a good measure of how prices will change. In other words, the tangent line (labeled "Cuspy" Coupon in Exhibit 3) is not a good proxy for the price/yield curve. At times, these types of securities trade at very attractive levels, but hedging only with Treasury notes or futures contracts may leave the investor exposed to more negative convexity than is desired. By purchasing options, the investor can shed unwanted negative convexity while benefiting from the cheapness of the security.

---

[8] Here, we define convexity as the price change of a security not explained by the equivalent position in Treasury futures.

Exhibit 4: Alternative Hedging Methods

Yield Curve Change	Price Change			Error	
	PHLMC 7.5	Duration Hedge	2-Bond Hedge	Duration Hedge	2-Bond Hedge
"Level" Up	-1.27	1.36	1.25	**0.09**	-0.02
"Level" Down	1.18	-1.34	-1.20	**-0.16**	-0.02
"Twist" Flat	0.24	-0.24	-0.25	-0.00	-0.01
"Twist" Steep	-0.26	0.24	0.25	-0.02	-0.01

Source: Miller Anderson & Sherrerd, LLP

TWO HEDGING EXAMPLES

At the end of February 1997, the effective duration of Freddie Mac 7.5% mortgages was 4.4 years and its price was 99-25.[9] Exhibit 4 compares the results achieved using two hedging strategies. The duration hedge strategy compares the security's performance with that of an equal-duration U.S. Treasury, while the 2-bond hedge strategy uses 2-year- and 10-year-note futures. By construction, the 2-bond hedge dominates because the amount in 2-year-note ($76 per $100 of MBSs) and 10-year-note ($44 per $100 of MBSs) futures is determined from price changes derived from the assumed level and twist yield-curve scenarios. However, Exhibit 4 demonstrates that duration is not a good measure of interest-rate risk because typical yield-curve shifts are not parallel.

If the duration hedge is used, it appears that mortgages do better in market selloffs and worse in rallies — apparently confirming a market belief that mortgages are "market-directional" investments (see the two bolded values in Exhibit 4). However, evidence using the 2-bond hedge suggests otherwise: because the yield curve seldom moves in a parallel fashion, properly hedged mortgages are not market-directional. When "likely" changes in the yield curve are accounted for, virtually all of the market-directionality is removed. The IRS of the 7.5% mortgage — 4.0 years — is derived from the IRS of the equivalent position in 2- and 10-year note futures. Assuming a "likely" yield-curve shift, mortgage passthroughs have about 10% less interest-rate sensitivity than duration measures imply.

The "error" in the 2-bond hedge is a measure of the negative convexity of the Freddie Mac 7.5% mortgage. For a 26 basis point move in the 10-year — assuming no rebalancing — the mortgage would underperform its Treasury hedge by two basis points (or two cents per $100 of face value). This loss is more than offset by the carry advantage of mortgages over Treasuries: over a 1-month holding period, this incremental yield would be worth about nine basis points. In practice, because more frequent rebalancing lowers the hedging error, we adjust our hedges daily.[10]

---

[9] All numerical calculations are based on closing prices as of 3/4/97.

[10] Over the past three years the daily standard deviation of the 10-year yield has been 6.7 basis points.

Exhibit 5: Hedging Negative Convexity with Options

| Yield Curve Change | Price Change | | Error | | Options+ |
	FHLMC 8.5	2-Bond Hedge	2-Bond Hedge	Option Pay-Off	2-Bond Hedge
"Level" Up	-0.98	0.93	-0.05	0.05	0.00
"Level" Down	0.85	-0.90	-0.05	0.05	0.00
"Twist" Flat	0.11	-0.12	-0.01	0.01	0.00
"Twist" Steep	-0.12	0.11	-0.01	0.01	0.00

Source: Miller Anderson & Sherrerd, LLP

"CUSPY"-COUPON MORTGAGES

At times, "cuspy"-coupon mortgages offer attractive risk-adjusted expected returns. However, they have more negative convexity than current-coupon mortgages. Using options enables us to offset some or all of this negative convexity. Exhibit 5 presents the same 2-bond hedge information (we have dropped the duration hedge) as Exhibit 4 for 8.5% Freddie Mac mortgages (duration = 3.3 years, IRS = 3.0 years, price = 103.50).

Because the prepayment option of the 8.5s is closer to the refinancing threshold than that of the 7.5s at the time of this analysis, the 2-bond-hedge error is greater. Buying calls and puts eliminates this drift. In Exhibit 5, we add two option positions[11] on the 10-year note that offset the 2-bond-hedge error, making the total package (MBS + 2-bond-hedge + options) insensitive to likely interest-rate movements. Of course, buying these options requires paying a premium which amounts to about seven basis points per month. Since the yield advantage of the 8.5s versus Treasuries is about 11 basis points, the expected excess return over Treasuries is about four basis points per month after we hedge out the negative convexity.

CONCLUSION

Successful MBS investing requires the ability both to find value and to extract it. Extracting value requires proper hedging of attendant risks. Understanding how the yield curve changes over time and how these changes affect mortgage prices allows a portfolio manager to use mortgages in client portfolios when mortgage spreads are attractive, thereby enhancing long-term returns. Careful hedging is the linchpin for separating the value decision from the duration decision so that mortgages can be used to construct attractive total-return portfolios without compromising the appropriate interest-rate sensitivity of the portfolio.

---

[11] Per $100 of MBS, $18 6-month call on 10-year U.S. Treasury (UST), strike = 99.5; $17 6-month put on 10-year UST, strike = 95; 10-year UST priced at 97-15.

Chapter 22

Portfolio Risk Management

H. Gifford Fong
President
Gifford Fong Associates

Oldrich A. Vasicek
Senior Vice President
Gifford Fong Associates

INTRODUCTION

Fundamental to portfolio risk management is risk measurement. Risk measurement can be thought of as the quantification of the characteristics of risk. Early attempts at risk quantification dealt with investments in relatively simple security types such as Treasury securities and equities. Risk was characterized by volatility of returns and measured by quantities such as variance, standard deviation, or mean absolute deviation.[1]

The development in risk management techniques introduced additional risk measures. In the case of fixed income securities, the concept of duration became a widespread tool for risk management. For equities, the beta coefficient[2] was introduced to provide further capability in managing the risk of equity portfolios. These analytical paths are indicative of the specialization by asset type since the earlier attempts at risk management. In addition, portfolio-oriented measures such as the concept of shortfall risk have been described.[3]

As derivative securities such as options or swap transactions with embedded options were introduced, the structure of marketable assets has become more complex. Derivative securities exhibit an asymmetric price distribution and, hence, cannot be adequately analyzed using the more traditional risk measures suitable for simpler investments. A number of recommendations have emerged to address the perceived need for additional risk analysis insight. The Group of

[1] Harry M. Markowitz, *Portfolio Selection* (New Haven, CT: Yale University Press, 1959) and Harry M. Markowtiz, "Portfolio Selection," *Journal of Finance* (March 1952), pp. 77-91.
[2] William F. Sharpe, "Capital Asset Prices: A Theory of Market Equilibrium Under Conditions of Risk," *Journal of Finance*, September 1964, Vol. 19 pp. 425-442.
[3] Martin Leibowitz and Roy D. Henriksson, "Portfolio Optimization With Shortfall Constraints: A Confidence-Limit Approach to Managing Downside Risk," *Financial Analysts Journal* (March-April 1989), pp 34-41.

Thirty[4] reviewed the derivative product industry practice and suggested value at risk as an appropriate risk measure. The Derivative Policy Group (DPG)[5]recommended stress testing under improbable market conditions.

Value at risk provides a useful summarization under prespecified conditions of the amount at risk given the risk characteristics of the portfolio. Stress testing complements the value at risk analysis by providing the results of extreme scenarios of risk factor changes. These two methods view risk from an overall portfolio standpoint rather than at the individual security level.

The focus of attention in this chapter will be the development of the methodologies appropriate for quantifying the risk of complex investments. The discussion concentrates for illustrative purposes on fixed income portfolios, as these contain typically the largest percentage of derivative securities and transactions. The principles of the analysis, however, apply to portfolios of all asset types.

RISK SOURCES

The total risk of a portfolio is represented by the potential decline in the market value of the portfolio. In order to measure this risk, it is necessary to quantify the possible market value changes, under probable as well as extreme circumstances, resulting from the individual risk sources and from their interplay. By identify individual sources of risk, the total and each component risk of the portfolio can be measured. These sources of risk include market risk, option risk, credit risk, foreign exchange risk, and security specific risk, etc.

In the area of fixed income derivatives, market risk arises from changes in the level and shape of the term structure of interest rates. Option risk results from uncertain future interest rate movement. The uncertainty in interest rate movement can be characterized by interest rate volatility. Credit risk stems from changes in the creditworthiness of issuers and can be quantified as the spreads over the default free government rates. Foreign exchange risk for foreign investments is due to exchange rate movements. Security specific risk is the remaining risk not explained by these principal risk factors.

In recapitulation, the principal risk factors for fixed income derivatives can be described as follows:

1. Interest rate level
2. Rates of benchmark maturities
3. Spreads over government rates
4. Volatility of interest rates
5. Exchange rates

---

[4] *Derivatives: Practices and Principles* published by The Group of Thirty, Washington, DC in July 1993.
[5] See Section 1 of *Derivatives: Practices and Principles*. Appendix I: Working Papers.

The investor may be able to hedge or otherwise compensate for some of these risks. For instance, the interest rate risk of the fund can be easily counterbalanced by short positions in interest rate futures contracts. Foreign exchange risk can be eliminated by forward currency hedges. In addition, the specific risk of the fund may be diversified away by the investor's other holdings. For proper risk management, therefore, it is necessary to measure the exposures to the sources of risk in such a way that these can be reduced or eliminated.

RISK EXPOSURES

An essential basis to risk measurement and management is determining the security and portfolio exposures to their risk factors. Suppose we denote the values of the risk factors by $F_1, F_2,..., F_n$. If P is the value of a security, then the change in the security value resulting from the change in the risk factors can, in the first approximation, be given as

$$\frac{\Delta P}{P} = -\sum_{i=1}^{n} D_i \Delta F_i \tag{1}$$

The quantities $D_1,..., D_n$ in equation (1) are the exposures of the security to each of the risk factors. They measure the percentage change in the value of the security due to a unit change in the value of the factors.

If we postulate a linear relationship between the changes in the value of the factors and the percentage price change represented by equation (1), then the exposures to the factors are defined by the partial derivatives as

$$D_i = -\frac{1}{P}\frac{\partial P}{\partial F_i} \tag{2}$$

For example, if F_i is the interest rate level, the expression (2) is the familiar definition of duration. If F_i is the volatility, the expression (2) gives the exposure to changes in volatility, which is sometimes referred to as "vega." It generalizes in the same form to other risk factors as well. Care needs to be taken that the duration and all other exposures are correctly measured on an options adjusted basis. Therefore, the price sensitivities will have already taken into account any embedded options affecting price changes.

Except as a first-order approximation, however, equation (1) is not a satisfactory representation for the price change of a security for several reasons. First, the price change is not a linear function of the factor change, particularly for derivatives. Secondly, the changes in the factors are not instantaneous, so that a change due to the passage of time needs to be incorporated. Third, there may be a specific component in the value of a security, not explained by the market move. And finally, it is more appropriate to characterize the dollar change, rather than the percentage value change, since derivatives such as swaps and other contracts often start with a low or even zero value.

We will therefore assume that the market value of each security is governed by the equation

$$\Delta P = A - \sum_{i=1}^{n} D_i X_i + \frac{1}{2} \sum_{i=1}^{n} C_i X_i^2 + Y \tag{3}$$

where

$$X_i = \Delta F_i \tag{4}$$

are changes in the value of each risk factor and Y is the risk specific to each security. The quantities D_i, C_i are then the *linear* and *quadratic exposures* of the security value to the factors. They are analogous to the dollar duration and dollar convexity measures of interest rate exposure. In order that the non-linear price response is properly approximated, however, D_i, C_i should be measured for a finite factor change, rather than the infinitesimal one given by equation (2). In fact, there are considerations (related to the theory of Hermite integration) that suggest that the exposures should be determined as

$$D_i = -\frac{P_i' - P_i''}{2\Delta F_i} \tag{5}$$

$$C_i = \frac{P_i' + P_i'' - 2P}{(\Delta F_i)^2} \tag{6}$$

where P_i' and P_i'' are the prices of the security calculated under the assumption that the risk factor F_i changed by the amount of ΔF_i and $-\Delta F_i$ respectively, and ΔF_i is taken specifically to be equal to

$$\Delta F_i = \sigma_i \sqrt{3} \tag{7}$$

where σ_i is the volatility of F_i over the interval Δt. With the definitions (5), (6), (7), the exposures characterize the *global* response curve of the security price rather than the local behavior captured by durations and convexities. Finally, the quantity A in equation (3) is equal to

$$A = \mu - \frac{1}{2} \sum_{i=1}^{n} C_i \sigma_i^2 \tag{8}$$

where μ is the expected return,

$$\mu = E\Delta P \tag{9}$$

With this representation of the price behavior, a risk analysis and measurement is facilitated. Both the linear risk exposures D_i and the quadratic risk exposure C_i combine for the portfolio as simple sums of those for the individual securities. Thus, if D_{ik} is the linear exposure of the k-th security to the i-th risk factor (and similarly for C_{ik}), then

$$D_{ip} = \sum_{k=1}^{m} D_{ik}$$

$$C_{ip} = \sum_{k=1}^{m} C_{ik}$$

would be the risk exposures for the portfolio.

A risk management process may then consist of a conscientious program of keeping all the portfolio risk exposures close to zero,

$$D_{ip} = 0 \qquad i = 1, ..., n$$

$$C_{ip} = 0 \qquad i = 1, ..., n$$

to eliminate an undesirable dependence on market factors. This is equivalent to hedging against all sources of market risk. The specific risks $s_k^2 = Var(Y_k)$ which combine by the formula

$$s_P^2 = \sum_{k=1}^{m} s_k^2$$

can only be reduced by diversification.

The overall variability of the portfolio or security value can be calculated from its risk exposures using the formula

$$\sigma^2 = Var(\Delta P) = \sum_{i=1}^{n}\sum_{j=1}^{n} D_i D_j \sigma_{ij} + \frac{1}{2}\sum_{i=1}^{n}\sum_{j=1}^{n} C_i C_j \sigma_{ij}^2 + s^2 \tag{10}$$

which is a consequence of the value change equation (3). Here σ_{ij} are the covariances in the changes of the i-th and j-th risk factor,

$$\sigma_{ij} = Cov(X_i, X_j)$$

To the extent possible, the variances and covariances should be obtained from current pricing of derivatives whose values depend on these variances (these are called the *implicit volatilities*). For instance, quotes are available in the swap market for interest rate volatilities, calculated from market prices of swaptions. These volatilities reflect the market's estimate of the prospective, rather than past, interest rate variability. Only when such implicit volatilities are not available for a given risk factor, a historical variability should be used. In this case, care should be taken that the historical period is long enough to cover most market conditions and cycles.

VALUE AT RISK

The *value at risk* (*VAR*) is a single most useful number for the purposes of risk assessment. It is defined as the decline in the portfolio market value that can be expected within a given time interval (such as two weeks) with a probability not exceeding a given number (such as 1% chance). Mathematically, if

$$Prob(\Delta P \leq -VAR) = \alpha \tag{11}$$

then *VAR* is equal to the value at risk at the probability level α.

In order that the *VAR* can be calculated, it is necessary to determine the probability distribution of the portfolio value change. This can be derived from equation (3).

Assume that the factor changes X_i have a jointly normal distribution with mean zero and covariance matrix (σ_{ij}), $i, j = 1,..., n$. Then the first three moments of ΔP are given by equations (9), (10), and (12), where

$$\mu_3 = E(\Delta P - \mu)^3$$

$$= 3 \sum_{i=1}^{n} \sum_{j=1}^{n} \sum_{k=1}^{n} D_i D_j C_k \sigma_{ik} \sigma_{jk} + \sum_{i=1}^{n} \sum_{j=1}^{n} \sum_{k=1}^{n} C_i C_j C_k \sigma_{ij} \sigma_{jk} \sigma_{ki} \tag{12}$$

Knowing the three moments, the probability distribution of ΔP can be approximated and the *VAR* calculated. There are theoretical reasons to use the Gamma distribution as a proxy. The resulting formula for the value at risk is then very simple:

$$AR = k(\gamma) \cdot \sigma \tag{13}$$

where σ is the standard deviation of the value of the portfolio or security, obtained as the square root of the variance given in equation (10) above. The quantity γ is the skewness of the distribution,

$$\gamma = \frac{\mu_3}{\sigma^3} \tag{14}$$

calculated using equations (9) and (11). Finally, the ordinate $k(\gamma)$ is obtained from Exhibit 1 (corresponding to the Gamma distribution). (Exhibit 1 only extends to the values $\gamma = \pm 2.83$, since this is the highest magnitude attainable for the skewness of the quadratic form in equation (3).)

Note that the value 2.33 in Exhibit 1 corresponding to $\gamma = 0$ is the 1% point of the normal distribution. In other words, if the portfolio value change can be represented by the symmetric normal distribution, the *VAR* at the 1% probability will be $VAR = 2.33\sigma$. For most derivative securities and portfolios, however, the probability distribution is highly skewed one way or the other and the normal ordinates do not apply. The numbers in Exhibit 1 represent the proper ordinate values.

Exhibit 1: 0.01 Ordinates as a Function of Skewness

γ	k(γ)
-2.83	3.99
-2.00	3.61
-1.00	3.03
-0.67	2.80
-0.50	2.69
0.00	2.33
0.50	1.96
0.67	1.83
1.00	1.59
2.00	0.99
2.83	0.71

Exhibit 2: Value at Risk (USD)

Security	Market Value	Interest Rate Risk	Derivative Risks	Specific Risks	Foreign Exchange Risks	Total Risk
USA						
TB 01/16/97	973,750	2,980	0	310	0	3,000
T 5.5 11/15/98	989,670	13,860	0	1,580	0	13,950
T 8.5 02/15/20	2,314,560	127,480	0	10,650	0	127,920
T 7.5 11/15/24	1,026,050	62,500	0	6,780	0	62,870
Floating rate loan	5,055,630	9,830	0	1,950	0	10,020
Cap sold	-85,790	46,940	5,540	5,510	0	47,590
USA Total	10,273,860	260,420	5,540	24,980	0	261,670
Germany						
DBR 8.5 08/21/00	80,430	920	0	110	3,220	3,350
DBR 9.0 01/22/01	797,260	10,180	0	1,320	31,900	33,510
DBR 8.0 07/22/02	742,100	12,640	0	1,240	29,690	32,290
DBR 6.0 02/16/06	661,130	16,980	0	1,580	26,450	31,470
Cross currency swap	-150,410	28,330	0	3,450	89,870	94,290
Germany Total	2,130,510	12,610	0	1,460	4,330	13,410
Portfolio Total	12,404,370	267,320	5,540	25,030	4,330	268,580

It may also be noted that equation (13) does not include the expected return μ. This is because the mean is of lower order of magnitude (namely Δt) than the standard deviation σ (which is of the order $\sqrt{\Delta t}$) and can be neglected.

The VARs can be calculated for individual securities, portfolio sectors, and the total portfolio, as well by the sources of risk. Exhibit 2 illustrates a VAR analysis with a global portfolio. This global portfolio consists of US Treasury securities, a floating-rate loan, a short position in an interest rate cap, and German government bonds hedged with a cross currency swap. The cross currency swap is composed of fixed rate DEM payments in exchange for floating rate USD receipts.

The numbers in Exhibit 2 do not necessarily add up, either down or across. The reason that they do not add up for the sectors and the total portfolio is that the value at risk due to, say, foreign exchange risk may come from rising exchange rate for German government bonds while for the cross currency swap, it comes from declining exchange rates. The reason the numbers do not add up across the sources of risk is that events of a given probability (say, 1%) do not add up: an interest rate change that can happen with 1% likelihood when considered alone is not the same as that which would happen together with, say, an exchange rate movement for a joint 1% probability.

STRESS TESTING

Although value at risk represents a useful assessment of the potential losses from various sources of risk and their interplay, it should be complemented by a series of stress tests. Value at risk is a proper measure of the instantaneous portfolio riskiness. This is all that would be necessary if all securities in the portfolio were perfectly liquid and if the portfolio risk was managed on a continuous-time basis. But in reality this is not the case. Thus, stress simulations of the portfolio's value response to market condition changes that are more extreme or persistent than those likely to occur in a short time interval are in order for comprehensive risk analyses. In this sense, stress tests are less systematic and somewhat ad hoc compared to the value at risk.

A stress test consists of specifying a scenario of extreme market conditions occurring over a specific time interval, and evaluating the portfolio gains or losses under such scenarios. This is useful for a number of reasons. First, such analysis allows for consideration of path-dependent events, such as cash flows on CMO securities. Second, it does not rely on a specific form of the value response curve, such as the quadratic form in equation (3). Portfolio values including derivatives with embedded options will not change in a linear or quadratic form. Depending on the structure of the portfolio, it may change by a large amount under extreme conditions. Third, it has an appeal to intuition that is lost in the VAR alone by showing the situations under which a loss can occur. And last but not least, it is required or recommended by the various oversight agencies and auditors.

Exhibit 3 is a possible stress test output table for the portfolio described in Exhibit 2. Scenarios 1 and 2 represent U.S. term structure movements, which affect USD denominated securities only. Scenarios 3 and 4 represent U.S. interest rate term structure steepening or flattening, which affects the cross currency swap through the floating-rate USD receipts. Scenarios 5 and 6 are exchange rates changes, which influence DEM denominated securities and the cross currency swap through the fixed-rate DEM payments. Scenarios 7 and 8 represent German interest rate term structure movements, which may affect DEM denominated securities only. Scenario 9 is a combination of a DEM/USD exchange rate change and a German interest rate change, which affects both German government bonds and the cross currency swap.

Exhibit 3: Stress Tests

Number	Scenario	Gain/Loss (USD)
1	USD interest rate up 100 bps	-451,950
2	USD interest rate down 100 bps	481,560
3	USD interest rate: 2 yr up 50 bps, 10 yr down 50 bps	112,490
4	USD interest rate: 2 yr down 50 bps, 10 yr up 50 bps	-103,640
5	DEM/USD up 10%	-9,840
6	DEM/USD down 10%	12,030
7	DEM interest rate up 30 bps	-137,710
8	DEM interest rate down 30 bps	140,300
9	DEM/USD up 10% & DEM interest rate up 30 bps	-2,290
	etc.	

CONCLUSIONS

Risk measurement of fixed income investments is a complex process due to the asymmetry of their return distribution. By utilizing value at risk and stress testing, an ability to evaluate non-symmetric return outcomes emerges. Each of these techniques has an important role. Value at risk is the expected loss from an adverse market movement with a specified probability over a stated time period. For example, value at risk is defined as the dollar amount that the total loss may exceed within 14 days with a 1% probability. On the other hand, stress testing determines how the portfolio would perform under stress conditions.

The market characteristics that affect the value of a security or portfolio are called risk factors. Risk factors that affect fixed income derivatives include interest rate level, benchmark maturity rates, spread over government rates, volatility of rates, and foreign exchange rates. To quantify the risk exposure to those risk factors, a quadratic approximation may be used and then a standard deviation may be calculated. The VAR number may be calculated by a Gamma distribution approximation. While value at risk gives a summary risk number, it does not tell the source or direction of the risk. To see the possible loss under extreme or least favorable market conditions, a series of stress tests must be performed. The value at risk and the result of a comprehensive stress test give a better risk picture than either one of them. In combination, they represent a comprehensive risk measurement necessary for portfolios with complex structures and interrelationships.

Chapter 23

Measuring and Forecasting Yield Volatility

Frank J. Fabozzi, Ph.D., CFA
Adjunct Professor of Finance
School of Management
Yale University

Wai Lee
Assistant Vice President
J.P. Morgan Investment Management Inc.

INTRODUCTION

There are two critical components to an interest rate risk management system The first component is an estimate of the price sensitivity of each fixed income security and derivative position to changes in interest rates. This estimate is typically obtained by changing rates by a small number of basis points and calculating based on a valuation model how the price changes. The result is an effective or option-adjusted duration measure. If the valuation model employed is poor, the resulting duration measure will not be a good estimate of the price sensitivity of an instrument to rate changes. A critical input to valuation models for cash market instruments with embedded options and option-like derivatives is the estimated yield volatility. The second component of an interest rate risk management system is the estimated yield volatility to assess the potential loss exposure. Consequently, yield volatility estimate play a dual role in an interest rate risk management system.

The previous chapters in this book discussed the measurement of interest rate exposure and the implementation of interest rate risk control strategies based on some expected yield volatility. The focus of the earlier chapters was not on the measurement of yield volatility. In this chapter, we look at how to measure and forecast yield volatility. Volatility is measured in terms of the standard deviation or variance. We begin this chapter with an explanation of how yield volatility as measured by the daily percentage change in yields is calculated from historical yields. We will see that there are several issues confronting a trader or investor in measuring historical yield volatility. Next we turn to modeling and forecasting yield volatility, looking at the state-of-the-art statistical techniques that can be employed.

We are grateful for the many constructive comments of George Chacko of the Harvard Business School.

CALCULATING THE STANDARD DEVIATION
FROM HISTORICAL DATA

The variance of a random variable using historical data is calculated using the following formula:

$$\text{Variance} = \sum_{t=1}^{T} \frac{(X_t - \bar{X})^2}{T-1} \tag{1}$$

and then

$$\text{Standard deviation} = \sqrt{\text{Variance}}$$

where

X_t = observation t on variable X
$\bar{X}$ = the sample mean for variable X
T = the number of observations in the sample

Our focus in this chapter is on yield volatility. More specifically, we are interested in the percentage change in daily yields. So, X_t will denote the percentage change in yield from day t and the prior day, $t-1$. If we let y_t denote the yield on day t and y_{t-1} denote the yield on day $t-1$, then X_t which is the natural logarithm of percentage change in yield between two days, can be expressed as:

$$X_t = 100[\text{Ln}(y_t/y_{t-1})]$$

For example, on 10/18/95 the Treasury 30-year zero rate was 6.56% and on 10/19/95 it was 6.59%. Therefore, the natural logarithm of X for 10/19/95 is:

$$X = 100[\text{Ln}(6.593/6.555)] = 0.5780$$

To illustrate how to calculate a daily standard deviation from historical data, consider the data in Exhibit 1 which shows the yield on Treasury 30-year zeros from 10/8/95 to 11/12/95 in the second column. From the 26 observations, 25 days of daily percentage yield changes are calculated in the third column. The fourth column shows the square of the deviations of the observations from the mean. The bottom of Exhibit 1 shows the calculation of the daily mean for the 25 observations, the variance, and the standard deviation. The daily standard deviation is 0.6360%.

The daily standard deviation will vary depending on the 25 days selected. For example, the daily yields from 8/20/95 to 9/24/95 were used to generate 25 daily percentage yield changes. The computed daily standard deviation was 0.8453%.

*Exhibit 1: Calculation of Daily Standard Deviation Based on
25 Daily Observations for 30-Year Treasury Zero
(October 9, 1995 to November 12, 1995)*

t	Date	y_t	$X_t = 100[Ln(y_t/y_{t-1})]$	$(X_t - \bar{X})^2$
0	08-Oct-95	6.694		
1	09-Oct-95	6.699	0.06720	0.02599
2	10-Oct-95	6.710	0.16407	0.06660
3	11-Oct-95	6.675	-0.52297	0.18401
4	12-Oct-95	6.555	-1.81311	2.95875
5	15-Oct-95	6.583	0.42625	0.27066
6	16-Oct-95	6.569	-0.21290	0.01413
7	17-Oct-95	6.583	0.21290	0.09419
8	18-Oct-95	6.555	-0.42625	0.11038
9	19-Oct-95	6.593	0.57804	0.45164
10	22-Oct-95	6.620	0.40869	0.25270
11	23-Oct-95	6.568	-0.78860	0.48246
12	24-Oct-95	6.575	0.10652	0.04021
13	25-Oct-95	6.646	1.07406	1.36438
14	26-Oct-95	6.607	-0.58855	0.24457
15	29-Oct-95	6.612	0.07565	0.02878
16	30-Oct-95	6.575	-0.56116	0.21823
17	31-Oct-95	6.552	-0.35042	0.06575
18	01-Nov-95	6.515	-0.56631	0.22307
19	02-Nov-95	6.533	0.27590	0.13684
20	05-Nov-95	6.543	0.15295	0.06099
21	06-Nov-95	6.559	0.24424	0.11441
22	07-Nov-95	6.500	-0.90360	0.65543
23	08-Nov-95	6.546	0.70520	0.63873
24	09-Nov-95	6.589	0.65474	0.56063
25	12-Nov-95	6.539	-0.76173	0.44586
	Total		-2.35020	9.7094094

Sample mean $= \bar{X} = \dfrac{-2.35020}{25} = -0.09401\%$

Variance $= \dfrac{9.7094094}{25-1} = 0.4045587$

Std $= \sqrt{0.4045587} = 0.6360\%$

Exhibit 2: Comparison of Daily and Annual Volatility for a Different Number of Observations (Ending Date November 12, 1995) for Various Instruments

Number of observations	Daily standard deviation (%)	Annualized standard deviation (%)		
		250 days	260 days	365 days
Treasury 30-Year Zero				
683	0.4902	7.75	7.90	9.36
60	0.6283	9.93	10.13	12.00
25	0.6360	10.06	10.26	12.15
10	0.6242	9.87	10.06	11.93
Treasury 10-Year Zero				
683	0.7498	11.86	12.09	14.32
60	0.7408	11.71	11.95	14.15
25	0.7092	11.21	11.44	13.55
10	0.7459	11.79	12.03	14.25
Treasury 5-Year Zero				
683	1.0413	16.46	16.79	19.89
60	0.8267	13.07	13.33	15.79
25	0.7224	11.42	11.65	13.80
10	0.8346	13.20	13.46	15.94
3-Month LIBOR				
683	0.7496	11.85	12.09	14.32
60	0.2994	4.73	4.83	5.72
25	0.1465	2.32	2.36	2.80
10	0.2366	3.74	3.82	4.52

Determining the Number of Observations

In our illustration, we used 25 observations for the daily percentage change in yield. The appropriate number depends on the situation at hand. For example, traders concerned with overnight positions might use the 10 most recent days (i.e., two weeks). A bond portfolio manager who is concerned with longer term volatility might use 25 days (about one month).

The selection of the number of observations can have a significant effect on the calculated daily standard deviation. This can be seen in Exhibit 2 which shows the daily standard deviation for the Treasury 30-year zero, Treasury 10-year zero, Treasury 5-year zero, and 3-month LIBOR for 60 days, 25 days, 10 days, and 683 days ending 11/12/95.

Annualizing the Standard Deviation

If serial correlation is not significant, the daily standard deviation can be annualized by multiplying it by the square root of the number of days in a year. That is,

Daily standard deviation $\times \sqrt{\text{Number of days in a year}}$

Market practice varies with respect to the number of days in the year that should be used in the annualizing formula above. Typically, either 250 days, 260 days, or 365 days are used.

Exhibit 3: Comparison of Daily Standard Deviation Calculated for Two 25 Day Periods for Various Instruments

Dates		Daily standard deviation(%)	Annualized standard deviation(%)		
From	To		250 days	260 days	365 days
Treasury 30-Year Zero					
10/8/95	11/12/95	0.6360	10.06	10.26	12.15
8/20/95	9/24/95	0.8453	13.36	13.63	16.15
Treasury 10-Year Zero					
10/8/95	11/12/95	0.7092	11.21	11.44	13.55
8/20/95	9/24/95	0.9045	14.30	14.58	17.28
Treasury 5-Year Zero					
10/8/95	11/12/95	0.7224	11.42	11.65	13.80
8/20/95	9/24/95	0.8145	12.88	13.13	15.56
3-Month LIBOR					
10/8/95	11/12/95	0.1465	2.32	2.36	2.80
8/20/95	9/24/95	0.2523	3.99	4.07	4.82

Thus, in calculating an annual standard deviation, the manager must decide on:

1. the number of daily observations to use
2. the number of days in the year to use to annualize the daily standard deviation.

Exhibit 2 shows the difference in the annual standard deviation for the daily standard deviation based on the different number of observations and using 250 days, 260 days, and 365 days to annualize. Exhibit 3 compares the 25-day annual standard deviation for two different time periods for the 30-year zero, 10-year zero, 5-year zero, and 3-month LIBOR.

Reexamination of the Mean

Let's address the question of what mean should be used in the calculation of the forecasted standard deviation. Suppose at the end of 10/24/95 a trader is interested in a forecast for volatility using the 10 most recent days of trading and updating that forecast at the end of each trading day. What mean value should be used?

The trader can calculate a 10-day moving average of the daily percentage yield change. Exhibit 1 shows the daily percentage change in yield for the Treasury 30-year zero from 10/9/95 to 11/12/95. To calculate a moving average of the daily percentage yield change on 10/24/95, the trader would use the 10 trading days from 10/11/95 to 10/24/95. At the end of 10/25/95, the trader will calculate the 10-day average by using the percentage yield change on 11/25/95 and would exclude the percentage yield change on 10/11/95. That is, the trader will use the 10 trading days from 10/12/95 to 10/25/95.

Exhibit 4: 10-Day Moving Daily Average for Treasury 30-Year Zero

10-Trading Days Ending	Daily Average (%)
24-Oct-95	−0.203
25-Oct-95	−0.044
26-Oct-95	0.079
29-Oct-95	0.044
30-Oct-95	0.009
31-Oct-95	−0.047
01-Nov-95	−0.061
02-Nov-95	−0.091
05-Nov-95	−0.117
06-Nov-95	−0.014
07-Nov-95	−0.115
08-Nov-95	−0.152
09-Nov-95	−0.027
12-Nov-95	−0.111

Exhibit 4 shows the 10-day moving average calculated from 10/24/95 to 11/12/95. Notice the considerable variation over this period. The 10-day moving average ranges from −0.203% to 0.079%. For the period from 4/15/93 to 11/12/95, the 10-day moving average ranged from −0.617% to 0.603%.

Rather than using a moving average, it is more appropriate to use an expectation of the average. Longerstacey and Zangari argue that it would be more appropriate to use a mean value of zero.[1] In that case, the variance as given by equation (1) simplifies to:

$$\text{Variance} = \sum_{t=1}^{T} \frac{X_t^2}{T-1} \tag{2}$$

Weighting of Observations

The daily standard deviation given by equations (1) and (2) assigns an equal weight to all observations. So, if a trader is calculating volatility based on the most recent 10 days of trading, each day is given a weight of 10%.

For example, suppose that a trader is interested in the daily volatility of the Treasury 30-year zero yield and decides to use the 10 most recent trading days. Exhibit 5 reports the 10-day volatility for various days using the data in Exhibit 1 and the formula for the variance given by equation (2). For the period 4/15/93 to 11/12/95, the 10-day volatility ranged from 0.164% to 1.330%.

---

[1] Jacques Longerstacey and Peter Zangari, *Five Questions about RiskMetrics^{TM}*, JP Morgan Research Publication 1995.

Exhibit 5: Moving Daily Standard Deviation Based on 10-Days of Observations

10-Trading Days Ending	Daily Standard Deviation (%)
24-Oct-95	0.757
25-Oct-95	0.819
26-Oct-95	0.586
29-Oct-95	0.569
30-Oct-95	0.595
31-Oct-95	0.602
01-Nov-95	0.615
02-Nov-95	0.591
05-Nov-95	0.577
06-Nov-95	0.520
07-Nov-95	0.600
08-Nov-95	0.536
09-Nov-95	0.544
12-Nov-95	0.600

In April 1995, the Basle Committee on Banking Supervision at the Bank for International Settlements proposed that volatility (as measured by the standard deviation) be calculated based on an equal weighting of daily historical observations using one year of observations.[2] Moreover, the committee proposed that volatility estimates should be updated at least quarterly.[3]

However, there is reason to suspect that market participants give greater weight to recent movements in yield when determining volatility. Moreover, what has been observed in several studies of the stock market is that high periods of volatility are followed by high periods of volatility.

To give greater importance to more recent information, observations further in the past should be given less weight. This can be done by revising the variance as given by equation (2) as follows:

$$\text{Variance} = \sum_{t=1}^{T} \frac{W_t X_t^2}{T-1} \qquad (3)$$

where W_t is the weight assigned to observation t such that the sum of the weights is equal to 1 (i.e., $\sum W_t = 1$) and the further the observation from today, the lower the weight.

The weights should be assigned so that the forecasted volatility reacts faster to a recent major market movements and declines gradually as we move

---

[2] The proposal, entitled "The Supervisory Treatment of Market Risks," is an amendment to the *1988 Basle Capital Accord*.

[3] RiskMetrics[TM] has a "Special Regulatory Dataset" that incorporates the 1-year moving average proposed by the Basle Committee. Rather than updating at least quarterly as proposed by the Basle Committee, the dataset is updated daily.

away from any major market movement. The approach by JP Morgan in RiskMetrics[TM] is to use an *exponential moving average*. The formula for the weight W_t in an exponential moving average is:

$$W_t = (1 - \beta)\beta^t$$

where β is a value between 0 and 1. The observations are arrayed so that the closest observation is $t = 1$, the second closest is $t = 2$, etc.

For example, if β is 0.90, then the weight for the closest observation ($t = 1$) is:

$$W_1 = (1 - 0.90)(0.90)^1 = 0.09$$

For $t = 5$ and β equal to 0.90, the weight is:

$$W_5 = (1 - 0.90)(0.90)^5 = 0.05905$$

The parameter β is measuring how quickly the information contained in past observations is "decaying" and hence is referred to as the "decay factor." The smaller the β, the faster the decay. What decay factor to use depends on how fast the mean value for the random variable X changes over time. A random variable whose mean value changes slowly over time will have a decay factor close to 1. A discussion of how the decay factor should be selected is beyond the scope of this chapter.[4]

MODELING AND FORECASTING YIELD VOLATILITY

Generally speaking, there are two ways to model yield volatility. The first way is by estimating historical yield volatility by some time series model. The resulting volatility is called *historical volatility*. The second way is to estimate yield volatility based on the observed prices of interest rate derivatives. Yield volatility calculated using this approach is called *implied volatility*. In this section, we discuss these two approaches, with more emphasis on historical volatility. As will be explained later, computing implied volatility from interest rate derivatives is not as simple and straight forward as from derivatives of other asset classes such as equity. Apart from assuming that a particular option pricing model is correct, we also need to model the time evolution of the complete term structure and volatilities of yields of different maturities. This relies on state-of-the-art modeling technique as well as superior computing power.

Historical Volatility

We begin the discussion with a general stochastic process of which yield, or interest rate, is assumed to follow:

---

[4] A technical description is provided in *RiskMetrics[TM] — Technical Document*, pp. 77-79.

$$dy = \mu(y, t)dt + \sigma(y, t)dW \tag{4}$$

where y is the yield, μ is the expected instantaneous change (or drift) of yield, σ is the instantaneous standard deviation (volatility), and W is a standard Brownian motion such that the change in W (dW) is normally distributed with mean zero and variance of dt. Both μ and σ are functions of the current yield y and time t.

Since we focus on volatility in this chapter, we leave the drift term in its current general form. It can be shown that many of the volatility models are special cases of this general form. For example, assuming that the functional form of volatility is

$$\sigma(y, t) = \sigma_0 y \tag{5}$$

such that the yield volatility is equal to the product of a constant, σ_0, and the current yield level, we can rewrite equation (4) as[5]

$$d\ln y = \mu'(y, t)dt + \sigma_0 dW \tag{6}$$

The discrete time version of this process will be

$$\ln y_{t+1} = \ln y_t + \mu' + \sigma_0(W_{t+1} - W_t) \tag{7}$$

Thus, when we calculate yield volatility by looking at the natural logarithm of percentage change in yield between two days as in the earlier section, we are assuming that yield follows a log-normal distribution, or, the natural logarithm of yield follows a normal distribution. σ_0, in this case, can be interpreted as the *proportional yield volatility*, as the yield volatility is obtained by multiplying σ_0 with the current yield. In this case, yield volatility is proportional to the level of the yield. We call the above model the *Constant Proportional Yield Volatility Model* (CP).

This simple assumption offers many advantages. Since the natural logarithm of a negative number is meaningless, a log-normal distribution assumption for yield guarantees that yield is always non-negative. Evidence also suggests that volatility of yield increases with the level of yield. A simple intuition is for scale reasons. Thus, while the volatility of changes in yield is unstable over time since the level of yield changes, the volatility of changes in natural logarithm of yield is relatively stable, as it already incorporates the changes in yield level. As a result, the natural logarithm of yield can be a more useful process to examine.[6]

A potential drawback of the CP model is that it assumes that the proportional yield volatility itself is constant, which does not depend on time nor on the yield level. In fact, there exists a rich class of yield volatility models that includes the CP model as a special case. We call this group the *Power Function Model.*[7]

---

[5] Equation (6) is obtained by application of Ito's Lemma. We omit the details here.

[6] See Thomas S. Coleman, Lawrence Fisher, and Roger G. Ibbotson, "A Note on Interest Rate Volatility," *Journal of Fixed Income* (March 1993), pp 97-101, for a similar conclusion.

[7] In the finance literature, this is also known as the *Constant Elasticity of Variance Model*.

Power Function Model

For simplicity of exposition, we write the yield volatility as σ_t, which is understood to be a function of time and level of yield. For example, consider the following representation of yield volatility:

$$\sigma_t = \sigma_0 y_{t-1}^\gamma \tag{8}$$

In this way, yield volatility is proportional to a power function of yield. The following are examples of the volatility models assumed in some well known interest rate models, which can be represented as special cases of equation (8):

1. $\gamma = 0$:   Vasicek,[8] Ho-Lee[9]
2. $\gamma = 0.5$:   Cox-Ingersoll-Ross (CIR)[10]
3. $\gamma = 1$:   Black,[11] Brennan-Schwartz[12]

The Vasicek model and Ho-Lee model maintain an assumption of a normally distributed interest rate process. Simply speaking, yield volatility is assumed to be constant, independent of time, and independent of yield level. Theoretically, when the interest rate is low enough while yield volatility remains constant, this model allows the interest rate to go below zero.

The CIR model assumes that yield volatility is a constant multiple of the square root of yield. Its volatility specification is thus also known as the *Square Root Model*. Since the square root of a negative number is meaningless, the CIR model does not allow yield to become negative. Strictly speaking, the functional form of equation (8) only applies to the instantaneous interest rate, but not to any yield of longer maturities within the CIR framework. To be specific, when applied to, say, the 10-year yield, yield volatility is obtained from the stochastic process of the 10-year yield, which can be derived from the closed-form solution for the bond price. To simplify the discussion, we go with the current simple form instead.

The volatility assumption in the Black model and Brennan-Schwartz model is equivalent to the previous CP model. In other words, yield is assumed to be log-normally distributed with constant proportional yield volatility.

Many of these functional forms for yield volatility are adopted primarily because they lead to closed-form solutions for pricing of bonds, bond options, and

---

[8] Oldrich Vasicek, "An Equilibrium Characterization of the Term Structure," *Journal of Financial Economics* (1977), pp. 177-188.

[9] Thomas S.Y. Ho and Sang-Bin Lee, "Term Structure Movements and Pricing Interest Rate Contingent Claims," *Journal of Finance* (1986), pp. 1011-1029.

[10] John C. Cox, Jonathan E. Ingersoll, and Stephen A. Ross, "A Theory of the Term Structure of Interest Rates," *Econometrica* (1985), pp. 385-407.

[11] Fischer Black, "The Pricing of Commodity Contracts," *Journal of Financial Economics* (1976), pp. 167-179.

[12] Michael Brennan and Eduardo Schwartz, "A Continuous Time Approach to the Pricing of Bonds," *Journal of Banking and Finance* (1979), pp. 133-155.

other interest rate derivatives, as well as for simplicity and convenience. There is no simple answer for which form is the best. However, it is generally thought that $\gamma = 0$, or a normal distribution with constant yield volatility, is an inappropriate description of an interest rate process, even though the occasions of observing negative interest rate in the model is found to be rare. As a result, many practitioners adopt the CP model, as it is straight forward enough, while it eliminates the drawback of the normal distribution.

One way to determine which yield volatility functional form to use is to empirically estimate the model with historical data. To illustrate, we use the 3-month, 10-year, and 30-year spot yields as examples. These yields are obtained by spline fitting the yield curve of Treasury strips every day within the sample period. We use the daily data from January 1, 1986 to July 31, 1997. To be consistent with the previous section, we assume that the average daily yield change is zero. Thus, the model to be estimated is:

$$y_t - y_{t-1} = \varepsilon_t$$

$$E[\varepsilon_t^2] = \sigma_t^2 = \sigma_0^2 y_{t-1}^{2\gamma} \tag{9}$$

where E[.] denotes the statistical expectation operator. The econometric technique employed is the Maximum Likelihood Estimation (MLE).[13] We assume a conditional normal distribution for changes in yield, after the dependence of volatility on level of yield has been incorporated. The details of this technique are beyond the scope of this chapter.[14] The results are reported in Exhibit 6, where an 8.00% yield is written as 0.08, for example.

Exhibit 6: Estimation of Power Function Models *

	3-month Treasury bill	10-year Treasury zero	30-year Treasury zero
σ_0	0.0019	0.0027	0.0161
	(12.31)	(11.00)	(5.58)
γ	0.2463	0.5744	1.2708
	(8.88)	(15.71)	(18.03)

* t-statistics are reported in parentheses.

---

[13] The model can also be estimated by Generalized Method of Moments (GMM), which does not impose any distributional assumption. We use MLE here in order to be consistent with the estimation of GARCH models to be discussed later. See K.C. Chan, G. Andrew Karolyi, Francis A. Longstaff, and Anthony B. Sanders, "An Empirical Comparison of Alternative Models of the Short-Term Interest Rate," *Journal of Finance* (July 1992), pp. 1209-1227, for a similar treatment. Also see Timothy G. Conley, Lars Peter Hansen, Erzo G.J. Luttmer, and José A. Scheinkman, "Short-Term Interest Rates as Subordinated Diffusions," *Review of Financial Studies* (Fall 1997), pp. 525-577, for a more rigorous treatment.

[14] Readers can consult James Hamilton, *Time Series Analysis* (Princeton, NJ: Princeton University Press, 1994). Also, there is some evidence that a conditional t-distribution is more appropriate for interest rate data. For simplicity, we maintain the conditional normal here.

Volatility of yields of all three maturities are found to increase with the level of yield, but to a different extent. As the results suggest, assuming the same value of γ for yields of all maturities can be inappropriate. For the 3-month spot yield, γ is found to be about 0.25, significantly below the 0.5 assumed in the CIR model. For the 10-year spot yield, γ is about 0.57, closed to CIR's assumption. Finally, for the 30-year spot yield, γ is about 1.27, significantly above the value of 1 assumed in the CP model. Furthermore, as the previous section mentioned, using different time periods can lead to different estimates. For instance, the behavior of interest rates in the late 1970s and the early 1980s were very different from those in the last decade. As a result, one should not be surprised that the dependence of volatility on the yield level might appear to be different from the last decade.

To illustrate the use of the Power Function Model, Exhibit 7 plots the forecasted volatility of the 30-year spot yield based on the estimates in Exhibit 6. For comparison purposes, we also plot the forecasted volatility when we impose the restriction of $\gamma = 1$. In the latter case, we are actually estimating the constant proportional yield volatility, σ_0, using the whole sample period. The value denotes the yield volatility on each day, annualized by 250 days.

As shown in Exhibit 7, using the CP model with constant proportional yield volatility ($\gamma = 1$) does not significantly differ from using the estimated value of $\gamma = 1.27$.

Exhibit 7: 250-day Annualized Yield Volatility of 30-year Spot Yield: Power Function Model

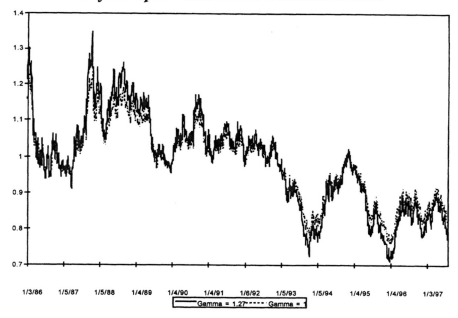

One critique of the Power Function Model is the fact that while it allows volatility to depend on the yield level, it does not incorporate the observation that a volatile period tends to be followed by another volatile period, a phenomenon known as *volatility clustering*. Nor does it allow past yield shocks to affect current and future volatility. To tackle these problems, we introduce a very different class of volatility modeling and forecasting tool.

Generalized Autoregressive Conditional Heteroskedasticity Model

Generalized Autoregressive Conditional Heteroskedasticity (GARCH) Model is probably the most extensively applied family of volatility models in empirical finance. It is well known that statistical distributions of many financial prices and returns series exhibit fatter tails than a normal distribution. These characteristics can be captured with a GARCH model. In fact, some well-known interest rate models, such as the Longstaff-Schwartz model, adopt GARCH to model yield volatility, which is allowed to be stochastic.[15] The term "conditional" means that the value of the variance depends on or is conditional on the information available, typically by means of the realized values of other random variables. The term "heteroskedasticity" means that the variance is not the same for all values of the random variable at different time periods.

If we maintain the assumption that the average daily yield change is zero, as before, the standard GARCH(1,1) model can be written as:

$$y_t - y_{t-1} = \varepsilon_t$$
$$E[\varepsilon_t^2] = \sigma_t^2 = a_0 + a_1 \varepsilon_{t-1}^2 + a_2 \sigma_{t-1}^2 \qquad (10)$$

where ε_t is just the daily yield change, interpreted as yield shock, E[.] denotes the statistical expectation operator, a_0, a_1, and a_2 are parameters to be estimated. In this way, yield volatility this period depends on yield shock as well as yield volatility in the last period. The GARCH model also estimates the long-run equilibrium variance, ω,, as

$$E[\varepsilon_t^2] = \bar{\omega} = \frac{a_0}{1 - a_1 - a_2} \qquad (11)$$

The GARCH model is popular not only for its simplicity in specification and its parsimonious nature in capturing time series properties of volatilities, but also because it is a generalization of some other measures of volatility. For example, it has been shown that equal-weighted rolling sample measure of variance and exponential smoothing scheme of volatility measure are both special cases of

---

[15] Francis A. Longstaff and Eduardo S. Schwartz, "Interest Rate Volatility and the Term Structure: A Two-Factor General Equilibrium Model," *Journal of Finance* (1992), pp. 1259-1282. Also see Francis A. Longstaff and Eduardo S. Schwartz, "Implementation of the Longstaff-Schwartz Interest Rate Model," *Journal of Fixed Income* (1993), pp. 7-14 for practical implementation of the model and how yield volatility is modeled by GARCH.

GARCH, but with different restrictions on the parameters. Other technical details of GARCH are beyond the scope of this chapter.[16]

Experience has shown that a GARCH(1,1) specification generally fits the volatility of most financial time series well, and is quite robust. The unknown parameters can again be estimated using MLE. The estimated models for the yields on 3-month Treasury bills and the 10-year and 30-year Treasury zeros are reported in Exhibit 8. Again, we plot the forecasted yield volatility, annualized by 250 days, of the 30-year spot rate in Exhibit 9 as an example.

One can immediately see that GARCH volatility is very different from the previous Power Function volatility. The reason is that GARCH incorporates the random and often erratic yield shocks as well as serial dependence in yield volatility into the volatility model; in contrast, the Power Function model only allows yield volatility to depend on the *level* of yield, without considering how past yield shocks and volatilities may affect the future volatility. The phenomenon of volatility clustering is well captured by GARCH, as revealed in Exhibit 9. On the other hand, the above GARCH(1,1) model does not consider the possible dependence of yield volatility on the level of yield. Thus, theoretically, GARCH volatilities do allow yields to become negative, which is an undesirable feature.

Power Function - GARCH Models

To capture the strength of both classes of models, one may consider combining the two into a more general form, at the expense of more complicated modeling and estimation, however. One way is to adopt the functional form of the Power Function model, while allowing the proportional yield volatility to follow a GARCH process. For example:

$$y_t - y_{t-1} = \varepsilon_t$$

$$\sigma_t = \sigma_{0,t} y_{t-1}^\gamma$$

$$\sigma_{0,t}^2 = a_0 + a_1 \varepsilon_{t-1}^2 + a_2 \sigma_{0,t-1}^2 \tag{12}$$

Exhibit 8: Estimation of GARCH(1,1) Models

	3-month Treasury bill	10-year Treasury zero	30-year Treasury zero
a_0	1.6467×10^{-8}	3.0204×10^{-8}	1.6313×10^{-8}
	(17.85)	(1.59)	(8.65)
a_1	0.0878	0.0896	0.0583
	(15.74)	(12.19)	(12.44)
a_2	0.8951	0.8441	0.9011
	(211.36)	(122.12)	(123.43)

[16] See, for example, Robert F. Engle, "Statistical Models for Financial Volatility," *Financial Analysts Journal* (1993), pp. 72-78; and Wai Lee and John Yin, "Modeling and Forecasting Interest Rate Volatility with GARCH," Chapter 20 in Frank J. Fabozzi (ed.), *Advances in Fixed Income Valuation Modeling and Risk Management* (New Hope, PA: FJF Associates, Pennsylvania, 1997), for an extensive discussion of GARCH as well as many other extensions.

Exhibit 9: 250-day Annualized Yield Volatility of 30-Year Spot Yield: GARCH(1,1) Model

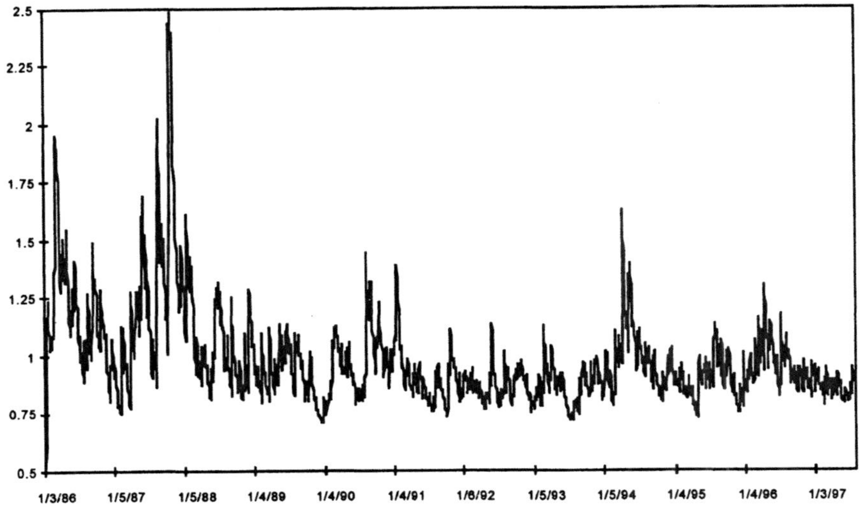

Exhibit 10: Estimation of Power Function - GARCH(1,1) Models

	3-month Treasury bill	10-year Treasury zero	30-year Treasury zero
a_0	8.6802×10^{-7}	3.6185×10^{-7}	3.8821×10^{-7}
	(1.59)	(1.23)	(1.37)
a_1	0.1836	0.0556	0.0717
	(12.73)	(11.07)	(14.20)
a_2	0.6424	0.8920	0.8015
	(34.53)	(48.52)	(5.40)
γ	0.2094	0.3578	0.3331
	(10.33)	(28.20)	(6.94)

With the above specification, yield volatility still depends on the level of yield, while past shocks and volatility affect current and future volatility through the proportional yield volatility, σ_0, which is now time varying instead of being a constant.[17] The estimation results are reported in Exhibit 10.

A noticeable difference between Exhibit 6 and Exhibit 10 is the fact that once the proportional yield volatility is modeled as a GARCH(1,1), γ assumes a smaller value than when yield volatility is only modeled as a power function of yield. In fact, γ for all maturities are all below 0.5, as assumed by the CIR model. This suggests that it is important to incorporate the dependence of current yield vol-

---

[17] See Robin J. Brenner, Richard H. Harjes, and Kenneth F. Kroner, "Another Look at Models of the Short-Term Interest Rate," *Journal of Financial and Quantitative Analysis* (March 1996), pp. 85-107, for a similar treatment and extensions.

atility on past information, or the sensitivity of yield volatility on level of yield may be overstated. For comparison purposes, Exhibit 11 plots the 250-day annualized yield volatility of the 30-year spot rate based on the estimated model in Exhibit 10.

Implied Volatility

The second way to estimate yield volatility is based on the observed prices of interest rate derivatives, such as options on bond futures, or interest rate caps and floors. Yield volatility calculated using this approach is called *implied volatility*.

The implied volatility is based on some option pricing model. One of the inputs to any option pricing model in which the underlying is a Treasury security or Treasury futures contract is expected yield volatility. If the observed price of an option is assumed to be the fair price and the option pricing model is assumed to be the model that would generate that fair price, then the implied yield volatility is the yield volatility that when used as an input into the option pricing model would produce the observed option price. Because of their liquidity, options on Treasury futures, Eurodollar futures, and caps and floors on LIBOR are typically used to extract implied volatilities.

Computing implied volatilities of yield from interest rate derivatives is not as straight forward as from derivatives of, say, stock. Later in this section, we will explain that these implied volatilities are not only model-dependent, but in some occasions they are also difficult to interpret, and can be misleading as well. For the time being, we follow the common practice in the industry of using the Black option pricing model for futures.[18]

Exhibit 11: 250-day Annualized Yield Volatility of 30-Year Spot Yield: Power Function - GARCH(1,1) Model

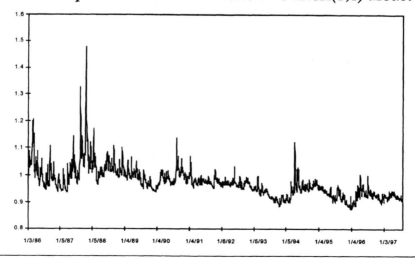

---

[18] Black, "The Pricing of Commodity Contracts."

Although the Black model has many limitations and inconsistent assumptions, it has been widely adopted. Traders often quote the exchange-traded options on Treasury or Eurodollar futures in terms of implied volatilities based on the Black model. These implied volatilities are also published by some investment houses, and are available through data vendors. For illustration purpose, we use the data of CBOT traded call options on 30-year Treasury bond futures as of April 30, 1997. The contract details, as well as the extracted implied volatilities based on the Black model, are listed in Exhibit 12.

Since the options are written on futures prices, the implied volatilities computed directly from the Black model are thus the implied price volatilities of the underlying futures contract. To convert the implied price volatilities to implied yield volatilities, we need the duration of the corresponding cheapest-to-deliver Treasury bond. The conversion is based on the simple standard relationship between percentage change in bond price and change in yield:

$$\frac{\Delta P}{P} \approx -\text{Duration} \times \Delta y \tag{13}$$

which implies that the same relationship also holds for price volatility and yield volatility.

Looking at the implied yield volatilities of the options with the same delivery month, one can immediately notice the "volatility smile." For example, for the options with a delivery month in June 1997, the implied yield volatility starts at a value of 0.98% for the deep in-the-money option with a strike price of 105, steadily drops to a minimum of 0.84% for the out-of-money option with a strike price of 113, and rises back to a maximum of 3.45% for the deep out-of-money option with a strike price of 130. Since all the options with the same delivery month are written on the same underlying bond futures, the only difference is their strike prices. The question is, which implied volatility is correct? While the answer to this question largely depends on how we accommodate the volatility smile,[19] standard practice suggests that we use the implied volatility of the at-the-money, or the nearest-the money option. In this case, the implied yield volatility of 0.91% of the option with a strike price of 109 should be used.

What is the meaning of an "implied yield volatility of 0.91%"? To interpret this number, one needs to be aware that this number is extracted from the observed option price based on the Black model. As a result, the meaning of this number not only depends on the assumption that the market correctly prices the option, but also the fact that the market prices the option in accordance with the Black model. Neither of these assumptions need to hold. In fact, most probably, both assumptions are unrealistic. Given these assumptions, one may interpret that the option market expects a *constant* annualized yield volatility of 0.91% for 30-year Treasury from April 30, 1997 to the maturity date of the option. Caps and floors can also be priced by the Black model, when they are interpreted as portfolios of options written on forward interest rates. Accordingly, implied volatilities can be extracted from cap prices and floor prices, but subjected to the same limitations of the Black model.

---

[19] Current research typically uses either a jump diffusion process, a stochastic volatility model, or a combination of both to explain volatility smile. The details are beyond the scope of this chapter.

Exhibit 12: Call Options on 30-year Treasury Bond Futures on April 30, 1997

Delivery Month	Futures Price	Strike Price	Option Price	Implied Price Volatility	Duration	Implied Yield Volatility
1997:6	109.281	105	4.297	9.334	9.57	0.975
1997:6	109.281	106	3.328	9.072	9.57	0.948
1997:6	109.281	107	2.406	8.811	9.57	0.921
1997:6	109.281	108	1.594	8.742	9.57	0.913
1997:6	109.281	109	0.938	8.665	9.57	0.905
1997:6	109.281	110	0.469	8.462	9.57	0.884
1997:6	109.281	111	0.188	8.205	9.57	0.857
1997:6	109.281	112	0.062	8.129	9.57	0.849
1997:6	109.281	113	0.016	7.993	9.57	0.835
1997:6	109.281	114	0.016	9.726	9.57	1.016
1997:6	109.281	116	0.016	13.047	9.57	1.363
1997:6	109.281	118	0.016	16.239	9.57	1.697
1997:6	109.281	120	0.016	19.235	9.57	2.010
1997:6	109.281	122	0.016	22.168	9.57	2.316
1997:6	109.281	124	0.016	25.033	9.57	2.616
1997:6	109.281	126	0.016	27.734	9.57	2.898
1997:6	109.281	128	0.016	30.392	9.57	3.176
1997:6	109.281	130	0.016	33.01	9.57	3.449
1997:9	108.844	100	8.922	8.617	9.54	0.903
1997:9	108.844	102	7.062	8.750	9.54	0.917
1997:9	108.844	104	5.375	8.999	9.54	0.943
1997:9	108.844	106	3.875	9.039	9.54	0.947
1997:9	108.844	108	2.625	9.008	9.54	0.944
1997:9	108.844	110	1.656	8.953	9.54	0.938
1997:9	108.844	112	0.969	8.913	9.54	0.934
1997:9	108.844	114	0.516	8.844	9.54	0.927
1997:9	108.844	116	0.250	8.763	9.54	0.919
1997:9	108.844	118	0.109	8.679	9.54	0.910
1997:9	108.844	120	0.047	8.733	9.54	0.915
1997:9	108.844	122	0.016	8.581	9.54	0.899
1997:9	108.844	124	0.016	9.625	9.54	1.009
1997:9	108.844	126	0.016	10.646	9.54	1.116
1997:9	108.844	128	0.016	11.65	9.54	1.221
1997:12	108.469	98	10.562	7.861	9.51	0.827
1997:12	108.469	106	4.250	9.036	9.51	0.950
1997:12	108.469	108	3.125	9.070	9.51	0.954
1997:12	108.469	110	2.188	9.006	9.51	0.947
1997:12	108.469	112	1.469	8.953	9.51	0.941
1997:12	108.469	114	0.938	8.881	9.51	0.934
1997:12	108.469	116	0.594	8.949	9.51	0.941
1997:12	108.469	118	0.359	8.973	9.51	0.944
1997:12	108.469	120	0.234	9.232	9.51	0.971
1997:12	108.469	122	0.141	9.340	9.51	0.982
1997:12	108.469	128	0.031	9.793	9.51	1.030

Limitations of the Black Model

There are two major assumptions of the Black model that makes it unrealistic. First, interest rates are assumed to be constant. Yet, the assumption is used to derive the pricing formula for the option which derives its payoff precisely from the fact that future interest rates (forward rates) are stochastic. It has been shown that the Black model implies a time evolution path for the term structure that leads to arbitrage opportunities. In other words, the model itself implicitly violates the no-arbitrage spirit in derivatives pricing.

Second, volatilities of futures prices, or forward interest rates, are assumed to be constant over the life of the contract. This assumption is in sharp contrary to empirical evidence as well as intuition. It is well understood that a forward contract with one month to maturity is more sensitive to changes in the current term structure than a forward contract with one year to maturity. Thus, the volatility of the forward rate is inversely related to the time to maturity.

Finally, on the average, implied volatilities from the Black model are found to be higher than the realized volatilities during the same period of time.[20] A plausible explanation is that the difference in the two volatilities represents the fee for the financial service provided by the option writers, while the exact dynamics of the relationship between implied and realized volatilities remains unclear.

Practical Uses of Implied Volatilities from Black Model

Typically, implied volatilities from exchange-traded options with sufficient liquidity are used to price over-the-counter interest rate derivatives such as caps, floors, and swaptions. Apart from the limitations as discussed above, another difficulty in practice is the fact that only options with some fixed maturities are traded. For example, in Exhibit 12, the *constant* implied volatilities only apply to the time periods from April 30, 1997 to the delivery dates in June, September, and December 1997, respectively. For instance, on May 1, 1997, we need a volatility input to price a 3-month cap on LIBOR. In this case, traders will either use the implied volatility from options with a maturity closest to three months, or make an adjustment/judgment based on the implied volatilities of options with a maturity just shorter than three months, and options with maturity just longer than three months.

Recent Development in Implied Volatilities

The finance industry is not unaware of the limitations of the Black model and its implied volatilities. Due to its simplicity and its early introduction to the market, it has become the standard in computing implied volatilities. However, there has been a tremendous amount of rigorous research going on in interest rate and interest rate derivatives models, especially since the mid 1980s. While a comprehen-

---

[20] See Laurie Goodman and Jeffrey Ho, "Are Investors Rewarded for Shorting Volatility?" *Journal of Fixed Income* (June 1997), pp. 38-42, for a comparison of implied versus realized volatility.

sive review of this research is not provided here, it is useful to highlight the broad classes of models which can help us understand where implied volatilities related research is going.

Broadly speaking, there are two classes of models. The first class is known as the *Equilibrium Model*. Some noticeable examples include the Vasciek model, CIR model, Brennan-Schwartz model, and Longstaff-Schwartz model, as mentioned earlier in this chapter. This class of models attempts to specify the equilibrium conditions by assuming that some state variables drive the evolution of the term structure. By imposing other structure and restrictions, closed-form solutions for equilibrium prices of bonds and other interest rate derivatives are then derived. Many of these models impose a functional form to interest rate volatility, such as the power function as discussed and estimated earlier, or assume that volatility follows certain dynamics. In addition, the models also specify a particular dynamics on how interest rate drifts up or down over time. To implement these models, one needs to estimate the parameters of the interest rate process, including the parameters of the volatility function, based on some advanced econometric technique applied to historical data.

There are two major shortcomings of this class of models. First, these models are not preference-free, which means that we need to specify the utility function in dictating how investors make choices? Second, since only historical data are used in calibrating the models, these models do not rule out arbitrage opportunities in the current term structure. Due to the nature of the models, volatility is an important input to these models rather than an output that we can extract from observed prices. In addition, it has been shown that the term structure of spot yield volatilities can differ across one-factor versions of these models despite the fact that all produce the same term structure of cap prices.[21]

The second class of models is known as the *No-Arbitrage Model*. The *Ho-Lee Model* is considered as the first model of this class. Other examples include the *Black-Derman-Toy Model*,[22] *Black-Karasinski Model*,[23] and the *Heath-Jarrow-Morton Model (HJM)*.[24] In contrast to the equilibrium models which attempt to model equilibrium, these no-arbitrage models are less ambitious. They take the current term structure as given, and assume that no arbitrage opportunities are allowed during the evolution of the entire term structure. All interest rate sensitive securities are assumed to be correctly priced at the time of calibrating the model. In this way, the models, together with the current term structure and the no-arbitrage assumption, impose some restrictions on how inter-

[21] Eduardo Canabarro, "Where Do One-Factor Interest Rate Models Fail?" *Journal of Fixed Income* (September 1995), pp. 31-52.

[22] Fischer Black, Emanuel Derman, and William Toy, "A One-Factor Model of Interest Rates and its Applications to Treasury Bond Options," *Financial Analysts Journal* (January-February 1990), pp. 33-39.

[23] Fischer Black and Piotr Karasinski, "Bond and Option Pricing when Short Rates are Lognormal," *Financial Analysts Journal* (1991), pp. 52-59.

[24] David Heath, Robert Jarrow, and Andrew Morton, "Bond Pricing and the Term-Structure of Interest Rates: A New Methodology," *Econometrica* (1992), pp. 77-105.

est rates of different maturities will evolve over time. Some restrictions on the volatility structure may be imposed in order to allow interest rates to mean-revert, or to restrict interest rates to be positive under all circumstances. However, since these models take the current bond prices as given, more frequent recalibration of the models is required once bond prices change.

The HJM model, in particular, has received considerable attention in the industry as well as in the finance literature. Many other no-arbitrage models are shown to be special cases of HJM. In spirit, the HJM model is similar to the well-celebrated Black-Scholes model in the sense that the model does not require assumptions about investor preferences.[25] Much like the Black-Scholes model that requires volatility instead of expected stock return as an input to price a stock option, the HJM model only requires a description of the volatility structure of forward interest rates, instead of the expected interest rate movements in pricing interest rate derivatives. It is this feature of the model that, given current prices of interest rate derivatives, make extraction of implied volatilities possible.

Amin and Morton[26] and Amin and Ng[27] use this approach to extract a term structure of implied volatilities. Several points are noteworthy. Since the no-arbitrage assumption is incorporated into the model, the extracted implied volatilities are more meaningful than those from the Black model. Moreover, interest rates are all stochastic instead of being assumed constant. On the other hand, these implied volatilities are those of forward interest rates, instead of spot interest rates. Furthermore, interest rate derivatives with different maturities and sufficient liquidity are required to calibrate the model. Finally, the HJM model is often criticized as too complicated for practitioners, and is too slow for real time practical applications.[28]

SUMMARY

Yield volatility estimates play a critical role in the measurement and control of interest rate risk. In this chapter we have discussed how historical yield volatility is calculated and the issues associated with its estimate. These issues include the number of observations and the time period to be used, the number of days that should be used to annualize the daily standard deviation, the expected value that should be used, and the weighting of observations. We then looked at modeling

---

[25] This by no means implies that the Black-Scholes model is a no-arbitrage model. Although no-arbitrage condition is enforced, the Black-Scholes model does require equilibrium settings and market clearing conditions. Further details are beyond the scope of this chapter.

[26] Kaushik I. Amin and Andrew J. Morton, "Implied Volatility Functions in Arbitrage-Free Term Structure Models," *Journal of Financial Economics* (1994), pp. 141-180.

[27] Kaushik I. Amin and Victor K. Ng, "Inferring Future Volatility from the Information in Implied Volatility in Eurodollar Options: A New Approach," *Review of Financial Studies* (1997), pp 333-367.

[28] See David Heath, Robert Jarrow, Andrew Morton, and Mark Spindel, "Easier Done than Said," *Risk* (October 1992), pp. 77-80 for a response to this critique.

and forecasting yield volatility. The two approaches we discussed are historical volatility and implied volatility. For the historical volatility approach, we discussed various models, their underlying assumptions, and their limitations. These models include the Power Function Models and GARCH Models. While many market participants talk about implied volatility, we explained that unlike the derivation of this measure in equity markets, deriving this volatility estimate from interest rate derivatives is not as simple and straight forward. The implied volatility estimate depends not only on the particular option pricing model employed, but also a model of the time evolution of the complete term structure and volatilities of yields of different maturities.

Section V:

Equity
Portfolio Management

Chapter 24

Investment Management: An Architecture for the Equity Market

Bruce I. Jacobs, Ph.D.
Principal
Jacobs Levy Equity Management

Kenneth N. Levy, CFA
Principal
Jacobs Levy Equity Management

INTRODUCTION

Anyone who has ever built a house knows how important it is to start out with a sound architectural design. A sound design can help ensure that the end product will meet all the homeowner's expectations — material, aesthetic, and financial. A bad architectural design, or no design, offers no such assurance and is likely to lead to poor decision-making, unintended results, and cost overruns.

It is equally important in building an equity portfolio to start out with some framework that relates the raw materials — stocks — and the basic construction techniques — investment approaches — to the end product. An architecture of equity management that outlines the basic relationships between the raw investment material, investment approaches, potential rewards and possible risks, can provide a blueprint for investment decision-making.

We provide such a blueprint in this chapter. A quick tour of this blueprint reveals three building blocks — a comprehensive core, static style subsets, and a dynamic entity. Investment approaches can also be roughly categorized into three groups — passive, traditional active, and engineered active. Understanding the market's architecture and the advantages and disadvantages of each investment approach can improve overall investment results.

The authors thank Judith Kimball for her editorial assistance.

Exhibit 1: Equity Market Architecture

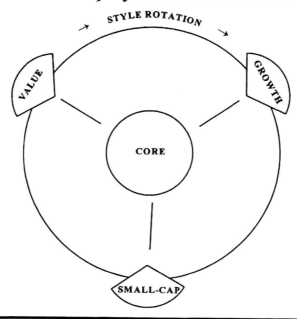

AN ARCHITECTURE

Exhibit 1 provides a simple but fairly comprehensive view of the equity market.[1] The heart of the structure, the core, represents the overall market. Theoretically, this would include all U.S. equity issues. (Similar architectures can be applied to other national equity markets.) In line with the practice of most equity managers, a broad-based equity index such as the S&P 500 or (even broader) the Russell 3000 or Wilshire 5000, may proxy for the aggregate market.

For both equity managers and their clients, the overall market represents a natural and intuitive starting place. It is the ultimate selection pool for all equity strategies. Furthermore, the long-term returns offered by the U.S. equity market have historically outperformed alternative asset classes in the majority of multiyear periods. The aim of most institutional investors (even those that do not hold core investments per se) is to capture, or outdo, this equity return premium.

The core equity market can be broken down into subsets that comprise stocks with similar price behaviors — large-cap growth, large-cap value, and small-cap stocks. In Exhibit 1, the wedges circling the core represent these style subsets. The aggregate of the stocks forming the subsets equals the overall core market.

---

[1] See also Bruce I. Jacobs and Kenneth N. Levy, "How to Build a Better Equity Portfolio," *Pension Management* (June 1996), pp. 36-39.

Exhibit 2: Small-Cap Stocks May Outperform Large-Cap in Some Periods and Underperform in Others

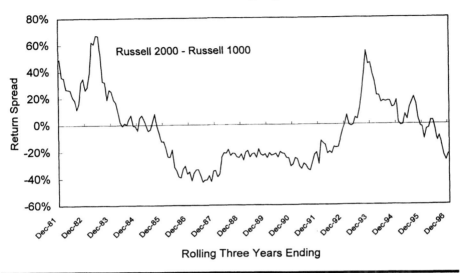

Rolling Three Years Ending

One advantage of viewing the market as a collection of subsets is the ability it confers upon the investor to "mix and match." Instead of holding a core portfolio, for example, the investor can hold market subsets in market-like weights and receive returns and incur risks commensurate with those of the core. Alternatively, the investor can depart from core weights to pursue returns in excess of the core market return (at the expense, of course, of incremental risk). Investors who believe that small-cap stocks offer a higher return than the average market return, for example, can overweight that subset and underweight large-cap value and growth stocks.

Over time, different style subsets can offer differing relative payoffs as economic conditions change. As Exhibit 2 shows, small-cap stocks outperformed large-cap stocks by 60 percentage points or more in the rolling 3-year periods ending in mid-1983 and by 45 to 55 percentage points in late 1993. But small cap underperformed by 20 to 40 percentage points in the rolling 3-year periods between early 1986 and December 1991.[2] Exhibit 3 shows that large-cap growth stocks outperformed large-cap value stocks by 30 to 40 percentage points in the rolling 3-year periods from mid-1991 to mid-1992 but underperformed by 20 to 35 percentage points in every rolling 3-year period from mid-1983 through 1986.[3]

---

[2] Exhibit 2 uses the Frank Russell 1000 (the largest stocks in the Russell 3000) as the large-cap index and the Russell 2000 (the smallest stocks in the Russell 3000) as the small-cap index.

[3] Exhibit 3 uses the Russell 1000 Growth and the Russell 1000 Value as the growth and value indexes; these indexes roughly divide the market capitalization of the Russell 1000. Results are similar using other indexes, such as the Wilshire and S&P 500/BARRA style indexes.

Exhibit 3: Large-Cap Growth Stocks Outperform Large-Cap Value in Some Periods and Underperform in Others

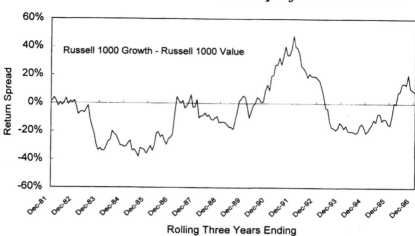

Just as some investors attempt to time the market by buying into and selling out of equities in line with their expectations of overall market trends, investors can attempt to exploit the dynamism of style subsets by rotating their investments across different styles over time, in pursuit of profit opportunities offered by one or another subset as market and economic conditions change.[4] The curved lines connecting the style wedges in Exhibit 1 represent this dynamic nature of the market.

The equity core and its constituent style subsets constitute the basic building blocks — the equity selection universes — from which investors can construct their portfolios. Another important choice facing the investor, however, is the investment approach or approaches to apply to the selection universe. Exhibit 4 categorizes possible approaches into three groups — traditional, passive, and engineered. Each of these approaches can be characterized by an underlying investment philosophy and, very generally, by a level of risk relative to the underlying selection universe.

TRADITIONAL ACTIVE MANAGEMENT

Traditional investment managers focus on "stock picking." In short, they hunt for individual securities that will perform well over the investment horizon. The search includes in-depth examinations of companies' financial statements and investigations of companies' managements, product lines, facilities, etc. Based on the findings of these inquiries, traditional managers determine whether a particular firm is a good "buy" or a better "sell."

---

[4] See Bruce I. Jacobs and Kenneth N. Levy, "High-Definition Style Rotation," *Journal of Investing* (Fall 1996), pp. 14-23.

Exhibit 4: Equity Investment Approaches

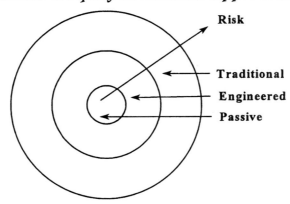

The search area for traditional investing may be wide — the equivalent of the equity core — and may include market timing that exploits the dynamism of the overall market. Because in-depth analyses of large numbers of securities are just not practical for any one manager, however, traditional managers tend to focus on subsets of the equity market. Some may hunt for above-average earnings growth (growth stocks), while others look to buy future earnings streams cheaply (value stocks); still others beat the grasses off the trodden paths, in search of overlooked growth and/or value stocks (small-cap stocks). Traditional managers have thus fallen into the pursuit of growth, value, or small-cap styles.

Traditional managers often screen an initial universe of stocks based on some financial criteria, thereby selecting a relatively small list of stocks to be followed closely. Focusing on such a narrow list reduces the complexity of the analytical problem to human (i.e., traditional) dimensions. Unfortunately, it may also introduce significant barriers to superior performance.

Exhibit 5 plots the combinations of breadth and depth of insights necessary to achieve a given investment return/risk level.[5] Here the breadth of insights may be understood as the number of independent insights — i.e., the number of investment ideas or the number of stocks. The depth, or goodness, of insights is measured as the *information coefficient* — the correlation between the return forecasts made for stocks and their actual returns. Note that the goodness of the insights needed to produce the given return/risk ratio starts to increase dramatically as the number of insights falls below 100; the slope gets particularly steep as breadth falls below 50.

[5] The plot reflects the relationship:

$$IR = IC \times \sqrt{BR}$$

where *IC* is the information coefficient (the correlation between predicted and actual returns), *BR* the number of independent insights, and IR (in this case set equal to one) the ratio of annualized excess return to annualized residual risk. See Richard C. Grinold and Ronald N. Kahn, *Active Portfolio Management* (Chicago, IL: Probus Publishing, 1995), Chapter 6.

Exhibit 5: Combination of Breadth (Number) of Insights and Depth, or "Goodness," of Insights Needed to Produce a Given Investment Return/Risk Ratio

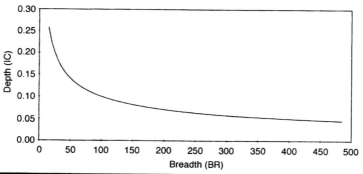

Traditional investing in effect relies on the ability of in-depth research to supply information coefficients that are high enough to overcome the lack of breadth imposed by the approach's fairly severe limitations on the number of securities that can be followed. As Exhibit 5 shows, however, the level of information coefficients required at such constricted breadth levels constitutes a considerable hurdle to superior performance. The insights from traditional management must be very, very good to overcome the commensurate lack of breadth.[6]

Furthermore, lack of breadth may also have detrimental effects on the depth of traditional insights. While reducing the range of inquiry makes tractable the problem of stock selection via the labor-intensive methods of traditional active management, it is also bound to result in potentially relevant (and profitable) information being left out. Surely, for example, the behavior of the growth stocks not followed by traditional growth managers — even the behavior of value stocks outside the growth subset — may contain information relevant to the pricing of those stocks that do constitute the reduced traditional universe.

Another inherent weakness of traditional investment approaches is their heavy reliance on subjective human judgments. An ever-growing body of research suggests that stock prices, as well as being moved by fundamental information, are influenced by the psychology of investors. In particular, investors often appear to be under the influence of cognitive biases that cause them to err systematically in making investment decisions.[7]

---

[6] Market timing strategies are particularly lacking in breadth, as an insight into the market's direction provides only one investment decision. Quarterly timing would produce four "bets" a year — a level of diversification few investors would find acceptable. Furthermore, unless timing is done on a daily basis or the timer is prodigiously skilled, it would take a lifetime to determine whether the results of timing reflect genuine skill or mere chance.

[7] See, for example, Daniel Kahneman and Amos Tversky, "Prospect Theory: An Analysis of Decision Under Risk," *Econometrica* (Number 2, 1979), pp. 263-292, and Richard H. Thaler (ed.), *Advances in Behavioral Finance* (New York, NY: Russell Sage Foundation, 1993).

Kenneth Arrow, for example, finds that investors tend to overemphasize new information if it appears to be representative of a possible future event; thus, if investors perceive a firm's management to be "good," and the firm has recently enjoyed high earnings, they will tend to place more reliance on the higher than the lower earnings estimates provided by analysts.[8] Robert Shiller finds that investors are as susceptible as any other consumers to fads and fashions — bidding up prices of "hot" stocks and ignoring out-of-favor issues.[9] We describe below four common cognitive errors that investors may fall prey to.

Cognitive Errors

Loss Aversion (The "Better Not Take the Chance/What the Heck" Paradox)
Investors exhibit risk-averse behavior with respect to potential gains: faced with a choice between (1) a sure gain of $3,000 and (2) an 80% chance of gaining $4,000 or a 20% chance of gaining nothing, most people choose the sure thing, even though the $3,000 is less than the expected value of the gamble, which is $3,200 (80% of $4,000). But investors are generally risk-seeking when it comes to avoiding certain loss: faced with a choice between (1) a sure loss of $3,000 and (2) an 80% chance of losing $4,000 or a 20% chance of losing nothing, most people will opt to take a chance. It's only human nature that the pain of loss exceed the glee of gain, but putting human nature in charge of investment decision-making may lead to suboptimal results. Shirking risk leads to forgone gains. Pursuing risk in avoidance of loss may have even direr consequences ("digging a deeper hole"), as recent episodes at Barings and Daiwa have demonstrated.

Endowment Effect (The "Pride in Ownership" Syndrome)
The price people are willing to pay to acquire an object or service is often less than the price they would be willing to sell the identical object or service for if they owned it. Say you bought a stock last year and it's quadrupled in price. If you won't buy more because "it's too expensive now," you should sell it. If you won't sell it because you were so brilliant when you bought it, you're sacrificing returns for pride in ownership.

The Gambler's Fallacy ("Hot Streaks, Empty Wallets")
Is it more likely that six tosses of a coin will come up HTTHTH or HHHTTT? Most people think the former sequence is more typical than the latter, but in truth both are equally likely products of randomness. In either case, the probability of the next flip of the coin turning up heads, or tails, is 50%. Market prices, too, will display patterns. It's easy to interpret such patterns as persistent trends, and tempting to trade on them. But if the latest "hot streak" is merely a mirage thrown up by random price movements, it will prove an unreliable guide to future performance.

---

[8] Kenneth J. Arrow, "Risk Perception in Psychology and Economics," *Economic Inquiry* (Number 1, 1982), pp. 1-8.
[9] Robert J. Shiller, "Stock Prices and Social Dynamics," *Brookings Papers on Economic Activity* (Number 2, 1984), pp. 457-510.

Confirmation Bias ("Don't Confuse Me with the Facts")

People search for and place more reliance upon evidence that confirms their pre-conceived notions, ignoring or devaluing evidence that refutes them. Four cards lie on a table, showing A, B, 2, and 3: What is the fewest number of cards you can turn over to confirm or refute that every card with a vowel on one side has an even number on the other side? Most people choose A, then 2. An odd number or a letter on the reverse of A would refute the conjecture. The 2, however, can merely confirm, not refute; the presence of a vowel on the reverse would confirm, but anything else would simply be immaterial. The correct choice is to turn A, 3, and B. A vowel on the reverse of 3 can refute, as can a vowel on the reverse of B. Investment approaches that do not have a method of systematically searching through all available evidence without prejudice, in order to find the exceptions that disprove their rules, may leave portfolios open to blindsiding and torpedo effects.

Investors susceptible to these biases will tend to take too little (or too much) risk; to hold on to an investment for too long; to see long-term trends where none exist; and to place too much reliance on information that confirms existing beliefs. As a result, the performances of their portfolios are likely to suffer.

The reliance of traditional investment management on the judgments of individual human minds makes for idiosyncrasies of habit that work to the detriment of investment discipline, and this is true at the level of the investment firm as well as the individual at the firm. It may be difficult to coordinate the individual mindsets of all analysts, economists, investment officers, technicians, and traders, and this coordination is even harder to achieve when subjective standards for security analysis differ from individual to individual.

Constructing Portfolios

The qualitative nature of the outcome of the security evaluation process, together with the absence of a unifying framework, can give rise to problems when individual insights into securities' performances are combined to construct a portfolio. However on target an analyst's buy or sell recommendations may be, they are difficult to translate into guidelines for portfolio construction. Portfolio optimization procedures require quantitative estimates of relevant parameters — not mere recommendations to buy, hold, or sell.

The traditional manager's focus on stock picking and the resulting ad hoc nature of portfolio construction can lead to portfolios that are poorly defined in regard to their underlying selection universes. While any particular manager's portfolio return may be measured against the return on an index representative of an underlying equity core or style subset, that index does not serve as a "benchmark" in the sense of providing a guideline for portfolio risk. Traditional portfolios' risk-return profiles may thus vary greatly relative to those of the underlying selection universe.

As a result, portfolios do not necessarily fit into the market's architecture. A traditional value manager, for example, may be averse to holding certain sectors, such as utilities. Not only will the portfolio's returns suffer when utilities perform well, but the portfolio will suffer from a lack of "integrity" — of wholeness. Such a portfolio will not be representative of the whole value subset. Nor could it be combined with growth and small-cap portfolios to create a core-like holding.

Because the relationship between the overall equity market and traditional managers' style portfolios may be ambiguous, "value" and "growth," "small-cap" and "large-cap" may not be mutually exclusive. Value portfolios may hold some growth stocks, or growth portfolios some value stocks. There is no assurance that a combination of style portfolios can offer a market-like or above-market return at market-like risk levels.

Because of their heavy reliance on human mind power and subjective judgment, traditional approaches to investment management tend to suffer from a lack of breadth, a lack of discipline, and a resulting lack of portfolio integrity. Traditional management, while it may serve as well as any other approach for picking individual stocks, suffers from severe limitations when it comes to constructing portfolios of stocks. Perhaps it is for this reason that traditionally managed portfolios have often failed to live up to expectations.

PASSIVE MANAGEMENT

The generally poor performance of traditional investment management approaches helped to motivate the development, in the late 1960s and the 1970s, of new theories of stock price behavior. The efficient market hypothesis and random walk theory — the products of much research — offered a reason for the meager returns reaped by traditional investment managers: stock prices effectively reflect all information in an "efficient" manner, rendering stock price movements random and unpredictable. Efficiency and randomness provided the motivation for passive investment management; advances in computing power provided the means.

Passive management aims to construct portfolios that will match the risk/return profiles of underlying market benchmarks. The benchmark may be core equity (as proxied by the S&P 500 or other broad index) or a style subset (as proxied by a large-cap growth, large-cap value, or small-cap index). Given the quantitative tools at its disposal, passive management can fine-tune the stock selection and portfolio construction problems in order to deliver portfolios that mimic very closely both the returns and risks of their chosen benchmarks.

Passive portfolios, unlike traditional portfolios, are disciplined. Any tendencies for passive managers to succumb to cognitive biases will be held in check by the exigencies of their stated goals — tracking the performances of their underlying benchmarks. Their success in this endeavor also means that the resulting portfolios will have integrity. A passive value portfolio will behave like its underlying selection universe, and a combination of passive style portfolios in market-like weights can be expected to offer a return close to the market's return at a risk level close to the market's.

As the trading required to keep portfolios in line with underlying indexes is generally less than that required to "beat" the indexes, transaction costs for passive management are generally lower than those incurred by active investment approaches. As much of the stock selection and portfolio construction problem can be relegated to fast-acting computers, the management fees for passive management are also modest. For the same reason, the number of securities that can be covered by any given passive manager is virtually unlimited; all the stocks in the selection universe can be considered for portfolio inclusion.

Unlike traditional management, then, passive management offers great breadth. Breadth in this case doesn't count for much, however, because passive management is essentially insightless. Built on the premise that markets are efficient, hence market prices are random and unpredictable, passive management does not attempt to pursue or offer any return over the return on the relevant benchmark. Rather, its appeal lies in its ability to deliver the asset class return or to deliver the return of a style subset of the asset class. In practice, of course, trading costs and management fees, however modest, subtract from this performance.

An investor in pursuit of above-market returns may nevertheless be able to exploit passive management approaches via style subset selection and style rotation. That is, an investor who believes value stocks will outperform the overall market can choose to overweight a passive value portfolio in expectation of earning above-market (but not above-benchmark) returns. An investor with foresight into style performance can choose to rotate investments across different passive style portfolios as underlying economic and market conditions change.

ENGINEERED MANAGEMENT

Engineered management recognizes that markets are reasonably efficient in digesting information and that stock price movements in response to unanticipated news are largely random. It also recognizes, however, that significant, measurable pricing inefficiencies do exist, and it seeks to deliver incremental returns by modeling and exploiting these inefficiencies. In this endeavor, it applies to the same company fundamental and economic data used by traditional active management many of the tools that fostered the development of passive management, including modern computing power, finance theory, and statistical techniques — instruments that can extend the reaches (and discipline the vagaries) of the human mind.

Engineered approaches use quantitative methods to select stocks and construct portfolios that will have risk/return profiles similar to those of underlying equity benchmarks but offer incremental returns relative to those benchmarks, at appropriate incremental risk levels. The quantitative methods used may range from fairly straightforward to immensely intricate. In selecting stocks, for example, an engineered approach may use something as simple as a dividend discount model. Or it may employ complex multivariate models that aim to capture the complexities of the equity market.[10]

The engineered selection process can deal with and benefit from as wide a selection universe as passive management. It can thus approach the investment problem with an unbiased philosophy, unhampered, as is traditional management, by the need to reduce the equity universe to a tractable subset. At the same time, depending upon the level of sophistication of the tools it chooses to use, engineered management can benefit from great depth of analysis — a depth similar to that of traditional approaches. Multivariate modeling, for example, can take into account the intricacies of stock price behavior, including variations in price responses across stocks of different industries, economic sectors, and styles.

Because engineered management affords both breadth and depth, the manager can choose a focal point from which to frame the equity market, without loss of important "framing" information. Analysis of a particular style subset, for example, can take advantage of information gleaned from the whole universe of securities, not just stocks of that particular style (or a subset of that style, as in traditional management). The increased breadth of inquiry should lead to improvements in portfolio performance vis-a-vis traditional style portfolios.

Engineering Portfolios

Engineered management utilizes all the information found relevant from an objective examination of the broad equity universe to arrive at numerical estimates for the expected returns and anticipated risks of the stocks in that universe. Unlike the subjective outcomes of traditional management, such numerical estimates are eminently suitable for portfolio construction via optimization techniques.[11]

The goal of optimization is to maximize portfolio return while tying portfolio risk to that of the underlying benchmark. The portfolio's systematic risk should match the risk of the benchmark. The portfolio's residual risk should be no more than is justified by the expected incremental return. Risk control can be further refined by tailoring the optimization model so that it is consistent with the variables in the return estimation process.

The quantitative nature of the stock selection and portfolio construction processes imposes discipline on engineered portfolios. With individual stocks defined by expected performance parameters, and portfolios optimized along those parameters to provide desired patterns of expected risk and return, engineered portfolios can be defined in terms of preset performance goals. Engineered managers have little leeway to stray from these performance mandates, hence are less likely than traditional managers to fall under the sway of cognitive errors. In fact, engineered strategies may be designed to exploit such biases as investor overreaction (leading to price reversals) or investor herding (leading to price trends).

---

[10] See Bruce I. Jacobs and Kenneth N. Levy, "Investment Analysis: Profiting from a Complex Equity Market," Chapter 25 in this book.

[11] See also Bruce I. Jacobs and Kenneth N. Levy, "Engineering Portfolios: A Unified Approach," *Journal of Investing* (Winter 1995).

Exhibit 6: Comparison of Equity Investment Approaches

	Traditional	Passive	Engineered
Depth of Analysis	Yes	No	Simple — No Complex — Yes
Breadth of Analysis	No	Yes	Yes
Free of Cognitive Error	No	Yes	Yes
Portfolio Integrity	No	Yes	Yes

The discipline of engineered management also helps to ensure portfolio integrity. The style subset portfolios of a given firm, for example, should be non-overlapping, and the style subset benchmarks should in the aggregate be inclusive of all stocks in the investor's universe. Value portfolios should contain no growth stocks, nor growth portfolios any value stocks. The underlying benchmarks for value and growth portfolios, or large and small-cap portfolios, should aggregate to the equity core.

Engineering should reduce, relative to traditional management, portfolio return deviations from the underlying core or subset benchmark, while increasing expected returns relative to those available from passive approaches. While judicious stock selection can provide excess portfolio return over a passive benchmark, optimized portfolio construction offers control of portfolio risk.

Exhibit 6 compares the relative merits of traditional, passive, and engineered approaches to portfolio management. Traditional management offers depth, but strikes out with lack of breadth, susceptibility to cognitive errors, and lack of portfolio integrity. Passive management offers breadth, freedom from cognitive error, and portfolio integrity, but no depth whatsoever. Only engineered management has the ability to construct portfolios that benefit from both breadth and depth of analysis, are free of cognitive errors, and have structural integrity.

MEETING CLIENT NEEDS

A broad-based, engineered approach offers investment managers the means to tailor portfolios for a wide variety of client needs. Consider, for example, a client that has no opinion about style subset performance, but believes that the equity market will continue to offer its average historical premium over alternative cash and bond investments. This client may choose to hold the market in the form of an engineered core portfolio that can deliver the all-important equity market premium (at the market's risk level), plus the potential for some incremental return consistent with the residual risk incurred.

Alternatively, the client with a strong belief that value stocks will outperform can choose from among several engineered solutions. An engineered portfolio can be designed to deliver a value-benchmark-like return at a comparable risk level or to offer, at the cost of incremental risk, a return increment above the value benchmark. Traditional value portfolios cannot be designed to offer the same level of assurance of meeting these goals.

With engineered portfolios, the client also has the ability to fine-tune bets. For example, the client can weight a portfolio toward value stocks while retaining exposure to the overall market by placing some portion of the portfolio in core equity and the remainder in a value portfolio, or by placing some percentage in a growth portfolio and a larger percentage in a value portfolio. Exposures to the market and to its various subsets can be engineered. Again, traditional management can offer no assurance that a combination of style portfolios will offer the desired risk-return profile.

Expanding Opportunities

The advantages of an engineered approach are perhaps best exploited by strategies that are not constrained to deliver a benchmark-like performance. An engineered style rotation strategy, for example, seeks to deliver returns in excess of the market's by forecasting style subset performance. Shifting investment weights aggressively among various style subsets as market and economic conditions evolve, style rotation takes advantage of the historical tendency of any given style to outperform the overall market in some periods and to underperform it in others. Such a strategy uses the entire selection universe and offers potentially high returns at commensurate risk levels.

Allowing short sales as an adjunct to an engineered strategy — whether that strategy utilizes core equity, a style subset, or style rotation — can further enhance return opportunities. While traditional management focuses on stock picking — the selection of "winning" securities — the breadth of engineered management allows for the consideration of "losers" as well as "winners." With an engineered portfolio that allows shorting of losers, the manager can pursue potential mispricings without constraint, going long underpriced stocks and selling short overpriced stocks.

In markets in which short selling is not widespread, there are reasons to believe that shorting stocks can offer more opportunity than buying stocks. This is because restrictions on short selling do not permit investor pessimism to be as fully represented in prices as investor optimism. In such a market, the potential candidates for short sale may be less efficiently priced, hence offer greater return potential, than the potential candidates for purchase.[12]

Even if all stocks are efficiently priced, however, shorting can enhance performance by eliminating constraints on the implementation of investment insights. Consider, for example, that a security with a median market capitalization has a weighting of approximately 0.01% of the market's capitalization. A manager that cannot short can underweight such a security by, at most, 0.01% relative to the market; this is achieved by not holding the security at all. Those who do not consider this unduly restrictive should consider that placing a like constraint on the maximum portfolio overweight would be equivalent to saying the

---

[12] See, for example, Bruce I. Jacobs and Kenneth N. Levy, "20 Myths About Long-Short," *Financial Analysts Journal* (September/October 1996).

manager could hold, at most, a 0.02% position in the stock, no matter how appetizing its expected return. Shorting allows the manager free rein in translating the insights gained from the stock selection process into portfolio performance.

Long-Short Portfolios

If security returns are symmetrically distributed about the underlying market return, there will be fully as many unattractive securities for short sale as there are attractive securities for purchase. Using optimization techniques, the manager can construct a portfolio that balances equal dollar amounts and equal systematic risks long and short. Such a long-short balance neutralizes the risk (and return) of the underlying market. The portfolio's return — which can be measured as the spread between the long and short returns — is solely reflective of the manager's skill at stock selection.[13]

Not only does such a long-short portfolio neutralize underlying market risk, it offers improved control of residual risk relative even to an engineered long-only portfolio. For example, the long-only portfolio can control risk relative to the underlying benchmark only by converging toward the weightings of the benchmark's stocks; these weights constrain portfolio composition. Balancing securities' sensitivities long and short, however, eliminates risk relative to the underlying benchmark; benchmark weights are thus not constraining. Furthermore, the long-short portfolio can use offsetting long and short positions to fine-tune the portfolio's residual risk.

In addition to enhanced return and improved risk control, an engineered long-short approach also offers clients added flexibility in asset allocation. A simple long-short portfolio, for example, offers a return from security selection on top of a cash return (the interest received on the proceeds from the short sales). However, the long-short manager can also offer, or the client initiate, a long-short portfolio combined with a position in derivatives such as stock index futures. Such an "equitized" portfolio will offer the long-short portfolio's security selection return on top of the equity market return provided by the futures position; choice of other available derivatives can provide the return from security selection in combination with exposure to other asset classes. The transportability of the long-short portfolio's return offers clients the ability to take advantage of a manager's security selection skills while determining independently the plan's asset allocation mix.

THE RISK-RETURN CONTINUUM

The various approaches to investment management — as well as the selection universes that are the targets of such approaches — can be characterized generally by distinct risk-return profiles. For example, in Exhibit 1, risk levels tend to

---

[13] See Bruce I. Jacobs and Kenneth N. Levy, "The Long and Short on Long-Short," *Journal of Investing* (Spring 1997), pp. 73-86.

increase as one moves from the core outward toward the dynamic view of the market; expected returns should also increase. Similarly, in Exhibit 4, risk can be perceived as increasing as one moves from passive investment management out toward traditional active management; expected returns should also increase.

Where should the investor be along this continuum? The answer depends in part on the investor's aversion to risk. The more risk-averse the investor, the closer to core/passive the portfolio should be, and the lower its risk and expected return. Investors who are totally averse to incurring residual risk (that is, departing from benchmark holdings and weights) should stick with passive approaches. They will thus be assured of receiving an equity market return at a market risk level. They will never "beat" the market.

Less risk-averse investors can make more use of style subsets (static or dynamic) and active (engineered or traditional) approaches. With the use of such subsets and such approaches, however, portfolio weights will shift away from overall equity market weights. The difference provides the opportunity for excess return, but it also creates residual risk. In this regard, engineered portfolios, which control risk relative to underlying benchmarks, have definite advantages over traditional portfolios.

The optimal level of residual risk for an investor will depend not only on the investor's level of aversion to residual risk, but also on the manager's skill. Skill can be measured as the manager's information ratio, or IR — the ratio of annualized excess return to annualized residual risk. For example, a manager that beats the benchmark by 2% per year, with 4% residual risk, has an IR of 2%/4%, or 0.5.

Grinold and Kahn formulate the argument as follows:[14]

$$\omega^* = \frac{IR}{2\lambda}$$

where ω^* equals the optimal level of portfolio residual risk given the manager's information ratio and the investor's level of risk aversion, λ. Increases in the manager's IR will increase the investor's optimal level of residual risk and increases in the investor's risk-aversion level will reduce it.

Exhibit 7 illustrates some of the trade-offs between residual risk and excess return for three levels of investor aversion to residual risk and two levels of manager skill. Here the straight lines represent the hypothetical continuum of portfolios (defined by their residual risks and excess returns) that could be offered by a highly skilled manager with an IR of 1.0 and a good manager with an IR of 0.5.[15] The points H, M, and L represent the optimal portfolios for investors with high, medium, and low aversions to residual risk. The point at the origin, P, with zero excess return and zero residual risk, may be taken to be a passive strategy offering a return and a risk level identical to the benchmark's.

---

[14] Grinold and Kahn, *op. cit.*

[15] In reality, no manager will offer a strategy for each possible risk/return combination. Furthermore, although *IR* is a linear function of residual risk when liquidity is unlimited and short selling unrestricted, in the real world *IR* will begin to decline at high levels of residual risk.

Exhibit 7: Risk and Return Change with Investor Risk and Manager Skill

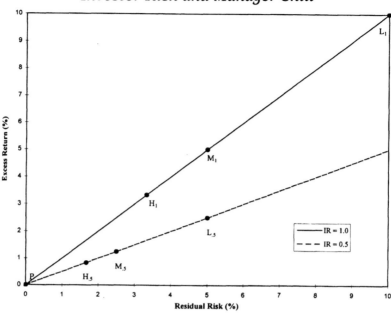

Several important observations can be made from Exhibit 7. First, it is apparent that greater tolerance for risk (a lower risk aversion level) allows the investor to choose a portfolio with a higher risk level that can offer a higher expected return. Second, the more highly skilled the manager, the higher the optimal level of portfolio residual risk, and the higher the portfolio's expected excess return, whatever the investor's risk-aversion level. In short, higher excess returns accrue to higher-risk portfolios and to higher-*IR* managers.

Within this framework, an investor who takes less than the optimal level of residual risk or who selects less than the best manager will sacrifice return.[16] Exhibit 8, for example, shows the decrease in return and utility (U) that results when an investor overestimates risk aversion. Here, an investor with a highly skilled manager, who actually has a medium level of risk aversion (M_1), chooses a portfolio suitable for an investor with a high level of risk aversion (H_1). The investor give-up in return can be measured as the vertical distance between M_1 and H_1. In somewhat more sophisticated terms, the higher-risk portfolio corresponds to a certainty-equivalent return of 2.500% and the less risky portfolio to a certainty-equivalent return of 2.221%, so the investor who overestimates his or her level of risk aversion and therefore chooses a suboptimal portfolio sacrifices 0.279 percentage points.

---

[16] See also Bruce I. Jacobs and Kenneth N. Levy, "Residual Risk: How Much is Too Much?" *Journal of Portfolio Management* (Spring 1996).

Exhibit 8: Sacrifice in Return from Overestimating Investor Risk Aversion

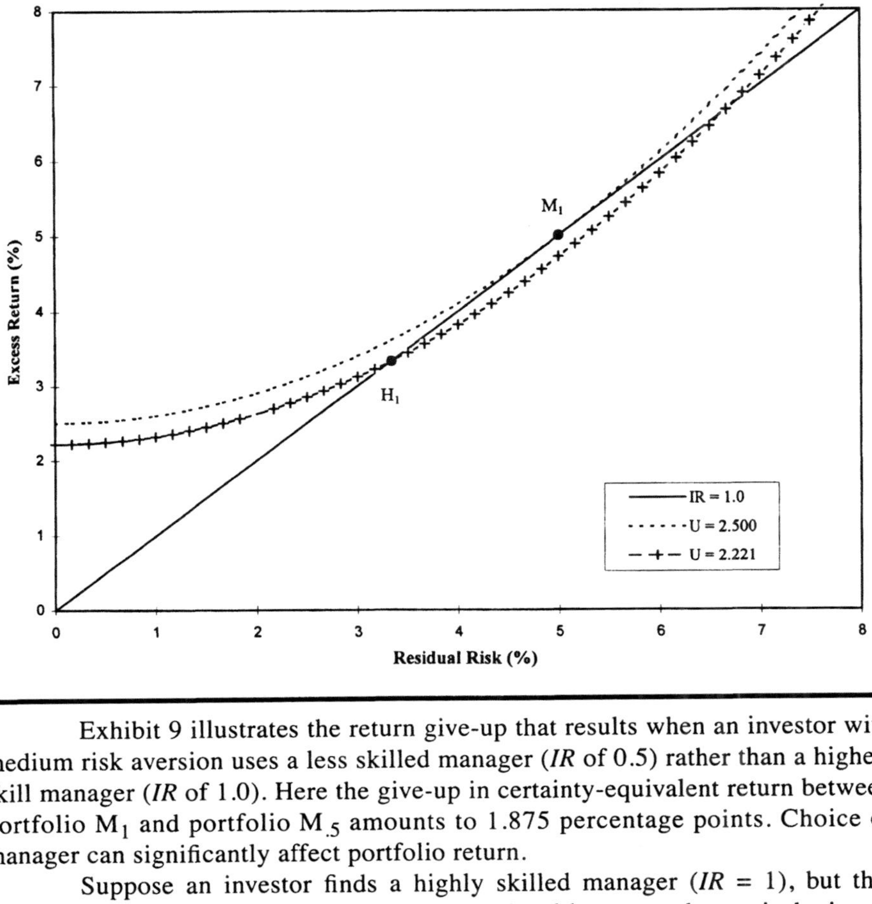

Exhibit 9 illustrates the return give-up that results when an investor with medium risk aversion uses a less skilled manager (IR of 0.5) rather than a higher-skill manager (IR of 1.0). Here the give-up in certainty-equivalent return between portfolio M_1 and portfolio $M_{.5}$ amounts to 1.875 percentage points. Choice of manager can significantly affect portfolio return.

Suppose an investor finds a highly skilled manager ($IR = 1$), but that manager does not offer a portfolio with a risk level low enough to suit the investor's high level of risk aversion. A less skilled ($IR = 0.5$) manager, however, offers portfolios $H_{.5}$ and $M_{.5}$, which do provide about the right level of residual risk for this investor.

The investor might try to convince the $IR = 1$ manager to offer a lower-risk portfolio. If that fails, however, is the investor constrained to go with the less skilled manager? No. The investor can instead combine the highly skilled manager's H_1 portfolio with an investment in the passive benchmark portfolio P, reducing risk and return along the $IR = 1$ manager frontier. Such combination portfolios will offer a higher return than the portfolios of the less skilled manager, at a level of residual risk the investor can live with.

Exhibit 9: Sacrifice in Return from Using Less Skillful Manager

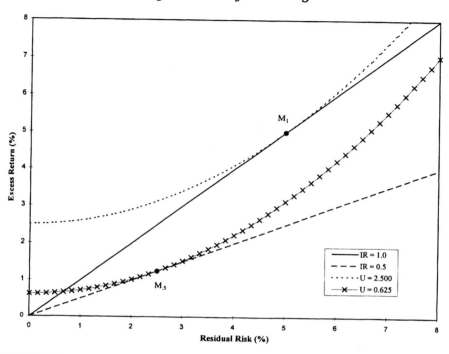

Finally, the manager's investment approach may affect the investor's optimal level of portfolio risk. Because engineered strategies control portfolio systematic and residual risk relative to the benchmark and take only compensated risks, they offer more assurance than traditional active strategies of achieving a return commensurate with the risk taken. Investors may feel more comfortable taking more risk with engineered portfolios, where risk and expected return are rigorously and explicitly assessed, than with traditional active portfolios.

THE ULTIMATE OBJECTIVE

The ultimate objective of investment management, of course, is to establish an investment structure that will, in the aggregate and over time, provide a return that compensates for the risk incurred, where the risk incurred is consistent with the investor's risk tolerance. The objective may be the equity market's return at the market's risk level or the market return plus incremental returns commensurate with incremental risks incurred.

This may be accomplished by focusing on the core universe and a passive representation or by mixing universes (core and static subsets, for example) and approaches (e.g., passive with traditional active or engineered). Whatever the selection universe and investment approach chosen, success is more likely when investors start off knowing their risk-tolerance levels and their potential managers' skill levels. The goal is to take no more risk than is compensated by expected return, but to take as much risk as risk-aversion level and manager skill allow.

Success is also more likely when equity market architecture is taken into account. Without explicit ties between portfolios and the underlying market or market subsets (and thus between market subsets and the overall market), managers may be tempted to stray from their "fold" (core, value, or growth investing, say) in search of return. If value stocks are being punished, for example, an undisciplined value manager may be tempted to "poach" return from growth stock territory. An investor utilizing this manager cannot expect performance consistent with value stocks in general, nor can the investor combine this manager's "value" portfolio with a growth portfolio in the hopes of achieving an overall market return; the portfolio will instead be overweighted in growth stocks, and susceptible to the risk of growth stocks falling out of favor. The investor can mitigate the problem by balancing non-benchmark-constrained, traditional portfolios with engineered or passive portfolios that offer benchmark-accountability.

When investors set goals in terms of return only, with no regard to equity architecture, similar problems can arise. Consider an investor who hires active managers and instructs them to "make money," with no regard to market sector or investment approach. Manager holdings may overlap to an extent that the overall portfolio becomes overdiversified and individual manager efforts are diluted. The investor may end up paying active fees and active transaction costs for essentially passive results.

Equity architecture provides a basic blueprint for relating equity investment choices to their potential rewards and their risks. It can help investors construct portfolios that will meet their needs. First, however, the investor must determine what those needs are in terms of desire for return and tolerance for risk. Then the investor can choose managers whose investment approaches and market focuses offer, overall, the greatest assurance of fulfilling those needs.

We believe that engineered management can provide the best match between client risk-return goals and investment results. An engineered approach that combines range with depth of inquiry can increase both the number and goodness of investment insights. As a result, engineered management offers better control of risk exposure than traditional active management and incremental returns relative to passive management, whether the selection universe is core equity, static style subsets, or dynamic style subsets.

Chapter 25

Investment Analysis: Profiting from a Complex Equity Market

Bruce I. Jacobs, Ph.D.
Principal
Jacobs Levy Equity Management

Kenneth N. Levy, CFA
Principal
Jacobs Levy Equity Management

INTRODUCTION

Scientists classify systems into three types — ordered, random, and complex. Ordered systems, such as the structure of diamond crystals or the dynamics of pendulums, are definable and predictable by relatively simple rules and can be modeled using a relatively small number of variables. Random systems like the Brownian motion of gas molecules or white noise (static) are unordered; they are the product of a large number of variables. Their behavior cannot be modeled and is inherently unpredictable.

Complex systems like the weather and the workings of DNA fall somewhere between the domains of order and randomness. Their behavior can be at least partly comprehended and modeled, but only with great difficulty. The number of variables that must be modeled, and their interactions, are beyond the capacity of the human mind alone. Only with the aid of advanced computational science can the mysteries of complex systems be unraveled.[1]

The stock market is a complex system.[2] Stock prices are not completely random, as the efficient market hypothesis and random walk theory would have it.

---

[1] See, for example, Heinz Pagels, *The Dreams of Reason: The Computer and the Rise of the Sciences of Complexity* (New York, NY: Simon and Schuster, 1988).

[2] See, for example, Bruce I. Jacobs and Kenneth N. Levy, "The Complexity of the Stock Market," *Journal of Portfolio Management* (Fall 1989).

The authors thank Judith Kimball for her editorial assistance.

497

Some price movements can be predicted, and with some consistency. But nor is stock price behavior ordered. It cannot be successfully modeled by simple rules or screens such as low price/earnings ratios or even elegant theories such as the Capital Asset Pricing Model or Arbitrage Pricing Theory. Rather, stock price behavior is permeated by a complex web of interrelated return effects. A model of the market that is complex enough to disentangle these effects provides opportunities for modeling price behavior and predicting returns.

This chapter describes one such model, and its application to the stock selection, portfolio construction, and performance evaluation problems. We begin with the very basic question of how one should approach the equity market. Should one attempt to cover the broadest possible range of stocks, or can greater analytical insights be garnered by focusing on a particular subset of the market or a limited number of stocks? As we will see, each approach has its advantages and disadvantages. Combining the two, however, may offer the best promise of finding the key to market complexity and unlocking investment opportunity.

AN INTEGRATED APPROACH TO A SEGMENTED MARKET

While one might think that U.S. equity markets are fluid and fully integrated, in reality there exist barriers to the free flow of capital. Some of these barriers are self-imposed by investors. Others are imposed by regulatory and tax authorities or by client guidelines.

Some funds, for example, are prohibited by regulation or internal policy guidelines from buying certain types of stock — non-dividend-paying stock, or stock below a given capitalization level. Tax laws, too, may effectively lock investors into positions they would otherwise trade. Such barriers to the free flow of capital foster market segmentation.

Other barriers are self-imposed. Traditionally, for example, managers have focused (whether by design or default) on distinct approaches to stock selection. Value managers have concentrated on buying stocks selling at prices perceived to be low relative to the company's assets or earnings. Growth managers have sought stocks with above-average earnings growth not fully reflected in price. Small-capitalization managers have searched for opportunity in stocks that have been overlooked by most investors. The stocks that constitute the natural selection pools for these managers tend to group into distinct market segments.

Client preferences encourage this Balkanization of the market. Some investors, for example, prefer to buy value stocks, while others seek growth stocks; some invest in both, but hire separate managers for each segment. Both institutional and individual investors generally demonstrate a reluctance to upset the apple cart by changing allocations to previously selected "style" managers. Several periods of underperformance, however, may undermine this loyalty and motivate a flow of capital from one segment of the market to another (often just as the out-of-favor segment begins to benefit from a reversion of returns back up to their historical mean).

In the past few decades, a market segmented into style groupings has been formalized by the actions of investment consultants. Consultants have designed style indexes that define the constituent stocks of these segments and have defined managers in terms of their proclivity for one segment or another. As a manager's performance is measured against the given style index, managers who stray too far from index territory are taking on extra risk. Consequently, managers tend to stick close to their style "homes," reinforcing market segmentation.

An investment approach that focuses on individual market segments can have its advantages. Such an approach recognizes, for example, that the U.S. equity market is neither entirely homogeneous nor entirely heterogeneous. All stocks do not react alike to a given impetus, but nor does each stock exhibit its own, totally idiosyncratic price behavior. Rather, stocks within a given style, or sector, or industry tend to behave similarly to each other and somewhat differently from stocks outside their group.

An approach to stock selection that specializes in one market segment can optimize the application of talent and maximize the potential for outperformance. This is most likely true for traditional, fundamental analysis. The in-depth, labor-intensive research undertaken by traditional analysts can become positively ungainly without some focusing lens.

An investment approach that focuses on the individual segments of the market, however, presents some severe theoretical and practical problems. Such an approach may be especially disadvantaged when it ignores the many forces that work to integrate, rather than segment, the market.

Many managers, for example, do not specialize in a particular market segment but are free to choose the most attractive securities from a broad universe of stocks. Others, such as style rotators, may focus on a particular type of stock, given current economic conditions, but be poised to change their focus should conditions change. Such managers make for capital flows and price arbitrage across the boundaries of particular segments.

Furthermore, all stocks can be defined by the same fundamental parameters — by market capitalization, price/earnings ratio, dividend discount model ranking, and so on. All stocks can be found at some level on the continuum of values for each parameter. Thus growth and value stocks inhabit the opposite ends of the continuums of P/E and dividend yield, and small and large stocks the opposite ends of the continuums of firm capitalization and analyst coverage.

As the values of the parameters for any individual stock change, so too does the stock's position on the continuum. An out-of-favor growth stock may slip into value territory. A small-cap company may grow into the large-cap range.

Finally, while the values of these parameters vary across stocks belonging to different market segments — different styles, sectors, and industries — and while investors may favor certain values — low P/E, say, in preference to high P/E — arbitrage tends to counterbalance too pronounced a predilection on the part of investors for any one set of values. In equilibrium, all stocks must be owned. If too many investors want low P/E, low-P/E stocks will be bid up to higher P/E levels, and some investors will step in to sell them and buy other stocks deserving of higher P/Es. Arbitrage works toward market integration and a single pricing mechanism.

A market that is neither completely segmented nor completely integrated is a complex market. A complex market calls for an investment approach that is 180 degrees removed from the narrow, segment-oriented focus of traditional management. It requires a complex, unified approach that takes into account the behavior of stocks across the broadest possible selection universe, without losing sight of the significant differences in price behavior that distinguish particular market segments.

Such an approach offers three major advantages. First, it provides a coherent evaluation framework. Second, it can benefit from all the insights to be garnered from a wide and diverse range of securities. Third, because it has both breadth of coverage and depth of analysis, it is poised to take advantage of more profit opportunities than a more narrowly defined, segmented approach proffers.[3]

A COHERENT FRAMEWORK

To the extent that the market is integrated, an investment approach that models each industry or style segment as if it were a universe unto itself is not the best approach. Consider, for example, a firm that offers both core and value strategies. Suppose the firm runs a model on its total universe of, say, 3000 stocks. It then runs the same model or a different, segment-specific model on a 500-stock subset of large-cap value stocks.

If different models are used for each strategy, the results will differ. Even if the same model is estimated separately for each strategy, its results will differ because the model coefficients are bound to differ between the broader universe and the narrower segment. What if the core model predicts GM will outperform Ford, while the value model shows the reverse? Should the investor start the day with multiple estimates of one stock's alpha? This would violate what we call the "Law of One Alpha."[4]

Of course, the firm could ensure coherence by using separate models for each market segment — growth, value, small-cap — and linking the results via a single, overarching model that relates all the subsets. But the firm then runs into a second problem with segmented investment approaches: To the extent that the market is integrated, the pricing of securities in one segment may contain information relevant to pricing in other segments.

For example, within a generally well integrated national economy, labor market conditions in the U.S. differ region by region. An economist attempting to

---

[3] See, for example, Bruce I. Jacobs and Kenneth N. Levy, "Engineering Portfolios: A Unified Approach," *Journal of Investing* (Winter 1995).

[4] See Bruce I. Jacobs and Kenneth N. Levy, "The Law of One Alpha," *Journal of Portfolio Management* (Summer 1995).

model employment in the Northeast would probably consider economic expansion in the Southeast. Similarly, the investor who wants to model growth stocks should not ignore value stocks. The effects of inflation, say, on value stocks may have repercussions for growth stocks; after all, the two segments represent opposite ends of the same P/E continuum.

An investment approach that concentrates on a single market segment does not make use of all available information. A complex, unified approach considers all the stocks in the universe — value and growth, large and small. It thus benefits from all the information to be gleaned from a broad range of stock price behavior.

Of course, an increase in breadth of inquiry will not benefit the investor if it comes at the sacrifice of depth of inquiry. A complex approach does not ignore the significant differences across different types of stock, differences exploitable by specialized investing. What's more, in examining similarities and differences across market segments, it considers numerous variables that may be considered to be defining.

For value, say, a complex approach does not confine itself to a dividend discount model measure of value, but examines also earnings, cash flow, sales, and yield value, among other attributes. Growth measurements to be considered include historical, expected, and sustainable growth, as well as the momentum and stability of earnings. Share price, volatility, and analyst coverage are among the elements to be considered along with market capitalization as measures of size.[5]

These variables are often closely correlated with each other. Small-cap stocks, for example, tend to have low P/Es; low P/E is correlated with high yield; both low P/E and high yield are correlated with DDM estimates of value. Furthermore, they may be correlated with a stock's industry affiliation. A simple low-P/E screen, for example, will tend to select a large number of bank and utility stocks. Such correlations can distort naive attempts to relate returns to potentially relevant variables. A true picture of the variable-return relationship emerges only after "disentangling" the variables.

DISENTANGLING

The effects of different sources of stock return can overlap. In Exhibit 1, the lines represent connections documented by academic studies; they may appear like a ball of yarn after the cat got to it. To unravel the connections between variables and return, it is necessary to examine all the variables simultaneously.

---

[5] At a deeper level of complexity, one must also consider alternative ways of specifying such fundamental variables as earnings or cash flow. Over what period does one measure earnings, for example? If using analyst earnings expectations, which measure provides the best estimate of future real earnings? The consensus of all available estimates made over the past six months? Only the very latest earnings estimates? Are some analysts more accurate or more influential? What if a recent estimate is not available for a given company? See Bruce I. Jacobs, Kenneth N. Levy, and Mitchell C. Krask, "Earnings Estimates, Predictor Specification, and Measurement Error," *Journal of Investing* (Summer 1997), pp. 29-46.

Exhibit 1: Return Effects Form a Tangled Web

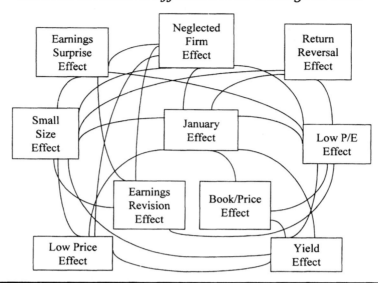

For instance, the low-P/E effect is widely recognized, as is the small-size effect. But stocks with low P/Es also tend to be of small size. Are P/E and size merely two ways of looking at the same effect? Or does each variable matter? Perhaps the excess returns to small-cap stocks are merely a January effect, reflecting the tendency of taxable investors to sell depressed stocks at year-end. Answering these questions requires disentangling return effects via multivariate regression.[6]

Common methods of measuring return effects (such as quintiling or univariate — single-variable — regression) are "naive" because they assume, naively, that prices are responding only to the single variable under consideration — low P/E, say. But a number of related variables may be affecting returns. As we have noted, small-cap stocks and banking and utility industry stocks tend to have low P/Es. A univariate regression of return on low P/E will capture, along with the effect of P/E, a great deal of "noise" related to firm size, industry affiliation and other variables.

Simultaneous analysis of all relevant variables via multivariate regression takes into account and adjusts for such interrelationships. The result is the return to each variable separately, controlling for all related variables. A multivariate analysis for low P/E, for example, will provide a measure of the excess return to a portfolio that is market-like in all respects except for having a lower-than-average P/E ratio. Disentangled returns are "pure" returns.

---

[6] See Bruce I. Jacobs and Kenneth N. Levy, "Disentangling Equity Return Regularities: New Insights and Investment Opportunities," *Financial Analysts Journal* (May/June 1988).

Exhibit 2: Naive and Pure Returns to High Book-to-Price Ratio

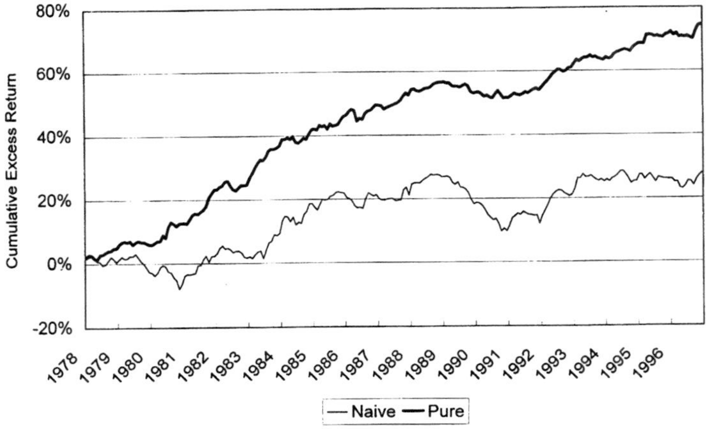

Noise Reduction

Exhibit 2 plots naive and pure cumulative excess (relative to a 3,000-stock universe) returns to high book-to-price ratio.[7] The naive returns show a great deal of volatility; the pure returns, by contrast, follow a much smoother path. There is a lot of noise in the naive returns. What causes it?

Notice the divergence between the naive and pure return series for the 12 months starting in March 1979. This date coincides with the crisis at Three Mile Island nuclear power plant. Utilities such as GPU, operator of the Three Mile Island power plant, tend to have high-B/Ps, and naive B/P measures will reflect the performance of these utilities along with the performance of other high-B/P stocks. Electric utility prices plummeted 24% after the Three Mile Island crisis. The naive B/P measure reflects this decline.

But industry-related events such as Three Mile Island have no necessary bearing on the book/price variable. An investor could, for example, hold a high-B/P portfolio that does not overweight utilities, and such a portfolio would not have experienced the decline reflected in the naive B/P measure in Exhibit 2. The naive returns to B/P reflect noise from the inclusion of a utility industry effect. A pure B/P measure is not contaminated by such irrelevant variables.

Disentangling distinguishes real effects from mere proxies and thereby distinguishes between real and spurious investment opportunities. As it separates high B/P and industry affiliation, for example, it can also separate the effects of firm size from the effects of related variables. Disentangling shows that returns to small firms in January are not abnormal; the apparent January seasonal merely proxies for

---

[7] In particular, naive and pure returns are provided by a portfolio having a book-to-price ratio that is one standard deviation above the universe mean book-to-price ratio. For pure returns, the portfolio is also constrained to have universe-average exposures to all the other variables in the model, including fundamental characteristics and industry affiliations.

year-end tax-loss selling.[8] Not all small firms will benefit from a January rebound; indiscriminately buying small firms at the turn of the year is not an optimal investment strategy. Ascertaining true causation leads to more profitable strategies.

Return Revelation

Disentangling can reveal hidden opportunities. Exhibit 3 plots the naively measured cumulative excess returns (relative to the 3,000-stock universe) to portfolios that rank lower than normal in market capitalization and price per share and higher than normal in terms of analyst neglect.[9] These results derive from monthly univariate regressions. The "small-cap" line thus represents the cumulative excess returns to a portfolio of stocks naively chosen on the basis of their size, with no attempt made to control for other variables.

All three return series move together. The similarity between the small-cap and neglect series is particularly striking. This is confirmed by the correlation coefficients in the first column of Exhibit 4. Furthermore, all series show a great deal of volatility within a broader up, down, up pattern.

Exhibit 3: Naive Returns Can Hide Opportunities: Three Size-Related Variables

Exhibit 4: Correlations between Monthly Returns to Size-Related Variables*

Variable	Naive	Pure
Small Cap/Low Price	0.82	−0.12
Small Cap/Neglect	0.87	−0.22
Neglect/Low Price	0.66	−0.11

* A coefficient of 0.14 is significant at the 5% level.

[8] See Bruce I. Jacobs and Kenneth N. Levy, "Calendar Anomalies: Abnormal Returns at Calendar Turning Points," *Financial Analysts Journal* (November/December 1988).

[9] Again, portfolios with values of these parameters that are, on average, one standard deviation away from the universe mean.

Exhibit 5: Pure Returns Can Reveal Opportunities: Three Size-Related Variables

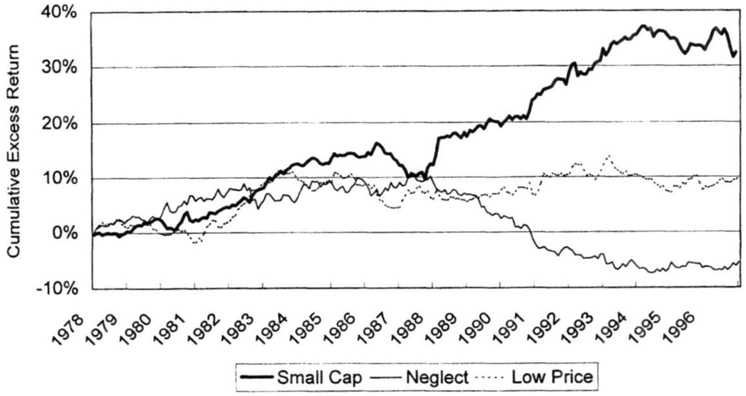

Exhibit 5 shows the pure cumulative excess returns to each size-related attribute over the period. These disentangled returns adjust for correlations not only between the three size variables, but also between each size variable and industry affiliations and each variable and growth and value characteristics. Two findings are immediately apparent from Exhibit 5.

First, pure returns to the size variables do not appear to be nearly as closely correlated as the naive returns displayed in Exhibit 3. In fact, over the second half of the period, the three return series diverge substantially. This is confirmed by the correlation coefficients in the second column of Exhibit 4.

In particular, pure returns to small capitalization accumulate quite a gain over the period; they are up 30%, versus an only 20% gain for the naive returns to small cap. Purifying returns reveals a profit opportunity not apparent in the naive returns. Furthermore, pure returns to analyst neglect amount to a substantial loss over the period. Because disentangling controls for proxy effects, and thereby avoids redundancies, these pure return effects are additive. A portfolio could have aimed for superior returns by selecting small-cap stocks with a higher-than-average analyst following (i.e., a negative exposure to analyst neglect).

Second, the pure returns appear to be much less volatile than the naive returns. The naive returns in Exhibit 3 display much month-to-month volatility within their more general trends. By contrast, the pure series in Exhibit 5 are much smoother and more consistent. This is confirmed by the standard deviations given in Exhibit 6.

The pure returns in Exhibit 5 are smoother and more consistent than the naive return responses in Exhibit 3 because the pure returns capture more "signal" and less noise. And because they are smoother and more consistent than naive returns, pure returns are also more predictable.

Exhibit 6: Pure Returns are Less Volatile, More Predictable: Standard Deviations of Monthly Returns to Size-Related Variables*

Variable	Naive	Pure
Small Cap	0.87	0.60
Neglect	0.87	0.67
Low Price	1.03	0.58

* All differences between naive and pure return standard deviations are significant at the 1% level.

Exhibit 7: Market Sensitivities of Monthly Returns to Value-Related Variables

Variable	Naive	(t-stat.)	Pure	(t-stat.)
DDM	0.06	(5.4)	0.04	(5.6)
B/P	−0.10	(−6.2)	−0.01	(−0.8)
Yield	−0.08	(−7.4)	−0.03	(−3.5)

Predictability

Disentangling improves return predictability by providing a clearer picture of the relationship between stock price behavior, fundamental variables, and macroeconomic conditions. For example, investors often prefer value stocks in bearish market environments, because growth stocks are priced more on the basis of high expectations, which get dashed in more pessimistic eras. But the success of such a strategy will depend on the variables one has chosen to define value.

Exhibit 7 displays the results of regressing both naive and pure returns to various value-related variables on market (S&P 500) returns over the 1978-1996 period. The results indicate that DDM value is a poor indicator of a stock's ability to withstand a tide of receding market prices. The regression coefficient in the first column indicates that a portfolio with a one-standard-deviation exposure to DDM value will tend to outperform by 0.06% when the market rises by 1.00% and to underperform by a similar margin when the market falls by 1.00%. The coefficient for pure returns to DDM is similar. Whether their returns are measured in pure or naive form, stocks with high DDM values tend to behave procyclically.

High book-to-price ratio appears to be a better indicator of a defensive stock. It has a regression coefficient of −0.10 in naive form. In pure form, however, B/P is virtually uncorrelated with market movements; pure B/P signals neither an aggressive nor a defensive stock. B/P as naively measured apparently picks up the effects of truly defensive variables — such as high yield.

The value investor in search of a defensive posture in uncertain market climates should consider moving toward high yield. The regression coefficients for both naive and pure returns to high yield indicate significant negative market sensitivities. Stocks with high yields may be expected to lag in up markets but to hold up relatively well during general market declines.

Exhibit 8: Forecast Response of Small Size to Macroeconomic Shocks

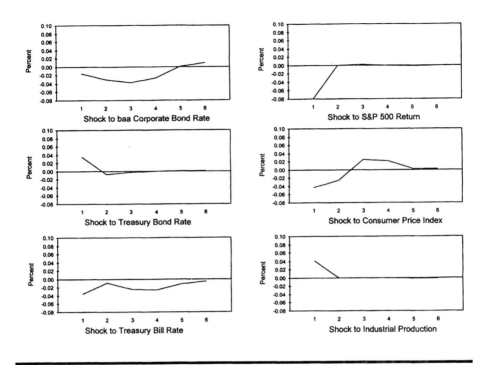

These results make broad intuitive sense. DDM is forward-looking, relying on estimates of future earnings. In bull markets, investors take a long-term outlook, so DDM explains security pricing behavior. In bear markets, however, investors become myopic; they prefer today's tangible income to tomorrow's promise. Current yield is rewarded.[10]

Pure returns respond in intuitively satisfying ways to macroeconomic events. Exhibit 8 illustrates, as an example, the estimated effects of changes in various macroeconomic variables on the pure returns to small size (as measured by market capitalization). Consistent with the capital constraints on small firms and their relatively greater sensitivity to the economy, pure returns to small size may be expected to be negative in the first four months following an unexpected increase in the BAA corporate rate and positive in the first month following an unexpected increase in industrial production.[11] Investors can exploit such predict-

[10] See also Bruce I. Jacobs and Kenneth N. Levy, "On the Value of 'Value'," *Financial Analysts Journal* (July/August 1988).
[11] See Bruce I. Jacobs and Kenneth N. Levy, "Forecasting the Size Effect," *Financial Analysts Journal* (May/June 1989).

able behavior by moving into and out of the small-cap market segment as economic conditions evolve.[12]

These examples serve to illustrate that the use of numerous, finely defined fundamental variables can provide a rich representation of the complexity of security pricing. The model can be even more finely tuned, however, by including variables that capture such subtleties as the effects of investor psychology, possible nonlinearities in variable-return relationships, and security transaction costs.

Additional Complexities

In considering possible variables for inclusion in a model of stock price behavior, the investor should recognize that pure stock returns are driven by a combination of economic fundamentals and investor psychology. That is, economic fundamentals such as interest rates, industrial production, and inflation can explain much, but by no means all, of the systematic variation in returns. Psychology, including investors' tendency to overreact, their desire to seek safety in numbers, and their selective memories, also plays a role in security pricing.

What's more, the modeler should realize that the effects of different variables, fundamental and otherwise, can differ across different types of stocks. The value sector, for example, includes more financial stocks than the growth sector. Investors may thus expect value stocks in general to be more sensitive than growth stocks to changes in interest rate spreads.

Psychologically based variables such as short-term overreaction and price correction also seem to have a stronger effect on value than on growth stocks. Earnings surprises and earnings estimate revisions, by contrast, appear to be more important for growth than for value stocks. Thus Intel shares can take a nose dive when earnings come in a penny under expectations, whereas Ford shares remain unmoved even by fairly substantial departures of actual earnings from expectations.

The relationship between stock returns and relevant variables may not be linear. The effects of positive earnings surprises, for instance, tend to be arbitraged away quickly; thus positive earnings surprises offer less opportunity for the investor. The effects of negative earnings surprises, however, appear to be more long-lasting. This nonlinearity may reflect the fact that sales of stock are limited to those investors who already own the stock (and to a relatively small number of short-sellers).[13]

Risk-variable relationships may also differ across different types of stock. In particular, small-cap stocks generally have more idiosyncratic risk than large-cap stocks. Diversification is thus more important for small-stock than for large-stock portfolios.

---

[12] See, for example, Bruce I. Jacobs and Kenneth N. Levy, "High-Definition Style Rotation," *Journal of Investing* (Fall 1996), pp. 14-23.

[13] See Bruce I. Jacobs and Kenneth N. Levy, "Long/Short Equity Investing," *Journal of Portfolio Management* (Fall 1993).

Return-variable relationships can also change over time. Recall the difference between DDM and yield value measures: high-DDM stocks tend to have high returns in bull markets and low returns in bear markets; high-yield stocks experience the reverse. For consistency of performance, return modeling must consider the effects of market dynamics — the changing nature of the overall market.

The investor may also want to decipher the informational signals generated by "informed agents." Corporate decisions to issue or buy back shares, split stock, or initiate or suspend dividends, for example, may contain valuable information about company prospects. So, too, may insiders' (legal) trading in their own firms' shares.

Finally, a complex model containing multiple variables is likely to turn up a number of promising return-variable relationships. But are these perceived profit opportunities translatable into real economic opportunities? Are some too ephemeral? Too small to survive frictions such as trading costs? Estimates of expected returns must be combined with estimates of the costs of trading to arrive at realistic returns net of trading costs.

CONSTRUCTING, TRADING, AND EVALUATING PORTFOLIOS

To maximize implementation of the model's insights, the portfolio construction process should consider exactly the same dimensions found relevant by the stock selection model. Failure to do so can lead to mismatches between model insights and portfolio exposures.

Consider a commercially available portfolio optimizer that recognizes only a subset of the variables in the valuation model. Risk reduction using such an optimizer will reduce the portfolio's exposures only along the dimensions the optimizer recognizes. As a result, the portfolio is likely to wind up more exposed to those variables recognized by the model — but not the optimizer — and less exposed to those variables common to both the model and the optimizer.

Imagine an investor who seeks low-P/E stocks that analysts are recommending for purchase, but who uses a commercial optimizer that incorporates a P/E factor but not analyst recommendations. The investor is likely to wind up with a portfolio that has a less than optimal level of exposure to low P/E and a greater than optimal level of exposure to analyst purchase recommendations. Optimization using all relevant variables ensures a portfolio whose risk and return opportunities are balanced in accordance with the model's insights. Furthermore, the use of more numerous variables allows portfolio risk to be more finely tuned.

Insofar as the investment process — both stock selection and portfolio construction — is model-driven, it is more adaptable to electronic trading venues. This should benefit the investor in several ways. First, electronic trading is generally less costly, with lower commissions, market impact, and opportunity costs.

Second, it allows real-time monitoring, which can further reduce trading costs. Third, an automated trading system can take account of more factors, including the urgency of a particular trade and market conditions, than individual traders can be expected to bear in mind.

Finally, the performance attribution process should be congruent with the dimensions of the selection model (and portfolio optimizer). Insofar as performance attribution identifies sources of return, a process that considers all the sources identified by the selection model will be more insightful than a commercial performance attribution system applied in a "one-size-fits-all" manner. Our investor who has sought exposure to low P/E and positive analyst recommendations, for example, will want to know how each of these factors has paid off and will be less interested in the returns to factors that are not a part of the stock selection process.

A performance evaluation process tailored to the model also functions as a monitor of the model's reliability. Has portfolio performance supported the model's insights? Should some be reexamined? Equally important, does the model's reliability hold up over time? A model that performs well in today's economic and market environments may not necessarily perform well in the future. A feedback loop between the evaluation and the research/modeling processes can help ensure that the model retains robustness over time.

PROFITING FROM COMPLEXITY

It has been said that: "For every complex problem, there is a simple solution, and it is almost always wrong."[14] For complex problems more often than not require complex solutions.

A complex approach to stock selection, portfolio construction, and performance evaluation is needed to capture the complexities of the stock market. Such an approach combines the breadth of coverage and the depth of analysis needed to maximize investment opportunity and potential reward.

Grinold and Kahn present a formula that identifies the relationships between the depth and breadth of investment insights and investment performance:

$$IR = IC \times \sqrt{BR}$$

IR is the manager's information ratio, a measure of the success of the investment process. IR equals annualized excess return over annualized residual risk (e.g., 2% excess return with 4% tracking error provides 0.5 IR). IC, the information coefficient, or correlation between predicted and actual results, measures the goodness of the manager's insights, or the manager's skill. BR is the breadth of the strategy, measurable as the number of independent insights upon which investment decisions are made.[15]

---

[14] Attributed to H.L. Mencken.
[15] Richard C. Grinold and Ronald N. Kahn, *Active Portfolio Management* (Chicago, IL: Probus, 1995).

One can increase *IR* by increasing *IC* or *BR*. Increasing *IC* means coming up with some means of improving predictive accuracy. Increasing *BR* means coming up with more "investable" insights. A casino analogy may be apt (if anathema to prudent investors).

A gambler can seek to increase *IC* by card-counting in blackjack or by building a computer model to predict probable roulette outcomes. Similarly, some investors seek to outperform by concentrating their research efforts on a few stocks: by learning all there is to know about Microsoft, for example, one may be able to outperform all the other investors who follow this stock. But a strategy that makes a few concentrated stock bets is likely to produce consistent performance only if it is based on a very high level of skill, or if it benefits from extraordinary luck.

Alternatively, an investor can place a larger number of smaller stock bets and settle for more modest returns from a greater number of investment decisions. That is, rather than behaving like a gambler in a casino, the investor can behave like the casino. A casino has only a slight edge on any spin of the roulette wheel or roll of the dice, but many spins of many roulette wheels can result in a very consistent profit for the house. Over time, the odds will strongly favor the casino over the gambler.

A complex approach to the equity market, one that has both breadth of inquiry and depth of focus, can enhance the number and the goodness of investment insights. A complex approach to the equity market requires more time, effort, and ability, but it will be better positioned to capture the complexities of security pricing. The rewards are worth the effort.

Chapter 26

The Use of Derivatives in Managing Equity Portfolios

Roger G. Clarke, Ph.D.
Chairman
Analytic/TSA Global Asset Management

Harindra de Silva, Ph.D., CFA
Managing Director
Analytic/TSA Global Asset Management

Greg M. McMurran
Chief Investment Officer
Analytic/TSA Global Asset Management

INTRODUCTION

The growth of the derivatives markets in recent years has given the investment manager an important set of tools to use in managing the risk and return characteristics of equity portfolios. In this chapter we will discuss some of the common strategies available using three different derivatives contracts: index swaps, futures, and options. Each of these derivatives has their own special characteristics which make them useful for adjusting the payoff profile of the portfolio to reflect a manager's expectations or view of the market.

One of the main characteristics of derivatives contracts is that little, if any, up-front money is required to initiate the contract. This feature allows the manager to maintain the principal involved in the transaction in other securities while increasing or decreasing exposure to the market through the derivatives contract. This separation of market exposure from the need for immediate cash outlays is what makes hedging possible, for example. Market exposure generated by holding underlying securities can be hedged with a derivative without having to sell the underlying securities themselves.

A major difference between the types of derivative contracts is the shape of the payoff structure that results when the market moves. Both index swaps and futures contracts have linear payoff patterns. That is, the payoff is symmetric around current market levels. The payoff as the market goes up or down mirrors the movement of the market itself. As a result, swaps and futures are often referred to as *portfolio substitutes* since their effects can substitute for the market return on a well-diversified portfolio of stocks. However, options generate non-linear payoff patterns. Put options are more sensitive to down market moves while call options are more sensitive to up market moves. This asymmetry allows options to create special effects in managing the risk of a portfolio not available by using swaps or futures contracts. The choice of the optimal derivative strategy is naturally a function of the manager's objectives, risk preferences, and market view.

This chapter is organized as follows. We first outline the use of derivative strategies which have linear payoffs including swaps and futures. Call and put options, along with other combination strategies which have non-linear payoffs are reviewed in the next section. In the final section we discuss the typical framework used to price options and the limitations of using this approach to select an optimal derivative strategy. We illustrate a basic framework for selecting a particular strategy given a manager's risk and return expectations. Examples are provided for one of the more commonly used derivative strategies — the covered call strategy.

LINEAR PAYOFFS: SWAPS

The simplest index swap contract is structured between two parties where the counterparties agree to exchange the return between an equity index and a fixed interest rate (usually LIBOR) scaled by the principal or notional amount of the swap. We shall refer to the investor who pays the fixed rate and receives the market return as the swap buyer; the counterparty is the swap seller. The swap allows the investor buying the swap to gain exposure to the market without having to purchase the underlying equities themselves. The investor's funds can be left in cash reserves earning interest which is exchanged with the counter party who has agreed to pay the investor the return on the equity index.

This arrangement is illustrated in Exhibit 1. Investor A who has purchased the equity index swap receives the equity index return from Investor B while paying the agreed upon fixed rate. No principal is exchanged between the two parties, only the agreed upon return tied to the notional amount of the swap is exchanged. This allows the investors to achieve returns in one market without actually having to hold securities in that market. Swaps are usually negotiated, private-party transactions. Though the specific terms of a swap may vary, it is not unusual for the maturity or *tenor* of a swap to run for a year or more with returns being exchanged at quarterly intervals.

A simple way to look at the impact of using a swap to achieve equity market returns is illustrated in Exhibit 2. The purchaser of the swap holds the notional amount of the swap in cash which earns interest. When the return on the investor's cash reserve is combined with the return on the equity index less the payment of the promised fixed rate, the investor is left with the return on the equity index plus the difference in return earned on the underlying cash reserves less the fixed return paid to the counterparty. The purchaser of the swap has created a synthetic equity return on the investment without having to actually purchase equity securities.

The seller of the swap receives the fixed return and pays the return on the equity index. If the seller holds underlying stocks which mirror the return on the equity index, the net return to the seller will be the fixed rate received plus any difference in return between the actual return on the stocks and the return on the equity index. The seller of the swap has effectively created synthetic cash while the actual underlying portfolio is invested in equities as illustrated in Exhibit 3. This is part of the power of using derivatives to manage portfolios. Since derivative contracts do not require the exchange of principal, underlying assets may be held in one type of security but the net result may be the return on another type of security.

Exhibit 1: Equity Index Swap

Buyer   **Seller**

```
Investor A    A pays fixed return  ──▶    Investor B
              B pays equity index return ◀──
```

Exhibit 2: Return Equivalency from the Purchase of an Equity Index Swap

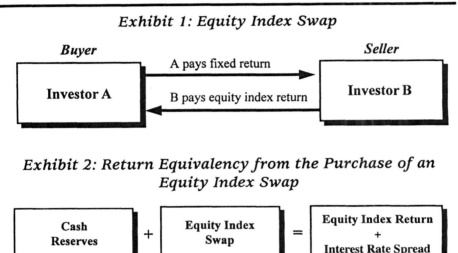

Cash Reserves + Equity Index Swap = Equity Index Return + Interest Rate Spread

└─── Synthetic Equity ───┘

Exhibit 3: Return Equivalency from the Sale of an Equity Index Swap

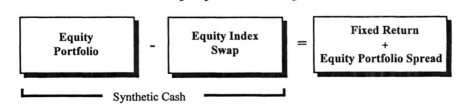

Equity Portfolio - Equity Index Swap = Fixed Return + Equity Portfolio Spread

└─── Synthetic Cash ───┘

Exhibit 4: Payoff of an Equity Index Swap as a Function of the Return on the Index

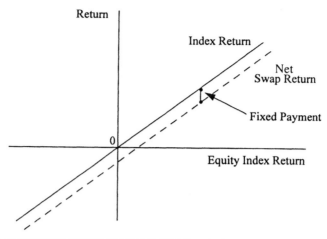

The return on the swap contract is referred to as being *linear* because it bears a straight line relationship to the return on the underlying equity index as shown in Exhibit 4. If the market goes up, the return on the swap contract will also go up. If the market goes down, the return on the swap contract also goes down. The difference between the index return and the swap return is the fixed rate the purchaser of the swap pays to the seller. When the swap return is added to the return the buyer earns on the underlying principal, the net result reflects the return on the equity index plus or minus the spread between what is earned on the cash reserve and what is paid to the seller.

Since swaps are usually entered into for an extended period of time, they are used primarily for either gaining or reducing market exposure. It may not be convenient or cost effective for the purchaser of a swap to buy actual equity securities. Entering into the swap agreement is an alternative for achieving equity exposure without the actual purchase of underlying equity securities. It has become popular in recent years to use swaps to create enhanced index funds. The investor may have a specific expertise in managing cash portfolios but no expertise in managing equity portfolios. If more can be earned on the cash portfolio than has to be paid to the seller of the swap, the investor ends up with an index-like return in the equity market but adds a spread generated by the difference in return between the actively managed cash portfolio and the fixed rate in the swap. This is sometimes referred to as *transporting alpha*. The alpha or differential return generated in one market can be converted to a differential return in another market.

Any type of equity index can be used in a swap as long as it is well defined and is agreed upon by both parties. It has become increasingly popular in recent years to use a swap on an international equity index. This saves the purchaser of the swap the difficulties of transacting in international markets and avoids directly paying for the accounting and custody fees. To the extent that the seller of the swap has potential economies of scale in assuming these costs and builds this reduced cost into the fixed return in the swap, the buyer of the swap may be able to generate international equity market returns at somewhat lower cost than purchasing the securities directly.

To illustrate an equity index swap transaction, suppose two investors agree to swap the return on the S&P 500 index in exchange for LIBOR plus 20 basis points on a $20 million notional value. The buyer of the swap pays the seller LIBOR plus 20 basis points in exchange for the total return on the S&P 500 index. If annualized LIBOR is 5.25% and the return on the S&P 500 index is 6.3% for the quarter, the buyer pays

$$\$20,000,000 \ (0.0545/4) = \$272,500$$

and the seller pays

$$\$20,000,000 \ (0.063) = \$1,260,000$$

In practice, the two amounts would usually be netted out against each other with the seller paying $987,500 to the buyer in this case.

Furthermore, suppose the buyer has invested $20 million in cash reserves earning an annualized rate of 5.85% for the quarter. The buyer of the swap has effectively earned a net return of

$$6.3\% + (5.85\% - 5.45\%)/4 = 6.40\%$$

or 10 basis points more than the index for the quarter. The extra 10 basis points comes from earning an annualized 40 basis points more per year than is required to be paid in the swap contract. If the seller of the swap has hedged the market obligation using a portfolio of stocks which has returned 6.5%, the seller's net return for the quarter will be

$$5.45\%/4 + (6.5\% - 6.3\%) = 1.56\%$$

or 6.25% at an annualized rate. The extra 100 basis points return over LIBOR with little market exposure is generated by receiving an extra 20 basis points from the fixed return in the swap plus an annualized differential return over the index of 80 basis points from the underlying equity portfolio.

LINEAR PAYOFFS: FUTURES

Futures contracts work much like swaps in their payoff pattern but there are some important institutional differences. One of the differences comes from the fact that futures contracts are traded on organized exchanges and are not negotiated directly between two counterparties. With a swap contract each counterparty is exposed to the credit risk of the other. With futures contracts the trading exchange and its members stand in the middle between two investors who have bought and sold futures contracts. The exchange plays the role of guarantor of the contract to ensure that all contract obligations are met. To help assure the financial integrity of the exchange and minimize the possibility that investors could build up losses beyond their ability to pay, investors initiating a position must deposit a performance bond with the exchange as *initial margin*. In addition, gains and losses are settled up on a daily basis between investors through the exchange (called *mark to market*) in contrast to swap contracts which are typically settled only quarterly. Finally, the interest rate which is fixed in the terms of a swap contract is embedded directly in the price of the futures contract so that it is not required to be independently specified up-front. The rate embedded in the futures contract is an implied market rate called the *implied repo rate* and matches the maturity of the contract in contrast to the fixed rate in the swap which usually resets each quarter when payments are exchanged

Exchange traded futures contracts typically carry a shorter term maturity than swap contracts. Maturities are usually staggered in three month segments with most of the liquidity found in the nearest maturity contract. There is often poor liquidity beyond the first two or three contracts. The shorter maturity of futures contracts allows them to be used with greater flexibility in managing equity portfolios, though like a swap, there are still only two things to do with a futures contract: buy it or sell it.

Applications of Buying Futures

The purchase of an equity index futures contract accomplishes the same thing as the purchase of an equity index swap. It adds equity exposure to the manager's portfolio. There are a variety of situations where a manager may want to add equity exposure. One of the most common is referred to as *cash equitization*. Equitizing cash through the purchase of futures contracts creates equity exposure synthetically without having to actually purchase underlying securities as illustrated in Exhibit 5. Many equity portfolios contain frictional amounts of cash that are difficult to keep fully invested. Dividends may be received from time to time or there may be new contributions that increase the cash in the portfolio. If the market moves up before these frictional amounts of cash can be invested in stocks, the portfolio performance will be exposed to *cash drag* and will not track the market as closely as it might. In a year when the market returns in excess of 25%, holding 5% cash would reduce portfolio performance by over 100 basis points. Since the market generally trends up over time, any frictional cash in the portfolio will tend to hurt performance.

Futures contracts might be purchased for more than just equitizing frictional amounts of cash. An entire portfolio could be left in cash reserves and futures contracts could be purchased to create a synthetic index fund. The combination of the cash reserve plus the futures contracts will behave as if a manager had purchased all of the stocks in the index. This creates tremendous liquidity in the portfolio. If funds are needed quickly, the futures contracts and the cash reserves are often easier to liquidate at lower cost than the underlying stocks. Furthermore, if the underlying cash reserve is actively managed to yield more than the implied repo rate in the futures contract, the index fund will have an enhanced return greater than the index itself. Futures contracts have been used to create enhanced index funds not only in the United States but in other countries that have actively traded equity index futures contracts. This achieves the same effect as purchasing a swap but with a shorter maturity.

Futures contracts are also useful in the trading process by helping manage the net market exposure of a portfolio as stocks are purchased or sold. It is not uncommon for slices of a portfolio to be traded involving multiple securities. These trades could be caused by the addition or withdrawal of funds in a portfolio or by a restructuring of positions internal to the portfolio. As long as the purchase or sale of securities leaves the portfolio temporarily overexposed or underexposed to the market while the trades are taking place, the portfolio manager can maintain market exposure until all of the security positions are in place by selling or buying the requisite number of futures contracts. The positions can then be closed out when they are no longer needed.

Applications of Selling Futures

The most common motivation for selling a futures contract in managing an equity portfolio is to temporarily hedge its market exposure. Like a swap, the sale of a futures contact against an underlying portfolio of stocks is equivalent to creating synthetic cash as illustrated in Exhibit 6. In essence, creating a hedged position is an attempt to counteract the market risk in the underlying securities and shift the risk to others willing to bear the risk. The risk can always be shifted by doing away with the underlying security position, but this may interfere with the nature of the investor's business or disrupt a continuing investment program. The futures market provides an alternative way to temporarily control or eliminate much of the risk in the underlying securities while continuing to hold the stocks.

Exhibit 5: Creating Synthetic Equity Exposure Using Index Futures Contracts

Exhibit 6: Creating Synthetic Cash Using Equity Index Futures Contracts: Hedging

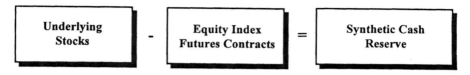

Exhibit 7: Return Profiles for Hedged Portfolios

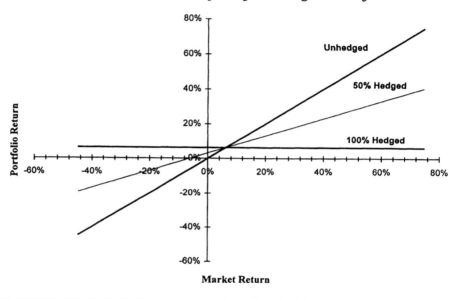

The impact of hedging can be seen by examining the effect of hedging on a portfolio's return profile and probability distribution. Exhibit 7 illustrates the return on the hedged portfolio relative to the return on the underlying market index. A partially hedged position reduces the slope of the return line, so that the hedged portfolio does not perform as well as the market when returns are high, but it also does not perform as poorly when returns are low. The greater the portion of the portfolio that is hedged, the less slope the line will have. A full hedge produces a flat line, indicating that the hedged portfolio will generate a fixed return no matter what the underlying market does. This fixed return should be equal to the riskless rate if the futures contract is fairly priced. The slope of the return line for an equity portfolio is often referred to as the portfolio's market sensitivity or beta. Hedging effectively reduces the market beta of the portfolio as it amounts to selling the equity exposure of the portfolio.

Exhibit 8: Return Distributions for Hedged Portfolios

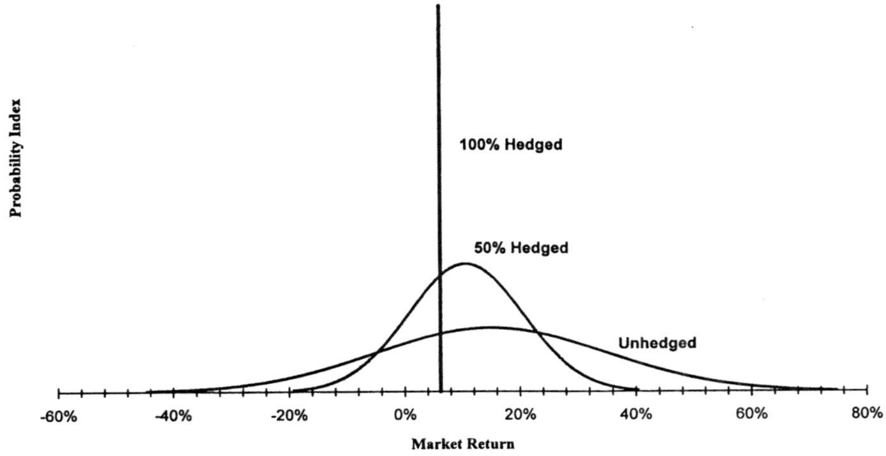

Exhibit 8 shows how the futures hedge changes the probability distribution of returns. If the return distribution for the market is symmetric with a wide dispersion, hedging the portfolio with futures gradually draws both tails of the distribution in toward the middle, and the mean return shrinks back toward the riskless rate. A full hedge draws both tails into one place and puts all of the probability mass at the riskless rate (the implied repo rate in the contract).

Hedging with futures will affect both tails equally. One of the main differences between options with their non-linear effects and futures is that options can affect one tail more dramatically than the other, so the distribution becomes quite skewed. Exhibit 9 illustrates the difference in the return distributions caused by a partial futures hedge versus a partial hedge created by using a put option. The put option hedge reduces the downside risk while leaving much of the upside potential. The use of options for hedging will be explained in more detail later.

Hedge Ratios Using Futures

A *hedge ratio* represents the amount of the futures used to construct a hedge relative to the amount of the underlying portfolio being hedged. In some cases there is a direct way to calculate the appropriate hedge ratio between futures and the portfolio. This technique can be used when the futures contract used for hedging is tied closely to the underlying portfolio being hedged as is the case when equity index futures are used to hedge a well diversified portfolio. Hedge ratios can be calculated easily because there is a direct link between the change in the value of the underlying portfolio and a change in the value of the associated futures contract.

To develop this idea, suppose an investor holds one unit of a portfolio containing securities S and wants to hedge it with a futures contract F. The change in the value of the combined position V as the portfolio value changes is

$$\Delta V = \Delta S + h\Delta F \qquad (1)$$

where h (the hedge ratio) represents the number of units of futures F used to hedge portfolio S. Solving for the hedge ratio directly from equation (1) gives

$$h = \frac{\Delta V - \Delta S}{\Delta F} \qquad (2)$$

For a complete hedge, or market neutral hedge ($\Delta V = 0$), the hedge ratio would be equal to the negative of the ratio of relative price changes between the portfolio being hedged and the futures contract. That is,

$$h = -\frac{\Delta S}{\Delta F} \qquad (3)$$

To illustrate this concept suppose S is a diversified equity portfolio, F is a futures contract on the S&P 500 Index, and $\Delta S/\Delta F$ is assumed to equal 0.95. That is, when the S&P 500 futures contract moves by $1, the underlying equity portfolio moves by only $0.95, indicating that the portfolio is slightly less volatile than the broad market represented by the S&P 500 Index. For a market neutral hedge, the hedge ratio is

$$h = -\frac{0.95}{1.00} = -0.95$$

Exhibit 9: Return Distributions for Hedged Portfolios
Options versus Futures

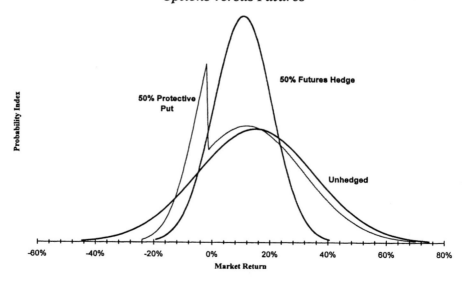

An investor would sell futures contracts worth 95% of the value of the equity portfolio to create the hedge. If the investor wanted only a partial hedge ($\Delta V = \frac{1}{3}\Delta S$, for example), the hedge ratio is

$$h = \frac{\frac{1}{3}\Delta S - \Delta S}{\Delta F} = \frac{-2}{3}\left(\frac{\Delta S}{\Delta F}\right) = -0.63$$

The investor would sell futures contracts worth only 63% of the value of the equity portfolio. With the hedge in place, the hedged portfolio would move only $\frac{1}{3}$ as much as the underlying portfolio.

Because the equity portfolio does not move one for one with the S&P 500 futures contract in the example, the investor does not want to use a hedge ratio of -1.0 to hedge the market risk in the underlying securities. A market-neutral hedge requires fewer futures contracts to be used because the underlying equity portfolio has only 95% of the movement of the futures contract.

The example above also shows what the hedge ratio must be if only a partial hedge is created to protect against the price movement in the underlying securities. If the combined hedged position is targeted to have $\frac{1}{3}$ of the movement of the underlying securities, a hedge ratio of -0.63 is needed. The investor would sell futures contracts worth only 63% of the value of the equity portfolio to create the partial hedge.

The arbitrage pricing relationship between the futures contract and the underlying market index links the two price changes together. This relationship can be used to calculate how the fair price of the futures contract will change as the price of the equity index changes. To see how this relationship can be used to estimate the hedge ratio directly, suppose that the price change of both the portfolio to be hedged and the futures contract are proportional to the change in the market index I in the following way:

$$\Delta S = \beta_S \Delta I, \text{ and } \Delta F = \beta_F \Delta I$$

where β_S and β_F represent the sensitivity to the index (market betas) of the portfolio being hedged and the futures contract, respectively.

Because portfolios and futures contracts are tied to the same underlying index, the hedge ratio is proportional to the ratio of their respective market betas. That is,

$$h = \frac{-\Delta S}{\Delta F} = -\frac{\beta_S}{\beta_F} \tag{4}$$

If the investor has an estimate of the market betas of the futures contract and the portfolio relative to the market index, the investor can calculate the appropriate hedge ratio directly.

For example, consider the calculation of the hedge ratio and the number of S&P 500 futures contracts required to hedge a $50 million equity portfolio with a beta of 1.05 relative to the S&P 500 Index. If the futures contract has a beta of 1.01 and the current level of the index is 900, the hedge ratio is

$$h = \frac{-1.05}{1.01} = -1.04$$

The contract size for the S&P 500 is 500 times the value of the S&P 500 Index, or \$450,000 (500 × 900), so the number of futures contracts required to be sold is

$$n = \frac{h(\text{Hedge value})}{\text{Contract size}} = \frac{-1.04(50,000,000)}{450,000} = -116 \text{ contracts}$$

Notice that the hedge ratio is slightly less than the beta of the portfolio. The short-term hedge ratio accounts for the slightly larger volatility in the index futures contract caused by its arbitrage pricing relationship. This additional volatility will shrink towards zero as the contract gets closer to maturity, reflecting a beta for the futures contract which converges to 1.0 at expiration. For longer term hedges with an investment horizon equal to the expiration date of the futures contract, a futures beta of 1.0 is typically used to calculate the hedge ratio.

NON-LINEAR PAYOFFS: OPTIONS

Simple options come in two forms: put options and call options. Unlike futures contracts and swaps, options require a small premium to be paid when purchased. Depending on the maturity of the option and the exercise price, the premium may range from less than 1% to more than 10% of the value of the underlying security or index. The payoff from an option at expiration depends on whether the security is above or below the level of the exercise or strike price. This lack of symmetry creates a non-linear payoff for the option at expiration. Put options have a non-zero payoff when the security price is less than the exercise price and call options pay off when the security price is greater than the exercise price. To see how options can be used in managing equity portfolios it is useful to review the payoff profile of put and call options.

Payoff Profiles for Options

Insight into the characteristics of options can be obtained by looking specifically at how options behave and what value they have at expiration. The matrix below is a simple technique for showing the value of option positions at expiration where S represents the value of the individual security or index and K represents the exercise price of the option:

	Payoff at Expiration	
	$S < K$	$S > K$
Call	0	$S - K$
Put	$K - S$	0
Security	S	S

At the expiration of the put or call option, its payoff depends on whether the security price is less than or more than the exercise price. The value of the underlying security is the same, S, whether it is below or above the option's exercise price. These payoffs form the basic building blocks for option strategy analysis.

Exhibit 10 illustrates the payoff pattern at expiration for a call option. On the horizontal axis is plotted the security price. The vertical axis measures the payoff at expiration. The trivial case representing the security's value is shown by the dashed line. For example, if the security ends with a value of K dollars, then the security will have a payoff of K dollars. The call option has a value of zero until the security price reaches the exercise price K, after which the call option increases one for one in price as the security price increases. The investor, however, must first purchase the option. So the net payoff from buying a call option is negative until the security price reaches the exercise price, and then it starts to rise (the dotted line). This line represents the payoff the investor receives net of the cost of the option. The investor breaks even with zero net profit at the point where the security price equals the exercise price plus the call option premium, C.

Note that the call option has a kinked or asymmetric payoff pattern. This feature distinguishes it from a futures contract. The future has a payoff pattern that is a straight line, as does the underlying security. This asymmetry in the option's payoff allows the option buyer to create specialized return patterns that are unavailable when using a futures contract.

Exhibit 11 illustrates the behavior of a put option. The put option has an intrinsic value of zero above the exercise price. Below there, it increases one for one as the security price declines. If an investor buys a put option, the net payoff of the option is the dotted line. The investor breaks even, with zero net profit, at the point where the security price equals the exercise price less the put option premium, P.

Exhibit 10: Payoff Profile of a Call Option

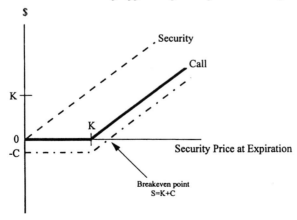

$ vertical axis

Security

Call

K

0
-C

Security Price at Expiration

Breakeven point
S=K+C

— · — · Net of option premiums

Exhibit 11: Payoff Profile of a Put Option

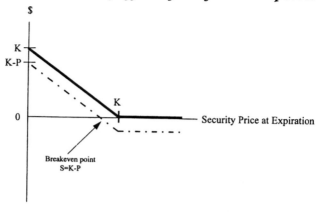

- - · - · Net of option premiums

Selling Call Options: Exchanging Appreciation for Income

One of the most popular option strategies is known as a *covered call*. A covered call is constructed by holding the underlying security and selling a call option. The payoff matrix at expiration for this strategy is

	Covered Call Payoff at Expiration	
	$S < K$	$S > K$
Security	S	S
Short Call	0	$-(S - K)$
Total Payoff	S	K

The value of the security is S whether it finishes above or below the exercise price. The value of the call option is zero below the exercise price and $(S - K)$ above the exercise price. Since the call option has been sold by the investor, the payoff of the call option is owed and serves to reduce the total payoff below the value of the security itself. The total payoff of the covered call is found by adding up the value in each column. Below the exercise price, the portfolio is worth S dollars since the call has expired worthless. Above the exercise price, the portfolio is worth K dollars since the short call neutralizes the appreciation in the security above the exercise price.

The covered call strategy is shown graphically in Exhibit 12. The dashed line again represents the security value. The solid line represents the value of the security plus the payoff from the short call option. Below the exercise price the investor is left with the value of the security. Above the exercise price the security's appreciation is capped at the exercise price. In exchange for this limit on the security's appreciation, the investor receives the premium of the call option. The investor has traded the possibility of upside appreciation above the exercise price for income in the form of the option premium. The break-even point occurs when the security price is equal to the exercise price plus the call option premium. Below this point the covered call strategy gives a better payoff than holding the security by itself.

To demonstrate the result of a covered call strategy, consider an investor who holds a position in a stock worth $10 million. Assume that the current stock price is $100. The following example illustrates the effect of selling call options if the stock appreciates or depreciates 10% over the next six months.

	Stock Price	Underlying Portfolio Value	Portfolio Percentage Change
Current	$100	$10,000,000	
After six months	$110	$11,000,000	10.0
After six months	$90	$9,000,000	−10.0

Suppose the investor sells 100,000 6-month call options, each covering 100 shares with an exercise price of $105 to bring in premium income of $300,000. If the stock price declines by 10% to $90, the call options will expire worthless and the investor keeps the income from the sale of the call options giving a portfolio value of

$$9,000,000 + \$300,000 = \$9,300,000$$

representing a decline of 7.0%. The value of the portfolio has declined by less than the 10% decline in the stock price because of the premium income received from the call options. If the stock price appreciates by 10%, the payoff of the call options owed by the investor will be

$$100,000 (105 - 110) = -\$500,000$$

Exhibit 12: Payoff Profile of a Covered Call

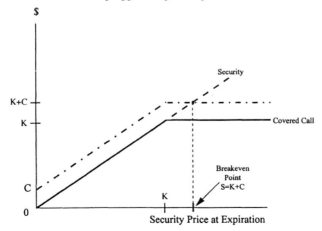

which when combined with the value of the stock and the premium income from the sale of the call options gives a portfolio value of

$$\$11,000,000 + \$300,000 - \$500,000 = \$10,800,000.$$

This represents a return of 8.0% on the value of the stocks in the portfolio compared to the stock price appreciation of 10.0%. The premium income from the call options has helped to offset the loss on the exercise of the options but the stock has appreciated beyond the break-even point so the net return on the portfolio is less than the appreciation in the stock itself.

Asymmetric Hedges: Protecting the Downside

The construction of an asymmetric hedge which responds to positive market returns differently than to negative market returns usually requires the use of an option. The most common strategies to hedge market exposure are (1) the protective put, (2) the protective put spread, and (3) the collar, range forward, or fence.

Protective Put

A *protective put* is constructed by holding the underlying security and buying a put option. The payoff matrix at expiration for this strategy is

Protective Put Payoff at Expiration		
	$S < K$	$S > K$
Security	S	S
Put	$K - S$	0
Total payoff	K	S

The value of the security is S whether it finishes above or below the exercise price. The value of the put option is $(K - S)$ below the option's exercise price and zero above the exercise price. The total value of the protective put is found by adding up the value in each column. Below the exercise price, the portfolio is worth K dollars at expiration. Above the exercise price, it is worth S.

This strategy is depicted graphically in Exhibit 13. The dashed line again represents the security value. The solid line represents the value of the security plus the put option. Below the exercise price, the put option compensates for the decline in the security price. Once the original cost of the put option is accounted for, the net payoff is represented by the dotted line. The break-even point occurs when the security price is equal to the exercise price less the cost of the put option. Below this point, the protective-put strategy gives a better payoff than holding just the security by itself.

The benefit of this strategy occurs below the break-even point. If the security price falls below this level, the portfolio is always worth more than the security itself. This protection is of great benefit if the market is going down. The market does not give this protection for free, however. Above the break-even point, the protected portfolio is always worth a little bit less than the security. The price paid for the option results in a slightly lower return on the upside. This strategy has sometimes taken on another name, portfolio insurance, because the put option protects the value if the security price falls while maintaining some market exposure if the price rises.

To illustrate the impact of put options to hedge equity exposure, consider the same investor who holds a stock position worth $10,000,000. Assume that the current stock price is $100 and can appreciate or depreciate by 10% over the next six months. Suppose also that the investor hedges the market risk by purchasing 100,000 6-month put options, each covering 100 shares with an exercise price of $100 at a cost of $600,000. If the stock price declines to $90, the payoff of the put options at expiration will be

$$\$100,000 \ (100 - 90) = \$1,000,000$$

The net value of the portfolio will be

$$\$9,000,000 + (\$1,000,000 - \$600,000) = \$9,400,000$$

representing a decline of 6%. The value of the portfolio has declined by less than the 10% decline in the stock price because of the net payoff of the options. The options will finish in the money and contribute some value to the portfolio. Without the option position, the unhedged value of the portfolio would have declined by the full 10%.

Exhibit 13: Payoff Profile of a Protective Put

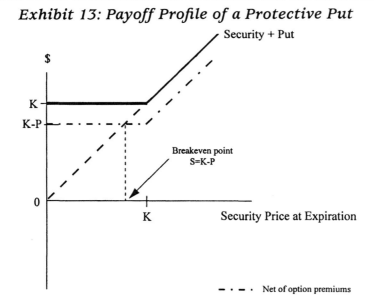

If the stock price increases to $110, the value of the put options at expiration will be zero giving a net value of the portfolio of

$$11,000,000 - \$600,000 = \$10,400,000$$

representing an increase of 4%. Due to the cost of the options, the hedged portfolio will underperform the unhedged portfolio which returns a full 10.0%.

Protective Put Spread

The *protective put spread* is constructed by purchasing a put option and selling a put option farther out of the money. The payoff matrix at expiration for this strategy is

Protective Put Spread Payoff at Expiration			
	$S < K_l$	$K_l < S < K_u$	$S > K_u$
Security	S	S	S
Put Purchased	$K_u - S$	$K_u - S$	0
Put Sold	$-(K_l - S)$	0	0
Total Payoff	$S + (K_u - K_l)$	K_u	S

The total payoff of the protective put spread is split into three pieces corresponding to whether the security price is below the lower exercise price (K_l), in between the two exercise prices, or above the higher exercise price (K_u). Below the exercise price the hedged portfolio is worth the value of the stock plus the difference between the higher exercise price and the lower exercise price. If the stock price falls in between the two exercise prices, the payoff is just equal to the higher exercise price. Finally, if the stock price is above both exercise prices, the payoff is equal to the stock price since both put options expire worthless.

The strategy is shown graphically in Exhibit 14. The dashed line represents the security value. The solid line represents the value of the security plus the payoff from the two put options. In between the two exercise prices, the put spread protects the value of the portfolio as before. Below the lower exercise price the portfolio is again exposed to the decline in the market price of the stock. Once the net cost of the put option spread has been accounted for, the net payoff is represented by the dotted line. The break-even point occurs when the security price is equal to the exercise price of the protective put less the net cost of the put option spread. The cost of the protective put option spread is less than that of the protective put by itself because of the premium brought in from the put option which has been sold. As a result the break-even point is higher. The stock has to decline less in order for the protective put spread to be better than leaving the security unhedged.

The previous example can be expanded to incorporate the put spread. Suppose that 100,000 put options with an exercise price of $90 were sold to bring in premium of $100,000 to help pay for the cost of the protective puts. Now the net cost of the option positions would be $500,000. If the stock price rises 10% to $110, the payoff of the hedged portfolio will be

Exhibit 14: Payoff Profile of a Protective Put Spread

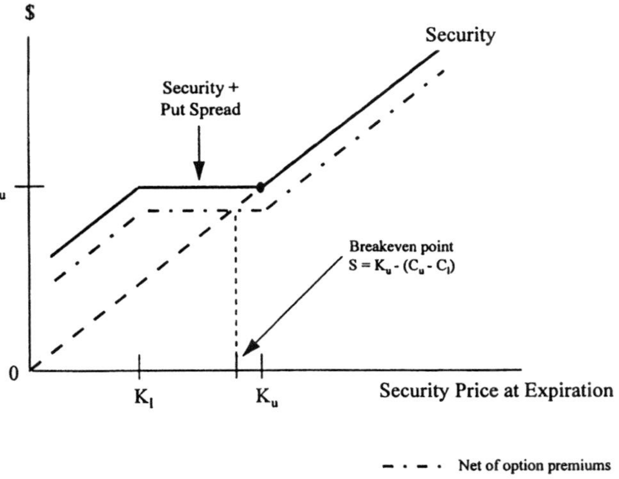

$$\$11,000,000 - (\$600,000 - \$100,000) = \$10,500,000$$

resulting in a portfolio return of 5%. If the price of the stock falls 10% to $90, the payoff of the hedged portfolio will be

$$\$9,000,000 + \$100,000 \,(100 - 90) - (\$600,000 - \$100,000) = \$9,500,000$$

resulting in a portfolio return of −5% compared to the 10% decline in the stock and the 6% decline if only the protective put is used. The additional benefits resulting from the protective put spread come because the portfolio is not completely protected if the stock price falls below the lower exercise price. For example, a 20% decline in the stock price would result in a 15% decline using the protective put spread while resulting in only a 6% decline using the protective put by itself.

Collar (Range Forward or Fence)

The *collar, range forward, or fence* is constructed by selling a call option in addition to the purchase of a put option. The sale of the call again brings in cash which reduces the cost of purchasing the put option. The maturity of the call option is typically the same as that of the put, but has a higher exercise price. The sale of the call option eliminates the benefit of positive security returns above the level of the call's exercise price. If the exercise price of the call option is set close enough to that of the put, the cost of the put option can be offset entirely by the sale of the call option. This is typically referred to as a *zero cost collar.*

   To accommodate the difference in exercise prices between the put and the call options, the payoff matrix must again be expanded. As a result, the payoff matrix for the collar is

Exhibit 15: Payoff Profile of a Collar

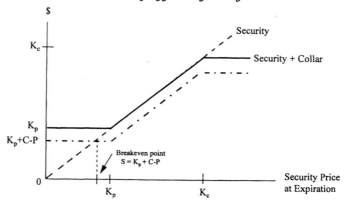

—·—· Net of option premiums

Collar Payoff at Expiration			
	$S < K_p$	$K_p < S < K_c$	$S > K_c$
Security	S	S	S
Put	$K_p - S$	0	0
−Call	0	0	$-(S - K_c)$
Total payoff	K_p	S	K_c

K_p represents the put exercise price and K_c represents the exercise price of the call option. If the security is below the exercise price of the put at expiration, the payoff will be equal to the exercise price of the put. If the security is above the exercise price of the call option, the payoff will be equal to the exercise price of the call option. In between the two exercise prices the payoff will be equal to the underlying security price.

The payoff of the collar is shown graphically in Exhibit 15. The solid line represents the value of the security plus the payoff from the options. The dotted line represents the value of the strategy once the net cost of the options is considered. A zero cost collar would have no net option cost so the dotted line would converge to the solid line. The dashed line represents the value of holding the security unhedged. The benefit of this strategy occurs below the exercise price of the option similar to the protective put. The exact break-even point depends on the price of the call option sold to truncate some of the upside potential. This loss of upside potential beyond the break-even point of the short call position is the disadvantage of using the collar.

To continue the previous hedging example, suppose that call options are sold with an exercise price of $105 for $300,000 in addition to the purchase of put options with an exercise price of $100. If the stock price declines to $90, the put options will have value, but the call options will expire worthless. The net value of the portfolio will be

$$\$9,000,000 + \$100,000\ (100 - 90) - (\$600,000 - \$300,000) = \$9,700,000$$

representing a decline of 3% compared to the stock price decline of 10%. The sale of the call option has helped offset the cost of the put option hedge which previously showed a decline of 6%.

On the other hand, if the stock price increases to $110, the put options will expire worthless and the value of the call option at expiration will detract from performance giving a portfolio value of

$$\$11,000,000 - \$100,000\ (110 - 105) - (\$600,000 - \$300,000) = \$10,200,000$$

representing a net increase of only 2% compared to the 10% increase in the stock price.

Comparing the protective put strategy with the collar shows that the investor is better off using the collar if the stock price declines, but could be worse off if the stock price increases sufficiently beyond the exercise price of the call option. In the example here the loss on the value of the call option is more than the premium received when the option was sold so the investor has done slightly worse than the protective put strategy even though the stock price increased. In general, the collar or range forward works well as long as the market does not increase beyond the exercise price of the call option. If the market rallies much beyond that point, the investor will not participate in the upside market gains.

Buying Call Options: Creating Market Exposure

Two common option positions used to create market exposure are buying calls and buying call spreads. To add equity market exposure to a portfolio, the investor can buy call options on an equity index. If, for example, extra exposure to the U.S. equity market is desired, the investor can buy call options on the S&P 500. If the market appreciates, the option will increase in value. If the market declines, all the investor can lose is the cost of the option. The cost of the call option is the price the investor must pay to participate in the upside market potential while avoiding a loss in a declining market.

An alternative strategy would be to buy a call spread to create the market exposure. With a call spread, an investor buys calls with a lower exercise price than the call options sold. For example, if the market has only moderate upside potential, an investor might buy a call option with an exercise price at current market levels and sell a call option with a higher exercise price — at an exercise price above where the market is expected to be at expiration. Using a call spread, the investor participates in the market only up to a point, but at a reduced cost because the sale of the out-of-the-money call option offsets the cost of the long call option.

Exhibit 16: Payoff Profiles from Buying Calls and Call Spreads

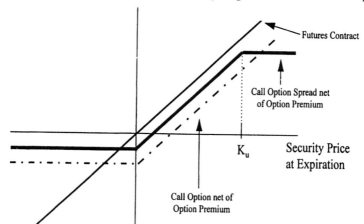

The payoff profiles at expiration for these two strategies, compared to buying a futures contract, are illustrated in Exhibit 16. If investors buy futures contracts, they will participate to the full extent of the market increase or decrease. If they buy a call option to create exposure, they participate if the market goes up, but if the market goes down, they will not suffer the full decline. The gap between the option and futures payoff on the upside represents the cost of the call option. If an investor's view about the market is positive, but not excessively bullish, the lower-cost call spread creates additional exposure but caps the market participation beyond a certain point.

Probability Distribution of Returns

In addition to using payoff diagrams to describe the effect of options, an investor can look at the probability distribution of returns for various strategies. Consider first the covered call strategy. Exhibit 17 shows the probability distribution of returns for an underlying security with and without the sale of call options. Note how the shape changes as an increasing proportion of call options are sold relative to the underlying security position. Selling call options draws the portfolio distribution back gradually on the right side and increases the chance that an investor will receive only moderate returns. Selling call options on 100% of the portfolio completely truncates the right-hand side of the probability distribution: the investor has a high probability of receiving moderate returns and no probability of receiving high returns. Most of the probability of receiving low returns is preserved, however.

Next consider the protective put strategy. Exhibit 18 shows the probability distribution of returns for an underlying security with and without the use of put options. Note how the shape changes as an increasing proportion of put options are purchased relative to the underlying security position. Purchasing put options draws the portfolio distribution back gradually on the left side and increases the chance that an investor will receive only moderate returns. Buying put options on 100% of the portfolio completely truncates the left-hand side of the probability distribution: The investor has a very high probability of receiving moderate returns and no probability of receiving low returns. Most of the probability of receiving high returns is preserved, however.

Exhibit 17: Return Distributions for Covered Calls

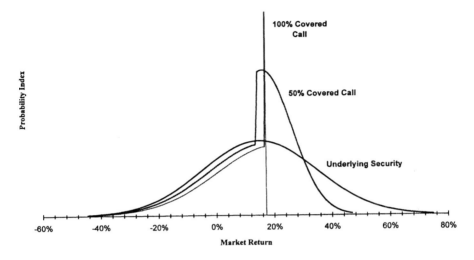

Exhibit 18: Return Distributions for Protective Puts

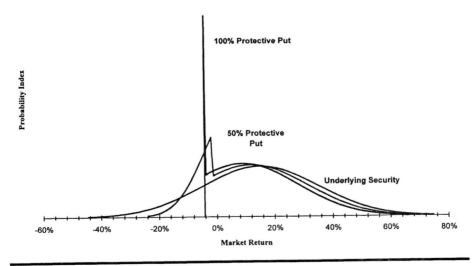

Exhibit 19: Return Distributions for Collars

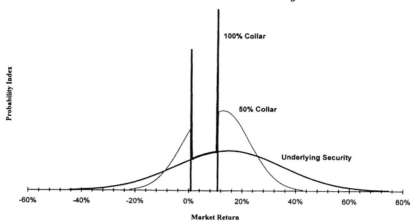

Exhibit 20: Creating a Synthetic Cash Reserve Using Options

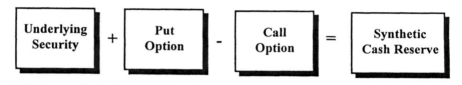

Exhibit 19 illustrates the effect of selling call options and buying put options simultaneously (a fence or collar). The combination causes quite a severe misshaping of the probability distribution in both tails. The distribution is no longer smooth and symmetric. The asymmetry of options allows an investor to shape and mold the probability distribution by truncating some parts and adding to others. Call options affect the right-hand tail most dramatically, while put options affect the left-hand tail.

Notice that the collar provides similar downside protection but loses its upside participation if the security return is positive beyond the level of the call's exercise price. Selling the call option with the same exercise price as the put option would protect against downside losses but would also eliminate any upside participation. This would make the hedge symmetric similar to selling a futures contract or swap. Indeed, the short call and long put position with the same exercise price creates a synthetic futures contract which produces a symmetric hedge. This can be seen from the stylized put/call parity relationship in Exhibit 20 which indicates that a combination of the underlying security, the purchase of a put option, and the sale of a call option with the same exercise price and maturity will behave the same as a cash reserve. The short call option and the long put option work to create a synthetic futures contract which offsets the risk in the underlying security resulting in a cash equivalent position.

Exhibit 21: Creating Synthetic Equity Exposure Using Options: Put/Call Parity

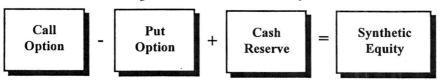

Exhibit 22: Creating a Synthetic Covered Call Strategy: The Collateralized Put

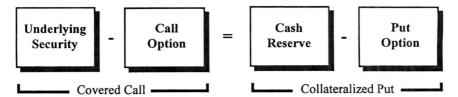

Exhibit 23: Creating a Synthetic Protective Put

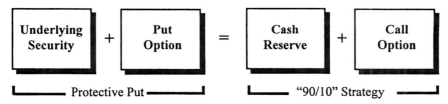

Rearranging the relationship to create a synthetic security instead of a synthetic cash reserve indicates that the combination of the cash reserve minus a put option plus a call option creates a market position as shown in Exhibit 21. In this case the long call option and the short put option work to create a synthetic futures position which adds market exposure to the cash reserve creating a synthetic security.

One last comment about the put/call parity relationship. Rearranging the components allows us to create the same payoff for the covered call and the protective put strategies in another way than previously described. The covered call strategy is normally constructed by purchasing the underlying security and selling a call option. An equivalent way to achieve the same payoff is to sell a put option and invest equivalent funds in an interest bearing cash reserve as shown in Exhibit 22. This alternative is sometimes referred to as a collateralized put and produces the same return profile as a covered call. In like manner, an equivalent way to create the same payoff as the protective put strategy is to purchase a call option and invest the remainder of the funds in an interest bearing cash reserve as illustrated in Exhibit 23.

This alternative is sometimes nicknamed the "90/10" strategy since roughly 90% of the investor's funds are held in a cash reserve with 10% used to purchase call options to give upside market participation. These configurations give equivalent payoffs because the arbitrage relationships between put and call options with the same maturities and exercise prices ensure that the payoff patterns will be preserved.

Automatic Changes in Market Exposure

Changes in market exposure can be triggered automatically as the market moves by selling options. The sale of a call option will truncate market participation above the option's exercise price. Selling some index call options against a long futures position or against exposure in the underlying stocks effectively pre-sells a portion of the exposure at the option's exercise price if the market reaches that level by the expiration date of the option. The receipt of the option premium effectively pays the investor for making the decision to sell in advance.

Conversely, the sale of a put option will allow the investor to prepurchase a position in the market at the put option's exercise price. The sale of options are frequently used in asset allocation and trading strategies to automatically reposition the portfolio if certain market levels are reached. Selling call options on 10% of the portfolio's exposure will automatically reduce the exposure by 10% if the market rallies up to the level of the call option's exercise price. Selling put options on 10% of the portfolio exposure will automatically increase the exposure by 10% if the market falls to the level of the put option's exercise price. At that point the investor can replace the option position by selling stocks for a gain and repurchasing the calls or by purchasing stocks at a discount and repurchasing the puts in order to make the shift permanent. The advantage is that the investor gets to keep the option premium for having made the decision in advance. The premium effectively increases the sale price of the appreciated stocks or reduces the purchase price of the depreciated stocks.

The purchase of additional market exposure by buying call options or the hedging of existing market exposure by buying put options can also be thought of as creating automatic changes in market exposure. The purchase of call options allows the investor to increase market exposure as the market rises while the purchase of put options allows the investor to decrease market exposure as the market falls. The options automatically adjust their levels of participation as the market reaches the options' exercise prices and go in the money. The non-linear payoff pattern of an option creates this automatic adjustment feature.

A VALUATION FRAMEWORK FOR SELECTING DERIVATIVE STRATEGIES

Since the advent of the listed equity option market in the United States in 1973, investors have used options both to reduce risk and enhance return. The majority of investors use options in combination with other securities — option covered-call writing strategies are an example of such a strategy, where options are sold on a portfolio of underlying stocks in order to generate incremental returns. In spite of the fact that options are used in such a fashion, there is no generally accepted framework to evaluate the impact the options have on the return of the overall portfolio. The most widely used option pricing models such as the model developed by Black and Scholes[1] or the model of Cox, Ross, and Rubinstein[2] are geared more to valuing options as opposed to computing the expected return from a combined stock and option position. These models do not help an investor in selecting an optimal choice of option or the optimal structure — i.e., how does an investor choose between the various covered call alternatives?

In this section we outline a framework which can be used to evaluate the combinations of stock and option positions. We do not cover the fundamentals of option pricing as there are a number of books that provide an introduction to this topic.[3] We do, however, briefly cover the assumptions underlying the Black-Scholes model in order to highlight the conditions under which actual option prices may significantly differ from their theoretical Black-Scholes prices. The primary focus of this section is to outline a valuation framework to be used in choosing the optimal trade-off between risk and return when deciding to invest in an option in combination with another security (such as a stock or bond). We focus on covered call or overwriting strategies in our examples, although the framework is applicable to any security and option combination.

The Problem with Black-Scholes

The typical investor has a specific view on the future outcome for an equity security in which he is considering making an investment. Option valuation models, however, take the current price of the stock as given and then price the security using the key assumption that it is possible to combine the option and the underlying security to form a risk-free security. This combination should in equilibrium earn the risk-free rate. These models, as we show using a simple example below, do not allow an investor to estimate the value or expected return from a particular option conditional on the investor's expected return distribution. In order to compute such an expected return it is necessary to compute the actuarial value of the option.

This actuarial value can then be used to compute the expected return from investing in a particular combination of stock and options. We illustrate this below using a simple example for a manager considering using a strategy of selling calls on stock he owns as a means of increasing the return on the portfolio.

---

[1] See F. Black and M. Scholes, "The Pricing of Options and Corporate Liabilities," *Journal of Political Economy* (May/June 1973), pp. 637-657 for the original derivation of this pricing model.

[2] This more general approach to option pricing was first presented in J. Cox, S. Ross, and M. Rubinstein, "Option Pricing: A Simplified Approach," *Journal of Financial Economics* (September 1979), pp. 279-263

[3] See for example R. Clarke, *Options and Futures: A Tutorial*, The Research Foundation of the Institute for Chartered Financial Analysts or J. Hull, *Options, Futures and Other Derivative Securities: 2nd ed.* (Englewood Cliffs, NJ: Prentice Hall, 1993).

Exhibit 24: Expected Stock Return

Current Value		Future Value	Probability	Future Price × Probability
		60	0.65	39
$50				
		40	0.35	14
Expected Value				$53
Return				6.00%

For example, consider a stock at $50 that can go up or down. This is shown graphically in Exhibit 24, where in a period of say one quarter the stock can move up to $60 or down to $40. Given this set of outcomes, how do we price a call option with an exercise price of $50. The Black-Scholes approach is to first create a riskless position — i.e., a position whose final value is independent of whether the stock price moves up or down. In this simple example, such a riskless position can be constructed by a buying one share of stock and selling two options. On expiration day, if the stock has appreciated to 60 the position will be worth the value of the stock less the value of the two call options (worth $20 at a price of $10 each) for a net position value of $40. Conversely, if the stock moves down, the two options expire worthless, so the net position is again worth $40. Given that this position is guaranteed to have a value of $40 at the end of the quarter, the current value of this position must be equal to $40 discounted at the risk-free rate. If we assume a risk-free rate of 5%, this amounts to $39.50. As the position is equivalent to buying the stock and selling two calls, both calls must be worth $10.50 — or $5.25 per option.

Notice that this does not require us to know the likelihood of outcomes to value options. The key observation in the Black-Scholes model and other risk neutral models is that information about the future outcomes is reflected in the price. From the perspective of a manager proposing to make an equity investment in a security about which he believes to have superior information, this valuation process is not very insightful.

One approach to overcoming this problem is to compute the actuarial return from investing in an option. Suppose in this case that the manager believes — based on his or her internal analysis — that the probability of the stock rising is 65% and the probability of the stock falling is 35% (the probabilities have to sum to one). Given the manager's analysis, the expected return from investing in the security as shown in Exhibit 24 is 6%. Using the Black-Scholes approach, if the manager observed the option selling at $6, he could sell the overpriced call option. However, selling the call would result in the expected return falling to 5.68%. (See Exhibit 25.)

The expected return is reduced because given the manager's expectations, the expected value of the call is $6.50. This is because there is a 65% probability that the option will be worth $10 and a 35% probability that it is worth zero. Note that this is more than the Black-Scholes value. This actuarial value is the criterion the manager should use in evaluating whether the option should be sold. Indeed, selling the option at a price less than the actuarial value will consistently reduce the expected return from the combined stock and option position *vis-à-vis* the stock position.

This does not imply that the Black-Scholes value is incorrect. However, it does highlight the notion that the Black-Scholes model is not useful when evaluating alternative option strategies given a view (in terms of expected return and risk) on a security. It also highlights the fact that an option's price being above that of the Black-Scholes does not assure that the seller should expect to gain from selling the option. The difference between the Black-Scholes value and the actual market price can only be earned if the seller of the option implements the complete Black-Scholes trade and re-balances the trade to maintain its risk neutrality until the expiration of the option. Transactions costs may often prevent such a strategy from being workable in the presence of limited liquidity and non-continuous markets or some of the other key assumptions underlying the Black-Scholes and other risk neutral models of option pricing as discussed below.

Why Observed Prices May Differ from Black-Scholes

The Black-Scholes model is one of the most widely used models to price securities. However there are key assumptions underlying the model which often result in observed option prices being different from their theoretical values. The factors which affect this usually arise from the violation of one or more of the economic assumptions underlying Black-Scholes. We discuss each of these briefly below.

Perfectly Liquid Markets

In order to construct the riskless hedge which underlies the Black-Scholes pricing model, we have to be able to buy or sell shares of the underlying stock and sell or buy a zero-coupon bond in the proportions required by the hedge. We must be able to trade at precisely the same price as we assumed in estimating the hedge parameters. In reality, when we actually make the purchase or sale, there is no guarantee that we will achieve our target price.

In addition, if the underlying stock is thinly traded the purchase or sale of shares will have a significant effect on the price. In such a case the cash flow of the purchase would not equal the amount required by the Black-Scholes formula.

Exhibit 25: Stock + Covered Call (at $6.00) Return

Current Value		Future Value	Probability	Future Price × Probability
$44		54	0.65	32.5
		40	0.35	14
Expected Value				$46.5
Return				5.68%

Constant Interest Rates

The risk-free rate of interest is not constant as assumed by the Black-Scholes formula. In other words, the costs built into the formula are not equal to the actual costs in carrying out the strategy. Whenever this happens it is no longer true that the total cost of constructing the hedge will be equal to the risk-free price.

Continuous Markets

The Black-Scholes hedging strategy works if the investor can continuously rebalance the hedge. This is seldom possible in the presence of transactions costs.

Geometric Brownian Motion

In computing the Black-Scholes hedge, it is necessary to assume that stock prices follow a geometric Brownian motion. In reality we observe serial correlation in stock prices and we also observe that the volatility of stock returns changes over time and often overreacts to new information. Stock returns also exhibit a tendency to "jump" — so Black-Scholes hedge positions will be susceptible to such jump risk.

Short Selling Assumption

The Black-Scholes hedge for an investor who is short call options consists of a bond sold short and a certain number of shares of the underlying security. The short position is used to finance the long position. If this money is not available, an opportunity cost (in terms of borrowing cost or foregone return) has to be incurred. In such a situation, the strategy will not be self financing.

Whenever one or more of these assumptions is violated, we would expect to see the implied volatility on an option being systematically greater than the expected actual volatility. Unless the assumptions are satisfied, however, it is not possible for an investor to attempt to capture the mispricing as he is unable to engage in the Black-Scholes riskless hedging strategy. The valuation approach identified here can then be used to identify the optimal option structure to exploit this mispricing without resorting to an active hedging strategy.

A Generalized Actuarial Model

In the example given above, we illustrated the concept of using an actuarial value approach. Here we outline a generalized approach under the usual assumption that stock returns follow a log normal distribution. We will use the following notation:

S_0	= initial stock price
C_0	= initial call price
W_0	= initial investment
D	= dividends received over the time period of the option
S_f, C_f, W_f	= values of the stock, call and investment on the expiry day of the option

$dS_f P_T(S_f/S_n)$ = probability density of stock price changing from S_0 to S_f in time T assuming log normal distribution

$$= \frac{dS_f}{S_f\sqrt{2\pi\sigma^2 T}}\exp\left(-\frac{\left(\ln\left(\frac{S_f}{S_0}\right) - \mu T\right)^2}{2\sigma^2 T}\right) \qquad (5)$$

T = time to expiration (T_{yr} = 1 year in same units)
σ^2 = variance of log of stock price return (ln (S_f/S_0))
μ = mean per unit time of stock log price return

Given this distribution, the expected return from an investment in the combination of stock and option is given by:

$$\int dS_f P_T(S_f/S_0)\ln\left(\frac{W_f(S_f)}{W_0}\right) \qquad (6)$$

For the covered call position:

$$W_0 = S_0 - C_0$$
$$W_f = S_f - \max[0, S_f - E] + D$$

The integral can be done numerically or approximated analytically. A similar approach handles any complex combination of stock, cash, and options, allowing an investor to identify the optimal security and option combinations. Note that using numerical techniques this same framework can be adapted to handle any arbitrary distribution. For example, the "fat tailed nature of stock price returns" can be taken into account. Transactions costs, including commissions and bid-ask spreads, are also easily incorporated into this valuation framework.

Examples of Actuarial Valuation

We illustrate the benefits of using the actuarial valuation approach to assess alternative covered call strategies — arguably one of the most popular option strategies. In this example, we assume that options on a $50 stock are priced at an implied volatility of 30% per annum. Given this assumption, call options with a maturity of one year on such a stock would take values similar to those shown in Exhibit 26. Our hypothetical investor forecasts the volatility on the stock to be 20% with an expected return of 12%. These forecasts can be derived using a variety of methods based on historical data, a factor model, or scenario forecasting. Obviously, given this volatility forecast, every option on the stock is overvalued because the implied volatility at 30% is greater than the forecast volatility of 20%. If the investor could trade the stock under the assumptions implicit under Black-Scholes, he could essentially engage in a continuous trading strategy to try and exploit the difference. However, for most investors this is not a feasible alternative — especially if the stock is not actively traded.

Exhibit 26: Call Option Prices

Strike Price	Call Price
40.00	13.19
42.50	11.42
45.00	9.80
47.50	8.35
50.00	7.06
52.50	5.93
55.00	4.95
57.50	4.11
60.00	3.40

Prices computed using Black Scholes model using a 30% annualized volatility, a risk-free rate of 5%, three months to maturity, and an underlying stock price of $50.

Exhibit 27: Gain from Alternative Stock Option Combinations
Expected Stock Return = 12% Standard Deviation = 20%

Strike Price	Stock + Covered Call Return (%)	Standard Deviation (%)	Negative Semi-Deviation (%)
40.00	7.8	3.6	2.4
42.50	9.3	4.6	2.9
45.00	10.3	6.3	3.8
47.50	11.4	7.2	3.8
50.00	12.6	8.8	4.3
52.50	13.8	10.2	4.4
55.00	14.6	12.4	5.4
57.50	15.0	13.7	5.5
60.00	15.3	14.8	5.5
Stock Only	12.0	20.0	7.5

The actuarial value approach described above, however, can be used to identify the preferred covered call position. Using equation (6), we compute in Exhibit 27 the expected return from the various covered call positions. Also computed is the standard deviation of the returns associated with each position, as well as the negative semi-deviation. Since selling the call "caps" the maximum return from the covered call position, this results in a non-symmetric distribution, and therefore standard deviation is not an appropriate measure of risk. To accurately capture the risk of loss, we compute the negative semi-deviation. This is a measure of downside risk. The data from Exhibit 27 demonstrate that the sale of an overpriced covered call should not necessarily be expected to generate incremental returns.

Selling of the calls with exercise prices of $52.5 or less actually decreases the expected return. However, it should be noted that the expected risk (assuming that negative semi-deviation is the appropriate risk measure for this investor) of each position is also lower. In contrast, the position with an exercise price of $60 has a higher expected return (15.3% versus 12%) and a lower downside risk (5.5% versus 8.5%) than simply investing in the stock.

Exhibit 28: Gain from Alternative Stock Option Combinations
Expected Stock Return = 12% Standard Deviation = 25%

Strike Price	Stock + Covered Call Return (%)	Standard Deviation (%)	Negative Semi-Deviation (%)
40.00	7.2	6.1	4.4
42.50	7.9	7.8	5.5
45.00	8.6	9.3	6.2
47.50	9.6	10.4	6.4
50.00	10.6	12.5	7.6
52.50	11.4	13.5	7.4
55.00	12.0	15.5	8.4
57.50	13.1	16.7	8.3
60.00	13.6	18.1	8.5
Stock Only	12.0	20.0	10.4

Differing expectations for the volatility and return of the security will obviously generate differing expected returns from following this strategy. Using the same example as before, the expected return under the assumption that the investor forecasts volatility to be 25% per annum is recalculated — i.e., closer to the implied volatility of 30%. The resulting returns and risk measures are shown in Exhibit 28.

In this case it is only the sale of those call options with an exercise price greater than $55 that can be expected to generate incremental returns. Changes in the expected return for a stock can also have a dramatic impact on the expected return from entering into a covered call position. For example, suppose that the investor has an expected return forecast of 8% with a volatility forecast of 20%. The resulting expected returns from a covered call position are shown in Exhibit 29. With the exception of the option with the lowest exercise price, every covered call strategy has the potential to generate incremental returns and reduce risk. The magnitude of the value added is also substantially greater in this instance.

In addition to highlighting the use of the actuarial valuation process, the examples in this section also illustrate the importance of forecasting both the mean and standard deviation when attempting to exploit option market mispricing though the use of covered call writing option strategies. In each example presented here, the options were overvalued; however, it was only in the case when the return on the underlying security was low (8% per annum) that the choice of any of the call options would have added value. Without such forecasts with some demonstrated predictive power, it is doubtful that value can be added though a traditional covered call writing strategy considered here.

The implication of the examples presented above is that managers considering the use of option strategies to enhance the performance of their equity portfolios cannot simply rely on using a simple Black-Scholes or risk neutral valuation approach to attempt to add incremental returns to a portfolio. As the analysis in this chapter demonstrates, the observation that the implied volatility on an option is greater than the actual volatility is not a necessary condition to ensure that the sale of the option will generate incremental returns to a portfolio.

Exhibit 29: Gain from Alternative Stock Option Combinations
Expected Stock Return = 8% Standard Deviation = 20%

Strike Price	Stock + Covered Call Return (%)	Standard Deviation (%)	Negative Semi-Deviation (%)
40.00	7.6	4.8	3.3
42.50	8.6	5.4	3.3
45.00	9.5	7.2	4.3
47.50	10.4	8.7	4.9
50.00	10.9	10.6	5.6
52.50	11.5	12.2	6.1
55.00	12.1	13.7	6.6
57.50	12.1	15.2	6.8
60.00	12.4	16.6	7.3
Stock Only	8.0	20.0	10.4

More generally, the valuation framework presented here can be utilized as a tool to identify optimal derivative strategies and test the implications of alternative return and volatility outcomes on expected returns. As outlined in this chapter, the potential for modifying the risk and return profile of a portfolio using derivatives is vast. Only by using such a formal valuation framework can managers systematically identify those strategies that efficiently exploit their risk and return forecasts of asset classes or individual securities.

Index

Valuation of Interest-Sensitive Financial Instruments

David F. Babbel and Craig B. Merrill

1997 Softcover $55

Published for the Society of Actuaries, SOA Monograph M-F196-1

BOOKS AVAILABLE FROM FRANK J. FABOZZI ASSOCIATES

BOND PORTFOLIO MANAGEMENT
FIXED INCOME SECURITIES
MANAGING FIXED INCOME PORTFOLIOS
VALUATION OF FIXED INCOME SECURITIES AND DERIVATIVES: THIRD EDITION
SELECTED TOPICS IN BOND PORTFOLIO MANAGEMENT
ADVANCED FIXED INCOME ANALYTICS
TREASURY SECURITIES AND DERIVATIVES
MANAGING MBS PORTFOLIOS
CORPORATE BONDS: STRUCTURES & ANALYSIS
COLLATERALIZED MORTGAGE OBLIGATIONS: STRUCTURES & ANALYSIS: SECOND EDITION
HANDBOOK OF CORPORATE DEBT INSTRUMENTS
HANDBOOK OF STRUCTURED FINANCAL PRODUCTS
ASSET-BACKED SECURITIES
THE HANDBOOK OF COMMERCIAL MORTGAGE-BACKED SECURITIES: SECOND EDITION
RENDS IN COMMERCIAL MORTGAGE-BACKED SECURITIES
HANDBOOK OF NONAGENCY MORTGAGE-BACKED SECURITIES
BASICS OF MORTGAGE-BACKED SECURITIES
ADVANCES IN THE VALUATION AND MANAGEMENT OF MORTGAGE-BACKED SECURITIES
VALUATION OF INTEREST-SENSITIVE FINANCIAL INSTRUMENTS
PERSPECTIVES ON INTERNATIONAL FIXED INCOME INVESTING
HANDBOOK OF EMERGING FIXED INCOME AND CURRENCY MARKETS
HANDBOOK OF STABLE VALUE INVESTMENTS
INFLATION PROTECTION BONDS
THE HANDBOOK OF INFLATION-INDEXED BONDS
BANK LOANS: SECONDARY MARKETS AND PORTFOLIO MANAGEMENT
HANDBOOK OF PORTFOLIO MANAGEMENT
ANALYSIS OF FINANCIAL STATEMENTS
INTRODUCTION TO QUANTITATIVE METHODS FOR INVESTMENT MANAGERS
MEASURING AND CONTROLLING INTEREST RATE RISK
DICTIONARY OF FINANCIAL RISK MANAGEMENT: THIRD EDITION
RISK MANAGEMENT: FRAMEWORK, METHODS, AND PRACTICE
PERSPECTIVES ON INTEREST RATE RISK MANAGEMENT FOR MONEY MANAGERS AND TRADERS
DERIVATIVES AND EQUITY PORTFOLIO MANAGEMENT
CREDIT DERIVATIVES
ESSAYS IN DERIVATIVES
ACTIVE EQUITY PORTFOLIO MANAGEMENT
APPLIED EQUITY VALUATION
HANDBOOK OF EQUITY STYLE MANAGEMENT: SECOND EDITION
FOUNDATIONS OF ECONOMIC VALUE ADDED
SELECTED TOPICS IN EQUITY PORTFOLIO MANAGEMENT
PROFESSIONAL PERSPECTIVES ON INDEXING
EQUITY MANAGEMENT
INVESTING BY THE NUMBERS
MODELING THE MARKET: NEW THEORIES AND TECHNIQUES
SECURITIES LENDING AND REPURCHASE AGREEMENTS
PENSION FUND INVESTMENT MANAGEMENT: SECOND EDITION
CREDIT UNION INVESTMENT MANAGEMENT
INVESTMENT MANAGEMENT FOR INSURERS
PERSPECTIVES ON INVESTMENT MANAGEMENT OF PUBLIC PENSION FUNDS
THE USE OF DERIVATIVES IN TAX PLANNING

FOR ORDERING INFORMATION, CALL (215) 598-8930
OR VISIT OUR WEB SITE AT:
WWW.FRANKFABOZZI.COM

Printed in the United States
83111LV00001B/22-48/A